Rita Laima

Skylarks & Rebels

A Memoir about the Soviet Russian Occupation
of Latvia, Life in a Totalitarian State,
and Freedom

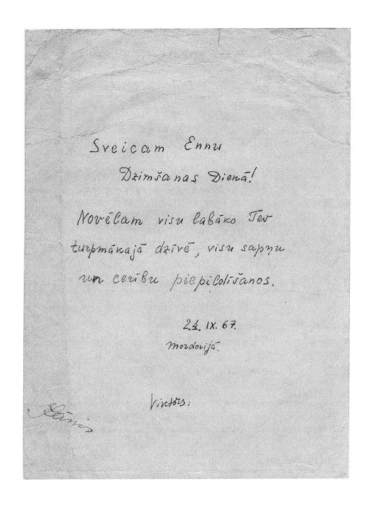

*

About the cover page illustration and its back (above): A birthday wish dated September 24, 1967 from two Latvian Soviet political prisoners, Viktors Kalniņš and one Jānis (surname unknown), to their prison mate, Estonian freedom fighter Enn Tarto (born in September 1938), on his 29th birthday in a prison camp in Mordovia. The card depicts the Latvian Freedom Monument, the Daugava River, and Rīga. The inscription on the back reads: "Greetings to Enn on his birthday! We wish you all the best in the future and the fulfillment of all your dreams and hopes. 24. IX. 67. Mordovia. Viktors. Jānis."

Illustration courtesy of Enn and Piret Tarto.

Rita Laima

SKYLARKS & REBELS

A Memoir about the Soviet Russian Occupation
of Latvia, Life in a Totalitarian State,
and Freedom

ibidem-Verlag
Stuttgart

Bibliographic information published by the Deutsche Nationalbibliothek
Die Deutsche Nationalbibliothek lists this publication in the Deutsche Nationalbibliografie;
detailed bibliographic data are available in the Internet at http://dnb.d-nb.de.

Bibliografische Information der Deutschen Nationalbibliothek
Die Deutsche Nationalbibliothek verzeichnet diese Publikation in der Deutschen
Nationalbibliografie; detaillierte bibliografische Daten sind im Internet über http://dnb.d-nb.de
abrufbar.

Cover design by Krišjānis Rozentāls.

Photograph by Andris Krieviņš.

ISBN-13: 978-3-8382-1034-6

© *ibidem*-Verlag / *ibidem* Press

Stuttgart, Germany 2017

The coat of arms of the Republic of Latvia designed by Rihards Zariņš and adopted in 1921. Source: Wikimedia Commons (https://commons.wikimedia.org/wiki/File:Coat_of_arms_of_Latvia.svg)

Country denoted for them not just a particular geographical environment known and cared for in every detail, but a cultural space alive with stories, myths, and memories. It furnished food, drink, and shelter, as well as every sort of sustenance for the mind and spirit.

—Iain McCalman, The Reef

Live Free or Die.

—The official motto of the US state of New Hampshire as coined by General John Stark

Deeper meaning resides in the fairy tales told to me in my childhood than in any truth that is taught in life.

—Friedrich Schiller

If you can't resign yourself to leaving the past behind you, then you must recreate it.

—Louise Bourgeois

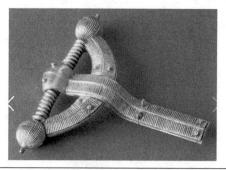

Photograph of a *stopa sakta* or crossbow fibula, traditionally worn by men in the eastern Baltic area, courtesy of Andris Rūtiņš, BalticSmith.com.

Cīrulīti mazputniņ, negul ceļa maliņā.
Rītu jāsi bargi kungi, samīs tavu perēklīti.
Samīs tavu perēklīti, iecels tevi karietē.
Iecels tevi karietē, novedīs vāczemē.
Novedīs vāczemē; tur tev liks mežā braukt.
Tur tev liks mežā braukt, tur tev liks malku cirst.
Kad tu malku sacirtīsi, tad tev liks guni kurt.
Kad tu guni sakurīsi, tad tev liks bruņas kalt.
Kad tu bruņas nosakalsi, tad tev liks karā iet.

•

Skylark, little bird, don't sleep by the roadside.
Tomorrow the harsh masters will come; they'll crush your little nest.
They'll place you in their carriage and take you to Germany.
They'll drive you into the forest and make you chop a lot of wood.
When you finish chopping, they'll make you build a fire.
When you build the fire, they'll make you hammer armor.
When you finish the armor, they'll make you go to war.

(Old Latvian folk song)

A map of the three Baltic States, Estonia, Latvia, and Lithuania, which lie on the eastern rim of the Baltic Sea. Source: Wikitravel (author Peter Fitzgerald) http://wikitravel.org/shared/File:Baltic_states_regions_map.png

With love to my children: Krišjānis (1984) and Jurģis (1990), born in Soviet-occupied communist Latvia; Tālivaldis (2001) and Marija (2005), born in the land of freedom and democracy, the United States; and to my grandson Teodors (2014) and my granddaughter Kirke (2016), both born in the free and independent Republic of Latvia.

In loving memory of my grandparents, Augusts and Emma Rumpēters and Jānis and Līvija Bičolis, who passed on the light and love.

I also dedicate this memoir to Latvians, Lithuanians, and Estonians around the world.

*"How many years can some people exist
before they're allowed to be free?"*

—Bob Dylan

"How could you live in communist Latvia?!"

—A question the author has often been asked.

Sweet sixteen: My older brother Arvils and I in Washington, DC in August 1976 to remind people of the notorious Molotov-Ribbentrop Pact signed by Nazi Germany and the Soviet Union on August 23, 1939, and to protest the ongoing Soviet occupation of Latvia, Lithuania, and Estonia. For many years the Baltic exile community remained strong, politically active, and dedicated to the cause of restoring the Baltics' independence. (Family photo)

Introduction

"I want to live in a free Latvia!" A photograph from 1991 and the "Barricades" time. (Unknown photographer)

These are the memories that I carried around inside of me for years after I left Latvia in 1999. For a while I simply could not find the time to sit down and write; I bore two more children into the world, and their needs consumed me. When my daughter was born in 2005, I realized it was "soon or never." Numerous unsuccessful job searches seemed to signal the urgency to turn to writing and try to capture the end of a dark era in Eastern Europe that many of my American compatriots knew little about. I had been there and lived through my "fatherland" Latvia's last decade under the brutal Soviet Russian occupation, but not that many people knew where Latvia was or what life in the Soviet Union had been like. And in spite of independence, the future of Latvia, Latvians, and our beloved language, the key to our identity, remained clouded by uncertainty and tough economic times. This situation added to my sense of urgency. Nor was I getting younger. Each year seemed to dissolve into the last, compressing my sense of time.

While I dug into my memory, Latvians continued to emigrate from their native land in droves. Each year, as I became one year older, Latvia's population diminished, with more people dying off than being born. There were many reasons for this, including the distant events of World War II and the Soviet occupation, which had a long-lasting, detrimental impact on the Baltic States. As I wrote, people of great significance to Latvia passed away, leaving a void. For a small nation each individual carries great weight. The oldest members of the former Latvian exile community (that is, my parents' generation, which experienced the war) are dying off these days. Latvia's demographic situation has become precarious. My story is about identity, language, patriotism, love, loss, and an archetypal landscape; it's also about being young, idealistic, and fearless. I was full of curiosity, longing, and love when I traveled to the "fatherland" (tēvzeme in Latvian), the land of my ancestors, the country my grandparents were forced to leave due to terrible events beyond their control. My story will resonate with the descendants of Balts and East Europeans whose countries ended up behind the Soviet Iron Curtain after the war, whose families became refugees, and who sought to preserve their ethnic identity while

9

becoming part of America. This is why I feel a deep kinship with my fellow Balts and with Poles, Ukrainians, Czechs, Hungarians, Jews, etc. Some of us still wonder where home is.

In this book I have retained diacritical marks to pay tribute to my mother tongue. Latvian, a very old Indo-European language, is the most basic and most important component of my identity. The United States of America is a country of immigrants, and Americans have come to accept all sorts of foreign names as part of their heritage. For this I love America.

As a first-generation American I am well integrated but not assimilated. I have no shame in speaking to my children in Latvian with Americans within earshot (I hope my fellow citizens do not consider me rude for doing so). I discovered that my fellow hockey, soccer, and school parents are a tolerant bunch. My Latvian language is a gift passed down through scores of generations, and I have no intention of breaking "the chain" of continuity. Our open American society makes me feel accepted. Our children's American public schools display Latvian flags alongside other flags representing the countries of their students' origins. What a great way to nurture American patriotism through the acceptance of its nation's amazing diversity!

My son in his American team's hockey uniform. (Family photo)

I enjoy reading the names on the jerseys of the hockey players we watch on the ice: it is also in those names that the diversity of America the Beautiful is revealed. Chinese, Finnish, French, German, Hungarian, Italian, Latvian, Polish, Russian, Swedish—names from all over the world—reflect the American nation's history and essence. Life in Latvia in turn exposed me to *its* multicultural history. I became acquainted with Russia's rich cultural and dramatic historical legacy and influence, even though in the Soviet era its positive effects on Latvian history were, mildly put, exaggerated and far-fetched. I was able to see a bit of Estonia and Lithuania while living in Latvia and realized again just how strategically important the relationship between the Baltic States is. In the 1990s I was able to easily travel to other countries in Europe. Stockholm, Amsterdam, Copenhagen, Salzburg, Helsinki, Vienna, Venice... So many beautiful, wonderful, and different destinations could be reached from Latvia within a couple of hours of air travel. Living in Europe was exhilarating, and it made me realize that I was an amalgam of European and American influences.

Although I am Latvian, this book is also dedicated to Latvia's Baltic neighbors, Lithuania and Estonia. The Latvian and Lithuanian (Baltic) languages are closely related. Old Prussian, now extinct, was once part of this language group. Estonian, the language of our hardy neighbor to the north, is a Finno-Ugric language and not at all like Latvian or Lithuanian. The Baltics are a distinct region of northeastern Europe with unique histories, cultures, and landscapes. My parents always spoke of Latvia, Lithuania, and Estonia as if they were members of a close family that had suffered the same fate in the 20th century.

Hello! *Sveiki!* (Latvian) *Labas!* (Lithuanian) *Tere!* (Estonian)

I am very proud of the fact that I know part of my lineage, and that I can trace my roots back in time to places on the map of Latvia: Vidriži, Aloja, Birži, Augstkalne... There are some places in the United States that bear names of Latvian origin, like Livonia (Michigan), Riga (New York), and Riga Lane (on Long Island). We Latvians get a big kick out of this. I am proud of my two flags: our Latvian red-white-red flag and the Star-Spangled Banner of the United States of America. Latvian Jewish artist Roman Lapp's hand from his exquisite series of drawings, "Hands for Friends," is a perfect illustration of what I am. These colors symbolize my belonging to two very different cultures, which have made me the person that I am. One flag represents an obscure region of the Old World; the other symbolizes the New World and the United States and its break from the colonial fold. The United States of America remains the world's brightest beacon of freedom and democracy: it has granted asylum to persecuted people from around the world. Among those were the Baltic refugees after World War II who could not return to their home-lands on account of the Soviet occupation. My dual identity has undoubtedly enriched me.

I love the American motto "Life, Liberty and the pursuit of Happiness" from the United States' Declaration of Independence. These words are loaded with meaning and connotations, especially when I think about the other half of my identity—the Latvian side. Latvia's quest for life, liberty, and the pursuit of happiness lasted a very short time, commencing in 1918 and coming to a violent end in 1940 with the Soviet invasion. While others rejoiced, World War II did not end happily for the Baltic States: for nearly 50 years these nations would be brutally oppressed by the Soviet communists. My grandparents barely escaped the "Russian bear." So many Latvian lives were lost in the 20th century, that it is a wonder that our nation survived into the 21st century.

I spent 17 years in Latvia—from late 1982 until March 1999. Part of that time was under the Soviet Russian occupation (until 1991). My charmed youth in the United States propelled me to the USSR in a strange state of euphoria and fear. I think that basic American freedoms, the American way of life, and my exposure to a lot of culture from an early age—art, music, litera-ture, theater, and cinema—went a long way in keeping me "charged" in the depressing Soviet era, when life was lived as if in an aquarium. American popular culture and humor also strength-ened me for what I was to endure in communist Latvia. "Hogan's Heroes" with Colonel Wilhelm Klink and Sergeant Hans Schultz had made us Latvian Americans laugh (although the Nazi occu-pation in Latvia had been exceedingly brutal and deadly). Totalitarianism would reveal itself to me in all its dark and dreary colors.

The words of many American and British rock songs would serve as a kind of buffer between my open and inquisitive mind and the oppressiveness of Soviet reality in the 1980s. "Where are you goin' to, / What are you gonna do? / Do you think it will be easy? / Do you think it will be pleasin'? / (...) / It's my freedom, / Don't worry about me, babe..." (Steve Miller, "Living in the USA") Unlike my compatriots in occupied Latvia, as an American citizen I had the freedom to travel, and I never took this freedom for granted. As soon as I was old enough, I wanted to get out of the house and see new places. First on the list was Latvia, which our family and Latvian American society had been talking about for years. Fantastically, my experience there would

11

correspond with history in the making: "The present now / Will later be past / The order is rapidly fading…" (Bob Dylan, "The Times They Are A-Changin'") You're young only once. Pumped up by the energy of the music I listened to and bored out of my mind by American suburban life, I felt I was ready for anything. Even adventures in a place that US President Ronald Reagan would deem "the Evil Empire."

Because so little was known about the Baltic countries during the years of the Soviet occupation, we were used to hearing many strange questions in the United States. For instance, my friend Gerry at Parsons School of Design wanted to know if people in Latvia wore clogs. "Is Russian Latvia's official language?" "Are you Latvians Russian?" This obsession with Russia grated on my nerves. Luckily, the Baltic States have clearly emerged from Russia's shadow, with many of my fellow Americans now recognizing the names of our countries. After independence in 1991, Latvian, Lithuanian, and Estonian athletes have been winning medals at the Olympic Games to the cheers of Balts all over the world. (For example: Latvians **Martins Dukurs** [SILVER, skeleton, 2010 Vancouver] and **Māris Štrombergs**—aka "The Machine" [GOLD, BMX, 2008 Beijing; GOLD, BMX, 2012 London]; Lithuanians **Rūta Meilutytė** [GOLD, breaststroke 100 m, 2012 London] and **Laura Asadauskaitė** [GOLD, Modern Pentathlon, 2012 London]; Estonians **Erki Nool** [GOLD, decathlon, 2000 Sydney] and **Heiki Nabi** [SILVER, Greco-Roman wrestling 120 kg, 2012 London], etc.) After years of being forced to compete under the despised Soviet flag, Baltic athletes could finally compete under their national colors and hear their anthems fill stadiums around the world.

As an American in Soviet Latvia in the 1980s, I was a curiosity and a mystery. My Latvian heritage did not seem that important to anyone; it was the fact that I was American that was initially so intriguing to the people I encountered. Yet most of them were too scared to ask questions. Most Latvians could not understand what I was doing in Latvia in the first place, and this nurtured wild rumors. CIA, KGB… "Why on earth was I lingering on a sinking ship?" was the question I heard from time to time in the early eighties. (*If the ship was sinking, that was a good reason to hang around*, I thought.) As time passed, the curiosity dissipated; people lost interest when they grew used to my presence. (Rīga is not that big.) My strange haircut—an extreme mullet of sorts—grew out, and I blended in. Soviet leaders came and went, the tide of history changed, and the great "upheaval" began. A trickle at first but then building into a torrent of emotion and daring protest … The late 1980s were an unforgettable historical period of "national awakening" in Latvia, Lithuania, and Estonia, prompted by Soviet leader Mikhail Gorbachev's policies of *perestroika* and *glasnost* after decades of repression, the numbing beat of Soviet communist ideology, and economic stagnation under the Politburo's heavy, all-controlling paw.

In my book I often refer to Latvia as the "fatherland," because Latvians traditionally refer to their native country this way. "I placed my head on the boundary / To defend my fatherland; / Better that they took my head / Than my fatherland" are the words of an old Latvian *daina* or folk poem/song. You won't find the word "motherland" in Latvian dainas and literature, but in artistic and especially sculptural representation Latvia is depicted as a woman. Latvia's Freedom Monument in Rīga is the figure of a woman—the mother who gave us life and defends her children, as we should defend her. The word *tēvzeme* evokes feelings of patriotism and protectiveness. Our history has been marked by so many tragedies, that we all feel protective of our beautiful country.

As the mother of three sons, I have thought a lot about all the Latvian boys and men who gave their lives for the idea and reality of a free and independent Latvia (in the Latvian War of Independence [1918–1920] and during WWII), and about those who were forcibly conscripted into foreign armies (Nazi Germany's and the Soviet Union's Red Army, for example) and died in wars they should never have been a part of. Their countless names are impossible to list. Their bones are scattered across Latvia, Russia, Belarus, Poland, Germany, and elsewhere. Some of Latvia's veterans from World War II still survive, cheered and cursed, their role in the last war misunderstood. The remnants of the Latvian Legion fought in the "Kurzeme Fortress" (also known as the "Kurzeme Cauldron") against the advancing Red Army in World War II, helping thousands of Latvian refugees, including my grandparents and parents, to escape across the Baltic Sea to freedom. We Latvians have a duty to explain our complicated history, in which allegiances were forced upon us at gunpoint.

I also reflected on the women of Latvia—mothers, sisters, daughters, sweethearts, and wives who had to hold Latvia together with their bare hands and survival instinct. In the early 1920s *National Geographic* reporter Maynard Owen Williams visited war-torn Latvia and wrote: "[… This country] owes a heavy debt to its women, who drive the wagons, harvest the flax, pile up the grain, tend the cattle, sweep the streets, pull the carts, run the hotels, tend the street markets, keep the stores, shovel the sawdust, and juggle the lumber." (Williams, Maynard Owen. "Latvia, Home of the Letts." *National Geographic Magazine* October 1924) My grandmothers were typical Latvian women: stoic and ingenious, patient and persevering. One led her children out of harm's way on a perilous flight across Europe from Stalin's "Red Terror." The other remained behind, cut off from escape by circumstance and responsibility: she and her young sons (my uncles) were among the millions of captives caught behind the Soviet Union's Iron Curtain.

The Baltic States' geography has not been kind to its human populations. Numerous waves of war leveled much of what human hands built in the Baltic lands. Those busy hands went back to work time and time again. Despite these cycles of destruction, my people survived, and they are a fascinating bunch. Latvia, shaped like a peasant's clog, is a repository of stories of tragedy and remarkable resilience: one only has to start digging, reading…

Ultimately, it is many people who made this book possible. My parents Baiba and Ilmārs Rumpēters and my grandparents, Līvija and Jānis Bičolis, and Augusts Rumpēters, instilled in me a deep love for the Latvian language and our cultural legacy. In my youth I basked in the light of my parents' friends, writers, poets, painters, and musicians, most of whom have passed away by now. I mourn their absence. My children, Krišjānis and Jurģis (born in Latvia), and Tālivaldis and Marija (born in the United States), made me realize how important it was to tell my story and to document a decade of Latvia's history under totalitarian oppression. My friends, especially in Latvia, helped me with my story by remembering certain details. The terrible suffering of the populations of Latvia, Lithuania, and Estonia in the last century was also a reason for working on my memoir. For too long the Baltic peoples had suffered without a voice.

INTRODUCTION

A bit about my work on this book: I did much of my research online; I have strived for accuracy but am not a historian; and this is a memoir. I wanted to give my people a voice. I had to translate just about every source from Latvian myself (marked as Tr. RL). It is an endeavor of creative non-fiction. Many of the subjects that I mention can and should be pursued separately. The Nazi German and Soviet Russian occupations of the Baltic States deserve continued serious study. My book is laid out in such a way as to introduce the reader to my youth, which paved the way for adventures in my "fatherland." I felt it was important to provide historical background information about Latvia in the 20ᵗʰ century; after all, events there explain why I was born in the United States.

So welcome to Latvia, a place I spend a lot of time thinking about, mainly because family and friends live there, and I think I would like to go back. My story is about being bicultural and exploring my family's European roots. It is also a memoir about Latvia in its last decade as a satellite republic of the militarily mighty and fearsome totalitarian state, the Union of Soviet Socialist Republics. In that unhappy union Latvia, Lithuania, and Estonia, independent and thriving countries before World War II, were reduced to the status of occupied provinces and nearly erased from world memory. I had the privilege of being in Latvia to witness firsthand the last decade of their oppression come to a much awaited end, as the "the Evil (Soviet) Empire" collapsed, and freedom was restored. Today that freedom is under threat again both from the outside and from within, and lessons learned in Latvia have provided a perspective on troubling times in Europe and, much to my surprise and dismay, in the United States.

Rita Laima

With gratitude

Gunārs Astra, Lidija Doroņina-Lasmane, and Juris Ziemelis: Their courage will always be an inspiration.

The Cultural Foundation of the World Federation of Free Latvians for its financial support
Toms Altbergs
Edmunds ("Edžus") Auers—For his mother's pastries and tea, for sharing his precious books from the pre-war era with us, and for all the Soviet jokes and many laughs
Tālivaldis Bērziņš for Tālivaldis Augusts and Marija Līvija
Parsla Blakis for her unwavering enthusiasm
Jānis Borgs
My mother Baiba Bičole for reading Latvian folk tales to me when I was little
Kārlis Dambītis
Sarma Dindzāne-Van Sant
Oļģerts Eglītis
Mārtiņš Grants
Ēriks Jēkabsons
Tija Kārklis
Arvis Kolmanis
Andris Krieviņš for Krišjānis and Jurģis and the beautiful photographs
Ēvalds Krieviņš
Juris Krieviņš for showing me the beauty of Latvia
Biruta Krieviņa for teaching me the value of hard work and persistence
Uldis Liepkalns
Ivars Mailītis
Mārtiņš Mintaurs
Karu Kuu
Valters Nollendorfs
Gunārs Opmanis
Valdis Ošiņš
My wonderful Raiņa bulvāris folks: Jāzeps and Ināra Lindbergs; Tamāra Legzdiņa; Māra Lindberga and Gunārs Lūsis; Inta and Ivars Sarkans; Daina Lindberga; Linda Lūse
Composer Steve Reich for his "Music for 18 Musicians" (1974–1976) – the sound of time collapsing
Kārlis Račevskis
Baņuta Rubess
Guntars Rumpēters
My father Ilmārs Rumpēters whose prolific artistic output has always been a source of inspiration
Reverend Visvaldis Rumpēteris
Anna Rūtiņa
Uģis Sprūdžs
Alfrēds Stinkulis
Jānis Stundiņš

Valdis and Inese Supe for their friendship and hospitality in Latvia
Tekla Šaitere
www.senes.lv
Kaspas Zellis
Mārtiņš Zelmenis
Ilze Znotiņa

October 1980: My first time in Latvia (then the Latvian Soviet Socialist Republic) visiting as a 20-year-old art student. This photo was taken on the roof of the 22-story Press Building (completed in 1978). The Press Building housed the editorial offices of most of Latvia's newspapers and magazines in the Soviet era. Construction of a new suspension bridge across the Daugava River is visible to the left. The work was completed the following summer (1981). The old floating pontoon bridge was eventually dismantled. On the day of this photo shoot I was painfully aware that my time in Latvia was running out. (Photograph courtesy of Gunārs Janaitis)

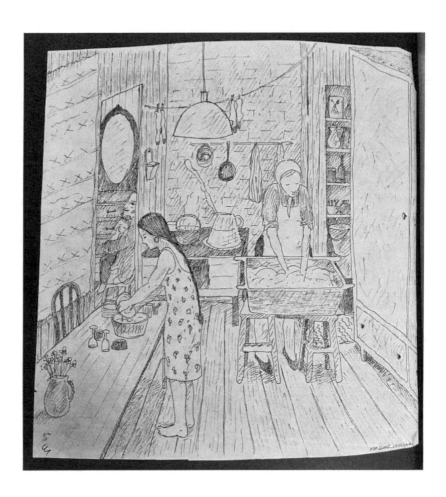

Latvia was and remains for me both a reality and a dream. This scene that I drew in the 1980s of our everyday life in the Latvian countryside in Piebalga—doing the dishes, baking bread, taking care of the children—is now a distant memory of something lost and something gained.

Table of Contents

Storks in the Latvian countryside in summer. (Photo by Juris Krieviņš)

Fond memories of life in Latvia: My sons Krišjānis and Jurģis with their cousins, Elīna and Alise, and a baby deer that their father rescued and raised on our farm in northern Latvia. Their "Omīte" (grandmother) Biruta Krieviņa can be seen walking to the barn, where she kept cows, pigs, and poultry. (Photo by Andris Krieviņš, 1992)

Glossary

Blats—A word from the Soviet era in Latvia that describes the system of connections, favors, and "who you know" in a centralized, impoverished economy, in which stores carried few attractive goods, and good services were hard to come by. For instance, if someone said, "I have *blats* at the butcher shop on Blaumaṇa iela," it meant "I know someone at the butcher shop on Blaumaṇa iela who can get me some quality meat'" (unavailable to walk-in customers). My father-in-law had this kind of *blats* at a butcher shop. He took portraits of the manager's family events and was reciprocated with good cuts of meat, which he shared with us. The decades-long system of *blats* promoted favoritism and spawned nepotism and corruption, problems that Latvia and all post-Soviet societies struggle with today. It also taught a part of society to calculate their relationships.

Cheka / chekist—The Soviet secret police, better known as the KGB. A chekist is a KGB operative.

Eastern Europe—I use the term Eastern Europe to describe the countries that found themselves behind the so-called Iron Curtain and under Soviet communist influence after World War II.

The Free World—A term used during the Cold War to describe countries with democratic political systems, freedom of speech, and free market economies, namely the United States, Canada, and Western Europe (as opposed to the Soviet Union and Eastern Europe).

Iela—The Latvian word for street

The Iron Curtain—"The political, military, and ideological barrier erected by the Soviet Union after World War II to seal off itself and its dependent eastern and central European allies from open contact with the West and other noncommunist areas. The term Iron Curtain had been in occasional and varied use as a metaphor since the 19th century, but it came to prominence only after it was used by the former British prime minister Winston Churchill in a speech at Fulton, Missouri, US, on March 5, 1946, when he said of the communist states, 'From Stettin in the Baltic to Trieste in the Adriatic, an iron curtain has descended across the Continent.'" (Encyclopedia Brittanica)

Laima—The Latvian goddess of fate and fortune. *Ej, Laimiņa, tu pa priekšu, / Es tavās pēdiņās, / Nelaid mani to celiņu, / Kur aizgāja ļauna diena.* (An old Latvian daina, which translates as: "Walk, Laima, ahead of me, / I'll walk in your footsteps, / Don't let me go down the path / Of the bad day."

Trimda—The Latvian word for exile. The word *trimda* stands for all the Latvians who left Latvia as political emigrants during World War II and then convened abroad to establish a temporary alternative Latvian society. The aim of the exile community was to preserve Latvian identity abroad while engaging in political activism to speed up the collapse of the Soviet Union. *Trimda* Latvians founded congregations, bought or built churches, established schools and camps for their children, published books, read their own Latvian language newspapers, organized concerts, theater performances, art exhibits, and other social activities, striving to preserve the memory of Latvia and the Latvian language and culture. The Soviet Latvian authorities mistrusted *trimda* Latvians and initiated smear campaigns against some of its leaders.

Prologue:
A Country the Size of West Virginia

THIRD ELEGY

Strange to hail from almost anonymous shores
in overexplored Europe where the Baltic
still hides a lunar side, unilluminated
except for subjugations, annexations
which continue unabated for centuries.
No problem for anyone to name the Nordic countries
from Iceland to Finland,
but how about the Baltic ones?
Surely one and the same language
is spoken there? If not Russian,
at least something akin to German?
You will never guess unless we unravel
the skein of Indo-European and Finno-Ugric
language families, ponder Babel
to clear up the Baltic,
and who has time for such marginal myths?
We persist with the subsoil. Grass is another
favored metaphor (trampled upon, it springs back),
or limestone cliffs filed away by gales
yet undefiled, withstanding millennia.
It is strange to hail from the dark side of the moon
while supposedly we inhabit the same planet.
There are Third World pockets inside Europe
one tends to overlook, anonymous shores
marked with an x or a mental question mark.
If only you incline in the Baltic direction,
you begin to hear the dirge of a beehive
and perceive in underwater outline
an amber chamber built with pollen of grief.

Ivar Ivask. *Baltic Elegies*.
Norman, Oklahoma: *World Literature Today*, 1987.
Translated by Valters Nollendorfs

So let it be known: my family hails "from the dark side of the moon" and "a Third World pocket inside Europe," from a country called Latvia. I am also American, born in the United States in 1960 as a child of refugees fifteen years after the end of World War II. My parents and all their predecessors were born in Latvia, as far as I know. I could claim to be 100% Latvian, but maybe there are some Liv, Estonian, Lithuanian, German, Swedish, Polish, or Russian genes mixed in there due to so many foreigners crossing Latvia over the course of history, breaching ethnic borders, and setting up camps or permanent bases on our lands, taking what they coveted and leaving the rest for my ancestors to subsist on. With all the wars and foreign occupations, fires, the bubonic plague, childhood mortality, waves of emigration, and deportations that went on for centuries years in Latvia, I consider myself and other Latvians alive today to be the survivors of the fittest and most fortunate. My parents' generation certainly seems to be robust, living to a ripe, old age.

Latvian musicians from Kurzeme in a photograph from the early 20th century. Many Latvian folk songs and melodies are hundreds of years old. Passed down from generation to generation, they symbolize my nation's resilience.

As a tiny link in a very long chain that stretches back in time, I cherish the ancient language passed down to me, as well as the rich treasure chest of Latvian culture: our delightful folk tales; our riddles rooted in everyday life; our witty, wise proverbs; our merry, foot-stomping folk dances and soothing, sometimes melancholic melodies played on the *kokle* (a wooden stringed instrument), the bagpipes, and the fiddle; the so-called dainas—our unique folk poetry that expresses all aspects of human existence; our traditional crafts; our ethnic jewelry with its ancient, mystical designs; our lovely folk costumes; our wooden architecture that merges so well with our northern landscape; and so on. It is a deep chest that we can be proud of, dip into for inspiration, and share with others.

A 19th century *pūra lāde* (dowry chest) from the Valka region. (Pauls Kundziņš, *Latvju sēta*, 1974.)

Latvia, a country slightly bigger than the state of West Virginia, lies on the eastern shore of the Baltic Sea opposite Sweden. Latvia's neighboring countries include Estonia to the north, Russia to the east, Belarus to the southeast, and Lithuania to the south. Latvia's geographical location as a country bordering northern Europe's Baltic Sea, a strategic waterway and transit route, and as a stepping stone between Europe and Russia, has been both a blessing and a terrible curse. A tasty geopolitical morsel, the territory of Latvia has tempted foreign armies to invade, raid, and occupy it, leaving lasting political, cultural, linguistic, and genetic imprints. (Perhaps this is why there are so many beautiful Latvian women and good-looking men.)

The peoples that preceded Latvia's modern nation.
Source: Wikimedia Commons https://en.wikipedia.org/wiki/Balts#/media/File:Baltic_Tribes_c_1200.svg
(© CC BY-SA 3.0 https://creativecommons.org/licenses/by-sa/3.0/deed.en)

Before German emissaries of the Holy Roman Empire and warrior monks began conquering the territory of ancient Latvia in the 13th century, it had been settled by numerous groups of peoples or tribes. These were: the Kurši (Curonians); Zemgaļi (Semigallians), Latgaļi (Latgalians), Sēļi (Selonians), and the Līvi (Livs or Livonians), a people linguistically related to the Finno-Ugric Estonians, Finns, and Hungarians. Like the ancient Vikings, the Kurši also took to the seas. One after the other, the local tribes ceded land to the Germans who named it Terra Mariana, the official name for medieval Livonia. The "castle hills" of our ancestors, pre-dating German arrival, can be found all over Latvia, many of them concealed by trees and bushes. The impressive stone ruins of the German invaders' ancient fortified castles still stand today, looking more and more like rocky outcrops of the earth. They are fascinating reminders of the distant past, when peoples and faiths collided under the northern sun.

The Latvian language belongs to the family of Indo-European languages. Latvian and Lithuanian are Baltic languages said to be distantly linked to Sanskrit. Old Prussian was once part of this "family" but died out in the late 17th or early 18th century. The Old Prussians were conquered by the Teutonic Knights in the 13th century. Latvian and Lithuanian are said to be among the oldest languages in Europe.

Janīna Kursīte, a Latvian linguist and literary scholar, says: "It's mostly true that Latvian and Lithuanian are among the oldest of Europe's languages. Russian philologist Vladimir Toporov, who was also very familiar with Baltic culture, once said that Latvian and Lithuanian enjoyed a unique status among European languages in that they were both a 'mother' and a 'daughter' to European languages. The richness of the (Latvian) dainas and their ancient, mythical motifs are unique and archaic; you won't find anything like the dainas among living languages and European cultures. At the same time, in terms of abstract notions of the modern world, the Latvian language is very recent, much more recent than German, English, and Russian; our modern-day Latvian was 'created' in the second half of the 19th century. Atis Kronvalds, Krišjānis Valdemārs, and Auseklis (Miķelis Krogzemis) were among those creating new Latvian words. We are both ancient and young; that is our blessing and our curse."

It is interesting to note the similarities between the two remaining Baltic languages, Latvian and Lithuanian, and then the Finno-Ugric languages, Liv, Estonian, and Finnish:

English	Latvian	Lithuanian	Liv	Estonian	Finnish
star	zvaigzne	žvaigždė	tēḑ	täht	tähti
sun	saule	saulė	pǟvaḷiki	païke	aurinko
sky	debess	dangus	tōvaz	taevas	taivas
river	upe	upė	joug	jõgi	joki
forest	mežs	miškas	mõtsā	mets	metsä
earth	zeme	žemė	mõ	maa	maa
brother	brālis	brolis	veḷ	vend	veli
hand	roka	ranka	kež	käsi	käsi

The territory around Rīga, the capital of Latvia, was originally settled by the indigenous Livs. Rīga was founded in 1201 as a political and military base for a holy war against the native pagans by Bishop Albert. The campaign was successful and established a powerful foothold for German rule for centuries to come.

Left: Rīga. Scene on the Daugava River. Original wood engraving by J. Koerner, 1878. Image courtesy of Mark Dechow Antique Prints, Maps, and Rare Books, Hamburg, Germany.

In 1282 the city of Rīga joined the Hanseatic League, an important economic alliance in northern Europe. Over the centuries Rīga was visited and settled by people of various nationalities and cultures. Artifacts from its colorful history—coins, furniture, tools, model ships, and silverware—are on display at the Museum of the History of Rīga and Navigation (1773) in the old town. The stories of the city's past are evident in its buildings and in Old Rīga's intriguing street names, which beg to be explained, as well as in its houses of worship. Over the centuries Rīga prospered and grew. The Daugava River served as a gateway between East and West. Other major cities in Latvia include the port cities of Ventspils and Liepāja on the Baltic Sea, Jelgava with its famous palace Rundāle, designed by

Francesco Bartolomeo Rastrelli (1700–1771), architect of St. Petersburg, and Daugavpils on the Daugava River.

I am lucky to have in my possession some faded photographs of my Latvian ancestors, my *senči*. I look upon their faces with love and like to imagine what their day and age in Latvia was like. These photographs, as well as a Bible printed in Rīga in 1794 that was passed down to me by my maternal grandmother, I count as my most precious material possessions. My Grandmother Līvija's and Grandfather Augusts' slim volumes of poetry in perfectly preserved bindings (his written between 1914 and 1925—a stormy period than includes World War I, Latvia's independence from Russia, an invasion by the Bolsheviks, and the first years of the newly independent Republic of Latvia) transcend time and space. We are linked through our mother tongue.

An old family photograph that my grandmother Līvija gave to me of a family wedding in Zemgale, circa 1900.

The language of my grandparents' poetry, Latvian, is not only ancient, it is beautiful, poetic, and evocative. It was the first language I heard as a child. I can speak and write it, and I am passing it down to my children. I cannot live without the Latvian language. It is as important to me as the air I breathe. It is the deepest part of my personal identity and a link to other Latvians around the world. Russian poet, exile, and Nobel laureate Joseph Brodsky (1940–1996) wrote: "I belong to the Russian culture. I feel a part of it, its component, and no change of place can influence the final consequence of this. A language is a much more ancient and inevitable thing than a state. I belong to the Russian language." (Poetry Foundation) I can say the same about the Latvian language: it is my spiritual home.

Latvia has been a multicultural country for centuries. Ethnic Latvians comprise its majority. Minorities include Russians, Belarusians, Ukrainians, Jews, Lithuanians, Poles, Roma, etc. Latvia's ethnic makeup was drastically altered under Nazi and Soviet rule. Its Jewish population was annihilated during the German occupation. Later under the Soviet policy of Russification, Latvia absorbed hundreds of thousands of Russian speakers. Latvia's Russian speaking population grew at an alarming rate under Soviet rule. This legacy remains a source of social and political tension in Latvia even today, especially in its relations with belligerent Russia.

Rīga Railway Bridge inauguration in May 1914. Until its declaration of independence in 1918, Latvia was part of the Russian Empire. Source: Wikimedia Commons https://commons.wikimedia.org/wiki/File:Riga_railway_bridge_inauguration.jpg (© Public Domain)

Prior to the Soviet occupation in 1940, Rīga was a thriving port city that enjoyed trade and commerce with many Western European countries. Around the turn of the 20th century Rīga had a small British community with its own Anglican Church, St. Saviour's, near the Daugava River. Soil was shipped from across the sea so that the church could be built on British soil. George Armitstead (1847–1912), born into a British merchant's family, became Rīga's mayor in 1901. Russian Orthodox churches throughout Latvia attest to Russia's influence in the region. The tumultuous and tragic events of the two world wars left a permanent impact on Latvia, its population, and its architectural legacy.

A fine son of Rīga's British community more than a hundred years ago: George Armitstead, Rīga's fourth mayor, at the turn of the 20th century. Armitstead was an engineer and entrepreneur. His magnificent neo-gothic hunting lodge, Jaunmoku Castle (Schloss Neu-Mocken) in Kurzeme, is a popular tourist attraction. Source: Wikimedia Commons https://commons.wikimedia.org/wiki/File:GeorgeArmitstead.jpg (© Public Domain)

Latvia's Baltic German population, once so powerful in Latvia, is long-gone, forced to repatriate under Hitler's orders starting in 1939. Germans had been around in Latvia for centuries as masters and commanders and had a great effect on on my ancestors' culture, customs, religion, character, and mentality. Not all of the influences were negative. Germans left us beautiful parks, churches, manors, and other notable buildings.

Latvia's synagogues before World War II reflected Jewish history in Latvia that could be traced back to the 16th century. Latvian literature and Latvian folk songs have references to Germans, Jews, Roma, and Russians. Many Jews who settled in Latvia after the war emigrated in the 1970s. The region of Latgale with its distinct Latgalian dialect or language (depending on whom you ask) has also been decimated over time.

The ruins of Eleja Manor in the 1930s. Built in the early 19th century in the style of classicism for Baron von Medem, the estate's buildings were torched in 1915 by the retreating Russian Army. Image courtesy of the National Library of Latvia collection "In Search of Lost Latvia."

Latvia's indigenous Liv population is nearly gone, and the Liv language on the verge of extinction. It may yet survive, thanks to the efforts of some fanatic Liv descendants. In his beautiful book of black and white photographs, *Līvieši* (2008), Juki Nakamura has documented the last of the Livs living in Latvia today.

"Vanishing voices": A group of Livs in their Sunday best photographed in their seaside village Sīkrags by Vilho Setele in 1912. "Vanishing Voices" was a compelling article published in *National Geographic Magazine* in October 2012 about the world's vanishing languages. Source: www.nba.fi/liivilaiset/Latvia/1Latvia.html

Latvians are "a small, thievish nation that lives in trees and eats mushrooms." In another version we are "a small, quarrelsome nation." Someone claimed that Winston Churchill coined this description. Others say it goes back centuries. Silly though it sounds, sometimes it describes us quite well. Our weakness is our infighting, especially in the political realm. We like to perpetuate the myth that our national character is marred by envy, jealousy, malice, and grudges. There are plenty of folk songs that seem to substantiate these claims. Supposedly we will do anything to trip up another Latvian: *"Latvietis latvietim gardākais kumoss"* ("A Latvian is a Latvian's favorite morsel"), and so on. These self-deprecating comments are funny up to a point. Yet events in history speak of our ability to consolidate, especially in the face of adversity, which has been our constant companion for centuries.

"Princess Bolete": a most perfect edible mushroom sitting in a soft carpet of green moss in Kurzeme, Latvia. (Photo by Aigars Adamovičs)

As for real mushrooms, in the late summer and early fall giddy Latvians don rubber boots and head into the forest with baskets and knives in search of glorious edible fungi, of which there is an astonishing abundance. For sautéing, marinating, and drying, mushrooms like King Bolete (*Boletus edulis* or *baravika* in Latvian), Slippery Jacks (*sviesta beka*), chanterelles (*gailene*), Saffron Milk Caps (*rudmiese*), Russula (*bērzlape*), etc. thrill Latvians young and old. In the spring, fungi connoisseurs also hunt for that special delicacy, morels (*Morchella sp.* or *murķeļi*). Most Latvians have a countryside retreat where they go to enjoy the outdoors, a bit of gardening, and culinary activities like berry picking and mushroom hunting. This is a marvelous way to stay in shape while enjoying the beauty and bounty of Latvia's nature.

Our ancestors built their homes with logs and planted oaks, lindens, and other trees around their houses for beauty and shelter. In ancient times their fortified castles on top of castle hills were constructed of timber before the advent of the crusaders. Even when the Germans started grabbing our lands, converting us to Christianity and making serfs of us, our ancestors stubbornly clung to their pagan ways and sought out oak trees, a symbol of male strength and courage, for worship and offerings. Other trees besides the oak were anthropomorphized. The linden symbolizes feminine beauty. Pērkons, our ancient god of thunder, rumbled and grumbled from his celestial perch. Our fates were determined by Laima, the goddess of destiny. Many ancient superstitions have survived into modern times, and some Latvians have sought to revive their ancestors' pagan religion, which is deeply rooted in nature.

Latvia's climate is similar to that of Europe's Scandinavia. Long, dark winters with considerable precipitation—sludge in the capital, snow in the countryside, dreary rainfall—are followed by short but brilliant summers with long days and short nights. Latvia's climate is excellent for raising crops, including grains, vegetables, fruit, and flowers. My personal favorite, the dahlia, thrives in Latvia's temperate summers.

The relatively shallow Baltic Sea never really warms up; swimming in it is a cold but refreshing experience. With the soft, white sands of the popular seaside resort Jūrmala next to the Gulf of Rīga, the picturesque, boulder-strewn beaches of the Vidzeme coastline, and Kurzeme's beautiful, quiet, relatively empty beaches and old fishing villages that stretch along the open Baltic Sea, Latvia's history has been defined by its meeting with the sea. Centuries ago it attracted foreigners who sought to claim it. At the end of World War II, departing from its shores, thousands of Latvians fled in fishing boats and German ships from the Red Army to Sweden and Germany. Under the communists, most areas along the sea were off-limits to the average Soviet citizen. The beaches were fastidiously patrolled by Soviet border guards, smoothed and combed to track the footprints of anyone attempting to escape from the USSR via the sea. Today the approximately 500-kilometer shoreline is open and accessible to the public. Latvians can still fish in their waters; however, rigid European Union quotas are endangering that age-old way of life captured in Latvian folk ditties: *The sea did roar, the sea did hiss, / What lies at the bottom of the sea? / Gold and silver / And some mothers' dear sons.*

A photograph taken at a Liv fishing village in Kurzeme in 1912 of fishermen sorting their catch near Miķeļtornis. Source: Vilho Setele, 1912. http://www.nba.fi/liivilaiset/Latvia

The Baltics have a way of casting a spell on people who have lived there for a longer period of time. American diplomat George Kennan (1904–2005), who worked at the American Legation in Rīga in the 1930s, took note: "(Visiting Stockholm), something in the light, the sunlight, the late Northern evening suddenly made me aware of (...) Latvia and Estonia, and I suddenly was absolutely filled with a sort of nostalgia for (...) the inner beauty and meaning of that flat Baltic landscape and the waters around it. It meant an enormous amount to me. You can't explain these things." (Costigliola, Frank. "Is This George Kennan?" The New York Review of Books. Dec. 8, 2011.) Latvia's gentle, verdant landscape dotted with gigantic boulders, many of them dubbed *velnakmeņi* or "Devil's Rocks," cast a spell on me, too, when I lived there.

"The Ruler of Vadakste" (Vadakstes valdnieks): a giant of a boulder in Ezere, Kurzeme near the Lithuanian border. The story goes that the last proprietor of Ezere Manor, Baron von Toll, ordered his peasants to move this boulder to his park. This task took the poor men ten years to complete, from 1845 to 1855.
Source: J. Sedols, Wikimedia Commons. https://commons.wikimedia.org/wiki/File:Vadakstes_vald nieks_-_akmens_Ezeres_park%C4%81_2000-11-04.jpg (© CC BY 3.0 https://creativecommons.org/licenses/by /3.0/deed.en)

A Latvian Folk Tale about Ezere

Several centuries have passed since that time when Ezere Manor was ruled by Baron von Nolcken. Back then it was simply called Nolcken. There was a terrace on the manor house's east side, where each morning the baron would sit and drink coffee. From the terrace the river, the Vadakste, which formed the border (between Latvia and Lithuania—RL), was well visible. The baron was a ruthless sadist. Beneath the manor, where the baron often dined with guests, he had constructed a maze of passages. These passages connected the manor house with the chapel and the river, which had once been deep and navigable by ships. It was said that these passages had been dug by slaves. Long, deep, and gloomy, they were filled with dangerous traps. According to the baron's instructions, secret cellars had been constructed beneath the passages to entrap hapless wanderers. One such passage was located right beneath the terrace. While the baron entertained his guests on the terrace, beneath it people sentenced to death for minor transgressions stumbled about trying to find a way out. At a certain point in the passage a large millstone had been set into the floor. If someone stepped on the stone, it tipped, propelling the victims into a dark and damp cellar filled with the bones of other victims.

The newlywed wife of the baron's son, the beautiful Ezere, fell into this trap, too. The young baron and Ezere had just celebrated their wedding. They and other young couples were playing the traditional game of hide-and-seek. Unsuspecting Ezere stepped on the millstone and fell into the cellar. But she was a sorceress. Outraged by what she discovered, she woke up the dead. They emerged above ground, chasing off the evil baron, and Ezere became ruler of the manor. That is how it came to be known as Ezere. (Latvian historical folk tale. Source: http://www.ezere.lv/35550/vesture1. Tr. RL)

Lielezere Manor. Source: © J. Sedols, Wikipedia. https://lv.wikipedia.or g/wiki/Att%C4%93ls:Ezeres_mui%C5%BEas_pils_2000-11-04.jpg (© CC BY-SA 3.0 https://creativecommons.org/licenses/by-sa/3.0/)

Ghost stories are attached to many of Latvia's old German manor houses, which remind me of the mansions of the American South. For some reason many of them feature a lady "in green" (*zaļā dāma*). Was there any truth to the Ezere tale? Had there once been a sadistic baron, a serial killer who had turned his manor into a house of horrors? Baron von Toll must have had a cruel streak in him as well, ordering his subordinates to roll a humongous boulder for ten years from the river to his park. Many of the old manor houses of the Baltic German landed gentry still stand in Latvia, some of them particularly ghostly in their state of neglect or abandonment.

Latvia, land of lore, boasts countless legendary "sacred" springs associated with tales of pagan worship and sacrifice. Our many castle hills inspired tales of mysterious passages and vanishing people and animals. Latvian peasants with lots of time to kill during the long, cold, dark winters spun yarns near the fire about hedgehogs becoming kings and orphans meeting God disguised as a beggar...

Groves of straight birch trees sweep the Baltic sky like gentle brushes. In the spring many Latvians tap into the sap, fermenting it for thirst-quenching, hangover-healing consumption after celebrating the summer solstice in late June. Ancient oak trees of enormous girth rise from the meadows and fields, their massive limbs and fingers providing a perch for birds, shaking down acorns in the fall for wildlife to feed on. Linden trees burst into fragrant bloom in early summer, attracting bees and other pollinators as well as humans in search of fragrant, healthy herbal teas. Latvia's magnificent forests are full of wildlife; its mysterios bogs beckon with shiny cranberries. If our planet Earth's biodiversity has diminished severely in the last half-century, then in Latvia it seems to be flourishing. According to Yale University's 2012 Environmental Performance Index, Latvia was ranked the second cleanest country in the world. Paradoxically, the backwardness of the Soviet economy and agricultural system just may have contributed to Latvia's "cleanness" and its high ecological rating. Most of Latvia's lakes are clean and full of fish.

My son Jurģis photographed at our house in northern Latvia with toys he made from acorns. (Photo by Andris Krieviņš)

What kinds of creatures call Latvia's open spaces and forests home? My people have whimsical dainas and folk songs about moose, elk, deer, bears, wolves, foxes, the gorgeous lynx, wild boar, polecats or fitchews, the hare, ermines, weasels, red squirrels with their cute tufted ears, flying squirrels, hedgehogs, badgers, otters, seals, and other animals, birds, fish, insects, and snakes, including the venomous *odze* (adder). The now extinct auroch or wild ox (*taurs*) and wisent or European bison (*sūbris*, *sumbrs*) once roamed across Latvia. Each summer storks from Africa visit Latvia to build their nests on chimneys and telephone poles; their clattering can be heard from far away. People in Latvia are close to nature, because they spend a lot of time outdoors sowing, planting, and harvesting. In the early 1990s wolves attacked and ate our beloved dog, Duksis... Latvia was a bit wild back then and still is.

Latvia is also a former battleground where men of various armies fought and died in many wars. The sounds of the skylark, cuckoo, corncrake, owl, and choruses of insects sang fleeting eulogies. Today it is hard to imagine that Latvia could sustain so much bloodshed, destruction, and human displacement in the conflicts of the previous century. Its quiet forests remind me of the quiet and peace of great cathedrals, and my generation has no personal recollection of these conflicts. Yet war has a way of rippling into the future. We are part of its aftermath. In the 1990s, when I first visited Kurzeme, I was enraptured by its beauty and sobered by thoughts of the war, the streams of refugees, and the tragedy of Latvia in the 20th century.

Ärmelband "Kurland," 1945. ("Army Group Courland Cuff Title.") Source: Wikimedia Commons. https://commons.wikimedia.org/wiki /File:%C3%84rmelband_Kurland.jpg (© Public Domain)

Latvia's highest mountain, Gaiziņš, which rises a mere 312 meters above sea level in the central part of Vidzeme, is more like a hill. The first time I climbed up its slope in the summer, I giggled. This was it? Our famous Gaiziņš "mountain"? However, the view from the top was breathtaking. Latvia's countryside provides no points of dramatic beauty like the Swiss Alps or New Hampshire's White Mountains. Its beauty is soft, a verdant velvet of rolling hills, forests, meadowlands, fields of ripening grain, and blue lakes that reflect a bright blue northern sky. Dusty roads cut through the scenic landscape dotted with old wooden buildings.

Lovely lakes, some quite deep like Dridzis in Latgale (65.1 meters), and smaller waterways add sparkle to the green landscape. Two large rivers wind through Latvia: the Daugava ("river full of souls"), emerging from the east in Russia and Belarus and flowing into the Gulf of Rīga near the Latvian capital; and the Gauja, which unfurls in the central part of the region of Vidzeme, loops northwards and then snakes south, depositing its waters into the gulf as well. Living in Rīga, the Daugava became a part of my life; I walked across it many times, always admiring the reflection of Rīga's centuries-old skyline. The only other city to occupy such a meaningful place in my identity is New York.

Latvia continues to change. with each generation encountering a new set of problems and challenges. My family's history reflects that of its country. My grandparents were born at the turn of the 20th century, when Latvia was still part of Tsarist Russia. They grew up against a backdrop of dramatic historical events and completed their higher education in the newly independent Republic of Latvia. As communist Russia underwent tumultuous and bloody changes that transformed it into an even more dangerous, unpredictable neighbor, my grandparents

started careers and families in the exciting years of free and independent Latvia. That brief 20-year period of independence was marked by the rapid dismantling of an old and unjust political system based on centuries of Baltic German minority rule, the redistribution of land, the rebuilding of Latvia's industry, which had been destroyed by World War I, and the steady growth of wealth, stability, and international recognition. But Latvia's independence, bought with blood, would be short-lived.

Four generations in Olaine, Latvia in 1984: on the wall a portrait of my great-great-grandfather Jānis Rumpēters (1831–1915); my paternal grandmother Emma (born Lejiņa) Rumpētere; my son Krišjānis and I. (Photo by Andris Krieviņš)

The Latvian economy has changed over time. Agriculture continues to play a big part in the life of Latvians, and farming seems to be second nature to them. As elsewhere, the Industrial Revolution would bring enormous changes, as new industries and factories attracted laborers from the countryside to the city. Then World War I razed much of Latvia's industry, mostly concentrated in Rīga, but there was an incredible resurgence and a rebuilding effort in the brief years of independence between the two wars. Forestry remains a precious resource and export for Latvia. After the collapse of the Soviet Union, most Soviet era industrial plants, including those based on Latvia's pre-war industry (such as VEF—*Valsts Elektrotechniskā fabrika*), were privatized, split up, and sold off, with the loss of thousands of manufacturing jobs. Today Latvia's farmers struggle to compete within the European Union's vast agricultural market, proving that each era brings a new set of challenges for my people to deal with.

Latvia has been a democratic parliamentary republic since 1991 and joined the European Union in 2004. Like many countries that once fell under the Soviet sphere of influence, it has deep-rooted problems, such as corruption, financial crime, a lagging economy, weak governmental oversight, and regional disparity.

There are wonderful positives about Latvia: its status as the 2nd cleanest country in the world; its status as the most beautiful country in the world (according to the *Daily Mail* of the United Kingdom, May 14, 2012, and other sources); the success of its cultural endeavors, including world class choirs (Kamēr, Balsis, The State Academic Choir Latvija) and opera singers of international fame (Elīna Garanča, Maija Kovaļevska, Kristīne Opolais, and others); its brilliant conductors (Mariss Jansons, Andris Nelsons), etc. Famous violinist Gidon Kremer grew up and went to music school in Rīga. Ballet legend Mikhail Baryshnikov was born and raised in Rīga. Latvia's artists regularly participate in the world's biennales. The music of Pēteris Vasks (b. 1946), Ēriks Ešenvalds (b. 1977), and other Latvian composers can be heard on American classical radio stations. Vasks' wife Dzintra Geka has made a name for herself promulgating via film and books the tragic stories of the children of Latvia deported to Siberia. In 2014 Rīga was the European Capital of Culture.

"Latvia/Baltic recognition" has improved in the United States in recent years. In 2011–2012 it was in the international financial news for its "successful" "austerity" measures. Over the years Latvia has been mentioned in film and on TV in mostly humorous references to an obscure European country, such as: the "Latvian Orthodox Church" episode on "Seinfeld"; the Latvian sneaker "Teslick" episode on "Family Guy"; etc. Latvia's problems have also propelled it into the

news, such as the collapse of the Maxima department store in Rīga in 2013, which killed more than 50 people. However, when Latvia, Lithuania, and Estonia were annexed by the Soviet Union in 1945, they were largely forgotten by the world.

My son Tālivaldis working on a batch of gingerbread cookies.

A small but resilient nation, it is miraculous that after all that Latvians have been through, we can still come together to sing, dance, and be merry. Wearing our traditional folk costumes, we are proud of our rich cultural heritage. I remain an idealist, even as modern-day Latvia struggles with its post-Soviet woes. Hopefully, things will improve. Recuperating from 50 years of foreign occupation and influence has been very difficult for many Eastern European countries.

I invite you, my reader, to visit my beautiful ancestral country Latvia, as well as its Baltic neighbors, Lithuania and Estonia. Good food and lovely cities, towns, countrysides, and unique monuments to fascinating histories and cultures await you. My sons and other members of my extended family live there, as do many dear friends. Latvia needs people; its schools need children; its cemeteries where our ancestors lie must be taken care of. Those of us who hail from Latvia must ask ourselves this question: who will take care of Latvia, if not us?

VECPIEBALGA
Paulēnkalns   ak

A winter wonderland… My first real "taste" of the beautiful Latvian countryside was in Piebalga, an area historically known for its artisans and writers. (Photo by Andris Krieviņš)

PART ONE:
New Jersey Latvian American Girl and *Trimda*
(Exile)

1962: Seventeen years after the end of World War II. Here I am, a two-year-old Latvian American girl playing in the sand at the Jersey shore. The first language to touch my ears was Latvian. *Jūra* ("sea"), *saule* ("sun"), *smiltis* ("sand")…

Hillside Haven

My grandparents (with the exception of my paternal grandmother) departed from Latvia in 1944 with aching hearts, singing the Latvian national anthem and hoping to return soon. Months in exile turned into years. After the Second World War my parents spent their teen to early adulthood years in DP ("displaced persons") camps in defeated Germany before sailing to the United States, which had granted their families political asylum. In the New World my highly educated grandparents worked in various low income jobs and socialized with other Latvian refugees.

My parents, Baiba Bičole (b. 1931 in Rīga, Latvia) and Ilmārs Rumpēters (b. 1929 in Daugavpils, Latvia), were married in 1953 in Baltimore, Maryland. America felt strange and even alien to them at first, and they clung to each other for comfort and companionship. When my father was released from military service in San Antonio, Texas in 1954, they settled down in New Jersey near my grandparents. My older brother Arvils was born in 1955, followed by me in 1960, and my younger brother Artis in 1963. Thanks to the GI Bill, my father graduated from the Newark School of Fine Art and Industrial Design and went on to work for many years for a leading packaging design company on Fifth Avenue in New York City. My mother gave up college to take care of us and expressed herself through poetry.

A photograph from November 10, 1944 of Latvian refugees on a fishing boat called Centība ("Endeavor") headed from Latvia to Sweden. Note the Latvian flag at the front of the boat and the woman in the shawl in the foreground. This shawl and this photograph are now part of the permanent collection of the Museum of the Occupation of Latvia 1940–1991.

I was born in East Orange, New Jersey in 1960, where my parents rented an apartment on Walnut Street. Later they moved into a rental property on Park Avenue (*Parkavēnija* in their tongue), which they shared with Mimmī and Tuks, my maternal grandparents, and Kārļonkuls (Uncle Kārlis), a relation on my father's side of the family. What I remember most about the Park Avenue house (perhaps referred to by the neighbors as "the place with all those foreigners") were the brilliant red climbing roses and dinnertime, when we all sat down together to eat.

I have early memories of Walnut Street and Park Avenue and their proximity to the church that Latvians rented in East Orange. In 1966 my parents bought a house in nearby Glen Ridge with a 10% down payment from money that my father had earned illustrating a Latvian "ABC" book commissioned by the American Latvian Association, an organization founded by Latvians in exile. In addition, his military service in the US Army entitled him to a lower mortgage. My parents were delighted to finally have a place of their own. East Orange, just south of Glen Ridge, would rapidly change in subsequent years, becoming a predominantly African-American community. American society was in a continuous state of flux, with immigrants climbing up the ladder of success.

My father painted our front door a bright crimson red, and we settled in. My brothers and I each had our own bedroom. My older brother later discovered some old documents hidden beneath the floor of our attic while snooping around: apparently our house was built around 1910 by a ship's captain. It was a wonderful house with lots of woodwork and simple charm. A round porthole window in our mudroom attested to the original owner's maritime adventures.

Glen Ridge is an affluent town wedged like a thin sliver between blue-collar Bloomfield and Montclair, a culturally diverse community with a lovely art museum, a university, and a wooded crest from which to gaze upon the skyline of Manhattan. Glen Ridge is famous for its antique gas lanterns, a good school system, and an excellent commute to New York City. It has its own Frank Lloyd Wright house, the Stuart Richardson house, a ten minute walk from where we lived. Our home, one of many Glen Ridge homes built in the early 20th century, was set on a shady, maple-lined street. Hillside Avenue runs beneath the Erie Lackawanna Railway and intersects Bloomfield Avenue, a busy street and bus route that connects depressed Newark with pretty suburban towns to the west, like Verona and Caldwell.

Life in white and predominantly white collar Glen Ridge provided my brothers and me with a large yard in which to play, exercise, and grow. There were trees and garage rooftops for climbing and feeling free. In his late teens, my older brother did crazy flips and stunts on the metal grape trellis. We played a lot of badmington in our yard. My father started a tomato and cucumber garden with the help of "the Senator" (my paternal grandfather). My parents planted a hedge of pink roses. Purple hyacinths, blue irises, and orange daylilies are some of the flowers I remember from the garden. Every summer my mother sowed zinnias for color. A lilac Rose of Sharon grew at the end of the garden path. Two dogwoods, pink and white, shaded our front veranda. In the summers there were cookouts with my parents' Latvian friends. On hot summer nights we sat on our back porch looking at flickering mosquito candles and fireflies. My older brother played the guitar, while the Cicadas rattled their maracas in unison. You could always hear the Garden State Parkway humming in the distance, a couple of miles away. The old, gray house was simple, modest, and cosy.

There was an attic beneath the roof. A brown bearskin coat that my Opaps had once worn in Latvia hung on the wall at the foot of the attic staircase. His old *smokings* ("tuxedo") from the fancy parties in Latvia before the war and my mother's dresses were packed into a wardrobe that smelled of mothballs. Our guests slept in the attic bedroom with its wonderful view of the evergreen trees. In my teens I went up to that room to smoke, opening the window to air out the evidence. Later my mother slept there, when my parents' marriage was disintegrating.

Our immediate neighbors were Americans of German and Italian descent, including a family allegedly linked to the Italian Mafia. The Schultes were a German-Italian union with four children. Mr. Schulte had all sorts of projects going on at home. At one time he kept geese in his garage. On occasion we raided his strawberry patch, so temptingly close. His wife, a teacher, had a very loud voice that could be heard calling the children home. In our household my mother used a small bell for that purpose.

Our other lively, loud Italian neighbors, Joe and Angie, had three daughters and a little white poodle named Shelly. The Schneiders next to us were a quiet, friendly couple who enjoyed the company of our wandering black tomcat Ūsiņš and fed our kitties when we were away. Then there was the spooky, white Victorian house on the corner occupied at different times by a Jewish family, the Braffmans, a bunch of hippies with a dog named Freak, and a large Venezuelan family. I remember Freak humping Shelly and getting stuck to her; what a scandal that was! Another time my mother caught one of the Venezuelan boys making out with Joe and Angie's youngest daughter in a tent in our yard. Lucky that grumpy ol' Joe didn't surprise them. The Venezuelans' youngest son Claude tried to kiss me under our porch. Sharon the ballet dancer lived across the street from us; she had once partnered with Rudolf Nureyev in Canada and had a big black and white photograph to prove it. The friendly, tidy Luises had a beautiful flower garden; when their son died, they moved away. There were neighbors of Irish, Scottish, and Jewish descent. Many people commuted to New York for work. Glen Ridge was a safe and pretty place to live.

When we were old enough, my mother took us into New York City. We rode the comfortable DeCamp bus line across the New Jersey Meadowlands and through the Lincoln Tunnel into Midtown Manhattan. The city's looming skyscrapers, loud traffic, and pungent smells—exhaust fumes, subway odors, roasting chestnuts, hotdogs, pretzels, and even human urine—always filled me with a strange excitement.

I still remember 42nd Street in its sleazy era, with porn shops, peep shows, titty clubs, and other X-rated venues and "dens of sin." My mother avoided it by shepherding us down other streets. From the busy Port Authority we traipsed around Manhattan, visiting the Museum of Natural History, the Museum of Modern Art, the Metropolitan, the Guggenheim, or going to concerts. Of course, when we were little, this was hard on us; the walking and looking at stuffy antiquities and modern art was exhausting. The Good Humor ice cream trucks and hot dog vendors were my mother's "carrot" to entice us in and out of these extraordinary repositories of history, art, and culture.

Glen Ridge is set on a gentle incline that rises up from a basin, which includes the swampy Meadowlands, towards a ridge that provides excellent views of the Manhattan skyline. From time to time we would drive up to Eagle Rock Reservation to get a really good view of the "Big Apple." Its jagged skyscraper silhouette was etched upon our developing brains. In the 1970s, when we were driving home from the city, we sometimes saw the World Trade Center's Twin Towers light up from the setting sun as if on fire.

Glen Ridge is named after a shallow glen with a creek called Toney's Brook that traverses the town from Montclair to Bloomfield and beyond. When I was little, the smokestack of an old factory between the creek and the train tracks still coughed up smoke that smelled of rubber. There were very few shops in Glen Ridge. We had one supermarket at the end of our street that changed owners several times. For shopping we walked down Washington Street to downtown Bloomfield, passing the Revolutionary War's Lt. Col. Thomas Cadmus House, site of some visits by President Washington in the late 18th century. Who knows: maybe it was seeing the historical marker by the Cadmus house that eventually got me interested in history and antiques.

I remember Bloomfield center as a safe and nice place for a kid to hang out in the 1970s. A great book shop and lots of mom and pop stores attracted pedestrian shoppers from the neighborhood. "The Last Straw" was a head shop. Its long-haired owners sold all sorts of neat stuff: silver jewelry; African imports; incense; clothes from India; stained glass; etc. I loved the scent of the store, which aroused me. Greeting cards featured depictions of marijuana and couples locked in cosmic orgasms. For a young teen like me "The Last Straw" was a magnet; its vibe was mysterious and alluring. Although I was too young to belong to the hippie era, its music, which continued to dominate the radio airwaves in the early 1970s, left a lasting impression on me: Joan Baez; Jimi Hendrix; Crosby, Stills, Nash, and Young; Jefferson Airplane/Starship; Richie Havens; Joni Mitchell; Janis Joplin; Creedence Clearwater Revival; The Band; etc. The Woodstock era's performers and their lyrics resonated with me, a budding teenager. I perceived them as bards of fun, freedom, change, tolerance, acceptance, peace, and erotic love, a subject I was growing increasingly interested in. There were two movie theaters and several "five-and-dime" stores, including Woolworth's, which I frequented. My childhood friend Barbara and I were apprehended prying candy out of a plastic container; I peed in my pants and immediately learned to respect the law.

The Beatles' movie "The Yellow Submarine"(1968) was a big event for our family, and we went to the movie theater to see it. Peter Max's psychedelic calendar lingered on my wall for several years. We grew up watching Charlie Chaplin, Buster Keaton, Laurel and Hardy, and the Marx Brothers, and humor would become a necessary part of my life. It would sometimes save me from depression.

Glen Ridge property taxes were high, and it is still considered a high-income commuter town. I remember only one black student in our school, Calvin, who lived all the way down at the south end, maybe even on the East Orange side. In other words, we grew up in a racial bubble. There was one Indian girl, Sandy, in our class. In America's multicultural society the Latvians of my grandparents' generation were mostly a conservative bunch, and they insulated themselves from the rest of American society in an attempt to preserve their "Old Country" identity. Acceptance of others required time, as the deep wounds of trauma and loss healed.

I can still remember the beautiful old mansion that was razed to build the new Glen Ridge high school. The first and last time we saw it was when we took our first walk around our new town; the next time I looked, it was gone. Many of Glen Ridge's homes were old, dating back to the turn of the 20th century, and well maintained, with green lawns and mature trees. Ridgewood Avenue was a parade of large, elegant dwellings with enormous yards owned by doctors, lawyers, and company executives.

Apparently Tom Cruise went to Glen Ridge High, though I never met him. Astronaut Buzz Aldrin was another Glen Ridge notable. Members of the Parker Pen family apparently lived there (a Parker girl and I graduated together). One of my favorite contemporary artists, Cindy Sherman (b. 1954), was born in Glen Ridge. *Sports Illustrated* writer Tom Verducci and I must have been in the same class. In terms of the social spectrum, we were somewhere in the middle and definitely not Glen Ridge Country Club material because of our last name and origin. As I was pedaling around the school playground on my tricycle one day, two boys asked me what my name was. When I answered "Rita Rumpeters," they burst into laughter. One of them asked me, "Do you eat rumps?" I pedaled away on my three-wheeler as fast as I could, confused and hurt by their laughter... Luckily, that was the first and last taunt I endured over our unusual surname.

When I was little, my father woke up early to take the bus into New York City. Later when I was a teenager, he began driving to a park-and-ride not far from the Lincoln Tunnel, thereby becoming a willing participant in the madness of New Jersey's morning hour rush. I remember commuting with him to my summer job in the city in 1978 and listening to his amusing curses aimed at other drivers. He drove like a maniac along the shoulder of the road, speeding by the stalled cars and never once getting caught.

On the weekends Tētis ("Daddy") worked on his paintings and pursued other artistic and creative endeavors, including photography and music. He created many of the superb cover designs for *Jaunā Gaita*, a quarterly devoted to Latvian culture and history. My mother, whose Latvian hips my grandfather "the Senator" judged to be perfect for childbearing, stayed home to take care of us and wrote poetry in the basement, leaning against the washing machine and smoking cigarettes. Her books were highly acclaimed by her peers—Latvian literati.

My mother was associated with a storied group of Latvian writers named after New York's Hell's Kitchen (*Elles ķēķis*), the neighborhood where beloved Latvian poet Linards Tauns (1922–1963) lived, and where they often congregated in his apartment or at the local taverns. These former refugees and fledgling Americans were brought together by their common language, identity, and love of poetry, art, music, and the vibe of New York City. They were a wonderful, unique group of Latvians who produced a rich legacy of art and literature.

My father's large, colorful paintings decorated the walls of our house, and the large, clunky stereo in the living room was always blasting some kind of music: opera; Woody Guthrie; the Kingston Trio; the Beatles; Bob Dylan; Joan Baez; Tom Paxton; Peter, Paul, and Mary; the Band; Simon and Garfunkel; et al. Later my brothers and I rocked the house with Led Zeppelin, Pink Floyd, the Allman Brothers, Kraftwerk, Jean Michel Jarre's "Oxygene," the Talking Heads, etc. My mother listened to New York's classical music station WQXR. In my late teens we tuned into WFMU, a public radio station at nearby Upsala College, to listen to the fantastic world music programming of "The Immigrant" (DJ Dan Behrman). We became friends with Dan and even visited him once in the studio to introduce Latvian music to his listeners.

Left: My parents, Baiba and Ilmārs Rumpēters in the center, with their friends, writers Astrīde and Ivar Ivask and painter Sigurds Vīdzirkste, in New York sometime in the late 1960s. Family photo.

Our shelves sagged with books about art and history, fiction, non-fiction, and poetry in English and Latvian. Needless to say, my brothers and I read a lot. In winter the old radiators hissed, rattled, and smelled delightfully of steam. Years of home cooking, mothballs in the coat closet, the industrial grade carpet where our feet walked and sometimes danced, cats and socks, traces of my mother's Shalimar perfume, sauerkraut at Christmas and hard-boiled eggs at Easter, rubber cement and magic markers and the scent from my dad's painting station in the basement: this was the potpourri of aromas that defined our house on Hillside Avenue. The old wooden floors creaked delightfully, and the curving front and back staircases added to the house's charm. It was full of slanting light and creative spirit. Latvian was the language of the house, and we were exposed to it from infancy through our parents, our extended family, Latvian school, books, and music. It was a wonderful home to grow up in.

My childhood was mostly uneventful, happy, and safe. My parents didn't fight, and my brothers and I got on fairly well. Arvils was a pack rat who collected books and military paraphernalia, including Nazi stuff. He even went to high school one year in a Nazi uniform for Halloween, when this sort of thing wasn't yet politically incorrect. Later he sold his collection for a good amount of cash and bought his first car. Nazi paraphernalia was of particular interest to military collectors. Arvils was a talented, self-taught guitarist who struggled with his Latvian identity on and off for years. My younger brother Artis was an athletic bookworm. As siblings we shared a love of "Tintin the Detective" by the Belgian writer and illustrator Hergé and good humor. I liked to draw and spent a lot of time hunched over a piece of paper lost in a fantasy world of horses and princesses. I was definitely influenced by my artistic father, and my mother in turn nurtured my interest in writing.

My maternal grandparents, Tuks and Mimmī, lived in nearby Montclair. My paternal grandfather Augusts Rumpēters, whom we called Opaps, called frequently and sometimes walked over from Bloomfield to visit. When he stayed overnight and slept on the couch, he put his false teeth in a glass of water, thus providing my brothers and me with an endless source of amusement. He brought us smoked whitefish, fruit slice marmalades, and Nestlé's Crunch bars.

I have wonderful memories of Opaps' storytelling: his imaginative tales were always about the ancient past and a place with deep, dark forests, people traveling on foot or by horse or carriage, lonely wayside taverns where they stayed, and the scary creatures they encountered, including a disembodied, floating hand. Opaps, the highly respected Latvian justice, apparently had a creative side to him. Opaps was always composed, dignified, and neatly dressed in a button-down shirt and neatly creased trousers, as befits a judge. But sometimes he crumpled a napkin and threw it at me at the dinner table, when I wasn't expecting it. The presence of my grandparents in my childhood taught me the value of the extended family.

My grandfather Jānis Bičolis' unique handwriting. Here he writes about the origins of the word "Lithuanian," February 2, 1935.

For many years Tuks and Mimmī rented the second floor of a large, old house in Upper Montclair owned by a Latvian family. Mimmī was not permitted to make stewed sauerkraut, a Latvian favorite, on account of the smell. But sometimes she did anyway in spite of the landlady's orders. Mimmī was very hospitable: when we came to visit, she would start bustling about the kitchen, taking food out of the refrigerator, even when we protested that we were not hungry. She often baked Latvian *pīrāgi*, caraway buns, and Latvian-style apple and Farmer's Cheese *plātsmaize* "pan-bread." My grandmother was a humble, self-effacing person, completely devoted to Tuks and his well-being and always in touch with us, her grandchildren, with kind and loving words. A graduate of the University of Latvia, she worked well into retirement as a cleaning lady at the Montclair Inn, supplementing my grandparents' meager pensions with a bit of cash. She, too, had once written poetry, as had Tuks, and their poems are poignant reminders of their youth and hopes and dreams. I loved Tuks' study, where the walls were lined with thousands of books and all sorts of knickknacks. Tuks and Mimi possessed so little in terms of wealth and yet owned so much: rich memories; knowledge, experience, wisdom, and love for their family and fatherland.

"Mr. Cool" ("the Senator") and "Mr. Hot" (my maternal grandfather the philologist) often argued about Latvian politics and history at our family get-togethers. It was quite amusing to see my grandfathers debating: the one calm and collected, the other turning red in the face and shaking from anger: two vastly different temperaments from the same country.

We children sometimes gently mocked our family members from the Old Country: we ridiculed their English pronunciation behind their backs, snickering and repeating it. "Vitch vey doo vee go, norse or souse?" ("Which way do we go, north or south?") Opaps' embarrassing use of the Latvian words *šitas*, pronounced *shitass* ("this here"), *šite* ("here"), *šito* ("this one") in stores and public places, with the emphasis on the first syllable *šit* or "shit-", made us cringe. Or the beloved *faktiski* ("in fact"): it made us squirm. My grandparents lost just about everything when they left Latvia, yet they were able to give so much of themselves to the Latvian exile community and us. With their heavy Latvian accents, they were exceptional people in my eyes, people of the book and of words, of culture, and history. They were my living connections to the Old Country that I would hear so much about: Latvia, a place far from New Jersey and its highways, malls, and congestion.

A vision of Latvia began to form in my mind at a very early age. I remember lying in bed as a child and listening to my mother read Latvian folk tales to me. It was like being teleported into another realm, another era, a place outside of time. My favorite was a funny story about the doomed friendship between a straw, a lump of coal, and a bean. I heard many whimsical yarns about animals and magical beings and places. Many of these folk tales had a didactic meaning. Printed in Soviet Latvia, this book featured superb illustrations by an artist named Pāvils Šenhofs. Latvia as I imagined it and Latvia as it was would later merge, when I was living there.

In my teens, slouching on the living room chair that swiveled back and forth, I began to read and enjoy Latvian books. I devoured works by the great Latvian classics Rūdolfs Blaumanis, Jānis Akurāters, Anna Brigadere, Ēriks Ādamsons, Jānis Jaunsudrabiņš, Jānis Ezeriņš, and other writers of the pre-war era. Reading these works expanded my Latvian vocabulary and deepended my sense of the place I knew I belonged to but had never seen.

Only now as a parent I can understand the reasons for my mother's rigid language rules and TV curfews. She could not stand American TV, hated commercial TV and radio stations, and controlled our TV time carefully. She pored through the weekly *New York Times* TV guide circling programs and movies that she approved of. Our television was in the basement, and we often snuck down there to watch TV without her permission.

Curled up in beat-up garden chairs, I watched a lot of World War II documentaries, thanks to my father's interest in the subject. The grainy black and white footage of German Luftwaffe planes zipping through the sky blasting their Allied targets; bombs crashing to earth and exploding in fiery blooms; tanks rolling over the scorched earth: these images of my parents' war became mine. I was drawn to my father's book *The Second World War* by Winston S. Churchill (Time Incorporated, 1959) with its illustrations of bloody soldiers, corpses, gore, and destruction.

No wonder my older brother became interested in military paraphernalia. Without realizing it, my parents passed their experience and legacy of World War II on to us. It was an inheritance of loss that we, too, had to process as young Americans of Latvian descent. We were attracted to the subject of the war.

In 1980 we huddled together in the basement to watch the Winter Olympics in Lake Placid. One of my greatest memories is seeing the underdog American men's hockey team beat the heavily favored Soviets in the game for the gold medal. How we screamed and jumped with joy when it was over, and Coach Herb Brooks and his players were crowned champions, stunning the Soviets into silence! We defeated those "Russian bastards"! I bet every single Baltic American was cheering like us. The young American boys who played their hearts out against the formidable Soviet team that included the famous Latvian player Helmuts Balderis were our heroes and true champions. We felt that the American team had righted some terrible wrong. My brother Arvils and his Latvian buddies had gone up to Lake Placid to protest Latvian athletes being forced to compete under the Soviet flag. It was a hard time for Latvians.

For many years our Hillside Avenue home was a gathering place for our extended family and Latvian friends. Christmas was the most memorable occasion, with great food, musical entertainment and games, and impromptu skits. It was mandatory for us children to recite poetry in order to receive our presents. Forty years later, I can still remember the words to some of these poems: *Balts sniedziņš snieg uz skujiņām / Un maigi dziedot pulkstens skan. / Mirdz šur tur ciemos ugunis / Un sirds tā laimīgi pukst man...* ("White snow falls on fir needles, / And the clock gently sings. / The lights come on in village homes,/ And my heart happily rings." (Jānis Poruks, 1871–1911)

Kārļonkuls (Uncle Kārlis), a cousin of my paternal grandmother Omamma, inevitably fell asleep after our three-course dinner. He lived on the third floor above my grandparents in Montclair. Kārlis Velme was born in 1891 in Dikļi Parish, where his father worked as a scribe. His mother, born Kristīna Cālītis, died while traveling back to Latvia from Ukraine, presumably after World War I. Kārļonkuls studied in Moscow. He was mobilized into the Russian Army during World War I and sent to Ukraine. He returned to Latvia in 1922 and began studying law at the University of Latvia. He worked as a judge in Daugavpils, Dagda, Subāte, and Rīga. In 1938 he became a judge at the Rīga Regional Court. In 1944 Kārļonkuls joined the mass of refugees bound for Germany. He came to America in 1949. He was a kind old soul, our "Humpty Dumpty" who never said much but who thrilled us at Christmas by giving each of us kids a real check, which made me feel grownup. We missed the golden opportunity to ask him about his youth. If Kārļonkuls' and my grandparents' memories could have been replayed like a video recording, they would have been great movies to watch. I remember Kārļonkuls sitting at our dining room table recounting how he and the last Tsar of Russia, Nicholas II, briefly locked eyes during the Tsar's visit to Rīga in 1910. This unexpected revelation, insignificant in the grand scheme of things, nevertheless startled me, for I had already read Robert Massie's riveting portrait of the doomed last tsar and his family, *Nicholas and Alexandra* (1967). My grandparents and Kārļonkuls were a bridge to the past. Years later the Internet provided me with the opportunity to view several historic photographs of the last Russian Tsar and his family strolling about Rīga. Kārļonkuls died in Montclair at the age of 94.

Opaps died at our home on Hillside Avenue on December 17, 1978, as we were celebrating my brother's 15th birthday. I stayed all night on our living room couch listening to Luciano Pavarotti's "O Holy Night," crying and staring at the winking lights of the Christmas tree. Every Christmas Eve since I could remember he had read the Gospel of Luke about the birth of Jesus (Luke 2: 1–20), emphasizing the words *"Gods Dievam augstībā, un miers virs zemes, un cilvēkiem labs prāts."* ("Glory to God in the highest heaven, and on earth peace to those on whom his favor rests.") My paternal grandfather was deeply religious and actively involved in the Latvian Lutheran Church in North America. My childhood was over, as death intruded in the shape of an old man's body slumped over in a chair. Born in Latvia at the end of the 19th century, Opaps and Kārļonkuls were witnesses to the tumultuous events that shaped the fates of my countrymen in the 20th century.

Some years later, standing on a hill and gazing across the undulating hills and valleys of central Vidzeme in Latvia, I felt the landscape keenly: it had been passed down to me through my genes, the folk tales read to me in my childhood, my grandparents' stories, and the Latvian literature that I had consumed in my youth. Under a sky filled with fluffy, quintessentially Latvian clouds a prickly hedgehog—just maybe a prince in the making—was scurrying across the road...

Chapter source:

(1) * Andersons, Edgars, Ed. "Kārlis Velme." *Latviju Enciklopēdija 1962–1982.* Rockville, Maryland: Amerikas Latviešu apvienības Latviešu Institūts, 2006. P. 319.

Programmed for Latvia

A caricature of a pupil attending Latvian school by Latvian actor Reinis Birzgalis (1907–1990) from his book *Letiņš trimdā* ("Latvian in Exile"). (New York: Grāmatu Draugs, 1977.) Illustration courtesy of Rasma Vītola.

Our parents spoke only Latvian to us at home, laying it down as the law. *"Runājiet latviski!"* ("Speak Latvian!") *"Šajā mājā runā tikai latviski!"* ("In this house we speak only Latvian!") For years this mantra was repeated, while our ears were glued to the radio spewing American and British pop tunes and our eyes to the television set, which was brainwashing us with commercials about squeezable toilet paper, a man named Mr. Clean, and "Snap, Crackle, and Pop" cereal. We were enrolled in a Latvian School in Newark, which held classes on Saturdays. From an early age our weekends appeared ruined; these were innumerable days of boredom and suffering, which managed to set us apart from our American peers early on, creating a sometimes uncomfortable schism in our youthful identities.

My brothers and I each reacted to this cultural indoctrination differently. Unknowingly, I absorbed it deeply, and it has manifested itself in my priorities and choices, including moving to Latvia. At one time my older brother rebelled: he was turned off by Latvian society's self-absorption and cliquishness. He succeeded in reconnecting with his Latvian side at the Latvian "2x2" camps and traveled to the International Latvian Youth Congress in Floreffe, Belgium in 1975. Much later in life he visited Latvia, where he felt like a reborn Latvian, blown away by the amount of history around him. My younger brother's best friends were all Latvian, and he remained strongly connected to Latvian American society through his positive experience at Latvian summer high school in Pennsylvania, his marriage to a Latvian American, and his children's school and camp. He embraced the life that the United States offered him. We were exposed to Latvian identity in the same way, yet we each chose a different route in life.

My parents and the vanguard of Latvian American society expected us to shoulder our legacy and carry it forward into the future, when the sun would rise over Latvia once more, figuratively speaking. They firmly believed this would happen, even as the decades of Soviet occupation wore on. Unfortunately, many of my peers of Latvian descent vanished into the American melting pot.

Our Latvian primary school, which moved from Newark to East Orange, provided a remarkably solid base for awareness of Latvia's history and culture. While American kids threw baseballs and Frisbees and rode their bikes, we were glued to the hard wooden seats of our classroom's chairs, where we practiced declensions and vocabulary, listened to lectures about Latvian history, wrote *domraksti* (essays) and endless *diktāti* (dictations), and took lots of tests. Latvian school improved my handwriting.

For someone like me, afraid of math and numbers, the memorization of important dates was torture. We were required to know the names of famous figures in Latvian history and when they lived, like Georgius Mancelius (1593–1654), Christoph Fürecker (1615–1685), Johann Ernst Glück (1652–1705), "Blind" Indriķis (1783–1828), Juris Neikens (1826–1868), Atis Kronvalds (1837–1875), Krišjānis Barons (1835–1923), etc. All of this, as well as poems and fiction and the rules of Latvian grammar, was stuffed into our pliable minds. Growing up Latvian was a lot of work and took up time that could otherwise have been devoted to leisure and fun activities.

Our Latvian history lessons ended abruptly with the year 1945. We were left with the impression that in 1945 Latvia was wiped off the map. All those cities, towns, ports, rivers, lakes, bogs, people, and bacon exports that we had to memorize seemed to vanish into nothingness. (Latvia's lucrative bacon exports really did vanish under the communists.) We were left with many questions. As I grew older, I found out about family members living in Latvia. My Omamma was still there, receiving parcels of leopard and tiger skin pattern fabrics from Opaps to help her get by. Perhaps this abrupt end to Latvian history was unintentional, or there wasn't enough time, or there simply wasn't enough information to tell us what life in Soviet-occupied Latvia was like. In fact, we knew very little about the "forgotten" or "hidden" war—"the war *after* the war"—in Latvia, Lithuania, and Estonia. This was the war of the "forest brothers"—our national partisans who valiantly resisted the Soviets by hiding in Latvia's deep forests. Outnumbered, they would eventually be defeated, flushed out, and shot or deported. Another wave of deportations in 1949 would send tens of thousands of Latvians to Siberia. Decades of arrests and imprisonment in our part of the world continued after World War II. This part of Latvian history remained veiled to us for many years because of Soviet repression, secrecy, censorship, and hindered contacts.

Our school's icy atmosphere and emphasis on memorization instilled us with fear and anxiety. Yet I still recall some stanzas from 40 years ago, such as Edvarts Virza's (1883–1940) poem *"Karogs"* ("The Flag")… *"Pūšat taures, skanat, zvani, saule plašu gaismu lej! / Karogs sarkanbaltisarkans vējos atraisījies skrej. / Skrej pa laukiem, skrej pa klajiem, sauc arvienu dzirdamāk, / Lai no mājām, lai no namiem, lai no kapiem ārā nāk."* ("Blow the trumpets, sound the bells, the sun is spreading light around! / A red-white-red flag races unfurled in the winds. / 'Cross fields and meadows it races, summoning ever louder / For all to emerge from houses, buildings, graves.") Virza's patriotic poetry was banned for the most part of the Soviet era. (Tr. RL)

Our Latvian school repertoire included dark, depressing songs about oppression, such as *"Ej, saulīte, drīz pie Dieva"* ("Hurry, Sun, to God") about a black snake grinding flour on a stone. The song was about slavery under our former masters, the Baltic Germans: "A black snake ground flour / On a rock in the middle of the sea / To be eaten by those masters / Who made us work at night." We also sang songs about abused orphans and war.

Many of the girls stayed after school to practice rhythmic gymnastics under our principal's scrutiny, stretching and bopping around with hula hoops and plastic balls. Luckily, my parents didn't sign me up. I was always very happy to scramble into the car and go home as soon as we were dismissed. One Saturday in my last year in school, as our principal was describing some dreary part of Latvian World War II history to us, I saw tears well up in her eyes. She struggled for composure. It was that fleeting moment, the crack in her steely armor, that made me realize she was human, that she had suffered, and that she had painful memories. That flash of emotion changed my perception of my teachers; I forgave them their "meanness," realizing that I owed them gratitude for their passionate, selfless devotion to the school and our education.

We had pored over the map of Latvia—that clog-shaped puzzle piece in Europe's northeastern corner—year after year, as our shoe sizes grew bigger. To us, Latvia seemed as remote as the Moon. Several times we listened to the story about Ivan the Terrible and the massacres in Vidzeme during the Livonian War in the 16th century.

> "Along the road from Rīga to Tartu not a rooster crows, not a dog barks." The chronicler (Matsey) Strykovsky described it with these words: "I myself have seen Latvians burying their dead accompanied by the blowing of horns, as they sing, 'Go, unfortunate one, from the world of misery into eternal happiness, where you will no longer suffer at the hand of the pompous German, the vicious Lithuanian, and the Muscovite.' An English traveler (…) paints a descriptive image of this time: "Alas, this terrible, inhumane massacre, drowning, and burning! Women and girls are caught, stripped in the freezing cold, and then in threes and fours tied to horses' tails and dragged alive or dead along roads and streets. Everywhere lie corpses, old people, children—some wealthy, dressed in velvet and silk, their jewels, gold, and pearls hidden. These people—the most beautiful in the world on account of their origin and climate—now lie cold and frozen. Many have been sent to Russia. It is impossible to calculate the wealth in money, goods, and possessions that are being sent out of the cities and countryside and from 600 plundered and sacked churches." (Dr. N. Vīksniņš. *Latvijas vēsture jaunā gaismā*. Oak Park, Illinois: Krolla Kultūras biroja izdevums/Draugas Publishers, 1968, pp. 112–113. Tr. RL)

We took our final exams, graduated, and grew up. Zinta married our Latvian camp's tennis coach and moved to Canada. Maijroze moved to California and back again. Marty turned into a serious man who drove a BMW and a shiny black Porsche, owned a nice house with a pool in northern Jersey, had two kids, and supported our Latvian school and camp. Many of my peers did not take to Latvian indoctrination well. The school felt like prison. Also, conservative Latvian society scared some people away. It is not easy to live in two parallel cultures. To get rid of the discomfort, many chose to block out one of two competing identities. Unfortunately, in many cases the Latvian identity was sacrificed.

Catskill Summers

Latvian Camp Nometne, 1974: your truly winning a race. Family photo.

When I was little, we spent our family summer vacations at the Jersey shore. I can still remember the feel of the hot sand grasping my little feet and dragging me down, the scent of the ocean's salty spray, and tar baking in the hot sun. When we got older, my parents packed us off to Latvian "Nometne" ("camp") in the beautiful Catskill Mountains. The trip was a nightmare for me, as I inevitably ended up vomiting in the back of the car or by the side of the road. With the introduction of Coca Cola and Dramamine into my life, these awful bouts of nausea ceased. Nometne filled me with excitement, anxiety, and even dread: would I have friends?

For our parents Latvian camp was a godsend. They could deposit us in a place where speaking Latvian was the rule, and where we would be occupied all day long for two to four weeks at a time. Who wants their kids at home in the suburbs in the summer, bored out of their minds? With Latvian school in the winter and Latvian camp in the summer, they had us "covered." Our parents hoped that camp would deepen our exposure to Latvian values, culture, the Lutheran faith, and lasting friendships. There was the added bonus of a gorgeous natural setting: tall, forested mountains; fields where Latvian kids could run around in the fresh air and sunshine; a lake fed by a mountain stream; and hide-and-seek and treasure hunts in the pristine woods around us. Evening candlelight services by the lake or up in the lovely *debesspļavas* ("Fields of Heaven") nurtured our spirituality.

The camp kitchen run by Latvian moms provided great meals. Sports were interspersed with Bible studies, art, music, song, dance, theater, and great hiking excursions. We began our mornings by raising the American and Latvian flags and singing an uplifting chorale. The sound of our young voices floated up and out into the beautiful valley between the mountains. We gazed at the mysterious lookout tower on Spruce Top, where our neighbors, German Americans, had established an exclusive residential club in the late 19th century. The words of many of these chorales have stayed with me: *"Rīta gaisma mūžīga, / Atspīdums no Dieva vaiga, / Tavu staru spožumā / Izzūd tumsas vara baiga! / Tavu spēku liec mums just, / Naktij zust.* ("Eternal morning sun, / Reflected from God's brow, / In your brilliant rays / Night's terror wanes! / Let us feel your power, / Let night fade." (K. Rosenrot, 17th century. Tr. RL) It was nice to start the day with a song.

While eating a breakfast of oatmeal of a glue-like consistency with cinnamon or the more preferable pancakes with sticky syrup, I would often gaze at Ēvalds Dajevskis' (1914–1990) fantastic painting of an ancient Latvian fortress on the Daugava River. Its dramatic orange sunset hues bathed the ancient scene in suspense and drama. And wasn't it so, that my people's history was full of suspense, drama, and never-ending conflict? Dajevskis' art was archetypal for Latvians, and in it we recognized ourselves.

In the Catskills summers were cooler with none of the awful humidity of New Jersey. These mountains were also popular with New York's Hasidic Jews who fondly called them Borscht Belt or the Jewish Alps. Sometimes we saw them walking along the roads outside of Tannersville. The streams that cut through the camp's territory seemed clean enough to drink from; on the weekends, as we waited for our parents to arrive, we hopped from rock to rock, studying the small pools in search of tiny fish.

Gvīdo, Andris, Ēriks, Pēters, Vidvuds, Andris, Aldis… We giggled, gawked, sighed, and blushed, and hoped to dance with our crushes. We stole glances at them, as we paraded around to Chopin's Polonaise. Our parents hoped that we would marry Latvians. They were uncomfortable with the idea that we might stray outside our Latvian bubble. They came to our *balles* and sat in the corner staring and smiling. It made us uncomfortable and even angry.

Nometne ran like a clock: we were responsible for keeping our cabins in order and clean, and we took turns sweeping and mopping the camp's facilities with PineSol and setting and clearing our tables at meal times. Campers were split into teams that competed against each other in sports and other activities. We chatted in English amongst ourselves but switched to Latvian around the counselors and managers. There were two main camp rules: *"Runājiet latviski!"* ("Speak Latvian!") and *"Akmeņi nelido!"* ("Rocks don't fly!").

Not everyone had sweet memories of Latvian camp. One summer, when my older brother was about 15, he begged our parents to take him home after his friends left camp. Some of the new camp arrivals were reputed to be bullies, and my brother suddenly felt very much alone. Our parents refused. They had signed him up for a month, and he was going to stay, no "ifs, ands, or buts." Shortly after our parents left, my brother famously "escaped" from camp, walking the 3.5 miles to to Tannersville, where he boarded a bus to New York City. He showed up on our block in Glen Ridge in the evening, striding past our house, too afraid to ring at the door. My mother, who had been alerted to the fact by the camp director and my grandfather (who was vacationing on the camp property), recalls standing in the veranda at dusk watching her son walk by, her heart breaking. When it got dark, he came to the door and rang the bell. As mother and son hugged, he said, "I told you I wasn't going to stay at camp!" The pain and guilt of this incident stayed with my mother for years: she blamed herself for inflexibility and insensitivity. "We were so obsessed with this Latvian thing!" she lamented more than 40 years later.

Latvian *Bohēma*

Raised in the countryside, in the city I fell in love with its lights,
Though the signs, languages, and sounds masked fright.
For example, the letters "Capri" in the nighttime sky—
Could easily devour it
With their loudness
And split that sky, which was one, into two.
Whether these letters advertised
Pigeon delicacies or nail polish,
I drew from their lights
As if from wells with a rustic clay pitcher.
These lights, these sounds offer me a new gospel,
But closing my eyes I see: the light falling from milky apples,
And in my blood pigeons
Like grandmother's tea kettle coo.

(From Linards Tauns' poem *"Plīvošana ar pilsētu"* ["Streaming with the City"] from his book *Mūžīgais mākonis* ["Endless Cloud"], 1958. Tr. RL)

As the children and grandchildren of exiles, we grew up hearing our mother tongue at home and English everywhere else. In addition to the thorough education provided by Saturday Latvian school and summers at Latvian camp, we were woven into the Latvian social fabric through my parents' circle of friends—Latvian writers and artists in the New York area. My family photographs have immortalized this ever shrinking circle. Poet Gunars "Gonka" Saliņš and his wife Jautrīte; poet and cultural activist Rita Gāle and her ever-present, always smiling husband Ansis Uibo; suave gold-and-silver-attired poet and Manhattanite with her large, shaded, chic eyeglasses, Aina Kraujiete, and her banker husband Viktors Neimanis; artist Daina Dagnija with her colorful canvases, head scarves, and penciled eyebrows, and her partner later in life, abstract painter Sigurds Vīdzirkste; poet and painter Voldemārs Avens and his wife Irēne, an art historian who worked for many years in the library of the Frick Collection on Fifth Avenue; translator and Shakespearean Bitīte Vinklere and her future spouse, Uldis Bluķis, active in BATUN (Baltic Association to the United Nations); painter and textile artist Ausma Matcate; handsome, bushy-eyebrowed composer Arnolds Šturms and his elegant, bubbly wife, art critic Eleonora Šturma; poet, historian, and bibliophile Jānis Krēsliņš; etc.: these were the unique, creative personalities I had the privilege of knowing in my youth.

My parents' friends were always present at Latvian cultural events and frequent guests at our house. There were parties and cookouts, serious discussions and witty repartee, laughter, the smoking of cigarettes and the clinking of glasses, and always the reading of poetry. Gunars and Jautrīte hosted many boisterous parties in their home off of staid Ridgewood Avenue. Other times everyone gathered at our house, and the floorboards rocked to the rhythms of Mongo Santamaria's "La Bamba," Nigeria's Olatunji, Mikis Theodorakis, and other world musicians.

They were a special bunch of people, the likes of which we will never see again here in North America. They treasured their old country's language and cultural legacy while absorbing America's novelty, freedom, and diversity. They sought to add new meaning to their lives, which had emerged from the traumatic experience of war and loss. They absorbed the dynamism of the city that they lived in or close to: New York was the heart of the world. Its shimmering skyscrapers and world-famous repositories of art, concert halls, and theaters enchanted these new Americans of European descent.

New York City was a beloved theme in the poetry of Linards Tauns, Gunars Saliņš, and my mother. Tauns lived in Hell's Kitchen, their group's namesake. It was a neighborhood on Manhattan's West Side near the Hudson River. Tauns' poetry in particular was a sensitive, tender amalgam of his rural past in Latvia and his new life in an alien but dynamic urban setting. "Let's turn New York into a forest," my godfather Gunars Saliņš wrote. "...Then hurry! Don't forget / to bring with you—besides plants and seeds—/ ten ships with premium top soil, / ten with clouds full of rain, / ten with fruitful moon phases, / a hundred with winds from the shores of Kurzeme!" (From *"Apmežosim Ņujorku."*)

Saliņš described Hell's Kitchen as "a port locale in Manhattan around the 40's, just a few blocks from Times Square and yet a world unto itself—with the smells of the port's slaughterhouses, with old six-story buildings, where the stairwells smell of poor people's apartments, with black and Puerto Rican kids hanging out on the corners, with hobos, with the Salvation Army, and 'Jesus Saves' establishments." In the 1950s and until Linards Tauns' death in 1963, the Latvian Hell's Kitchen poetry devotees scrunched together in Tauns' tiny apartment in the vastness of New York and the New World..

"We come to renew our faith that we are not yet dead," Saliņš wrote in a poem called *"Atjaunošanās"* ["Renewal"]. To cope with the loss of their native land and their new existence in an exile of an unknown length of time, these young Latvians needed each other's company and shared their creative endeavors. Their friendship kept them alive spiritually and sustained them. When Tauns died in 1963, the spirit of Hell's Kitchen was transplanted to this group's suburban New Jersey kitchens, living rooms, and leafy gardens. There was a great exchange of ideas, constructive criticism, and moral support. They were rebuilding their lives, for the most part successfully. Like many recent immigrants, they lived parallel lives. They were employed in the American workforce, but they devoted their free time to Latvian social life and culture, the glue that bonded them.

Gunars and Jautrīte Saliņš and their three children, Laris, Laila, and Lalita, lived at the north end of town and remained among my parents', especially my mother's, closest life-long friends. Gunars' poetry of magical realism remains a singular, critically acclaimed voice of the Latvian diaspora. It was always fun to know that there were other kids like my brothers and me, Latvian Americans, in our neighborhood. If I bumped into them on the street near school, I experienced a sense of joy, an unspoken recognition, a visceral connection.

Baltic poets in New York in the 1970s. From the left: Rita Gāle; Aina Kraujiete; an unidentified Lithuanian poet; Lithuanian filmmaker Jonas Mekas; my mother Baiba Bičole; poet Gunars Saliņš; Voldemārs Avens; Estonian poet Alexis Rannit. Family photo.

Another Latvian family residing in Glen Ridge was that of Kārlis and Klāra Osis; they lived about four blocks away. Dr. Kārlis Osis (1917–1997) was a well known parapsychologist who dealt with the paranormal and things like ESP and out-of-body experiences. His wife Klāra, a woman with intense blue eyes, was a poet and painter. Klāra's daughter Gunta worked for Penguin Putnam as a book designer. She also lived nearby. In the 1980s, when I was away in Latvia, Arnis Balgalvis, an electrical engineer, data communications expert, and avid audiophile and his wife Aina, an accomplished photographer, purchased a house by my elementary school. For a small town like Glen Ridge, this number of Latvians seemed like a small wonder. There were Latvians in neighboring towns and throughout New Jersey.

If I close my eyes, I can even still hear these individuals' voices after more than 30 years. According to my mother, Jānis Krēsliņš and my grandfather Jānis Bičolis competed in acquiring rare Latvian books and publications for their personal libraries. Krēsliņš, a thin, wiry, geeky-looking fellow with spectacles, knew how to propel himself forward on his butt. He liked to bake and never ate sugar. His house in New York, which he shared with his wife Skaidrīte and their three children, Zuze, Māra, and Jānis, was, as I was told, packed with old books, porcelain, and other art finds. He liked to remind us that the Germans had introduced us, Latvians, to civilization.

And then there were those friends who "dropped in" from time to time while traveling: the Latvian Canadian writer Aina Zemdega; actress Rasma Birzgale and her architect husband Vitolds Vītols from Boston; the chain-smoking prosaist Ilze Škipsna (Ilse S. Rothrock) who headed the library of the Kimbell Art Museum, designed by Louis Kahn, in Fort Worth, Texas; the writer Astrīde Ivaska and her Estonian husband Ivar Ivask, editor of *Books Abroad* (later *World Literature Today*), a journal published by the University of Oklahoma. Ivar Ivask introduced a section on the Baltic States to the journal and was instrumental in setting up the so-called Neustadt International Prize for Literature. Astrīde and Ivar were a handsome, worldly couple who visited our house several times and were always very kind to us children. We knew they rubbed shoulders with famous writers, and I looked up to them.

The Garden State Parkway, the New Jersey Turnpike, the Lincoln Tunnel, and other routes in the New York City area were pulsing arteries that connected these "transplants"—Latvian Americans. In the second half of the 20th century Latvian American society in the New York area was very active. There were so many Latvians, that they could rent New York's finest concert halls for cultural and Independence Day events.

There were many Latvians in exile who left a life-long impression on me. One such person was Juris Kļaviņš, a World War II veteran with a wooden leg. Juris always showed up at social events wearing a traditional gray Latvian ethnographic "suit" adorned with some silver pin or other of his own design; he was a master silversmith. A pipe tucked into the corner of his mouth finished off the charming ensemble. Juris was a great storyteller and Latvian "neopagan." I wore his silver bracelet when I went to Latvia for the first time in 1980 and kept it on for many years as a kind of talisman.

We took many trips across the George Washington Bridge to get to the Daugavas Vanagi ("Daugava Hawks") building in the Bronx near the old Stella D'oro cookie factory. Daugavas Vanagi is a Latvian veteran's organization that was founded in 1945 in Belgium by the surviving members of the so-called Latvian Legion. We attended many Latvian gatherings at the organization's beautiful, old building in a deteriorating neighborhood populated by Hispanics and African Americans. From time to time elegantly dressed Latvians were pelted with eggs from above, as they walked to the building.

Every Latvian get-together had lots of good food. The aroma of stewing sauerkraut and sausages floated up from the DV building's basement kitchen, as we listened to music or lectures, our stomachs rumbling. All diasporas cling to their culinary traditions for comfort. We couldn't get enough of *pīrāgi* (bacon buns) and real rye bread, which was impossible to buy in any American supermarket. My Latvian mother forbade us to eat enriched white bread; no self-respecting Baltic woman would be caught dead with a loaf of Wonderbread in her pantry. So we ate Jewish rye and pumpernickel. We all knew that Latvian bread was the best in the world.

Latvian social gatherings often featured bowls of *rosols* (a salad made of diced boiled potatoes, hard-boiled eggs, peas, ham, marinated pickles, sour cream, and mayonnaise) and other cold salads laid out on the long tables covered with white tablecloths (basically a Latvian Smörgåsbord). Beet salad was very popular, as were open-faced sandwiches with smoked salmon and ham, hard-boiled eggs, anchovies, mushroom salad, etc. for toppings. Scrumptious deviled eggs sprinkled with paprika were always appreciated and vanished quickly.

In winter my mother served us sauerkraut soup, a hearty peasant stew made with stringy sauerkraut, chunks of pork, and potatoes. Latvians loved *galerts* or "meat jello" (a head cheese or boiled meat in aspic) and ate it with vinegar or horseradish. My mother made it with pigs' feet she bought at the local European deli.

Hailing from countries by the sea, we Balts love our herring with sour cream and smoked salmon. We were sometimes lucky to savor some smoked eel, a special, hard-to-find treat. Adults would pine for *lucīši* or lamprey, which was popular in Latvia before the war. So-called *Aleksandra kūka* (Alexander cake), *biezpienmaize* ("Farmer's Cheese bread"), and Latvian-style apple pie were sweet staples of all Latvian social gatherings. For birthdays Latvians made *kliņģeris*, a delicious pastry flavored with saffron and shaped like a giant pretzel topped with almonds and powdered sugar. At Christmastime gingerbread cookies packed with an assortment of expensive spices were baked. As a special Christmas treat, my mother used to buy blood sausage from a German butcher. Old habits, customs, and recipes die hard.

Latvian comfort or soul food: (from the left, back) deviled eggs; pīrāgi or bacon buns; "gray" peas; rye bread; and caraway cheese. Family photo.

In addition to food, exiles and immigrants in the New World found other ways to express their longing for the Old Country and their youth. Latvians planted trees such as birches, oaks, and lindens, which reminded them of their native land. Flowers like rudbeckias, daisies, dahlias, phlox, mums, and Michaela daisies were popular in flower beds, because these were the "traditional" flowers of Latvia. Lilacs brought back the scent of Latvia in May. Nostalgia was also evident in the colors and interior design accessories many expats chose for their living rooms: earthy browns; grays; mustard yellow; beige... Latvian ceramicists churned out green and brown pottery that harked back to the the (President) Ulmanis era (the late 1930s) of "national romanticism." Some of this pottery was rather garish.

Ethnic dolls batting their eyes, decked out in miniature Latvian folk costumes, sat on couches and fireplace mantels. Pillows embroidered with Latvian ornaments were another popular, nostalgic accessory for the Latvian home away from home.

Certain artists' art was especially popular in the exile community. Lūdolfs Liberts (1895–1959) was known for his romantic Rīga and Parisian cityscapes and his *tautu meitas* ("folk women") in ethnic garb. Jānis Kalmīte (1907–1996) painted so many versions of Latvian threshing barns, that they began to resemble large American sedans with glowing headlights. Margarita Kovaļevska's (1911–1999) whimsical paintings of Roma girls were popular. Some Latvian artists clung to their past, while others such as Edvīns Strautmanis, Sigurds Vīdzirkste, Daina Dagnija, Voldemārs Avens, and my father absorbed the influences of modern art on view in New York's museums and galleries. Life in the United States and near a city like New York left a profound effect on those who chose to explore its cultural wonders.

A colorful map of Latvia published by Latvia's Ministry of Social Affairs in 1938. The map features details of our country's history, traditions, and way of life. I grew up looking at this map, which was reprinted by the Latvian exile community.
Source: Vidzeme.com and ACADEMIA / Latvian National Library

All of these experiences—linguistic, cultural, culinary, and social—would draw me to the image of what felt like a place that had fallen out of time into some deep, dark void, dark like the settings of my grandfather's fantastic tales. For years a map of Latvia called "Apceļosim dzimto zemi!" ("Let's Travel In Our Native Land!") on my bedroom wall drew me into a landscape both familiar and foreign. The wonderful drawings by Alfrēds Švedrēvics (b. 1887) showed Latvia to be a country with interesting natural features, charming architectural monuments, and historical landmarks.

Left: With my brothers Arvils and Artis and our grandfather ("Opaps"), the storyteller, in Glen Ridge in the 1970s.

As I grew older, I became more aware of the tragedy of Latvia. As a little girl, I had made a birthday card for my Omamma (grandmother) in Latvia. I drew a castle with the Latvian national flag. As I handed it to my grandfather Opaps for appraisal, I was shocked to see him look at it and then suddenly rip it up and toss it into the trash can. Then he proceeded to scold me: "You could cause a lot of trouble for your Omamma with this!" I stared at him in shock and disbelief, feeling ashamed and hurt. It was the first time I realized there was something "wrong" with Latvia.

I would absorb what my parents told me and what was taught at Latvian school, that communism was the great evil that had the Baltic States and Eastern Europe in a stranglehold. Americans of Eastern European descent were rightfully upset when only Hitler was mentioned as World War II's "bad guy." What about Stalin? He was just as bad, but no one in America mentioned the crimes of the Soviet Union. It was a bit strange. Even Anne Applebaum would write about this in her book *Gulag* "[…] While the symbol of one [Nazi] mass murder fills us with horror, the symbol of another [Soviet] mass murder [Soviet] makes us laugh." (Anne Applebaum. *Gulag*. 2003: Anchor Books, New York) Latvians, Lithuanians, and Estonians felt that much of the world had forgotten about their tragic fate during and after World War II and the ongoing occupation.

In American school we learned about the Holocaust, reading *The Diary of Anne Frank* and Eli Wiesel's *Night* and watching disturbing documentaries. Emaciated, skeletal-like Jewish prisoners in prison garb, naked corpses robbed of all human dignity being bulldozed like heaps of firewood: who could forget thoses horrific images? Yet the subject of Soviet atrocities and murders and the slave labor camps of the Gulag were never mentioned. Why? Eli Wiesel himself wrote: "To forget the dead would be akin to killing them a second time." Soviet communism and its criminal prison state persisted.

The summers without air conditioning in Jersey were unbearably hot, and if I was not away at Latvian camp in the Catskill Mountains, I often lay like a limp rag on the couch between two open windows, perspiring and looking thirstily at pictures of pools or trying to forget the heat between the covers of a book. The Seals and Croft song "Summer Breeze" filled me with longing. The soft cocoon of my childhood slowly peeled away, and my room started to feel small and cramped. By the time I reached my late teens, I felt bored and cramped in our comfortable suburban home in Essex County. My hormones had kicked in.

My four years at high school were uneventful and at times boring. I was not part of the "popular crowd" and had few friends due to my painful shyness. I did well, but nothing interested me academically other than French, although art class was a nice place to hang out and listen to Pink Floyd and the Grateful Dead. It probably did not help that my parents steered our social life towards exclusively Latvian events and society. In many ways I felt like an outsider. I did not belong to any of the distinct cliques: the jocks; the geeks; or "the deadheads." My best friend from childhood, Barbara, abandoned me in the first year of high school. It was a traumatic experience, as I was socially timid but loyal. But there were a lot of kids who did not belong to any cliques, and I found a new best friend in a girl named Donna. She was pretty, smart, and witty, a bit mischievous, and totally cool with my Latvian side. On Friday nights we cruised along the empty streets of our little town in her Cadillac Seville. We got drunk on rum and coke at a middle school play. We talked about guys, books, art, and music. Occasionally we puffed on cigarettes and felt cool. Suburban life seemed like *such a drag. We were so over it.*

After graduating from Latvian elementary school, I attended Latvian high school in Yonkers, New York on Friday nights. It was there that I met my other best friend from my high school years, Laura Padega from Hastings-on-Hudson, New York. We became inseparable almost immediately. Laura played the violin, as did her sisters, Ilze and Silvija, and the Padegs family was active in the Latvian community. Although the drive from Glen Ridge to Yonkers was a drag, and the classes were not particularly stimulating, I looked forward to meeting my new friend, funny, bright, and so like me. We called each other "Pupa" ("Bean").

My classmate Andris V. had a crazy habit of clicking on a lighter behind the back of our un-suspecting Latvian literature teacher. The three-inch flame had us convulsing in suppressed laughter. There was only one teacher who made a lasting impression on me and whose class I looked forward to, and that was Dzintra Bungs, gracious, friendly, and supportive of my creative writing. Evenutally she moved to Europe to work for Radio Free Europe/Radio Liberty and penned numerous important papers about the Baltic region.

Everyone in our class looked forward to the short moment of fun and freedom when classes ended, and we were allowed to run across the street to get a slice of pizza, Carvel ice cream, or a Chinese spring roll. Driving home in the dark, we listened to songs on the radio and dreamed our teenage dreams. The Eagles, the Bee Gees, Rod Stewart, ELO, Boston... "Night Fever" was out there; our hormones were bubbling. Laura and I often had sleepovers after school, and we began to venture into New York City together, meeting up at Grand Central Station. For the first time in our young lives we were truly on our own: two long-haired, giggling Latvian American girls in love with life. New York was the humming backdrop for our talks about the future and what we wanted. I looked forward to art school; Laura would pursue a degree in music.

Best friends in the Big Apple: With Laura Padega in front of the New York Public Library on Fifth Avenue, late 1970s. Photo by Japanese tourist.

Laura's father Juris Padegs worked for a New York law firm. The Padegs' beautiful house near the Hudson River was a delight to visit. Juris was related to the fa-mous eccentric Latvian artist Kārlis Padegs (1911–1940) whose unusual work I would become acquainted with in Latvia. Laura's mother Gita ran a gallery and was a great cook. Music, food, and Latvian hospitality made me feel at home among the remarkable Padegs clan.

The core of the Latvian expatriate community in the United States, people like the Padegs family, was astonishingly busy and committed to the goal of raising awareness about the Baltics' lost independence while preserving Latvian language and culture. Latvian organizations like the World Federation of Free Latvians, the American Latvian Association, and Daugavas Vanagi were involved in supporting Latvian schools, churches, research projects, song and dance festivals, and lobbying US government representatives to condemn the illegal Soviet annexation of the Baltic States. The Latvian diaspora stayed connected through various Latvian publications, and Latvians drove enormous distances to see other Latvians. My lengthy trips across the Hudson to be with Laura were a good example of this need to be together. We were soulmates.

Assimilation took a great toll on the Latvian diaspora. Schools and jobs often landed Latvians in communities where there were few or no Latvians. Marriages to non-Latvians speeded up the assimilation process. And then there was assimilation by deliberate choice. For many an "extra" identity was a burden. Some felt ashamed of their Latvian identity. There were Latvians of my grandparents' generation who chose to forget their native language and spoke only English to their children for fear of arrested development, thus robbing them of the gift of a second language. For my own grandparents and parents, preserving their native language and culture and passing it down to us was of utmost importance, and I will always be grateful to them.

In her immediate family my mother was the only daughter who nurtured her ethnic roots, writing in her mother tongue and socializing with Latvians. It wasn't that she was an ethnocentric snob; she and my father felt most comfortable in the company of people like themselves. My mother's sisters drifted away from Latvian society for various reasons. My cousins grew up as Americans with practically no connection to the Latvian community. Life in the New World was not easy for immigrants. The United States was so different from Europe, and adapting was often a struggle. With Latvians prone to self-censorship, we heard about personal tragedies only in passing whispers.

My father's immediate family in the United States consisted of his elderly father, Senator Augusts Rumpēters, and his older brother Visvaldis, a Latvian minister in Milwaukee, Wisconsin. We met our Wisconsin relatives only once. My great uncle Arkādijs died before I had the chance to meet him. The United States was vast, with Latvians scattered across it like dandelion seeds.

Here I am (second row, right) in 1976 with my Latvian folk dancing peers. Family photo.

In my senior year at Glen Ridge High School, when I was named one of "the most creative students" in our class, I was accepted to the only school I applied to, Parsons School of Design, which was located in Downtown New York. Prestigious Parsons was famous for its fashion design department, which produced Donna Karan, Anna Sui, Tom Ford, and other top-notch designers. I chose to focus on illustration. I began commuting by train in the fall of 1978. I loved the ride through the Meadowlands, a dreamy landscape of resilient marshes and industrial blight. Art school thrilled me, as did the energy of the city. At the end of the day I would grab a croissant at Balducci's or a Greek gyro on 14th Street and begin my trip back to Glen Ridge. After dinner I got busy doing homework, drawing, reading, and writing. Despite its steep price tag, I loved Parsons and was crazy about New York.

It was an exciting time to be in Lower Manhattan. The music and art scenes were hopping. It was the era of punk. The songs of groups and musicians like the Clash, the Ramones, the B52's, Patti Smith, Bruce Springsteen, the Cars, Blondie, Laurie Anderson, the Talking Heads, the Police, etc. accompanied me into early adulthood. Wandering the streets of Lower Manhattan, I felt "Gloria"-alive and open to the world. Artists like Jennifer Bartlett, Jenny Holzer, Robert Longo, Chuck Close, James Rosenquist, and others were exhibiting in the large, open spaces of Soho galleries. The whole area was changing, with artists moving into empty lofts followed by businesses and commerce. Most of my instructors had lofts. Greenwich Village and the surrounding areas were teeming with music clubs, cafés, and interesting shops. The Jersey suburbs were dull in comparison to this plethora of culture and hip retail.

Robert Mapplethorpe was in the limelight with his erotic photographs of male nudes and elegant flowers. Many of Parsons' male students were gay and struggling with their identity. A gay classmate told me about the Anvil, as he sketched a column of ants marching into a woman's vagina. The Anvil, located from 1974–1986 in the meat-packing district of Lower Manhattan, was a club for gay men. If you met a guy you liked at Parsons, you had to wonder if he was gay or straight. The AIDS epidemic was about to explode.

In her poignant memoir *Just Kids* about her years together with Robert Mapplethorpe and the 1970s-1980s Downtown New York scene, poet and punk queen Patti Smith mentions Dovanna, a popular model photographed by Mapplethorpe. I bumped into Dovanna in one of the bathrooms at Parsons in 1979. Tall and spaghetti thin, with dark eyes and jet black hair cut in a stylish bob, Dovanna was a Latvian American just like me. She hailed from Michigan. I knew her brother from Latvian gatherings. At the time he was on a passionate mission to establish a full-time Latvian school somewhere in the United States. I found out time and time again that chance encounters with Latvians, a rare breed, were surprisingly commonplace. I seemed to be seeing Vija Vētra, a performer of classical Indian dance, just about everywhere in New York.

In my first year at Parsons I fell madly in love with a Soviet Russian Jew named David. He was a dancer, and I met him at a party at the loft of a Latvian couple, Uģis and Laila, on West 18th Street. David seemed worldly; I found that attractive. He and his friends, also recent Jewish immigrants from the USSR, lived in an apartment on the Upper West Side close to Central Park. The location was fantastic, but the one-bedroom apartment was run-down, dusty, and barely furnished. The young men seemed to be in transit. Aside from a couple of mattresses on the floor, there was nothing to grant the place a semblance of home. Cockroaches scurried about in the kitchen. We made love in the soft glow of Manhattan's street lights and then watched the sky turn from orangey-black to pink at dawn. I adored this tall, slim Jew with the long-lashed, soulful brown eyes, wondering what my parents would say if they found out. My first real relationship was short but sweet, a mere three months. David and his friends moved away. On his way south he stopped at our house to say goodbye to me. Just a couple of years later I would find myself traveling toward the prison state he had left behind.

"Hey, Nineteen!" (Steely Dan): 19 in 1979. My friend Anthony, who took this photograph at Parsons, did not understand my obsession with Latvia.

When I hooked up with a Venezuelan in my second year at Parsons, my mother nearly had a nervous breakdown. I escaped from the house to join him in the city and later at his parents' apartment in Queens. My mother turned into a hysterical "tigress" waiting to pounce on me with unsheathed claws when I got home from the city. She wanted to meet my Latino beau in person and tear him to shreds. From a soft-spoken, sensitive, loving parent she had turned into what felt like a paranoid tyrant, raging about my choices, shaking her finger, and screaming. At one point she threatened to disown me. (Ironically, my parents were not present at my fairytale wedding to a "full-blooded" Latvian just a few years down the road.) Living with my parents, I was at their mercy. Years later my mother was embarrassed about this episode in her life.

Like Patti Smith, I was also attracted to poetry and even dabbled in it for a while in Latvian, writing pretentious stream-of-consciousness verse that later sounded like gibberish. I felt compelled to write on account of my mother and her literary friends. Writing was in my genes; surely I had some talent. Some of my stuff was published in the Latvian quarterly *Jaunā Gaita*. I was toying with a very old and rich language that I knew quite well but not well enough. It would take many years of living in Latvia for me to feel comfortable with my Latvian.

In the late 1970s my father became involved in a new association of New York area Baltic artists called Baltia. Until then our contacts with our fellow Balts were nil. A couple of art shows that were organized were lovely events. Another time New York Balts gathered at the beautiful Ukrainian Institute of America on Fifth Avenue for a reading of Baltic poetry. This was one of the very rare Baltic get-togethers that I experienced in my youth, yet it left a lasting impression of kinship. My parents became good friends with Vladislovas and Ida Žilius, recent émigrés from Lithuania. Vladas was painting large, colorful abstractions at the time. We visited them at his studio in the Bronx where Ida had prepared *cepelinai* dumplings for us, a traditional Lithuanian dish. Baltia folded when the Soviet Union collapsed.

My mother's 1978 encounter with the enigmatic, charismatic, famous Latvian poet from Latvia named Imants Ziedonis (1933–2013) opened up a remote possibility for me to travel to Latvia. Ziedonis had attained rock star status in Latvia, and for my mother and her literary and artistic friends meeting him in New York was a huge event. He represented "the other side"—the "real Latvia." Ziedonis played it safe with the Soviet authorities while pursuing his own agenda; he wanted to improve life in Latvia by raising Latvians' sense of responsibility and ownership toward their fatherland, urging them to become involved in grassroots efforts to ensure Latvia's future while avoiding open confrontation with the Communist Party. Ziedonis was a party member, but he chose to focus on the issues and problems of rural life, Latvian folklore, our natural wonders, and life as it was in Soviet Latvia, without any overt criticism. By the end of Ziedonis' visit, my mother and the famous poet had devised a plan: his son Rimants and I should be pen pals, and I should try to go to Latvia to study art.

It was very strange to hear about the phobias of some members of the exile community who saw "red" and "communist" in anyone from Soviet-occupied Latvia. There was the incident at the premiere of the film "Pūt, vējiņi'" ("Blow, Wind") in the 1970s in Manhattan; someone was urging Latvians to boycott the movie, saying it was laced with subliminal Soviet propaganda. The movie was based on a play by Jānis Rainis (1865–1929); Imants Ziedonis had co-authored its script. Set in Latvia's folkloric ancient times, it was about a brash suitor named Uldis who arrives in a boat on the Daugava River to marry a wealthy girl named Zane but falls in love with Baiba, the shy and elusive servant girl instead. We went to the movie and enjoyed it greatly; I developed a crush on actor Ģirts Jakovļevs. Someone even showed up to snap photographs of the moviegoers, "commie sympathizers." My grandfather Tuks referred to these people chasing communist phantoms as *tumšie ļautiņi* or dimwits. A part of Latvian society in exile would remain conservative and suspicious of their compatriots in communist Latvia. Ironically, these people were a mirror image of some people in Latvia.

And so it was set in motion: my "return" to the land of my ancestors. It commenced with a regular exchange of letters between the children of poets, one in New Jersey, the other in Soviet-occupied communist Latvia. My correspondence with Rimants made the idea of visiting Latvia seem real, possible, and irresistible. Despite my exciting and fulfilling time at Parsons in the city I loved, I was itching to leave. Latvia was pulling on my heartstrings. How did Latvia fit into the formula of youth, "sex, drugs, and rock and roll"? Drugs did not appeal to me, punk rock had energized me, and sex…? My mother was probably hoping that a trip to Latvia might hook me up with a Latvian suitor.

My first and only pen pal Rimants Ziedonis (left) in the late 1970s with his cousin. In 2012 Rimants became the first editor of the Latvian edition of *National Geographic Magazine*. He is the author of several lovely travel books about Latvia.

It took almost two years to finalize my travel papers and arrangements. Rīga's so-called Cultural Liaison Committee with Countrymen Abroad, a branch of the KGB, must have been very surprised to receive my petition to study at the Latvian Art Academy. The Cold War was at its zenith with no thaw in sight. The zombie-like Leonid Brezhnev still fronted the Central Committee of the Communist Party of the Soviet Union at Moscow's Kremlin, which ruled over a vast territory that included Latvia, Lithuania, and Estonia. The Soviets blamed the West (especially the United States) for everything, especially imperialism. In their eyes, spies and saboteurs were everywhere, attempting to derail the Soviet Union's impending victory over the hearts and minds of the world's proletariats. Specks like me, the descendant of bourgeois nationalists, traitors, and opportunists, were to be examined closely for the risk of contamination.

School was out. In the summer of 1980 I worked cleaning houses in Glen Ridge, Montclair, and Bloomfield. I shopped for my trip, buying clothes and gifts for my relatives in occupied Latvia. As my anticipation grew, so did my apprehension. I had never been abroad (with the exception of Canada), and the USSR resembled a huge splotch of darkness on the world map. Somewhere

on its western fringe was Latvia. There were real people *there*, my blood relatvies, waiting for me. Latvia was real, and I was going there!

Flying out of John F. Kennedy International Airport in September 1980, I realized I was flying toward the past, my own past, the one described to me in the history books of Latvian school and the stories of my grandparents and the poetry of my mother and other Latvian writers. In a sense, I was returning to my cradle. As "the big ol' jet airliner" (Steve Miller) climbed up through the clouds into the darkening sky, "Hillside haven" and my childhood receded. Below me lay the Atlantic Ocean, once traversed by scores of European refugees seeking asylum and a new life in the United States. Ahead of me lay the Old World and inevitable transformation. Was this not the culmination of all those years of my indoctrination? I was fulfilling a part of my grandparents' and parents' deepest and most fervent wish to go back home.

PART TWO:
Latvia as a Battlefield—World War II

Soviet leader Joseph Stalin and Nazi Germany's Foreign Minister Joachim von Ribbentrop in Moscow. A "non-agression" treaty signed on August 23, 1939 by von Ribbentrop and Soviet Foreign Minister Vyacheslav Molotov included a secret protocol that carved up parts of Europe, including Latvia, Estonia, and Lithuania, into Soviet and Nazi "spheres of influence." Source: Wikimedia Commons. https://commons.wikimedia.org/wiki/File:Bundesarchiv_Bild_183-H27337,_Moskau,_Stalin_und_Ribbentrop_im_Kreml.jpg (© Bundesarchiv, Bild 183-H27337 / CC BY-SA 3.0 https://creativecommons.org/licenses/by-sa/3.0/de/deed.en)

In the middle of Europe in the middle of the twentieth century, the Nazi and Soviet regimes murdered some fourteen million people. The place where all of the victims died, the bloodlands, extends from central Poland to western Russia, through Ukraine, Belarus, and the Baltic States. (...) The victims were chiefly Jews, Belarusians, Ukrainians, Poles, Russians, and Balts, the peoples native to these lands. [...] Though their homelands became battlefields midway (...), these people were all victims of murderous policy rather than casualties of war.—Timothy Snyder. *Bloodlands.* New York: Basic Books, 2010. vii-viii

Soviet (Russian) tanks entering Rīga in June 1940. Occupied by the Soviets in 1940–1941, Latvia was re-annexed by the USSR in 1945 with little protest from the Allied Forces. The illegal Soviet occupation lasted for nearly half a century.
Source: Wikimedia Commons https://commons.wikimedia.org/wiki\File:Riga_1940_Soviet_Army.jpg (© Public Domain)

Nazi Germany drove the Soviets out of Latvia in July 1941, and the Nazi occupation lasted from 1941–1944/45. Already by the end of 1941 most of Latvia's Jews had been murdered. This photograph, dated February 15, 1944 and taken at the Rīga Central Station, includes Otto-Heinrich Drechsler, Hinrich Lohse, Friedrich Jeckeln, and other high-ranking Nazi German officials.
Source: Wikimedia Commons. https://commons.wikimedia.org/wiki/File:Bundesarchiv_Bild_146-1970-043-42,_Lettland-Riga,_Ankunft_von_Hinrich_Lohse_mit_Offizieren_am_Bahnhof.jpg (© Bundesarchiv, Bild 146-1970-043-42 / Unknown Photographer / CC BY-SA 3.0 https://creativecommons.org/licenses/by-sa/3.0/de/deed.en)

Exhibit presented at the Wannsee ("Final Solution") Conference on January 20, 1942 indicating that only 3,500 Jews remained in Latvia out of about 60,000 in the country at the time of the Nazi takeover.
Source: Wikimedia Commons. https://en.wikipedia.org/wiki/The_Holocaust_in_Latvia#/media/File:WannseeList.jpg (© Public Domain)

The double occupation, first Soviet, then German, made the experience of the inhabitants of these lands all the more complicated and dangerous. A single occupation can fracture a society for generations; double occupation is even more painful and divisive. It created risks and temptations that were unknown in the West.—Timothy Snyder. *Bloodlands*. New York: Basic Books, 2010. P. 190

August 23, 1939: A "non-aggression treaty" between the Soviet Union and Nazi Germany was signed in Moscow by Soviet Foreign Minister Vyacheslav Molotov and Nazi German Foreign Minister Joachim von Ribbentrop. The Molotov-Ribbentrop "spheres of influence" pact partitioned the Baltic States, with Latvia and Estonia assigned to the Soviet Union, while Lithuania was slated to be occupied by Germany. After the Soviet invasion of Poland in September 1939, the Soviets pressured Latvia to sign a military mutual assistance treaty that would allow the USSR to set up military bases in Latvia. Latvian President Kārlis Ulmanis did not dare oppose the Soviets; fearing a bloodbath, in 1940 he ordered his army not to resist the impending Soviet occupation. According to Ēriks Jēkabsons, while the Latvian military consisting of 28,000 military personnel was well trained, its available arsenal would have been used up in one month. Countries like Great Britain, Sweden, and Germany had declined to sell Latvia meaningful armaments during its independence years. Prior to the full-scale Soviet invasion of the Baltic countries in 1940, the USSR had encircled them with its naval fleet on the Baltic Sea, and along the land borders it had amassed 541,000 soldiers, 3,938 tanks, and 2,516 fighter planes. (Source: Ēriks Jēkabsons, *"Latvijas okupācijas hronika. Aculiecinieka vēstījums."*)

June 17, 1940: Soviet tanks rolled into Rīga. Soviet authorities took control of the Latvian government, replacing it with a puppet government controlled from Moscow. President Ulmanis was deported to Stavropol in Soviet Russia in July 1940. He allegedly died of dysentery in prison in 1942 in Krasnovodsk (in present-day Turkmenistan).

June 14, 1941: The Soviets arrested and deported more than 15,000 Latvian citizens to far-flung outposts in Siberia. With little time to prepare for their grueling journey, packed into cattle cars without food or water, many of the weak—the elderly, infants, and children—died, and their bodies were discarded along the way. Men are separated from their families and sent to slave labor camps. Women and children were dispersed in settlements throughout the Soviet Union, sometimes in the middle of nowhere.

My great-aunt and great-uncle, Velta and her husband Eduards Rapss, a decorated Latvian war veteran, were among the many Latvians arrested on June 14 and deported to Siberia. Neither returned. In July 2014, when I was visiting my paternal uncle who lives at Vīganti, the family's ancestral farm, he described how Soviet chekists caught Uncle Eduards who tried to hide in the nearby forest. Velta was taken away in a summer dress.

June 22, 1941: Nazi Germany launched "Operation Barbarossa," attacking the Soviet Union.

July 1, 1941: Nazi Germany occupied Rīga and then the rest of Latvia, replacing Soviet terror with its own reign of terror. The burning of the Great Choral Synagogue on July 4, 1941 symbolized the start of the Holocaust in Latvia and the methodical murder of Latvia's Jews, Roma, communists, the mentally disabled, and other "undesirables." Latvian workers were sent to Germany. Anyone criticizing or opposing the Germans was severely punished.

My great-uncle on my mother's side, Alfrēds Bičolis, was among the patients at Jelgava's psychiatric hospital murdered during the Nazi occupation, possibly in January 1942 by the notorious Latvian Arājs Commando.

January 1943: Hitler ordered the formation of the Latvian Legion to help Germany fight the Soviet Red Army. The legion was comprised of Latvian forced conscripts and a handful of volunteers. The Latvian legionnaires did not subscribe to Nazi ideology. They fought solely for their country, Latvia. In their popular wartime song "Every Saturday night" (*"Ik katru sestdien's vakaru"*) they promised to beat up the *utainos* (lice-infested Russians) and then "trounce the blue-grays" (a reference to the Germans and their uniforms).

July 18, 1944: The Soviets breached the Latvian border.

> In 1944 I had finished my second year at Rīga's 1. ģimnāzija (Rīga Secondary School No. 1) and was staying at my paternal grandfather's farm in Vidriži. On my birthday, July 24, when I turned 17, I was informed by mail that I had been conscripted into the German Luftwaffe's auxiliary staff. At the beginning of August, along with many other Latvian youths I was evaluated by a medical

commission on Alberta iela in Rīga and deemed fit for military duty. Along with several of my classmates we were sent to an anti-aircraft gun battery in Sarkandaugava for training.—*An excerpt from an essay by Visvaldis Rumpēteris, my paternal uncle, about his terrifying wartime adventures that ended in Germany in the summer of 1945. (Latviešu karazēnu un meiteņu stāsti II. Rīga: Fonds Latvijas vēsture, 2001. pp. 16–17)*

July 27, 1944: The cities of Daugavpils, Preiļi, and Rēzekne fell to the Soviets.

On July 28 my maternal grandparents Jānis and Līvija Bičolis and their three daughters including

my mother, who had been living in Birži during the German occupation, packed up their most essential belongings and began their uncertain flight westward away from Sēlija, which was turning into a dangerous war zone.

Soviet soldiers of the First Baltic Front in Jelgava on August 16, 1944. Wikimedia Commons. Source: https://commons.wikimedia.org/wiki/File:19440816_soviet_so ldiers_attack_jelgava.jpg (© Public Domain)

July 29, 1944: The Red Army continued its assault from the south in Lithuania, advancing on the German forces in Latvia and taking over the beautiful old city of Jelgava, which was subsequently nearly destroyed. By this time Latvians had been forcibly conscripted both by the Germans and Russians and were often unwittingly and tragically fighting against each other.

My paternal grandfather Augusts Rumpēters and my father Ilmārs (age 15) left Rīga on September 24, traveling west to Kurzeme.

"(The streets in Rīga) were lined with anti-tank barriers and long columns of the German Army retreating through the city in a westerly direction. The bridges were being mined. Rīga had become a frontline city."—Ilmārs Rumpēters

October 11, 1944: The Red Army shelled Rīga, intensifying its aerial assault, and on October 13 Latvia's capital fell to the Soviets. Although the Red Army attempted to penetrate and seize Latvia's westernmost region Kurzeme, it did not succeed until the end of the war. The fierce battles over control of the so-called "Kurzeme cauldron," the last bastion of Latvian resistance to the Soviet occupation, have survived in Latvian consciousness as truly epic and tragic. More than 100,000 refugees would leave Latvia before it was swallowed by the Red Army.

End of 1944–1991: Latvia was occupied by the Soviet Union.

Another wave of devastating Soviet arrests and deportations took place on **March 25, 1949,** when about 43,000 people, including children, "kulaks," "nationalists," and other "enemies of the Soviet state," were arrested and deported to Siberia.

A Latvian woman and former Gulag prisoner (deported in 1949) and her daughter visiting a field of graves just outside a slave labor camp (in the distance) in Jezkazgan (Dzezkazgan), Kazakhstan in 1957 shortly after it was shut down. Hundreds of mounds and crosses mark the graves of inmates who died there. Photograph courtesy of Maija Miesniece, Latvia.

Chapter sources:

(1) Edgars Dunsdorfs. *Latvijas vēstures atlants*. Melbourne, Australia: Kārlis Goppers Foundation, 1969.
(2) Pēteris Dreimanis, *Latvju tautas vēsture*. Winds Bogtrykkeri Haderslev, Denmark: Amerikas Latviešu Apvienības Izglītības birojs, 1969.
(3) Kārlis Dambītis, Latvian War Museum
(4) Museum of the Occupation of Latvia 1940–1991

The Two Wars' Long Shadows

Using women for archery target practice: a rendering by Dariusz Kupisz of Russian atrocities during the Livonian War (1558–1583).
Source: Wikimedia Commons https://commons.wikimedia.org/wiki/File:Russian_atrocities_in_Livonia_ib_XVI_century.jpg
(© Public Domain)

War has been a part of Latvia's history for centuries. Latvians have many dainas and songs about war. In tsarist times men could be called up for military duty for 25 years. In the mournful song "Es karā aiziedams" ("I went off to war") a young conscript bids farewell to his sister in the cradle, only to see her again when she is a young woman who has embroidered a military flag for him.

The bloody 1905 Russian Revolution spilled into the territory of Latvia, which was part of the Russian Empire at the time. Workers went on strike in the cities to protest economic hardship and the lack of political rights. Latvian peasants revolted against their despised German overlords' privileges and called for an end to Russification efforts. Over 400 German-owned manors were destroyed in the violent uprising. The Russian government sent in military forces to protect the German landed gentry and quell the unrest. Bloody conflicts ensued. Military tribunals run by Russian officers were set up in the countryside; almost all ended in death sentences. Punitive expeditions fanned out, rounding up and shooting suspects without a proper trial. The 1905 uprising claimed the lives of about 2,500 people in Latvia. Thousands of revolutionaries were deported to Siberia, while others emigrated, never to return. Some of these events are described by my great-grandfather Augusts Rumpēters in his unpublished memoir. My grandparents' lives had just begun in this era of dramatic transformation in Latvia.

According to Latvian historian Ēriks Jēkabsons, a large number of Latvians went to the United States at the turn of the 20th century and right after the 1905 Revolution. Primarily left-leaning, they comprised the first wave of Latvian immigrants to the US. According to Jēkabsons, about 40,000 Latvians had settled in the Unites States prior to Latvia's declaration of independence in 1918. Today the old building of the Philadelphia Society of Free Letts stands as a reminder of those times of upheaval in our nation's history.

Left: Volunteers from Kurzeme's 3ʳᵈ Latvian riflemen's battalion in a photograph dated August 7 (20), 1915. Source: Wikimedia Commons https://lv.wikipedia.org/wiki/Att%C4%93ls:Brivpratigie_latviesu_strelnieki.JPG (© Public Domain)

World War I began in the summer of 1914. Many Latvians conscripted into the Russian Army would die fighting against the Germans in Prussia and elsewhere. The Germans invaded Lithuania and Kurzeme (Courland) in the spring of 1915. The Russian Army retreated in panic, as their commanders ordered the countryside razed. About 400,000 refugees from Kurzeme fled eastward. People from Rīga, Vidzeme, and Latgale joined the exodus, including my paternal grandmother. Latvia's refugees were mostly unwelcome in Russia; they were saved by their compatriots' skill in creating hundreds of refugee organizations under the auspices of a central committee for Latvian refugees steered by Vilis Olavs, Arveds Bergs, and Jānis Čakste, who would become the first president of the Republic of Latvia.

In August 1915, as German forces drew closer to Rīga, the Russian military leadership allowed for the establishment of Latvian voluntary battalions to defend the city. By October the first Latvian battalions, poorly prepared, were dispatched into battle. The first three Latvian soldiers to die were laid to rest in Rīga's *Meža kapi* ("Forest Cemetery"), which would become the permanent site of Latvia's national memorial, the Brothers' Cemetery.

World War I ended on November 11, 1918. Latvians declared independence from Tsarist Russia on November 18, 1918. Germany and its allies were defeated. But Russia, too, was imploding; the Bolsheviks had deposed the last Russian Tsar Nicholas II in the violent 1917 revolution and instated Vladimir Ilyich Lenin as the country's leader. The Russian Revolution swept many Latvians into its blood-spattered fold, including revolutionary idealists, communists, and the so-called Latvian Red Riflemen, some of whom served as Lenin's trusted guards. Many Latvian communists and red riflemen would perish in the Stalinist purges of the 1930s.

During Russia's civil war (1917–1920) Latvians fought on the side of "the reds" and "the whites." Russians even say that the Bolsheviks won the battle thanks to Russian stupidity, Jewish brains, and Latvian brawn, or something like that. However, for those back home independence did not come right away with the Declaration of Independence. Latvians plunged into yet another war to stave off Lenin's Bolshevik forces.

After their accession to power in Russia, the Russian Bolsheviks declared that nations had the right to secede and establish independent states. This declaration proved to be a propaganda move to secure the help of non-Russian nations in building, fortifying, and cementing the Soviet state. Ignoring this promise, the Red Army invaded the newly independent Baltic republics at the end of 1918. On this occasion *Izvestia*, the Soviet newspaper wrote on December 25, 1918: "Estonia, Latvia, and Lithuania are directly on the road from Russia to Western Europe and therefore a hindrance to our revolutions... This separating wall has to be destroyed." The newly established Baltic States (...) were forced to take up arms in order to liberate their countries from the red aggressors, which they managed to achieve in 1919–20."

(Augusts Rumpēters, LL.M. *Soviet Aggression Against the Baltic States*. Published by the World Federation of Free Latvians, 1974.)

After declaring independence in 1918, Latvians fought in the War of Independence (1918–1920). They succeeded in driving both the Germans and the Bolsheviks out of Latvia with the help of Estonian forces. In 1919 Latvia's population had endured "red" and "white" terror, which nearly killed my great-grandparents, Augusts and Amālija Rumpēters. About 1,000 people were executed in revolutionary war tribunals or troikas. The clergy were ruthlessly persecuted and massacred. Many Baltic Germans were arrested and deported to Siberia. On the other side, "white" terror was waged by the Germans against Soviet and communist sympathizers, also resulting in thousands of executions. Hundreds of American army officers, physicians, privates, and civilians attached to various US missions saw a bit of action in Latvia during the War of Independence. Latvia signed a peace treaty with Soviet Russia on August 11, 1920.

Needless to say, Latvia suffered terribly in the first two decades of the 20th century. In 1914 Latvia's population was 2.6 million. In 1920 it had contracted to 1.6 million. (After 1920) about 250,000 people returned to Latvia from Russia, where they had been surviving as refugees; many refugees had perished there, too. Besides huge demographic losses, Latvia's economy was devastated. As they retreated, the Russians destroyed Rīga's factories and confiscated many items of cultural value. Many buildings near the front were destroyed by enemy fire or burned down by the Russian Army. A 1920 survey counted 78,000 completely destroyed and 105,000 partly destroyed buildings. For several years after the war Latvian peasants were forced to live in dug-outs and other temporary shelters. The people of Latvia began rebuilding their newly independent, war-torn country with enormous energy. (Edgars Dunsdorfs. *Latvijas vēstures atlants*. Melbourne, Australia: Kārļa Zariņa Fonds, 1998. P. 164. Tr. RL)

The two world wars of the 20th century nearly bled Latvia to death. My grandparents lived through the dramatic events of the 1905 Revolution and survived World War I and Latvia's War of Independence, which plunged their country into chaos, bloodshed, and terror. They entered adulthood when the Republic of Latvia was a fledgeling independent state. Those brief years of sovereignty and freedom, a mere two decades, would be their golden years, and they were our nation's "gold generation." Theirs was the generation that rebuilt Latvia into a thriving European export country. Their children, including my parents, were born in the short-lived republic. Starting in 1940, their dearly cherished homeland Latvia would be crushed by Soviet Russian and Nazi German tanks and boots.

Chapter source:

(1)   Edgars Dunsdorfs. *Latvijas vēstures atlants*. Melbourne, Australia: Kārļa Zariņa Fonds, 1998. Tr. RL.

Latvian riflemen from Vidzeme in 1917 with flags typical of that time following Russia's February Revolution: "Long live an autonomous Latvia!" and "Glory to freedom! Glory to Latvia! In a free Russia!" Source: Wikimedia Commons
https://lv.wikipedia.org/wiki/Att%C4%93ls:Latviesu_strelnieki_1917.jpg
(© Public Domain)

Refugees, Immigrants, Exile

Baltic refugees: My maternal grandparents, Līvija and Jānis Bičolis, leaving Traunstein for Munich, Germany on May 23, 1950 (their first step towards a new life in the US). Their daughters Baiba, Gundega, and Laila are with them although not pictured.

From generation to generation, my ancestors' old and beautiful language, Latvian, was passed down to me. My grandparents hailed from different regions of Latvia—Vidzeme, Zemgale, and Sēlija. Their words sounded like a soothing brook in my childhood: *"meitiņ"; "māsiņ"* ("daughter," "sister"). Their lives in the United States were forever permeated by a deep longing for all that was lost to them: the independence of their beautiful European country; their scattered family and friends; their lost homes; and their disrupted professions. Their identity was defined by their language and culture. Unlike economic migrants, my grandparents were political refugees; as such, they could not let go of their past, of Latvia, which they left unwillingly.

Baltic immigrants and their American offspring in the early 1960s... Here I am (bottom right) with my parents, brothers, cousin Marīte, and grandparents in East Orange, New Jersey.

My grandparents' stories explain why I was born in the United States. Had there been no Second World War, Latvia would have turned out like modern-day Finland, Sweden, or Denmark: a thriving, wealthy country. Latvia's population would have been much bigger than today, stronger, healthier. Judging by the remarkable achievements of Latvia in the short years of independence in the interbellum period (1920–1940), Latvia would have made great strides in education, science, research, and economic development. And I would have recognized many more faces in my family tree. But it was not to be.

My grandfather Jānis Bičolis in Latvia in the summer of 1928.

My fingers have sifted through old photographs given to me by my mother and father. Group photos of Latvia's young women and men in the 1920s and 1930s are especially haunting. I can't help but sadly wonder what happened to them. Did they wind up dead on the battlefield, in Siberia, or in exile?

Shattered cities. Smoldering ovens. Stacked corpses. Steeples like cigar stubs. Such are the images of Europe in 1945, images of a civilization in ruins... Never had so many people been on the move at once. Millions upon millions. Prisoners of war, slave laborers, concentration camp inmates, ex-soldiers, Germans expelled from Eastern Europe, and refugees who had fled the Russian advance— a congeries of moving humanity."—Modris Eksteins, *Walking Since Daybreak*, 1999

American General George S. Patton was my father's hero. He should have been allowed to "finish the job" by invading the the Soviet Union and defeating Stalin. The deaths of millions, including many Balts, Latvians, and members of our family, would have been spared, he would say at the kitchen table, when the subject of the war came up. At the time we kids, forking our *kotletes* (Latvian meatballs), potatoes, and peas, only vaguely understood what he was talking about, but his monologues and grumblings about Russia became our worries too.

A Dream in Lilacs

... At last no more did arms have we

but wings

to carry us over the blossoming earth.

We flew

and flew

and sank into the sky --

Our souls fused together in bloom

and then—disintegrated.

(Līvija Bičole. Tr. RL)

My maternal grandmother Līvija Bičole (b. Sproģe), whom we called Mimmī, was born in 1905 in Mežmuiža (later Augstkalne or "High Hill," named after the ancient Semigallian tribe's Silene castle hill) near the Lithuanian border. Sliding down the Google map and across the border, the soft sounds of our Baltic sister tongue, Lithuanian, emerge in place names like Daukšiai, Žagare,

Žučiai. Mimmī was the daughter of the overseer of Mežmuiža (aka Augstkalne) Manor. Orphaned at 15, my grandmother was raised by her uncle and aunt.

Līvija studied Baltic philology at the University of Latvia. There she met my grandfather Jānis Voldemārs Bičolis (b. in 1904 in Zīlēni), a young man from Birži Parish in Sēlija in the southeastern part of Latvia. Līvija and Jānis married in 1930. They were both active in Ramave, a student organization dedicated to Baltic philology. From 1933–1939 my grandfather was editor of *Ceļi*, a journal published by Ramave about Baltic philology, folklore, ethnography, and etymology.

By the time World War II rolled around, my grandmother had given birth to three daughters, Baiba, Gundega, and Laila, and the philologists were living in a small apartment in Pārdaugava, a suburb of Rīga. My mother remembered trips to Lielmaikaiši, her great-uncle Albis' (Alberts Ābelītis, b. 1894) farm near the Lithuanian border; her aunt Elza's farm in Bukaiši; *Tante* ("Aunt") Zeta's *jaunsaimniecība* ("new farm") in Eleja; as well as her paternal grandparents' Pēteris and Dārta Bičolis' farm in Birži near Jēkabpils. Mostly my mother remembered Zemgale, Latvia's "bread basket," for its open sky and scary summer thunderstorms. She recalled Tante Elza's enormous "honey" linden full of aromatic blooms and bees.

After Latvia was annexed by the Soviet Union in 1940, a state of terror ensued. Mimmī's maternal uncle, Alberts Ābelīte, a village elder, *aizsargs* (home guard), and farmer ("kulak" in Soviet terminology), was arrested in 1941 and sentenced to 25 years of hard labor in Siberia. According to my mother, after he was deported the local school children planted a grove of birch trees to honor him. By the time he came home after Stalin's death, the birch trees had grown tall, as had his own children. Latvia's "bread basket" was devastated during and after the war; its hard-working, proud farmers were scattered or mowed down by the Soviet scythe. Under the Soviets, once flourishing farms fell into a state of ruin.

Uncle Albis remains for me just a story, a vague family figure from whom I was separated by time and historical events. Had there been no war in Latvia, I presume I would have known much more about him, his family, and his farm called Lielmaikaiši, which now belongs to a stranger. I discovered that Uncle Albis had a rather distinguished biography, which would explain why the Soviets punished him so severely. According to Nekropole.lv, a Latvian website devoted to my nation's departed, Alberts Ābelīte served in the Russian artillery from 1915–1918. In 1915 he was decorated with Russia's Cross of St. George III and IV Class. From 1919–1921 he was a sergeant in the Jelgava infantry battalion. From 1921 until 1940 Uncle Albis was active in the Latvian Home Guard organization, and from 1923 until 1939 he was commander of the Jelgava Home Guard battalion's VI Cavalry Squadron. In 1928 he was decorated with the Home Guard's Merit Cross. On November 14, 1936 he was decorated with Latvia's Order of the Three Stars V Category #4059. In 1939/1940 Alberts Ābelīte served as commander of the Jelgava Home Guard Battalion's V Cavalry Squadron. His obituary also lists him as a doctor and proprietor of Lielmaikaiši. Uncle Albis had brothers whom my mother vaguely recalled: Teodors, owner of a pharmacy in Zemgale and a large farm; Roberts (who bequeathed his nursery to my grandmother's brother Fricis Sproģis); Zamuēls, an entrepreneur (?)... The names of these men have faded from the annals of Latvia's history; their fates remain unknown to us.

When the Soviets invaded Latvia in 1940, my mother and her sisters had no idea what was going on around them. They could sense their parents were very worried: they were crying and whispering. As the news of arrests spread and people vanished, my grandparents lived in an agonizing state of suspense, trying to maintain an air of normalcy for their children. My mother's paternal grandmother Dārta Bičole was shocked when the school curriculum suddenly changed, and her granddaughters were forced to recite and sing communist propaganda poetry and songs.

When the Germans drove the Soviets out and occupied Latvia (1941–1944/1945), my grandfather Jānis Bičolis ("Tuks") discovered that his name had been on the list of people to be deported to Siberia. Somehow they had missed him. The German occupation was equally savage. The Nazis allegedly murdered Tuks' brother Alfrēds, an inmate at the psychiatric hospital in Jelgava, along with other patients in early 1942. I was sure that hearing about the slaughter of their Jewish neighbors induced a deep, life-long trauma in my grandparents' generation, which they seemed unable to talk about.

In the summer of 1944 the Soviet Red Army advanced into Latvia, battling the Germans and the Latvian Legion. The terrifying military activity, which included aerial bombardments, sent shock waves and panic throughout the country. My mother's family readied itself for escape from Birži. For my grandfather it was difficult to leave his native Sēlija. His parents lived there, and it was the birthplace of numerous notable people, including writers Jānis Rainis (Dunava, 1865–1929), Jānis Jaunsudrabiņš (Nereta, 1877–1962), Aleksandrs Grīns (Birži, 1895–1941), and Velta Toma (Nereta, 1912–1999). Jaunsudrabiņš ended up in West Germany. Toma settled in Canada. Grīns was arrested at the Latvian Army camp in Litene in 1940, deported to Soviet Russia, and shot in Astrakhan in 1941. Professor, physician, and surgeon Dr. Pauls Stradiņš (Viesīte, 1896–1958), Holocaust historian Andrievs Ezergailis (Rite, 1930), photographer Mārtiņš Buclers (Sauka, 1866–1944), and famous painter Mark Rothko (Daugavpils, 1903–1970) also hailed from that corner of Latvia.

In his autobiographical notes my grandfather Jānis Bičolis describes how his family's life in exile began in the summer of 1944. "Before we reached refuge abroad, we were refugees for three months and two weeks in Latvia. This was, in fact, a lengthy farewell to Latvia. There was no hope that Latvia could remain standing, only hope for a miracle. Sustained by hope, we clung to our country as long as possible." The fact that there was an airport near Birži precluded my grandparents' and their children's safety, where they had hoped to 'weather the storm' on my great-grandparents' farm ("Labieši" in Biķernieki).

> That summer (1944) we were living with my parents in Sēlija, in Birži Parish in the district of Jēkabpils. We were taking care of my father's property while working at the local agricultural school and pursuing various social activities. Already the spring had brought a sense of unrest and change, and our life as we knew it began to disintegrate at the beginning of the summer. It was impossible to hope for a peaceful existence because of the airport at one end of the parish. The Russians had established the airport in 1940, confiscating our arable land, and now the Germans had claimed it. Increasingly, we began to feel like we were living on the edge of a battlefield: we could hear the sound of sirens as well as bombing. We had already moved out of the house and were living at the other end of the parish. Soon it became all too clear that the Germans were losing the war, and that Latvia faced another Soviet invasion.

Our refugee journey commenced on July 28 (1944), when we drove out of Žeikari in Birži in the afternoon. We had a one-horse cart that served us well until the middle of October, when we found ourselves in a completely different part of Latvia. As refugees we crossed our own parish, spending the night at our neighbors' the Zambarnieks' house. The next morning we passed by our own house; I went in, looked around, took a couple of photographs, gave some instructions to those who were staying there, and bid farewell. Then, traveling on lonely forest roads, we reached Sunākste. From the hills of Sunākste we looked back towards home. One of Latvia's most impressive views: in the blue haze of summer the seemingly endless forests of Sēlija. But at that moment the airport at Birži was being bombed. The muffled bursts of exploding bombs, the fire of anti-aircraft artillery, and the distant roar of airplanes; the windows of our house facing the garden had already been knocked out in a previous air raid. What was going on at home? I had left a great portion of my library there; I had moved the most important sections elsewhere and was taking three boxes with me. In the winter (of '44) I had seen German soldiers who were staying in our house using books from my library for kindling; still, it's not that easy to burn a large library. There is so much to regret, but mostly I regret that our lifetime coincided with such terrible events. I regret leaving a few things behind: the two blocks of apple wood that I had saved from our lovely orchard, which was killed off by the great freeze of 1940. These blocks of wood gave off a sweet aroma, each of its distinct apple tree, and I had hoped to ask a wood carver to make a memorial to our orchard using these blocks." (Jānis Bičolis. *Pašportreti.* New York; Grāmatu Draugs, 1965, pp. 45–46)

Latvians had hoped and believed that the Allied Forces would come to Latvia's rescue, forcing the Soviet Union to retreat. But this hope faded quickly. As thousands of Latvian soldiers melted into the forests to become national partisans, hundreds of thousands of refugees abandoned their homes—farms, houses, and apartments—and made their way westward, seeking refuge from the tyranny of Soviet communist rule. They knew what to expect after having survived the first Soviet occupation. My grandparents' "long farewell" from Birži to Sunākste, Sece, Sērene, Aizkraukle, Lēdmane, Sigulda, Līgatne, Straupe, Lielstraupe, Rīga, Kalnciems, Džūkste, Irlava, Zante, Varieba, and Vārme towards the setting sun took them and their daughters further and further from their familiar places and home.

In November 1944 my grandparents and their girls sailed from Liepāja to Gotenhafen (now Gdynia in Poland). A seething mass of disoriented people disembarked from the ship onto the foreign shore, grateful that their vessel of freedom had not been torpedoed or bombed by the Soviets. In Gotenhafen they were packed into a building along with hundreds of other dazed refugees and slept on the floor. Later they were funneled into a horrible holding camp, filthy and primitive, with barbed wire fences and watchtowers. Bedbugs, diarrhea, and malnourishment are what my mother remembered most from this first stop on their flight away from the Soviet menace. She also recalls the terror of seeing Allied planes high up in the sky, and the rumbling, whining sound of their engines that sent the camp's inmates into a wild panic. The gates were opened only in the event of a possible air raid, and everyone scattered for cover into the nearby forest. This was a filtration camp where Germans decided who would be sent where to accommodate what type of Nazi war effort. In early December 1944 my mother's family was sent to work in a parachute factory in Bensen (Benešov nad Ploučnicí) in Sudetenland in Nazi-occupied Czechoslovakia. My mother recalled the Christmas dinner at the factory that year. A plate with a single sausage swimming in yellow mustard sauce was set before each worker and family members. The factory's bosses in their mustard-yellow shirts came in and saluted everyone with a forceful "Heil Hitler!"

When the war ended in the spring of 1945, it became terrifyingly apparent that Czechoslovakia would come under Soviet influence. My grandparents along with many other refugees sought to find a way out and away from Soviet reach. Rumors of the Russians' mass rape of women and girls fueled fear among refugees. My grandparents learned of a form of illegal transport to the west and the American zone in Germany, which my mother believes was organized by a Catholic organization from Prague. It was in Prague, waiting for the train to Plzen (Pilsen), that my mother's family was nearly separated.

My mother recalled: "We had arrived at the Prague railway station and found out that we had several hours to spare before the train departed at 17:00 in the afternoon. Because she still had some food coupons, my mother decided to go in search of provisions. I watched my mother and another Latvian woman named Marta, who was traveling with us, board a tram. My father remained with us children in a nearby park to wait for Mimmī and the train's departure. Shortly after my mother left, we got word that the train would be departing at 14:00 instead of 17:00! For 30 agonizing minutes we waited for my mother to return; with no sign of her, my father made the gut-wrenching decision to board the train. At two o'clock the train started to move. Crammed together on the train's open platform, we girls continued to look desperately for our mother, hoping to see her. I cried and cried and cried for what seemed like hours. Then suddenly I was overcome by a sense of peace. We were nearing Pilsen. Our train was diverted onto a different set of tracks to make way for a passenger train arriving from Prague. A short while later we spotted our mother and Marta stumbling along the tracks, racing for their lives to get to us. We pulled them up into our car just as our train was about to depart!"

My mother's family was able to escape from an area that came under Soviet control. "We made it safely to Amberg, a beautiful medieval town in Germany. We heaved an enormous sigh of relief at our first sight of convoys of American trucks with their white stars. Freedom!" After the war Amberg was located in the so-called American Sector, and it was there that the Bičolis family was interned in their first displaced persons camp in 1946, where people of many different nationalities were assembled. They spent the next four years until 1950 in two other DP camps in Hersbruck and Traunstein. The displaced persons camp era helped consolidate Latvians and thwart assimilation, which would become a problem in later years, when Latvians had established themselves in their new homelands outside of Latvia.

So much had been lost, but they were now safely out of reach of communist terror. As the Iron Curtain enveloped the Baltics and Eastern Europe in decades-long gloom, the Bičolis family set their sights on the New World on the other side of the Atlantic Ocean. They set sail in December 1950, enduring bouts of seasickness and pangs of anxiety about the future, the persistent pain of separation from their fatherland, and worries over its future and the fate of their loved ones who did not make it out. Five days later, they disembarked at their port of entry in

New York and traveled south to Baltimore, where a job at an egg farm awaited them. My grandparents eventually settled permanently in New Jersey, residing for many years in Montclair, their home away from home.

Right: Fricis Sproģis in his youth.

Mimmī's brother Frīdrichs ("Fricis") Sproģis and his family were not so lucky. They tried to depart from Sudetenland a week after my grandparents on a "secret" train but were intercepted by the Czechoslovakians or Russians and sent back to Soviet-occupied Latvia. Before the war Fricis had owned and operated a successful nursery on Vienības gatve in Pārdaugava, but his commercial enterprise was shut down by the communists. Miraculously, he and his family were not deported to Siberia and were even allowed to continue to live in their small wooden house on Vienības gatve (the old road from Rīga to Jelgava). From it they could watch years of work go to waste, as the greenhouses fell into disrepair...

Uncle Fricis died in the 1970s. For years he and my grandmother did not correspond for fear of attracting unwanted attention from the ever vigilant Soviet KGB. My grandmother's older sister Elza managed to get through to him in later years in a circuitous manner.

My grandfather's in-depth knowledge of Latvian, one of Europe's oldest living languages, had no practical application in his life in exile: he worked as a janitor at Hahne's department store in Montclair. He was frequently invited to give lectures about Latvian literature at various Latvian events in the New York area. In his spare time he wrote for Latvian exile publications about the Latvian language and literature. Tuks died of a heart attack in August 1982, four months before I moved to Soviet-occupied Latvia. I was able to record an interview with him about his life. My grandfather's library was eventually shipped to Latvia, its rightful place, and is now part of the collection of the Latvian Academy of Culture in Rīga. His ashes were buried in Leimaņi Cemetery in his native Sēlija in the summer of 1983. Mimmī died in 1998 in Colorado, and her ashes were scattered in the mountains nearby.

Opaps (Paternal Grandfather)

Courtship: My Opaps and Omamma in the 1920s.

When I was growing up, I heard my paternal grandfather Augusts Rumpēters' peers in North America address him as Senator Rumpēters. Up until the Soviet occupation of Latvia in 1940, he served as a senator of the Latvian Supreme Court. Even in exile Latvians of his generation respected his former status. My grandfather became a senator at the age of 39 and was the second youngest Latvian senator. He was the last living senator of the Republic of Latvia. "The Senator" was our dearly beloved "Opaps."

My grandfather was born March 13, 1899 in Turaida Parish. He had one older brother, Arkādijs Rumpēteris (1890–1962), and an older sister named Velta (1895–1956). His father Augusts Jānis Rumpēters worked at the famous "Swiss House" in Turaida as an innkeeper. In the 1920s under Latvia's agricultural reform program he had acquired the inn but sold it in 1927 in order to spend more time at his farm "Vīganti" in Vidriži Parish.

Right: Augusts Rumpēters, center, and classmates from Rīgas pilsētas ģimnāzija (Rīga City Secondary School), circa 1915.

My grandfather began studying law at the University of Tartu in Estonia. In 1919, when he was 20, he enlisted in the so-called First Student Company of the Kalpaks Battalion and took part in the Latvian War of Independence in Latgale. After the war he went back to school at the University of Latvia and graduated from the Department of Law and Economics in 1926. He served as a justice of the peace in Daugavpils. On September 1, 1938 Augusts Rumpēters was appointed senator to the Supreme Court's Department of Civil Cassation and worked there until the Senate was liquidated by the Soviets on November 26, 1940.

My mother said that my grandfather considered his time in the Senate as the most interesting period in his professional life, when he could devote himself to questions of judicial interpretation. He possessed an impressive legal library with more than 2,000 books. My mother recalled how her father-in-law criticized the events of 1934 in Latvia, when President Kārlis Ulmanis staged a coup and dismissed the Saeima (parliament), arrested his opponents, and instituted a brief quasi-dictatorship. My grandfather had lamented the loss of Latvia's parliamentary democracy, and he and other Supreme Court justices had been unanimous in their opinion that the (Latvian) Republic had to return to a democratic system of governance. Ultimately, their opinions didn't matter. They would end up running for their lives.

Left: Rīga's so-called Palace of Justice, where Augusts Rumpēters worked until the Soviet occupation in 1940. This photograph was in his photo album.

When the Soviets relieved him of his duties in 1940, my grandfather went to work in a pharmacy. In 1941, alerted to the fact that he was to be arrested by the NKVD or Cheka, as it was known, my grandfather hid in the forest ("Majags") near Vīganti. On June 14, 1941 his sister Velta and her husband Eduards Rapss were arrested at the farm and deported to Siberia.

During the Nazi German occupation my grandfather worked in the Department of Civil Cases. He also became involved with the underground Latvijas Centrālā padome ("Latvian Central Council" or LCC), a resistance organization that sought to establish contact with Latvia's allies in the West and to rally support for the renewal of Latvia's independence and democracy, condemning any form of dictatorship. The secret consolidation of Latvia's democratic forces had already started during the Soviet occupation and lead to the founding of the LCC on August 13, 1943 during the German occupation. In addition to political efforts, the LCC organized Latvian fishermen's boats to transport refugees to the shores of Sweden, so that they could relay news about the German occupation in Latvia.

The LCC's memorandum of March 17, 1944, an impassioned appeal to Western governments that was addressed, as a precaution under the Nazi occupation, to Latvian General Rūdolfs Bangerskis, sought to rally the nation and the Latvian military (or what was left of it) around the restitution of Latvia's sovereignty and defense of the country against another Soviet invasion. The LCC coordinated its efforts with resistance movements in Estonia and Lithuania. In April 1944 the German Gestapo intercepted a Lithuanian courier. As a result, some of the LCP's members were arrested. Arrests were also made in Lithuania and Estonia. The memorandum was drafted and signed by a group of desperate but determined individuals. The story of the Latvian Central Council is dramatic, tragic, and worthy of a book or film: Latvia was doomed, as were many of the LCC's members. The story of this remarkable Latvian resistance organization, which based its efforts on the principles of national sovereignty and democracy (thereby disassociating itself from the Ulmanis regime), involved covert, dangerous get-togethers, perilous journeys across the Baltic Sea, intercepted escapes, arrests, trials, deportations, and death: that is, lost hopes and dreams. The LCC was dissolved in 1951.

Number 42: Augusts Rumpēters' signature under the March 17, 1944 LCP Memorandum.

I have written about my grandfather Augusts Rumpēters' and my father Ilmārs' escape from Latvia in the foreword to my father's book of drawings, which was published in Rīga in 2013:

> By the fall of 1944 Germany was on the verge of collapse. Many Latvians, overwhelmed by fearful memories of the Soviet occupation of 1940–1941 and a sense of impending doom, decided to flee west. It had become quite apparent that nobody was going to save the Baltic States from re-occupation by the USSR. On September 22, 1944, as artillery fire resounded in the distance, 15-year-old Ilmārs said goodbye to his mother at the end of the road to Vīganti and hurried back to Rīga to join his father. There was no way he could have known that day that 40 years would go by before he saw his mother and brothers again.
>
> Back in Rīga Ilmārs saw the streets lined with anti-tank barriers and long columns of the German Army moving through the city in a westerly direction. The bridges were being mined. Rīga had become a front line city. Beginning in 1944, Ilmārs documented his wartime experiences in a diary that he later called "Ten Months." Two days after returning to Rīga, my father and Senator Rumpēters were forced to abandon the capital; along with countless other refugees they traveled west to the region of Kurzeme, across the Baltic Sea and beyond, away from the horrors of the Red Army and the encroaching wave of Soviet communist domination. Ilmārs' older brother Visvaldis, who had turned 17 in 1944, had been conscripted by the Nazi German authorities that summer to serve in an anti-aircraft artillery unit. As Russian tanks rumbled toward Rīga, the Rumpēters family was painfully split apart. With the Red Army advancing deeper into Latvia, Ilmārs' mother and two younger brothers were stranded in the countryside, unable to leave because of the retreating German Army with its heavy armored vehicles, and because of the old folks at Vīganti.

My grandfather and my father left Latvia by ship from the port city of Liepāja, reaching Germany on October 12, 1944. They were later re-united with Visvaldis in Germany; he had barely escaped death's clutches. Inspired by his war-time experiences, my father's older brother later studied theology in the United States, was ordained, and served in a Latvian Lutheran congregation in Milwaukee, Wisconsin.

My grandfather Senator Augusts Rumpēters penned an important tractate, *Soviet Aggression Against the Baltic States*, which was published by the World Federation of Free Latvians in 1974. The tractate is still considered "one of the best sources extant examining the Soviet-Baltic relationship regarding mutual agreements and international law—and how the Soviet Union abrogated those agreements and violated international law in coercing the Baltics into accepting Soviet troops and then invading and annexing them." (www.Latvians.com) Stuck in exile in the United States, my grandfather remained politically active and devoted to the work of the Latvian Lutheran Church and his fraternity Lettonia. With my grandfather's passing in 1978, "the Latvian Senate's living history had ended." It was the end of an era. (Ed. R. Zvejniece. *Latvijas Senāts 1918–1940*. Rīga: Latvijas Republikas Augstākā tiesa, 2008)

Omamma (Paternal Grandmother)

Emma Lejiņa in Omsk in 1919.

On September 22, 1944 my maternal grandmother Emma Rumpētere waved to her second-born son, as he walked down the road away from his grandfather's farm. He vanished from her view for 40 years, and little did she know that day that she would never see her husband again. Omamma was a tower of strength. Born in 1896 in a house called Liel-lāles in Aloja Parish, Emma Elfrīda Lejiņa graduated from a girls' secondary school in Valmiera in 1917. She enrolled in the private Serkov Secondary School in Rīga, which was evacuated to St. Petersburg with the outbreak of World War I. Young Emma moved to St. Petersburg to continue her studies and lived with her uncle, Hamilkārs Lejiņš, who owned a cafeteria there. In her free time she worked the cafeteria's cash register. She graduated from the Serkov School with a gold medal and enrolled in St. Petersburg's Bestuzhev Courses for women to study natural sciences. When Uncle Hamilkārs vacationed in Finland in summertime, she visited him there, retaining lovely memories of the Nordic country.

When the Russian Revolution heated up and the situation in St. Petersburg became too volatile, Omamma and her sister Paulīne headed deeper into Russia to Ufa. There she was hired as a tax inspector, while her sister found work in a pharmacy. As the Bolsheviks drew near, an uncle who owned a mill in the Latvian farmers' colonies in the Ural Mountains arrived by horse carriage to fetch my grandmother and her sister. With Bolsheviks causing unrest in the colonies, Omamma moved to Omsk, where she worked in the office of a Latvian-owned cosmetics factory. When Latvia and Soviet Russia signed the 1920 Peace Treaty, Omamma returned home. She entered the University of Latvia to study agronomy. In her third year in school she began working in the *Lauksaimniecības ekonomiskā sabiedrība* (Agricultural Economics Society) as an assistant accountant while attending school. It was at this time that she met my grandfather, Augusts Rumpēters. My grandparents were married by my great-uncle Arkādijs Rumpēteris, a Latvian minister, on November 11, 1926 in Daugavpils. My grandmother gave birth to four sons, Visvaldis, Ilmārs, Ģirts, and Andris.

Three of four: My father Ilmārs (1929) and his brothers Visvaldis (1927) and Ģirts (1931) Rumpēters. The family's *pastarītis* (youngest child) Andris, born in 1936, is not in the photograph.

Omamma wrote: "I spent the greater part of my youth outside of my family, beginning with my school years in Mazsalaca, Valmiera, and Rīga, and then I ended up far away in Russia. Once back in Latvia, I married, started a family in Daugavpils, and lost touch with my parents for a while." Her early independence would help her later in life, when she ended up without a husband in Soviet-occupied Latvia with two young sons in her care. For many years Omamma worked as an accountant at the local kolhoz. My grandfather remained faithful to her until the end of his life.

My uncle Visvaldis told me: "Our mother raised us with sensitivity and patience. She taught us to pray at a very early age and to put our trust in God. Every night when we went to bed, she would recite the prayer "Nu es gribu gulēt iet"("Now I Lay Me Down to Sleep"). She talked to us about God and answered all of our questions. On Christmas Eve she accompanied our Christmas songs on the piano. She was an accomplished pianist." Visvaldis was also separated from his mother and younger brothers for four decades.

The year 1940 marked the end of the Republic of Latvia and a good life of work, family, and pleasure. Uncle Visvaldis: "In June of the 'Year of Terror' (1941), when the communists started arresting and deporting people en masse, there was nobody at home at our apartment on Āgenskalna iela in Rīga. My mother had gone to Jūrmala with (my brothers) Ilmārs and Ģirts. My little brother Andris and I were at Vīganti, when Aunt Velta and Uncle Eduards (Rapss) were arrested by chekists and taken away. My brother and I and two old women and one old man were left in the house crying. My immediate family was lucky to escape the deportations. We found out later that the NKVD had been looking for us at our apartment in Rīga." Miraculously, the Senator and his family had slipped through the Cheka's net.

A family photograph taken in the home of my great-uncle Arkādijs Rumpēteris (1890–1962), seated far left with his son Jānis in Daugavpils, Latvia in 1926, either before or after the marriage of my grandparents, Augusts and Emma Rumpēters, center. On the right: my great-aunt Velta and her husband Eduards Rapss.

A small, slim, blue notebook in almost perfect condition contains my grandfather Opaps' poems written in pencil, some of which are dated 1914. His handwriting remained the same throughout his life. A section titled "Emšukam" ("To Emmie") contains love poems dedicated to my Oma. Tucked into the very back of the notebook is a poem by Elza Stērste (1885–1976) written in my grandmother's handwriting:

Veltījums. *Plaukst mežrozīte jūras priedēs, / Drīz ūdenslilja ziedu vērs. / Kā senāk, mīļā, viss Tev ziedēs, / Tik dzīve neies vecās sliedēs, / Tik kopā nebūsim vairs mēs. // Kā mākoņi, kas, vēja dzīti, / Pie Tevis steidz, tā domas steidz. / Kaut nesniedzamā tālē mīti, / Tev mani vakari un rīti, / Un viss, kas paliek neizteikts.*

(**Dedication.** The briar rose flowers in the seaside pines, / The waterlily will open soon. / Like before, my love, all will bloom for you, / But life won't be as before, / We won't be together anymore. // Like clouds pushed by the wind / My thoughts hurry to you. / Though you dwell far away, / All my evenings and mornings / And unspoken words are for you.—Tr. RL)

Dimmed Lights (Great-Grandparents)

My great-grandparents Pēteris and Dārta Bičolis with their sons Jānis (my grandfather) and Alfrēds.

Pēteris and Dārta Bičolis of Sēlija

My great-grandfather Pēteris Bičolis was a locomotive engineer turned farmer whose farm "La-bieši" in Biķernieki in the region of Sēlija was intersected by a narrow-gauge (light rail) railway line. My mother Baiba Bičole said that her grandfather had the soul of an artist. "He had thick hair and bushy white whiskers. When we came to visit, he would greet us playing on his fiddle. He had also learned to play the clarinet and dance the Russian *kazachok* in Russia. My sister and I had to sing for him to demonstrate our musical ability. He enjoyed telling us stories. My grand-parents often quarreled. Grandfather was a dreamer, Grandmother was a workhorse." Pēteris Bičolis' father, whose name my mother no longer remembers, was reputed to have been a sought-out healer.

Dārta Bičole graduated from a secondary school for girls with a gold medal. Like many women of her time, the practical aspects of life prevented her from continuing her education. According to my mother, she was petite, with fair skin and light-blue eyes. Like in the Latvian folk song *"Adatiņa maza sieva, lielu darbu darītāj"* ("The needle's a little woman, doer of great works"), Dārta was always busy, practical and sensible, and accomplished in every farm chore there was. She could shear sheep, spin wool, weave, knit, sew, bake bread, and take care of her livestock. "Very loving, always busy, always worried about the little things in life. When she came to visit, she always brought us homemade butter cookies and apples. She was always nagging my grandfather to go and do something; she must have thought he was lazy, because he day-dreamed a lot": this is how my mother remembers her grandmother, who managed a household and farm.

My mother's grandparents Pēteris and Dārta chose to stay put in Latvia in 1944, when the world around them seemed to be disintegrating. Perhaps they felt too old to venture into the unknown. Pēteris Bičolis died soon after the war. Dārta went to live with relatives and passed away in the 1950s. Her oldest son Jānis (my grandfather) had emigrated with his family. The Nazis had murdered her youngest son Alfrēds in 1942. The farm she worked so hard to maintain fell into disrepair.

Augusts Jānis and Amālija Rumpēters of Vidzeme

My great-grandfather (my father's paternal grandfather) Augusts Jānis Rumpēters (*left*) lived from 1862 until 1938. My father recalled: "I remember my grandfather from childhood, when I spent summers at his farm called Vīganti in Vidriži Parish. I mostly remember him in his study, seated at his desk, sometimes smoking. His enlarged prostate caused him considerable suffering. He died of blood poisoning from a urinary tract infection. He was a calm, self-possessed man."

My great-grandfather acquired Turaida's famous *Šveices māja* ("Swiss House"), where he had previously worked as an innkeeper, in the 1920s under Latvia's agricultural reform program. According to the website *Zudusī Latvija* ("Lost Latvia"), the Swiss House was built as a replica of an Alps hotel. A second-story balcony wrapped around the inn; slender columns carved from wood, eight-paned windows, and exterior staircases were some of its decorative features. A large sign on the façade of the inn, which faced the road, was emblazoned with the following text in Latvian and German: 'This Swiss house / Stands here with God's blessing. / This house when it was built / Was dated from Christ's birth / The year 1828.' The inn was frequented by wealthy clients from Rīga, St. Petersburg, Warsaw, and elsewhere. Between 1848 and 1886 many (Latvian) teachers' conferences took place at the Swiss House. Atis Kronvalds (one of the Latvian National Awakening period's best known figures—RL), gave speeches there in 1869 and 1870. In 1919 the so-called landless workers' council met at the inn. In the 1930s it became a post office and telephone central. The inn burned down in World War II as the German Army was retreating.

According to my uncle Visvaldis Rumpēteris, my ancestor Kārlis dreamed up with the surname "Rum-peter," which he wrote into his Bible. This must have happened when serfdom was abolished in Vidzeme, which resulted in a name-giving campaign in the early 19th century: former serfs could claim surnames.

Here is an excerpt from my great-grandfather Augusts Jānis Rumpēters' memoir about how people from various locales acquired nicknames: "(In our dark ages) there was a tradition of giving people and places nicknames. (...) People from Turaida were called '(barrel) hoop thieves.' People from Krimulda were known as '(church) collection thieves.' People from Mazstraupe were 'flies.' People from Sigulda were 'corpse thieves.' People from Rauna were 'cat hangers.'" Apparently each funny nickname was baed on a true story. People from Sigulda were called "corpse thieves" on account of this story: Some robbers heard that a pig had just been slaughtered at a certain farm. So they broke into the farm's granary at night, saw something covered with a white sheet, carried it out, placed it in their wagon, and took off. They found out soon enough that it was the body of a dead man who had just passed away; his body had been wrapped in a sheet and placed in the granary. In the old days all the parishes had nicknames. For instance, people from Rauna were also called 'bucket shitters.'" This quaint tradition has not survived into modern times.

Augusts Jānis Rumpēters married Amālija Plūme ("Plum"). My great-grandmother was born in 1866 and died in 1938. According to my father, she spent her days at Vīganti sitting motionlessly in the same chair. "She was paralyzed during World War I, when her husband was arrested by the Bolsheviks and thrown into Rīga Central Prison, where everyone thought he would be shot. She suffered a nervous breakdown from which she never recovered. As she sat in her chair, I often whispered in her ear, although she had lost her speech. In spite of her disability, I could sense how much she loved us, her grandchildren. Her appearance was most kindly and loving," my father remembered.

Amālija's sisters and brother, Anna, Marija, and Kārlis, none of whom married, came to live at Vīganti in the 1930s. They saw Uncle Eduards and Aunt Velta arrested and taken away by Soviet chekists in the summer of '41. My great-grandparents passed away before the terrible events that engulfed Latvia starting in 1940.

Great-Grandparents Antons and Matilde Lejiņš of Northern Vidzeme

My great-grandparents, Antons and Matilde Lejiņš.

My grandmother Emma Lejiņa's father Antons Lejiņš (*left*) was born in 1861 and died in 1940. He owned a farm called Liel-lāles near Nikšas in Aloja Parish. Uncle Visvaldis said he could barely recall his maternal grandparents, because as children he and his brothers rarely visited: Aloja was far away in the northern part of Vidzeme close to Estonia. Antons' father was one Jānis Lejiņš (1833–1899) lived on a farm called Rimeikas in Vecate Parish near Mazsalaca. Antons' mother Līze (Liise Kruusman) was Estonian. Jānis and Līze Lejiņš had 16 children: 12 sons and four daughters. Five of the children died in childhood. One son, Pauls Lejiņš (1883–1959), became a famous Latvian agronomist. (Source: Nekropole.lv)

According to family stories, Antons was a passionate hunter and walked around with a shotgun slung over his shoulder, providing his family with an ample supply of meat. He made his living growing and selling flax, barley, and horses. He was crazy about horses and raised them for profit. His horses were very fast, and he did not let anyone pass him on the road. He took his horses to shows, where they won many awards.

According to Uncle Visvaldis, my great-grandmother, Antons' wife Matilde Cālītis (1868-1947), was a workaholic who even at moments of rest kept her hands busy knitting. A prolific weaver, she always had something going on the loom. She sewed simple clothes for herself and her daughters. She was the one who pushed for better education for her children, better than what she had received in her lifetime. She was quiet and patient and devoted herself entirely to her family. She toiled not to hoard wealth but out of a sense of responsibility towards her family and especially her children.

In learning more about the people who came before me, I am struck by how hard-working they were. Lazy is not a word that describes most Latvians. Destined to live in a country that was often beset by misfortune and war, they struggled to school their children and take care of the land that fed them. Out of people like them emerged the Republic of Latvia, free and independent and prosperous. To them I feel indebted.

Enemies of the Soviet State:
A Latvian Hero and His Bride

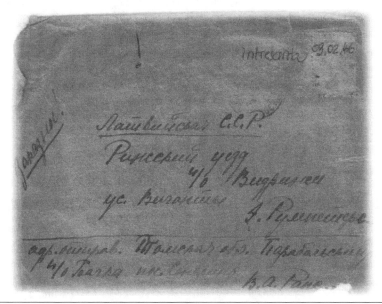

A letter from Great-Aunt Velta Rapss addressed my grandmother, sent from Tomsk Oblast in 1946.

Time won't trace its old path this summer, / Flowers will sorrow, the honey turn bitter, / The horse won't be harnessed for faraway visits, / The jasmine won't bloom in May. / Sunlight won't shatter the days' deep darkness, / Midsummer will be jilted by joy, / And a blossom just picked will wilt in the hand, / A fearful expanse, a fear past each shrub. / The wind will drive a red fog o'er the fields, / The trees will shed their fruit too soon, / A burden will be what is and what isn't. / Even the depths of the earth lie mute: / Your betrayal has turned / The water into wormwood.— "Baigā vasara" ("The Terrible Summer"), a poem by Edvarts Virza (1883–1940). Tr. RL.

This popular Latvian poem, "The Terrible Summer," was almost prophetic with its stanza about a "red fog" rolling over the land, causing ripening fruit to fall prematurely. Edvards Virza wrote it in 1939, the year when Nazi Germany and the USSR signed a secret pact that paved the way for events of epic violence in Latvia and elsewhere. Virza died in 1940, when Latvia was occupied by Soviet Russian forces. Had he lived a bit longer, his patriotism, nationalism, and favor with the last Latvian President Kārlis Ulmanis would have ensured his arrest and deportation or execution. Regardless of its original intent, for Latvians the poem came to signify their country's suffering under the Soviet Russian occupation. Any mention of Virza and his poetry was unwise during this time. His life and literary legacy were repressed like so much of Latvia's historical and cultural legacy. His beloved home in Zemgale, Billītes, was nationalized and turned into a communal dwelling for kolhoz families. By the end of the 1980s the once charming house with its columned entrance looked unrecognizable in its state of neglect.

Surely my great-aunt Velta and her husband Eduards Rapss had read this sinister-sounding poem; Latvians adored poetry. Foreboding as it was, could any Latvian in the late 1930s possibly imagine the horror—"the red fog"—that would bear down on them from the east, or the psychopathic terror that Nazi Germany would soon import? When Jews seeking refuge in Latvia from Poland were telling their stories, few wished to believe them. And President Ulmanis had muzzled the press.

When I was a child, I did not know that my grandfather had a sister. Many questions went unasked and therefore unanswered, typical of childhood. Nor did I know much about my Omamma in Latvia other than that we sent her aid packages from time to time. My father did not talk to me about her or what had happened. As for my great-aunt Velta, she died in Tomsk Oblast four years before I was born. The war severed natural ties, and family members scattered across continents drifted apart.

Left: Velta in her childhood.

Velta Rumpētere was my grandfather's older sister, born in 1895. She attended school, but what she studied my uncle Visvaldis could no longer say. Velta married Eduards Rapss, a dashing young soldier who had taken part in Latvia's War of Independence and was a recipient of the Order of Lāčplēsis, Latvia's highest military honor.

"Eduards Rapss, son of Pēteris, was born on January 1, 1890 in Allaži into a family of farmers. He attended Alexander Secondary School in Rīga and became a tutor. He was recruited into the Russian Army in 1915 and served in the 149th Reserve Battalion of Penza. In 1916 he was transferred to the 3rd Division's 9th Regiment, in which he fought against the Germans, including at the Rīga front near Koknese. Eduards Rapss joined the Latvian Army as a volunteer in December 1918 and took part in the first battles against the Bolsheviks near Cēsis in Vidzeme. On December 21, 1918 Rapss offered to cross enemy lines: he arrived in Valmiera and established himself in a building housing Bolshevik headquarters, where he succeeded in obtaining intelligence about the enemy. On December 23 he arrived in Rīga and passed this information directly to the Defense Minister.

Right: The Order of Lāčplēsis No. 850 that Eduards Rapss received in 1921 for reconnaissance behind enemy lines in Valmiera, Latvia. Source: Latvian War Museum / Guntars Rumpēters.

"In Rīga Rapss joined a student company of the Kalpaks Battalion and took part in battles in Kurzeme. After Rīga's liberation he was promoted to the rank of lieutenant and transferred to the so-called War Economic Authority (Kaŗa saimniecības pārvalde) as Assistant to the Chief of Supplies. Rapss was decommissioned in June 1921. For his military service he was awarded Griķu Inn in Inčukalns Parish. Eduards Rapss was a member of Latvia's Home Guard organization from 1921 (...) and moved up its ranks. By 1931 he was Chief of the Home Guard's Department of Organization. (...)

In June 1941 (Eduards Rapss) was deported from Vīganti in Vidriži Parish to the Soviet Union. He died on November 7 (of that year) in Usollag (Perm Oblast, Russia)."[1]

In 1995 a Latvian expedition of four men, Ilmārs Knaģis, Ainārs Bambāls, Zigurds Šlics, and Alfreds Puškevics, set out to Russia to visit the sites of the former Stalinist death camps, Vyatlag and Usollag, to erect memorials to the Latvians who perished there. The following is an excerpt from the expedition's notes about my great-uncle's death in Usollag:

> It's time to head to Usollag's administrative offices. Along the way (walking past 20 Let Pobedy Street) we are shown the spot where the old administration building burned down. The archives were not damaged; nothing of the Cheka's is ever lost. Behind a high metal fence decorative bushes conceal the new building. The gate is wide open. There is now a bed of bright flowers where (Felix) Dzerzhinsky's monument once stood. (Felix Edmundovich Dzerzhinsky, 1877–1926, was the founder of the Bolsheviks' feared secret police, the Cheka.—RL) Entering the building, we jump at the sound of a praporshchik's/officer's bark: "*Stoi! Kuda?* (Halt! Where are you going?)" Our guide V. Belkin talks to the fellow. We stand around waiting for the officer on duty.
>
> The walls in all the rooms are decorated with shiny Lenin bas-reliefs. "Iron Felix" (Dzerzhinsky) is nowhere to be seen. We recall Vyatlag, where two Felixes and one Lenin bas-relief had been removed from the façade of the main building. Go figure! Maybe someone got the instructions mixed up? In an office we are approached by General A. Yaborov who wears a uniform shirt with epaulettes. His jacket hangs off the back of his chair. This means our conversation won't be strictly official. Ilmārs informs the General of our mission. Ainārs surprises the General with his knowledge of the archives, asking him to show us the file cards documenting Latvians (who were imprisoned at Usollag): Lāčplēsis Order recipients and officers. Soon enough 20 cards appear on the table. The ones we had hoped to see are not among the cards placed in front of us. There's an easy explanation: they can't show us the cards with the verdict "death by shooting." Instead, we are shown these. The general's explanation: the cards we want to see are too hard to find!
>
> I pick up one of the cards on the table. Who did the Soviet authorities consider their most dangerous enemies to be liquidated? "No. 60561 Usollag. 1. Surname—Rapss. 2. First name, patronym—Eduards Petrovich. 3. D.O.B.—1896. 4. Social origin—landowner. 5. Ethnicity—Latvian, citizenship—(blank). 6. Education—Secondary. 7. Former party affiliation—Home Guard Organization. 8. Place of residence—Vidriži Parish, Latvia. 9. Profession—(blank). 10. Occupation—Teacher. 07. 16.41. (Signature of card's preparer.) Arrived from where: 07. 10.41., Latvia (in stages). Location: Surmog, 07. 13.41. Died: 11.8.41." A 45-year-old teacher of farming origin dies in the lager just after four months. Without an investigation or proper trial. Socialism is the victor here: there's one Latvian teacher less to deal with.
>
> (...) In the afternoon we are introduced to a physician and NKVD veteran, one Peter Nikitovich who remembered the events of 1941. (...) According to him, most of the deaths at Usollag were the result of starvation. The prisoners who worked

---

[1] Source: LKOK.com

in the forest should have received 4,000 calories of nourishment a day; instead, the lager's daily norm was barely 3,000 calories. For a while people survived on their inner reserves, but then those ended, and they expired. (...) In 1942 the food supplies dwindled even more, as the war raged on. (2)

Aunt Velta died in 1956 in the tiny, remote village of Senkino in Tomsk Oblast, Russia. According to Wikipedia, "Tomsk Oblast is largely "inaccessible because it is covered with taiga woods and swamps." A dreary image is lodged in my brain of a godforsaken place in the middle of nowhere. Or rather, in the middle of Siberia's frightening vastness. The bones of Balts are scattered all over Siberia. Had Velta and Eduards chosen to leave Latvia as soon as the Soviets invaded, they probably would have survived. Their fate took them in the opposite direction, away from civilization into a brutal system of repression that dated back to the Russian tsars.

The following is a partial list of recipients of Latvia's highest military decoration, the Order of Lāčplēsis, who were murdered by the Soviets in 1941 (3/1150) **Andersons, Krišjānis,** died on October 2, 1941, Vorkutlag/Vorkuta, USSR ; (3/2007) **Anšmits-Anšmidts, Jānis,** discovered murdered at Rīga Central Prison in July 1941 after the arrival of the Germans (other sources allege that he was shot in Katlakalns on February 21, 1941); (3/1899) **Bachs, Žanis,** shot in Moscow on October 16, 1941; (3/2056) **Balodis, Nikolajs,** died of heart failure at Surmog Camp, Usollag; (3/640) **Blaus, Eduards,** allegedly executed on June 22, 1941 in Rīga; (3/495) **Blaus, Jānis,** shot on June 22, 1941 at Rīga Central Prison; (3/1317) **Blūmfelds, Paulis,** shot on November 8, 1941 in Astrakhan; (3/1032) **Blūms, Paulis,** shot on November 8, 1941 in Novosibirsk; (3/414) **Broders, Alberts,** shot on June 22, 1941 by the NKVD at Baltezers; (3/279) **Celmiņš, Hugo,** shot on July 30, 1941 in Moscow; (3/97) **Ceplītis, Rūdolfs,** shot on October 16, 1941 in Moscow; (3/1520) **Cielēns, Otto,** discovered shot near Babīte in July 1941 after the arrival of the Germans; (3/1933) **Dālbergs, Artūrs,** shot on October 16, 1941 in Moscow; (3/282) **Dannenbergs, Artūrs,** shot on October 16, 1941 in Moscow; (3/312) **Ērglis, Jūlijs,** shot on June 22, 1941 (body found near Baltezers after the arrival of the Germans in July); (3/1449) **Ērmanis, Valdemārs Jēkabs,** shot on June 22, 1941 (body found near Baltezers after the arrival of the Germans in July); (3/253) **Gāršnieks, Mārtiņš,** died in 1941 or 1942 in Sverdlovsk Oblast, Siberia; (3/1153) **Goldfelds-Zeltiņš, Otto,** shot on July 28, 1941 in Moscow; (3/101) **Goppers, Kārlis,** shot on March 25, 1941; (3/198) **Greble, Jānis,** shot on December 8, 1941 in Sol-Iletsk; (3/98) **Grīslis, Eduards,** died on October 24, 1941 in Siberia; (3/1935) **Hartmanis, Mārtiņš,** shot on July 27, 1941 in Moscow. Source: www.LKOK.com.

Death by shooting appears to have been the Soviets' preferred method of ridding Latvia of its defenders and military heroes. General Mārtiņš Hartmanis was the father of writer Astrīde Ivaska who stayed at our house in Glen Ridge a couple of times with her husband Ivar. Tragically for millions of people, the gravesites of their loved ones remain unknown: Russia's Siberia is a terrifyingly vast territory that is difficult to traverse.

Chapter sources:

(1) Eduards Rapss and the Order of Lāčplēsis > LKOK.com
(2) Eduards Rapss > Alfreds Puškevics. Crimes Against Humanity. Latvian Site. "Ekspedīcija Vjatlags-Usoļlags '95." ("Expedition Vyatlag-Usollag '95") http://lpra.vip.lv/puskevics.htm Published 11/6/2010.

Victims of Soviet Repression:
Photographs of Velta (b. Rumpētere) and Eduards Rapss

Great-Aunt Velta was also a good storyteller, according to my father Ilmārs.

Velta the young Latvian lady..

Velta and her Eduards.

Latvia in the 1930s: Uncle Eduards examining the bounty of the earth at Vīganti, where he was arrested in 1941.

1930s: Members of Latvia's Aizsargi (Home Guards) and their four-legged companions. Aizsargi was a voluntary paramilitary organization established in 1919 as a self-defense force and to help the fledgling Latvian government maintain law and order. The Soviets liquidated the Home Guards in 1940. Many of its members were arrested, shot, or deported. Second from right: Eduards Rapss.

Just a few more years together: this photograph looks to have been taken in the late 1930s, when Velta and Eduards Rapss were in the prime of life.

PART THREE:
Return to Terra Incognita

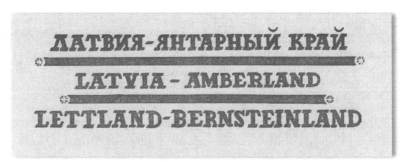

An insert from the book *Dzintarzeme Latvija* published in 1960, the year I was born.

A "punishment" or "humiliation" sign that was hung around the neck of Latvian children at the end of the 19th century, when the territory of Latvia was part of the Russian Empire, and a policy of Russification was in effect. The sign says, "I spoke Latvian today."
Source: Ivo Briedis, Latvian Museum of National History

As the plane droned towards Europe, my thoughts swung back and forth between reverie and practical concerns. I was an inexperienced traveler, and it was my first time crossing the Atlantic. The Union of Soviet Socialist Republics still lay far to the east, shrouded in darkness and Cold War "007" mystery. The Robert Ellyn Travel Agency in New York had taken care of my travel arrangements; I just had to stay on track. The distant stars seemed to be winking at me, as I thought about about my grandparents Tuks and Mimmī and my mother. They were the three people who had exhibited the most enthusiasm about this opportunity. Tuks had been giddy like a child, picturing his granddaughter in his native land. Sadly, my paternal grandfather did not live to see this day. I was certain, though, that he was watching over me.

A rosy light in the sky ahead of us signaled that my flight was approaching its destination, Europe (the Old World), and the dawn of a new day. About thirty years ago my grandparents and their children, my parents, had left war-torn Europe for their new home in the United States with remnants of their former life squeezed into their luggage; family photographs, cherished books, and small souvenirs of the homeland were tucked in among clothes and other necessities. How agonizing it must have been to choose what to bring and what to leave behind, when each hour was precious! The photographs that survived their escape from Latvia would offer us, their descendants, a glimpse into our own ever darkening past.

I knew very little about what had happened in Latvia after "zero hour" (*Stunde Null*), which marked "the end of the war, the retreat of Germany, the arrival of the Soviet Union, the moment the fighting ended and life started up again." (Anne Applebaum, *Iron Curtain*) Our Latvian school history books ended with the year 1945, and for decades the exile community wrote and spoke of Latvia primarily in the past tense. The Republic of Latvia had ceased to exist, yet it was a vivid memory in the minds of the people who had experienced it. Latvia's people weren't all gone, but so many were. Latvia lost approximately one third of its inhabitants because of the war and the Soviet and Nazi occupations. The losses, both human and economic, continued after the war under the Soviets, and they became systemic, a kind of chronic hemorrhaging that went on for almost half a century. Still, the large "coffee table" books that my uncle in Latvia had sent us from Soviet-occupied Latvia, and which I had carefully studied, told me that Latvia's European legacy was not completely destroyed.

I knew very little about the people who lived in Soviet-occupied Latvia, and even our family in Latvia, the people I would soon be meeting, was a group of strangers to me. I barely knew anything about Latvia's "famous" people of the Soviet era and its intelligentsia—writers, artists, composers, etc. I was aware of Russia's Gulag system in Siberia, that for Latvians Siberia had no other connotation than slave labor, and Russia's role in my people's history in the 20th century and prior to that. I had read Alexander Solzhenitsyn's *One Day in the Life of Ivan Denisovich*, as well as works by other Russian writers, Bulgakov, Chekhov, Dostoevsky, Gogol, Tolstoy, Turgenev... I had read Mikhail Bulgakov's *Master and Margarita*, and I thought of the Soviet Union, particularly Russia, as a place ruled by Satan's dark forces. Anna Akhmatova's poems captured the essence of the dark era that followed Imperial Russia's demise: madness; chaos; darkness; and death. I knew that Latvia and Russia were now inextricably linked; my country and its people were a captive nation, despite the Soviet Union's claims of liberating our country. But post-war life in occupied Latvia was a mystery to me. The Soviet propaganda and lie machine had started up in the first days of the "re-occupation," and state censors were kept busy for decades. Strange captions in Soviet Latvian books about Lenin, "bourgeois Latvia," the mighty Red Army, the "friendship" of Soviet nations, and inescapable communist victory signaled that Latvia was different than I imagined it.

What exactly happened in Latvia when Germany lost the war, and the Baltic States were ceded to the Soviet Union?

> After World War II, when the murders, deportations, and repressions had been carried out, the Soviet Union had three main objectives to achieve in the Baltic States: their colonization by Russians; the Russification of the populations of the Baltic States; and the total integration of the Baltic economies, which were formerly oriented to the West, into the the Soviet Union's economic structures. This included the nationalization of all private property except for a limited amount of personal possessions. The property of hundreds of thousands of deportees was confiscated, because these people were considered politically suspect or were simply designated as enemies of the Soviet state. In practical

terms, the USSR resumed implementing the same repressive measures it had initiated in June 1941.

Soviet/Russian colonization was closely linked to mass murder, deportations, and repressions against the indigenous people of Latvia, Estonia, and Lithuania. After each mass deportation people from other Soviet republics, mostly ethnic Russians, were sent into the Baltic States. The deported Balts—those who had not already been murdered by the Soviet Russian NKVD in their countries—were permitted to bring with them to Siberia only the minimum amount of personal belongings including food for the long trip. All of the deported Balts' property and their personal belongings, as well as the contents of their homes and apartments, were handed over to the settlers—the colonizers. At first these colonizers were USSR (Russian) military personnel, NKVD personnel, and communist functionaries, as well as many economic refugees fleeing Russia's kolhozes who were later joined in Latvia by their families. In the first 12 years after World War II more than 400,000 such colonizers arrived in Latvia to occupy the apartments and homes of deported and murdered persons. Over the next 40 years this number reached 708,000. The region of Kurzeme suffered the most right after the war: the Soviet Union set up filtration camps and incarcerated Latvian men between the ages of 16 and 60; many of these men were then sent to Siberia (according to estimates about 50,000). They were deported on the sole basis of being Latvian.

On March 25, 1949 the Soviet NKVD executed a "top secret special operation" code-named *Krasta banga* ("Shoreline Surge"). This special operation was implemented by the Soviet Union's NKVD-MVD (Ministry of Internal Affairs)-MGB (Ministry of State Security) internal forces, which deported approximately 95,000 people from the Baltic States (from Estonia 20,713, from Latvia 42,149, from Lithuania 31,917). Of those deported from Latvia, 72.9% were women and children. The colonization (of Latvia) as it had commenced in 1940–1941 continued during the entire Soviet occupation up until 1991. The data shows that the number of immigrants who arrived in Latvia from 1945 until 1955 reached 535,000; they were mostly from Russia. This number does not include Soviet military personnel who served in the occupation forces and lived in Latvia. It was Soviet policy to encourage army personnel to retire in Latvia: that is, to stay in Latvia after retirement or to move to Latvia to retire with their families, for which they received special compensation and privileges.

The Soviet Union's Russification program was simply structured but strictly enforced. It was mandatory for the local population's children to learn Russian, and all official business had to be conducted in Russian, although 99% of Latvians did not speak Russian (at the outset of the Soviet occupation—RL). The Russian language dominated all situations and all occasions—at meetings, the movies, etc. If there were ten Latvians and one Russian, the conversation usually had to take place in Russian; nobody thought to protest because one could end up in Siberia over a minor issue. Moscow's goal was to diminish the role of Latvian, which Russian chauvinists referred to as the language of "dogs" or "fascists." Latvia was especially vulnerable to this Russification program because of its large number of colonists. (...) Settlers who did not speak Latvian assumed leading roles in Rīga and in regional offices. These officials refused to learn to speak Latvian and issued all of their directives and reports in Russian. Farmers for the most part did not understand the Russian edicts. The ousting of the Latvian language from daily life was so extreme, that even some high-ranking (communist) officials protested it.— Andrejs Mežmalis. "Rusifikācijas politikas izraisītie zaudējumi Baltijā." (Losses Sustained by the Baltic States Under a Policy of Russification) Ed. Juris Prikulis. *The Soviet Union's Losses Inflicted on the Baltic States: Material from an International Conference in Riga*. Rīga: Latvijas Okupācijas izpētes biedrība, 2012. Excerpt: Tr. RL.

In 1980 I was flying to a country that had undergone enormous political, economic, and social transformation since my grandparents' departure in 1944. I knew that there would be a disconnect between how I imagined Latvia and what I would see and experience. This in and of itself was a reason to go. I wanted to witness Soviet-occupied communist Latvia to be able to tell my family and friends what it was like. It bothered me that, according to the exile community, Latvia seemed to have vanished into thin air in 1945. Yes, the Republic of Latvia no longer existed. But Latvia remained a distinct ethnic (albeit changing) and geographic entity. I also hoped to get a whiff of Latvia's past, the one that my grandparents belonged to.

Latvians in exile who had read George Orwell's dystopian novel *1984* (first published in 1949) understood that the Soviet state was based on the same sort of principles described in the novel: perpetual war; government surveillance; the manipulation of public opinion; a government jargon (like Orwell's "Newspeak"); a privileged Party elite; the persecution of individualism; independent thinking as "thought crime"; historical revisionism; and the tyranny of Big Brother "always watching you." All of these frightening aspects of Orwell's imaginary society were actually integral components of the Soviet political system, as I was soon to discover. In the Soviet Union every aspect of life was controlled by the Communist Party in Moscow. It is one thing to read a book of fiction about a totalitarian state; it is another to experience such a state in real life. My personal experience with totalitarianism was through the lens of documentary films, books, and eye-witness accounts.

The Cold War had inspired some great books and films, like some of my favorite James Bond movies. I had packed Hedrick Smith's 1976 book *The Russians* to read during my travels. I knew I was going to hear a lot of Russian in Rīga. I was bracing myself for the shock. I hoped my friend Gerry at Parsons wasn't right when he asked me, "Is Russian the official language of Latvia?"

Crossing the Border

"Vakars vēl tāls, Rīga vēl ļoti, ļoti tālu prom..." ("Evening's still far, Rīga's still far away...") In the 1970s I sang along to the songs of Dundurs ("Horsefly"), a Latvian Swedish band. The song *"Visi ceļi"* ("All Roads," 1970) had an urgent, almost desperate sound to it: *"Ātrāk!"* ("Faster!")... For Latvians around the world, all roads seemed to lead back to their ancestral homeland. The band's drummer Juris Kronbergs would emerge as a highly acclaimed poet and translator of Latvian literature into Swedish. Lead singer Pāvils Johansons was the son of émigré writers Andrejs Johansons and Veronika Strēlerte who found refuge in Sweden.

In late September 1980, clutching a large, bulky purse especially weighed down by my father's Minolta camera, I boarded a Finnair flight bound for Helsinki. I was traveling with two enormous suitcases and a large camping backpack stuffed with clothes and gifts for the numerous relatives I knew were waiting for me in Rīga. In Helsinki I proceeded by taxi to the Georg Ots ferry bound for Tallinn, the medieval capital of Soviet-occupied Estonia (the Estonian Soviet Socialist Republic) on the other side of the Gulf of Finland. The ferry route seemed more appealing than flying through Moscow, the seat of our enemies. I wandered around on the decks of the ferry looking at the churning, slate-gray water of the Baltic Sea and the seagulls following us above the ship's wake.

What did the Finns and Swedes know of their Soviet-occupied neighbors, with whom they shared this sea? Many Finns traveled to Tallinn on this ferry spending their money on Soviet booze. They were somewhat informed, I guessed. As I strolled about on the deck, I enjoyed listening to the musical sound of the Finnish language, which was related to Estonian. The Finns had their own unpleasant experience with the Russians, losing part of their country to the Soviets. To the east lay Leningrad (St. Petersburg), former seat of the House of Romanov—the dynasty of Russian tsars. As for "neutral" Sweden, ever since I had read about Sweden's illegal extradition of Baltic soldiers to the Soviets in 1945–1946, I felt a sense of disgust and deep resentment toward this wealthy country on the other side of the Baltic from Latvia. While the spoiled Swedes flourished, the Balts were withering away in the stranglehold of their Russian occupiers.

The Baltic Sea was one of the most polluted seas in the world: chemical weapons and toxic industrial waste had been dumped into the Baltic by various states. Its bottom was littered with thousands of airplane wrecks, sunken ships, and other debris. Yet on the surface it was lovely, a cool, blue-gray mirror of deception.

Ahead of me lay the world's largest prison state—the Union of Soviet Socialist Republics. Behind its "bars," the Iron Curtain, entire countries, nations, peoples, languages, and cultures languished. The tentacles of Moscow reached far and wide holding vast territories in their steely suction grip. In the 20th century communist Russia expanded like a ravenous ogre gobbling up vast territories and nations and regurgitating them as Soviet republics: the Byelorussian Soviet Socialist Republic; the Ukrainian Soviet Socialist Republic; the Uzbek Soviet Socialist Republic; the Kazakh Soviet Socialist Republic; the Georgian Soviet Socialist Republic; the Turkmen Soviet Socialist Republic; the Tajik Soviet Socialist Republic; the Kirghiz Soviet Socialist Republic; the

Armenian Soviet Socialist Republic; the Azerbaijan Soviet Socialist Republic; the Moldavian Soviet Socialist Republic; and lastly, the Baltic countries—the Latvian, Lithuanian, and Estonian
Soviet Socialist Republics, once prosperous and proud, sovereign states with market economies
integrated with Western Europe.

Borders did not exist between the Soviet republics; Soviet citizens could travel within the
Soviet Union freely. But the Iron Curtain kept them within Soviet borders; travel abroad was not
permitted, with a few exceptions. Under Soviet dictator Joseph Stalin vast numbers of peoples
of different nationalities had been scattered across a seemingly endless Siberia. Later, to escape
the Soviet prison state, some famous people defected to the West: the Russian ballet dancers
Rudolf Nureyev, Mikhail Baryshnikov, and Alexander Godunov are among the best known Soviet
defectors. Baryshnikov, who was born in Rīga, starred in the movie "White Nights" (1985), a film
about defection from the Soviet Union. Nureyev's biography *Dancer* by Collum McCann (2009)
describes the grim world that the famous dancer chose to leave behind.

The Baltic Sea lapped against the invisible Iron Curtain. The land of my ancestors was now
occupied and guarded by Russian tanks and armed soldiers who did not speak Latvian, as well
as by the secretive, omnipresent KGB. At the Tallinn customs checkpoint I felt my first pangs of
unease, observing the sullen Soviet officers with their withering stares. Apparently they had
been trained to look mean and to creep out friendly, naive westerners like me. However, to my
immense relief, I slipped through easily. So there I was, on the other side of the Iron Curtain, on
"the Dark Side of the Moon." "Welcome my son, welcome to the machine. Where have you
been? It's alright, we know where you've been..." (Pink Floyd, "Welcome to the Machine") I
quickly discovered that no one in Tallinn spoke English. I left my luggage at Hotel Viru to walk
around the old town. In the late afternoon I took a taxi to Tallinn's central train station, dreading
the moment I would be left at the curb. Dragging my luggage behind me, I located a train sched-
ule in the station and was able to make out the word Рига ("Rīga") in Russian on the announcement board. The train was scheduled to depart later in the evening.

I looked around. Everyone seemed to be speaking Russian, and everyone was drably dressed.
I sat for a while near some women wrapped in shawls, their hair tucked under faded kerchiefs,
chattering mouths revealing missing teeth. Potato women, I thought, imagining gray fields and
hard, dirt-caked, cracked fingers prying round, dirt-covered potatoes out of the ground. They
glanced at me from time to time, as did other people sauntering by. My foreign-looking luggage
was excessive, my attire stood out: I was wearing a bright purple beret with some sort of yellow
star on it, purchased in a Manhattan boutique, as well as a pair of cowboy boots. Where were
all of these people traveling to? Moscow? Leningrad? Rīga? Minsk? A banana from the previous
day was moving through my bowels. Had the potato women ever tasted a banana?

I was thinking apprehensively of the stairs leading to the departure and arrival platforms, as
I squirmed on my bench. How would I ever surmount them with my entire luggage? I would
have to leave something at the bottom of the stairs. As far as I could see, there were no
escalators or elevators to help passengers with small children, lots of luggage, or the disabled. I
tried not to stare at the people around me, not wanting to draw attention to myself. I realized I
was completely alone on alien "turf," cut off from the rest of the world. Anything could happen
to me. As my watch's hands inched towards departure time, I felt helpless. The stairs looked

miles long by this time. Would some kind Soviet citizen help me? Would I be robbed as I lurched up the staircase dragging suitcases stuffed with Western goods? My first impression of the Soviet Union was that it was drab, Russian, and intimidating.

Don't ever judge anyone at face value, I learned. The dilemma of the steep staircase and my belongings was solved when my entire luggage was carried up and into the train by two friendly Russians who realized I was in dire straits. I thanked them profusely in English, as they grinned and departed. The Tallinn train station receded, as my train called the *Chaika* ("seagull") pulled away. Rīga was next, with Minsk its second and final destination. It was already cold in this part of the world; I was traveling in and grateful for my long wool coat.

I was overjoyed to be on the train, which was picking up speed. I could finally enjoy the fact that I had made it this far without any real problems. Cell phones had not been invented yet, and this journey felt like a "coming of age" ritual. My three compartment mates were all Russian speakers: two men and a woman who lived in Rīga. We conversed a bit, she in broken Latvian. These strangers were exceedingly kind to me: they prepared my top berth for the night, were friendly, polite, and discreet, and made me feel completely safe and welcome. The train's clickety-clack sounds and rhythm were soothing. We all enjoyed a glass of hot *chai* (tea) together, and then it was time for me to climb up and try to sleep.

As the hours passed, I suspected that I was the only one awake. I drifted in and out of semi-consciousness, sometimes turning and craning my neck to look out the window. I was too excited to fall asleep. It was pitch black. I wondered at what hour we would cross the invisible border into Latvia. The anticipation of this moment thrilled me to my soul. I dozed off enjoying the rhythm of the train. At some point I woke up with a start and realized that we were in Latvia. I turned over on my stomach and gazed out into the darkness. I was overwhelmed by indescribable feelings. As the other passengers slept, I lay in the dark shivering with emotion. "Mother Latvia"! I was home! I tried to grasp the landscape outside my window with my eyes: Vidzeme! Out there somewhere were places linked to my family history!

The Latvian Soviet Socialist Republic

The coat of arms of the Latvian Soviet Socialist Republic. Source: Wikimedia Commons.
https://commons.wikimedia.org/wiki/File:Emblem_of_the_Latvian_SSR.svg

The spring of 1940 burst into bloom, bringing the Latvian working people the fulfillment of their cherished dream, the happiness that they had fought for with bitter perseverance: Soviet rule. The people rose up and overthrew the bourgeois government. The prison gates opened; brilliant sunshine and freedom welcoming the champions of revolution who exchanged their prisoners' uniforms for work clothes and joined the new front. The barriers fell. Latvia joined the great family of nations of the Soviet Union.

A period of large-scale construction of a new life and of vast social transformation set in. But the powerful rhythm of this work of creation was soon interrupted. During the next summer, on one of the lovely Whitsun nights, when dusk joins hands with dawn, the country was shaken by the thunder of war from the West. Like an avalanche the army of Hitler's Germany swept across the frontier of the Soviet Union, trampling beneath its feet the free Soviet Latvian Republic. The wreaths and garlands of St. John's Day remained unmade, the oaken barrels of sweet beer untouched. Again the Latvian people, old and young, took up their weapons, and together with all Soviet nations they joined the ranks of the Soviet Army. The thick fir and pine forests were shelter and ambush for daring partisans. Those were hard times. (…)

Under the powerful blows of the Soviet Army, the Hitlerite war machine eventually crashed. The occupied nations saw the hour of liberation. Liberty also dawned for Latvia. The ruins of houses destroyed by the retreating occupants were still smoldering when the first units of the Red Guard troops entered Rīga. (Ed. K. Bērziņa. *Dzintarzeme Latvija.* Rīga: Latvijas Valsts izdevniecība, 1960.)

Cold Light in Rīga

A portrait of Lenin hangs from a building near Gorkija iela (Gorky Street) in Rīga. Russian officers stroll nearby. A typical scene in Soviet-occupied Latvia that was a shock to my senses at first. Unknown photographer.

After a night of fitful sleeping I was up and looking out and about with curiosity as our "seagull" squeaked into the Rīga train station. Rīga! Rīga! I had heard its name touted in folk songs since I was little: "Rīga dimd!" ("Rīga resounds!") I eased myself and my luggage down the train's dangerously steep steps and was immediately surrounded by a large group of smiling faces: my Latvian relatives whom I'd only seen in photographs (and some of them for the first time that day). Members of my father's brother Uncle Ģirts' and my father's cousin Uncle Jāzeps' families. Uncles, aunts, cousins. Bright, inquisitive, friendly looks. Hugs and laughter. *Our girl from America! Such long braids! Her Latvian is pretty good!* Glances around. *Anyone spying on us? Let's talk while walking to the hotel!* A good idea. It was a chilly morning.

How my luggage made it to the hotel, I don't recall. I suspect that somebody from the Cultural Liaison Committee with Countrymen Abroad was there to welcome me and handle the arrangements. "Local" Latvians weren't usually permitted inside the Intourist hotel, which was reserved for foreigners, a dangerous breed.

I was to reside at Hotel Latvija for ten days before moving in with Uncle Jāzeps' family. This arrangement was probably designed to observe my first movements, behavior, and the people I met with. None of my relatives had a car at the time. We chattered happily passing through the grungy train station in a large group and out into the pale sunshine and the streets of downtown Rīga.

I felt physically tired but mentally alert. Surely trailed by some "tails" (the Latvian term for KGB agents), I glanced around, taking in the city I had heard so much about. Merķeļa iela, named after Garlieb Helwig Merkel (1769–1850), a Baltic German writer and publicist, looked grimy and uninviting. Close to the station that brought in masses of Soviet shoppers from all over the USSR, seedy-looking hotels were ensconced in once-elegant, pre-war buildings. In his book *Die Letten* ("The Latvians") Merkel outlined the abuses inflicted upon the Latvian peasantry by their masters the Baltic German barons, whose power and abuses lasted some 700 years. When would we Latvians ever get a break? Clunky, Soviet-built cars in drab colors and taxi cabs hurtled past

111

us, as did various vehicles of public transportation—smelly yellow buses and humming trolley-buses. I noticed an interesting building with a sign that indicated that it was the Rīga Circus, which dated back to 1888. Apparently the Soviets, especially Russians, were wild about the circus. Little did I know that real elephants were in my proximity. Nor did I know that the circus building had been constructed of railway ties. An old city is full of mysteries, I would soon discover.

Hotel Latvija was under the Soviet tourism agency Intourist, and the KGB carefully controlled Western tourists, their movements, and their actions. The KGB allegedly occupied a bunch of rooms at the top of the hotel. At the entrance to the hotel my relatives, second-class citizens in their own country, declined to come inside. They felt the invisible hand of Soviet authority waving them away. A Pit-bullish doorman shot them a dirty look; we hugged, and then my relatives dispersed. We would get in touch by telephone. It was a rude awakening for me: most Latvians lived in a state where "all were equal but some more equal than others." (George Orwell, *Animal Farm*)

As a tourist I knew I had to behave and follow Soviet rules and regulations. There were severe travel limitations for Western tourists, which was a particularly painful affront to people born in Latvia or of Latvian descent. my prospects were confined to the seaside in Jūrmala, picturesque Sigulda, and Salaspils with its Nazi concentration camp memorial. To travel anywhere else in Latvia, foreigners had to submit written requests that in most cases were denied. After all, Latvia was dotted with military bases.

I checked into the hotel and rode an elevator to the 12th floor. A hallway monitor nodded her head curtly. She would be around most of the time seated at her desk during my stay, watching me come and go. When I went out, I had to leave my room key with her. I knew immediately that this was a way of monitoring guests' actions. Such inspector *zhenzhshchinas* (women) controlled each and every floor of the hotel. She or perhaps someone else would probably rifle through my stuff for a peek at the capitalist Western world. Maybe she was trained to search for forbidden literature. My hotel room faced north towards Vidzeme, my father's native region, admitting a cool light. It was a pleasant and comfortable room, rather stark, with wooden furniture stained black. It was probably as modern as any accommodations you could find in the Soviet Union. I assumed the room was bugged.

Later that morning I was whisked away from the hotel on a walk accompanied by a representative of the Cultural Liaison Committee with Countrymen Abroad. Seeing Rīga for the first time left me strangely cold. I had to pinch myself to accept that this was one and the same Rīga that I had heard about for years, the city where my grandparents went to school, worked, and led a social life. It looked clean but colorless. The multitude of signs in Russian brought home the reality of the occupation of Latvia. Posters, announcements, the shop signs: the Cyrillic alphabet was everywhere. A huge Russian Orthodox Cathedral near the hotel turned out to be a planetarium, exhibition hall, and café. Its crosses had been sawed off.

We passed the former Palace of Justice, where my paternal grandfather had once worked serving his country and Themis. A building characterized by severe lines, it looked positively cheerless, as if it were hissing, "Go away! Mind your own business!" Yet in photographs from before the war it looked modern and efficient. Apparently a political system could taint the appearance of just about anything. The sound of Russian was everywhere, alienating. I noticed Rīga's beautiful, old architecture, but the crowds of Russians everywhere diminished my pleasure.

My ten days at the hotel were enjoyable. The food was delicious and plentiful, and I liked the peace and quiet of my room. I spent my first days visiting with my relatives, going to art exhibits and museums, and getting to know the layout of Rīga. I was a big walker and enjoyed going everywhere on my own. Luckily, this didn't seem to be a problem for anyone.

In 1980 Hotel Latvija was just two years old. Touted by the Soviets as a paragon of modernity and comfort, it was similar to Tallinn's Hotel Viru—"modernly" bland. The pale blue Hotel Latvija was a 27-story rectangular monolith that towered over Komunāru laukums ("Communards' Square"), the so-called Esplanāde before the war where Latvian military parades and song festivals were held, and the Russian Orthodox Cathedral designed by architects Nicolai Chagin and Robert August Pflug. The hotel stood on the corner of Kirova iela ("Kirov Street," now Elīzabetes) and Ļeņina iela ("Lenin Street," now Brīvības ["Freedom"]) facing the Lenin monument and caddy-corner from "Opaps'" Palace of Justice. It also faced a "political" book store.

Pre-war Rīga was a city of graceful, unique architecture. Luckily, much of it survived the war, though a part of Old Rīga was obliterated. To be fair, Hotel Latvija was similar to the modern and rather ugly high-rises that cropped up in European cities after World War II.

At least at meal times it was possible to hear the Latvian language. The brusque waiters in their red shirts spoke Latvian, and there were some Latvian-speaking guests. In the evenings the locals lined up at the hotel's side entrance to try to get into the nightclub at the hotel. This was where *blats*, the Soviet system of connections, played out. The door attendants filtered the people at the door much like the famous Studio 54 in New York. I met with my relatives at their apartments to spare them the shame of being barred from entering the hotel lobby.

The hotel complex included a *valūtas veikals* ("hard currency store"), a source of fascination for the average Soviet citizen, as well as a large art gallery called *Izstāžu zāle Latvija* ("Exhibition Hall Latvija"). The *valūtas* store was for foreign tourists or those who could flash *valūta*—US dollars, West German Deutsch Marks... I purchased coffee and chocolates there as gifts. Other hard-to-find items were available at the store, such as washing machines and various electronic gadgets, as well as shoes, clothes, and merchandise manufactured in Eastern European countries like East Germany, Hungary, Romania, and Yugoslavia. Despite demanding pay in hard currency, there was nothing available from the US or other capitalist countries.

The social equality that the communists had touted had never materialized. This was a segregated society of haves and have-nots based on *blats*, a system that divvied up scarce consumer goods to those with direct access to it, while the rest suffered. Expatriate Latvians flush with cash from capitalist countries could bring their poor and humiliated relatives to the store, yet I found it surprisingly lacking in a broad range of goods.

There were plenty of Russians in the hotel though. This strengthened my conviction that Russians made up the "ruling class" in Latvia and throughout the Soviet Union, pushing their way in and about everywhere they went. Like unwanted guests, they had barged into many countries both before, during, and after the "Great Patriotic War," displacing local populations, taking things and taking over, and savoring their victor's status.

As I made my way around Rīga, celebrated for centuries in Latvian folk songs, I began to warm up to it. The city's parks were lovely, with magnificent oaks, lindens, and other specimen trees and quiet paths. I gazed upon buildings with towers and turrets, whimsical design motifs, sculptures, stained glass windows, and tiled stairwells, many of them vandalized, unfortunately. Under the Soviets large single-household apartments had been turned into communal flats; subsequently nobody cared about anything anymore. With no private property, no one had a sense of ownership and concern. And it showed. Upon closer inspection, the wear and tear was evident.

While exploring beautiful Friča Gaiļa iela (named after Fricis Gailis, a revolutionary who committed suicide by jumping out of a window), which was lined with exquisite examples of art nouveau architecture, I was appalled to see the brilliantly hued tiles of many stairwells smashed or missing, broken windows, garbage, and filth out in the back. Lifting my Minolta to take a picture of an astoundingly ornate building on the corner of Alberta and Strēlnieku, I was interrupted by the gruff sound of a Russian in a military-style uniform barking at me to put my camera away and get lost. Unbeknownst to me, the building at Alberta iela 13 was occupied by some Soviet establishment, and taking photographs of it was not permitted. Many of the stunning buildings in the area had been designed by famous Russian architect Mikhail Eisenstein (1867–1921). In 1980 their fate seemed precarious.

I quickly turned and ducked into a building on the other side of the street. I didn't want any problems with the Russian military. After all, I was at a distinct disadvantage: I did not speak Russian. Ascending a magnificent spiral staircase, I reached a set of double doors that opened up to the memorial museum of Latvian artist Janis Rozentāls or Jan Rosenthal (1866–1916). It was perfectly preserved with examples of his work, period furniture, and a small memorial room where the famous Latvian writer Rūdolfs Blaumanis had once stayed. Museum tickets were cheap in the Soviet era—just a few *kapeikas* (kopecks). Like many Latvians, Rozentāls had studied art in St. Petersburg. He had married a Finnish singer, Elli Forsell, portrayed in numerous paintings.

Rozentāls is considered one of the founders of the Latvian school of painting. He painted portraits and landscapes. His painting "Girl with a Monkey" (1913) was popular before the war, and reproductions of it hung on the walls of many households, including my grandparents'. As for Blaumanis whose fur coat and other personal items were on view, his main body of work, plays and short stories, is a national treasure and remains a big part of my Latvian upbringing. We read a lot of Blaumanis in Latvian elementary school. This small memorial museum, which employed an elderly, very friendly Latvian woman, felt like a sanctuary in the shadow of Alberta iela 13, occupied by some intimidating Soviet establishment.

The condition of the buildings on this and many other Rīga streets was heartbreaking. Possibly many of the large apartments on this street had belonged to Rīga's wealthy Jews who had once played such an important role in Latvia's economic life between the two world wars. Rīga had changed in so many ways...

On my jaunts I noticed that Rīga lacked luster, bright lights, and cheer—the sparkle that apparently only capitalism, private ownership, and a competitive market could bestow upon a city. A generic sign over a store, "Gaļa / Myaso" ("meat" in Latvian and Russian), left little to the imagination. People in gray—gray jackets, gray coats, gray hats, gray trousers, gray skirts, gray shoes, and gray faces—added to the city's withered, faded, grungy, unhealthy look. Disgruntled customers lined up in stores waiting for their chance to buy something. I avoided going into most stores, because the throngs were unbearable, the air heavy. Alberta iela with its jeweled tiles, sphinxes, lions, and other mythical figures was a brilliant contrast to the grayness of Soviet life, which was immediately apparent to the western tourist.

The overbearing sound of the Russian language in my grandparents' city was chilling. Already in my first days in my fatherland I was beginning to sense that language was being used as a weapon. Russian to my ears sounded harsh and angry; my anti-Russian sentiment only sharpened this perception. I quickly learned to tell Latvians apart from Russians. Latvians were quiet and even obsequious; Russians were louder and more noticeable.

Rīga's street names had undergone numerous changes under different occupying authorities. The Nazi Germans had also displayed a penchant for changing history. Ļeņina (Lenin) iela under the Soviets (Brīvības or Freedom before WWII) had been Adolf-Hitler-Strasse during the Nazi occupation. Valdemāra iela named after Krišjānis Valdemārs (1825–1891), one of the "fathers" of the Latvian National Awakening in the second half of the 19th century and founder of Latvia's first maritime school for Latvians in 1864, became Hermann Goering Street in 1942. When the Soviets occupied Latvia, they changed Valdemāra iela to Gorkija (Gorky Street). Ģertrūdes became Kārļa Marksa iela (Karl Marx Street). Stabu iela turned into Engelsa iela (Friedrich Engels Street). Marijas iela (Maria's Street) was given the name of Russian Field Marshal Alexander V. Suvorov (1729–1800) under the Soviets. Before the war it was known for its brothels and Jewish shops. But the Jews were nowhere to be seen. The famous Latvian poet Aleksandrs Čaks (1901–1950) once wrote: "O, Marijas iela, / Monopoly / of silk / and moths,—let me / sing of you / in verses long and slender / like giraffes' necks (...)" (Tr. RL). As a young Latvian American tourist I was struck by how Russian Rīga felt. I was stunned. This was ... the capital of Latvia?

I also immediately noticed that the situation of "Mother Latvia" or "Milda," as our Freedom Monument was fondly called, was precarious. Inaugurated on November 18, 1935 at the intersection of Raiņa and Brīvības (Ļeņina under the Soviets), the monument had remained miraculously unscathed by the war. The monument was designed by sculptor Kārlis Zāle (1888–1942); it had been financed by public donations. At the base of the monument various figures portrayed our people's historical struggle for freedom. But in 1980 it was ensnared by the electric cables of trolleybuses that rumbled around its base picking up and dropping off passengers. I could feel the vehicles shaking the foundation beneath the monument, endangering its very existence. Latvians could only walk by and watch helplessly. It was clear that lingering near the monument was unwise. Mother Latvia stood above us in a state of solitary confinement, so to speak. All alone. I walked past the monument looking carefully at the sculptural figures of our warriors and eyeing the trolleybus cables. They reminded me of a noose. Mother Latvia was slowly being strangled, while Russian tourists were being told that she symbolized Mother Russia and the three Soviet Baltic republics, an egregious insult to injury!

Rīga's artsy crowd frequented *Dieva auss* ("God's Ear"), a café in the cathedral with the sawed off crosses on Ļeņina iela. They sat at tables in comfortable semi-darkness, drinking, munching on cookies and pastries, cracking jokes, and people-watching. During my month-long stay I would pop in there from time to time with my relative Gunārs. After being introduced as a Latvian American, I noticed that people seemed to freeze, unable to muster anything more than a polite "Priecājos" ("Pleased to meet you"). Understandably... Perhaps a "comrade" was sitting nearby listening...

Reminders of Soviet communist ideology and history were everywhere. Latvian communist Pēteris Stučka's (1865-1933) name was also associated with the University of Latvia, the alma mater of my grandparents: *Pētera Stučkas Latvijas Valsts Universitāte*. A monument to Stučka, whose name sounded a lot like the word "stukačs" ("informant"), stood in the park near Rīga Castle. My Latvian school teachers in New Jersey had referred to Stučka as a traitor and an enemy of free and independent Latvia: he headed the short-lived Bolshevik government in Latvia in 1918–1920. In Soviet-occupied Latvia he was an officially celebrated historical figure. My fatherland had been turned upside down, I quickly learned. White was black, and black was white.

In Old Rīga I wandered into an old church that had been turned into a youth club affiliated with the Rīga Polytechnical Institute. It was also used as a discotheque and concert hall. Built between 1857 and 1859, the neo-Gothic Anglican Church was designed by architect Johann Daniel Felsko (1813–1902), Rīga's chief architect from 1844–1879. According to the website *Cita Rīga*, in 1891 about 180 registered Anglicans, mostly merchants, lived in Rīga. In 1980 there were none. English was a language one simply did not hear in Rīga in the communist era; our capital had gone from being a well known Baltic port city to an obscure Soviet outpost that was difficult to reach and no longer of any commercial interest to Western Europe. The steps to the church were dilapidated, the small churchyard untended, but the view toward the Daugava River was spectacular.

One of the first monuments that I encountered with a sense of pure delight and immediate recognition was that of writer Rūdolfs Blaumanis, already mentioned. The monument, an almost life-size portrait in stone, was by famous Latvian sculptor Teodors Zaļkalns (1876–1972). It was located in the park next to Raiņa Boulevard, where my uncle and his family lived. On the pedestal were inscribed these famous words by Blaumanis: *"Mans zelts ir mana tauta, / Mans gods ir viņas gods"* ("My gold is my nation, / My honor is her honor"). Someone had placed a bouquet of yellow mums at the writer's feet. This was Latvia *and not Russia*.

In Komunāru parks ("Communards' Park") I gazed upon a large granite monument dedicated to our poet Jānis Rainis (1865–1929), which was designed by Kārlis Zemdega (1894–1963). As Latvian American school children we had read Rainis' poems and plays, which were often performed in North American Latvian centers. Rainis' plays were laced with symbolism that reflected our nation's growing self-awareness and longing for freedom in the early 20th century. A social democrat, Rainis was an advocate for Latvian independence. When he returned to Latvia in 1920 after 15 years of self-imposed exile in Switzerland, he and his wife, the legendary writer Aspazija, were given a heroes' welcome. These monuments belonged to the Latvia that I had been taught to love. I realized that there was only one Latvia in the world; our Latvian exile bubble could never fully replicate it. Latvia was here beneath my feet and all around me, yet it was clearly endangered, fragile, and vulnerable to an aggressive foreign influence. To understand Latvia's complicated history and Latvian culture fully, it seemed natural and necessary to spend time in Latvia, occupied or not. Standing next to Rūdolfs Blaumanis hewn from stone, I looked toward 3 Raiņa bulvāris, where I would soon be living. All around me the linden trees cast a golden light.

3/5 Raiņa bulvāris

So long, Hotel Latvija! Finally, after being monitored, I was permitted to move in with my relatives, the Lindbergs family. They lived in a handsome apartment building from 1881; its designer was none other than Jānis Frīdrichs Baumanis (1834–1891), Latvia's first architect of Latvian descent. The building's central location was fantastic. My father's cousin Jāzeps Lindbergs (1922–1994) was a conductor at the Latvian National Opera. He lived with his wife Ināra, their three daughters Māra, Inta, and Daina, Māra's husband Gunārs Lūsis, granddaughters Linda and Zane, Ināra's mother Ida Legzdiņa and her sister Tamāra Legzdiņa, as well as an old woman named Ženija Finks in an impressive third floor apartment. Somehow all of these people could co-exist there in relative comfort.

Left: Rīga's Otto Schwarz Restaurant in the 1930s. Image courtesy of the National Library of Latvia collection "In Search of Lost Latvia."

Restaurant Otto Schwarz, Rīga

The building's main doors, which exhibited traces of fine workmanship, were dilapidated. They no longer closed properly and swung shut with a bang. Some of the mailboxes in the stairwell were broken. Apparently the theft of mail was a big problem in Soviet Latvia. Still, it was possible to imagine the stairwell in its better days, when (as I liked to imagine it) elegant couples descended to stroll at a leisurely pace to the opera or step into a horse-drawn carriage or open car to go to a fancy restaurant, like the once famous Otto Švarcs Restaurant and Café.

The Lindbergs' apartment was vast, with five bedrooms, an enormous living room with tall, arched windows that faced the boulevard and park, a dining room full of antique cabinets packed with imported pre-war porcelain, a bathroom and lavatory, a maid's room, and a kitchen with an exit to the cellar, where my relatives kept perishable root vegetables and firewood. In 1980 the apartment was still being heated with wood; its solid woodstoves were a marvel. Central heating had not yet come to this magnificent building on one of Rīga's most prestigious boulevards.

Some of the rooms were filled with valuable antique furniture. A grand piano, which Jāzeps played from time to time, stood near the living room's lace-curtained windows. My uncle's family had "inherited" this apartment and its fine furnishings through a series of twists and turns of fate triggered by World War II. A beautiful, quintessential Vilhelms Purvītis (1872–1945) landscape hung above an elegant antique sofa on which we often sat drinking coffee or tea, nibbling treats, and chatting. The old, creaking parquet floors had lost their sheen but were, for all their wear and tear, still a marvelous vestige of the pre-war era. Apartments with parquet floors were

117

highly coveted. All in all, it was a cozy home for this large, friendly, talented, and dynamic extended family.

How did the Lindbergs family end up living in such a comparatively luxurious apartment in this fantastic location? Initially I thought it was because Uncle Jāzeps was a conductor at the opera and had earned it. This was not the case. As my cousin Inta later explained, her great-aunt Magdalēna Kilbloka, a well known dentist in the 1930s who even fixed President Kārlis Ulmanis' teeth, was acquainted with one Konrāds family that owned the building and fled to Italy when the Soviets occupied Latvia in 1940. Before their departure, the Konrāds family invited Ms. Kilbloka to occupy their apartment while they were abroad. Because she was single, and the apartment was very big, her sister Ida Legzdiņa and her family moved in with her. Ida's daughter Ināra married Jāzeps Lindbergs, my father's cousin.

Ida Legzdiņa's husband Jēkabs Legzdiņš, a commander of Rīga's Home Guards and a high-ranking official at the Interior Ministry when the Soviets occupied Latvia in 1940, was allegedly betrayed by his acquaintance, the popular writer turned Soviet collaborator Vilis Lācis (1904–1966). Lācis was a communist and was allegedly responsible for the deportation of many of his compatriots. According to my cousin, Lācis relieved Jēkabs Legzdiņš of his duties and advised him to go to his house in the countryside, suggesting he would be safe there. Legzdiņš was arrested the next day. For a while nobody knew what had happened to him. Then the family received news that Legzdiņš had hung himself in prison. Badly tortured, he had taken his own life.

Right: Here I am seated on the steps leading up to No. 3 Raiņa bulvāris, a beautiful building in desperate need of restoration in 1980.

That was the beginning of the "Lindbergs era" in this magnificent apartment two blocks from the Freedom Monument. Magdalēna Kilbloka practiced dentistry in the apartment. Her niece Ināra Lindberga also became a dentist and was able to supplement her family's income for many years "on the sly." The old dentist's chair was still there in 1980 tucked behind an antique screen, and once or twice I detected Aunt Ināra fussing over a private patient. This was a risky venture, as private enterprise was forbidden under the Soviets. After the war, afraid that the authorities would install strangers in the apartment, the family invited friends of theirs, Ādolfs Skadiņš and his wife Līza, to live with them. The Skadiņš couple moved in with their devoted maidservant Ženija. She continued to live in the maid's room at the back of the apartment for years, even after her employers had passed away. In fact, in 1980 she was still living there, a tiny woman with a kindly "apple doll" face. Most of the fancy antique furniture and china had come with the apartment. It was a pleasure to sip coffee from the dainty, gold-rimmed cups manufactured in England and France.

Even if the apartment was very big, it was always teeming with people. It was basically a communal apartment, even though just about everyone living there was related. There were pluses and minuses to this sort of "village" life. There was always somebody there to mind the children; everyone worked as a team to put a decent meal on the table and take care of practical matters, like fixing something or heating the apartment; there was little privacy for the couples; these once magnificent single-household apartments suffered from endless wear and tear.

Art was in our extended family's genes, it seemed. My cousin Māra Lindberga, Jāzeps and Ināra's oldest daughter, worked in advertising at the Latvian Drama Theater (later—the Latvian National Theater) just a few blocks away. Her sister Inta was studying architecture. The youngest sister, Daina, was studying landscape design. Māra's husband Gunārs Lūsis was a designer, and Linda, their oldest daughter, was already attending art school. Art was a family affair for most Latvian artists, I discovered.

Uncle Jāzeps, a handsome man with a high forehead and a strong, masculine profile, had studied piano at the Latvian Conservatory. He was arrested in 1950 during his final exams based on a denunciation that he had refused to speak Russian. He was sentenced to five years of forced labor, where his pianist hands were ruined. Upon returning to Latvia, he studied conducting and was allowed to work at the "White House"—the Latvian Soviet Socialist Republic State Opera and Ballet Theater. However, Uncle Jāzeps was told that because of his "stint" in Siberia, he could never hope for a "big" career at the opera. "Which is why he was such a wonderful, devoted father to us," his daughter Inta said to me.

The Latvian National Opera at the turn of the 20th century. Photograph: Wikimedia Commons. https://commons.wikimedia.org/wiki/File:National_Opera_House_Riga.jpg (© Public Domain)

The Latvian National Opera was housed in a white neo-classical building designed by Ludwig Bohnstedt (1822–1885), an architect from St. Petersburg, Russia. It was located in the park between Raiņa and Padomju (Soviet) bulvāris (now Aspazijas). It was fronted by pretty, formal flower beds and a large water fountain that had also survived the war. In 1980, though still majestic, the White House (as it was fondly called) was in obvious need of restoration. Several times I heard Uncle Jāzeps murmur this in my presence, as if he were ashamed and apologetic for the landmark building's faded looks.

I had read Mariss Vētra's (1901–1965) entertaining autobiography *Mans baltais nams* ("My White House") a year or two in advance of my trip. Before the war Vētra was a popular tenor and well-traveled soloist. His charming voice can still be heard on the old Bellacord recordings (YouTube). He ended up in Canada after the war. His descriptions of the intrigues that went on at the opera were highly amusing. The scratchy recordings of Vētra singing popular Latvian "oldies" still bring on an overwhelming feeling of loss in me... "The sky so dark and cloudy, / The sea churned by the storm; / Through its waves and crests / My boat, my life, ploughs ahead. / Darkness and danger everywhere. / Only far to the west / On this night of gloom / A single star does shine. (...)" Those are the lyrics from a popular old song called *"Debess tumša mākoņaina."* Who could in the 1930s predict the trials and tribulations the people of Latvia would be subjected to during and after World War II?

The Latvian Art Academy was just one block away. The University of Latvia, my grandparents' citadel of learning, was also nearby on Raiņa bulvāris. Everything was within reach, often within walking distance, and Rīga's public transportation, which included trams, trolleybuses, yellow Ikarus buses, and trains, was simply marvelous. From a small balcony next to their bedroom my uncle and aunt could enjoy the view of the trees in the nearby park. Old Rīga with its architectural marvels was just on the other side of that park. A trolleybus stop was conveniently situated right across from our apartment building.

My cousin Daina kindly gave up her bedroom for me and moved in with her sister, so that I could enjoy some privacy. The window in her room faced a dark, narrow courtyard and the windows of the building next door, which, in fact, was occupied by the Soviet Latvian Interior Ministry. Daina's bedroom contained a few pieces of sturdy, ugly Soviet furniture. I inspected her souvenir pins from places she had visited and knickknacks with interest. I had immediate access to the lavatory and bathroom just across the hallway. A window in the lavatory seemed to be permanently open to let in fresh air; it looked out over a narrow, inaccessible shaft. A thick stack of neatly torn newspapers to be used as toilet paper was mounted on a large nail. The bathroom had a large bathtub and a multitude of towels and hygiene items. I inspected the Soviet-made toothbrushes, toothpaste, and toiletries. The brown soap that I used several times to wash with turned out to be cheap laundry soap. To me it looked like the popular natural oatmeal soaps touted in the US.

I quickly adjusted to some of Soviet life's inconveniences, washing my long hair only once a week instead of every day, using a small basin of warm water to rinse it as I sat in the bathtub, like a bather in a Degas painting. The building did not have central heating, nor did it have hot running water. People had adjusted to these nuisances. Central heating would come, Uncle Jāzeps said... People were patient. There was little they could do to speed things up. The men took turns carrying firewood up from the cellar to heat the stoves; the thermometer was dipping, hinting at the approach of winter.

I marveled at the long row and variety of slippers near the front entrance; everyone moved around the apartment sounding like a broom sweeping the old parquet floor. Slippers were for keeping one's socks and the floors clean.

I quickly became good friends with Māra's daughters Linda and Zane, my adorable, inquisitive, well-behaved nieces. They liked to come into my room to look at my things and me. Children are quick to spot differences in attire, appearance, and personal belongings. All my small accessories were a source of utter fascination for the girls: my makeup; my hair elastics; my tiny flasks of aromatic Indian attars. I greatly enjoyed talking with them as well as with the adults. They were all busy but also very hospitable and helpful, as was just about everyone I was introduced to in Rīga. It was touching.

In the mornings I was awakened by an extraordinarily loud alarm clock. One of my aunts would usually be in the kitchen puttering around. I had breakfast at the enormous oval dining room table, often by myself, as mostly everyone had already left the house for work, school, or to run errands. Aunt Ināra's sister Tamāra, fondly called Nūmīte, prepared a pot of chicory coffee every morning, which sat on the table covered with a clean towel; infused with her "special" sweet cream from the market, it was absolutely delicious. Real coffee was reserved for the high and mighty in the Communist Party or the Soviet military. A thick slice of Latvian rye bread with butter and farmers' cheese was a filling, nutritious breakfast. The Latvian cheese, homemade liver pâté, and sausage were also tasty toppings.

Nūmīte would often regale me with stories of her shopping exploits at the central market, about her special contacts there, and all the delicious items she could obtain. Shopping was a kind of obsession for everyone in the Soviet Union. With no competition or private incentive, Soviet manufacturing had become a cumbersome state-run, problem-ridden operation, and distribution was hobbled by corruption and theft. I believe my relatives went to great lengths to keep me well fed. Thus in 1980 I had no direct experience with the economic hardships and large gaps that stalled the supply chain in Soviet Latvia, although I took note of the fact that no imports from the capitalist world were available in Rīga.

When I came home from school, some of us ate lunch. I fell in love with *klimpu zupa*, a milk soup filled with sweet dumplings. Once we had delicious roasted carrots that Daina brought home from her school's *brīvprātīgi obligāti* ("voluntary mandatory") harvest work at a kolhoz. (Every fall Soviet students had to take part in the harvest at Latvia's collective farms. This wasn't necessarily a bad thing, I thought.) My taste buds were aroused. Gunārs was an avid recreational fisherman; he was well acquainted with Latvia's waterways, preferring the method of underwater spear-fishing. Instead of oranges and bananas, I enjoyed Latvia's delicious organic apples. Nūmīte complained about the long lines and the shortage of goods.

The Lindbergs' household's industrious women ensured a steady supply of food products, and they were expert cooks. Everything I tasted was delicious, fresh, and sometimes new to my palate, including Uncle Jāzeps' beloved *kaņepsviests* or hemp butter, a Latvian specialty, which he slathered on rye bread and ate with gusto, smacking his lips. Its taste reminded me slightly of peanut butter. In 1980 the economic aspects of life in Soviet-occupied Latvia did not interest me, although I noticed many deficiencies, the lack of toilet paper being one of them. I didn't actually grasp how time-consuming and stressful shopping was. It was the people and the historical city that I wanted to get to know. I had no idea how much the lack of goods and services affected people's behavior and values. When people stared at me on the street, they were staring at my western "exotic" looks (multiple long braids, black eyeliner) and my clothes. My cowboy boots were a source of fascination, as was my purple and pink shawl from Africa. Such vibrant colors stood out against Rīga's drab hues of proletarian gray.

And then came my first day at the Latvian Art Academy, located one block away on Communards' Boulevard. The neo-Gothic building was designed by Baltic German architect Wilhelm Bockslaff (1858–1945). With some trepidation, I opened the school's heavy doors and stepped into the poorly lit vestibule, which was illuminated by a huge stained glass window above the stairs. It was very quiet; there were no signs of any student activity. They were already in their classes working. I proceeded to the main office. Nobody there seemed to know who I was. The secretary vanished into the rector's office. After an uncomfortable pause, a tall man emerged; his piercing black eyes betrayed an involuntary sign of recognition. Comrade Rector Valdis Dišlers shook my hand and then escorted me up to the third floor to meet Professor Pēteris Upītis (1899–1989), my assigned instructor. In our first slightly awkward encounter I detected an element of surprise: I had the uncomfortable feeling that no one had prepared Comrade Upītis for my arrival.

Professor Upītis was a master of miniature graphics, especially woodblock printing, and specialized in the art of the ex libris—personalized bookplates. Upītis had been present at the Latvian Art Academy's founding ceremony in 1921. He was polite and friendly, but I could tell that he was unsure how to handle my presence, as were most of the instructors in the *Grafikas katedra* ("Graphic Arts Department") whom I was introduced to. I had imagined that I would be working in a classroom setting. I found out that I was to receive individualized instruction, which would make it harder for me to get to know my fellow students.

I was told that as a "guest student" I was free to come and go as I pleased. Thus I set my own hours, attending school every weekday from 10:30 until 3:00, all the while feeling slightly like an unexpected intruder. It was obvious that the school staff had been alerted to my intentions and arrival at a very short notice. The school had not bothered to set up any kind of individual work program for me; that was immediately apparent and a bit embarrassing for all concerned. I was given a preliminary introduction to etching and started work on a woodblock. I encountered very few students while I was at school. Professor Upītis enjoyed talking to me. He had concentrated his artistic endeavors on the art of the ex libris and tirelessly created new designs for friends and acquaintances. Despite his years, my mentor's eyesight seemed to be remarkably good. He looked healthy, trim, and happy with himself and life. I also quickly discovered that the academy was a bastion of the Latvian language. Free to establish my own routine, I began to alternate my hours at school with walks around Old Rīga sketching its buildings. The weather was still warm enough. Nevertheless, I was sad to be so isolated from my peers. And yet—what else could I expect? In the eyes of the communists, I was a "contaminant" from the "decadent" and dangerous capitalist West.

The other instructors and people working in our department were friendly but reserved. Later, when I had put them at ease with my friendly demeanor, a couple of them would invite me in for coffee and cognac (!). As cigarette smoke wafted into the air, jokes would tumble out of Aleksandrs Stankēvičs' mouth like mischievous imps; this guy was a real character! The very talented Stankēvičs (b. 1932) contributed cartoons to the humor magazine *Dadzis*. His companions, Jānis Reinbergs (b. 1937) and Dainis Rožkalns (b. 1928), also staff members, were always present at these seemingly spontaneous gatherings. Professor Upītis usually did not participate in our cognac chats; perhaps he did not approve of them. Were any of these guys a snitch? To me it didn't matter. Mostly I listened to their humorous banter and giggled: Stankēvičs and Reinbergs were a couple of very funny guys. Humor, I was discovering, was a trait my brethren in Soviet-occupied Latvia had sharpened into a fine art. Rožkalns was the reserved one; he sat back and peered at me with his dark, impenetrable eyes.

Two other people, Comrade Celms, a gaunt man with large, blue eyes behind thick Soviet glasses, and Comrade Līce, a bespectacled, matronly woman in her sixties always neatly attired in a white blouse and gray frock, assisted in the department and were most forthcoming and helpful. Comrade Līce did not let me hold jars of acid, saying I would ruin my marvelous (American) clothes. Sometimes these two sat down with their comrades Stankēvičs, Reinbergs, and Rožkalns to listen in. None of them dared ask me any questions about where I came from or what life in America was like; I guess they possessed the common sense *not to go there*. Oh, but if we could have talked from the heart! It would probably have led to tears… or a bitter argument.

Then Gunārs Krollis, another accomplished artist, took me under his wing. With his goatee and mustache, he reminded me a bit of Lenin. He seemed to be genuinely interested in my efforts. Much of the work produced by the staff seemed stodgy and bland. There was a definite Soviet feel to the work, which was characterized by chunky stylization and robust figures and shapes. Many artists had adapted to this conformist style. Most of the art of the Soviet era feels dated today, reflecting the ideological constraints under which it was produced.

Artists were weighed down by the constraints of Soviet ideology and the constant push to produce political and ideological work, for example: glorifying the "Great Patriotic War"—World War II; power to the proletariat; labor and industrialization; collective farming; and the hackneyed Soviet notions of "work," "peace," "victory," "May" (a reference to International Labor Day and Victory Day and the end of the war). Some artists were able to successfully incorporate these Soviet demands while preserving their artistry and even hinting at another truth. Bruno Vasiļevkis' (1939–1990) painting "My passport" from 1979 remains a perfect example of this: a simple but riveting rendering of the artist's red Soviet passport, which could trigger different thoughts and emotions in viewers. This painting made me think of the concept of a captive nation; it made me reflect on Latvia's history and how it had been turned into a satellite state, its citizens' passports issued in a foreign alphabet, their lives at the mercy of a foreign occupying power that ruled from a distant city, Moscow. The red Soviet passport was a grim symbol of the restrictions the Soviet state imposed on captive nations; it was useless for travel beyond the Iron Curtain.

By 1980 only the most fawning individuals chose to go down the beaten track by producing art glorifying aspects of Soviet history and ideology. For decades, espousing Soviet rule, the Soviet version of history, and the validity of the Soviet occupation had been a way to get a studio, an apartment, a comfortable position, a car, or a state commission. Soviet era art remains a reminder of an historical era that many of us Balts would like to forget.

From what I was able to see of students' work, I found it to be technically remarkably good. Masterful renderings of ancient Greek and Roman busts and the human figure told me that there was a sturdy academic foundation in place: the school provided the technical instruction to turn students into excellent draftsmen. My own school in New York, Parsons, sought to wring individuality from each student. At the Latvian Art Academy technical skills came first. One had to master perspective, proportion, anatomy, light and shade, and materials before taking creative liberties, which were discouraged anyway. I was impressed.

Sometimes I walked about the hallways trying to get a glimpse of what other students were doing. No one offered to show me around; no one paid attention to me. Enormous marble sculptures occupied the ground floor hallway. Who had made these, and how long had they been there? It was strange to stand by the mirror in the ladies' room and never be greeted by anyone, not even with a friendly smile. I felt painfully out of place, like an alien on Mars. I heard students speaking in my mother tongue, yet an invisible abyss kept us apart. Spontaneous smiles and greetings were hard to come by in the workers' paradise.

I realized that it was important to judge Soviet Latvian art within the context of the political parameters: the demands and restrictions imposed on artists by a totalitarian state. Thanks to my connections, I would meet some extraordinary Latvian artists whose work made me realize that Latvian (and Baltic) art was not stagnant. In fact, it was bubbling.

Latvian Poster Art

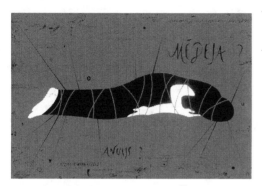

Left: A poster by Ilmārs Blumbergs from 1975 for a production of Jean Anouilh's *Medea* at the Leons Paegle State Valmiera Drama Theater. Image courtesy of Ilmārs Blumbergs.

My cousin Māra and her husband Gunārs were both graduates of the Latvian Art Academy, and most of their friends were artists. I was able to visit some of them during my month-long stay and enjoyed their warm hospitality, delicious food, and the ever-present popular Armenian cognac. Several of them, designers Gunārs Kirke, Laimonis Šēnbergs, Georgs Smelters, and Juris Dimiters, lived comfortably in their own "private" homes. Artistic talent was a valuable commodity, if you knew how to adapt to the conditions set by the state. Art was also a refuge, of course. Artists could bury their heads in their art to escape the reality around them.

Poster art had become a popular form of visual communication in Eastern Europe in the 1970s. Colorful, eye-catching posters advertised theater and opera productions. In spite of the Iron Curtain, theater was alive and well in Eastern Europe. Latvian artist Ilmārs Blumbergs produced some especially unusual and memorable posters for Latvian theater. There were signs and posters plastered on billboards and pillars all over Rīga, but most of them were black and white announcements, many of them in Russian. Anything in color and/or with an image attracted attention, and I often paused on the street to examine posters and advertisements.

By the end of the decade, Eastern European and Baltic posters would be addressing issues of government bureaucracy, rigged elections, thought control, pollution, materialism, shoddy workmanship, and sensitive subjects related to Soviet history. I had arrived in Latvia in the "golden age" of Latvian poster art.

The poster as an artistic medium has been around in Europe and Russia for a long time reflecting the countless historical, political, social, and cultural changes that took place there. Latvia has a rich collection of posters reflecting several historical eras, including the two world wars and Latvia's brief independence between those wars. Posters advertising Latvian-manufactured Ērenpreiss bicycles or promoting local tourism were succeeded by anti- and pro-Nazi, anti-Semitic, and pro- and anti- Bolshevik/communist/Soviet posters, which reflect the tragic years of Latvia's occupation by foreign armies and ideologies. All of these posters serve as compelling illustrations of various periods in Latvia's history.

While I was getting acquainted with life behind the Iron Curtain, change was stirring elsewhere in communist Eastern Europe. Around the time of my first trip to Latvia, Solidarity (*Solidarność*), the first trade union not controlled by the Communist Party, was founded in Gdansk,

Poland. It would receive much attention in the Western press in its early years and serve as a catalyst for change in Poland and elsewhere. That golden autumn in Rīga, I sensed an eddy, a barely perceptible, murmuring undercurrent of alternative thought, insight, and reflection, like the first movement of water beneath early spring's ice. 1980 was less than a decade away from the great historical changes that would lead to the implosion of the USSR, but none of us could imagine it then. Although we never discussed politics in Rīga during my stay, they and historical events were part and parcel of all Latvians' consciousness. In 1980 the Soviet status quo remained firmly entrenched, seemingly unbreakable, impermeable, and permanent. Yet the human mind and spirit cannot be fettered.

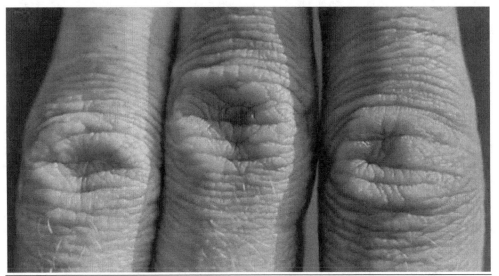

Miervaldis Polis, "My Fingers," 1974. 120 x 70 cm. Oil on canvas. Image courtesy of Miervaldis Polis.

While some painters in Soviet-occupied Latvia continued to play it safe, a few individuals pursued a different path. One day Gunārs Lūsis and I took a trolleybus up Ļeņina iela to visit an artist couple, Līga Purmale and Miervaldis Polis, both born in 1948, who were experimenting with photorealism, a style of painting that began in the United States in the late 1960s and which I had seen many examples of in New York City. Līga Purmale was a striking woman with thick, curly brown hair, blue eyes, and a lovely smile; she embodied the essence of Latvian feminine beauty. Her partner Miervaldis Polis with his blond hair, mustache, and goatee appeared to have stepped out of a Rembrandt painting. (I was thinking of "The Anatomy Lesson of Dr. Nicolaes Tulp"). Polis' hyperrealistic paintings, such as his magnified fingers, his scrupulously rendered self-portraits, and Purmale's delicate landscapes and studies of interiors were refreshing, to say the least. I was blown away.

In the early 1970s Miervaldis Polis completed a series of twelve paintings on the pages of a book about Venice. Some of the images appeared singed in reference to a fire in the famous "city of water"; others appeared to have been immersed in water. Some are Polis' self-portraits with Venice as a backdrop. The series' reference to a place in no way associated with the Soviet Union, Soviet history and ideology, or even Soviet-occupied Latvia is startling for the time period in which it was made.

To Polis, who grew up under the Soviet occupation, Venice must have felt as far away as the Moon. After the Soviets entrenched themselves in the Baltics, artists of these countries were cut off from the rest of Europe. Latvia, Lithuania, and Estonia were reoriented to the East. With limited access to news about art and culture in the Free World, they lived in a peculiar vacuum. This did not mean that these artists were in any way inferior to their counterparts in the West. On the contrary, talent was abundant.

It was these touching encounters with Latvian artists that granted me a glimpse into a creative domain that existed outside of the unnatural bubble of Soviet communist ideology. One day I accompanied a friend across the floating Pontoon Bridge to tour the recently built ceramics studio on Ķīpsala, a picturesque island once inhabited by fishermen, raftsmen, and sea captains. I was introduced to Pēteris Martinsons (1931–2013), an extraordinary ceramicist and human being who moved me deeply: I walked out of his studio with several ceramic jackdaws. Later we visited him at home; I was surprised to learn that he was a vegetarian. In a society where meat was such a sought-after commodity, this was a refreshing revelation. Soft-spoken, industrious, kind, hospitable, generous: Martinsons embodied the best qualities of my people on the dark side of the Iron Curtain.

Life at Raiņa bulvāris was calm and enjoyable. Standing by the windows of the living room, I could look down at Rigans waiting for the trolleybus or hurrying along with their cloth shopping bags. I could look out at the park and the trees, which were quickly losing their foliage. Would I get to see some snow? On sunny afternoons the living room filled with the receding sun's amber-colored light. Golden particles of dust danced on the slanting rays. New Jersey seemed so very far away. I didn't want to go anywhere. I loved this room and the view. I loved these people. I loved Rīga. I wanted to stay in my fatherland.

An antique wooden clock ticked away the time, chiming sonorously on the hour. It had lived through rough times yet faithfully fulfilled its duty. In the mornings my uncle stood by a large mirror in the living room exercising his muscular body. He was a remarkable man, full of warmth, joy, and love for his family, his profession, and Latvia. Despite his miserable experience in the Gulag and suppressed sadness and anger over his country's occupation, Uncle Jāzeps was vivacious and had a great sense of humor. I enjoyed listening to his funny stories and jokes. He had spirit, that man. The Latvian spirit. I also liked to listen to him play the piano. The sounds of Beethoven and other beloved composers filled the apartment with a sense of timelessness.

Although everyone seemed to get along splendidly, I knew that Gunārs longed for a place of his own. He and Māra and their daughters slept, worked, entertained friends, and developed photographs at night in their bedroom. Gunārs' calm, steady nerves and sense of humor served him well. He cracked me up all the time with his funny jokes.

Sometimes with the permission of Aunt Ināra I would take one or both of my nieces for a walk in the afternoon. Linda and Zane seemed wise beyond their years; with so many adults around them, this came as no surprise. For a few kopecks I bought them ice cream near the Freedom Monument, and then we headed into the park or Old Rīga, where we enjoyed running through the quiet cobblestone streets, exploring mysterious alleys, and chasing pigeons. Old Rīga was hurting! The gray skies of autumn accentuated the old town's emptiness. This former Hanseatic pearl now seemed to be lying in a pile of soot, unnoticed, forgotten. A Cinderella!

Our wanderings took us all over Old Rīga and even beneath the Gorkija iela (Gorky Street) overpass into Citadele, a once massively fortified area established in the 17th century to thwart attacks from the sea. Citadele had been designed as part of Rīga's defense system but was separated from Rīga Castle and moved further out by the famous Swedish engineer Erik Dahlberg (1625–1703). By 1769 Citadele was a separate military garrison with a central plaza surrounded by various buildings. In an engraving from 1867, Citadele was a distinct star fort surrounded by water. In 1980, with no guide book to educate me, I failed to grasp the historical depth of what I was looking at.

St. Peter and St. Paul Orthodox Church in Citadele in a photograph that predates World War II. Image courtesy of the National Library of Latvia collection "In Search of Lost Latvia."

The centerpiece of this small, seemingly abandoned quarter was an old blue-green church, which stood empty and shuttered in 1980. From all appearances, it was being used for storage. This was the old St. Peter and St. Paul Orthodox Church commissioned by Russian Empress Catherine the Great, designed by Kristof Haberland, and built in 1780–1785. Designed expressly for the garrison, at the time it was considered one of the best examples of classicism in Rīga. St. Peter and St. Paul Church was Rīga's first Russian Orthodox Church and fulfilled this role until the Nativity of Christ Cathedral was built in the late 19th century.

In 1790 Johann Christoph Brotze made a faithful drawing of the blue-green church in Citadele, immortalizing its significance in Latvian history. Brotze was an extraordinary artist and ethnographer who documented life in Livonia in his *Sammlung verschiedner Lieflandischen Monumente*, a collection of thousands of drawings, descriptions, and documents, documented life in Livonia, a historical region that encompassed present-day Latvia and Estonia. By the beginning of the 19th century, Citadele's wooden architecture had been largely replaced by brick and mortar. A charming guardhouse (1775), a couple of old warehouses from the 1720s, the soldiers' barracks (late 18th century), and the church were still standing in 1980. The area's history included dramatic sieges and attacks. The church was shuttered in 1940 after the Soviet invasion. When I first came upon Citadele, it barely resembled Johann Christoph Brotze's drawing. Citadele was a great example of how history dismantled history.

By 1875 Citadele's ramparts, visible in Brotze's drawings, had been leveled, its moats filled in. Under the Soviets, some of the area's older buildings had been knocked down. From what I could see, the Red Army had occupied Citadele's old *kazarmas* (barracks), and I saw troops and army vehicles parked there. Nearby drab Soviet apartment buildings nicknamed "The Crow's Nest" typified the blandness of the "modern" era. A large, ugly Soviet "skyscraper" nicknamed *Skābbarības tornis* ("the Silo"), which housed the Soviet Latvian Ministry of Agriculture, loomed over the historic area.

In 1977 St. Peter and St. Paul Church had been handed over to the choir Ave Sol to be turned into a concert hall. However, in 1980 there were still no signs of any work being done to salvage the historic church's former grandeur. I worried about the overall neglect of Old Rīga while day-dreaming about its potential. (Sources: Tournet.lv; AveSol.riga.lv; Wikipedia [http://lv.wikipedia.org/wiki/R%C4%ABgas_citadele]. Tr. RL)

Linda and Zane were enthusiastic troopers. A bit pale-faced, I don't think they got out of the apartment much to run around. Aunt Ināra didn't want the girls eating ice cream in the fall, so we kept it a secret. Cheap ice cream like "Plombīrs" (packaged like a sausage) and "Pols" (similar to Good Humor's "Eskimo Pie" bar) was sold by pushcart vendors on various street corners. Soda water dispensers were also something new to me: they were set up throughout the city along with *granonkas*, thick glasses designed by Latvian-born sculptor Vera Mukhina. How clean could they be? People in Rīga didn't seem to be as concerned as Americans about hygiene.

I noticed that other food items were sold on the street, such as bags of frozen *pelmeņi*, a traditional meat-stuffed dumpling that was boiled in water and eaten with sour cream, for example. Or greasy *pončiki*, little dough balls filled with some sort of ground meat: these were quite popular in cold weather. *Pončiki* were filling but left a bad aftertaste on account of the nasty sunflower oil in which they were fried. Vegetable oil as I knew it, not to mention aromatic olive oil, was nowhere to be found in Latvia in the Soviet era. In 1980 I observed all of these small details of daily life with great interest.

One of the symbols of the Soviet era in Latvia: the kvass barrels of the warm season. Kvass is a fermented beverage made from rye bread. Photo: Silvija Vecrumba, 1977

I saw people enjoying *kvass,* a popular fermented beverage, which was sold in the summertime from large, yellow barrels carted in and parked on various street corners. Judging by the number of people lined up near the barrels, it must have been good. I heard a couple of horror stories though about the barrels being filthy and full of dead bugs and grubs, so I never did try the stuff in that manner. The *kvass* sold in bottles was tasty.

Sometimes we walked along the Daugava River, which flowed into the Gulf of Rīga. Ancient hub of trade Rīga, which was close to the mouth of the river, was once a settlement of the native Finno-Ugric Livs. They were the first to encounter German merchants who would eventually set into motion a successful strategy of "divide and conquer." Latvian historian Jānis Straubergs (1886–1952) wrote in his 1936 book *Rīgas vēsture* ("History of Rīga") that a ship from Bremen en route to Gotland was blown off course by a northwesterly and ended up sailing into the mouth of the Daugava River. "When the uncouth pagan people saw such a big ship approaching, they flocked (to the shore) in droves to get a better look at it because of its strange appearance. They wondered what to make of the ship and its crew, which they knew nothing about. The Christians stayed on board the first night, trying to decide what to do." (Tr. RL) I like to imagine this ancient scene: a sailing ship on the Daugava with a crowd of curious and worried Livs on the bank of the Daugava gawking in amazement.

A new bridge was going up next to the pontoon bridge. The Daugava River inspired all sorts of thoughts. Walking back towards downtown, I gazed at Old Rīga's distinctive skyline: Rīga Castle on the left; St. James' Cathedral; Our Lady of Sorrows; the Anglican Church; St. Mary's; St. Peter's... Rīga's skyline reminded me of the image of a heartbeat on a vital statistics monitor: the soaring peaks of its churches symbolized the human spirit; the dips represented daily life, strife, and toil. Centuries of it. I looked eastward. The Daugava River flowed into Latvia from Belarus and Russia. An ancient trade route, it had been a bone of contention for centuries between everyone fighting for power and authority in this part of Europe. In his marvelous biography *Catherine the Great: Portrait of a Woman*, Robert K. Massie described the 14-year-old future empress of Russia crossing the frozen Daugava in 1744 in a sled filled with warm, luxurious furs on her way to St. Petersburg.

World War II destroyed part of the Old Town. Unique buildings like the 14th century Schwarzhaupter Haus (House of the Blackheads) and the elegant Rathaus were gone, and European merchant ships hadn't docked in Rīga in decades. The Latvian flag, which had once flown from the top of Rīga Castle, was also absent. In 1980 Rīga was a changed place, heavily Russified, its air thick with the exhaust of diesel fuel, and Soviet slogans everywhere. I couldn't get used to them. And even though Rīga had always been a multicultural city, Latvians had become a fragile minority in their own capital with little say in matters of strategic national importance. Moscow's shadow lay across the land. I absorbed Old Rīga's skyline, and then we raced across the bridge towards home, those wonderful Latvian girls and Latvian Yankee me!

My relatives advised me not to walk around in Old Rīga at night, where young Russian punks allegedly gathered to drink and cause trouble. One evening as we were walking past Freedom Monument, my friend Juris O. was accosted by three young Russians who yanked his guitar out of his hands and ran off with it. We had just been walking around the old town talking and singing. A delightful evening of song and laughter with a rude ending. Juris was not only shaken but ashamed.

Right: Rīga at the turn of the 20th century. Source: Wikimedia Commons / Library of Congress, Prints and Photographs Division. Source: Wikimedia Commons https://commons.wikimedia.org/wiki/File:Riga_old.jpg (© Public Domain)

I realized that my "expectations" of Rīga were largely unrealistic; they were based on the sentimental memories of my grandparents' generation of the "Ulmanis era," which was marked by national romanticism. I had always pictured Rīga as a pristine, shimmering citadel of *latvietība* ("Latvianness"), a bastion of the Latvian language, culture, and society. For some reason I had also imagined it to be crimeless. Spotless, so to speak.

How silly! How naïve! In fact, Rīga was a place that had experienced terrible bloodletting, many untold tragedies, and suffering.

In addition, I wasn't fully aware of Latvia's multicultural history, as my Latvian upbringing only focused on our ethnicity. Russians had been around for centuries in Rīga, although not in such numbers. However, the incident with the guitar underscored the unsavory characteristics of the Soviet Russian occupiers. Their roots in Latvia were shallow, their memory clipped. Latvia was Russia's *Pribaltika*—just a territory that they had "liberated." Many of them believed Latvia to be theirs anyway, part of Peter the Great's historical conquests. When I told my relatives about the unpleasant incident, they gave me looks of "we told you so."

I went to several theaters and enjoyed the plays immensely. The Lindbergs had *blats*, which ensured a seat at one of the popular shows. Latvians *and* Russians seemed to love the theater. The Russians had their own in Old Rīga, the Russian Drama Theater.

But it was also nice to stay at home and hang out with my relatives, a lively, interesting bunch. We drank tea at 20:00 (8:00 pm) and occasionally watched Soviet Latvian television, an interesting experience for me. There were no commercial interruptions. News anchors read the Soviet news in a cool, detached, expressionless manner. We enjoyed several concerts and ballet performances on TV. I even enjoyed a couple of excellent Russian films, such as "Father Sergius," a silent film from 1918. At the beginning of October we chuckled over exalted reports about the excellent, ever increasing harvest yields. I discovered that in the Soviet Union all harvests were splendid and plentiful, and each year cows continued to produce more and more milk. I noticed with surprise that cynicism was a part of my Soviet Latvian compatriots' nature. The radio shows were eclectic. In an hour-long music program one could hear a composition by Handel, the Belgian punk rock singer Plastic Bertrand, and Russian folk music. I still remember the sound of a soft, purring voice announcing the news: *"Runā Rīga"* ("This is Rīga speaking").

Much to my delight, I was unexpectedly introduced to several young artists, Andris Breže, Ojārs Pētersons, and Juris Putrāms. These guys, all good friends, were a blast to hang out with. They amused me to no end with their crackling dry wit, sarcastic banter, and fondness for black humor. Sarcasm, like cynicism, I was discovering, was another by-product of the pressures of Soviet ideology. My new friends were amused by my American good humor and naiveté, I by their intellectually stimulating humor. It was subtle and hilarious.

Besides amusing me to no end with their jokes and anecdotes, they wanted to know more about contemporary American art. In fact, art was what we mostly talked about. My friends were interested in my school and the New York art scene. I suppose to them I appeared like a colorful Bird of Paradise landed in the tundra. The very fact that I could freely travel to a place like occupied Latvia must have been food for thought. Andris was Baltic blonde, handsome, and cryptic. He dabbled in poetry, his ironic verse reflecting the darker side of Soviet life and the grungy, proletarian beauty of Rīga. Ojārs Pētersons, tall with a baby dumpling face and soulful blue eyes, was especially funny; he would look at me with a deadpan expression and then utter something that just cracked me up. Soft-spoken but intense, Juris reminded me of a raven with his protuberant proboscis, dark Gypsy eyes, and punk-spiky black hair. Wonderful guys! So unlike anyone I'd met in the United States. So intense and full of intellectual curiosity!

I have come to the place / where we once drank beer / I watch the dark current / crooking round the island's tip / where our matchsticks paused / and grew into weeping willows / their branches bending over the river / they'd forgotten the image on their box / the sun sets through their branches / I take a piss / the birds chirp (Andris Žebers, *Šņabji*, 2007)

One day Andris, Ojārs, Juris, and I took the train out to Dubulti in Jūrmala by the sea to the Writers' House, a retreat for people of the pen from Latvia and other Soviet republics. First we visited Māris Melgalvs (1957–2005), a young writer whose poetry was making waves. He was staying in a room with a great view of the pine-covered dunes. Just beyond them was the beach and the Gulf of Rīga. It was a cool, blustery day: the tall, straight pines that our famous poet Jānis Rainis wrote about in his 1905 poem "Lauztās priedes" ("Broken Pines") were swaying in the windy blasts. The famous poem had been set to music by Latvian composer Emīls Dārziņš (1875–1910). A staple of our popular Latvian song festival, its mood was dramatic but by the end hopeful.

The wind broke the tallest pines / That stood in the dunes by the sea,—/ Their gazes yearning for what was afar. / They could neither hide nor bend their spines. / "You broke us, hateful enemy force, / The battle against you has not ceased, / Even the last moan utters its longing for the horizon, / Each branch hisses hatred toward (your) rule!" / Though broken the tallest pines / Resurfaced as ships on the water—/ Their breasts proudly heaving against the storm, / The fight in them stirring once more: / "Raise your swells, you hated oppressor, / We will reach the horizon where happiness dwells! / You can divide us, you can break us—/ We will reach the horizon where the sun does rise!" (Tr. RL)

It appeared that the retreat was a great place for writers to socialize, their tongues loosened by spirits and nicotine. Poetry was very popular in Latvia, even among the youth, as I discovered. Melgalvs' room was filled with cigarette smoke and dirty coffee cups. The pale, disheveled poet seemed surprised by our visit, shy and introverted, and kept shooting inquisitive looks at me with his dark eyes. His appearance belied his growing popularity.

> Stepping over the threshold into the 1980s, the first of the young Latvian poets to make his debut was Māris Melgalvs with his 1980 book *Meldijās iešana* ("Walking into Melodies"), which attained instant success, as he became one of his generation's most popular authors. Young people could relate to his maximalist approach to life, his rebelliousness, his irony, and his tongue-in-cheek stance towards the negative phenomena of his day and age. (They appreciated) his bravura, which masked his real feelings, frailty, vulnerability, and helplessness. Melgalvs' poetry with its artistic playfulness, its uncomplicated poetic phrasing, and organic simplicity, as well as its innate melodiousness and rhythm, were set to music and became part of the repertoire of the popular Latvian rock group Pērkons ("Thunder"). Melgalvs' poetry revealed the poet's underlying (...) compassion for his fellow human being (...). (Melgalvs') poetry was an attempt at harmonizing the world around him."—Elīna Gailīte. 2004: http://eng.atlants.lv/research-papers/mara-melgalva-dzejas-ipatnibas/199684. Tr. RL.

After hanging out with Melgalvs, we went back downstairs, where Latvian filmmaker Ansis Ep-ners (1937–2003) was about to introduce his film *Lielvārdes josta* ("The Lielvārde Belt") about

Estonian artist Tõnis Vint (b. 1942) and his research on ethnic ornaments. Produced by the Rīga Film Studio in 1980, the film was about Vints' hypothesis that ancient geometric ornaments shared by many cultures around the world point to some sort of cosmic language. For instance, how could one explain that the ancient swastika symbol (*ugunskrusts* or "fire cross" in Latvian) appears in so many ancient cultures around the world? The film's focal point was the beautiful, intricately woven belt that is part of the traditional women's folk costume of Lielvārde. The red and white belt consists of subtly changing patterns of geometric ornaments that are similar to those found in other cultures around the world. The film, which was so *un-Soviet* for its time, was enhanced by an ambient music soundtrack by composer Svens Grīnbergs. We certainly felt mystified. "The Lielvārde Belt" would draw large crowds of people looking for an alternative to Soviet reality. Such mysticism was attractive in a society whose leaders had banned all forms of religion except the cult of Lenin. (The film is available on YouTube.)

Gustavs Klucis. "USSR—Shock Brigade of the World Proletariat." 1931. Source: Wikimedia Commons / Google Art Project https://commons.Wikimedia.org/wiki/File:Gustavs_Klucis_USSR_%E2%80%93_shock_brigade_of_the_world_proletariat_Google_Art_Project.jpg (© Public Domain)

We then watched a 1977 documentary called *Plakāts—Laiks* ("Poster—Time") about the Latvian constructivist Gustavs Klucis (1895–1938) who was part of the Russian avant-garde art scene in the early 20th century and studied under Kazimir Malevich. An idealistic communist, Klucis' experimental abstract art morphed into Soviet propaganda art that was eventually forced to sing praises to Soviet dictator Stalin. Despite his "credentials" and flattering homage to the ruthless Soviet leader, Klucis was executed during the Stalinist purges in the late 1930s. In 1980 the Stalinist purges were not open for discussion in the Soviet Union, and the film did not mention them. Tens of thousands of Latvians living in Soviet Russia at that time had been murdered, yet their senseless deaths were silenced. The Russian Revolution spawned an orgy of terror and death that lasted for decades, yet the film was officially dedicated to the October Revolution's 60th anniversary. I had never heard of Gustavs Klucis and was fascinated to discover that such an artist had existed.

Lastly, we saw a 1979 film called "Atmoda" ("Awakening") about the famous Russian filmmaker Sergei Eisenstein born in Rīga in 1898, when Latvia was part of the Russian Empire. The film was directed by Herzs Franks (1926–2013), one of Latvia's brilliant Jews who would later move to Israel. Eisenstein earned international acclaim with his films *Battleship Potemkin* (1925), *October* ([1927] also known as *Ten Days That Shook the World*) about the Russian Revolution, *Alexander Nevsky* (1938), and others. Eisenstein also suffered as an artist under Stalin, although his life was spared. Already an avid consumer of culture, I was delighted to sit back with my new friends and take in culture from a different world. I knew little about the Latvian victims of the Soviet "Great Terror," and Rīga's history was still unfolding before my hungry eyes.

The day had been magical. We left the building to stroll down to the beach. Then the wind—the wind that tried to break the straight, tall pines—threw itself at us and lifted us off our feet. Yes, we hovered in the air for a moment in eternity. I can still remember it 35 years later!

As the commemoration of the October Revolution approached, heavy Soviet Russian tanks and armored vehicles thundered down 3 Raiņa bulvāris in preparation for the "festivities." Uncle Jāzeps stood near the window looking down on the machines of war with a pensive frown on his handsome face. A victim of Soviet repression, he watched quietly as the tanks of occupation belched their exhaust, their cold caterpillar tracks grinding the asphalt, Russian soldiers sitting up in their turrets looking smug and invincible. Our "liberators"...

I took the train to Olaine to visit my grandmother, Omamma. In the Soviet era Olaine was known for its large pharmaceutical plant said to emit toxic pollution. Omamma shared a tiny, shabby one-bedroom apartment with my uncle Andris who had studied art at the Latvian Art Academy. Andris was her *sāpju bērns* ("child of sorrow"). In her early 80s, she was in relatively good health. She must have been endowed with enormous stamina to get through the post-war years with two young boys. I was the physical link with her husband, now deceased. We sat on the couch in her tiny apartment holding hands, as if it could make up for the years of painful separation.

Most people were not as lucky as the Lindbergs clan. Uncle Ģirts, my father's younger brother, lived with his wife Dzintra and their two young daughters, Ruta and Vita, in a small two-room apartment in one of the seedy Ķengarags neighborhood Soviet high-rises. Ķengarags, an ugly, sprawling housing development, was situated to the east of Rīga near the Daugava River. It was predominantly Russian; my relatives informed me of that right away, as if to prepare me. These Russians were post-war immigrants, and Latvians described Ķengarags as a Slavic ghetto. My poor uncle, he was deeply nationalistic and didn't hide his feelings about the Russian colonists. He was a land surveyor and had traveled all over the Soviet Union for his work. He knew Russia well and could attest to the differences in the standard of living between the Baltics and their gigantic neighbor.

After we had eaten a delicious meal prepared by Dzintra, Ģirts produced a hidden stash of precious pre-war memorabilia: old postage stamps and money from the Republic of Latvia. Apparently this was my grandfather's collection or at least part of it: Opaps had been an avid numismatist. Uncle Ģirts was about ten when he last saw his father and two older brothers. He had grown up in communist Latvia, but the communists had failed to brainwash him. I was sure that my Omamma was to thank for that. Ģirts was proud of Latvia's pre-war era and of his father's accomplishments. Uncle Ģirts lived under the Soviet Russian occupation in quiet defiance like so many Balts. I could see that he was happy to vent his anger in my presence. He did not seem to be afraid to speak his mind. He spoke angrily of the hordes of Russians moving to Latvia and of their lack of respect for the Latvian language and culture. He wanted me to know that ethnic Latvians were disadvantaged compared to the immigrants and their future in doubt. I believed him. I could tell.

Even though Uncle Ģirts' apartment in Ķengarags was tiny, his family were lucky. They did not live in a communal apartment. My cousin Videmārs' friend Pāvils lived in a communal apartment on Stučkas iela in downtown Rīga; his family occupied two rooms in a large apartment that they shared with at least one other family. A curtain draped across one of the rooms divided it into two spaces for privacy. For someone like me for whom privacy was so important, communal apartments seemed like one of the worst aspects of Soviet life.

By the end of my stay, I saw that many consumer goods that we took for granted in the United States were simply not available in communist Latvia. Hot water was a luxury in many buildings in the 1980s. So was clean tap water. Fluoride was absent from water and toothpaste, and people's smiles were often marred by missing teeth. The easiest solution for tooth decay was quick but painful extraction. This procedure also led to bad teeth, because people were afraid of the dentist. There was no preventive care. Parents borrowed shoes from one another for their children; the hand-me-down culture was one of necessity. For women there were special problems: no sanitary napkins. As I had brought sanitary napkins and tampons along, I didn't have to deal with this icky problem, nor did I ask what my cousins used. No toilet paper either, at least not freely available. This was a common complaint of western tourists. None of this diminished my enthusiasm for Rīga. I was a happy trooper fueled by idealism and armed with an eye for detail. Below the sooty surface Rīga was exquisitely beautiful. There wasn't much in the stores, but my friends and family had lots of funny and interesting stories to tell. I was thrilled to be taking it all in—the good, the bad, the ugly, and the eternal.

One day I ventured out to Pārdaugava on the other side of the Daugava River on my own, my backpack weighed down by my camera and chocolate and coffee from the hard currency store. I disembarked near Irbenes iela and began looking for the little wooden house where my mother's cousin Imants Sproģis supposedly lived. Irbenes iela, which ran parallel to my great-uncle Fricis' property, was a small side street immortalized in the paintings of Konrāds Ubāns (1893–1981). Pastendes iela, where my mother was born and spent her early childhood, was nearby. This was a quiet, sleepy suburb of Rīga that I immediately liked, having grown up in green Glen Ridge.

I approached a tiny wooden house with the right number provided by my grandmother. I was, of course, hoping to meet Imants, even though he had no idea I was coming. And meet him I did. He was home, as was his wife, and we ended up sitting inside for a couple of hours chatting about this and that—making small talk. It was difficult to relax and converse freely. After all, it was 1980. I had no idea what Imants' life had been like, or if my visit could somehow cause problems for him. It wasn't unusual for people who had met their western relatives to be summoned by the KGB for a talk. Communist Latvia was a freaky place.

Like all Latvians, Imants and his wife immediately served me something to eat and drink, as we struggled to navigate our conversation past the "mines" of history, the occupation, and family fates. It was awkward and exhausting. I would have liked to get a good look at Uncle Fricis' house, its nooks and crannies, and the garden my mother had told me about. After all, she could remember the types of flowers he grew, and how her aunt prepared a homemade red berry dessert with whipped cream. The past was tulips, sweet peas, roses, and chrysanthemums and close family ties. The present was a sad estrangement and the fear to talk openly about what had happened, why we were still there in America, why we couldn't come home.

By the end of October the branches were bare and winter was fast approaching. One day the phone rang. Uncle Jāzeps picked up the receiver. Someone was calling to tell me that my visa would not be extended, and that I had to prepare to leave shortly. I was devastated, my uncle ashamed. The initial plan was for me to spend the entire school year in Rīga. Perhaps my informal, "uncontrolled" meetings with various people around town had caused the KGB to change their mind about me.

Uncle Jāzeps, a proud man of exceptional integrity, put on his cap and jacket and walked out the door, telling me he was going to go argue with "the visa people" and plead on my behalf. Of course, he was back an hour later, defeated, deflated, and humiliated. Like the vast majority of my compatriots in the Latvian Soviet Socialist Republic, Uncle Jāzeps was just a prisoner with no say in a totalitarian state.

Farewell, Latvia!

Atbalss ("""Echo") was part of the Soviet Latvian publication *Dzimtenes balss* ("""Voice of the Native Land"), a tendentious Soviet publication aimed at the Latvian exile community.

End of October 1980. Leaves fell, scattered, and whirled in *sudmaliņas* and *kazachok* dances across Old Rīga's skull-smooth cobblestones and the city's boulevards and parks. As I packed my suitcase and backpack, I mourned my departure, which I was unprepared for. *Latvia! I don't want to leave you!* Rīga did not reply. Its people did not know me, its ghosts were silent.

I layered boxes and bars of Laima chocolates, books, records, posters, and postcards between my clothes. Everything that I could do without and that was of any use to my relatives I left in Latvia. A month in the fatherland had flown by. I wanted to hold on to Rīga's church steeples, the limbs of its old trees, and the Freedom Monument's hands to keep myself there. My last days went by in a haze of talks, laughter, tears, and Armenian cognac, which seeped into my taste buds and olfactory receptors. Forever and ever its aroma would bring back memories of Rīga and Latvia in 1980. My dear cousin Māra had offered to accompany me on the train to Tallinn, from which I would sail back to the Free World.

The Cultural Liaison Committeee invited me to do an interview for their propaganda newspaper, *Dzimtenes Balss*, which I agreed to. We did not discuss the painful subject of my premature departure, but regardless of their allegiance, the people I spoke to were kind to me (or trained in dissimulation). I refused to be confrontational, and they were grateful for that. Certainly it was humiliating to be asked to leave one's ancestral homeland for unspecified reasons; I had traveled there with a naive sense of entitlement, which was rudely dashed. One of the committee's employees took me to lunch at the charming restaurant "Pūt, vējiņi" ("Blow, Wind"—named after a popular Latvian folk song) in Old Rīga, a place where the average Soviet citizen had little chance of getting in. We ate pork chops, a food that I would associate with that era and Latvia (often served at Hotel Latvija). Again, I wondered what to talk about, as the main subjects—the existential ones—were off the table, so to speak. Even back then I wasn't good at shallow pleasantries. My intensity scared some people. I was guarded, knowing that this neatly-groomed fellow worked for the KGB. As an American, I was unused to filtered language. But I was fully aware of the fact that some of my compatriots were not what they seemed. They were Latvian, but in Soviet-occupied communist Latvia and anywhere else, for that matter, being Latvian did not guarantee integrity and trustworthiness. My rose-tinted glasses were forever shattered.

Pēc pusotra mēneša uzturēšanās Rīgā ļoti apmierināta mājup devās Ņujorkas mākslas skolas audzēkne RITA RUMPĒTERE. Ar Latvijas kultūras sakaru komitejas gādību viņai, ārzemju latviešu jaunās paaudzes talantīgajai pārstāvei, bija radīta iespēja papildināties Latvijas Valsts Mākslas akadēmijā. Viņas skolotājs bija Tautas mākslinieks Pēteris Upītis, pie kura mācījušās daudzas ievērojamu Latvijas grafiķu paaudzes. Tieši sirmais profesors bija tas, kas Rigā pamudinājis Ritu izšķirties savas jaunās māksliniece nākotnes nodomos — viņa būs grafiķe. Protams, vēl priekšā nopietni studiju laiks, un tāpēc viņa ļoti cer atkal būt Rīgā, kur pavisam neilga laikā guvusi daudz vērtīgu atziņu un iemanu dažādās grafikas tehnikās. Mājup viņa devās ar trīs pabeigtiem saviem darbiem.

A t t ē l ā: Rita Rumpētere pie Latvijas Mākslas akadēmijas ieejas.

A photograph of me – a contagious speck of capitalism and freedom— in *Dzimtenes balss*, November 1980.

After our pleasant meal in the oddly empty restaurant, we had coffee at Pētergailis, a small café near St. Peter's, and I was interviewed. After the interview a staff photographer snapped the picture on the left. I had fallen in love with Rīga, its architecture and artists, and its spirit, which eluded the grasp of Latvia's oppressors. Resilience, obstinacy, pride, dignity, and lots of humor existed beneath the gloom of the Soviet occupation. I had bonded with Latvia through my mother tongue. That bond could never be broken.

Then came the day when my cousin Māra and I boarded the Rīga-Tallinn train, as a crowd of relatives and friends stood on the platform to wave goodbye. I was free to go back to the Free World; they remained in Latvia—hostages of an unjust 1945 agreement that slated them and their successors to captivity. It was in that moment, gazing upon the pale faces of my Latvian relatives in their drab Soviet clothes deprived of the freedom to travel outside of the USSR, that the terrible outcome of World War II for the Baltic States became painfully clear to me. I had already decided that I would do everything in my power to return soon. Latvia had captivated me.

Interlude
(November 1980–September 1981)

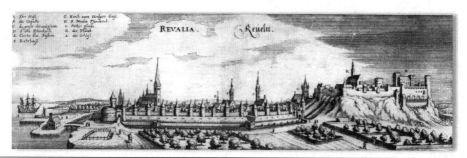

A view of Tallinn (or Reval, as it was once called) in the 17th century. Engraving by Adam Olearius (1603–1671). Source: Wikimedia Commons. https://commons.wikimedia.org/wiki/File:Tallinn_Olearius.jpg

In Tallinn Māra and I had some hours to walk around the Old Town before the departure of my ferry. The Estonian capital, founded in 1248, was smaller than Rīga. Just like Rīga, Tallinn had endured its share of foreign occupations. I enjoyed listening to the Estonian language, which is similar to Finnish. Estonian is also a sister language to Latvia's nearly extinct Liv language, so I pricked up my ears. "Minu nimi on Rita…" Tallinners were used to a lot of Finnish tourists in their town; their rich, free neighbors came over on the ferry to spend their money on cheap booze.

It was so kind of Māra to accompany me! Ten years older than me, my cousin Māra was an extraordinary woman: talented; industrious; kind; attentive; dutiful; and a wonderful daughter, sister, wife, and mother to her children. She impressed me with her inner strength, calm demeanor, and practical wisdom. Solid as a rock, Māra Lindberga was one of the many extraordinary women I would meet in Latvia.

The trip to Helsinki on the Georg Ots ferry was memorable due to all the drunken Finns—men and women—staggering about and mumbling. I was befriended by a small group of Finnish students: they were very interested to hear about my exploits in communist Latvia. Our camaraderie was so enjoyable, that I stayed an extra two days in Helsinki at one of the girl's apartments and got to see Helsinki itself, including its main art museum. I got to see the extraordinary art of Akseli Gallen-Kallela (1865–1931) and Hugo Simberg (1873–1917). Gallen-Kallela's extraordinary illustrations for the Finnish epic *Kalevala* still mesmerize me, but the subjects of Simberg's symbolist paintings reminded me of Latvian folklore, especially Latvian devils. Walking around in pretty downtown Helsinki, again I was forced to think about the predicament of my people. Up until the war Latvians had traveled freely to Berlin, Paris, London, Rome, Stockholm, Helsinki, New York, you name it… President Kārlis Ulmanis had studied at the University of Nebraska. What kind of paranoid state put up an "iron curtain" to keep their citizens from seeing the rest of the world? How would long-term isolation affect the prisoners? Gazing at the Finns who looked healthy and content, my heart ached.

Entering the airspace over New York, I gazed down at the vast maze of this wonderful city and its throbbing congestion, my hot tears dripping into an airplane napkin. I was miserable over my ejection from Latvia, so cruel and unfair. I had hoped to be there for at least three months. What crime had I committed? I had only visited friends and family, moved about obediently like a tourist, and attended school, according to plan. *Those communists are fucking bastards!*—I snorted, wiping my nose. They had turned Latvia upside down and inside out: white was black; black was white; logic was illogical; dimwits ruled over bright minds and consciences; God was Satan, and Satan was Comrade. A positively evil system. What right had they to throw me out like that? Latvia was my fatherland! I wasn't a dissident or firebrand agitator! But the voice of reality gently prodded my brain: the chekists didn't like me visiting all those Latvians and running around with young artists. I carried the germs of democracy and free speech.

Life in in the Free World no longer seemed interesting. I had missed the beginning of the school year at Parsons because, unwisely, I had not planned for the (very real) scenario of an early return to the US. I was convinced that the Soviet authorities would let me stay in Latvia until the spring. I also realized that if I wanted to go back to Latvia as soon as possible, I needed money, which meant finding a job. Pushing aside my regrets about missing school, I found a house-cleaning job and began planning my next trip. To feel better about leaving Parsons and full-time studies, I enrolled at the Art Students League in New York City and took drawing classes. I also had a project underway: to obtain funds to purchase a synthesizer for a young composer named Jānis Lūsēns. In this I was quickly successful. A wealthy Latvian entrepreneur in Venezuela sent me a check for $1,500 no questions asked, no strings attached.

Left: My brother Arvils and I goofing around on train tracks in New Jersey in 1981.

My cleaning job was uninspiring, but my savings grew. I also got a great workout. Looking back, it is hard to believe that I walked such huge distances—from four to seven miles each day—to get to work and back. With no car and no one to drop me off or pick me up at my destinations (my father was at work and my mother did not drive), I had to rely on my own two legs. I longed for a bike. As I scrubbed my fellow Americans' toilets and bathtubs, vacuumed, wiped, and sprayed, breathing in the smells of Mr. Clean, Comet, and Windex, my mind traveled to Latvia. On weekends I went into New York to see art exhibits and soak up the city's energy. I was full of nervous energy.

I greatly enjoyed writing letters to my friends and family in Latvia. Snail mail was all we had back then, and I waited for the mailman eagerly, hoping to spot his truck at the end of our street. Letters from my artist friends Andris, Juris, and Ojārs were funny, poetic, and creative. Ojārs had been shipped off to some faraway Soviet republic for military service. His self-portraits in a Russian soldier's uniform, which I put up on my wall, raised the eyebrows of some of my Latvian American friends.

In December 1980 I traveled to Chicago to join a small group of Latvian American writers for a poetry reading. Sniedze Runģe, Jānis Imants Sedliņš, and Mārtiņš Grants were my companions that weekend: we were the offspring of refugees, born in America but carrying the torch of our mother tongue forward into the hazy future. We stayed up all night listening to music from Latvia, mostly Imants Kalniņš and Raimonds Pauls. At daybreak beautiful, mysterious Sniedze took a razor blade and sawed off my long, thick braid, the one people in Latvia had admired so much. It was an eager parting with my childhood.

In the winter of 1981 I sat down at our old typewriter and wrote about my trip to Latvia. I called the piece "Atgriešanās vēl neredzētā zemē" ("Return to Terra Incognita") and dispatched it to the American Latvian Youth Association's (ALYA) journal *Vēja zvani* ("Wind Chimes"). Unfortunately, the Soviet Latvian KGB also read the magazine...

Summer of 1981, "Endless Love" (Lionel Richie and Diana Ross), and "O Superman" (Laurie Anderson) rolled around. New Jersey perspired in the sweltering heat, as I counted the days.Scrubbing toilets had gotten me to where I felt comfortable about traveling abroad, with money in my pocket. In August I began packing, this time with a synthesizer in tow. My travel route was different than last time.

Here come the planes. They're American planes. Made in America. (Laurie Anderson)

Instead of flying to Helsinki, I flew to Moscow via Warsaw, with the last leg of the trip being absolutely miserable, as the small plan bucked and pitched, overwhelming me with motion sickness. Green and shaken, we landed at Sheremetyevo Airport, a big, scary place teeming with nervous foreign travelers and mean-looking Soviet Russian airport personnel. "Psycho Killer" by the Talking Heads described this place well. "Run run run away..." The Soviets'/Russians' ill will towards us westerners was palpable. It was there that I encountered my first real trouble.

While standing in line and inching towards a booth with some scowling Russian customs officers, I was surprised to be greeted by a couple of smiling, giggling, slightly intoxicated, long-haired friends of Jānis Lūsēns. One of them turned out to be Latvia's soon-to-be-crowned "King of Rock" Juris Kulakovs. The other was Rauls Zitmanis, a young artist who looked like he belonged in the Allman Brothers Band. Not your average Soviet citizens. Lūsēns had sent them to Moscow as his "emissaries" to pay off the synthesizer's import duty and take possession of the instrument. Although these Latvian fellows seemed pleasant, amusing, and perfectly innocent, their presence made me nervous. The Soviets didn't like non-conformists and especially those from the fascist hinterlands. Add long hair, shameless giggles, the scent of alcohol, and you were asking for trouble. The airport teemed with apparatchiks looking to bust someone.

Standing at the booth, I was informed that the synthesizer was appraised at a sum so high that it barred me from "importing" it (or something absurd like that). I was not allowed to take it with me to Latvia. As I struggled to contain my composure, Juris and Rauls started arguing with the Russian customs officials about the matter, making things even worse. As the two unruly Latvians vanished into an airport security room, I was forced to hurry to join my tour group to get to the hotel, leaving the prized instrument in an airport holding area. The Latvian "bums" were thrown out of the airport after being detained and interrogated. Yikes! Now *that* situation did not bode well for my stay in Rīga.

That evening before going to bed, I stood by the window of my Intourist hotel room looking out at the lights of Moscow, the capital of the Union of Soviet Socialist Republics. Moscow seemed enormous, cold, and unfriendly. The incident at the airport had left me pretty shaken.

My well-intentioned efforts had bounced against a wall of Kafkaesque absurdity before knocking me over. I was made to feel guilty of a crime I had not committed. Would my punishment be meted out in Rīga?

Before leaving Moscow, someone let me know I could pick up the synthesizer on my way back to the United States. I was nervous about what lay ahead of me. Instead of joyful anticipation, I experienced a sense of mounting dread and anger at the stupidity of the Soviet bureaucracy. I was helping a Soviet musician, goddammit! This time I was not a guest and protégé of Soviet Latvia's Cultural Liaison Committee; I was a mere tourist, and some adventurous young Latvian men had just made a small mess at Moscow's international airport because of me. I was sure there would be repercussions. Someone in Rīga wasn't happy with me.

Of course, this time my visit was a bit different. As I began running around visiting my relatives and friends, I was waiting, anxiously waiting... for that call. Da... Moscow had contacted Rīga. I was expected at the Visa Department for a chat. Entering the building on Anrija Barbisa (Henri Barbusse) iela, I marveled at how empty and eerily quiet it was. The communists sure didn't mind taking over buildings built by the kind of people they despised—successful capitalists. The so-called Visa Department (for foreigners) was tucked away in a building that had probably once belonged to a wealthy Rīga German. Traces of the building's ornate interior contrasted with the cold aura of Soviet bureacracy.

I walked up to the second floor and sat down in the waiting area. Before long I was ushered into a small room with a desk, two chairs, one barred window, and a portrait of Lenin on the wall. There was a conspicuously bright red telephone on the desk. A man in a black leather jacket stood up and extended his paw. "*Vot, vot, sveiki*," he said, introducing himself as Comrade (Jānis) Rucinš, his Latvian betraying a heavy Russian accent. My skin prickled, because for the first time in my life I was in the same room with someone whom I perceived to be a true villain. I felt like a mouse in the presence of a fat, hungry cat.

After preliminary chitchat Comrade Rucinš reached into a drawer and fished out a copy of *Vēja zvani*, the journal that contained my candid article about my first trip to Latvia. I looked up at Lenin. What kind of paternalistic preaching would I be subjected to? I wondered how these slimebags had gotten their grubby hands on such a small, peripheral publication distributed to just a few hundred people. Perhaps ALYA, the American Latvian Youth Association, sent copies to the Cultural Liaison Committee? Comrade Rucinš zeroed in on my negative comments and chided me for them, as if I'd taken advantage of Soviet hospitality. Then he proceeded to ask about some expatriate Latvians—people involved in the American Latvian Youth Association and other Latvian organizations. I said I didn't know these people (and really I didn't). Lastly, Comrade Rucinš brought up the subject of history, asking me how I knew things were better before the Soviet occupation, and why did I think people were unhappy now. It was a dangerous moment.

Squeezed into a corner, I proceeded to lie myself out of the tight spot, claiming I had no interest in politics and Latvian American political activity. Having gained zero "intelligence" from me, Comrade Rucinš and I parted with an insincere handshake, and a couple of days later I was summoned to the office of a high-ranking KGB officer named Bruno Šteinbriks. This meeting was definitely more serious, as it took place in "Stūra māja," the Soviet Cheka building where people had been tortured and shot in 1940-41. Again I was overcome with a feeling of absurdity, as I failed to grasp my transgression. It was precisely the absurdity of the KGB's interest in me that also saved me from despair; deep within some voice was giggling, and Ruciņš and Šteinbriks reminded me of the loutish devils in Latvian folk tales. He immediately brought up the subject of the synthesizer and how the commotion at the airport had caused problems for him. Scandalous! Comrade Šteinbriks pressed me for information regarding the young musician Jānis Lūsēns and his friends—the ones who had caused the *tracis* (ruckus). My session with Comrade Šteinbriks was certainly unpleasant, but I knew nothing about Kulakovs and Zitmanis and wasn't even sure why all of this was even an issue. I answered his sharp questions reluctantly and evasively. Truth be told, I had little to say. What do you say to a person who suspects you of something you're not guilty of and accuses you of importing a musical instrument? The meeting was an affront to my Western sensibilities. Was bringing an instrument to the Soviet Union a crime? They should have been happy. Šteinbriks was a big *šiška* ("boss") in the Latvian KGB, but I didn't find him particularly scary. More like annoying. And a waste of time for him and me: our conversation dead-ended because—*really*—there was nothing to divulge.

I ended up getting to know the long-haired miscreants after all. Rauls and his beautiful wife Kira were art students at the Latvian Academy of Art. They lived in a terribly run-down apartment on Karl Marx Street, which they shared with Rauls' parents. They had a small room to themselves and a little boy named Otto. Rauls' paintings and drawings reminded me of rock n' roll album covers. Big, tall, handsome Rauls with his shaggy locks would have looked good in an ancient Latvian warrior's get-up with a war ax in his hand. Many buildings on Karl Marx Street were in bad condition. You had to sell your soul to the Devil to get out of these hell holes, but many of my Latvian compatriots weren't prepared to do that, no matter what. Many sought escape in alcohol and drugs. Latvians were prone to alcohol abuse: I had seen it myself in America. In Latvia, where people felt trapped, some took it to a whole new level.

The music of Jānis Lūsēns (b. 1959) was quite popular in the early 1980s. His album "Zodiac: Disco Alliance" (LEFT) was successful not only in Latvia but elsewhere in the Soviet Union. It was reminiscent of the synthesizer music of Frenchman Jean Michel Jarre and the group Space. It was one of the albums I brought back to the United States in 1980. Despite Lūsēns' growing fame, for some reason the Soviets did not want him to have his Moog.

One evening Juris Kulakovs pulled up beside me on a bike in the shadows of the park and offered me a ride to Hotel Latvija. Not only was this the first bike I had seen in town, but Kulakovs was such a character—the quintessential rock star with no inhibitions. It seemed like a crazy and fun thing to do because *nobody* rode around on a bike in Rīga back then except for this grinning Cheshire Cat. And then out of the blue, near the hotel, he proposed. Our marriage would be mutually advantageous. He could go abroad and study, I could come and live with him in Latvia and get to know life there. I giggled; he grinned slyly. Juris waved his hand, asked me to think about it, and pedaled off into the darkness. In the morning I'd already forgotten about it.

And then it *really* happened just a few days later shortly before my departure. I really did fall in love, unexpectedly. Poet Imants Ziedonis led me down a set of narrow, winding stairs into the musty basement of the Small Guild on Amatu iela in Old Rīga, which operated as a house of culture. There in a rather dark and mysterious space filled with antiques and clutter I was introduced to a short, bearded man named Juris Krieviņš who ran a youth photo club called Īriss ("Iris"). Club activities included trips to the countryside, from what I could see. After Imants' departure, Mr. Krieviņš invited me to come see his personal studio located just a couple of blocks away. Yowza! Was this place cool or what? The little man's hideout was built into the roof of a marvelous Art Nouveau building, and it was breathtaking. Through one window I could see St. Mary's Cathedral towering over the rooftops of charming buildings in this oldest part of Rīga; from another window I could see St. Peter's majestic spire.

It was there in that most romantic setting that I was introduced to the photographer's son Andris who had stopped by for a visit. Friendly, funny, and handsome, he made me laugh and excited me. That very same evening Andris and I went out to eat with filmmaker Ansis Epners and then had a very enjoyable evening of talks and tea at Epners' place. We walked back to my hotel holding hands. It felt so natural, as we leaned into each other. In the park we fell into a passionate embrace. We promised to write to each other. And then, just like the cat from the previous evening, Andris melted into the darkness. I sent my first letter to him on a napkin from Hotel Latvija.

For the next 15 months Andris and I exchanged many letters: pages filled with drawings, photographs, poetry, and longing. We constructed our relationship and our future based on these letters, which the voyeuristic Soviet censors touched, handled, and registered. These letters caused problems for Andris who was serving in the Soviet military in Rīga. But he was a wild one; he didn't care. Like his father, Andris was a photographer. He wrote his letters and poetry on the back of black and white photographs of himself, Rīga, the beautiful Latvian countryside, and the people around him. I marveled at the exquisite Soviet postage stamps—charming envoys of a corrupt, totalitarian state.

Back in the US, I decided to enroll in a new Latvian language studies program at Western Michigan University in Kalamazoo. A special residential building was going up to house the students. The program was a pet project of Dr. Valdis Muižnieks. For me the decision to enroll was a no-brainer: I was riding on a wave of patriotism and interest in Latvia.

That fall (1981) we students spent our free time helping build our future dormitory. In school we studied Latvian history, literature, grammar, and phonetics with our friendly mentors, Lalita Muižniece, historian Jānis Peniķis, and linguist Anda Libere. While the building took shape, I lived at the Muižnieks' house, went running after school, read Latvian poetry, and wrote long letters. Some poetry, like Vizma Belševica's (1931–2005), made me cry. My experiences in Latvia had left a profound impact on me, and I was feeling in love. After Christmas break we moved into the brand new dormitory, where we each had our own room. Our schoolwork was inspiring, as were were our friendships. I ran to the mailbox each day to look for letters from Latvia. I taped Andris' black and white photographs to the walls of my room. I fell for a classmate and felt confused and guilty. I listened to Ricki Lee Jones and Bruce Cockburn and enjoyed the cold Kalamazoo winter with snowdrifts and icicles. It was a time of introspection, learning, and anticipation.

I graduated in May and went back home to New Jersey to clean houses and stash away money. I informed my parents of my decision to go to Latvia *again*. Third time's a charm, they say. This time they knew it was a matter of the heart. In July I spent a couple of days interviewing my maternal grandfather Jānis Bičolis about his life, making a tape recording of his narrative. On the second day I rode home from his house on my bike only to find out that he died of a heart attack right after I left. Furiously, I pedaled the five or so miles back to Tuks' place. I saw my grandfather sprawled out face-down on the floor. My beloved Tuciņš—so kind, loving, and wise! At his funeral we danced to recall his passion for music. He was such a down-to-earth, free soul with no interest in material things other than books.

My grandfathers' influence on my life is apparent to this day. I grew up listening to their voices, their conversations, their speeches, and their arguments over history and politics, which I could barely understand. In 1982 I was 22. After the funeral I focused on everything related to my trip to Latvia. I wanted to believe that my grandfather's soul was finally back in Latvia. For years he had wanted to go home, to lie down in a meadow, and to feel Latvia's soil beneath him. No wonder there were Latvian tourists who brought small bags and jars of soil from Latvia back with them; the attachment was deep-rooted.

Fall came and shorter days. On November 10 General Secretary of the Central Committee of the Communist Party of the Soviet Union Leonid Brezhnev (b. 1906) died. Brezhnev had presided over his party since 1964, when I was four years old. With his bushy eyebrows, mongoloid features, and robotic speech, he was the butt of many hilarious Soviet era jokes. Brezhnev's demise was big news. Who would succeed him? What changes in the Soviet Union could the world expect, if any? Singing along to Foreigner's "Urgent," I folded my clothes into my suitcase: "You wanna fly, don't want your feet on the ground / You stay up, you won't come down..."

The Black Time

Hardly a green, just a faint airborne premonition
That soon a green-tinged mist will envelop supple birches
The timorous northern love of the slow greening of birch trees.
The waiting. The breathlessness. The almost choking tenderness.

Unseen. Unheard. The buds of birch unfurl. There's still
A lull between the owl's moan and the lark's trill. It's still
A black time— a pulsing streak between the white and the green.
Hardly a green, just a faint airborne premonition.

Vizma Belševica
Translated by Māra Rozītis

PART FOUR:
The 1980s

Winter of '83: With Omamma, Uncle Andris, and my cousins Ruta and Vita in Olaine.

Tuk! Tuk! I'm Home!

Top: A Christmas greeting sent in December 1982 in Rīga.
Bottom: A postcard to my relatives in Latvia telling them I'm cleaning houses in New Jersey to pay for my ticket to Latvia, and that I've cut off my long hair. Postcard sent summer of 1982.

A few days before Christmas of 1982 my mother and I stuffed my suitcases into my godfather Gunars Saliņš's Honda. We climbed in and took off for JFK Airport, hurtling through the New Jersey Meadowlands in a dreamy state of laughter, excitement, and suspense. My father suffered from commuter burnout and had squirmed his way out of driving me to the airport, so "Gonka" had offered to help. For him, too, it was an adventure. He was a great companion for this manic trek to the airport. His humor, wit, and magical take on things helped dispel my anxiety. Gonka knew that my love interest was waiting for me in Latvia. He was a ladies' man and inquisitive about matters of love. My mother and my godfather were very excited for me. None of us was immune to the pull of Latvia, even in its undignified state of captivity.

"Don't let the sun go down on me…" (Elton John) One reality was dissolving into another as the sun went down in the west. The Meadowlands, the Verrazano-Narrows Bridge, the Atlantic Ocean: familiar sights… My flight to Moscow was scheduled to depart in the early evening. I checked in, and then we had some time to kill, so we went back to the car to huddle, talk, giggle, and sip elixir vitae (cognac) from Gonka's pocket flask. We were giddy like children. We were part of a conspiracy, forging a plan to defeat the USSR through the simple act of love. This would be the greatest miracle: love would defeat tyranny. The lights of JFK twinkled in the early evening darkness. How much I loved New York City! The minutes were ticking. Twenty-four hours to go until my meeting with destiny.

Departure. Big hugs. Bright, teary smiles. I walked away from my mother, looking back from time to time to see her waving and waving and waving. My mother. Motherland. It was my mother whose personality and principles had left such a great impact on me as a Latvian. Her poetry, written in her mother tongue, explored her past, her identity, and Latvian archetypes.

She is the bowl and the spoon, / her husband, her children, her brood / dip into and ladle from her, / she is a white, soft, steaming potato, / white milk, and a tiny grain of barley, / butter's golden eye / and a dark-green, pungent scallion, / she is a table, and she is a bed / from which, as the seasons turn, / her tribe rises / and the symbols of dainas and shawls (Baiba Bičole, Senmāte ["Ancestress"] Tr. RL)

How is it that a place can come to mean so much to a person? It has remained a mystery for my entire life. What was the draw? Was it a need to confirm some part of me? Was it a longing to repair something? A hope to connect to a patch of earth that held the remains of my ancestors? In December of 1982 I was willing to step off the edge of the Free World to tumble into the murky darkness of my family's past, hoping I would land on my feet.

Moscow: that cold, scary city. It was one of the few routes to reach the western periphery of the Soviet Union, which included Latvia. It was an unpleasant, uncomfortable detour, which underscored Latvia's political situation. Unlike New York, Moscow seemed busy yet devoid of life. After enduring the gauntlet of cold, suspicious Russian eyes, we westerners were herded like a bunch of sheep by our Latvian Intourist agent from the airport to our bus and the hotel. Nothing was left to chance and spontaneity. Moscow Radio's eerie midnight chimes, set to the tune of the popular Russian song "Podmoskovnye Vechera" ("Moscow Nights"), captured the mood of that era. I still get goosebumps hearing this melody, which reminds me of the enormous failed communist experiment. Beyond Moscow lay an enormous landmass. Russia was big. Scary big. Siberia had swallowed the bones of millions of victims of communism, including Balts and my family members. I wanted to leave Russia as quickly as possible. It felt cursed and dark.

Rīga (1201)

Riga's Architecture

I

One Riga—a city of friendly cobblestoned streets from days gone by, of
stone walls, of crumbling stone steps, of towers and steeples, -
the other—a city of fear,
fear in the steeples, in walls, in crumbling stone steps, in cobblestone streets, -
coursing in eyes and fingertips
fear

II

We're walking—
coming towards us, the Laima clock and the lindens, swans on the canal and
the Opera, the Statue of Freedom—as though in a postcard. But then
we cross Lenin Boulevard—and the asphalt crackles, caves in, we drop
down into an underground world.
Those are shafts,
those are coal mines—and in the center of Riga, we're suddenly
at a vast distance from Riga. We're walking
through mines, in the Arctic—stooping, signaling to each other,
whispering.
The lindens, the Statue of Freedom are a vast distance away—as though on an old
postcard.
As though on an old
postcard that faded years ago, somewhere at a distance,
At a vast distance somewhere above our heads—
Riga?

Gunars Saliņš
Translated by Ilze Kļaviņa-Mueller

Bastejkalns in winter in a photograph taken before WWII. The scene was the same in December 1982. Image courtesy of the National Library of Latvia collection "In Search of Lost Latvia."

December's bone-chilling cold and darkness wrapped around me as I left Hotel Latvija in the early evening, walking towards Bastejkalns. It was a popular meeting place for lovers. Andris and I had agreed to meet on top of this romantic elevation, from which in daytime you could see the Freedom Monument, our national symbol of sacrifice and freedom. As I reached the top of the hill, my sweetheart stepped out from from the shadows, and we fell into each other's arms, laughing.

Latvia's wintry gloom suited us just fine: cloaked in its darkness, we felt safe from the prying eyes of the shadowy figures that had stalked us and now stood nearby, lurking behind the trees and bushes like wolves, trying to keep sight of us. Separated for 15 months, we hugged and laughed and then, hand in hand, quietly descended from Bastejkalns. We crossed Padomju bulvāris (Soviet Boulevard) and plunged into the winding streets of Old Rīga, hoping to put some distance between ourselves and the beasts.

We raced beneath St. Mary's gaze, our feet pounding the icy cobblestones, and continued down Jauniela, where we turned and hurled ourselves through the doorway of Krāmu iela 10. The old door slammed shut behind us with a loud bang. We scrambled up the many steps to the top, laughing like children, enjoying the sense of danger and escape. I did not feel afraid with my companion at my side. At 21, Andris was a young buck, wild and free.

Without even discussing it in detail, we both immediately realized that we would have to marry *now* or part ways again for a very long time. Talk about a whirlwind proposal! We were both by nature impatient and impetuous; these traits would be tempered by time. I had come to Latvia on a typical Soviet tourist visa good for a mere two weeks. The urgency of the situation was apparent. It seemed like *now or never*, and neither of us wanted to wait. The Soviet Union did not issue visas freely, and I was sure that my previous "behavior" was already part of a file with the relevant authorities. Andris had no interest in leaving Latvia for a new life in the United States. He was a Latvian patriot; this, of course, made him even more appealing.

The tiny apartment adjacent to Juris Krieviņš's studio was occupied by Andris' sister Gita, her husband, and their newborn daughter, Elīna. They were not home at the moment; perhaps that had been arranged. Juris Krieviņš was also conspicuously absent. I gazed at the magnificent architecture of St. Mary's, a church that dated back to the early 13th century. At that moment, Rīga looked like a Christmas postcard. The rooftops were white, the sky low and promising more snow. It was no wonder that Andris did not want to leave Rīga! The location of his father's studio was priceless. We talked in earnest about *here* and *there* and who we were and what we wanted. I did not want to leave Latvia. The decision was mutual and fantastically simple. I would stay. We would marry. We would overcome any hardships together. This was the land of our ancestors, occupied or not. The KGB freaks could go to hell.

I spent my first Christmas in Rīga attending mass at St. James' (1225), a Catholic church in Old Rīga illuminated with candles and open to those who sought light in the heart of darkness. Many Latvians celebrated Christmas secretly at home with a small Christmas tree, simple gifts, and food in spite of the communists' ban of organized religion. On New Year's I was introduced to some alien characters at a couple of Latvian public events and on TV: "Salavecis" (or Ded Moroz, the Russian version of Santa Claus) and "Snegurochka" ("Snow Maiden") were imported from Russia, and I was shocked to see my fellow Latvians involved with these Slavic characters. We ushered in 1983 by partying at the Latvian Music Conservatory and the Latvian Art Academy, where Juris Kulakovs and his band Pērkons were performing.

I wrote a letter to my parents about my decision to remain in Latvia and gave it to my hotel roommate Gunta Dreifelde, a Latvian Canadian, to mail from Canada. I also dispatched a telegram announcing my decision to stay: "I'm not coming back. Spring wedding. Come to *mičošana."* (*Mičošana* is a traditional Latvian wedding ritual.) My mother shared this news with her Latvian friends at a New Year's party in Glen Ridge. It was all everyone could talk about, apparently. "Shock, amazement, dismay, so many questions…" My visa was extended; the "comrades" were intrigued. Our plans were moving ahead. My family, our relatives, and friends were surprised, to put it mildly. My original departure day came and went; in January I was still in Rīga.

Seventeen years in Latvia began with a simple, spontaneous decision, because there was no other way. Andris liked my middle name so much that, while I lived in Latvia, most people except for my relatives called me Laima, which is a quintessentially Baltic name. Laima was a Baltic female deity from pre-Christian times, the goddess of fate and fortune, and she is invoked in many Latvian dainas. However, there were few Laimas in Latvia in the Soviet era. Latvian mythology had no place in communist ideology. Rīga's famous chocolate factory was named after Laima.

My visa was extended on the grounds that I was getting married and had expressed my intent to reside in the Latvian Soviet Socialist Republic. Juris Krieviņš, my future father-in-law, was understandably fearful of the consequences of our decision. In fact, later he confided that a "friend" of his, Ivars Ķezbers (1944–1997), a historian who sometimes appeared on television and had friends in high places (namely, people in the Latvian Communist Party's Central Committee), had explicitly warned him of possible problems, if we—his kids—did not "behave."

A wedding date was set for March 4. The Krieviņš family had to make room for us as a couple, because there was nowhere for us to go. Neither Rīga nor any other Soviet city had a housing market with apartments for rent. It was decided that Andris' sister and her family would move back in with Biruta Krieviņa, my future mother-in-law. She lived in a tiny apartment in Pārdaugava, which Gita had "escaped" from. How this difficult arrangement ultimately affected Gita's private life, I'll never know. It was never discussed, but I quickly realized how stressful her living conditions must have been. I felt guilty for pushing her out of her fragile "private space," which was hardly private, as I would soon discover. Gita's choices in later years made me wonder how adverse living conditions—small, cramped apartments shared with parents and other family members—could shape a person and determine their actions.

An old postcard depicting Krāmu iela (Kramerstrasse) at the beginning of the 20th century. Image courtesy of the National Library of Latvia collection "In Search of Lost Latvia."

My new life in Latvia began on the corner of Krāmu and Jauniela in Old Rīga. Our building had miraculously survived the bombs dropped in World War II. Our firstborn son would be conceived there. I would translate and illustrate my first book there. It was a good place for a while. I was surrounded by a history I wanted to know more about.

Letter dated January 4, 1983 to my parents in New Jersey

Čau (Ciao), mīļiši (loved ones)! It's snowing. We are drinking tea. Tomorrow morning I have to go get my visa and then walk over to the Foreign Ministry to clarify some formalities regarding my future here. I may have to go to Leningrad and stay there for a few days (with the Consul's family—ha!). I'm itching to get busy doing something. I typed out my poems and plan on showing them to Uldis (Bērziņš) to discuss future possibilities. Andris promised to find a book on how to learn Russian. I went to the Central Market today and bought two  *large cod and some carrots, my first attempt at making a meal! I cleaned the kitchen, but the bathtub is full of dirty dishes, and Andris refuses to touch them. Blah! Tomorrow night we are going to see a play by Rūdolfs Blaumanis, which commemorates his 120th birthday. We have our first art up on the wall, thanks to Ojārs Pētersons ("With R. in the Cafés of Rīga"). Tomorrow we will hang a portrait of Andris by Uldis Zemzaris. I'm doing OK. Please send: 1) An English language tutorial. 2) My Indian blanket. 3) A skirt. 4) Some pants. 5) My jogging suit. 6) Some money— hehe. 7) My Luma watercolors. Love, Rita Laima*

Everyone in Rīga younger than 30 used the word "čau!" as a greeting, so that stuck with me, as would other local words and expressions, like the funny "johaidī!" (pronounced *yo-hi-dee*), an expression apparently derived from a German student drinking song, and "jopcikbumbiņ" (pronounced *yop-tsyk-boombeen*). Both of these were old expressions for heightened emotions. My ears were turning into radars, tuning into how the people around me spoke, the words they used, the jokes they cracked.

I had arrived in Latvia with practically no experience in the kitchen. I knew how to boil an egg, peel vegetables, and make a sandwich. My mother had always done all the cooking and had never asked me to help her, thinking it was better that I spend my time reading, drawing, and studying. I was a complete novice when it came to measurements, oven temperatures, preparation times, and any dish that required being made from scratch. What made things worse was that all the cookbooks in Latvia prescribed their measurements in metric weights and volume. And our oven did not have a temperature gauge.

In January 1983 I started writing letters to my family in the United States, sharing my observations, minor complaints, regrets, hopes, and enthusiasm. My letters also included lots of pathetic wheedling, as I very quickly discovered how difficult it was to get by without certain useful products that one took for granted in a market economy: American toothpaste and dental floss; hair elastics (rubber bands tore hair); shavers (women in Latvia had hairy legs and armpits); all types of clothing, including underwear and outerwear; running shoes (nobody in Rīga jogged); art supplies; books in English (some I discovered in second-hand bookshops); etc. Had they been rich, I could have asked my family to ship us toilet paper, Kleenex, and other such handy items, but that would have been ridiculous. One simply got used to using *Literatūra un Māksla* and *Padomju Jaunatne* (the newspapers *Literature and Art* and *Soviet Youth*) as toilet paper and blowing one's nose into a damp, snotty handkerchief. I washed and ironed these handkerchiefs dutifully.

How was it that the USSR, which prided itself in its bloody revolution, the righteousness of communism and the dictatorship of the proletariat, and its military might, did not live up to its propaganda posters featuring lean, grim-faced factory workers churning out... Yes, what exactly were they churning out, if so much was in demand and impossible to find? Smokestacks spewed smoke and workers streamed in and out of factories, but people complained about all sorts of shortages.

> In addition to the tremendous humanitarian losses under the Soviet occupation, the Baltic States sustained great losses in the industrial sector. Soviet propaganda devoted a great deal of effort to prove that the Soviet system "had clear advantages" (over capitalism—RL) and claimed to have "made enormous investments" in the development of manufacturing and improvements in workers' living conditions, especially in the new Soviet Baltic republics. (...) Compared to the West, the Baltic States, as well as the rest of the Soviet Union, despite several major scientific and technical achievements (mostly in the fields of military and space exploration), were sinking into technological stagnation with sharply disproportionate development among Soviet regions. This, however, was kept secret from the people of the Soviet Union and the (Soviet) Latvian Republic.—Juris Prikulis. "Latvijas rūpniecība 1940.-1960. Pēckara gados: Ekstensīva paplašināšana PSRS reģionālo disproporciju pieauguma apstākļos." (Latvian Industry in the Post-War Years 1940–1960.) *Padomju Savienības nodarītie zaudējumi Baltijā.* (Losses Sustained by the Baltic States under the Soviet Occupation.) Rīga: Latvijas Okupācijas izpētes biedrība, 2012. Tr. RL.

According to the news on Soviet Latvian radio and TV, which reported a continuous increase in industrial and agricultural output, Latvia's stores should have been full of all sorts of goods and merchandise. But they weren't, and Soviet citizens spun jokes about the perpetual shortages. Fruitless searches for adequate shoes, certain types of medicine, toilet paper, etc. could at least be turned into a joke.

> As a result of World War I (1914–1918) Latvia was Europe's most plundered and devastated country: ¼ of all its buildings had been razed; its railroads, factories, and commercial fleet were completely destroyed. In 1914 Latvia's population was 2.5 million; at the beginning of Latvia's independence (early 1920s) the population did not exceed 1.5 million. As a result of the war, Latvia had lost almost a million people. No other country in Europe had suffered such losses. Newly independent Latvia had to rebuild its industry and national economy from scratch. (Ibid, p. 104. Tr. RL)

In the US we had read about the extraordinary surge in economic activity and development in the Republic of Latvia between the two world wars (that is, in a very short period of 20 years). Latvia became a prime exporter of agricultural products to other European countries. *Bekons* (bacon) and *Latvijas brūnā* ("the Latvian Brown Cow)" are the two words I remember well from my days in Latvian school. Prior to World War II, Latvia was a huge exporter of bacon, and the "Latvian Brown" was an excellent bovine developed at the turn of the 20th century. Professor Pauls Lejiņš, a relative of Omamma's, was one of the first to begin work on pedigree cattle breeding in Latvia in 1910. The Brown Cows were still around in the 1980s in Latvia, but I heard that the breed had deteriorated.

Many other Latvian products were shipped to markets in Western Europe before World War II: timber; flax; butter; cheese... Latvia's economy was thriving in the 1930s, and tax revenue contributed to numerous significant public investment projects. According to Prikulis, "Latvia experienced a swift renaissance after 1920. New factories sprang into action, expanding their range of products and importing equipment from the West. An impressive "re-industrialization" took place after years of war and displacement of the population. It is especially important to note that Latvia's industry developed faster than its agricultural sector in the 1920s and 1930s. The output of radio apparatus, telephones, photography equipment, buses, bicycles, and other means of transportation, as well as cement, electricity, and other goods and commodities grew exponentially. " (Ibid p. 104. Tr. RL)

> Latvia's State Electrotechnical Factory (*Valsts elektrotechniskā fabrika* or VEF) began producing the world famous miniature Minox camera invented by Walter Zapp. The pocket-size camera became popular with spies and is now a collector's item. By the end of the 1930s Latvia's industrial output had increased five times over the early 1920s. These were rather impressive achievements even on a global scale, taking into account the Great Depression. By 1940 and the Soviet occupation, Latvia was a developed European country, and its standard of living and industrial and agricultural output far exceeded that of its neighbor, the USSR. (Ibid p. 104. Tr. RL)

VEF's Kārlis Irbītis had even designed planes in the 1930s. The Soviets put an end to that in 1940. Kārlis Irbītis ended up in Canada after the war, where he designed the experimental Canadian vertical landing and take-off airplane, the CL-84 (1950).

Prikulis notes that the so-called "first post-war five-year period" (1946–1950), as it was known in the Soviet Union's official economic lexicon, was a time of enormous economic losses for the surviving population of pre-war Latvia. Soviet statistics from that era would eventually disclose that in that "five-year period" Latvia was stripped almost bare, shrinking to the development level of the "old" Soviet republics. An enormous gap would emerge between the new Soviet reality and Latvia's many positive economic achievements before the war. (Ibid, p. 105. Tr. RL)

According to Prikulis, under the Soviet occupation "more than 70% of industrial manufacturing in Latvia was linked to the USSR military-industrial complex (...). In addition, converting manufacturers or their parts into non-military manufacturing plants and service providers was possible only through enormous capital investments, which were out of reach." (Ibid, p. 113)

I did not know who manufactured what in Latvia for the Soviet military, but names like Alfa, Biolar, and Komutators were linked to it. The Soviet military sector was like an enormous dragon with a bottomless belly. The dragon was fed at the expense of other sectors and the health and well-being of Soviet society. I did not want to know anything about the military industry in Soviet Latvia for obvious reasons. Like Sergeant Schulz, I chose to "know nothing and see nothing." If 70% of Soviet Latvia's industrial output was devoted to serving the needs of the Soviet military, it was well concealed. No wonder the KGB were skittish about Latvian tourists from the West. No wonder there were so many travel restrictions.

After World War II Latvia experienced a massive influx of Russian economic refugees fleeing from their impoverished kolhozes and villages. This, along with the influx of the Russian military, triggered widespread housing shortages. These shortages had not diminished by 1980, when I first visited Latvia, despite the construction of new apartment buildings meant to entice and house *new* Russian immigrants. Young Latvian couples like us were at a disadvantage, when it came to apartments.

As I began my new life in the USSR, I was only vaguely aware of Soviet Latvia's manufacturing sector and its "brands" and products. I was interested in brands, because my father was a packaging designer. As I started to make my rounds, I became more familiar with what was available and what was not. The once famous VEF factory still manufactured stuff like telephones and radios. These were simple but sturdy apparatus, rather primitive in appearance. Soviet products were better known for their physical toughness than their refinement. It was said you could kick a Soviet TV to make it work better. By 1980 the famous Minox camera was a legend of the past. Little or no investments seemed to be going towards product innovation and modernization, judging by their appearance. Going up Ļeņina iela, we would drive past the plant'ssprawling corpus. The factory looked tired. The old VEF was just an old-timer's memory of independent Latvia's economic status, accomplishments, and work ethic.

I quickly became familiar with the products of Dzintars ("Amber"), a Soviet Latvian company founded on the remnants of expropriated and nationalized pre-war private cosmetics manufacturers. Dzintars exported its perfume, eau de cologne, and skin, hair, and oral hygiene products to the rest of the Soviet Union and to some Eastern European countries. Its perfumes' were rather overpowering, its packaging inferior to similar products in the West. Used to American toothpaste, I failed to find a Soviet toothpaste that appealed to me. There was even a toothpaste of dubious origin that I used briefly in 1983: it coated my teeth with a green scum, much to my horror.

However, everything is relative. Dzintars products were highly coveted in the Soviet Union. The Baltics remained the most modern part of the Soviet Union, their European/German legacy evident in their architecture and work ethic. Both were damaged under the communists.

Many other Soviet Latvian factories originated in the pre-war era, when they were privately owned. When the Soviets occupied Latvia in 1940, these factories were nationalized. For instance, after the Soviet invasion in 1940, entrepreneur Helmārs Rudzītis was forced to relinquish his famous "Bellaccord Electro" record factory in Pārdaugava, founded in 1931. The factory assumed various labels under the Soviets, its last being "Melodija." It continued to produce records, which we bought and listened to in the 1980s. Rudzītis fled to Germany in 1944. Eventually he ended up the United States, where he founded *Laiks*, a Latvian language newspaper that is still published.

(My mother was one of the newspaper's editors.) Many of Bellaccord Electro's recordings are available on YouTube.

The famous Laima chocolate factory was founded in 1870 by an entrepreneur named Theodor Riegert. The "Laima" name was adopted in 1925 following a merger. Uzvara ("Victory"), once known as L. W. Goegginger, produced hard candies in the Soviet era. I remember stashing Uzvara candies in my coat pockets in the 1980s; sometimes I'd forget about the little suckers and then fish them out months later covered in lint. The children of Soviet Latvia sucked on and crunched the hard candies of Uzvara voraciously, which probably contributed to a high incidence of caries. Another popular candy, especially with children, was the *Īriss*—a tiny, chewy caramel. The factory of Vilhelms Ķuze (1875–1941), founded in 1910, became "June 17" under the Soviets; it manufactured wafers, cookies, and cakes. Ķuze died in a Soviet prison camp.

Laima remains a viable exporter to this day. Its popular chocolate products are even available at Russian delis in the United States. When I lived in Old Rīga in the 1980s, I bought Laima chocolates at the bread shop near St. Peter's. Laima chocolates were sold by weight and in bars. I can still recall  how the saleslady pulled out a sheet of coarse paper, rolled it into an elegant cone, and then, plunging a metal ladle into one of the chocolate bins, poured rustling, individually wrapped chocolates into the cone, weighing them according to my specifications... A delightful moment in an economy otherwise plagued by shortages.

> (Before WWII) Laima was successful due to a sound credit policy. (From its start in 1925) as a small enterprise in which products were hand-crafted, it grew into a large confectionery manufacturer that employed about 790 workers by 1938. Laima used Latvian sugar for its products. Its production capacity swiftly increased with the completion of a modern production facility at Miera iela 22. The new plant manufactured chocolates, candy, cocoa, cookies, and marmalade. Laima not only supplied the local market but also exported its products to England, Norway, France, Holland, and even Palestine, Morocco, and India. Up until World War II the name Laima ensured quality and attractive packaging. The war made some corrections. During the German occupation the factory also produced barley coffee, jams, and dried yeast. The Nazis confiscated Laima's manufacturing equipment and sent it to Germany. Everything had to be rebuilt under the Soviets. (www.ogresvestisvisiem.lv / Tr. RL)

Like VEF, by the 1980s the old Laima factory on Miera iela looked stressed. Nevertheless, it still perfumed the air with the sweet scent of cocoa. Its products were primarily shipped east to Soviet Russia and its hungry satellites. Its high-end products were not for sale in Rīga shops; the alcohol-infused "Prosit" was only for sale at the hard currency shop, it seemed. In 1983 we came upon Laima's delectable truffles in a regular town shop in Vilnius, Lithuania. This surprised and angered us, because these delicious, powdery chocolates were nowhere to be found in Rīga. Or rather, you could obtain them if you had *blats*.

Ogres Trikotāža, located in Ogre, produced knitwear and other textiles: sweaters; skirts; dress ensembles; shawls; and blankets. Many of the products were quite appealing. In the mid-

1980s the plant "imported" Vietnamese workers who lived in Zolitūde, a Soviet housing development in Pārdaugava.

It was common knowledge and a source of constant complaint voiced in private that the "cream" of Latvia's economic output was being sent to Moscow to feed the "fat cats" of the Soviet capital. Latvians secretly described Russians as lazy and incompetent. If before the war Latvia had matched countries like Denmark and Sweden in exports, then by the mid-1980s Soviet Latvia's already dimished output had stalled because of the overall failure of the Soviet Union's command economy. The gap between the quality of Soviet products and Western goods was evident to most Latvians, many of whom had relatives in the Free World who visited and brought gifts.

In 1983 I stepped into the role of Homo Sovieticus played by millions from Rīga to Magadan. In the 1980s, from time to time, my father sent us cardboard-framed photographs in the mail, which, when unsealed (he used rubber cement), would reveal a fifty or hundred dollar bill. This eased our monetary hardships, yet it was more important for us to stabilize within this strange economy, which no one could get used to.

New Beginnings at Krāmu iela 10/4a, Tel. 211951

My new home in Rīga, Latvia beginning in 1983. This building at the corner of Jauniela and Krāmu iela (to the left) in Old Rīga was designed by Wilhelm Ludwig Bokslaff (1858–1945) and completed in 1903. Today it is a privately owned luxury hotel.
Photo by Jānis Krastiņš.

Our tiny apartment was situated on the last floor of a building from the turn of the 20th century. It is one of Rīga's many outstanding examples of art nouveau, a distinct decorative style of architecture. Our entrance was from Krāmu ("Junk") iela, a short, narrow, cobblestone corridor that ran between Jauniela ("New Street") and Kaļķu ("Lime") iela, one of Old Rīga's main arteries. Our address was in the very heart of Rīga, in a city with a dramatic history that stretched back to the murky 12th century, when the Liv people fished in the Daugava River.

In the 1980s the lives of the people who lived in picturesque Old Rīga (also hailed by the Soviets as a tourist attraction) were fraught with unpleasant problems related to water and sewage. Old Rīga had been largely neglected for years, with only a few renovations taking place since the war. It was true that the Soviet government had rebuilt magnificent St. Peter's Church, which could be traced back to the early 13th century and sustained heavy damage in 1941. Yet Rīga's precious architectural legacy was, for the most part, not being conserved and restored properly because of the priorities of the Soviet economy. The roof of our building leaked; apparently it had been damaged by shrapnel in World War II and had never been fixed. In the early

1980s a Polish restoration company began working in Old Rīga to patch things up. I could attest to the shoddiness of their work when I saw Polish workers slapping pieces of lumber into the dilapidated chimney in place of bricks.

Left: The restaurant "Pūt, vējiņi" on Jauniela. Unknown photographer.

In the early 1980s Old Rīga often felt deserted. My footsteps re-sounded on strangely empty, quiet streets. From time to time groups of tourists from other Soviet republics would bustle through. Two of Rīga's finest Soviet era restaurants—"Pie Kristapa" ("*Chez* Kristaps") and "Pūt, vējiņi" ("Blow, Wind")—were nearby. In fact, "Pie Kristapa" was on the ground floor of our building, and its operations prevented water from reaching our floor during the day. Both of these restau-rants were exclusive; people stood in long lines to try to get in and were often rejected. In 1980 I had enjoyed a delicious meal at "Pūt, vējiņi" with a KGB operative. In 1983 I was looking down from my father-in-law's window at the haggling going on at the restaurant: from time to time the front door would open, an elderly doorman (reputed to be an old chekist) would stick his head outside, causing a *ņigu ņegu* ("commotion") to erupt. Funny was one way to describe it.

The door of our entrance was usually unlocked, unfortunately. From time to time a lock was installed to try to prevent unwanted trespassers from coming in and urinating in the stairwell. These locks were quickly broken. I discovered that there were no public restrooms in Rīga, nor did stores or restaurants offer such basic amenities to their clients. When nature called, Homo Sovieticus urinated and defecated where he/she could, and Rīga's elegant buildings smelled like outhouses.

One evening in 1983 we were coming home after spending a delightful evening at the Drama Theater. Ascending the last flight of stairs, we gasped as we spotted a ginormous turd—a mas-sive coil of odoriferous, brown horror right by our door. My husband cursed in Russian. Hearing the commotion, our Russian neighbor opened the door, and her eyes grew big as saucers. It was, in retrospect, the most perfect turd I had ever seen: it coiled around majestically, tapering off into an upturned salute. "Velcome, Comrade Ilmarovna!" it seemed to say. As perfect as a gag toy. And gag we did. I was pregnant at the time, and our neighbor took pity on me. She removed the giant stool and scrubbed the floor. As we discussed the foul incident, giggling and "yukking," we figured that a KGB snoop had been ordered to hold his bowels for three days and then march up our stairs and stoop and poop. Perhaps this was payback for the fact that we were misbehaving—that is, not cooperating with "the comrades."

It was a tiring jaunt up to the sixth floor but good for one's heart and health. As far as I could tell, most of the apartments in our building were communal. About four times a year a *sētniece* ("female custodian") would arrive with a broom, bucket of water, and large rag. She would then proceed to sweep and wash the entire staircase from top to bottom. Unfortunately, the smell of piss persisted near the entrance. Otherwise, our stairwell was bright due to large windows on every landing. At night it was mostly illuminated, although there were occasions when all the lights were out, and we had to grope our way up the stairs. Someone had stolen the light bulbs.

There was a wooden closet on our landing. Juris kept it locked, even though it was just filled with glass jars from all the preserves—jams, juices, and pickles—he had hauled to his studio at one time or another. In the Soviet era there was no plastic packaging in Latvia. Cheese, meat, fish, and other products were wrapped in paper at the store. You could get money for turning in glass *tara* (glassware), which was recycled. Boozehounds snooped around looking for beer and vodka bottles, which they could redeem at collection points for money. Our door had a tiny peephole that I appreciated.

Stepping across the threshold, you entered a small room with a window, which revealed two of our building's rear exterior walls. From the window you could look up at the old roof, a chimney, and the blue-eyed jackdaws, as well as see part of the Akmens ("Stone") Bridge, the Daugava River, and the southeastern sky, which provided enough light for the apartment to be deemed somewhat cheery. Peering down into what could be described as a large, semi-open shaft, you could spot a couple of small balconies, where people often stored vegetables and other perishable food items in the cold weather. (Soviet refrigerators were very small.) In the mid-1980s one of the balconies collapsed: the old cement bottom simply dropped out. Thank God, no one was standing on it at the time. This sort of event was not uncommon in Rīga, a city neglected by its communist proprietors. People even fell to their deaths this way. The bottomless balcony looked creepy. It reminded me of how little communists cared about safety, and how run-down Rīga's everything was in this historic city.

Juris Krieviņš had his own entrance to his studio from another stairwell at the back of the building. The window of the top landing of that stairwell was directly opposite our apartment: it was at this window that we caught KGB agents spying on us a couple of times. They would remove the top landing's lightbulb, thinking that the darkness could conceal them, but we could see their shadowy outlines. I went down that stairwell to take out the trash: there was a large garbage bin behind the Rīga Polytechnical Institute nearby.

Compared to the United States, Soviet consumers produced less garbage. I already mentioned the recyclable glass containers and paper wrapping. In addition, everyone had a collection of cloth shopping bags, which could hold a kilogram or two of potatoes or carrots and other heavy items. Ironically, these reusable cloth bags were "greener" than the plastics-crazy American packaging system. And Soviet citizens seemed brawnier, tougher, toting their heavy sacks across town, on to public transportation, and up flights of stairs.

In 1982 our apartment was partitioned into two small rooms by a wall. An old tiled stove in the corner could provide emergency relief in the event that we lost heat. We needed to use it only once. While I lived there, the apartment was cosy and warm. Our living room was small, so when friends came over, we were really packed in. But nobody cared. The Soviet era was also a time of friendly visits, sharing food, and anecdotes. I refused to view our guests as KGB stooges. I did not succumb to any sort of paranoia in this regard. We liked to have people over, and everyone came bearing flowers, chocolates, or some other goodies. Our couch served as a bed at night. I must have been very skinny back then, because it was the size of a single bed. With its slightly rounded surface it was narrow and uncomfortable. But people in love are just happy to be scrunched up next to each other. The size of everything in Latvia was smaller than in the

US: smaller beds; smaller refrigerators; smaller apartments; smaller cars; and smaller (skinnier) people.

We started out our new life with very little. We had a couch, a desk, a small shelf, and a simple wooden wardrobe in which to store our clothes, blankets, towels, linens, and other belongings. We put my suitcase on top of it. Life in Latvia taught me not to hold on to too much; things took up room; things collected dust; things could hold a person down. When I thought about my grandparents, I also began to see things as a burden, perishable and transient. Another war could come...

The floor was covered with ugly Soviet linoleum that had to be painted from time to time. When the snow melted or it rained, the outer wall by the window became damp. Drab curtains concealed the peeling, cracking wall. Charming. It was.

The small kitchen was painted in a mustard yellow. There was a window with a wide sill, a shallow sink with a mirror above it (where I could watch my face transform, as pudgy American cheeks melted to reveal high Liv cheekbones), a small Soviet stove hooked up to a gas canister that needed to be changed from time to time, and a small, collapsible, blue-green table. The gas canister caused me considerable worry, but hey, this was Soviet life. You just had to accept it.

Thanks to the restaurant downstairs, it was usually impossible to wash dishes during the day. Sometimes I got lucky: the pipes would start squeaking and clanging, and then I would rush into the kitchen to turn on the faucet, which would release a sudden, precious gush of water. A small moment of happiness: I could wash or rinse something! Initially I handled these nuisances with stoicism...

Chimney sweeps in the town of Strenči in the 1930s. Image courtesy of the National Library of Latvia collection "In Search of Lost Latvia."

The back area of the kitchen was taken up by an old wood stove once used for cooking and baking. It hogged precious space, so we used its surface for storing things like pots, pans, and vases. It was only later, when we moved to Zolitūde (a new Soviet apartment complex), that I realized what a blessing such old stoves were (of course, if they were tested and the chimneys were cleaned). I did see chimney sweeps walking around Rīga dressed in black. If you saw a chimney sweep, you were supposed to touch something black on your body for good luck. When the nasty *Rīgas Siltums* ("Rīga Heat") heating company delayed turning on the heat in November, people with wood stoves were lucky.

A low door in one corner of the kitchen opened up to a narrow corridor, from which the bathroom (shared by us and Juris) was accessible. The corridor connected our apartment with Juris' studio. The bathroom was tiny but quaint and wonderfully warm in the winter. There was a toilet and a small, deep bathtub with a ledge that you could comfortably sit on. A wooden shelf ran along the length of one of the walls, which were covered with wood paneling. Above the paneling the walls were painted white. The wall behind the the tub was covered in pretty light blue and white tiles. Someone had hand-painted a mermaid with flaming red hair (Ariel!) on one of the tiles.

Poster courtesy of Prague Museum of Communism.

We stored our toiletries on the long shelf alongside Juris' belongings—toothbrushes, shavers, and Soviet hygiene products. Compared to the United States, hygiene in communist Latvia was at a basic level. No deodorants, no nail clippers, no Q-Tips, no problems... Right above the bathtub a hole in the wall, literally, ventilated the bathroom. If you stood up in the bath and took the rag out of the hole, you could actually see the Rīga Polytechnical Institute. The bathroom was very warm; it was nice to relax in it late at night, when we finally had water at our disposal.

We did not have "the luxury" of toilet paper; the proletariat had no need for it apparently, because, as this funny poster from the Museum of Communism reminds us, "luckily there was not much food either." I was well acquainted with the toilet paper deficit since my visit to Latvia in 1980. I discovered pink napkins in an office supply store on Stučkas iela, and we used those instead of newspaper. I hoped the pink dye wasn't toxic. Toilet paper really was a hot commodity. A couple of times I saw someone walking down the street with toilet paper rolls strung together on a string. Passersby stopped to stare; some even trailed after the lucky duck making inquiries. The lack of toilet paper was a popular subject of ridicule of communism amongst expatriate Latvian tourists getting a glimpse of Soviet life in the fatherland.

Juris' frequent guests hung up their coats, jackets, and hats in the narrow corridor that lead from our apartment to the spectacular studio. I say spectacular, because it really was. Most people's jaws dropped when they entered that space. Juris and Andris had done much of the construction work themselves. The studio was built into part of the historic building's enormous attic space. With white walls and wooden floors, it was bright, clean, uncluttered, Scandinavian, and serene. It was quite large, with a high, sloping ceiling. It was also very comfortable, with the space split into three sections. The smallest section, directly beneath the slant of the roof, was taken up by Juris' dark room, which was protected by a heavy curtain, and a work table where he sat to eat, drink, and read the newspaper. There was also an unheated storage space where we could safely store our valuable potatoes, carrots, yams, jams, juices, pickles, and other preserves in the winter (the fruit of Biruta's labor of love).

Summer of 1983: entertaining guests from the US and West Germany in Juris Krieviņš's studio. From the left: me; artist Valdis Kupris; a couple of German actors; and Andris Krieviņš. Photo: Juris Krieviņš

A skylight framed St. Mary's massive tower and belfry. One wall was lined with shelves filled with books, photographs, and memorabilia. There was a large storage unit where Juris kept antique photo albums, rare photographs, a collection of old postcards, his own photographs, negatives, and contact copies, as well as a couple of bottles of home-brewed liquer, the famed local concoction *Rīgas Melnais balzāms* (Rīga Black Balsam), dainty coffee cups and saucers, sugar, and cookies for his numerous guests. The skylight flooded this space with a bright, indirect light. Juris Krieviņš was very hospitable and invited me to join him from time to time to meet his visitors. Our relationship began on a friendly note and would remain one of mutual respect.

Another large window granted a view eastward, revealing old, lopsided buildings, tiled roofs, the rather ugly shape of the Soviet era Rīga Polytehnical Institute, and St. Peter's Church with its magnificent steeple topped by a golden rooster. After reconstruction in 1690, the steeple of St. Peter's was the tallest wooden structure in all of Europe. According to the website *CitaRiga*, St. Peter's was the first church in Rīga to install a clock on its steeple (in 1352). A sentry had once manned the steeple to warn the city's residents of danger, such as fire. The church was reconstructed after the war. A new rooster was placed on the spire in 1970. (It was the seventh in a long line of roosters to gaze upon Rīga and witness its changes.) In the Soviet era St. Peter's was an exhibition hall. Tourists could take an elevator to the top of the steeple to get a panoramic view of the city. I came to associate the old folk song "Rīga dimd" ("Rīga resounds") with St. Peter's, because it was played as a recording from the steeple.

From this window you could also see, at an angle, the windows of our apartment. Once as I was standing there looking out, I detected a blurry of commotion through the dirty glass of the windows of the apartment below us: our Russian neighbor was chasing his screaming wife around a table. This couple was a great example of the Latvian saying *"Kas mīlējas, tas ķivējas."* ("Who loves also quarrels." In other words, squabbles and arguments were a part of love.) These were the people who would sometimes blast the music of Boney M and Russian bard Vladimir Visocky for days at a time. The songs "Rasputin" and "Rivers of Babylon" were my soundtrack of the 1980s in Rīga. Visocky enjoyed a cult following in the Soviet Union; his gravelly voice floated up in the summer like a mostly unwelcome visitor. In Visocky's case, it must have been an acquired taste, like "our" Tom Waits. When this Russian couple welcomed a son into the world, the music quieted down.

Our immediate neighbors were all Russian, but I cannot say what the overall ethnic breakdown of the tenants of this particular building was. Our Russian neighbors did acknowledge us with a nod or greeted us in their language (none of them spoke Latvian), and I always greeted them in Latvian with a smile. They seemed pleasant enough. There was a Latvian family on the third floor, and I enjoyed hearing them conversing on their landing in our mother tongue.

The Russian family next to us—a babushka, her son and daughter-in-law, and a grandson— was quiet and polite.They had a wonderful apartment with spectacular views of St. Mary's Cathedral and access to the picturesque tower on the corner of the building.

Besides Boney M and Vladimir Visocky, another musical (or not) companion to our days beneath the eaves were the blue-gray, beady-eyed *kovārņi* (jackdaws) that landed on our rooftop and flew in droves in circles around St. Mary's tower. Oblivious to human suffering, they had built their nests in Rīga for centuries. Their chattering was a part of this old city's soundscape.

Juris' studio was sparsely furnished, with a chartreuse-green settee and two brown otto-mans. There was a fireplace tiled in green, and a window with decorative columns opening to an unforgettable view of Old Rīga, the northwestern sky, and St. Mary's. The cornerstone of this church was laid in 1211. I enjoyed the privilege of looking at it each and every day.

I could also see in the distance the new cable bridge across the Daugava, popularly called the "Voss balalaika." Augusts Voss was another heartily disliked Latvian Communist Party leader who had endeared himself to the Russians by suppressing his ethnicity: he refused to speak Latvian in his own country. Officially the bridge was named after Maxim Gorky (1868–1936), the Soviet Russian writer and political activist allegedly murdered in 1936. Gorky Bridge extended from Gorkija (Gorky) iela (now Valdemāra) across the Daugava River to Pārdaugava, a green suburb of Rīga. Nowadays it is simply known as Vanšu ("Cable") Bridge. It was sleek and modern-looking and replaced the old pontoon bridge that I got a chance to cross in 1980.

At night I loved to stand by the window and look out at the dark silhouettes of Old Rīga's buildings. Rīga, once a pearl of the Hanseatic League, a historic trading alliance, was now all but forgotten by the rest of Europe and the world. The rooftops of this part of the city were ravishing with their timeworn, uneven appearance. Old Rīga's architectural legacy spoke of a unique his-tory, of centuries of busy international trade and ships coming and going, as well as of fire, war, and jolting transformations, including military occupations. And we would survive the ordeal of the Soviet occupation, just as these old buildings had survived countless calamities. St. Mary's for me was a beacon of hope and endurance. The lyrics of the Drifters' song "Up on the roof" would pop into my head from time to time: up there beneath the roof I felt peaceful and at ease. It was there, looking out over our capital's oldest area, that I sensed the passing of time and knew that someday this unjust era would end. Yes, I really did feel it.

After Krišjānis Barons' 150th anniversary celebrations in 1985, Juris decorated his studio with pre-war photographs depicting Latvia's beautiful countryside and farmers at work. Each was captioned with a Latvian *daina*. He also put up a portrait of Krišjānis Barons with his long white beard, oval spectacles, and benevolent gaze. Barons was famous for continuing the work of folklorist, poet, and translator Fricis Brīvzemnieks (1846–1907), launching a nationwide cam-paign in the late 19th century to collect, organize, and preserve the dainas of our nation for pos-terity. Barons' portrait was a comforting reminder of our nation's perserverance and strength, as well as the Latvian work ethic.

Juris Krieviņš was a work horse who divided his time between photography, instructing his students, looking after the needs of his family, and taking care of his summer residence in the countryside. He also read a lot. He let me go through his contact sheets, which were neatly stacked by the hundreds in boxes, and I could see that he was a Latvian patriot: in addition to capturing the beauty of our country, he took photographs of Latvian writers, actors, artists, con-ductors, etc. Juris was also "good with his hands," having started his career as a carpenter in a furniture factory. He spent his whole life fixing things and cherished anything that was from "the good old days."

I quickly noticed that most Latvian men were handymen, able to fix and build things them-selves without relying on outside help. This skill was probably a result of the backwards "econ-omy" they lived in. And most Latvian women could sew, knit, crochet, darn, and stitch. Biruta was very good at crocheting. She made elegant gloves, which she sold at a souvenir store on Vaļņu iela. I marveled at the women and men who knew how to work a loom and produced beautiful traditional blankets and textile art. The skillfulness and practical agility of the Latvians whom I met over the years was a never-ending source of admiration for me. I certainly felt inferior, having arrived in the Soviet Union with little more than an experience in freedom. I was a girl from a capitalist country where everything was available, every problem had a fix offered by companies X, Y, and Z, and goods were dispensible. Clothes were cheap and easy to come by, and nobody had the time or willingness to sit down and sew on a button, or darn a sock or a mitten.

An extremely dusty area that extended over the rest of the building lay beyond Juris' studio. There must have been a broken window somewhere, because I could see and hear pigeons cooing and flapping their wings. To avoid soiling the studio with the dust of the attic, Juris had laid down planks on the floor. His double doors were bolted and secured. There were many bureaucratic hurdles to overcome to acquire a studio like Juris' and possibly bribes to be paid. This is how the Soviet economy functioned. Building materials were hard to come by. One needed connections, one needed *blats*.

Despite her burning stares aimed at my haircut and unusual clothes, Biruta was helpful and sent us food once in a while. Or we would visit her at the family apartment in Pārdauagava for a delicious dinner and to play with Gita's baby Elīna who became my goddaughter. My fiancé quickly saw how inexperienced I was in matters of cooking, so from time to time we would go out to eat in one of Rīga's cheap cafeterias, where you had to take your chances with greasy borsch, solanka, plov, or *klopsis* (ground meat). I came down with food poisoning several times. Since everything was owned by the state, Soviet citizens improvised on ways to make extra money and embezzle. The borsch and solanka I ate in the 1980s was covered with a ½ inch layer of liquid grease, which made me feel queasy and produced unpleasant burps. I think the locals' stomachs were used to the griminess of the Soviet eating establishments; they were immune to the bacteria simmering in the pots, pans, and storage areas.

Despite my overall apprehension, there were items that were absolutely delicious, like fresh pastries and buns. Fast food was non-existent, and I didn't miss it. I frequented the Vaļņu iela cafeteria called Pulvertornis "Powder Tower" for many years, even when I worked around the corner in the late '90s. As my cooking skills improved, we ate out less and less. I longed for a peeler, as I scraped carrots and peeled potatoes with a knife. Latvia's salt and sugar were coarse, and dairy products spoiled quickly. I took the new challenges in stride, although my culinary experiments could not compete with Biruta's delicious concoctions. I envied my cousins who seemed so skilled at everything they did. It took me a long time to absorb the lessons and feel confident about what I was doing in the kitchen and elsewhere. My new life was teaching me life-long skills, even if I didn't realize it at the time.

Living in such close proximity to my father-in-law inevitably caused friction. Our privacy was fragile, our boundaries unclear. Father and son argued. What started out as a romantic roost turned into an almost claustrophic closet. Intimacy was soon lost. Soviet housing, which was characterized by small or communal apartments, wreaked havoc on people's sex lives and family relationships.

Andris and his sister had grown up in a small two-room apartment in Pārdaugava, which they shared with their parents and an old aunt. One of the rooms was a walk-through. There were many young Latvian couples who were forced to cohabit with their parents because of the apartment shortage (many people waited for years to get an apartment), and because in Latvia the housing sector was characterized by ethnic favoritism. One of the first nagging problems I grappled with was the housing shortage, and why were Russian immigrants moving into new apartments, while many Latvians rotted away in sub-standard housing? I began sweeping many unpleasant realizations under the rug, so to speak. Realizations that had to do with powerlessness.

The feeling of being trapped in the system, unable to improve one's living conditions and other aspects of our life, affected people in different ways. As an alien, initially I accepted the first of many challenges with humor and an open mind. I had fallen in love with an angry young man, however. Financial matters, especially his wages, taxed his nerves. There seemed to be hurdles to getting ahead everywhere we looked. My partner simmered for about a decade, sometimes exploding. In spite of the outcome, our first years were happy in Old Rīga. My interest in history and art immediately helped me deal with the many unpleasant aspects of everyday Soviet communist life that I was encountering. I arrived in Latvia as a true idealist. Early on I found that the rampant negativity was being countered by my meetings with many interesting people, most of whom seemed to be doing alright in spite of it all. They (like I would) had learned to partition their brains for self-preservation. Life in Old Rīga was not only a gateway into the past; it would be a test of my endurance.

During my years in Old Rīga time seemed to drag, because the occupation dragged, seemingly endless. The church clocks were broken, the "real world" was elsewhere, and I had entered a strange non-reality with many walls. Some of them I could break down; others remained standing, impossible to breach because of the political system. The non-reality was communism, a destructive Utopian theory. The living conditions I was forced to learn to accept had already rigorously tested my compatriots with varying results. The gorgeous building that we lived in had withstood the test of time and the total destruction that took place one block away in 1941 of hundreds of years of history. I leaned on history for survival.

Letters

Excerpts from a letter dated January 15, 1983 to my parents

I'm sitting by an open window so that the floor will dry faster; I'm watching the daylight fade. It was sunny today, but we were busy inside all day—cleaning, dusting, and washing. Now everything looks nice and cosy. (...) I've started a self-portrait.

Self-portrait "Eyes." January 1983, Rīga, Latvia.

Yesterday we came back from Leningrad. I spent the afternoon washing our clothes and shopping and even went jogging. I purchased some sneakers here, but they're pretty awful compared to the ones I left in New Jersey. I hate to ask you, but could you send them as well as some sweat pants? Next week we plan to register our impending marriage. I would love to get married in Piebalga, if possible. Of course, that is probably unrealistic. As long as I'm not a Soviet citizen, my movement here is limited. I've been offered Soviet citizenship right after getting married with permission to hold on to my American citizenship for one year. Sounds complicated. Mammiņa, remember the poem I wrote for you? I've visualized you here so many times: on the street; in the market; on the train; by the canal; near the Daugava River...

Our short two-day trip to Leningrad (St. Petersburg) to settle some matters with the American Consulate was an exciting excursion for me. A consumer of the Russian classics, I looked forward to seeing the famous city of Peter the Great and the Russian tsars. I adored trains, their clickety-clack sounds, and rhythmic movement. In the evening we were served a glass of *chai* in a metal holder emblazoned with the hammer and sickle. Russia, here we come! I half expected the music of "Lara's Theme" from "Dr. Zhivago" (1965), a favorite film of mine, to begin.

There was a joke based on the famous Russian television spy serial "Seventeen Moments of Spring" (1973) about World War II (some of it filmed in Rīga)... The hero, spy Maxim Isaev, aka Max Otto von Stierlitz in Nazi Germany, is sipping tea at a Nazi reception. As he brings the teacup to his mouth, one of his eyes keeps winking. His cover is blown. How? Everyone knows Russians don't take the spoon out of their *chai* when drinking it. The popular series spawned many funny jokes.

The lavatory on the train was atrocious. Before attempting to maneuver myself safely over the gaping hole without avoiding touching the filthy rims of the "toilet," I could actually gaze down at the tracks going by below us and feel the frigid air swirling upward into my face. Gosh, someone could be murdered and pushed down into that hole and end up in pieces on the tracks, I thought ... How wonderful to be young and carefree! I was 22, and life was an adventure.

The train attendant brought us our sheets, and we made our berths. Early in the morning we were roused from sleep by the sounds of a marching band playing an energetic Russian melody, which sounded military. The music was being blasted at us from the train's loudspeakers. Talk about a rowdy welcome to the cradle of the Russian Revolution! Leningrad, as it was known then, was a marvel and a gem. Unlike Moscow, old St. Petersburg charmed me to no end.

Left: The famous Latvian newspaper *Pēterburgas Avīzes*, published in St. Petersburg in 1862–1865 by *jaunlatvietis* or "New Latvian" Krišjānis Valdemārs.

After visiting the American Consulate, we began our tour of the city. Occasionally harassed by Russian *spekulanti* (speculators), we crisscrossed Leningrad's majestic boulevards, passing over canals, and lingered near the Winter Palace and the State Hermitage Museum. We walked along the Neva River to marvel at the scene that unfolded before us and gazed at the Peter and Paul Fortress in the distance. St. Petersburg had attracted many Latvians when Latvia was part of the Russian Empire, including my paternal grandmother who had studied there.

We purchased a record by Zhanna Bichevskaya from a crowded record shop and had a decent meal on Nevsky Prospect, amazed at our luck in getting in, finding a seat, and being served bowls of hot dumplings. Bichevskaya's soulful voice stirs up memories of Leningrad/St. Petersburg and its architectural splendor, its dark canals and bridges, and the wisps of human breath in the cold Russian winter.

Rīga up Close

A light in winter... A drawing by me from 1983 of an antique candleholder in Juris Krieviņš's studio. The light we kept ourselves alive in came from within. Love, hope, and spite...

It was the dead of winter in 1983 in my 23rd year in life. In January I noticed that the days were becoming longer and that the light was returning. Snow fell, blanketing rooftops, and then quickly turned into a dark sludge that slopped into stores and made a mess of shoes. My American snowboots handled the cold porridge well. Despite the frigid temperatures, I bundled up and hit the streets each day.

My new life with my fiancé had settled into an easy routine. Our wedding was scheduled for March 4. Andris worked at the Latvian Art Foundation just a few blocks away as a photographer. I discovered an art supply store there and picked up some India ink, pencils, and paper. It looked like a busy space with studios and artists coming and going. I began exploring my surroundings in earnest. I was in "beginner's mode" to learn the techniques of the Soviet shopper to track down food and other necessities, although Juris and Biruta helped out from time to time with food products. I accepted the challenges as part of the package of living abroad in a different culture, economy, and political system.

A wonderful woman from the Chamber of Commerce signed me up as a freelance translator of marketing materials for Soviet Latvian enterprises, such as the cosmetics giant Dzintars. Andris made a pittance at his job, so the assignments made me feel useful, and the roubles came in handy. Those were hard times, when we sometimes raided Juris' piggybank or redeemed glass bottles and jars for money.

I had a pair of sweats, a sweatshirt, and sneakers to go jogging, a form of exercise I had committed to in the USA. I established a route that I stuck to for a while, running to keep in shape and to get to know Rīga. I started out by running across June 17 Square (now Dome Square) and down Komjaunatnes ("Komsomol") iela (now Jēkaba) past the magnificent Supreme Council of the Latvian Soviet Socialist Republic, which was a historic building constructed for the Landtag of the House of the Livonian Noble Corporation in the Governate of Livonia. (It is now the seat of the Latvian Saeima or Parliament.) I continued on past Pioneer Square, the Drāma (later—National) Theater along Kronvalda bulvāris (once called Pushkin Boulevard in 1899 in honor of the famous writer's 100th anniversary), and down Ausekļa iela past (Jānis) Fabriciuss Square. Rīga was under a spell. June 17, the Komsomol, the Pioneers... None of this "alternative reality" meant anything to me. In fact, June 17 was the day the Soviet Union occupied Latvia in 1940. It was a day of sorrow for our nation.

In 1931 the square had been renamed to honor President George Washington's (1732–1799) 200th anniversary. In the 1930s the American Legation was located next to the square at 22 Ausekļa iela; John F. Kennedy had stayed there in 1939 as a Harvard student. Prior to 1931 it was known as Hanzas laukums (Hanza Plaza). Rīga's history was multi-layered, yet in the Soviet era only historical plaques and monuments related to communism and the history of the Soviet

Union were permitted. In the Soviet era the nearest American diplomatic missions were in Moscow and St. Petersburg. In the 1980s it was difficult to imagine that there had once been a strong foreign diplomatic presence in Rīga. Had I known about Washington Square, it would have warmed my heart. But all traces of this history had been eradicated, nor did I have access to literature about it. Our heads were being twisted eastward towards Russia, and Latvia had been poisoned by the fallout of Russia's history in the 20th century. According to my upbringing, Fabriciuss was the "wrong" kind of Latvian. Yet he was a Latvian, and his biography was part of Latvian history.

As a jogger I was conspicuous in those days running in my sweats in the middle of winter. Soviet trucks rumbled by on Hanzas and Sverdlova streets belching acrid fumes, their rough-and-tough drivers staring down at me. Women stopped to gape; their snide remarks petered out as I put distance between them and me. Few people saw exercise as necessary, it seemed. I guess they got enough of it walking around the city and shopping and lugging purchases. I hadn't seen a single obese person in Rīga.

I wondered about Jānis Fabriciuss, the namesake of the tiny, neglected square that I whizzed past several times a week. It looked more like a shabby dog-pooping area (not that I saw any dogs in Rīga). Fabriciuss (1877–1929) was a Latvian revolutionary, Bolshevik, rifleman, military commander, communist, and commissar of the Red Army. I knew very little about the Latvian "Red Riflemen" who retreated to Russia in 1918 and fought in the Red Army. When Latvia and Soviet Russia signed a peace treaty in 1920, some of these riflemen repatriated; others stayed in Russia and were later executed in the Stalinist purges. I had never heard of Jānis Fabriciuss; nor had I ever heard of Linards Laicēns or many other Latvian communists. For various reasons many Latvians chose to stay in Soviet Russia, even when they could have returned to their free and independent homeland after the successful War of Independence. They paid with their lives for that decision: the Stalinist purges liquidated this minority in the late 1930s. A superb illustration of their fates is the tragic story of Skatuve, the Latvian theater in Moscow (1919-1938). Latvians had been involved in the Russian Revolution, and many had been swayed by Marxist philosophy and communist ideology. It was undeniable. It was hard to accept, however, in light of the horrendous crimes of Soviet communism.

The longer I lived in Latvia, the more I came to realize how spotty my knowledge of Latvian history was. The same could be said about my compatriots in Latvia. We, the Latvian exile community, had our version of Latvian history, somewhat accurate but with significant gaps (our "bad boy" communists and home-grown perpetrators of the Holocaust, etc.). Latvians in Latvia were "fed" a version of Latvian history that had been pressed through the sieve of Marxism-Leninism. The story of Latvia's riflemen and their "red" brothers in the struggle for Latvia's independence is fascinating and typical of Latvia's history in the 20th century, marked by a halving and then splintering of Latvia's population.

Rīga's handsome pre-war architecture hinted at close ties with Western Europe. Yet most of its monuments and commemorative plaques in the Soviet era were rooted in the history of Russia, glorifying the Great October Socialist Revolution (1917) and the Great Patriotic War (World War II). Rīga was like a giant cabbage with many layers of history waiting to be peeled away.

Fabriciuss' biography and George Washington Square were tucked in among those layers. However, in the 1980s the older layers were harder to get at due to Soviet censorship.

My beat spun me back towards Old Rīga along busy Sverdlova iela (now Pulkveža Brieža) and Komunāru bulvāris (now Kalpaka). I passed the modern, admittedly attractive building that housed the Central Committee of the Communist Party. There were always lots of Volgas parked out front with drivers hanging around talking and smoking. (Lots of people Latvia smoked, puffing on cigarettes such as Elita, Rīga, Kosmoss, Prīma, and Belomorkanal, which was named after Stalin's wild White Sea-Baltic canal project that killed thousands of slave workers...) As far as I could hear, everyone spoke only Russian, the lingua franca of Soviet communist Latvia.

I dove into Kronvalda Park, pounding the pavement and passing the massive monument to Latvian writer and hardcore communist Andrejs Upīts (1877–1970) who fared well under the Soviets. As a result, the Latvian exile community ignored Upīts and his work. A *persona non grata*, he was never mentioned in our Latvian literature classes. In his 1967 book, *Bezsaules noriets latviešu buržuāzijai un tās literatūrai emigrācijā* ("A Sunless Sunset for the Latvian Bourgeoisie and its Literature in Emigration"—RL), Upīts described Latvian writers in exile as *"garā pavāji spalvas grafomāni"* ("mentally retarded graphomaniacs of the pen"), "more pitiful than despicable," "servants of the bourgeoisie," "a twice-atrophied layer of degenerate escapees," etc. Upīts belonged to the upper crust of Latvian communist society and as such could ill afford to praise or positively acknowledge any Latvian writers in exile. (Eva Eglāja-Kristsone, *Okupētās Latvijas un latviešu trimdas saskarsme un tās dinamika—VIII daļa* [http://zagarins.net/jg/jg263 /JG263_Eglaja-Kristsone.htm]. Tr. RL).

The big, bulky bronze monument to Latvian writer and communist Andrejs Upīts (1877–1970) was inaugurated in 1982. The monument was designed by sculptor Alberts Terpilovskis and architect Gunārs Asars. Photo: Kaspars Zellis

Rather quickly I got tired of people staring at me and making remarks. Oh well, I never really liked jogging anyway. Also, Old Rīga's cobblestones and the city's gravel-covered, icey sidewalks were not kind to my sneakers. I put them away and resumed my explorations at a slower pace, walking sometimes for miles a day to get to know Rīga. I was restless and unsure of my place in Latvia. As I became acquainted with Rīga's neighborhoods, I discovered where many stores were and what they offered. I can still picture them now, the *maizes / hleb* ("bread"), *gaļas / myaco* ("meat"), and *piens / moloko* ("milk/dairy") shops scattered throughout downtown Rīga. Their signs were in Latvian and Russian. I still remember the red, white, and blue pyramid-shaped ½ liter *moloko* cartons and the soggy Farmer's Cheese packets stacked in plastic bins with their sour aroma. Sensitive to smell, to me 1980s Rīga smelled of diesel fuel, Russian *papirosi* (cigarettes), deep-fried *pončiki* and sunflower oil, sour whey, and flowers. Even on the

coldest days in winter, you could buy flowers from vendors keeping them warm in candlelit boxes at the flower market. It was a strange concoction of aromas, of industrial toxicity interspersed with traces of bittersweet chrysanthemums, roses, and carnations. We bought a lot of flowers in our first winter in Rīga, because we visited a lot of people.

In the winter of 1983 I wandered about Old Rīga exploring its empty courtyards, some with stiff, hanging laundry. Old doors creaked open revealing dark, steep stairwells. Who lived there? So much potential, so much neglect. Ancient warehouses on Miesnieku ("Butcher") iela looked as if they'd been untouched for centuries. Bundled up in my long wool coat, hat, and mittens, I relished the opportunity to be out on my own. The wind whistled in from the Daugava River carrying a mournful tune. A street map with notations would have come in handy, but no such map was available in the tourist shops. Too dangerous, according to the comrades.

As a young American I was enthralled by the antiquity of the Old Town and its architectural details and asymmetry. I longed for a knowledgeable companion who could tell me stories about these old streets, the significance of their names, and the architecture itself, such as "the Three Brothers"—three narrow, ancient-looking buildings in a row on Mazā pils ("Small Castle") iela. The oldest of them, No. 17, dated back to the 15th century, when Rīga established ties with Dutch traders. Rīga was a German city, although until then I had never thought of it that way.

I was immediately concerned about preserving historical buildings as a legacy for future generations. There was so much in Rīga to admire and be proud of. The so-called Bobrov House (1902) at 8 Smilšu ("Sand") iela was just one of many stunning examples of Art Nouveau in our vicinity. The building's entrance hallway was breathtaking, decorated with friezes of nymphs bearing flowers, vases of irises, and antique lamps. I wondered who, if anyone, lived in the building, which looked like it was in good condition. Luckily, nothing appeared vandalized, yet the ground floor was empty, in spite of the ornate interior. I gazed through the dusty windows in awe of what I was seeing. Another Cinderella. Our capital was full of such wonders.

Other than its charming, sagging buildings, Rīga's Old Town offered few attractions, such as pubs, cafés, and shops. There were a couple of eateries on Smilšu iela. One of them, "Pelmeņi," served hot, greasy Soviet sliders (dumplings), which tasted very good in the winter when you were famished. Latvian and Russian food was hearty and rich. Sometimes I ducked into Doms, a pretty café on the corner of Smilšu and Komjaunatnes, to warm myself with a cheap cup of coffee and a delicious pastry. There were a couple of other cafés close to St. Mary's—*Zilais putns* ("Blue Bird") and *Trīspadsmit krēsli* ("Thirteen Chairs"). The quality of service depended on the mood of the personnel. Nobody smiled.

Because everything was owned by the state, no one enjoyed ownership, and nobody cared about competition. Store employees' attitudes towards their eager clients ranged from mediocre to poor. Waiters and salespeople treated most clients with a poorly concealed contempt, unless they knew they could get something in exchange or if the customer was a "big shot." Many of the hopefuls standing in line to get into these establishments were often spurned. Even we as a young family were once rudely told by the doorman of the restaurant "Pie Kristapa" to go somewhere else, because "this restaurant isn't for kids." These places were run by a kind of mafia, it felt like. I blamed the communist system for the lack of manners in people and tried not to judge them. I tried to imagine what their lives outside of work were like, if they lived in a communal apartment, and what pressures they had to withstand in the centralized command economy.

Right: one of Old Rīga's popular bars in the last Soviet decade in Latvia: "Thirteen Chairs."

Jauniela, which ran past our apartment building, was actually somewhat lively in the late afternoons. There were a couple of souvenir stores, which sold the usual Latvian tourist stuff: knitted mittens; socks; shawls; Latvian town souvenir pins; tacky wooden and ceramic knick-knacks; postcards; linen towels and runners; etc. Traditional Latvian jewelry in silver and gold was impossible to find, because the state hoarded precious metals. There was a tiny gallery on Jauniela that offered paintings and other examples of fine art and crafts. Even in roubles the prices were exclusively high. Occasionally groups of boisterous Russian tourists bustled by, picking up speed when they saw the shops. *Bistro! Bistro!* ("Faster! Faster!")—I often heard them exclaim.

Old Rīga's streets enchanted any tourist. Most of them had retained their original names, which hinted at the activities of Rigans of previous centuries: Tirgoņu ("Merchants'") iela; Zirgu ("Horses'") iela; Kalēju ("Blacksmiths'"); Miesnieku ("Butchers'"); etc. Why was our street called Krāmu ("Junk") iela, I wondered? Were there a lot of junk shops there at one time?

The communists got rid of some of Old Rīga's historical street names. Grēcinieku ("Sinners'") iela became Imanta Sudmaļa iela. Sudmalis (1916–1944), *left*, was an editor, communist, and partisan. He was involved in a terrorist attack on a large demonstration at Dome Square that killed three people, including an architect, a worker, and a young boy. Sudmalis was arrested and executed by the Nazis. Kungu ("Lords'") iela became Daugavas iela. Poļu gāte ("Polish Alley") became Tūristu ("Tourists'") iela in 1950. There was no room for sinners or lords in the workers' paradise. "Polish" hinted at the notion of nationality, something communists planned to do away with; that is, with the exception of the Russian language and culture. Thus I mused... Later I discovered that many of Rīga's streets had been changed numerous times; this wasn't just a Soviet thing. The changes reflect Rīga's long history.

Grandfather Tuks had mentioned a former fellow student by the name of Aleksandrs Jansons (1916–1991), an expert on the history of Old Rīga and its architecture. One bright day in February I went on a long walk with the erudite and amiable Mr. Jansons. In 1983 Jansons would have been 67 years old; he appeared trim and fit, with a sparkle in his eyes, a slight lisp to his speech, a bashful laugh, and a head full of facts and stories. It was an altogether wonderful, unforgettable excursion, as we meandered through Old

Rīga, the ice crunching beneath our feet and long, jagged icicles dangling above our heads. Maybe because I had such a warm and loving relationship with my grandparents, I was fond of elderly people, but in Latvia I was particularly drawn to them and studied their faces with interest, believing them to be walking story books. Each one surely had some dramatic yarn to share. How could they not? The older they looked, the more I would have loved to ask them questions about their survival. In the 1980s most old people in and outside of Latvia were witnesses to the terrible events of World War II; they carried crazy memories and dramatic stories around inside of them. They were living connections to the "old days," when my grandparents still lived in Latvia. Aleksandrs Jansons knew more than ordinary Rigans; he could make the past come to life by rattling off all sorts of facts and stories about the area we were exploring.

Mr. Jansons lived in Bišumuiža (*Bienenhof* in German, "Beesmanor" in English) in Pārdaugava near Bauskas šoseja ("highway"). Pārdaugava, a historical gateway to Rīga from the south, was full of wonderful places like Bišumuiža. According to the website Zudusī Latvija, Bienenhof, which dated back to the 1770s, was also at various times known as Brandenburg, Schilder, and Catherine Manor. In 1792 the estate had nine buildings, including two residences, three stables, a barn, and a coach house. The manor or "Lord's house," built at the beginning of the 19th century, had been richly decorated with painted walls.

Johann Sebastian Bach's last student Johann Gottfried Müthel (1728–1788), a virtuoso pianist and harpsichordist, spent the second half of his life at Bišumuiža, where he wrote and published his compositions. From 1767 until 1788 he was an organist at St. Peter's Church in Rīga.

According to a publication prepared by the Bišumuiža Library, Aleksandrs Jansons' grandfather, a cabman, purchased some land in Bišumuiža at the end of the 19th century. Jansons' parents were simple working folks who, like many Latvians, made a tremendous effort to provide their children with an education. Aleksandrs flourished in school. In 1941 he graduated from the University of Latvia with a master's degree in Baltic philology. He was fluent in several languages. In 1944, a year of turmoil and uncertainty in Latvia, he became a deputy director of the National Historical Library (*Valsts Vēsturiskā bibliotēka*). With another Soviet occupation bearing down on Latvia, many members of the Latvian intelligentsia chose to go into exile rather than risk their lives under the communists. Aleksandrs Jansons bid farewell to his wife and son who joined the tide of refugees. He had decided to take his chances and stay in Latvia and concentrate on his work.

Presumably some time in the late 1940s, while researching the history of "the Great Patriotic War" (World War II), Jansons came upon some publications that the Soviet communist authorities would have considered dangerous to the state. He carried these "nationalistic" publications with him, afraid to leave them in his desk at work. But despite his precautions, someone was on to him. Jansons was apprehended and searched; the material was confiscated. The "crime" was grave: he was accused of possessing and disseminating anti-Soviet literature. Aleksandrs Jansons was sentenced to eight years in a slave labor camp in Archangelsk, Russia, where he endured hunger and extreme cold.

After Aleksandrs Jansons was freed and returned to Latvia, he was not allowed to reclaim his previous position at the library. Despite this setback, he made every effort to get closer to books and research. At first he worked in a book store. Eventually he was able to participate in the preparation of the first volume of works by the famous German ethnographer Johann Christoph Brotze (1742–1823), *left*.

By digging into Latvia's historical archives and unearthing the fascinating history of his country, Aleksandrs Jansons was able to achieve some measure of peace and shut out the harsh reality of the political system he was living in. He took part in ethnographic expeditions and was devoted to preserving the history of Latvia's architecture and Bišumuiža. According to the Bišumuiža Library's tribute, Jansons, "a quiet man of a plain, nondescript appearance, greatly enjoyed taking people on tours around town": "the inconspicuous historian came to life, relating stories about Rīga's buildings and historical events with passion." I was one of the lucky people to experience Jansons' presence, which reminded me of the strength and perserverance of my nation in the face of adversity.

Aleksandrs Jansons' spirit was not broken in the Soviet Gulag. Ultimately, he made meaningful contributions in his field ofstudy. Like so many Latvians that I had the honor of meeting, he was a quiet, humble "workhorse." Jansons was reunited with his long lost family only once after the war, in the last year of his life. He was "rehabilitated" in 1990. (Source for Jansons' biography: *Jaunās vēstis* [7/105], A Publication of the Rīga Central Library. July 2011.)

Bišumuiža Manor. Image courtesy of the National Library of Latvia collection "In Search of Lost Latvia."

I wish I had visited Aleksandrs Jansons at home in Bišumuiža, a suburb of Rīga with its own interesting history that the historian strove to preserve. Then again, in the early 1980s I hesitated to call on many people, worried that my intrusion might cause them problems with the Latvian KGB.

I hoped to get in touch with some of my grandparents' old friends from before the war. So many years had passed since the war, and these people, if they were still alive, were getting old. What had they experienced in the mayhem of the occupations and afterwards, when Latvia was sealed behind the Iron Curtain? During that dreamy walk I never dared ask kindly Aleksandrs Jansons about his past. I wondered how he felt about my presence in Latvia.

St. Mary's Cathedral, commonly known as "the Dome," towered above our house on Jauniela like a magnificent queen. The church's first foundation stone was laid in 1211 by Bishop Albert who established his residence there. Before the arrival of the Germans, the area had been populated by the local Liv people. The cathedral was the main part of an ensemble of buildings with an enclosed garden area. The former cloister houses the marvelous collection of the Museum of the History of Rīga and Navigation. Image courtesy of the National Library of Latvia.

I walked past St. Mary's just about every day, gazing up at the windows of the sanctuary, which faced Jauniela. The Soviets had converted the cathedral into a concert hall, turning its wooden pews in the opposite direction to face the magnificent organ installed in 1882–1883 by the German company E. F. Walcker and Sons, which also built the organ of the Boston Music Hall in Massachussetts. The cathedral's original organ, once the largest in the world, was destroyed in a fire in 1547. Viewed from Juris Krieviņš's studio windows, St. Mary's—the largest medieval church in the Baltic States—emanated a calm, resolute presence. Its clock had stopped ticking, and no one knew when it would be repaired; the giant hands stood frozen in time. (According to the Kremlin, there were more important things to spend money on, like the manufacture of Kalashnikovs and missiles.) Always the cathedral reminded me of the passage of time and the inevitability of political change. People, wars, and occupations had come and gone, yet St. Mary's still stood in its spot relatively unscathed. It remains my favorite church in Rīga.

Jackdaws hung out near St. Mary's enormous belfry, beggars at its doors. One of those poor people nearly made me jump the first time I encountered him: the flesh on the poor man's face was in tatters. Like a Hollywood zombie, he reminded me of how I pictured lepers in my Latvian Bible studies class. He managed "to shock" centimes (Soviet pennies) and even roubles out of tourists without speaking. A spectral apparition, he came and went. I continued to see him from time to time in the vicinity of St. Mary's; the sanctuary was his and the other unfortunates' "mother."

The interior of St. Mary's was stunning with its soaring vaulted ceilings, enormous pillars, and relics from previous centuries. The names of German nobles painted on wooden plaques reminded me of how the Germans had held Latvian territory in a steely grip for centuries. I would have liked to see the cathedral's churchyard, but it was closed to the public and looked messy through the windows. It was another sign that all was not as it should be.

Herder Square with a bust of Johann Gottfried Herder (1744–1803), a German philosopher, theologian, poet, and literary critic who came to Rīga to teach, was next to St. Mary's. Herder wrote his first major works in literary criticism in Rīga, emphasizing "the importance of the concept of nationality and of patriotism": "He that has lost his patriotic spirit has lost himself and the whole worlds about himself." (Wikipedia: Johann_Gottfried_Herder) I suspected that Soviet Latvia's youth knew little about Herder and his life. I remembered Herder's name from my Latvian school in New Jersey. According to Latvian historian Edgars Dunsdorfs, Herder was the first person in Europe to draw attention to the unique Latvian form of folk poetry known as the daina.
Source: Wikimedia Commons https://commons.wikimedia.org/wiki/File:Johann_Gottfried_Herder.jpg (© Public Domain)

A Strange Incident at the Rīga Bourse

One day in February 1983, dressed warmly with my breath billowing in the frigid air, I crossed June 17 Square to start another long walk. I loved the cold: it invigorated me. As I neared Komjaunatnes iela, I looked up at the striking old Rīga Bourse building, designed by German architect Harald Julius von Bosse (1812–1894) and built in the mid-19th century. Its restoration had been dragging on since the 1970s, and nothing in its shuttered appearance spoke of hurried work or deadlines. The building was simply divine, with rows and rows of arched windows and ornate sculptures across its facade. In 1983 it was closed to the public, its windows covered with a grimy film. Once this building had been at the center of Rīga's thriving economy fueled by international trade and links with Western Europe.

> Maintenance of the (Bourse) building required capital, so in the 1880s rooms at the Bourse were rented out to firms and private clients; various services were rendered there. At the time the Bourse was in the very center of town, surrounded by hotels (e.g. Central Hotel, Krepša Hotel, Hotel Petersburg), pastry shops, and cafés. The 1888 publication *Vadonis pa Rīgu* ("Guide to Rīga") informed the reader that tickets to a concert at St. Mary's Cathedral could be purchased at the Krepša Hotel or at the telegraph office in the Rīga Bourse. In 1913 the Bourse

committee established an office for managing the facility and coordinating its usage. Because the Bourse had ample room, auctions, conferences, and meetings were organized there. According to old advertisements, the office of August Dombrovsky, a violin maker, was located at the Bourse. In 1924 the first Latvian chess convention took place at the Bourse. (Source: Banga, Vita. *Mākslas muzejs Rīgas birža*: "Doma laukums un biržas ēka laika plūdumā." Rīga: Jumava, 2010. Tr. RL)

Exactly 100 years prior to my arrival in Rīga, the Bourse was humming like a beehive and had become a symbol of Rīga as a city of commerce and trade. According to historian Vita Banga, after World War II the Bourse was used as a large-scale exhibition hall and housed a couple of libraries. In 1973 the building was slated for renovation without a clear idea of what purpose it would serve. In January 1980 a devastating fire broke out on the top floor: "(The fire) destroyed the beautiful upstairs rooms; the ceiling collapsed, and much of the interior and furniture were ruined." (Banga) New plans were adopted, but all work ground to a halt in 1982. The building was, for lack of a better word, abandoned. In 1983 the palazzo-like Bourse was just another lovely, empty, neglected building in an obscure country behind the Iron Curtain.

I glanced over and noticed a worker entering the building. On the spur of the moment I decided to follow him inside. I was dying to see what the interior looked like. On previous walks I had taken note of the Bourse's windows, which, despite the scaffolding and grime, hinted at a spectacular interior. A natural light emanated from within, indicating that there was a huge skylight. The entrances to most buildings remained unlocked in the Soviet era, and I had already been in and out of many old buildings exploring.

Cautiously, I opened the heavy door and slipped into the foyer. The building was very quiet, the floor covered with a film of dust. As I looked around, a door in front of me opened, and a middle-aged man emerged; he greeted me in Latvian, his eyes friendly and inquisitive. I explained who I was (a Latvian American), and that I simply wanted to take a look around. "*Ak tā*, come with me," he said, looking around quickly and then motioning with his hand for me to follow.

We ascended a flight of winding stairs to the second floor and entered a room, which was empty except for a beautiful antique wood stove covered in tiles. The man walked over to it and retrieved a package from the top of the stove. Strange, I thought! As I stood there looking on with curiosity, he peeled away the paper wrapping, and I was stunned to see an old Latvian flag folded in his outstretched hand. Caught by surprise, I was unsure of what to do or say. The enormity of the gesture was staggering for *those times*.

Here was a seemingly ordinary citizen of Soviet Latvia in 1983 in the Cold War era offering me—a complete stranger (and meddlesome Latvian American mistrusted by the Soviet authorities)—a symbol of the Republic of Latvia. Our flag and our national colors had been repressed for years under the Soviets. The flag looked old, its colors slightly faded. "We found it right here on top of the stove. We don't know what to do with it. Do you want it?" the man asked in earnest. I thought for a moment and then politely declined the crazy, wonderful offer. I had to refuse this temptation! Was this a provocation? I didn't think so. My decision to visit the Bourse was completely spontaneous and lightning-quick. But if I were to take the flag home, who knows what kind of trouble it might bring us. Juris would freak out, throw a fit, collapse from a heart attack: he had already been warned...

I told my unexpected "co-conspirator" that I could not accept such a precious gift; he nodded wordlessly and placed it back on top of the stove, out of sight. And that was that. It all transpired as if in a dream. The man and I left the room, walked back down to the first floor, bid each other thank you and goodbye, and that was that. I didn't get to see the rest of the building, but it didn't really matter. All day I walked around in a wonderful daze, as if someone had let me get a peek at a precious ruby in the palm of his hand.

What happened to the flag at the Rīga Bourse? Did this kindly Latvian eventually take it home with him? Did it make its debut six or seven years later as a source of pride and defiance, when freedom of speech was threatening to bring down the once mighty Soviet Union? Who had stashed it there? I wish I knew.

I never saw this man again. As for this beautiful building, it took many more years for it to finally be restored to its original grandeur (in 2011). Today the stunning Rīga Bourse houses Latvia's Foreign Art Museum. In 2014, when I was in Latvia, I went to the Bourse and sought to identify the stove from which the flag emerged that day so long ago in 1983. I still remember this strange and touching event like it was yesterday. It unfolded so quickly, yet the casual encounter was loaded with emotions: an immediate, instinctive trust; an unspoken conviction; silent, mutual understanding; love (of the fatherland); and the ethereal, shining thread that binds people of a nation and a language together...

In 2014, I shared my story of this encounter with Mārtiņš Mintaurs, a young historian. He offered this comment: "That man could have been from the so-called *Zinātniskās restaurācijas darbu pārvalde* (Scientific Restoration Project Administration), which was famous for its skilled artisans... Many of them had biographies that the Soviets frowned upon. Perhaps this is why he trusted you. He was just as surprised to encounter a young Latvian woman from America... Very touching; this man was courting danger with his spontaneous gesture. Obviously he wasn't afraid." Mārtiņš also told me that in January 1980, a few months after my first visit to Latvia, a suspicious fire had broken out at the Bourse causing a huge setback, because restoration work had been nearly completed. What I saw in February 1983 was the aftermath of that fire. The place seemed dead.

Puppets and Masters

The so-called Latvian SSR Supreme Council building, the former (and future) seat of the Latvian Saeima (Parliament), was just down the block from the Bourse on Komjaunatnes iela. Black and gray Volgas stood parked on the cobblestones near the impressive building, while their drivers in simple suits chatted on the street in Russian and Latvian. A statue of our mythical hero Lāčplēsis ("Bearslayer") had once decorated a niche near the entrance. That niche was now empty. Lāčplēsis was banished in the 1950s. Nobody except for the communists took this legislative body seriously, as nothing it did affected anyone in a positive way, nor could the average Soviet citizen do anything to affect its work and decisions. The Party made all the decisions for everyone. The Supreme Soviet was *de jure* Latvia's highest organ of power, but everyone knew who was really in charge. The Council had little authority of its own: it catered to Moscow's needs and whims. The Soviet election system was a joke. I even received an election ballot in the mail in the fall of 1983 but never thought of going to vote because (1) maybe the ballot was a provocation; (2) I obviously couldn't vote, because I wasn't a Soviet citizien; and (3) my vote couldn't possibly change anything anyway, because the results of any Soviet elections were pre-determined.

According to the website Saeima.lv, during the Nazi occupation the high command of the German police and the SS organization in Ostland occupied the building and destroyed part of its interior. The Nazis, known for their penchant for looting, sent many of the building's books, artifacts, and paintings to Germany. Some of the building's artistic valuables continued to vanish after the war under the Soviet regime.

The Catholic St. James Cathedral (Svētā Jēkaba) from 1225 was located right next to the Supreme Council. Its immediate neighbor, St. Mary Magdalene's Church (1260) and its old cloister, formed a Roman Catholic quarter in Old Rīga. According to LiveRiga.com, "(Mary Magadelene's) first wooden building was constructed around 1260 as a monastery church for Cistercian nuns. According to legend, the church was dedicated to the first baptised pagan girl from a Liv family." The Livs were gone. Latvians were also close to being an endangered species. Several times a week I would walk around in this very old part of town looking at the history around me in amazement. It was just me, the pigeons, and ghosts. St. James' clock had also stopped ticking. Rīga reminded me of Snow White...

The doors to Old Rīga's churches were open during the day, and it was possible to step inside and get a look at their interiors and become lost in time. Only old ladies attended church, it seemed. Although church attendance was discouraged by the Soviet authorities, Latvians in the fatherland didn't seem particularly devout anyway, at least not in the way that the Lithuanian Catholics appeared to be. Latvians seemed to value the churches more for their historical and architectural significance. Christianity had set foot in Latvia in tandem with political and military conquests followed by hundreds of years of German oppression. Historically, Latvians had no love for the German Catholic priests preaching to them in Latin. Even after Martin Luther's Reformation, the light of ancestral pagan fires still glimmered in the Latvians' eyes. Soviet Latvia was atheist; the empty and desecrated churches of the 1980s demonstrated that. I also heard that many ministers were in cahoots with the Soviet authorities.

The Soviet occupation contributed to the destruction of many churches in Latvia. In 2014 when I was visiting Latvia, my children and I came upon Siguļu Church in Carnikava. It is the only wooden church near Latvia's coastline in Vidzeme. Built in 1728, it is one of a handful of wooden churches in Latvia. The church's interior suffered in both world wars. In the Soviet years it was used for grain storage. According to legend, the church's clock fell and rolled into a nearby lake, which is how the lake got its name "Pulksteņezers" ("Clock Lake"). Thanks to decades of neglect, the lovely 280-year-old church looked like a shabby warehouse..

Construction of Rīga Castle, a massive medieval structure with several imposing towers near the Daugava River, was commenced in 1330. Initially the castle served as the seat of the Livonian Order. It was destroyed and rebuilt several times. Over the course of history the castle was occupied by Germans, Lithuanians, Poles, Swedes, and Russians seeking to expand their power by controlling the Daugava River, a strategic gateway between East and West. The robust, fortress-like castle suffered from fires, catapult assaults, and other scourges. When the Latvians finally became masters of their country in 1920, the castle served as the seat of the Latvian President. An indelible part of the classic Rīga panorama from the Daugava River, Rīga Castle reminded me of a gigantic block of Swiss cheese.

In 1941 the Pioneers, a Soviet youth organization, established their seat at the castle, which was named "Pioneer Castle." This is how everyone referred to it in the 1980s. It also housed several art collections, including art of antiquity (Roman and Greek busts and sculptures) and Latvian traditional handicrafts (woven belts, knitted mittens, intricately embroidered shawls, etc.). There were rooms for various clubs and activities, such as folk dancing and art classes. A real but shabby mummy lay by the entrance looking permanently offended. Wrong country! And it's cold and drafty here! The Egyptian mummy, which dated back to 30–100 B.C., had traveled to Rīga in its sarcophagus in 1902.

It was very difficult to get a sense of the castle's original interior or full size due to its many rooms, but it felt big. I certainly saw only a part of it. Apparently there was a huge, creepy cellar down below. Grungy neon lights cast a cool pall on the interiors. Tickets to get in were cheap, and I went there often.

On the outside, a magnificent wrought-iron gate designed by Latvian artist Ansis Cīrulis (1883–1942) and hammered out by Augusts Bormanis and installed in 1939 remained intact as a superb example of the artistry of the past. As the seat of the President of Latvia before the war, this must have been where our last President Kārlis Ulmanis came and went in his official car: through Cīrulis' splendid gates. Ansis Cīrulis was also known for his pseudo-ethnic furniture, popular in the 1930s. In 1940 President Ulmanis was arrested and deported to Siberia, possibly leaving his post for the last time through these gates. Along with passionate disputes among Latvians about Ulmanis' rule and legacy, these fancy wrought iron gates were really all that remained of his era and his "benign" dictatorship. The courtyard was littered with junk and bricks.

Well, after many centuries of suffering under foreign rule, the revolutionary Latvians had finally moved into the castle. In the 1980s I spent many an hour there, and I can't imagine Rīga without this citadel, which, like Rīga's old churches, survived so many crazy conflicts and brutal assaults.

An old photograph of Rīga Castle's Tower of the Holy Spirit in 1919, pounded by Russian artillery. Source: Wikimedia Commons https://commons.wikimedia.org /wiki/File:Riga_castle_ww1_shelling.jpg (© Public Domain)

With time I got to know downtown Rīga quite well. What the Soviets had added to Rīga in their almost 40 year rule did not impress me, with the exception of the suspension bridge and the Latvian Communist Party headquarters, which looked modern, neat, and comfortable. Soviet architecture reflected the regime's heavy-handed approach to just about everything. There was no finesse. The Daile Theater on Ļeņina iela was touted as a paragon of modernity, but all I saw was an ugly cement block. The so-called Agroprom and Press buildings on opposite sides of the Daugava River were eyesores.

"*Staļina kūka*" or "Stalin's cake," originally called the Kolhoz Workers' Building, was Soviet Latvia's first "skyscraper" and stuck out like a sore thumb. It housed the Latvian SSR Academy of Sciences. A 21-story building, it was built between 1951 and 1961. Similar buildings in the style of Socialist Classicism or the Stalinist Empire style can be found elsewhere in the former Soviet Union and in Eastern Europe. Rīga's building was a copy of Moscow's "Seven Sisters" Stalinist style skyscrapers. Comrade Stalin also "gifted" such a "cake"—the Palace of Culture—to Warsaw, Poland. In Latvia the unpopular building was referred to as "Stalin's birthday cake," "Stalin's tooth," "the Kremlin," etc. I have read that an old church, its cemetery, and an ensemble of wooden buildings once considered an architectural monument were razed to make room for the Kolhoz Workers' Building.

Left, a drawing of the Kolhoz Workers' Building by architect Osvalds Tīlmanis. Courtesy of the Latvian Museum of Architecture.

The building, a legacy of the brutal Stalin era, looms above the Rīga Central Market near streets named after the great Russian writers, Gogol, Pushkin, and Turgenev. This is where Maskača, the so-called Moscow (or Latgale) suburb of Rīga, with a colorful history and heavily Russified, begins. In my wanderings all over the central part of Rīga and later on the other side of the Daugava River, I was attracted to everything from the pre-war era—my grandparents' era. Even the most humble of wooden cottages evoked tender feelings in me. I could never warm up to "Stalin's cake," built at a time when my great aunt and countless others were suffering in exile in Siberia.

Even uglier than Rīga's "skyscrapers" in downtown Rīga were the public housing "massives" on the outskirts of the capital (some of these were going up in the 1980s): Ķengarags; Purvciems; Pļavenieki; Imanta; Mežciems, Zolitūde; etc. These cookie-cutter neighborhouds, touted in all Soviet era books as huge accomplishments, were indeed massive, sprawling neighborhoods of ugly poured concrete apartment highrises that made a person feel lost and small. They were Rīga's blight, specifically built to accommodate Latvia's swelling Russian population. Latvians could only helplessly look on as these mega-blocks went up, absorbing the Russian military and Russian migrant workers. Rīga was turning into an enormous *sādža* (Russian village).

These apartment buildings were attractive to the average Soviet citizen: they beckoned with the promise of new plumbing, hot water, loggias for parking babies, produce, and other stuff, and relative privacy (compared to communal apartments). How well were these Soviet highrises constructed? Soviet era "coffee table" books touted these apartment building canyons as paragons of modernity, practicality, and social equality. Canyons for the common man. Luckily, we lived in one of Latvia's most romantic places, Old Rīga, and we rarely ventured out to any of the Soviet "massives." There was nothing to do there anyway nor anything to see. An avid walker and seeker, I absorbed Rīga's architecture happily, tracing my grandparents' footsteps while observing with what heavy, dirty strokes an alien political system was marring and leaving scars on Rīga's beautiful features.

Practicum

Once we had settled into our Krāmu iela apartment, I had to learn to deal with some of the basic aspects of Soviet life. While living with my parents, I had taken things like food and meals, clean laundry, and financial support for granted. Like many of my American middle class peers, I had grown up in a bubble, accustomed to a certain level and way of life. My father earned a respectable wage, and my mother made sure we were healthy and well fed and dressed. All of my observations in communist Latvia were processed from that perspective, of an average American youth from the suburbs. Like most middle class Americans, our family had a house, a car, a great choice of privately owned, well stocked stores to shop in, clean running cold and hot water at home, and a spacious yard. I grew up in a market economy where everything was available and customer was king. This, of course, is *not* how most of the world lives. My first year in Latvia was a rude awakening: I was woefully unprepared for the rigors of Soviet life. Instead of climbing trees, devouring books, and drawing in the USA, I should have learned to sew, knit, darn, and cook.

The Soviet era Laundromat and sauna called Varavīksne ("Rainbow") in Old Rīga. Image courtesy of the National Library of Latvia collection "In Search of Lost Latvia."

On a cold day in January 1983 we loaded our dirty clothes, towels, and sheets into large bags and set off for a Laundromat called Varavīksne ("Rainbow") about three blocks from our house. It was situated in a badly constructed Soviet era red brick building that also accomodated a public *pirts* (sauna) for those without a bath or hot water at home, or who just liked to feel like a steamed *pelmenis* (dumpling) from time to time. The bricks used to complete this shoddy construction were manufactured in Lode, reputed to be of poor quality. The Lode brick would come to symbolize "Soviet quality."

I could not believe that we were going to an actual Laundromat. It sounded too good to be true in this run-down place where some people in downtown Rīga went without running water for hours at a time (like us), and the stairwells smelled like piss. My excitement was deflated when I saw how filthy "Rainbow" was. Half of the machines were out of order. A grumpy technician was busy trying to resuscitate them. Did we really want to set our bags down on the scummy floor? The place looked like it hadn't been washed since the day it opened.

Interestingly, the machines did not operate on coins. Instead, you paid a scowling attendant, and she handed you a grooved plastic strip that was inserted into a slot; this procedure jumpstarted the machine. Soviet laundry detergent, although similar in appearance to American detergent, had a sharper, more pungent smell; we dispensed it into an opening at the top of the machine and then stood back and watched the plastic script scroll through the slot, somehow controlling the washing cycle. Funky!

We eyed the other clients, all women, and we observed the dryers. Laundromats everywhere make me feel like I'm in a race. At "Rainbow" I was thinking: who'll be the first to get to the *two* functioning dryers? Water from *māmuliņa* ("Mommy") Daugava had turned the white detergent into a wonderful white froth that scrubbed our clothes, tossing and turning them. In the rinse cycle a bubbling brook of chemical suds drained from the machine directly onto the floor, streaming towards a drain hole that I imagined sent this and other local wastewater straight to the nearby Daugava. I observed all of this with fascination. I was suspicious of the Daugava as one of Rīga's main sources of drinking water. I always boiled it; this was recommended for everyone whose water source was the river. We kept an old silver five lat coin from before the war in our pitcher of water; supposedly it acted as a purifier. Oldsters remembered Rīga as reputedly having the best water in Europe before the war...

I marveled at the engineering of the Soviet washing machines with their grooved plastic strip. So primitive, and yet they worked. Once the plastic strip had scrolled down all the way, the cycle came to an end. Andris and I hurriedly emptied the machines and whisked our stuff to the centrifuges (spin dryers), which cranked up loudly, spun furiously, and expelled excess moisture. Then it was time to dry everything in the cavernous dryers. While our clothes spun, we took our spots on either side of an enormous, hot ironing roll and began feeding our towels, handkerchiefs, and bed linens into it. The roll turned, pressing and flattening everything in a wonderful way.

When we removed our clothes from the furnace-hot dryer, I realized that I had destroyed my beautiful orange Peruvian wool sweater: it had shrunk by 30%. It smelled of singed wool, and I threw it out at home, thinking myself an idiot for not reading the label and not knowing such things. Trial by error, they say. Despite this loss, it was nice to come home with bundles of crisp, clean laundry, which we then sorted and stacked away into our wardrobe. My beau was efficient and neat. I was quickly learning to maximize the use of my clothes, wearing slacks and skirts numerous times before throwing them into the dirty laundry heap. I washed my underwear and socks in the bathtub on a daily basis (late nights, usually) and hung them to dry in our kitchen in a discreet spot on the pipes.

Our humble abode was supplied with bedsheets and towels, thanks to Biruta Krieviņa, soon to be my mother-in-law. There were no paper towels, kitchen sponges, or dishwashing detergents to be had, so I improvised, using rags and hot water (when it was available). I became acquainted with Soviet household chemical goods. In lieu of Ajax or Comet, I used a stinky, gooey, abrasive paste called Skaidra to scrub the sink, tub, and toilet. Most American household chemicals had Soviet/Latvian equivalents, although I never did find a product like Windex for windows. In Latvia I learned to clean glass with newspapers and water, which left no fuzzy residue.

Packaging in the Soviet Union was practical but primitive. With no private manufacturers and no competition, product design was bland. Some products did have names, such as "Lavanda" soap. Others had generic labels, such as *peldu* ("swim soap") or *bērnu* ("children's") soap. The environmental impact of Soviet cleaning products was unknown, but I suspected it wasn't good. Ecology and environmental protection were at the bottom of the list of Soviet priorities. The Baltic Sea was and remains one of the most polluted seas in the world.

There were Soviet-made appliances to make people's lives easier, but they were primitive and hard to come by. Some people, including   Biruta, had a simple laundry machine at home. Soviet laundry machines were small, basic devices, half the size of a regular American washing machine. Some were even as small as a laundry basket. Most models were cylindrical, with an opening at the top. Biruta preferred brown laundry soap, already mentioned, as a detergent; she shaved it into thin slivers with a knife. Some models featured a combined laundry receptacle and centrifuge or spinner. The receptacles were quite small, so you had to wash your laundry frequently and then hang it up to dry somewhere. Biruta rinsed her laundry in the bathtub, which was backbreaking work. Driers did not exist in the Soviet Union (or, if they did, only high-level Communist Party officials had them).

Bathrooms in Rīga reminded me of photographs of old Italian cities and drying laundry draped from wall to wall. When I visited my cousin Guntars in 1981, he and his wife and baby daughter were living in an old, wood-heated house in Pārdaugava; we sat in a room that was partitioned by a "wall" of ropes covered with drying laundry. Small Soviet-era apartments could not accommodate any large American-style appliances; these were not on the market anyway. In addition, private homes built under the Soviets had to comply with strict size regulations. For seventeen years in Latvia I washed our laundry at various Laundromats around town or in the countryside, which was a major physical undertaking—a two or three day affair, really. Centrifuges were a godsend. Just try expelling water from a pair of jeans with your hands!

People cooked on small gas stoves. Some, like ours, were hooked up to a gas canister, which, when empty, was replaced by a worker from the gas company whose job it was to haul these things up and down many flights of stairs. Sometimes the new canister arrived bright red and shiny; other times it arrived old, beat up, and greasy, and I had to sponge it down. It worked well enough.

The refrigerators from Soviet Lithuania's Snaige factory were dimunitive, the size of American bar fridges. This is why so many people stored meat and other perishables on window sills and balconies in winter. It wasn't uncommon to see a large chunk of wrapped up meat or a sack of potatoes hanging on the outside of a window (of course, higher up and out of reach) in the cold season. I shopped every other day, and the food perished quickly, indicating it was free of preservatives (a good thing).

We had an electric coffee bean grinder made in Latvia by the Straume factory, and I even used it to make confectioner's sugar and pulverize oatmeal. Someone once told me that the caffeine in the coffee beans for sale in the Soviet Union had been removed before sale. Who knew? Our sturdy blender, also manufactured by Straume, served up delicious ice cream "cocktails," and later I used it to puree fresh vegetables, meat, and fruit for our baby. I missed my American toaster.

I boiled water for coffee, tea, and general consumption on the stove or in a pitcher with a "boiling wand"—an appliance that looked very unsafe to me. I never got used to and comfortable with this thing; it looked like a KGB torture device.

One thing I have to say about Soviet appliances: what they lacked in sophistication, they often made up for in ruggedness and simplicity of design. Your TV didn't work: hit it with your fist. Car's not moving? Kick it. Since design and aesthetic appeal were the aspects of manufacturing that the Soviet Union was not good at, Soviet citizens *immediately* noticed anything that was manufactured outside of the USSR.

Although I was a novice at home-making, there was no time for dawdling! Our young and restless stomachs were growling. My fiancé was also unwilling to be a full-time cook for us. I would have to learn how to operate with pots and pans, ingredients, and heat. My first meal ever was some sort of meat and vegetable stew. I purchased the meat at the Rīga Central Market and retrieved carrots and potatoes from Juris' "pantry" at the back of his studio. The result served with white rice, which I boiled the best I could (there were no instructions on Soviet food packaging, and many products were sold by weight), was edible (that is, passable). Andris wasn't one to dispense compliments freely, and I never did find out what he thought of my first effort to please. He cleaned his plate though.

We drank kefir with the meal, which I acquired a taste for; it went well with many foods. Tangy and refreshing, we drank it often. From that day on, my role as the "scavenger" increased significantly: I was the one who ventured forth into the city to scope out shops for food and other items. As I did more exploring, shopping, and analyzing, my eyes and mind opened to new needs and possibilities; as it is with everything in life, the "hands on" approach proved to be the best.

In the Soviet era most stores were limited to a certain type of product, as I already mentioned (milk, meat, bread, etc.). Thus, to do all your shopping you had to march around to various stores that sold different types of goods, as if you were visiting "mom and pop" bakeries, butcher, and specialty cheese shops. For instance, the store next to St. Peter's Church sold *maize* ("bread"), cakes, and confectionary goods only. There I could buy soft white bread, rye bread, wheat bread, a multi-grain bread called *karaša*, the popular *ķieģelis* ("the brick"), the moon-shaped *radziņš*, and delicious *barankas* (small, round, bagel-type of bread with a hole in the middle, delightful to chew on and popular with children). In addition to baked goods, this store also sold certain Laima chocolates, cookies, waffles, boxed cakes, and hard candy.

A tiny store on Šķūņu iela offered meat products: *gaļa* or *myaso* (in Russian). Contrary to the bread shop, this place was more or less a joke and a good example of what was wrong with the Soviet economy. The only meat for sale were cow udders, slabs of white fat, and sometimes random chunks of bloody, sinewy beef. Yes, from time to time I saw a carcass being carted in, but where did all the parts go? Store managers ran their own private business selling or bartering choice cuts to their family, friends, and acquaintances and displaying whatever was left over for random customers like me. For meat, I ended up going to the market. It was expensive, but Soviet Rīga's meat shops were simply too unpredictable; in other words, a waste of time.

The lowly sausage had become a symbol of the Soviet consumer, the Soviet economy, and Soviet life. A marvelous painting from 1979 by Latvian artist Auseklis Bauškenieks (1910–2007)—"Rindā pēc prieka" ("In Line for Happiness")—depicts a long line of drably attired Soviet customers waiting in a "roller-coaster" to purchase sausages. Most East Europeans who grew up in the communist world could relate to the painting.

Auseklis Bauškenieks. "Rindā pēc prieka," 1979. ("In Line for Happiness.") Image courtesy of Ingus Bauškenieks.

Why this love affair with the sausage—a product made from grist, grease, offal, and slime? Apparently sausage was still better than no meat at all; it was wildly popular. After all, carnivores crave the smell and taste of meat, even if an approximation. I myself shied away from sausage; it seemed suspect. On rare occasions I bought "Hunter's Sausage" at the market. One of the sausages popularly known as "suņa prieks" ("doggie joy"), pale gray in color, reminded me of sun-blanched dog poop. It was at the bottom of the price list, which was also a red flag for me. I tried it exactly once with mustard. Nothing bad happened, but fear was enough to keep it off of my plate permanently.

Milk and other dairy products were sold in dairy shops, at the markets, and at Universālveikals—Old Rīga's popular, hectic department store. I preferred the small shops to the madness of Universālveikals ("Universal Store"), which was close to the train station and attracted Homo Sovieticus storming Rīga from other Soviet republics. There was a rather nice dairy shop near Pioneeru laukums (Pioneer Square) that carried an assortment of products: milk; kefir and ryazhenka; farmer's and other cheeses; and sweet and sour cream. Specialty cheeses like Brie, Roquefort, Feta, Stilton, etc. were unavailable, because they were expensive to import. Latvia's "Cheddar" cheese was nothing like the orange cheese I grew up with in the US in terms of appearance and taste. Despite the absence of such European delicacies, local cheese was tasty. Latvijas ("Latvia's") cheese came closest to replicating the pungent specialty cheeses of Europe: it stank and was delicious!

Most products were available by weight and poured directly into the customer's own jar, such as cream. Milk and other liquid dairy products were sold in glass bottles capped with an aluminum seal that could easily break. These containers weighed down our our shopping bags considerably. This was another reason why I shopped so frequently: I could not carry a lot home in one trip.

One managed with what one could find. Shopping in those days was like an adventure: you were out on a hunt and never knew what you might stumble upon. Sometimes you came back empty-handed, sometimes with the same old stuff, and sometimes your sack contained some small, exciting treat. Rīga's amazing pastries were such a treat: I was addicted to *biezpienmaize*, a cake made from Farmer's Cheese. Ice cream made me happy, too.

I remember seeing a banana peel on a sidewalk in the early 1980s. It was a surreal sight both for me and other passers-by who also stopped for a moment to look in amazement. If the sausage symbolized the Soviet economy, then the happy yellow banana smile symbolized the world of free market capitalism for me. *Where?! Who?! How?!* Some Soviet consumers were willing to spend hours and days tracking down such exotic imports.

From time to time I did venture into Universālveikals, the famous department store in Old Rīga. Universālveikals attracted shoppers from all over the Soviet Union in search of valuable local products. The occupied Baltic countries were the most economically advanced area of the Soviet Union.

Before the war Universālveikals was known as *Armijas ekonomiskais veikals* ("Army General Store"). Designed by architect Artūrs Galindoms (1894–1966), the construction of this landmark building commenced in 1936; that is, shortly before the first Soviet occupation of Latvia in 1940. When the store opened, its shoppers could ride up and down brand new escalators. By the early 1980s, however, there was no sign of escalators, as tens of thousands of pairs of tired Soviet feet pounded the store's creaking, badly worn wooden stairs. By the time I arrived in Latvia, this once magnificent five-story building, which my mother's generation remembered from childhood as "modern and beautiful," was badly run-down from years of neglect and overuse. In fact, on the inside it looked so unattractive, that the story about its escalators was almost hard to believe.

Universālveikals was a great example of the economic regression that the Soviet occupation had caused in Latvia. I felt sorry for the building. In winter the Soviet masses pushed a tide of slush into the store, which slopped around like porridge and spread out, coating the floor. Like so many Balts, the architect Mr. Galindoms escaped to Germany, where he was severely wounded in an air raid; he ended up in the United States after the war and worked in the Boston, Massachussetts area as an architect.

Food and beverages were sold on the first floor. The upstairs floors offered clothing and housewares. How many times I wandered about on those upper floors in search of something wearable and remotely flattering. No wonder the people around me looked so drab: the colors of Soviet-manufactured clothes were gray, brown, black, or some other muddied hue. Even the reds, blues, and greens looked ugly or even garish, like the upholstery of Soviet furniture. No wonder many women learned to sew and made their own clothes, using their imagination and skilled fingers to produce elegant attire. Latvian women had a knack for looking good even in the impoverished Soviet economy, where everything was in short supply! No wonder so many Latvian women wanted to leave Latvia when given the chance.

When my mother visited in May 1983, her new shoes were so uncomfortable, that we had to go find her something to wear. We visited the shoe section at Universālveikals, where she bought a pair of "granny" shoe-sandals. Dowdy and ugly, they did serve her well during her stay, ironically. It was a comical sight.

The large number of pushy people hustling and bustling through the drab store and the tedious purchasing process kept me away from Universālveikals. The communists had set up a kind of control system in which easy shelf-to-cashier purchases in the store were impossible. In just about any store my shopping procedure was as follows: (1) Comrade Ilmarovna stands in line to place her purchase order with Grumpy Lady (aka counter operator); (2) Grumpy Lady takes customer's order, weighs product, and scribbles price on piece of paper; (3) while Grumpy Lady wraps up order (cheese, socks, chocolate, etc.), (4) Comrade Ilmarovna stands in another line to pay for purchase at a cashier's "booth"; (5) after paying and receiving a receipt, Comrade Ilmarovna pushes her way back through the throng to the cheese, socks, chocolate, etc. counter to pick up her order from Grumpy Lady. I suppose this was a way of dealing with shoplifters, but it was damn annoying and terribly time-consuming. No wonder people skipped work to shop.

I rarely bothered to look at the meat section at Universālveikals, as it was almost always empty, as was the seafood section. That is, there was no fresh fish. Only canned. Cans were stacked in pretty pyramids. This seafood deficit seemed absurd, of course, because Latvia was a country by the sea, the Baltic Sea, and Latvians and Livs had once fished in their own sea. There were scores of folk songs and dainas about the beauty and perils of the sea, Here is one from Ventspils near the sea: *Jūra šņāca, jūra krāca, / Ko tā jūra aprijuse? / Aprijuse zvejniecinus / Ar visām laiviņām.* ("The sea hissed, the sea groaned, / What has the sea devoured? / She devoured the fishermen / With all their boats." With the Iron Curtain stretching along Latvia's western border, the Baltic Sea was off limits to private fishermen. Fishermen worked in kolhozes like Sarkanā bāka ("Red Lighthouse"), Brīvā Venta ("Free Venta"), Bolshevik, etc. The Soviet Union used canned fish to barter with other socialist countries. However, the Baltic Sea was badly depleted. When I was growing up, from time to time we enjoyed sprats packed in Latvia. As a child, I was absolutely thrilled by these little black and gold tins from Latvia. They seemed to confirm Latvia as a real place in time and space. However, "Rīga Sprats" were impossible to buy in Rīga in the Soviet era, as they were considered a lucrative export to be sold for hard currency.

"Employees on the flotillas of the seas and rivers! Hurry to bring in your cargo for the needs of the state economy! Fight for exemplary navigation in 1947! Soviet railroad workers! Fight to increase the loading of freight, for renewing the railways, and building new facilities! Improve passenger service!" A clipping from *Brīvā Venta* ("Free Venta"), a Ventspils newspaper, about increased output in the fishermen's kolhoz "Sarkanā bāka" ("Red Lighthouse"), May 1, 1947. (Source: Arhīvi.lv)

Thirty years had passed since Stalin's death, and Latvia's economy was in a shambles. Under Stalin, Latvia had been crushed with mass arrests and deportations. Yet Stalin's death was not the end of communist rule, and the Communist Party had lived on, continuing to govern the Soviet economy with an iron fist. Like everyone else, I ventured to Universālveikals hoping that maybe, just maybe I'd find something special there. Alas, I almost never did. If any attractive goods were being delivered to the store, they were probably being siphoned off by the management. From all those years of wandering around like an alien in that Soviet consumers' mecca, the only items that I remember with delight are: *šokolādes kartupelīši* ("chocolate potatoes"), a soft, chocolaty doughball resembling a small potato powdered with confectioners' sugar; and "Kārums," a chocolate-glazed dairy treat made from sweetened Farmer's Cheese. It tasted a lot like cheesecake.

Officially, there was no unemployment in the Soviet Union. Everyone and anyone, even a lazy drunk, could find and hold on to a job and, unofficially, take time off from work to stand in line to shop or run errands. (Alcoholics often worked as *sanitāri* or orderlies "cleaning" hospitals. No wonder the hospitals were a mess.) The Soviets, who claimed they were the "workers' paradise," were not a very productive society. Or maybe people in paradise don't work very hard. So many types of goods were in great demand and short supply. When hardliner Soviet KGB chief Yuri Andropov succeeded Leonid Brezhnev as General Secretary of the Communist Party of the Soviet Union in 1982, he pledged to get people off the streets and out of stores during working hours to increase productivity. This attempt at changing people's habits failed miserably, much to everyone's amusement, and spawned more jokes. No, nothing would change under Andropov. Or Chernenko.

Shopping at that madhouse, Universālveikals, was an excuse to walk over to a little café on Padomju ("Soviet") bulvāris and order a delicious Soviet-style milkshake made from Plombīrs ice cream and a fruit nectar. Like anyone living in that communist society, I enjoyed what I could.

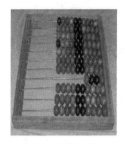 Most stores did not have cash registers. Instead, salespeople (who happened to be mostly women) used an abacus (*left*), a handmade calculator from ancient times. I enjoyed seeing nimble fingers manipulating and clicking the beads. All transactions were executed in cash; personal checks and credit and debit cards were nonexistent. People could keep their money at the one and only savings bank, Latvijas PSR Krājbanka ("Latvian SSR Savings Bank"), or at home in "the sock." Utility bills could be paid at the bank. I read that the abacus is still popular in Asia and Africa, and that it is a great tool for teaching children math. Of course, the abacus did not keep records of transactions. Those ubiquitous scraps of paper, Soviet receipts, were impaled on a sharp implement next to the abacus. No wonder it was so easy to steal from the state.

There were many newspaper kiosks scattered throughout Rīga selling newspapers, magazines, tickets, pens and pencils, paper, combs, cigarettes, postcards, etc. They were located near transportation stops, so that people could purchase their transportation tickets right before boarding.

With time I learned to improvise to make up for the lack of certain items. For instance, I fashioned Q-tips out of cotton and wooden matches manufactured in Liepāja. The small, blue matchboxes (*right*) were indispensible in my kitchen, because I couldn't light the range without a match.

The Liepāja Match Factory, as it was known in modern times, was not always a match manufacturer. In 1890 a factory was built in Liepāja for the production of wooden laths for export. The laths were sent to (the town of) Kuldīga for further processing. (The Liepāja and Kuldīga factories, owned by one and the same entrepreneur, were called Vulkāns ["Volcano"]. Liepāja's Vulkāns factory was known as the Liepāja Match Factory in the Soviet era.) In 1891 output was increased and included the manufacture of matchsticks. (...) In 1906 the Kuldīga and Liepāja factories were united under a single shareholding company called Vulkāns. By the end of the 19th century the factory was producing 250,000 matchboxes a day, 91,000,000 annually. A large percentage of the output was exported through London to Great Britain's colonies.

The Saturday edition of the May 2, 1942 newspaper *Kurzemes vārds* ran a story called "Neuzvarēs nedz Londona, nedz Ņujorka, nedz Maskava, bet—Ādolfs Hitlers" ("Neither London, nor New York, nor Moscow, but Rather Adolph Hitler Will Triumph"), as well as an article about a May meeting at the Liepāja Match Factory: "Workers employed in the woodworking sector (...) gathered in their cafeteria, which was decorated with both Great Germany's and Latvia's national colors, as well as green boughs. (...) The meeting was opened with an address by the director of the factory. After that a representative of the regional kommisar outlined future work assignments for the large crowd of workers and stressed the importance of National Labor Day. With a triple 'Sieg Heil!' salute to Great Germany's Führer and New Europe's creator, the meeting was adjourned."

But when World War II ended, on September 6, 1946 the Jelgava newspaper *Zemgales Komunists"* ("Zemgale Communist"), which featured the slogan "Proletariats of the World,

Unite!" above its masthead, ran the following news: "The Liepāja Match Factory will resume work. The match factory, which was destroyed by the German occupants, is being renewed. The production of matches must begin on December 1. The occupants took the factory's equipment with them to Germany. Now the most modern equipment from other Soviet republics is being installed. In 1947 the factory will produce 50 million match boxes. In the following years output will increase, and at the end of the five-year period, working in two shifts, the plant will be producing 141 million matches a year." (Source: "Liepājas sērkociņu fabrika." Diggers.lv. 2 February, 2014. <http://www.diggers.lv/v2/index.php/industrialie-objekti/rupn/51-liepajas-serkocinu-fabrika>. Tr. RL)

So you see, even a tiny matchbox has a story to tell about Latvia's crazy history. Those matchboxes served me well over the years lighting many fires. Today the Liepāja Match Factory is gone, its grounds deserted and vandalized.

Zeppelin: Rīga Central Market
(Central Kolhoz Market)

When I lived in the old town, Rīga Central Market quickly became my favorite "go to" place for groceries. Later in the 1990s, when I lived on Ģertrūdes iela, I went to Matīsa tirgus (market) on Brīvības iela, because it was closer. The first time Andris and I went to Rīga Central Market to shop in the winter of '83, it was jampacked with enormous crowds. I could not believe how many people were milling about. And all I could hear was the Russian language. Huge lines stretched towards vendors selling… lemons? Oranges? I don't recall the products, but I remember long lines. Soviet citizens appeared to have all the time and patience in the world to stand in line, even with small children in tow.

It must have been a weekend. It was a very cold day, and people were bundled up snugly in warm coats, wearing all sorts of hats like the popular and practical zaķene (a rabbit fur hat with long, furry flaps to keep the ears warm), hand-knit shawls, and mittens. Unlike in the USA, people in Rīga took the cold seriously. Hundreds if not thousands of plumes of human breath rose up into the frigid air. It had snowed, and the snow was ploughed and pushed into mounds along the walkways.

I had heard all about Rīga Central Market in Latvian school. Latvians were very proud of it. Rīga, like all European cities, had always had several markets. Prior to 1930 Rīga's old market, which dated back to the 16th century, was located right near the Daugava River: "Merchants' booths took up 22,000 square meters. They were unhygienic, and because of poor sanitary conditions products spoiled quickly, especially in the summer, causing major losses," According to historian Arveds Švābe in *Latvju Enciklopēdija*, 1950-1951. Following an international competition, the design of the new market was awarded to architect Pāvils Dreimanis (1895–1953). Work on the modern market was commenced in 1924 and completed in 1930. The new market featured five pavilions partially constructed from old German Zeppelin hangars that had once stood at a German air base in Vaiņode. The market featured modern freezers and storage cellars, which were connected to the city canal by three tunnels, so that boats carrying products could easily reach the market from the Daugava River.

According to Juris Dambis, Head of the Latvian State Inspection for Heritage Protection, "When Rīga Central Market was first opened on November 2, 1930, it was the largest and the most modern marketplace on earth." "During the 1930s the pavilions were one of the market's main tourist attractions. A wide array of inexpensive produce was available for degustation. Tourists from Germany and England highly appreciated the butter and bacon. The fish pavilion was especially attractive with large, colorful aquariums. The large number of tourists furthered Rīga Central Market's reputation as one of the more grandiose buildings in Europe." (Source: Wikipedia [en.wikipedia.org/wiki/Riga_Central_Market]) The Rīga Central Market is a UNESCO World Heritage Site.

The famous market was a 15–20 minute walk from where we lived. It was a hustling, bustling, fascinating center of commerce. While state vendors stood around looking bored, their private counterparts competed for attention. Bundled up warmly, they stood by their sacks of potatoes and apples, tubs of sauerkraut, cranberries, and other appetizing products, their cheeks ruddy from the cold. They were quick to respond to a customer's question, weigh the goods, and complete a transaction. Even delicate flowers were sold at the market in winter, protected by boxes heated with candles. Some "entrepreneurs" even tried sweet talk to attract passers-by. For me, a young American who had never seen a European market, it was all absolutely delightful. Even under communism one could sense private enterprise at work. Rīga Central Market attracted visitors and vendors from faraway places in the Soviet Union who would fly in or take the train. It was conveniently located only a couple of blocks from the train station.

The market was laid out next to five airy pavilions: meat; dairy; "gastronomy"; produce; and fish. Latvia's kolhozes leased stands and booths inside the pavilions. Private or individual vendors, such as the little old ladies with their flowers, sold their products outside on long tables. Every time I went to the market, I visited all the pavilions. I found them to be endlessly fascinating. I liked to discreetly observe, and at the market there were hundreds of interesting faces.

In the meat pavilion bright red slabs of beef, pink veal and pork, poultry, rabbit meat, and sausages lay on display on metal counters attended to by vendors in blood-smattered smocks. To prove that it was an actual rabbit and not a cat, vendors had to leave one leg covered in fur. The meat, sold by various Latvian kolhozes, was surprisingly expensive. In fact, it was a luxury that neither we nor others could easily afford. Customers walked back and forth, eyeing the meat and swallowing hungrily. For deprived carnivores like us, it all looked delicious, but I could purchase only very small pieces, it was that expensive. And even then I always hesitated, wondering what I would do with the meat, once I got home. As I walked past the rows of vendors, I wondered if I should fry the meat in the stinky sunflower oil or use the smelly yellow margarine sold by weight in stores. What about plain old butter? Or should I just boil it? My lack of culinary experience filled me with anxiety, as I pondered the possibilities for dinner for us hungry. skinny Latvians.

Gazing at the red meat, I felt my mouth salivating. I was growing thinner from all the walking and our frugal meals. Smoked *mednieku* ("Hunter's") sausages, layed out in rows, beckoned with their fantastic aroma. My stomach rumbled.

Next up was the dairy pavilion, where vendors in pure white aprons sold fresh milk, sweet and sour cream, Farmer's Cheese, cottage cheese, honey, and delicious-looking loaves of rye bread and *saldskābmaize* (sweet and sour bread). Some honey vendors also sold aloe vera leaves for medicinal use. Everything was sold by weight, so customers had to provide their own glass jars and jugs, although some vendors had a few containers on hand for the forgetful and unprepared. Vendors readily offered customers samples of their products for appraisal and comparison. This was one of the market's main attractions.

Cookies, chocolate, caramels, hard candy, various grain products like flour, oats, *prosa* or millet, barley, kasha, etc., locally made pasta, and canned goods of dubious quality with drab labels were sold in the so-called *gastronomijas* (gastronomy) pavilion, bathed in a dull, yellowish light. Gray, sullen-looking people huddled in booths stocked with products that no one seemed to want. Did rats run this joint at nighttime, I wondered, looking at the open sacks of flour. I knew they lurked just below our point of vision, probably in the tunnels that ran beneath the market to the Daugava River. The lords of night and Rīga's underworld were audacious enough to scamper about on the banks of the canal in daylight. The grandchild of a Latvian writer died after contracting a rat-borne disease. At any rate, anything I brought home from the market I scrubbed and washed carefully before using.

The produce pavilion was remodeled. This was my favorite pavilion. Here customers could walk around the large kolhoz stands and booths to examine produce for freshness and variety. All sorts of goodies like potatoes, carrots, beets, turnips, cabbage heads, cauliflower, onions, garlic, apples, and herbs were heaped in mounds, producing a colorful, appetizing effect. The market was seasonal. In the winter of 1983 I began buying fresh cranberries, apples, and sauerkraut to replenish my depleted Vitamin C. Private vendors sold pickled vegetables. Sauerkraut and marinated and salted pickle vendors near the side entrance received a steady stream of "tasters." Sauerkraut, loaded with Vitamin C and iron, was sold from large barrels, and the customer was welcome to taste all the different varieties. The best sauerkraut and dill pickles are in Latvia! A dill pickle was a great way to tame one's appetite; often I would eat one on the way home. Steeped in salty brine flavored with garlic, dill, and the leaves of black currants, these ordinarily bland gourds were a crunchy snack that all Rigans enjoyed. A pickle in my belly improved my mood.

During a salmonella outbreak I started buying my brown eggs from a kolhoz vendor in the vegetable pavilion. Eggs were a cheap protein alternative to meat. My mother-in-law advised me to always wash eggs with warm water and soap before using them, and I continue to do this in the United States.

Canned "Pork in Aspic" from the Soviet era.

The last pavilion closest to the Daugava River offered fish. The large aquariums for freshwater fish were usually empty, but from time to time a delivery of live carp would attract delighted customers and children and me, the ever inquisitive American girl. Mostly though, (saltwater) fish was sold in large, frozen blocks. If you wanted some, a brawny-armed woman would pick up her sledgehammer and whack the frozen fish out of the block for you, as chips of ice scattered about. It appeared that many older women had a fondness for stray cats; I often saw them purchasing bags of shiny silver sardines for their kitties. The Soviet Union did not manufacture pet food, as far as I know. The fish pavilion was well stocked with canned fish, and my husband and I took a liking to canned calamari, combining it with hard-boiled eggs, Latvian mayonnaise and sour cream, and other variable ingredients for a tasty seafood salad. By the mid-1980s smoked fish would become increasingly available, and items like "Rojas gardums"—smoked flatfish—was a big hit.

On the east side of the pavilions the outdoor market space was lined with long tables, where private vendors stood or sat offering their produce for sale. They were competing with the state, the kolhozes and sovhozes, and with the city's state-owned stores. The vendors came in all shapes and sizes. They spoke Latvian and Russian and other languages as well. They came from near and far, sometimes very far. Aside from local Latvians and Russian speakers, there were Georgians, Azerbaijanis, Tadjiks—you name it. Exotic-looking vendors from the Central Asian republics with black skull caps and narrow, dark, piercing eyes set in wide faces invited me to their tables. They sold dried melon, fruits, nuts, and dates, and fresh exotic fruits, like the orange hurma and the red pomegranate. They infused the market with a special atmosphere. When they laughed, they revealed mouths full of gold. Their Mongoloid faces spoke of the steppes, of craggy mountains, of the Wild East, where Ghenghis Khan and his Golden Horde once roamed.

Raised on uniform American supermarket apples, bananas, oranges, grapes, and iceberg lettuce, I enjoyed discovering new foods at Latvia's premier market. Food in Latvia tasted raw, unadulterated, and wholesome. Ironically, I was so inexperienced in the kitchen. I embarrassed myself, when I bit into a pomegranate that a friend had given me. Knowing nothing about this strange fruit, which I had never seen before, I clamped down on it with gusto and immediately shuddered, gagging on the bitter pulp that enveloped the sweet red seeds. Since in Latvian it's called *granātābols* ("granate apple"), I assumed I could eat it like an apple.

I loved visiting the market's outdoor vendors. In the summer they offered fresh home-raised vegetables and fruit. With the advent of spring, people flocked to the market to buy planting material: flower and berry plants; tree saplings; seed potatoes; and seeds. Over time potatoes had become an important staple of the Latvian diet, and my mother-in-law was always trying new varieties in her garden. In Soviet Latvia one's diet adjusted to the seasons, and I thought it was a healthy way of eating.

In the summer the market produce was incredibly fresh and straight from the garden, ripe and ready to eat or preserve, grown without expensive pesticides and herbicides. (These poisons simply weren't readily available in the backwards Soviet economy.) By July people were buying, eating, and preserving delicious strawberries and raspberries. Even tiny wild strawberries, which perfumed the air, were for sale. Latvia's bounty was revealed in vendors' offerings of sweet, crunchy snap peas, young carrots, lettuce, pungent dill, green onions, parsley, cherries, plums, boysenberries, black currants, red currants, cranberries, hazelnuts, scrumptious mushrooms, etc. Popular herbal teas like chamomile, peppermint, spearmint, *asinszāles* (*Hypericum*), *pelaški* (yarrow), diligently picked in meadows, dried, and tied into bunches, were also for sale. The markets were a foodie's paradise. And most Latvians were foodies!

The private flower vendors in Latvia were (and still are) unlike anything I have ever seen in the United States; the blooms were always fresh and offered in dazzling arrangements. In early spring (primarily) women sold bunches of dainty, sky-blue hepatica, *purenes* (marsh marigolds), and glorious butter-yellow *sviesta bumbas* ("butter balls" [*Trollius europaeus* or globeflowers]), gathered somewhere out in the woods and wet meadows. The spring blockbusters crocuses, narcissus, and tulips in all shapes, colors, and sizes, and chubby bouquets of brilliant primroses paved the way for spectacular peonies. In May lilacs filled the parks and outskirts of Rīga with their heady aroma, and Latvians cut sprigs of the exquisite blooms to put into vases. Summer arrived with daisies, blue Bachelor's Button, and sumptuous roses. As the 1st of September and the new school year drew near, the market beckoned wth tubs of tall, majestic gladiolas.

Some market booths offered hot-house flowers and houseplants for sale; the first house-plant we purchased for our apartment was a Bird-of-Paradise plant, which we couldn't resist buying because of its exquisite orange blooms. Andris was an aesthete.

Some flowers in Latvia are special, and thinking of them triggers bittersweet memories. Few people stateside are familiar with the amazing, gorgeous *puķuzirnis* (*Lathyrus odoratus* or sweet pea), which filled our apartment with the scent of heaven in summer while mesmerizing with its soft pink, purple, and peach ruffles. Dahlias of brilliant hues, which enjoy Latvia's cool summers, spilled forth in August from the simplest of gardens like stars, like planets. But mums with their unique bittersweet aroma still evokes images of Latvia's park-like cemeteries, where people gather in late November with candles and flowers to remember the deceased and their heroes.

Rīga Central Market was a place that you could not easily leave without a flower bouquet! But speaking of flowers, Rīga's flower shops weren't bad either. And all year round, even on bitterly cold, snowy, dark days and evenings, private vendors stood by their booths near the Sakta store on Ļeņina iela hawking precious, fragile blooms in hand-made boxes warmed by flickering candles. It was magical: life, light, and beauty persisted despite the terrible darkness and cold of the Soviet winter.

Rīga Central Market also featured a bazaar, where all sorts of random household stuff—clothes, shoes, and what not—was for sale. Clothes strung up beneath canopies swayed in the wind. There was little that interested me in this part of the market, but perhaps people from faraway, more impoverished republics found something of use to bring back home. Soviet communist rule had been very unkind to many countries, cultures, and millions of people. Many people had and would continue to suffer under the Russian yoke, unfortunately. If they made it to Rīga, they saw Europe for the first time.

In February of '83 I timidly ventured into a kolhoz booth at the market, which sold high-quality fur hats, jackets, and coats. I was afraid the saleswoman didn't speak Latvian (and she didn't). Leather and fur were extremely popular in the Soviet Union, particularly among Russians, not so much among Latvians. Of course, these were expensive materials. After looking around, I overcame my timidity and purchased a black Qaraqul (or Karakul) hat. It wasn't cheap, but I had noticed the unusual material, which was said to be very warm. Qaraqul "is a hat made from the Qaraqul breed of sheep, often from the fur of aborted lamb fetuses." (Wikipedia) Accord-ing to Wikipedia, Qaraqul means "black fur" in Turkik. My hat was a version of the tall Qaraqul hats that Soviet army generals wore in winter. Qaraqul, distinguished by its brain fold look, was also popular as coat material. In this photograph from 1974, former Communist Party Central Committee General Secretary Leonid Brezhnev is wearing a Qaraqul hat. Mine was the warmest hat I have ever had, and it brought me endless enjoyment and satisfaction in the cold Rīga winters.

Not only were the market's "Zeppelin" pavilions impressive, but there were also a couple of rows of old brick warehouses called *spīķeri* nearby and on the other side of Maskavas iela near the Daugava River that attracted my attention: solid and well built, these buildings definitely held vintage appeal and were apparently still used for storage.

According to Spikeri.lv, a website devoted to the warehouse quarter near Rīga Central Market, since the 14th century this area served as a location for the loading/unloading of cargo from ships. The German word for these buildings was Hanf-Ambaren or "hemp warehouses." The warehouses were constructed mostly in the 1860s-1880s after the demolition of Old Rīga's fortified walls. Of about 55 warehouses only 13 have survived. The tan brick structures were designed in one of the more formal styles of the 19th century, eclecticism, which at that time was very popular for industrial and storage buildings. The Spīķeri quarter was developed according to designs by architects Karl Felsko, Friedrich Hess, Robert Pflug, Reinhold Schmaeling, and Jānis Baumanis. (Over time) the warehouses lost their functional role. (...) There was a plan to redesign the remaining warehouses into residential buildings, and in 1929 building engineer Teodors Hermanovskis (1883–1964) converted one warehouse into a five-story residential house. (It was later torn down along with two other warehouses.) The Spīķeri quarter changed completely when the construction of the market commenced. Most of the warehouses were demolished to make room for the market. Some of the warehouses were altered to meet the needs of Rīga Central Market.

Our Latvian world was quite small. I'm quite sure I was in the same cabin at Latvian camp with Teodors Hermanovskis' granddaughter in 1976... Hermanovskis was yet another Latvian forced to abandon his native land during World War II; he ended up in United States and settled in the New York area. He died in New Jersey in 1964. According to Wikipedia, Hermanovkis helped design about 100 buildings in Rīga. In the 1980s these old warehouses, lined in neat blocks that stretched toward the Daugava, looked abandoned. Maybe they weren't. When I strolled past them, I pictured their potential.

As I shuffled through the market's busy pavilions, slowly making my rounds and adding purchases, my cloth sack got heavier and heavier. Soviet citizens were certainly in better shape than many Americans just from carrying heavy shopping bags long distances. They did this on an almost daily basis, as they rushed from store to store or from the market to home. Ironically, this was a greener society; plastic bags were hard to come by and were washed and reused. Many people did not own a car, so they made use of their feet and the cheap, excellent public transportation. I became used to lugging home two sacks of market purchases, building up my muscles and stamina. Often I felt a great sense of accomplishment: shopping was hard physical work in Rīga! I was growing up quickly.

Even on my first Latvian winter's bleakest days my outlook remained bright. Everything in Rīga was so different, that there was no time to dwell on the easy life I had left behind. I had to "grab (Soviet) life by the horns," so to speak, to adjust as quickly as possible. My stomach was adjusting to the local food, too. No more bananas and yogurt. Now it was apples and kefir. On the whole, for the 17 years that I was there, my diet in Latvia was healthy, natural, and wholesome. We did not consume processed foods, which are full of sugar and sodium. Most of what we ate was homemade with fresh, perishable ingredients. Fresh-pressed cranberry juice was an excellent substitute for orange juice and probably a lot healthier; cranberries were harvested in small quantities, sometimes by a single person squishing about in a bog. I bought the berries at the market and then squeezed them through a piece of cheesecloth, wringing out their thick, brilliant-red juice, the color of the Latvian flag.

Days of bounty: Rīga Central Market in the 1930s. Image courtesy of the National Library of Latvia collection "In Search of Lost Latvia."

We ate *a lot* of garlic. When I had a cold, my husband taught me to cut up a clove of garlic and insert tiny slivers in my nostrils. This procedure tickled my nose, triggering sneezing episodes that brought me considerable relief. In the winter of 1983 my husband also introduced me to briar rosehip syrup, touted as a Vitamin C supplement, and to a popular supplement called *Buļļa asinis* ("Bull's Blood" or Hematogen), which was great for anemic people. It looked like a snack bar, tasted like chocolate, and was made from cow's blood. I had no qualms about eating it and quickly overcame my American leeriness of "strange" foods, even acquiring a taste for cow's tongue with tangy horseradish sauce. On my long walks I popped sweet glucose tablets into my mouth; these helped me with my hypoglycemia. I was losing weight from all my walking and our simple diet; I felt great. Honey, bee pollen, garlic, cranberries, carrots, cabbage, and other natural market products became my new sources of vitamins. We drank a lot of herbal teas gathered over the summer by Biruta.

I did miss good coffee, which was impossible to find in Soviet Latvia, and I missed Nesquik and Swiss Miss for making chocolate milk and hot cocoa. But then I discovered that I could improvise: I combined confectioner's sugar and cocoa powder in our coffee mill and whipped it into a fine powder. Voilà! The powder didn't dissolve as nicely as Nesquik did, but who cared. It tasted good.

I continued to visit the so-called *valūtas* (hard currency) store on Ļeņina iela from time to time. By now the salespeople and the sullen doorman knew me well. I was the weird foreigner who didn't leave. Despite what "outsiders" (that is, the "excluded," meaning your average Soviet citizen) thought, the store wasn't that great. Many of the products, including souvenirs and chocolates, could also with luck or connections be purchased in "regular" local stores with roubles, so why spend precious dollars? I bought instant coffee at the *valūtas* store, as well as shoes (although the store's selection was limited and not to my liking). Everything was expensive. My dollars ran out at the end of January, and my father began sending us money from time to time through the mail. And I picked up more translating work. I quickly realized that more important than an expensive pair of Italian shoes and Crest toothpaste was a sense of belonging and purpose. I also discovered that so much of life is just about watching, listening, and observing. (And I don't mean TV.)

Desecration

January 1983. We have left a tiny wreath at the foot of the monument to Latvia's first Foreign Minister Zigfrīds Anna Meierovics (1887–1925) in Rīga's Meža ("Forest") Cemetery. Photo: Andris Krieviņš

If it's one thing I won't ever forgive the Soviet communist authorities (with plenty of Latvians in their ranks), it was their barbaric attempt at altering, desecrating, and purging Latvia's past—our history, our heroes, our monuments, our culture, and our achievements from the time before the war. It wasn't enough to murder or deport our brightest minds, patriots, and women and children to Siberian death camps and settlements; our people were extinguished post-mortem, their graves vandalized or even destroyed, their biographies erased from history books. And there were many people in Latvia—ethnic Latvians, Latvian Jews, Poles, etc.—that the Soviet communists didn't like.

While I was growing up in the United States learning about the Holocaust, the Baltic peoples and millions of other people and whole nations continued to suffer under Soviet totalitarianism. The crimes of Stalin and the Soviet communist state were mostly ignored in the West for decades. Why? *Why?* I had chosen to live in a criminal state ruled by hypocritical self-seekers and KGB thugs. In 1983 I began my life in *1984*, an Orwellian state not fully understood by the Free World. Communism was an ideology that could not exist in the real world without the application of brute force, that much was clear to me. It was an unnatural, unrealistic ideology that crippled the societies it penetrated, warping minds and destroying decades and centuries of progress. These realizations dawned on me very quickly as I looked around. Freedom was as important to human beings as oxygen and water. I knew.

On a very cold day in January 19 we boarded Tram No. 11 to ride out to the famous Meža ("Forest") Cemetery on the northeast side of Rīga that I had heard so much about. Andris wanted to show me around and take photographs of some monuments. Along the way we disembarked to get a look at an old and spooky graveyard called Lielie kapi ("Great Cemetery"). Andris warned me that the notable cemetery had suffered greatly under the Soviets. It became quickly evident that this cemetery deserved hours of investigation. The more we looked, the sadder we became. Sadness and shock turned into anger.

(Left) The cemetery of Rīga's German Lutheran churches and the Reformierte (Reformed) Church, now known as Great Cemetery, in a drawing by Johann Christof Brotze in 1796. Depicted is the cemetery's first so-called Green Chapel. The same chapel as it looks today. (Image courtesy of the National Library of Latvia collection "In Search of Lost Latvia.")

According to Wikipedia, Rīga's Great Cemetery spans 22 hectares and includes Jēkaba ("St. John's Catholic") Cemetery and the Russian Pokrova Cemetery. Great Cemetery was established in 1773. It was the final resting place of many of Rīga's Baltic Germans who died between 1773 and 1944, including famous Livonian documentalist and artist Johann Christof Brotze (d. 1823). Many famous Latvians were also laid to rest there, including: "the father of the Latvian daina" Krišjānis Barons; first Latvian architect Jānis Frīdrichs Baumanis; painter Jāzeps Grosvalds; linguist Kārlis Mīlenbachs; writer Andrejs Pumpurs; and spiritual leader of the first Latvian "Awakening" in the 19th century, Krišjānis Valdemārs. Soldiers of the German Wermacht who had died in Soviet captivity were also buried in a corner. Yet the old graveyard, a sacred sanctuary and embodiment (literally) of Rīga's history and culture, looked deserted and spooky. Shadowy entrances to abandoned, vandalized mausoleums yawned like the gaping mouths of the dead: a perfect setting for "Tales from the Crypt." I would not have been surprised if the eerie place was haunted.

Great Cemetery's list of "illustrious bones" gives us an idea of just how important this graveyard is to history of Rīga and Latvia. The following are random excerpts from a fascinating Wikipedia article about the cemetery (Tr. RL):

Origin
Great Cemetery started out in 1773 as a burial ground for the victims of the bubonic plague, which killed off many people in Russia's Baltic provinces in 1770–1772.

Famous people
Tens of thousands of Rigans have been laid to rest in Great Cemetery, although it is impossible to determine the precise number, because the cemetery's books have not survived in full. Among the notables: Latvian folklore researcher, writer, translator **Fricis Brīvzemnieks**, *left* (1846–1907); writer, teacher, and Lutheran minister **Juris Neikens** (1826–1868); composer and conductor **Nikolajs Alunāns** (1859–1919); famous architects **Christoph Haberland**, *right* (1750–1803), **Jānis Frīdrichs Baumanis**, **Kristaps Morbergs** (1844–1928), **Johann Daniel**

Felsko (1813–1902); painter and renowned portraitist **Jānis Staņislavs Roze** (1823–1897); members of the **(Friedrich Wilhelm**, 1779–1862) **Brederlo** family whose art collection would become the basis for Latvia's Foreign Art Museum (now part of the Art Museum "Rīga Bourse"); art historian and Latvian National Art Museum founder and first director, architect, and art historian **Johann Wilhelm Carl Neumann**, *left* (1849–1919); Africa specialist and explorer, botanist, and geographer **Georg August Schweinfurth** (1836–1925); botanist and author of the atlas *Baltische Landeskunde* (1910) **Karl Reinhold Kupffer**, *left* (1872–1935); zoologist **Carl Greve** (1854–1916), first director of the Rīga Zoo; physician and historian **Otto von Huhn** (1764–1832); **Karl von Löwis of**  **Menar** (1855–1930), an expert on Latvia's castles from the Middle Ages; 1909 Nobel Laureate in Chemistry **Wilhelm Ostwald** (1853–1932); Russian painter **Sergey Vinogradov** (1869–1938); president of the Rīga Society of Naturalists at the end of the 19th century, **Gothard Schweder** (1831–1915); the mayors of Rīga; clergymen murdered by Latvian communist Pēteris Stučka's Bolshevik government; (Russian Orthodox) Archbishop **Jānis Pommers** (1876–1934), canonized in 2001; Vilnius and Lithuanian Metropolitan **Sergey Voskresensky**; Rīga merchant, mayor, art collector **Ludwig Wilhelm Kerkovius** (1831–1904); engineer, entrepreneur, and fourth Mayor of Rīga and the city's modernizer **George Armitstead** (1847–1912); famous Roma clairvoyant **Eižens Finks** (1885–1958), *right*, said to have correctly predicted numerous events, etc.

Apparently Finks lived at Raiņa bulvāris 3 from 1932 on; this was the same building in which my relatives lived and with whom I stayed in 1980 during my first visit to Latvia. Finks' fame and reputation live on; I heard the soothsayer mentioned numerous times, as if Latvians were relying on him to destroy the Soviet Union.

> For decades following World War II, Great Cemetery was vandalized: gravestones, fences, monuments, and wrought-iron decorations simply vanished, believed to have been stolen to decorate private homes or to be melted down. These losses included unique stone sculptures, the likes of which can't be found anywhere else in Latvia.
>
> The destruction of the cemetery already began during World War II when graves were dug up and family vaults were vandalized in search of valuables; granite and marble monuments were broken off and hauled away. Right after the war a large group of robbers established themselves in the cemetery's "brick vaults," terrorizing people in the surrounding neighborhood. When their hideout was discovered, the bandits repelled the militsiya (Soviet police) with machine guns, which inflicted damage on the surrounding monuments. The destruction of the cemetery continued unabated for years despite an ongoing investigation. Soviet law enforcement officials turned a blind eye to the desecration of German soldiers' graves.
>
> Burials at Great Cemetery ceased completely in 1969 following a Rīga Executive Council order. What followed were years of systematic and individually inflicted

destruction of the cemetery. The (Latvian) press has associated the destruction of Great Cemetery with Soviet (Russian) immigration. (Russian) immigrants could not relate to local cultural and historical traditions. In addition, they did not represent their own Russian society's learned segment. Even if they did not harbor a distinct hatred towards all things German, they lacked the "moral brakes" (to abstain from vandalism) and interest in preserving their surroundings. Gravestones and metal fences were carted away and re-installed in nearby private gardens. In 1953 the director of Great Cemetery was put on trial for selling gravestones and monuments.

On April 23, 1969, following the adoption of Decree No. 153, it was decided that Great Cemetery would be partly leveled to make room for a memorial park called "Great Cemetery," which would span 34 hectares. A special commission was set up to classify the cemetery's monuments into "protected" and "unprotected" (read "worthless") objects, with the latter slated for destruction.

Following Decree No. 331, issued by the Latvian SSR Council of Ministers on June 14, 1982, Great Cemetery was placed under the Society for the Protection of Nature and Monuments. Under the society's leadership the cemetery was turned into a semi-official quarry and source of iron for professional and amateur sculptors. (Many sculptures produced during this time period were made from material procured at the cemetery.) The society sanctioned the demolition of three crypts and petitioned to tear down an additional 11 crypts.

Dendrological material
More than 60 species of trees and bushes can be found on the grounds of Great Cemetery; of these 39 are so-called introduced species, including Japanese larch (*Larix kaempferi*), dwarf almond (*Amygdalus nana*), Crimean lime (*Tilia x euchlora*), northern white cedar (*Thuja occidentalis*), Siberian elm (*Ulmus pumila*), etc.
(Source: Lielie kapi. Feb. 2017. < https://lv.wikipedia.org/wiki/Lielie_kapi>)

Need I stress the historical, cultural, and artistic value of Great Cemetery? Besides the interesting crypts, many of its beautiful monuments were produced in the studio/workshop of sculptor August Volz (1851–1926), as well as at the iron foundry of L. Lācis (founded in 1897) and other firms. That day my fiancé told me that at one point many graves were simply bulldozed, and countless grave markers were lost in the brutal, careless process. A small, headless angel would end up at Paulēni, the Krieviņš family's summer place in the countryside, rescued from a pile of rubble by Juris and Andris.

Great Cemetery in its eerie, abandoned state was a silent indictment of the Soviets' crude and barbaric destruction of Latvia's historical memory, art, architecture, and culture. Vandals and drunks continued to inflict damage on what was left. Desecrating the final resting places and memorials of the deceased was an egregious offense, in my opinion. Although the monuments to most of the famous Latvians were still intact, much of the cemetery had been razed. Apparently the paranoid communists were even afraid of the dead.

Rīga's Great Cemetery once was and could have been an extraordinary monument to our capital's unique and illustrious history; it could have been Rīga's Père Lachaise. Of course, in a way it still was, but from all appearances the cemetery had been left to fend for itself. And the dead are defenseless, as we know. Many of the people laid to rest there had been unique Rigans with notable biographies and important roles in the life of the city, as I would later learn in my research. In the winter of 1983 the fate of Rīga's Great Cemetery appeared tragic.

The following is an excerpt from Anita Zvirgzde's interview with Eižens Upmanis, Director of the Supervisory Board of the Brothers' Cemetery and the Freedom Monument, in the daily *Neatkarīgā Cīņa*, June 17, 1994:

> While at school, I was working at the Ministry of Culture, and I took part in the meetings of the Ministry's Methodological Council, which was discussing what (historical) monuments to preserve. I clearly remember one H. Verners, Deputy Minister of Culture, who emphasized that *we shouldn't preserve too many monuments in Great Cemetery, because we would eventually have to explain why certain monuments were saved.* This was the idea that set the tone of our discussion, and everyone adhered to it. I remember how the reactionaries crossed the monument to Matīss Ārons off the list. (Ārons, 1858-1939, was a Latvian teacher, journalist, bibliographer, and literary critic.—RL) Mostly the graves of historical persons were discussed. (…) This was the approach to Great Cemetery in 1975.
> (Source: http://kristusdraudze.lelb.lv/?ct=rakstsnckapi)

Time and time again I was forced to think about Homo Sovieticus, a term used to describe the average Soviet person, a product of Soviet communist indoctrination. Rootless, restless, and hungry for a higher standard of living in another people's space, hordes of Homo Sovieticus were pouring into Latvia from Russia, trampling our history and cultural legacy. Sneeringly, they called Latvians fascists; according to them, we Balts were undeserving of our own space and our dignity. Latvians, of course, attached a nationality to this unfortunate people, the spawn of generations that had suffered under their society's organs of repression. These migrants had no clear sense of home, history, or culture. By and large they were fortune seekers. In the Soviet grand scheme of things, places like Great Cemetery were not worthy of attention and thus better destroyed. The vandalism was tolerated, if not openly welcomed. Great Cemetery was a perfect contrast between the order and flow of the past and the organized chaos of the Soviet world, in which nobody owned anything and nobody owed anything to the history that predated the Soviet occupation. (Source: Wikipedia. "Lielie kapi." <<http://lv.wikipedia.org/wiki/Lielie_kapi>> 2/10/2014. Tr. RL)

As we boarded the tram to continue our excursion, again I felt sad. Latvian men had been emasculated under the Soviets communists. It started with President Ulmanis' order to the Latvian Army in June 1940 not to resist the Soviet Red Army, which was rolling in: in other words, a full-scale invasion was underway, but the army would turn a blind eye. An agonizing decision for the President, no doubt: despite his "dictatorship," often called fascist, Ulmanis was a patriot. By noon the following day Russian tanks had reached Rīga. Ulmanis' infamous words to the people of Latvia, "I will stay in my place, you stay in yours," are still divisive. Four decades later I saw that my countrymen were mostly helpless and weak, robbed of any say in matters of vital importance to our nation and its future.

The Soviet totalitarian system sucked in the weak in spirit and individuals whose moral compass was damaged; at least that was how I saw it. The system was brutal and effective. All around me I was seeing signs of decay and amnesia. Those people with the resolve to remember, cherish, and try to preserve the past were heroes to me. There were many such people despite outward appearances. But did an old cemetery really matter? Questions about the preservation of history and historical landmarks in Latvia continue to haunt me.

Art in the Forest

A couple of stops later, we disembarked near the Aizsaules ("Afterworld") iela entrance to Forest Cemetery and purchased a tiny wreath from the flower ladies. Andris jokingly said he hoped the wreath was "fresh": that is, that the flowers weren't recycled from freshly dug graves... We then proceeded into the enormous compound, which was established in 1913, because Great Cemetery was running out of space. Andris seemed to know his way around. We were not being followed; we made sure of that.

Gently winding paths led us into a vast, green oasis. We passed beautiful headstones with poetic inscriptions and sculptural monuments marking the final resting place of Latvian artists, composers, musicians, actors, writers and poets, and public figures. And ordinary people. *My people*. As we walked in soft silence, I was suddenly overcome by a wonderful sense of communion. Of course, this was what I had been missing in my life until now. Robert Frost's quiet poem about the woods came back to me. Here all was lovely, dark, and deep.

Forest Cemetery was an active cemetery with fresh graves, flowers, and signs of tender care, evident in the carefully raked sand. We spent time reading some of the epitaphs inscribed in our mother tongue. Forest Cemetery was a tranquil sanctuary. It was also very green, even in winter, with an enormous variety of evergreens, undulating hills covered with ivy, vinca, and other ground covers, ornamental bushes, trees, and the pines, which towered above us, sighing. Forest Cemetery is an astounding repository of art, with hundreds if not thousands of beautiful sculptures and monuments crafted out of stone and metal.

Andris was interested in showing me the cemetery's "forbidden" parts: those that were linked to Latvia's pre-war political past and to Soviet atrocities. The latter included the "White Cross" burial site, where about 120 victims of Soviet atrocities were laid to rest in 1941. The crosses remained standing until 1969, when the Soviet authorities had them removed. New burials were made on top of the remains of the victims of the Soviet NKVD. But Latvians remembered their history and knew their cemetery. According to historian Uldis Neiburgs, the Soviets did not like the fact that the gravesite had been established during the Nazi occupation of Latvia, and that people continued to place flowers in the area, marked by a large pine tree, which the Soviets cut down.

Left: A photograph from July 6, 1942 of the White Crosses, which mark the burial spot of victims of Soviet terror. Source: Museum of the Occupation of Latvia 1940–1991.

Sixty of the 98 victims discovered at Rīga Central Prison at the beginning of July, 1941 were on the so-called Shustin List, now on display at the Museum of the Occupation of Latvia. This document contains the names of 78 people and LSSR State Security Chief Semyon Shustin's June 26, 1941 written order "to shoot them all on account of their threat to (Soviet) society."

This list was discovered at Rīga Central Prison after the Red Army had been driven out. The list of names of the victims also reveals the absurdity of the charges. Several of the people had been arrested on the night of June 23–24, 1941: their only "crime" was the celebration of Līgo— the Latvian summer solstice.

> The Soviet NKVD alleged that 56-year-old retired Latvian Army Colonel Nikolajs Fogelmanis had "started a bonfire in his yard, which helped the German aviation direct its bombs and destroy objects," but Viktors Somovičs "was singing fascist songs on the street, thereby mocking the Soviet system." Well known Latvian School Department Deputy Director Arnolds Čuibe and his son, architect Arnolds Nikolajs Čuibe, were "engaging in espionage by signaling to the German aviation during an air raid." Actually, on the day of their arrest, June 27, father and son had been standing by an open window smoking. Minna Elerbuša and Kazimirs Burneiko were accused of possessing "fascist swastikas," but four Jews—Jāzeps Kagans, Eduards Genohs, and Nisons and Dina Trubeka—were accused of "supporting the German Army." They were sentenced "for high treason" according to Paragraph 58 of the Criminal Code of the Russian Soviet Federative Socialist Republic, although as Latvian citizens they had "become" Soviet citizens only after Latvia's occupation and annexation to the Soviet Union in 1940. (Source: Uldis Neiburgs. "Baltie krusti čekas upuriem." ["White Crosses for the Cheka's Victums"] Tvnet.lv. Published June 30, 2006. Retrieved 2/10/2014 <http://www.tvnet.lv/zinas/latvija/186648-baltie_krusti_cekas_upuriem> Tr. RL)

Thus we made our way along the winding paths, until we came upon a lovely memorial dedicated to Latvia's first Foreign Minister Zigfrīds Anna Meierovics (1887–1925). The monument depicted a woman in mourning, dressed in a traditional Latvian folk costume, her hair pleated in two thick braids, her head bowed and hands clasped... Mother Latvia... Meierovics was born in Durbe, Latvia to a Jewish doctor, Chaim Meierovics, and a Latvian woman, Anna Filholde, who died while giving birth. Sickened by grief, the father was unable to care for his son. Meierovics was raised by his maternal uncle.

Schooled in business and finance, Meierovics became an active and very important participant in the formation of the new Latvian Republic, eventually serving as the fledgling country's first Foreign Minister and lobbying European states to officially recognize Latvia's independence from Soviet Russia. Latvia along with its Baltic neighbors, Estonia and Lithuania, was admitted to the League of Nations in 1921. Meierovics felt that "Latvia should serve as an economic transit country between East and West, but in the political and military sense it must act as a barrier to discourage an alliance between Russia and Germany, which would give rise to new world war." Meierovics actively pursued cooperation between the three Baltic States, Poland, and Finland. Tragically, his life and good intentions were cut short on August 22, 1925 in a car accident in Kurzeme. The Republic of Latvia lost an exceptionally talented and devoted statesman that day. The Soviets frowned on the memory of this man. Andris took a photograph of me standing by the monument. (Source: Arveds Švābe. *Latvian Encyclopedia, Volume II Kangari-Piegula*. Stockholm: Trīs Zvaigznes, 1952–1953. P. 1654)

Next we visited the monument to Latvia's first President Jānis Čakste (1859–1927), a brick semi-circle with Čakste's portrait in in the center. Latvians were still placing candles near the monument on All Souls' Day in late November in spite of KGB thugs lurking nearby, waiting to round up and haul away these "nationalists." It was a game of cat and mouse. That day in January there was nobody around and we were able to get a good look at the memorial, which showed obvious signs of neglect.

Our final destination was the Brothers' Cemetery (or Cemetery of the Brethren), *left*, a national monument designed by sculptor Kārlis Zāle (1888–1942) and architects Aleksandrs Birzenieks (1893–1980) and Pēteris Feders (1891–1980), as well as garden architect Andrejs Zeidaks (1874–1964). (Zāle also designed the Freedom Monument in downtown Rīga.) The memorial incorporated the original design of Zeidaks, Rīga's chief landscape artist, for the graves of Latvia's fallen soldiers who were laid to rest there in 1915. As the military conflict had escalated, more and more soldiers were buried side by side. An old photograph shows a field of white crosses in what would later become the Brothers' Cemetery.

With its first fallen, Latvian *strēlnieki* ("riflemen") and freedom fighters Andrejs Stūris (1895–1915), Jēkabs Voldemārs Timma (1896–1915), *right*, and Jānis Gavenas (1895–1915), the Brothers' Cemetery would grow into a national memorial of enormous symbolic significance for Latvians. It would come to represent our nation's sacrifices in the struggle for freedom and self-determination. The cemetery was consecrated on November 11 (Lāčplēsis or Bearslayer Day), 1936. It is the final resting place of about 2,000 Latvians killed between 1915 and 1920 during World War I and the Latvian War of Independence (1918–1920). The remains of some soldiers of the Latvian Legion, a World War II formation, and some recipients of the Latvian Order of Lāčplēsis (conferred on individuals for extraordinary military merit and valor during the War of Independence), were also moved to the site. Kārlis Zāle and architect Aleksandrs Birzenieks are interred there. It is a beautiful, powerful, stirring memorial, with large sculptures of Latvian warriors and their steeds and the tall figure of Mother Latvia standing over her fallen sons. These men's sacrifices ensured Latvia's freedom from Russia and Germany, our historical archenemies. (Source: "Rīgas brāļu kapi." Retrieved 2/11/2014. <http://lv.wikipedia.org/wiki/R%C4%ABgas_Br%C4%81%C4%BCu_kapi> Tr. RL)

We approached the cemetery along a walkway lined on both sides by linden trees. The Soviets had buried high-ranking Russian military officers along the walkway in a grassy area never intended for burials. This action essentially defiled the grounds near the "Eternal Flame," an urn with a perpetually burning flame, and the memorial itself. Typical Soviet Russian style: an unabashed alteration of historical truth...

It was telling that later that year in autumn (1983), when we returned to this spot on the evening of All Souls' Day, not a single candle burned near the graves of the Soviet military brass.

Yet hundreds of candles shimmered and flickered in the darkness by the graves of the Latvian soldiers who had given their lives for our freedom so long ago. They were not forgotten by their grateful nation.

> In October 1944 Nazi Germany's regime in Rīga was replaced by the Soviet occupying forces. Rīga's Brothers' Cemetery was again subjected to an ideological transformation. All activities at the cemetery that were not sanctioned by the new communist authorities were strictly forbidden. With a few exceptions, up until 1958 there were no new burials at the Brothers' Cemetery. Word leaked out that the Soviet authorities were planning on turning the Brothers' Cemetery into a "proletariats' recreation park," similar in concept to what would transpire at Rīga's historical Great Cemetery. At this time Soviet authorities were removing or destroying many monuments and memorial places in Latvia that had something to do with the War of Independence and Latvia as a sovereign state. (Miraculously) the Soviet authorities did not (bulldoze) the Brothers' Cemetery; however, they removed several symbols that were incompatible with Soviet ideology.
>
> One of the first alterations was done at the entrance to the memorial. The coat of arms of the Republic of Latvia and two crosses were removed in 1959 and replaced by a wreath of oak leaves. The inscription "1915–1920" was changed to "1915–1945." The (Christian) cross at the foot of the monument of Mother Latvia was filled in; until then it had been concealed by the flag of the Latvian Soviet Socialist Republic during public events.
>
> In 1958 the Soviet authorities passed a new statute, which declared that henceforth only Soviet military and Communist Party functionaries would be interred at the Brothers' Cemetery, thereby degrading the original concept of the memorial.
>
> The Soviet authorities never ceased to regard Rīga's Brothers' Cemetery as an ideologically dangerous memorial. Any gatherings there were interpreted as insubordination, which is why public gatherings at the memorial were simply forbidden, as well as the lighting of candles and the placement of flowers at the "wrong" graves. Officially, the Soviet authorities acknowledged the great cultural and historical significance of the memorial, yet in reality, up until independence, they continued to degrade it. Their aim was to make Latvians forget the importance of this memorial to the freedom of Latvia. Despite these attempts, Latvians continued to visit the memorial on dates associated with the Republic of Latvia, leaving candles and flowers (to honor their heroes). (Source: Ciganovs, Juris. "Rīgas Brāļu kapu memoriālajam ansamblim — 75." Tēvijas sargs. Published October 26, 2011. Retrieved 2/11/2014. <http://www.sargs.lv/Vesture/Vesture/2 011/10/26-01.aspx#lastcomment> Tr. RL)

I will always remember my years of Latvian schooling in the US and our teachers' emphasis on August 11, 1920 as the signing of the Latvian-Soviet Peace Treaty, by which (communist) Russia (aka the USSR) swore to "forever" abandon any territorial claims on Latvia. Latvia's War of Independence was an enormous and truly heroic effort on the part of an army of young, scrappy volunteers to defeat the Germans on one side and the Russian Bolsheviks on the other. In these valiant efforts the Latvians succeeded brilliantly. Their sacrifices paved the way for the birth of the Republic of Latvia. Their earthly remains at the Brothers' Cemetery and elsewhere in Latvia reminded Latvians of their heroes' valor and sacrifice. Thus this cemetery, a national memorial, was an unpleasant reminder to the Soviet communist authorities of the will of the Latvian people, as well as of their own broken promise.

Another concrete example of this Soviet denigration of Latvian history was the disappearance of a modest monument by the side of the Pskov (now Vidzemes) Highway near the town of Ieriķi. Dedicated on May 6, 1934, it marked the grave of an unknown Latvian soldier. It was carved out of stone by a forest ranger named A. Kaņeps. In 1983 it was still standing: I perchanced to spot it in a brief flash, as we drove by on our way to Piebalga. In the summer of 1984 it vanished. The empty spot grated on our nerves each time we passed it; the memorial's removal seemed positively indecent. Juris Krieviņš said that some overzealous locals were to blame: they did the dirty work for the Soviets. This sort of treasonous behavior made me cringe.

In the 1980s I would hear many disturbing stories about Soviet (read Russian) vandalism and intentional destruction, especially within the confines of the many Soviet Army firing ranges and training grounds scattered throughout Latvia, in which houses and even churches were used for target practice. At the Soviet firing range in Zvārde, Kurzeme the Soviet military used the Zvārde and Ķērkliņu churches as targets and bulldozed the cemetery.* Although nearly powerless, there were vigilant Latvians who took note and saved what they could.

Monument to the Latvian fallen in the War of Independence in Jaunpiebalga. Image courtesy of the National Library of Latvia collection "In Search of Lost Latvia."

I saw other memorials that had remained miraculously unscathed, such as the memorial to Latvia's freedom fighters who had been members of the St. Thomas' Lutheran Church in Jaunpiebalga (*left*). The memorial was dedicated on June 29, 1930 by then Latvian President Alberts Kviesis (1881–1944). According to the Latvian Ministry of Defense, it was designed by sculptor Kārlis Zāle and architect Aleksandrs Birzenieks, the authors of the Brothers' Cemetery. On that day in June the people on hand for the dedication had planted 500 young oaks in remembrance of their local heroes. An inscription on one side of the memorial says: *"Mūžam nerims varoņu gars"* ("Heroes' souls will never die"); on the other side *"Brīvības cīņās kritušiem"* ("To those who fell in the War of Independence"). St. Thomas', consecrated in 1804, was repeatedly vandalized in the Soviet era, its windows smashed, its organ broken, its attributes stolen, according to the Latvian Evangelical Lutheran Church website (www.LELB.lv).

Chapter sources:

* Pētersone, Ilze. "Kā aviācijas bumbas krita no skaidrām debesīm." Lauku Avīze Online. December 6, 2013. Retrieved February 11, 2014. <http://www.la.lv/bumba-no-skaidram-debesim>

"Old Friends" (Bookends) and
the Magic of Ramave

Can you imagine us / Years from today, / Sharing a park bench quietly? / How terribly strange / To be seventy. / Old friends, / Memory brushes the same years, / Silently sharing the same fear...—Simon and Garfunkel

---

Right: Jānis Endzelīns in his youth. (Family photograph archive)

"Neviens, kas grib latviski pareizi runāt un rakstīt, nedrīkst neinteresēties par tautasdziesmu valodu tai apjomā, kādā tā vēl tagad mums der par paraugu. Jo mūsu vecās tautasdziesmas ir vienīgais latviešu valodas gluži dzidrais avots, tās valodas, ko izbijušos laikos ir runājuši latvieši, kas nei paši pratuši kādu svešu valodu, nei bijuši ciešos sakaros ar ļaudīm, kuru runā ieviesušies dažādi ģermānismi un slavismi."

("Nobody who wants to speak and write Latvian correctly can afford not to take an interest in the language of our folk songs, which still serve as an example. Our old folk songs are the only pure wellspring of the Latvian language, of the language that Latvians spoke when they knew no foreign languages, when they had no contact with people whose speech was permeated by certain Germanisms or Slavisms.")—Jānis Endzelīns

"Vietvārdi ir it kā kāds zemes archīvs, kas līdzīgi dokumentu archīvam var sniegt ziņas par bijušiem laikiem."

("Place names are like an archive of the land, which, just like an archive of written documents, can provide us with information about the past.")—Jānis Endzelīns

A letter to my family in the US, February 8, 1983:

The window is open. A fat chimney is spewing smoke; it feels like Old Rīga is sitting in a cloud. I can hear pigeons cooing on our windowsill, city noises rising up from the street. Today I could finally go outside without a hat. We ran out of money and have tightened our belts. For two weeks we have subsisted on white food: Farmer's Cheese; milk; kefir; sour cream; rice; pale butter. Our only dark morsels are rye bread. Eleven kopecks for half a loaf, but boy is it good! I hope to find translating work to bring in some money. Until now my work has all been pro bono. Uldis Bērziņš's text for sculptor Ojārs Feldbergs' catalogue. An application form to a show for artist Gunārs Zemgalis. Of course, I'm happy to help out where I can. Thanks for the thesaurus! Yesterday I ran over to the Academy to hand Professor Upītis our wedding invitation. My talks with the Art Academy are at a standstill. Everything hinges on citizenship. They tell me that as a foreigner I am not allowed to study here or in Tallinn. I guess I'll wait a year and see what happens. March 4 is bearing down on us. I'm still here! I haven't left! I can't wait to see Piebalga! From the photographs I've seen, it looks like the most beautiful place in the world. Please send me some hair elastics! And photographs from home, of New York, of yourselves! Oh, and I met some of Mimmī and Tuks' old friends. Gosh, they're a wonderful bunch! Laima

Left: Ancient Romuva. Source: https://commons.wikimedia.org/wiki/File:Romuva_sanctuary.jpg © Public Domain

"Romuva or Romowe (known as Rickoyoto in the writings of Simon Grunau) was an alleged pagan worship place (a temple or a sacred area) in the western part of Sambia, one of the regions of pagan Prussia. In contemporary sources the temple was mentioned only once by Peter von Dusburg in 1326. According to his account, Kriwe, the chief priest or 'pagan pope,' lived at Romuva and ruled over the religion of all the Balts. According to Simon Grunau the temple was central to Prussian mythology. Even though there are considerable doubts about whether such a place actually existed, the Lithuanian neo-pagan movement Romuva borrowed its name from the temple." This drawing was created after the 16th century account of Simon Grunau, a Dominican priest and the author of *Preussische Chronik*, a history of Prussia. (Source: "Romuva—Temple." Wikipedia: <https://en.wikipedia.org/wiki/Romuva_%28temple%29>)

Left: The University of Latvia in a photograph from the late 19th century. Image courtesy of the National Library of Latvia collection "In Search of Lost Latvia."

In 1983 some of my maternal grandparents' old-time friends from Ramave were still alive. Ramave was an academic organization founded in 1929 at the University of Latvia for students of Baltic philology. In fact, my maternal grandfather Jānis Bičolis was one of its founders. "It was an organization that was active (…) until 1940, with about 70 members and later, beginning in the 1950s, with about 200 members in exile. Ramave organized lectures, published journals, and promoted the scientific research and social life of students of philology." Its motto, according to Kārlis Zvejnieks, was: "Friendship, aspiration, work." (Rīgas latviešu biedrība, www.RL.lv).

Unlike Latvian fraternities, Ramave was for men and women. And unlike Latvian fraternities, which were modeled on German fraternities and their traditions, including many German student songs, Ramave turned to Latvian traditional folk songs for inspiration.

Growing up in the company of my grandparents, I heard them mention some of the old *ramavieši* ("Ramavians") from time to time. Even in exile, my grandfather furthered the aims of the organization, which the communists had destroyed with the stroke of a pen in 1940. The eminent professors Jānis Endzelins, Jānis Kauliņš, Ludis Bērziņš, Anna Ābele, and other renowned Latvian linguists had been Ramave's honorary members, and my grandparents had known them personally. I have a couple of photographs of this tight-knit, lively group of Latvians who devoted their time to the study of the Latvian language and Baltic philology. I sensed that they had shared a warm camaraderie.

According to my mother, Ramave was like a friendly "club": members met in informal settings for discussion, debates, and to socialize. Students were active in field work interviewing people throughout Latvia, especially old folks, to track down old words and their meanings. At the end of each school year the *ramaviesi* took excursions to the countryside, visiting the birth places/homes of people notable for their contributions to Latvian culture. Many of them became friends for life. Ramave even produced new couples who married and started families, like my grandparents. *Ramaviesi* Krišjānis Ancītis and Kārlis Kurcalts were my mother's godfathers. Ramave published the journal *Ceļi* ("Paths"), devoted to academic discourse on Baltic philology, folklore, and ethnography. My grandfather Jānis Bičolis was one of the journal's founders, a regular contributor, and would later become its editor in exile.

Like other Latvian non-governmental organizations and associations, Ramave was shut down in 1940 by the communists who had an inherent distrust of any organizations other than their own. According to Kārlis Zvejnieks, "Several *ramaviesi* were arrested, many perished in Siberia, the organization was liquidated, and any association was strictly forbidden." Many of Ramave's members sought refuge in exile in the West. No doubt the Soviet occupation was a very frightening time for my grandparents. (Zvejnieks, Kārlis. "Ramaves 70 gadi." *Universitātes Avīze.* November 5, 1999. <http://foto.lu.lv/avize/19981999/ua16/ramave.htm>)

> (...) Everywhere the Red Army went, Soviet and local communists harassed, persecuted, and eventually banned many of the independent organizations of what we could now call civil society: the Polish Women's League, the German "anti-fascist" groupings, church groups, and schools. In particular, they were fixated, from the very days of the occupation, on youth groups: young social democrats; young Catholic or Protestant organizations, Boy Scouts and Girl Scouts. Even before they banned independent political parties for adults, and even before they outlawed church organizations and independent trade unions, they put young people's organizations under the strictest possible observation and restraint.—Anne Applebaum, *Iron Curtain*. (Applebaum, Anne. Iron Curtian. New York: Doubleday, 2012. P. xxix.)

Ramave was renewed in exile, its far-flung members tried to keep in touch, and *Ceļi* was published outside of Latvia. *Ramaviesi* pursued their interests and published their findings in books and periodicals in exile. However, Ramave's central figure Jānis Endzelīns, an academic revered by his students for his intellect, encyclopedic memory, and unforgettable lectures, suffered humiliation in the new era of the proletariat in Latvia:

The Soviet communist authorities' attitude towards Endzelīns deserves a separate story to describe how superficial praise in fact masked his ousting from the University of Latvia, the liquidation of the Department of Baltic Philology that he founded, and the systematic erosion of his legacy. In the early 1940s Endzelīns had prepared a revised and expanded edition of his book *Lettische Grammatik* ("Latvian Grammar"), but the Soviet authorities did not allow him to send it to German publishers, questioning the need for publishing the book abroad. At the same time they refused to publish it in Latvia, claiming there was no need for such a tome in the German language. According to Pēteris Kļaviņš, the Soviet authorities urged Endzelīns to translate this work into Latvian, but the author declined, saying he had other work to do, and that he no longer had the strength to undertake such an endeavor. Translators at the Liesma publishing house assumed this task. Some of the translations were bad. (...)

After the war Endzelīns' former colleague and and a contributor to the expanded edition of the (Kārlis) Mīlenbachs Dictionary, Edīte Hauzenbera-Šturma, who was working at Bonn University, was contacted by Vinter, a German publishing house. They wanted to know how they could get in touch with Endzelīns, as they were receiving repeated requests for his (*Lettische*) *Grammatik*. The publishing house sent a letter to Endzelīns in 1960 but never received an answer. "Of course, the Soviet censors weren't passing this 'unnecessary' mail on to Endzelīns," said Pēteris Kļaviņš, who would later go through Endzelīns' entire correspondence but failed to find such a letter. Hauzenberga-Šturma received another letter from the publisher in 1969, which requested her help in finding Endzelīns' heirs, because another large scientific publishing house in Paris had published a translation of Endzelīns' comparative study of Baltic languages into English and wished also to publish *Lettische Grammatik*. This letter, too, went unanswered. („Mazrunīgais valodnieks Endzelīns." Sestdiena. Published February 22, 2013. Retrieved February 12, 2014. http://www.diena.lv/dienas-zurnali/sestdiena/mazrunigais-valodnieks-endzelins-13994948> Tr. RL)

My friend, historian Mārtiņš Mintaurs, told me that in 1952 someone allegedly proposed that Latvia switch entirely to the Russian alphabet, Cyrillic. Apparently this dastardly suggestion met with too much local resistance. Luckily for Latvia, Comrade Stalin died the following year. The outcome of World War II shattered my grandparents' professional pursuits and social life, evidenced by old photographs of happy gatherings and field excursions. Exiled in the West, separated by continents and oceans, or banished to Soviet prison camps, the members of this once active and vital student organization were like branches ripped from a young sapling by a ferocious storm. Recently planted, the damage would kill it. Professor Endzelīns was demeaned not only by representatives of the new Soviet order, but even by some overenthusiastic students of the new communist generation. Unable to accept this new order, Endzelīns, a recipient of the Order of Lenin in 1958, eventually parted ways with his beloved University of Latvia, transferring to the Latvian (SSR) Academy of Science, where he quietly continued his work in relative solitude.

Endzelīns corresponded with some of his former students who had been deported to the Siberia, even sending care packages and money to them and keeping their spirits up with his letters. Some of my grandparents' former acquaintances, including Aleksandrs Jansons, already mentioned, were deported to remote, primitive penal outposts in Siberia, like Tomsk, Taishet, Amur, Bichura, etc. If my grandparents had stayed in Latvia, would they have been arrested and deported? According to my mother, they had been slated for deportation in 1941 but managed to evade the NKVD's clutches, because the Germans invaded Latvia, thereby preventing the Russians from "fulfilling their quotas."

Eventually my grandfather managed to renew ties with some of his old friends in Rīga. Accompanied by Aleksandrs Jansons, Andris and I visited a small group of these oldsters at the apartment of Nellija Zālīte, a spry lady my grandparents' age, in an old building in Pārdaugava in the winter of 1983. Part of the building, which took up a block on the corner of Meža iela and Raņķa dambis, was in rather shocking shape. Sections of its eastern wing looked like a fire or bomb had gutted it: a huge hole in the exterior wall revealed empty apartment spaces, parts of a dangling ceiling, caved in floors. Yet the rest of the building was inhabited. It remained standing in this state for years (and still stands), an eyesore and fire hazard.

It was there that I was introduced to Milda Grīnfelde (1909–2000), legendary last companion and muse of the great Latvian poet Aleksandrs Čaks (born Aleksandrs Čadarainis, 1901–1950). His last book of poetry, *Debesu dāvana* ("Heaven's Gift"), was allegedly dedicated to Grīnfelde. Čaks died of a heart attack at the age of 48; his literary accomplishments were trashed by Soviet critics; he was hounded for spurning "Marxist values." The following year Čaks' muse Milda was arrested, convicted, and deported to Siberia for her involvement in the so-called French Group—a loosely knit association of enthusiasts who met from time to time after the war in the late 1940s in informal settings, usually apartments, to discuss France and French culture and literature. Grīnfelde and her "associates"—Kurts Fridrihsons, Ieva Lase, Miervaldis Ozoliņš, Maija Silmale, Elza Stērste, and others—were convicted of treason, which automatically implied a 25-year-sentence.

> The profound suspicion of civil society was central to Bolshevik thinking, far more so than is usually acknowledged. (...) Even while the Soviet leadership was experimenting with economic freedom in the 1920s (during Lenin's New Economic Plan) the systematic destruction of literary, philosophical, and spiritual societies continued unabated. Even for orthodox Marxists, free trade was preferable to free association, including the free association of apolitical sporting or cultural groups. This was true under Lenin's rule, under Stalin's, rule, under Khrushchev's rule, and under Brezhnev's rule. Although many other things changed, the persecution of civil society continued after Stalin's death, well into the 1970s and 1980s.—Anne Applebaum, *Iron Curtain*, pp. 151–152.

Milda Grīnfelde in her youth.

Born on April 20, 1909 in Novosibirsk, Russia, where her father had been deported after the 1905 Russian Revolution, Grīnfelde was a prolific, highly respected translator of more than 60 books, including the works of Honoré de Balzac, Albert Camus, Alain René-Lesage, and Romain Rolland. She had studied Romance and Baltic philology at the University of Latvia (1927–1940) and worked at Zelta Ābele, a publisher of serious literature, and at the Academy of Sciences' Department of Languages. Grīnfelde was a Latvian language purist who also loved Russian, English, French, and German.* (Source: Rūmnieks, Valdis. "Milda Grīnfelde." Diena. Published October 3, 2000. Retrieved April 10, 2013. <http://www.diena.lv/arhivs/milda-grinfelde-10814200> Tr. RL)

Grīnfelde was one of several Latvians deported to Siberia with whom Professor Jānis Endzelīns corresponded out of deep sympathy and concern. In a letter dated January 19, 1956 from Taishet, Irkutsk Oblast, Grīnfelde wrote to her mentor: "(...) Permit me to express my sincerest gratitude to you for your postcard, which brought me so much joy in this remote corner of the earth. Dear Professor, like children we delight in each and every word that we receive from our native land, but your letters move us beyond compare, and we hold on to them like treasures."* When I was introduced to Milda Grīnfelde in the winter of 1983, she was a slim, elderly woman in a dark dress that accentuated her girlish figure. She rose from her chair and came up to me, took my hands into hers, and smiled. Thirty years later, I realize that that moment still means a lot to me: in a single touch of warm flesh generations and experiences seemed to click and lock into place." (Source: Dzidra Bārbare, Brigita Bušmane. *Jānis Endzelīns atmiņās, pārdomās, vēstulēs.* Rīga: Latviešu valodas institūts, 1999. Tr. RL)

Grīnfelde's friend, actor Miervaldis Ozoliņš (1922–1999), *right*, was also part of the „French group" that was crushed by the communists. Ozoliņš survived his ordeal at forced labor camps in Inta and Vorkuta by performing with a puppet for his fellow prisoners and playing the violin in the camp orchestra. I saw Ozoliņš in several performances at the theater.* The stories these people could have told us, but I did not know to ask. Nor was I bold or shameless enough to ply my host and her other guests with questions about Latvia's history at a time when it was dangerous to do so. (*Source: Krūze, Velta. „Miervaldis Ozoliņš 1922.g. 17.III—1999.g. 8.V." *Diena.* May 12, 1999. <http://www.diena.lv/arhivs/miervaldis-ozolins-1922-g-17-iii-1999-g-8-v-10446960>)

In late winter of 1983 Andris and I paid a call on the painter Līvija Endzelīna (1927–2008), daughter of Jānis Endzelīns from his first marriage to the beautiful and accomplished Marta Grimma, a poet and literary critic who had worked on a Czech-Latvian dictionary. Endzelīna lived in a drab Soviet "block" building just down the street from the Drāma Theater, close to the Daugava River. The cluster of white brick buildings, built in the 1950s, was popularly referred to as "the crows' nest." Endzelīna lived a quiet life, shunning publicity and social gatherings. She was an extraordinarily gifted painter who produced painstakingly rendered realistic still lifes in oil: old clocks, jugs, antique items, glass containers, and objects of the natural world that hinted at the passage of time, of art's purpose as a reflection of time. She was a quiet, withdrawn host who treated us to tea and biscuits and showed us some of her father's photographs from the 1930s. I was deeply moved to spot in some of those photographs my maternal grandparents in their youth, posing together with their friends and their beloved Professor Endzelīns. This visit was another link to my past. I wish we could have afforded to purchase one of Ms. Endzelīna's remarkable paintings, which are now regarded as national treasures.

Today Jānis Endzelīns seems to have faded from many Latvians' memory. His Latvian language "rules" are, if not openly derided, then simply disregarded. The spirit of that era, of the First Republic, and the enormous energy of those who were part of it has been difficult to replicate in today's Latvia. We know that language changes over time. However, Endzelīns, his colleagues, his contemporaries, and his followers laid down crucial groundwork for the Latvian literary language based on meticulous historical research and ongoing fieldwork, which was devoted to preserving unique words, place names, expressions, manners of speech, and dialects from all corners of Latvia. Endzelīns' so-called language commission, an open forum for discussing the mother tongue, brought together young and old, seasoned experts and enthusiastic novices who shared their linguistic discoveries. My own grandfather's life-long devotion to the Latvian language and Latvian literature was a continuation of the work started in the First Republic—a short-lived time of freedom and independence in the history of the Latvian people.

Ramava, Romuva... this ancient Baltic name evokes the image of a grove of enormous oak trees, of a place of worship. The ancient Balts were once spread over a large area that included ancient Prussia. Many traditions and even very old songs live on today in the 21st century, handed down from generation to generation. The Midsummer solstice, Jāņi, is Latvia's best known traditional and ancient festival; it is a celebration of the longest day, and of light and fertility. In a sense, the summer and winter solstices symbolize Yin and Yang. One of the foods that every Latvian expects to eat at Jāņi is the solstice cheese, *Jāņu siers*, round and yellow like the sun, full of caraway seeds, the goodness of the earth, happiness, and hope. Solstice cheese is bound tightly to give it shape and drain excess moisture. The solstice marks the year's longest day and shortest night, after which the sun gradually retreats from the Baltic lands. The Latvian American folk ensemble Lini sing a song about this cheese, but is it about how the cheese is made or about something else, something more sinister about the fates of the peoples of this part of Europe?

Jāņu māte sieru sēja deviņiem stūrīšiem; / Es nevaru atminēt, kāpēc tieši deviņiem. / Es prasīju Jāņu mātei: kāpēc tieši deviņiem; / Man sacīja Jāņu māte: Es nevaru atcerēt. / Es prasīju leišu mātei: Kas tā licis stūri siet; / Man sacīja leišu māte, lai prasot prūšu mātei. / Tā gan būtu sacījusi, kas tā licis stūri siet; / Nevarēja pasacīt, ar zobenu sakapāta.

Translation: The Jāņi hostess bound the cheese with nine corners; / I can't remember why exactly nine. / I asked the Jāņi hostess: why nine? / But she replied: I don't remember. / I asked a Lithuanian woman: Who made you tie the corners so? / The Lithuanian woman replied: Go ask the Prussian woman. / The Prussian woman would have told my why, / But she couldn't: she was hacked to pieces by the sword. (Tr. RL)

The Old Prussians, a Baltic tribe, were conquered in the 13th century by the German Teutonic Knights. Reading up on their history, I am thrilled to recognize similarities between Old Prussian and Latvian words, although Old Prussian is now officially exctinct. We Latvians share words like "Dievs" ("God"), "Pērkons" ("Thunder"), "druva" ("field"), "medus" ("honey"), "saule" ("sun"), "upe" ("river"), and others with this now extinct people. This haunting song makes me think of our Baltic memory's far reach into the past and toward distant borders, across the lands of Lithuania into ancient Prussia and Ramave, the magical grove.

Ramavieši in their caps and colors at their fifth anniversary and 300th get-together on March 4, 1934 at Skolas iela No. 27, Apartment 1 in Rīga. Professor Jānis Endzelīns is seated in the middle of the second row (fifth from the left). My maternal grandmother Līvija Bičolis is in the front row holding my mother in her lap. My grandfather Jānis Bičolis is seated at the end of the second row, right. My grandmother's handsome brother Fricis is in the back row, second from the right. Family photograph.

In the summer of 2014, when I visited my uncle in Vidriži, Latvia, he told me that many of the old farms in the area had "Liv-sounding" names. An old map called "Westliches Russland" (Western Russia) from the early 20th century shows the house called Rumpēter from which my predecessors moved to Vīganti, where Uncle Ģirts now lives. After visiting my uncle, I came home, found the map, and began exploring it to see what he was referring to. Indeed, I did find some interesting names that sound more Liv than Latvian: Kidrik; Lalle; Kügul... If indeed they are Liv place names, they would indicate the centuries–long presence of this nearly extinct Finno-Ugric nation in Latvia. Like my grandparents, I liked to dig into the past. Like them, I loved the semantics of our language. Being separated from their native country was very painful for my grandparents. Realizing that as I have gone through my grandfather's notes, which are devoted to the Latvian language, I have felt a nagging, existential sorrow.

Aleksandrs Čaks

Varoņu piemiņas dienā ("On Heroes' Remembrance Day")

On Heroes'
Remembrance Day
a stranger
a simple worker on the street
invited me
to drink with him.
We spent the whole evening
and the night until morning
drinking
with whores
coarse sailors
and vagabonds.

We drank
to the fallen
at Tīrelis*
and the Carpathians,**
we drank
to abandoned wives,
mothers,
and children.

We drank
with bitterness
and pain
as caustic as the voices of drunks
we drank
and sang a song
about ourselves
and our lost lives.

(Translated by Rita Laima)

* Tīrelis—Tīrelis is a large bog in Latvia where the dramatic "Christmas Battles" of World War I took place in 1917 (Julian calendar). Many Latvian riflemen fighting on the side of Russia perished in the battle against German forces. Aleksandrs Čaks' epic poetic eulogy *Mūžības skārtie* (1937–1939) to the Latvian soldiers, most of them average young men from the streets, suburbs, and countryside, was criticized and then banned in the Soviet communist era.

** Carpathian Mountains—Latvians also fought on the side of Russia in the Carpathian Mountains before fighting for Latvia.

1983: A Wedding in Snow

Happily ever after? My father, ever the creative genius, depicted my fiancé and me in Latvian traditional folk costumes. (Illustration by Ilmārs Rumpēters)

Just married: on my wedding day in Turaida with my cousin Inta and her husband Ivars, our "sponsors." Photo: Juris Krieviņš

March 1983. Four months had passed since General Secretary Leonid Brezhnev's demise in November, but the Cold War dragged on, even as a new spring dawned. There was a new man in Moscow, Yury Andropov, a KGB strongman who had played a significant role in crushing the Hungarian revolution in 1956. Nothing had changed since the robotic Brezhnev gave up the ghost, despite Andropov's pathetic efforts to curb the illicit sale of alcohol and get people off the streets during working hours. Homo Sovieticus was a crafty species, finding a way around each new law, limit, and hurdle. Andris had his connections and had squirreled away a large stash of booze for the upcoming bash.

We had worked tirelessly in advance of our big day, buying products for the wedding feast. We shopped at Rīga Central Market and then lugged our purchases, including a bag of herring, to the Small Guild, where the banquet was to be prepared and served. The fact that my immediate family would not be attending (for financial and logistical reasons) had cast a slight shadow on our preparation for the joyful event. Latvian American girl meets and marries native Latvian boy. They live happily ever after. But without Mamma and Tētis ("Dad") and my brothers there, everything felt a bit off-kilter.

March 4 dawned as a cold and blustery Friday. In the morning, with the attentive help of my future mother-in-law and my cousin Inta I dressed at Biruta's apartment in Pārdaugava. My traditional white dress and white shoes were from a store called Pavasaris ("Springtime"), which sold items related to weddings and newborns. To be able to shop there, you had to register your wedding and/or pregnancy in advance. Because the state controlled the sale of everything, items such as wedding dresses and swaddling cloth were available only to those who could prove they really needed these items. I was quite happy with my dress and veil, and the shoes were surprisingly nice, too, even though a tad uncomfortable. With my kohl-lined eyes framed by the folds of the veil, I looked quite exotic; that is, not at all Latvian.

The sweet scent of my wedding bouquet of orange freesias still lingers in my memory. At our official union at the so-called ZAG (an abbreviation for the Russian term for the vital records office—*Zapis Aktov Grazhdanskogo Sostoyaniya*) on Slokas iela the presiding official ended the brief ceremony by declaring that the Soviet state would ensure our well-being. Or something like that. Andris sniggered and I giggled as a handful of smiling guests looked on. We knew what this attentive (KGB) care was like. And that was it, at least where Soviet law was concerned. We signed the papers and admired the gold bands on our fingers. Our marriage license was issued in Russian, an indication that Russian was, in effect, Soviet Latvia's official state language.

After hugging our guests, we bounded out to my father-in-law Juris' Lada. He would serve as our chauffeur and photographer. We made a stop to have our "official" (Soviet style) wedding portrait taken at a nearby "photo salon." Then together with my cousin Inta and her husband Ivars, our sponsors, we drove out to picturesque Turaida near the Gauja River, where we walked through the snow laughing, shivering, and embracing, while Juris Krieviņš took photographs of us. It was wintry, cold, and simply lovely. The ancient, scenic river valley was powdered in white. We left flowers at the grave of the "Rose of Turaida" (1601–1620) who was murdered by a Polish nobleman or soldier. We had coffee and cognac in the nearby café. My toes were numb.

It was my impression that for many young people in communist Latvia weddings were a way to escape boredom. It seemed that many couples married young, for the fun of it, to try to improve their living conditions, or due to an unexpected pregnancy. Weddings were a good reason to throw a party and receive gifts, I speculated. Latvia's divorce rate in the Soviet era was high, however, and would remain high. Living conditions were stressful. Our union resulted in my sister-in-law having to move back into the tiny apartment that she had escaped from, but now with a family in tow. How was sexual intimacy possible with one's parents within earshot?

Our wedding took place in the heart of Old Rīga, in a large vaulted hall in the Small Guild (*right*), which dated back to the 16th century. In the Soviet era it was called Kultūras nams (House of Culture), and Juris was able to reserve the hall because he worked there. We had a great number of guests and apparently a couple of snoops: chekists who snuck in to see who was there. Our relatives and friends arrived dressed in their finest, with inquisitive stares, because I was still something of a novelty. People in Soviet Latvia did not smile readily, nor did they laugh lightly in public. Or maybe my guests recognized the presence of the KGB...

There were stiff speeches and toasts, a lot of staring, a good meal heavy on meat, and a bit of dancing. I sat through all of it in a daze, emotionally detached. Then we were put through a Latvian wedding ritual called *mičošana*. None of it seemed real; it was a far cry from what I had imagined would be one of the most joyful days of my life. I felt like I was part of a performance, a play, or a pawn in someone's hand—but whose exactly? The next morning I woke up feeling depressed and spent the day crying, much to the chagrin of my new husband. I attributed my post-wedding blues to the absence of my family and to the fact that we weren't married in a church. As I wiped my eyes and blew my nose, I looked at the beautiful flowers that filled vases, buckets, and our tub. We even had to give some of our flowers away to family and friends, there were so many. My flower nation: why was I so sad? Perhaps I cried because I was bidding farewell to my happy childhood and teenage years. The future seemed bleak, even though I was in love. I had stepped into adulthood, but I was not sure who I was, or what my role should be. I felt a bit lost in Latvia.

We had our *atkāzas* ("post-nuptial feast") on that teary day in Juris' cosy basement studio at the Guild. We ate and drank and socialized with young people I did not know. These were friends and acquaintances of my husband, all nice people, of course. We listened to music that I did not recognize, nor did I like it. My rock and roll wedding never transpired. The sappy music of the Latvian group Credo did nothing to lift my spirits. I stared at our guests hopping to the "Funky Chicken" and felt glum. It was my first encounter with cultural alienation. I had to settle for sappiness, when in fact I wanted to scream and shake to "Whole Lotta Love" by Led Zeppelin or "Gloria" by Patti Smith or "Once in a Lifetime" by the Talking Heads. I wanted to burn and go crazy: "I walk in the room and I look so fine..." Heat! Happiness! Craziness! Dancing! Shaking! Screaming! Instead I would simmer, for years.

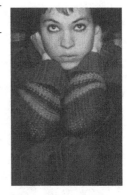

Right: Brooding Latvian American in the Soviet Union in 1983. I am confused, because not much is as I expected.

There was no *medusmēness* ("honeymoon") for us. We unpacked our gifts and put them away. Ceramicist Pēteris Martinsons' large, decorative vase and Imants Ziedonis' large purple pot were among the many lovely, hand-crafted gifts we received and admired. Ziedonis had also dedicated a wonderful poem to us, which lifted my spirits. The marvelous flowers brightened our rooms for several days before wilting. Our lives resumed just like before, except that now I was a Mrs. Or was I? No, I was Comrade Krieviņa. From now on each day would be a lesson of life and acceptance for me. I was 23; my impetuous husband was a year younger than me. I had seen little of the world and had chosen to get married and live in a totalitarian state controlled by a communist dictatorship. It was my choice and no one else's. And thus I resigned myself to this life calmly, with Latvian stoicism. For all those years that I lived in Latvia under the communists my philosophy was: *if they can do it, so can I*. My wedding blues faded, and real life set in with all of its problems and bright moments. Life was every day!

In-Laws

My new family (that is, my in-laws) was getting used to me. Of course, Juris saw a lot of us. Sometimes we even ate together. We caused him considerable anxiety. If ever our conversations strayed in the direction of the Soviet authorities, Juris demanded that we put a pillow on the phone. He was convinced that our phones were bugged, and probably they were. Could a pillow somehow help?

Gaujiena before World War II. Image courtesy of the National Library of Latvia collection "In Search of Lost Latvia."

Juris had experienced his share of terror growing up in Latvia after the war. He was born in Gaujiena, a small town on the Gauja River close to the Estonian border. As a young boy he saw the ravages of war: the mangled, bloody bodies of German and Russian soldiers were strewn across the Gauja meadows. A childhood friend and his dog were blown up by abandoned explosives; playing with grenades and other weapons was apparently a popular but risky sport for boys right after the war. Juris' father was shot by "bandits." Banditry and marauding men were a common phenomenon all across Eastern Europe in the wake of the war. The communists were clever to lump marauders together with national partisans; Latvia's national partisans were referred to as "bandits" and criminals.

Juris was a Latvian patriot with no interest in cultivating ties with the Soviet communist elite. However, he observed the status quo, as did most Latvians. Courting trouble with the KGB was not his cup of tea. Juris was worried about us, because we were both very young, temperamental, and naïve, especially me.

My father-in-law was shorter than me, about 5 ft. 5", with thinning hair combed back from his high brow. With his gray goatee beard and large, cool-blue eyes, he reminded me of an elf. He was a workaholic, always running somewhere with his camera bag or lugging something home—potatoes, apples, a slab of valuable meat, or a rare and exciting find at the "black book market," which took place on weekends in some always changing secret location that only a select few knew about. Who frequented the black book market? I never found out, because Juris never invited me along. It was too risky. How did Juris know when and where to go? Obviously it was word of mouth. According to Juris, at the market one could find rare pre-war books, photographs, and postcards from the "bourgeois" era, as well as other "forbidden fruit."

Sometimes Juris and Andris argued loudly, but I got along with my father-in-law just fine. I tried not to intrude on him, and he tried to do the same. We did share a refrigerator, so he came into our kitchen from time to time. Juris was willing to share his studio space with us, and he let me look at his books and photographs. Although our relationship was never affectionate, it was mutually respectful. He was a good man despite his "bristles." I also discovered that, although my compatriots in occupied Latvia were not generally affectionate, they were remarkably hospitable. Human beings are intricately designed and affected by their experiences and social and political environment. The lives of people growing up behind the Iron Curtain were unimaginably different from what people in the Free World experienced. It was important to understand that, although some expatriates refused to. What Latvia was like during and after the war, I could only guess.

Juris Krieviņš cared deeply about Latvia's history; he cared about the preservation of its endangered cultural, historical, and architectural legacy. He was interested in philosophy and read a lot. Juris was acutely aware of what was going on around him and proceeded cautiously, working towards his goals within the parameters set by the Soviet communist regime. He was driven and had concrete goals. He knew how to skirt obstacles. Juris was a "passive opponent" (Applebaum) who engaged in passive resistance to the Soviet communist system, as did most people in Latvia the prison state.

Juris lived in his studio, working, eating, and sleeping there. My mother-in-law remained in their apartment on Dreiliņu iela. The Soviet era apartment buildings had been built into the so-called Āgenskalna Pines, which can be seen in an old photograph (*left*). My father used to live down the street from these pine-covered dunes, when he was a boy. The few pines that were left appeared to be dying.

The Krieviņš apartment was on the second floor of a five-story, white brick building. The front door of the apartment opened to a tiny foyer next to a tiny bathroom crowded by a bathtub and toilet. There was no sink. The tiny kitchen was on the other side of the bathroom wall. There was a "living" room and a small bedroom. Growing up there, my husband and his sister had shared the apartment with three adults. Some of the nearby buildings had one-room apartments where entire families lived; my husband said that they had been meant as temporary workers' flats, which turned into permanent occupancies. What was that like, I wondered: growing up in a one-room apartment?

My mother-in-law Biruta Krieviņa, born Liepiņa, was a slender woman with beautiful, luminous, green eyes. She was an emotional person who teared up easily. She had also worked as a photographer, first in a studio that specialized in family portraits and then later at the Art Foundation. She retired soon after my arrival, supplemented her pension crocheting gloves, and looked after her baby granddaughter Elīna.

Biruta hailed from Taurupe in Vidzeme, where she grew up on her parents' farm. She learned all the farm chores from an early age and loved life in the countryside. She felt confined and unhappy in Rīga. During the war her family was expelled from its house by the Germans and then by the Russians. According to Biruta, before leaving, the Russians defecated in every single cupboard and drawer of the house—a strange, bestial, barbaric thing to do. Was this a tradition passed down by the Mongol Horde? Biruta's brother vanished in 1941 while pedaling home on his bike. The family never found out what happened to him. My husband made me a gold ring from Biruta's father's wedding band. The design resembled two rams butting their horns together. Andris and I were both born in the sign of Aries.

Biruta was an excellent cook and *saimniece* or homemaker. In fact, she was a typical Latvian woman: always busy; always working; always doing something with her hands. She did not know how to sit still, just like my graandmothers and great-grandmothers. Like all Latvian women, she could do it all: she had held a job and then cooked and cleaned and cared for her children when she got home. She was practical, and her long, slender fingers were nimble, darning socks and mending holes. I learned a lot about cooking from her. She was an old-fashioned kind of home-maker for whom shirts, linens, towels, and even handkerchiefs had to be ironed and pressed. She told me that ironed handkerchiefs were a sure sign of a good *saimniece.* Subsequently I took to ironing our bed linens, towels, and handkerchiefs to please her. I was a dutiful daughter-in-law. Although we never became close, I am grateful to Biruta for teaching me many practical skills by example. I respected her devotion to the task at hand. Her work ethic was in no way damaged by communism, an ideology that robbed many Soviet citizens of willpower and an attention to detail.

Biruta was a very attentive grandmother to Elīna, my sister-in-law Gita's beautiful daughter; she took great pains to purchase, clean, and squeeze fresh fruit and vegetable juice for the baby. At one point Elīna turned almost orange from all the carrot juice her grandmother was giving her. Biruta knitted Andris and me warm mittens and socks and often sent us something tasty via Juris. Sometimes we went to eat with her. We always looked forward to these meals. We were always hungry, and everything she prepared was delicious. Biruta simply did not know how to make a bad meal.

My parents-in-law lived parallel lives. Juris obiously needed his personal space to pursue his creative endeavors. If Biruta was more interested in domesticity and country life, then Juris' calling was photography, art, literature, philosophy, history, and legacy. He came and went as he pleased. It was an uneasy relationship, yet it lasted.

My sister-in-law Ligita (or Gita) was a year older than me. She could sew and took great pains to dress well like many of the Latvian women I met. Like her parents and her brother, she was talented and dexterous. Gita was an excellent seamstress, and I was always amazed by what she could fashion for herself "from nothing." She had attended a secondary school for the applied arts. She knew how to work a loom and wove several beautiful traditional Latvian blankets that I tried to find customers for. By the time she was 30, Gita had gone through four marriages. I believe the Soviet housing problem was one of the causes. The lack of private space pressed down on communist Latvia's youth like permanently overcast skies. Like so many Latvian young people, Gita felt confined by her income and her lack of choice. Beautiful, talented, unhappy Gita: she sought simple pleasures to beat away the drudgery of the Soviet economy. We had some fun times together.

As for my young husband, he was handsome, funny, witty, charming, stubborn, irascible, and always in a state of conflict with someone: his father; his employer; or the Soviet state. He was a nationalist and could barely hide it. For nine precious years we made our home a happy one, and there is much to remember and cherish. Together we made two wonderful sons. There were many things he taught me: to appreciate and recognize nature—that is, plants, birds, and animals, and to embrace the rural way of life. He loved natural beauty and always seemed hap-piest in the countryside, working outside or caring for his animals. He had an eye for beauty, a gift he put to great use in his photographs.

Comme des Communistes:
Trying to Look Chic in a Command Economy

Rīgas Modes (Rīga Fashion House) on Ļeņina iela with Hotel Latvija in the distance, 1980. Image courtesy of the National Library of Latvia collection "In Search of Lost Latvia."

Soon after the wedding I had an uncomfortable talk with my mother-in-law. I needed new clothes. My stockpile of American apparel had dwindled, and I was convinced that there was *nothing* in Rīga's stores that I liked. I was disoriented in my new surroundings and unhappy, but my mother-in-law wished to tame my exotic look. Rīga wasn't New York City with displays of Parisian and Milanese haute couture in the windows of a Saks Fifth Avenue, Henri Bendel, or Lord & Taylor, nor did it have a hip downtown like Greenwich Village with its punks with purple mohawks, pierced noses, black lips, and black leather (not that I was a punk). Forty years after the war Rīga, once called "the Paris of the North," was a dim blip on the western perimeter of the Soviet Union. It was a city of faded glory populated by gray masses trudging through shabby stores that lacked choice, color, and the *cool* factor. As an ideology, communism had no need for fashion, elegance, individuality, or *hip*.

I did not sew, nor was I interested in sewing, knitting, or crocheting. The same went for my mother who had always been more interested in books, writing, and trips to the Big Apple. I recall my 6th grade home economics class experience as a failure: I was barely able to complete a simple apron, as the thread in the Singer sewing machine jumbled up into an ugly mess under my sloppy guidance. I felt very inadequate in the fatherland, where almost all women knew how to sew and displayed dexterity in everything they did.

Soviet people with their probing eyes were always on the lookout for something, anything that looked "Western" (that is, not Soviet). Jeans were all the rage, even "fake" ones. In 1981 Gita couldn't stop staring at my shoes; I took them off before leaving and gave them to her. Wherever I went, I felt those deprived Soviet eyes latching on to me, scurrying up and down, appraising... Certainly I was no style icon, yet Homo Sovieticus could tell what was made in the Soviet Union and what was imported. The fabric, the pattern, the cut, the style, the color: all these elements added up to huge differences between Soviet and Western apparel. The Soviets' eyes and noses were fine-tuned to spot something different. And Western products even had a pleasant scent, something I had taken for granted when living in the US. From what I could tell, products made in Soviet Russia were apparently at the bottom of everyone's "wish list." Old-style capitalism had been killed off in Russia in the revolution. Other than Kalashnikovs and other weapons, the quality of Russian goods was notoriously low.

227

Balts were different than the other Soviet republics. Their roots lay in the West and the Western European way of life, which was fueled by market economies, private ownership, and competition, factors which accelerated research and development. Private Western companies were also liable for the quality they promised consumers, whereas the Soviet state was an amorphous manufacturing giant that carried no liability. I remember how in the spring of '83 my husband bought me a bike manufactured in Soviet Ukraine. It broke on the way home, and the store refused to take it back, even though we could provide a receipt.

Although nearly 40 years had passed since the Soviet annexation of the Baltic States, memories of the old way of life persisted. By the 1980s many Latvian families were being reunited, as émigrés ventured to Latvia to visit their fatherland and reconnect with their kin. They hauled enormous suitcases, which were stuffed with coffee, candy, cigarettes, clothes, shoes, lingerie, toys, and even pornography to butter up the Soviet Russian customs officials. Western goods were so superior in packaging and design, that their recipients could see the difference between the propaganda they were subjected to and the material quality of the world that the Soviets constantly denigrated. In addition, person to person contacts and the exchange of stories would also impact Latvians in occupied Latvia. Comparing prices, wages, and opportunities in communist Latvia and the Free World did wonders in deepening Latvians' disillusionment with and cynisism toward communism. I don't believe for a minute that a majority of Latvia's population ever wanted to be annexed by a murderous regime, contrary to the claims of Soviet history books.

It was arranged that Gita would accompany me on a shopping expedition, which I was dreading. My in-laws wished to help me by dressing me. I already knew that our trip would yield nothing to my liking; I had done some scouting myself. We walked here and there, up and down, in and out ambling about, as my mood sank into the Soviet quagmire of hopelessness. After many hours, all we had to show for our efforts was a drab skirt and jacket ensemble and an ugly red and black dress, which I accepted unwillingly and wore with extreme reluctance for about a year before stuffing it deep into our wardrobe. Yes, there were clothes in Rīga's shops, but they were neither attractive nor remotely stylish. And they weren't cheap! This surprised me the most. Not only were clothes prohibitively pricey, they never went on sale. Because there was no competition between stores in the Soviet economy, there were no discount wars. And the consumer suffered. In the 1980s we struggled to make ends meet.

Thus my dispatches to my parents were peppered with "wish lists," which, luckily, they ignored for the most part. (It's embarrassing to think about how much I whined and begged.) When my mother came to visit in May 1983, she brought a suitcase of clothes that I made maximum use of. If anything, life in Soviet Latvia made me permanently hate shopping. I would be happy with just one black dress, a pair of black pants, and black boots. And a bottle of good perfume.

Ironically, despite being cut off from the West and the merchandise glut of the Free World, many Latvian women had an innate sense of chic. How did so many women in communist Latvia, especially artists, pull off their stylish appearance in a country with such empty stores? The ultrapopular West German magazine *Burda*, which offered patterns and designs, circulated among many of my Latvian acquaintances, many of whom were expert seamstresses. The magazine was obtained through connections (*blats*) and then passed from hand to hand. In 1987 it was the first Western magazine to be published in the Soviet Union due to its immense popularity and Raisa Gorbachev's efforts. Aside from *Burda*, Latvian women like my sister-in-law were very talented and had a good eye for fashion. Not only did Gita know how to sew, she also had a great figure and long legs and looked good no matter what she wore, despite the empty store shelves.

Sometimes I purchased Soviet Latvia's fashion magazine *Rīgas Modes* ("Rīga Fashions" [1948–1992]) at the kiosk and examined the clothes and pretty models with interest. The magazine itself was printed on newspaper-quality paper (no glossies in the Soviet era), which dulled the overall presentation. The clothes featured in this popular magazine were not particularly exciting, nor were they readily available in stores. The content of the magazine was a far cry from the reality of Rīga's empty store shelves and unappealing apparel. Yet many Latvian women were magicians at copying from sight and improvising, and in the early 1980s I met some young women (all of them artists) who looked positively smashing: Frančeska Kirke; Ieva Iltnere; Laima Kaugure; and others. Handsome painter Džemma Skulme (b. 1925) was the essence of northern European elegance

Rīga's typical street scene in the Soviet era was positively dull. Store windows were full of stuff no one wanted. The city looked bleak. Living in Rīga was like living in a cage; as a Balt stuck behind the Iron Curtain, you knew there was a "more beautiful" world out there, but it was out of reach. In the 1980s people in Latvia were one generation removed from capitalism. Stories of fancy shops and shiny things were passed down by grandma and grandpa or by a visiting aunt or uncle. Decades of deprivation warped the nation's character, I'm sure. No wonder that this system turned so many Soviet women into gold-diggers and manipulative opportunists!

Despite the drab street scene, Rīga's opera and theater crowds revealed many Latvian women to be neatly or even elegantly dressed. Attending the opera and theater was a special occasion, so everyone got dressed to the nines. During intermission the public would rush to the refreshment stand or promenade in a circle, eyeing and appraising each other. And many Latvian women were so pretty as to look good in anything! I admired their ability to get dressed up in spite of the disastrous Soviet economy. They dressed their children neatly, too, with boys in spiffy little vests and hand-sewn bow ties, their hair slicked back, and girls with pigtails tied with big bows. The look was a bit archaic, but the need to dress up as a display of reverance to high culture was touching.

Attractive, well made foot apparel—shoes, boots, and sneakers—was a painful deficit in Soviet Latvia. Yet I noticed that there were some women, especially a few notable artists, who sported sexy shoes and boots. I assumed that these goods were available through that murky Soviet system of barter and clout called *blats*. Some Soviet citizens were lucky enough to visit the Warsaw Pact countries of Eastern Europe, where the quality of clothes and shoes was better than in the USSR. They brought back goods for themselves and/or for barter or sale. Apparently deficit goods changed hands in warehouses and behind counters, never reaching the actual shelves of stores. Soviet roubles could purchase little. Deficit goods also circulated on the black market, available through connections. So-called *spekulanti* ("speculators") thrived in this zone beneath the radar of the Soviet authorities, although who knew what the relationship between *spekulanti* and the authorities really was. The Soviet economic system was very corrupt.

Homo Sovieticus was adept at sniffing out deficit goods and patient when it came to waiting in line for a shipment of something. In 2013 always charming and elegant Latvian journalist Tekla Šaitere reminisced about the Soviet years and what it was like to try to look good in Rīga in an era of economic stagnation and chronic shortages.

The downtown Rīgas Modes building on Ļeņina iela was an atelier that took up multiple floors with many fitting rooms and workshops that designed and manufactured clothing for re-tail and made-to-measure apparel. According to Šaitere, "I was never a fashionista, but I always wanted to dress well. I was not a client of Rīgas Modes, because I didn't have the patience to stand in the long lines, and I couldn't stand the master seamstress' arrogance. Who was dressed there? Party functionaries, men and women with money and connections, and the 'indispensa-bles'—doctors, dentists, butchers, retail managers (who had direct access to incoming goods), the wives of Soviet sailors, etc. My neighbor's husband was a sailor. She used to work at VEF (*Valsts Elektrotehniskā fabrika*); she's now 75 and still wears a coat that was made by Rīgas Modes. They made all sorts of clothes at Rīgas Modes, and coveted customers paid in dollars and deutsch marks. I don't sew. When I made my debut in Rīga society, I was lucky to find several good seamstresses. I had a friend in Minsk, Belarus, a journalist and model for the Minsk Fashion House. Through her I met a model with my measurements, so beginning in the 1970s I traveled to Minsk on a regular basis to purchase two or three pieces of the model's wardrobe each year, as well as Belarusian shoes, which were very good in the Soviet era.

"It wasn't possible to buy anything really nice in Rīga's stores, but everyone got everything from somewhere: from packages sent from abroad by relatives or friends, or by standing in long lines at the GUM (*Glavnyi Universalnyi Magazin* or State Principal Department Store) and CUM ("Central Universal Department Store") in Moscow, which everybody in the Soviet Union was familiar with, just like Lenin's Mausoleum. These were Moscow's big department stores near Red Square. If you went there, if you were patient, and if you stood in line (which thousands of visitors did), then you could get your hands on French and Polish perfume, winter boots, leather gloves, French make-up, silk stockings, and crockery. My husband and I went to Moscow from time to time to enjoy the theater, especially the Taganka (Theater), and I remember standing in a long line to buy the Polish perfume *Mozhet byt* ('Maybe')." Soviet store lines were famous: they were a way of life.

Soviet citizens traveled far and wide in search of merchandise, especially anything related to fashion and beauty. Good shoes for children were especially hard to find; when our son was born, my parents began sending us shoes and baby and toddler clothes. I remember stories of Latvian families going to Lithuania, apparently "better stocked," to shop. If we ever visited a small Latvian town, I always took time to visit the main store. One never knew what one could find in the "provinces." Consumers from other Soviet republics flocked to Rīga with sacks (yes, large sacks) to scour its stores and markets. Demand drove Homo Sovieticus to go to great lengths (literally) in search of basic consumer goods.

Tekla Šaitere: "Rīga's women were dressed quite well and some even stylishly. I used to or-der my shoes from the highly respected shoe shop, *Elegants*, which was located on Krišjāņa

Barona iela near Vērmaņa Park. Not all mortals were admitted, however. I was granted admittance only because I arrived with a popular Russian actress, Ludmilla, who had the same shoe size as me. That time at *Elegants* she ordered five pairs of shoes for herself and then gave them all to me; I wore them for years. I struck up a friendship with the store manager, and from then on I felt right at home there. Unfortunately, he later emigrated to Israel. I still visit the store, because one of its old shoemakers still works there." *Elegants* was a few doors down from the Latvian Writers' Union. I never did muster the courage to open the door and go inside; communist Rīga's store personnel were haughty, cold, unfriendly beings. Their behavior exemplified the Soviet economy, in which the customer was *not* king: rather, the store manager and employees were. And they could treat you like dirt.

According to Šaitere, "(Soviet era) stores had nothing nice to offer: no nice fabrics, no pretty shoes, no attractive handbags. Nothing remotely appealing. If anything was available, it was at the big (Soviet Latvian) manufacturing plants, like VEF, Radiotehnika, Zvaigzne ('Star'), Sarkanā Ausma ('Red Sunrise'), etc., but there was no equality in distribution there either: the bosses got first pickings. And that went for food products, too. The Ministry of Culture sometimes made sausage and instant coffee available to us. But whatever—we were young, in love, and now, looking back, everything seemed lovely."

Many Latvian (and Russian) women were extraordinarily good-looking: tall and slim, with great facial structure, lovely eyes, and super-long legs. In fact, many women in Latvia were drop-dead gorgeous, and today quite a number of Latvian models are walking the runways of famous fashion houses and are featured in their advertisements. By the late 1980s there were fashion designers with a name and a following, such as popular model-turned-fashion-designer Asnāte Smeltere. Elita Patmalniece is still one of Rīga's funkiest fashionistas and a jazzy painter; she sports a beehive hairdo, dresses in loud colors, and paints bright, happy paintings. In the late 1980s Patmalniece was like a splash of neon pink against Rīga's drab gray tones. Beneath the dull veneer of communism all sorts of colors were bubbling.

My look in the early 1980s: a mullet! Photograph/illustration: Andris Krieviņš and Rita Laima

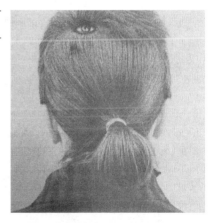

I went to Latvia in 1982 with my hair cut in a mullet (!): very short hair on the top of my head and a ponytail at the back. It must have shocked my mother-in-law. For many years my only make-up was (and still is) black kohl eyeliner and lipstick. I don't recall many women in Rīga with painted nails. Maija M. recalled a nail polish made by Florena of East Germany. "You could find foreign-made nail polish in second-hand shops for exorbitant sums, and the wives of sailors sold cosmetics in private." Ieva L. remembered locally manufactured nail polish that was sold in so-called *galantērijas* shops (haberdasheries) and peeled quickly: "Iridiscent nail polish was described in literature as something especially bourgeois-decadent." Egida P. recalled that the brushes of the domestically manufactured nail polish were of poor quality; the "hairs" fell out and got stuck in the nail polish. Iveta G. said that women used black shoe polish as mascara.

And oh those lines (Egida P.): "When people stood in line to purchase subscriptions to the theater, or for the newest books, or for boots at *Elegants*, then they stood in line for several days and nights. Family and friends helped out by taking turns. Everyone wrote down their number in line. It was 'fun'..." As with everything, even if stores had small batches of quality cosmetics and nail polish, it was reserved for "special customers." One needed *blats* for access to these. As with all Soviet products, packaging was of poor design and quality, which is why so many people were obsessed with Western cosmetics and goods. The appearance of Western products was already a sign of superiority.

Ilze Z. remembered: "The so-called *spekulanti* (speculators) were people with *blats.* They frequented sewing shops, stores, and hair salons, offering all sorts of deficit products at high prices: boots; shoes; make-up. In the 1980s Russian cosmetics were available in Rīga's stores, as well as nail polish. I remember a dry mascara kit that you had to spit into to wet the mascara."

Some older women, especially Russian *ghenshine*, sported garishly red and orange lipstick and three hair colors, piss yellow, proletariat purple, and revolution orange, which made me cringe. Many women bleached their hair with hydrogen peroxide, which gave them a cheap "Playboy bunny" look; I called them *urīngalvas* (urine heads). Egida P.: "Hair was bleached with hydrogen peroxide, which was mixed with whipped egg whites and then smeared into the hair. The hydrogen peroxide was a biting skin irritant." Believe it or not, according to my friends the purple hair color was obtained by using stamp dye. The orange color was obtained from henna. I was a bit surprised by my fellow Latvian women's obsession with blonde hair. Were they trying to live up to some sort of stereotype?

When it came to accessories like jewelry, the Soviet state had a monopoly on gold and silver, and therefore "private" jewelry makers had to use cheaper metals and alloys for their creations. Gold and silver jewelry was for sale only in state stores for exorbitant sums. Despite its claims, Soviet society was just as stratified as capitalist society, with "equals" and "more equals."

In spite of this obsession with beauty products, women in Latvia seemed more relaxed when it came to their looks and their body image. Hairy legs and armpits were a normal sight in the summer, as were mustaches and facial hair. People weren't as obsessed about personal hygiene as in the United States. Skinnydipping was natural; people were less prudish. I learned to accept my body in Latvia. Girls there did not struggle with serious conditions like anorexia and bulimia. Many girls were slender, and even those with a more robust figure looked natural. Greasy hair could be explained by a lack of hot water. There were many natural beauties in Latvia. Leonīds Tugaļevs' photographs of women from the late 1970s and early 1980s were absolutely striking.

The Controller Is Coming!

A trolleybus in Rīga in 1963. Photograph courtesy of Rīgas Satiksme.

In Rīga you could travel from one end of town to the other and beyond on an intricate web of tram, trolleybus, bus, and train lines. A network of electrical cables for powering trolleybuses and trams was draped over the capital. Trams, my favorite mode of transportation, were clean, comfortable, and efficient though often packed. Running on electricity, they were odorless, quiet, and smooth. Not many people had personal cars, as those were a Soviet deficit. People waited years for cars.

Transportation in Rīga in "the old days." A scene from Kaļķu iela in Old Rīga from the turn of the 20th century.

The rubber tires of the trolleybus gently swallowed Rīga's bumps and ruts in soft gulps, and the hum of its electric motor was soothing. Sometimes the cable detached from its overhead feeder, and the driver had to jump out with a pair of thick gloves to maneuver it back into place. Idle passengers looked on with interest, as the driver struggled with the cable. Would he/she succeed in reconnecting it? Small thrills...

Once on board, passengers had to validate their tickets by "punching" them in a special ticket puncher. Ticket "controllers" boarded public transportation randomly and stealthily, usually taking everyone by surprise. They wore no uniforms, only a concealed badge, so that no one could ever predict their intimidating surprise visit. If you were caught hitching a free ride, you had to get off at the next stop and pay a minor fine and wait for the next mode of transportation. I tried to avoid such confrontations by punching my tickets, because these people were not very nice. They took their job seriously and seemed to enjoy harassing delinquents and freeloaders. "Hurry up! The controller is coming!" Most people squirmed nervously.

233

Public transportation was cheap in the Soviet era, and the system operated smoothly, with very few delays. In the morning and late afternoon rush hours buses, trolleybuses, and trams were packed full like cans of sardines. Some passengers could also get to downtown and ride home on the minibus Latvija, a van manufactured by Rīgas Autobusu Fabrika (Rīga Autobus Factory) or RAF in Jelgava, a city just south of Rīga. In the 1990s I sometimes took advantage of this option; as we hurtled through the downtown streets and across the Daugava River towards Pārdaugava, smooshed together and wearing no seat belts, the little bus quivered, jolted by each and every rut and bump. I prayed.

The RAF 2203, also called "Latvija." Source: Wikimedia Commons https://commons.wikimedia.org/wiki/File:Latvija_RA F.JPG (© CC BY-SA 3.0 https://creativecommons.org/licenses/by-sa/3.0/deed.en)

Rīga's pushiest, rudest passengers were the little old ladies, especially Russian babushkas who had learned to get what they want, a cozy seat, by switching into "offensive" mode. They startled dozing or unsuspecting teenagers, lecturing them on the rights of the elderly. After successful dislodgement, they plopped down with their shopping bags grinning smugly, as the victim moved away, cursing under his/her breath.

From our trolleybus stop near the Red Riflemen's Memorial the ride to Dreiliņu iela in Pārdaugava to visit my mother-in-law was about 20 minutes. I always enjoyed that ride, which took us through the quaint streets of Pārdaugava with their old trees and wooden houses, fences, and yards full of lilacs blooming in May. My mother was born and grew up in Pārdaugava, a green and special part of Rīga that Aleksandrs Čaks lovingly described in his poems. "Ciao, Pārdaugava!" was the title of one of those. Other notable writers, including Jānis Akurāters, Andrejs Upīts, and Ojārs Vācietis and Ludmilla Azārova had also called Pārdaugava their home.

An elegant private residence in Mežaparks before the war. Image courtesy of the National Library of Latvia collection "In Search of Lost Latvia."

I could also easily walk to Tram No. 11, which went to Mežaparks ("Forest Park"), known as Kaiserwald in the "German era." Mežaparks was a beautiful, old suburb of Rīga with elegant houses from the pre-war era. What I didn't know was that during the Nazi occupation of Latvia the Germans had established the Kaiserwald concentration camp there. According to the Jewish Virtual Library, on account of its harsh conditions thousands of Jews died at Kaiserwald shortly before the Germans evacuated the camp in 1944, transporting its inmates to Poland.* In the 1980s Mežaparks was a pretty place that clearly showed the superiority of capitalism over Soviet Russian communism. In the 1980s some of Mežaparks' marvelous formerly private residences looked run-down; some were occupied by multiple families. Still others were occupied by the Soviet nomenklatura. The Rīga zoo and an amusement park were Mežaparks' main attractions. (*Source: https://www.jewishvirtuallibrary.org/jsource/Holocaust/Kaiserwald.html)

I quickly learned to get around the city and always appreciated the convenience of public transportation. A car seemed like an impossible dream for us in 1983. Juris had a car, a Lada that he kept locked up in a garage in Pārdaugava. He took good care of it and got a lot of mileage out of it. Car mechanics made a lot of money in Soviet Latvia. In fact, they were part of the Soviet Union's upper crust. Car parts were hard to come by. Mechanics' impressive private homes were evidence of their important position and leverage in Soviet society.

Right: An Art Deco poster from 1927 advertising the Rīga-Paris line. In the Soviet era the possibility of boarding a train in Rīga and traveling to Paris seemed like science fiction.

I have always loved and been fascinated by trains, marveled at the power of locomotives, enjoyed the mournful whistle sound of a train in the distance (a childhood memory), and appreciated them as a relaxing mode of transportation. Trains were a popular and valuable form of transportation in Latvia, with tracks branching out in all directions, connecting Rīga with other towns and cities and the countryside, as well as with foreign cities and countries. Before the war Latvians had been enthusiastic travelers who explored Europe and studied in cities like Berlin and Paris.

Rīga's Central Railway Station, the point of my first arrival in Latvia in 1980, was constructed between 1959 and 1965. It was a dreary box with tall windows and an uninviting, stark interior. The absence of benches discouraged loitering. A tall clock tower with colored lights in the large square in front of the station was a feeble attempt at imparting an aesthetic component to the box. A chapel in front of the old station to commemorate the miraculous survival of Russian Emperor Alexander III and his family in a train wreck was removed in 1925, because it was an unpleasant reminder of the tsarist era. Rīga was a cabbage head, an onion, with so many layers.

The square attracted all sorts of shady characters—hustlers and *spekulanti* who stood around smoking, leering, and trying to attract the attention of passers-by with hisses. Thousands of passengers streamed through the station on a daily basis, many arriving from Moscow, Minsk, Vilnius, Tallinn, Leningrad, and elsewhere. Tickets could be purchased at windows or from ticketing machines. Kiosks sold print media, cigarettes, candy, and odds and ends. I always purchased an ice cream at the station. Ice cream was irresistible in an economy with few perks and pleasures. The rest rooms were another story; I went in once, paled, and promptly exited, never to return.

From what I have read, in the years after World War II the station was a hub for *maišeļnieki* ("bag people"); that is, poor immigrants from other Soviet republics, especially Russia, who arrived in Rīga with their earthly possessions stuffed in sacks in search of a better life. After the USSR annexed the Baltic States, the border between Latvia and Russia was thrown wide open, admitting all sorts of traffic, including unsavory criminal characters. In the 1980s the station was full of shoppers and visitors from other Soviet republics.

In the summer the rails beckoned with a short ride to the beach, to Jūrmala and seaside towns in Vidzeme, which promised sunshine, warm, soft sand, and cool, refreshing water. Or you could take the train out to the beautiful town of Sigulda and enjoy a hike through the scenic Gauja River valley. The breathtaking Gauja National Park was within reach by train, as were many small rural towns.

The history of Latvia's railway system reflects Latvia's occupations by foreign powers. Latvia's original rail system was linked to Imperial Russia. During World War I the Germans came in and changed the rails, linking Latvia to Germany and the West. During the era of the First Republic (1918–1940) "Train No. 1" was the train to Berlin. "When we visited my mother's family in Zemgale, we took the Berlin train to Meitene, the last station in Latvia before Lithuania. I enjoyed these trips, because I could hear different languages being spoken," my mother recalled. When the Soviets occupied Latvia, the rails were switched back to the Russian gauge. When the Germans pushed into Latvia in 1941, the rails were switched back to the German system to help with the war effort. After World War II, Latvia's rail system was again linked to that of the Soviet Union, in effect disconnecting it from the West.

Right: The Viesīte "choo-choo" train. Could this be the same train my mother rode as a girl?

Once popular narrow gauge train lines for the cute little *mazbānītis* ("mini- train"), installed in the Tsarist Russia era for the transportation of cargo and people throughout the Latvian countryside and then by the Germans during World War I, were all but gone. My mother remembered the Jēkabpils-Viesīte narrow gauge line that cut through Biķernieki, her grandfather's property. "The tracks were very narrow, and the train chugged ahead slowly, rocking back and forth. It went up an incline so slowly that you could jump off safely, which is what my mother, my sisters, and I did."

During World War I the region of Sēlija was crisscrossed by narrow gauge rails installed by the Germans for bringing in ammunition and provisions. The front was near the Daugava River, with the Russians on the other side. The trains and tracks were an important lifeline for the Germans. When they retreated, the tracks, locomotives, and cars remained and were used for peaceful purposes during the First Republic. Today only one narrow gauge railway—the Gulbene-Alūksne line—remains in operation in Latvia. A souvenir from the past, it is a popular tourist attraction, offering its passengers a trip along a scenic route in northern Vidzeme. You can take a virtual ride on this line on YouTube and see a real choo-choo train—"the little engine that could"—in action.

The design of Soviet Latvia's locally built trains with their steep steps coupled with the lower than usual station platforms made embarking and disembarking difficult, awkward, and even a bit dangerous. If you had a child in a stroller or a baby carriage, you had to hope that some helpful fellow passenger would reach down and help lift the carriage up the steps into the train. These trains could not accommodate the disabled: for someone with a serious disability it was impossible to board such a train.

Over the years we rode trains out to Jūrmala, Sigulda, Tukums, and other sleepy Latvian towns. In the summer the open windows pulled in the heat and the sweet country air. I remember one of our trips to Ērgļi. We had purchased a chunk of "Latvijas" ("Latvia") cheese, the stinkiest cheese available on the market. Thirty minutes into the trip we realized that the entire car smelled toe cheese. Our delicious cheese was "fumigating" the car with its dirty sock aroma.

Left: A photograph from June 1941 of cattlecars stuffed with human cargo getting ready to depart from Rīga for Soviet Russia.

The train tracks going east towards Russia were once tracks of tears, despair, horror, and in many cases death for Latvia's citizens arrested and deported in 1941 to Soviet Russia's Siberian slave labor camps and forced settlements. Our friend Mārtiņš Bisters (b. 1924) was arrested by the Soviet Cheka (NKVD) at the age of 17 for being a Latvian Boy Scout leader. He told us of the anguish of the people stuffed into cattle cars that brought them closer and closer to Latvia's border with Soviet Russia and the point of no return in the summer of 1941. Mārtiņš told us that near Jēkabpils they spotted German tanks far off in the distance: however, those tanks failed to intercept the train, which rumbled on, crossing the border into Soviet Russia, where most of these innocents, "enemies of the Soviet state," would perish in inhuman conditions.

I met Mārtiņš Bisters in 1983. He lived in the seaside town of Asari with his wife Mērija and young son and grew tulip bulbs for a living. He was a sprightly senior with bright eyes and a sparkling wit. As a youth Bisters was an active member of (Latvia's) Boy Scouts, and the Soviet authorities did not like this. In January 1941 four chekists showed up at Bisters' door to arrest him: this was the beginning of his long journey to and from Siberia.

"I was 100% fanatically convinced that I would return, that nothing could happen to me; as I was leaving the room and my father came up to me, I said, 'I'll be back.' On the threshold I repeated it: 'Wait for me, I'll be back. No matter when.' And I did come back, the only one out of 900 to make it out alive."

After half a year of torture in the Soviet Cheka's cellars in Rīga, the prisoners were driven and forced into cattle cars. Seventeen-year-old Mārtiņš knew right away that they were being sent to Russia. Yet Mārtiņš was born lucky; he found a piece of paper from a pack of cigarettes and scribbled a note to his parents. Despite his fear of being shot, he dropped the paper through a hole in the floor to be used as a toilet. On the paper he wrote: "M. Bisters, Rīga, Stabu iela 116. We are being taken to Russia. I feel good and am well, don't worry. Please pass this on. 06/24/1941."

Someone found the note and published it in the *Tēvija* newspaper. Mārtiņš's parents saw it. Today after 70 years the note has been preserved. (It is now part of the collection of the Museum of the Occupation of Latvia.—RL)

(In Siberia) Mārtiņš saw how people sentenced to death lost their minds and died of starvation and disease, yet he says he survived because he was stubborn, shrewd, and fervently wished to go home. Many prisoners died of tuberculosis working in the copper mines. Mārtiņš's health suffered too, but he proudly claimed that he was not sick for even a day in Siberia.

In 1955 Mārtiņš was summoned to court. Someone in Rīga had negotiated the release of the youngest prisoners. After 14 years in exile he was given a train ticket home. From Moscow he sent his parents a telegram that he would soon be back in Rīga.

Mārtiņš remembered: "The train rolled into Rīga in the morning; my mother and father were there to meet me. It was a beautiful moment. My mother was crying, my father wiped a single tear from his cheek, and we started to walk back to Stabu iela. That evening relatives and friends came over to see me." (Source: "Šodien piemin komunistiskā genocīda upurus." TVNET. Published June 14, 2009. Retrieved February 16, 2014. <http://www.tvnet.lv/zinas/latvija/323346-sodien_piemin_komunistiska_genocida_upurus> Tr. RL)

In Latvia, stories can spout from trolleybuses, trams, and trains. Today the train to Ērgļi no longer exists, another memory dismantled. Thousands of miles of train tracks and memories associated with them have vanished. Latvia's choo-choo trains are all but gone. What remains are old photographs and documents that tell the tale of a nation that has been to hell and back.

Leniniana

Vladimir Ilyich Lenin, "Father of the Russian Revolution," boxed up in Cēsis, Latvia in April 2013. This particular Lenin was chiseled by Kārlis Jansons (1896–1986), a famous Latvian sculptor from Cēsis. Photograph by Kaspars Zellis.

"The subject of Vladimir Ilyich Lenin in Soviet fine arts has branched out in our times. It is explored in monumental art, painting and drawing, poster art, book design, and the decorative applied arts. Representatives of all the Soviet multinational art schools, including Latvian artists, have contributed to its enrichment.

It is safe to say that the subject of V. I. Lenin is one of the central subjects of Soviet art and at the same time one of its most complicated. The subject is made complicated by the simultaneously multi-faceted and uniform nature of Lenin's personality. According to A. Lunacharsky, V. I. Lenin was "a man who embodied both historical eminence and an unusual personal charm, whose moral and intellectual aspects were bound together in remarkable harmony."

In the last forty years, since Soviet rule was renewed in Latvia, the Leniniana of Latvian artists has widened; it has illuminated many of Lenin's brilliant facets in stone and bronze, on canvas and paper, reaching for a psychologically comprehensive portrait that will reflect historical truth. The subject of V. I. Lenin surged in Latvian art in preparation for his 100th birthday, and it continues to be explored today, as the Soviet nation celebrates the immortal genius' 110th anniversary." (Cielava, Skaidrīte. *Latviešu tēlotāja māksla*. Rīga: Liesma, 1980. Tr. RL)

The ghost of Vladimir Ilyich Lenin (1870–1924), the "Father of the Russian Revolution," hovered in the Soviet-occupied Baltic States and across the great expanse of the USSR. Depictions of the famous Bolshevik's head, bust, and body dominated the squares and centers of villages, towns, and cities. Big, small, flat, monumental, you name it: he came in all shapes, sizes, and materials. An enormous Lenin head looked out over Ulan-Ude, the capital of Buryatia in Russia. In Rīga,

Lenin stood at the intersection of Ļeņina and Kirova pointing east to the source of all our problems. He was on Soviet stamps; he lived in offices, parks, on building walls, and gazed down on school children in classrooms. Omnipresent. Young children in Latvia recited poems about him. My visits with the KGB were conducted in his presence; that is, he stared at me from his portrait on the wall.

His embalmed corpse, a major Russian tourist attraction, lay in a casket in a mausoleum on Moscow's Red Square, on view for the whole world to see. His mortal remains were the brunt of political jokes. It was a morbid business. The corpse had been there since 1924. During World War II it was whisked away to Siberia in the event of a Nazi invasion of Moscow and then returned to its permanent spot. Decades-old dead flesh. The probing eyes of countless visitors. Somehow it seemed indecent.

Ms. Cielava's eulogy to Lenin was a typical example of the academic literature published in communist Latvia. Just about everything was interpreted through Marxism-Leninism, even history that predated communism. In his marvelous travel journal *Rīga retour*, expatriate and history buff Andris Kadeģis, while visiting Latvia in 1960, is surprised to learn at the State Rīga History Museum that Latvians have been engaged in class warfare since the era of feudalism, and that Beethoven, too, was a fighter for the communist cause.* More than twenty years after Kadeģis' visit nothing in Latvia had changed: I read the Soviet communist spin on history everywhere. The emphasis was always on the same issues: evil capitalism; the exploited worker; class warfare; the historical role of Russia in setting things right; the friendship of nations, etc. Soviet communist ideology seemed to pervade every aspect of life. For me as a Latvian American, it was all new, alien, and totally silly. Unlike the Russians, for whom Lenin was a God, Latvians had no love for him; they saw Lenin as a bloodthirsty tyrant and oppressor. Nobody mentioned Stalin anymore, except in jokes. The trauma of Stalinism had barely healed. (*Klāns, Pāvils. *Rīga retour*. New York: Grāmatu Draugs. 1961. p. 225)

In the Soviet era the subject of Lenin and Soviet history kept Latvian sculptors employed. In marble, granite, and metal, they produced an army of stiff, severe-looking Lenins and other communist figures. Over time Lenin's features seemed to harden, because they were exaggerated.

In January 1919 the bodies of 27 supporters of a Soviet Latvia—the so-called *komunāri* (communards)—were buried behind the Russian Orthodox Cathedral. Under the short-lived (1918–1920) Bolshevik government of Pēteris Stučka, Esplanāde was renamed Komunāru laukums (Communards' Square). When the Bolsheviks were defeated, the bodies were dug up and moved to a cemetery, and the park became Esplanāde again. Esplanāde was also the setting for Latvia's song festivals from the late 18th century until the 1950s. The Latvian Army held their parades there in the 1920s and 1930s. After the war the Soviets changed the name back to Communard Square. A public skating area there had once kept Rigans happy in winter, but there was no trace of it in the 1980s.

In 1960 a Heroes' Alley was created next to the Latvian Art Academy near Communards' Square. Bronze busts of notable Latvian communists, Augusts Arājs-Bērce (1890–1921), Jānis Jansons-Brauns (1872–1917), Otomārs Oškalns (1904–1947), and others were mounted on granite pedestals and placed in two rows on either side of a walkway framed by linden trees and decorative shrubs. By the 1980s the trees had grown tall and formed a shady canopy over the "gallery" of bronze busts, which nobody seemed to take notice of. Nobody gave a rat's a-- about

the old Latvian communist vanguard. Nobody placed flowers by the pedestals. I looked at the busts from time to time but instinctively dismissed them as part of Soviet ideological warfare. The Soviet version of history was so one-sided, that it revolted me.

Soldiers of the Latvian Army in Esplanāde in 1936. Image courtesy of the National Library of Latvia collection "In Search of Lost Latvia."

Communards' Square Plaza underwent more changes following World War II. Between 1950 and 1952 plantings were made, thereby getting rid of the sandy parade field. Architect Kārlis Plūksne (1906–1973) and dendrologist Alfrēds Kapaklis (1889–1971) came up with the park's new design. Cement paths were put down, lawns were seeded, and trees, bushes, and perennials were planted. Plūksne had two water fountains installed. The paths were laid out in such a way as to lead towards a prominent area of the park, a sunny, open spot, where the monument to (poet) Jānis Rainis is now located near a large, rectangular flower bed. All of this was done to pave the way for a monument to Joseph Stalin. Rīga lacked a grandiose monument to Stalin, so the race was on to find the right spot. Without the appropriate spot, a competition for the monument's design could not proceed.

The first thought was to get rid of Rīga's Freedom Monument and put Stalin there. It was Vera Mukhina (1889–1953), born in Rīga, who opposed this idea, maintaining that the Freedom Monument was of high artistic caliber. In addition, experts noted that the area near the Freedom Monument was too small for Stalin. These two reasons saved the Freedom Monument from destruction. Once the decision was made, it was necessary to prepare Communards' Square for the great honor. Experts claim that the remains of the concrete base intended to support the Stalin monument are still buried beneath the large flower bed.

The competition to submit designs was announced in January of 1952. The design of Aleksandra (1901–1992) and Jānis Briedis (1902–1953) won first place. The produce pavilion at Rīga Central Market was vacated, so that the artists could commence their work there. A monument to Stalin could not be designed by just any old artist. It was a privilege reserved for the special few. Aleksandra and Jānis Briedis were superb sculptors, but it is highly unlikely that they wished to work on a monument to Stalin. To turn down the honor would be dangerous. There were quite a number of Stalin monuments in Latvia at the time, yet none of them was big enough or in a prominent central location. There was a large Stalin monument, two to three meters high, in the seaside town of Dubulti.

The main Stalin monument was to be seven meters tall, cast in plaster, split into sections, and shipped to Leningrad to be cast in bronze. The huge monument really needed a large area, which is why Communist Party officials worried that Communards' Square would be too small. Some party boss came up with the idea of connecting Communards' Square with Kirov Park (now Vērmanes) to make more room for the monument, and to call the new area Stalin Park. Because two streets, Ļeņina and Stučkas, were in the way, the plan included bulldozing those and connecting the two parks with paths and flower beds near the Supreme Court building. The nightmarish project was scrapped when Joseph Stalin died on March 5, 1953. On the day of Stalin's funeral his bust in Kirov Park was buried under mounds of flowers. After Stalin's death this bust was promptly forgotten: it remained in its spot until 1962 despite changes in the Soviet Union, the denouncement of Stalinism, and the removal of his body from Lenin's mausoleum. (Šidlovska, V., Mauriņa, B. "Esplanāde (no franču vārda esplanāde) Glacis." IAptieka.lv. Published November 5, 2008. / Retrieved October 10, 2012. <http://iaptieka.lv/?lapa=raksts&raksts=611> TR. RL)

Vera Mukhina is famous for the Soviet monument "Worker and Kolhoz Woman" in Moscow and for designing the *granonka*, the popular Soviet glass used for drinking vodka and also available at soda water dispensers. May Vera Mukhina rest in peace: she saved our Freedom Monument from destruction!

Generally speaking, Soviet era monumental sculpture was anything but creative or artistic: it was static, repetitive, boring, and even creepy. The many monuments to Lenin, the revolutionaries and communists, the fallen Komsomol fighters, and other Soviet heroes looked lifeless, no matter how talented the artist was. For someone like me who had been nurtured on modern art and loved the sculptures of Alexander Calder, George Rickey, Louise Nevelson, Louise Bourgeois, and other great modern sculptors, Soviet monumental sculpture appeared heavy, monolithic, and depressing. The ideological constraints robbed these works of life.

Left: A monument to revolutionaries at Matīsa Cemetery, Latvia. Source: Rīga. Latvijas Valsts Izdevniecība: Rīga, 1961.

The best in Soviet art—its true avant-garde—had happened a staggering 60 years prior to my arrival in Latvia, in the early 20th century; "non-objective" Suprematism and its astonishing artists and thinkers Kazimir Malevitch (1879–1935), El Lissitzky (1890–1941), and others produced art with lasting value. And then there was Constructivism, fueled by the revolution, with artists like Vladimir Tatlin, Naum Gabo, Liubov Popova, Alexander Rodchenko, Vladimir Mayakovsky, (Latvian) Kārlis Johansons (sometimes transcribed as Karl Iaganson), Valentina Kulagina, and her Latvian husband Gustav Klutsis (or Klucis), another victim of the Stalinist purges in the 1930s. The Russian Suprematists and Constructivists were the true avant-garde of Russia; their light was extinguished under Stalin with the introduction of socialist realism in 1934 and the terrible purges that followed.

The Russian avant-garde of the early 20th century remains a phenomenon to this day. None of the "official" Soviet art that I saw in the 1980s could compare to Russia's exciting and novel Suprematist and Constructivist art in the early 20th century. I experienced a depressing and maddening sense of regression and backwardness in all aspects of life in Soviet-occupied Latvia. It was as if everything had been turned upside down: old (as in pre-war) seemed new (as in novel and remarkable), while everything related to the Soviet era seemed bland and already dated.

Monuments to Stalin disappeared after the tyrant's death, but Lenin lived on, although Latvians knew stories of his cruelty and terrorism. In the 1980s Russian school teachers and their pupils visited monuments to Lenin to lay red carnations at his feet, whereas Latvians abstained when possible. Latvia's communist leaders assembled near the Lenin by Hotel Latvia on official Soviet days of commemoration, surrounding the monument with their Volgas and chauffeurs. I was appalled by this idolatry of a bloodthirsty tyrant who sent millions to their death. The Russians were a strange people, I concluded.

Left: Latvian Red Riflemen in Moscow, circa 1918. Source: Latvianhistory.wordpress.com.

Lenin's stature in Russia is not to be underestimated; he is still worshipped. There is a Latvian connection to Lenin. For a while Latvian "Red" Rifleman served as Lenin's bodyguards. For years a story circulated alleging that they executed the last Russian Tsar Nicholas II and his family. This story has been disproved. Latvians wished to sever their ties from Russia and its bloody state. Nobody I knew personally in Latvia had any affection for Lenin. In fact, I was convinced that, given the opportunity, most Latvians would have gladly taken a sledgehammer to Lenin and other Soviet era monuments, which represented a false narrative of history.

"Communism's Victory is Inescapable!"

Living in Soviet-occupied communist Latvia, I became acquainted with Soviet slogans and catchphrases, which could be found all over Rīga and in other towns and cities. Essentially, Soviet propaganda in Latvia replaced commercial billboards. I had grown up absorbing American commercial advertising, which pounded our brains from the TV, the radio, print media, and ugly roadside billboards. Whereas American capitalism reminded us of the the cheesiest pizza, the best "dentist recommended" toothpaste, and the squeeziest toilet paper, the Communist Party's self-glorifying signs relentlessly reminded the Soviet masses of communist ideology's utopian ideas and (ever elusive) rosy future.

Like the steady sound of a sledgehammer that one gets used to over time, these slogans were hackneyed and even absurd (judging by Soviet reality) and spawned comic spin-offs. For example, there was a slogan, "Partijas plāni—tautas plāni": "The Party's plans—the people's plans." According to my friend Oļģerts, some comedian at the Oktobris (October) kolhoz in Valka made subtle changes to the slogan, so that it read: "Pārtijai—plāni, tautai plāni," which means: "The Party has plans, (while) the people are bad off." (The word "plāni" has two meanings: "plan" and "bad.")

Left: A forced demonstration during the first Soviet occupation of Latvia, 1940–1941. "Long Live Latvia as a Soviet Republic!" "We demand Stalin's Constitution!" Photo: Museum of the Occupation of Latvia 1940–1991.

In the era of "High Stalinism," when the glorification of Joseph Stalin had reached its apex, manifesting itself in all walks of life, Latvian writers composed ghastly poems glorifying Stalin and Lenin. Many of these poems not only eulogized the mass murderer Stalin but groveled at the feet of Russians, singing praises to the Russian language and culture without which, apparently, Latvia and my people would be nothing. By the 1980s such humiliating stooping had subsided, but Soviet communist propaganda was still very much a part of everyday life in Latvia.

Jānis Grots

Tautu draudzība ("The Friendship of Nations")

The great, noble Russian people, dear to my heart, / And their language, which echoes far and wide, / Waking us in the morning and shimmering in the late hour, / It gave me Pushkin and Mayakovsky—

And many, many more. There is no end to them, / My heart hears new things, my thoughts wander far, / And leafing through a book, it feels like a nightingale / In the roses by the Volga is singing a song to Rīga.

The Russian language is giant bridges of rays / On which the Latvian word will ascend to higher horizons, /—Its brilliance envelopes our clan of workers / And lifts their spirits to their lifetimes' zenith. (Tr. RL)

Latvians who grew up in Soviet-occupied Latvia remember ideological "jingles"; many of them were direct translations of Russian slogans. They took on a life of their own and often morphed into hilarious jokes, which Latvians had the knack for telling with a straight face. I laughed a lot in the 1980s. The Party's promises of living in communism were twisted into anecdotes: if this deficit-ridden life was the bumpy road to communism, what would communism finally look like? How else to survive the madness if not with humor? The Russian Revolution, which had promised equality and happy days to all the working people, happened a long time ago, but you couldn't even buy toilet paper at the store.

While American youth munched on chips and fast food, absorbing jingles created by American advertising gurus, such as "Morris, Time for Din Din" (9-Lives cat food), "America's Cookie Jar" (Nabisco), "I am the Frito Bandito" (Fritos Corn Chips), "Mr. Whipple, Please Don't Squeeze the Charmin" (Charmin toilet paper), "Those Dirty Rings" (Wisk), etc. and watching the Lucky Charms leprechaun and "Snap, Crackle, and Pop" at work, communist Latvia's youth was raised on a completely different set of images and "values." They marched in unison, albeit unwillingly, in parades for the glory of the Communist Party and toiled in beet plantations in the summer. Their "jingles" were coined by Soviet ideologues.

Right, a Latvian poster from the 1950s for May 1st (International Workers' Day): "Long live May 1st!"

Visu zemju proletārieši, savienojaties! **(Proletariats of the world, unite!)**

Miers. Maijs. Darbs. **(Peace. May. Work.)**

Ekonomijai jābūt ekonomiskai. **(The economy must be economic.)**

Komunisma uzvara ir neizbēgama! **(Communism's victory is inescapable!)**

Tagadējā cilvēku paaudze dzīvos komunismā! **(This generation of humanity will live in communism!)**

Partija—mūsu laikmeta prāts, gods un sirdsapziņa. (The Party—our era's mind, honor, and conscience.)

Left: "PSKP slava!" ("Glory to the Communist Party of the Soviet Union!") This sign was on top of a building near the Latvian Freedom Monument, foreground.

Lai dzīvo PSRS tautu draudzība! (Long live the USSR peoples' friendship!)

Partijas plāni—tautas plāni. (The Party's plans—the people's plans.)

Komunisms = Padomju vara + visas zemes elektrifikācija. (Communism = The power of the Soviets + the whole country's electrification.)

Zem Marksisma-Ļeņisma karoga, komunistiskās partijas vadībā—uz priekšu uz komunisma uzvaru! (Under the flag of Marxism-Leninism and the Communist Party's leadership—onward to communism's victory!)

Partija un tauta ir vienota! (The Party and the people are united!)

Komunisma idejas dzīvo un uzvar! (The ideas of communism live and are victorious!)

Mums maizi nevajag—darbu dodiet! Mums saules nevajag—mums Staļins/Ļeņins/partija staro! (We don't need bread—give us work! We don't need the sun; Stalin/Lenin/the Party shines upon us!)

Needless to say, this is an older slogan, recalled by a friend of mine Ēvalds, a Soviet Army veteran.

Pasaulei mieru! Slava PSKP! Partija svinīgi pasludina: nākamā padomju cilvēku paaudze dzīvos komunismā! (Peace to the world! Glory to the Soviet Union's Communist Party! The Party solemnly announces: the next generation of Soviet peoples will live in communism!) Of course, Latvians both tittered and shuddered at such promises...

Piecgadi trijos gados! (The Five Year Plan—in three years!)

Fresh Air in the Latvian Countryside

Spring 1983. My first time in the "real" Latvian countryside: that is, beyond the confines of Soviet-imposed travel restrictions for tourists from the Free World. Here I am leaning against an old building in Piebalga. This farmstead was just one of many abandoned properties that I would see in the years to come. Photo: Andris Krieviņš.

We had passed the cold winter months prior to our wedding in Rīga in the company of friends and family. We also attended concerts and plays and dealt with the issues of practical life. Unlike my mother who did her grocery shopping once a week, I shopped nearly every day, because the food in Latvia was perishable, produced without additives and preservatives, and our refrigerator, which we shared with Juris, was very small. I had gotten the hang of shopping and was lugging home heavy purchases, doing the dirty laundry, and coping with our chronic water shortages while Andris was at work. In other words, I was being domesticated. My early translation work helped boost my self-esteem.

Rīga had a thriving culture scene, with artists, writers, actors, and musicians plying their talents and keeping the public entertained. I was getting used to some of the local popular music, such as Eolika with its bouncy lead singer Olga Rajecka, a great band called Sīpoli ("Onions"), the composer Imants Kalniņš and his ensemble Menuets, and Pērkons ("Thunder"), Juris Kulakovs' famous band. Used to American music radio stations, I was very disappointed to discover that there was nothing of the sort in communist Latvia. We had a small tape recorder/radio, which I turned on from time to to time, catching a drift from Warsaw, Poland. Nobody seemed to know anything about American or British rock and roll, and I was forced to adapt to this different world of music.

What lay beyond Rīga, this city of more than a million that was Latvia's capital and center of political, social, and cultural activity? Rīga ended where the Latvian countryside began, and we were itching to see it. Rīga's air was heavy with the fumes of motor vehicles; I needed fresh air. With my visa situation resolved and a residency permit in hand, shortly after our wedding I received permission to take a trip to Paulēni, my in-laws' place in Piebalga.

The Krieviņš family spent much of their spring, summer, and early autumn at their beloved cottage gardening, entertaining, and enjoying the fresh air, beauty, and tranquility of the Vidzeme countryside. I assumed I was the first American (under the Soviet occupation) to venture out to Piebalga, a very scenic part of Latvia known for several famous Latvian writers and public figures, like Atis Kronvalds (1837– 1875), the Kaudzīte brothers, Reinis and Matīss (1848–1926 and 1839– 1920, resp.), "King of the Latvian Fairy Tale" Kārlis Skalbe (1879–1945), and Antons Austriņš, *right* (1884–1934). I had cared for Austriņš's  widow in Astoria, Queens in the months preceding my departure for Latvia in 1981; their daughter Mudīte had been one of the muses of the Hell's Kitchen writers in New York and was a good friend of poet Imants Ziedonis. Austriņš's birthplace, Kaikaši ("Foot Scratchers"), was on the way to Paulēni. Mudīte would have been thrilled to hear that I was going to go by her father's "old place."

Packing ourselves and our provisions into Juris' small but sturdy Lada, we drove out of Rīga with a sense of relief and anticipation, heading up the Pskov (now Vidzemes) Highway, a two-lane strip stretching from Rīga to Veclaicene near the Estonian border in a northeasterly direction. I looked out at the landscape with interest and emotion. We passed a couple of charming, crumbling old taverns. What a shame! Latvia's countryside was like seeing the fatherland for the first time. Rīga was one thing; the Latvian landscape triggered a different set of emotions.

At the old *Bērzkrogs* ("Birch Tavern") we took a right turn, heading southeast towards Vecpiebalga and Madona. Solitary wooden dwellings dotted the otherwise empty, hilly landscape. Despite kolhoz villages, many people were living in the old houses where they could keep a cow, a pig or two, sheep, chickens, and grow their own vegetables and flowers. Most Latvians appeared to like the solitary *viensētnieka* ("farmsteader") life. The *viensēta*—the Latvian farmstead—has been part and parcel of our history and our ethnic way of life, even under the German barons, although Latvians were always present in German Rīga.

The word *viensēta* seemed to hark back to those times when our ancestors had to build *sētas* ("fences") around their homes to keep out wild animals. So firmly entrenched was the *viensēta* in our consciousness, that even Latvian painters in exile, like Voldemārs Avens (b. 1924) and Jānis Kalmīte (1907–1996) referenced it in their semi-abstract works. American architect Frank Lloyd Wright would have appreciated the Latvian *viensēta's* organic appearance: constructed primarily of timber and stone, often with thatched roofs, the old buildings blended with the Latvian landscape.

Architect Pauls Kundziņš summed it up this way: "The Latvian *viensēta* has existed for nearly 2,000 years. In this span of time the Latvian nation pursued its way of life on farmsteads generation after generation. If someone for some reason was separated from their native farmstead, experiencing a different way of life, they still felt deeply connected to their father's farmstead." Most of the Latvian classical literature that I had read was set in the countryside in works by Rūdolfs Blaumanis, Anna Brigadere, Jānis Akurāters, the Brothers Kaudzītes, Jānis Poruks, Augusts Saulietis, Kārlis Skalbe, Edvards Virza (*Straumēni*), and others. We had sung folk songs about the beauty of the Latvian farmstead: "*Skaista mana brāļa sēta tik cēlai vietiņā*" ("Beautiful is my brother's farmstead in such a lovely spot"). Thus my first experiences outside of Rīga were significant, because preconceived, sketchy impressions suddenly materialized into actual settings in what was an archetypal landscape. (Pauls Kundziņš, *Latviju sēta*. Stockholm: Daugava, 1974.)

It was said that Latvians shunned village life. *Sādžas* or *derevnyas*—rural villages typical of Russia—could be found in Latgale, which borders Russia. The clumps of apartment buildings that kolhozes had built in the small rural centers all over Latvia were drab and claustrophobic in appearance. Yet there were people who preferred to live there, where they could enjoy the luxury of running water and small town gossip.

On the way to Piebalga: Taurene in a photograph from the 1930s with the bridge over the Gauja River. The buildings pictured here were still standing in 1983. Image courtesy of the National Library of Latvia collection "In Search of Lost Latvia."

The late winter palette of brown and patchy white imbued the Vidzeme landscape with a sense of cold loneliness. I was surprised to be feeling underwhelmed. Accustomed to summers in the magnificent, picturesque Catskill Mountains of New York State, Latvia's puny hills and muted March colors, as well as the hint of mud and the shabby look of buildings did not trigger any feelings of excitement for me. As Juris extolled the beauty of the landscape we were driving through, I wondered guiltily why I wasn't "feeling it." It would take several years for Latvia's beauty to grow on me. Still, the trip was, literally, a breath of fresh air. We could feel the difference immediately. There was a joke that the air in the countryside was so fresh, that one had to lie down and inhale a car's exhaust fumes from time to time to lessen the shock to the lungs.

Unlike New Jersey, where roadsides in congested areas were "littered" with gawdy billboards, garish signs, and millions of glaring lights competing for attention, Latvia's rural roadsides were devoid of commercial signage. At night the countryside was pitch black. In the absence of private enterprise and initiative, state-owned stores were inconspicuous and carried a very limited quantity of merchandise. In the evening these stores were closed. The three small shops that we passed and would later frequent in the villages of Taurene, Vecpiebalga, and Ineši were announced by plain, barely noticeable signs with the word *Veikals* ("Store") written on them. All of these stores had a specific, sour smell to them. Stacked canned goods—peas in a layer of white fat, colorless diced vegetables—were a prime component of their offering. Fresh bread, cheese, sausage, candy, crackers, cookies, beverages, cigarettes, booze, beer; one never knew what one was going to find at the store. Sometimes there was a nice surprise, which kept people talking for days. Many remote areas were serviced by an *autoveikals*, a truck stocked with provisions that stopped at regular intervals along certain routes.

Some of the people standing in line at these stores out in the boondocks had risen from the soil: brown and gray; mouths missing teeth; rough, red, and calloused hands; broken fingernails crusted with dirt and machine lubricants; prematurely wrinkled skin; dirty clothes. Some of them smelled. Even some women wore ugly *pufaikas*, practical, batted jackets used by the Soviet military. They stood by their kolhoz men like androgenous beings. They could straddle a tractor like a man and easily compete in emptying "granonkas" (shot glasses) filled with *Kristāldzidrais* ("Crystal Clear" vodka). Drinking was a big part of Soviet social life, especially in the countryside. Because what else was there to do? There were no malls, no movie theaters, and no American-style recreation centers. Homo Sovieticus drank vodka, the mother of inebriation, smoked, and coupled. Alcoholism was rampant. It shortened the life expectancy of many Soviet-born men. But Latvians were prone to alcoholism anyway. *Bērnu nami* or children's homes (orphanages) had also proliferated, adding to Latvia's misery.

A liter of vodka, called a *polšs*, was like liquid cash back then. Many men weren't interested in helping out for money; they demanded a *polšs*. So my father-in-law had a stash of the *baltais dzidrais* ("white and clear") stuff on hand for tractor drivers and handymen whose skills were needed from time to time, for ploughing the soil, fixing the roof, masonry work, etc. According to narcologist Dr. Jānis Strazdiņš, the old Straupe Manor in Vidzeme was renovated by recovering alcoholics who were mostly skilled carpenters.

Many of the country folks looked like the salt of the earth: oldsters and simple folk. Their roots ran deep in the Piebalga hills. Quiet people, like the gray boulders that lay in the fields and meadows. Women with a *lakatiņš* (kerchief) tied beneath their chin; simply but neatly dressed, tireless workers. They looked like they had been around forever, timeless.

When I became a regular visitor to the countryside, I enjoyed my trips to these stores. When there is nothing else to be had, you begin to enjoy the few items that avail you of any sort of pleasure: tiny Īriss caramels; a fresh loaf of white bread; cheese; a bottle of *kvass*. Strangely, wine was an alcoholic beverage that was not readily available in the Soviet era; few people remembered or drank it. One item these stores rarely carried, if ever, was fresh fruit; an irony considering that tons of fresh fruit were rotting in kolhoz orchards. Kids were crazy about a toxic-green soda called Tarhūns, which reminded me of Mountain Dew. Chewing on sweet little caramels and topping them off with Tarhūns probably contributed to widespread caries in Latvia's countryside.

Trips to the store were a big outing. Every item's "desirability" index value was determined by its availability. Homo Sovieticus learned to scope out a store's supply in a glance and then swoop in for the "kill." (I acquired this skill, too.) Luckily, the atmosphere in rural stores was more laid back, because there were a lot less people. Our eyes hungrily roamed along the shelves in hopes of spotting something desirable, something needed, something hard to find... Stores in the provinces were often stocked with items that were hard to find in the Rīga metropolis, where visitors from Russia and beyond flocked to shop. In the Soviet command economy it was impossible to keep up with demand.

With the permission of Communism Road, the local kolhoz in Ineši, in 1980 or so Juris Krieviņš purchased part of an old farm on top of Paulēnkalns, a hill with a pretty view, for 50 Soviet roubles. That sum bought him what was left of an old granary and a barn/shed, which had once been part of an old farmstead called Paulēni. There were strict limits on how much land Soviet citizens could utilize for their personal needs; Juris' "share" was basically a small patch on a hilltop but with a stupendously gorgeous view all around. He was entitled to use that patch for his needs, such as subsistence gardening. The kolhozes and local town councils were essentially proxies of the Soviet state; you wanted to be on good terms with their bosses, not exactly the most forthcoming people.

Most of the farmhouses around Paulēni were occupied. The famous composer Imants Kalniņš (b. 1941) was our closest neighbor. He was a bit of a recluse, so we barely saw him. Our other neighbor, old Vīksnas *māte* ("Mother" Vīksna), lived alone like so many old Latvian women whose spouses had passed away. She hobbled around with difficulty, her backbone bent into a boomerang. She had a cow and tottered between the house and barn supported by a cane. Her farmhouse was old and lovely, with apple trees that bloomed white and pink in the spring. The large shed by the road, which had been part of her homestead, had been appropriated by the kolhoz, which had dug a smelly silage pit alongside it.

Another neighbor was nosy, beady-eyed "Tante" ("Auntie") Lida. My husband called her "Pithecantropus" for her primitive personality. Lida was an "outsider" who harked from Belarus. She was a marvel of endurance, walking for kilometers just to gossip and tell on us, which is why Juris and Biruta advised me not to talk to her. It had not occurred to me that gossip could be such a big part of country life. Then again, there were many Latvian folk songs about gossip and slander.

Left: Evening light at Paulēni. Photo: Andris Krieviņš.

Allegedly one of the wealthier farmers in the area, the original owner of Paulēni, Jānis Skrābāns, his (?) mother Marija, and his (?) sister, also Marija, perished under the Soviets. According to "These Names Accuse," Jānis Skrābāns (born in 1900, son of Pēteris Skrābāns, a book publisher who taught in Vecpiebalga) was arrested in 1941 and died en route to Siberia at the age of 41. His mother died in Siberia in 1945; she was 80 at the time of her death. Skrābāns' sister (?) died in Siberia in 1944, aged 44. The site states that Alīda Skrābāns (his wife?) and a baby, Leons, survived and were eventually released and returned to Latvia. We never saw them.

Juris and Andris had worked diligently to restore the old granary, straightening it and putting on a new roof. They also put up a new shed, which covered one third of the old barn's foundation. Juris installed a smokehouse on the east side of the shed. (I can still remember the delicious taste of his home-smoked chicken, pork, and bacon.) Stacks of firewood were kept at the other end, and a small chicken coop was installed by the stone wall. Juris paid somebody to excavate a delightful pond, which he stocked with fish. Lastly, he and Andris built a traditional Latvian *pirts* (sauna), which attracted the interest of our neighbors.

The old granary, which had been transformed into a summer cottage by the time of my arrival, was fronted by two rows of tall, magnificent ash trees that provided pleasant shade in hot weather. The driveway leading up to the house was lined by old maple trees, which reminded

251

me of New England. Somewhere father and son had discovered and hauled back three magnificent old millstones. Two of these were set upright into the lawn as garden art, welcoming our visitors. The third millstone was laid flat between the pond and house and could be used as a place to sit and lunch. A headless angel covered in downy moss, saved from the senseless destruction of Rīga's Great Cemetery, knelt by the table, its hands clasped in prayer. A small, round boulder—a substitute for its lost head—was perched on its shoulders.

An enormous lilac bush brushed up against the south side of the house, perfuming the air in late spring. The granary, which was traditionally used to store harvested grains and other products and household items, now functioned as a small but cosy cottage, thanks to the men's vision and diligent hands. A small, nicely sheltered veranda was flanked on both sides by tiny antechambers, once used for storage, which now served as bedrooms: one for Juris; one for Andris (and now me). A large dowry chest had been placed in the middle of the veranda as a decorative element, no doubt retrieved from some abandoned farmstead. The veranda was a nice place to hang out to take in the beautiful view towards the pond and Lake Inesis in the distance. When it rained, you could see the pond quiver and the fishes jump.

Our tiny bedroom accommodated a simple bed made of planks of wood and topped by a thin mattress, and a window that could be opened for fresh air. My husband's black and white photographs and some dried summer solstice wreaths hung on the walls—roughly hewn logs. Juris slept in the other chamber on a mattress stuffed with hay.

An old, low door fit for elves opened from the veranda to a cosy kitchen. A lovely antique buffet for dishes, spices, paper, and other supplies stood against one wall. Products like salt, sugar, tea, coffee, and flower vases were lined on a shelf. The cottage did not have running water, so several times a day we had to walk to the well to draw water in a pail and carry it back to the house. A compact wood-burning stove heated the kitchen and adjacent bedroom. The stove was efficient, and we used it for all of our cooking and baking, as well as for heating water for washing dishes. The only drawback was that the flames singed the bottoms of the pots and kettles black, making for messy cleanup. Preparing meals and washing dishes was a time-consuming affair. Water could also be quickly boiled in a jug with an electric prong. A small refrigerator held some of our most perishable provisions, like meat, eggs, and dairy products.

A small outhouse with a splendid view was situated a short stroll from the cottage; it was a nice place to sit for a moment and gaze through the tiny window at the Piebalga treetops. In the summer I sometimes walked out into the yard in the middle of the night and peed in the grass beneath the stars. If it was bitterly cold, we had chamber pots tucked beneath our beds.

Juris eventually replaced the sturdy round table in the kitchen with a rectangular wooden table with an ethnic Latvian design and with benches. Biruta and her charge, Elīna, slept in a small bedroom off of the kitchen. And then there was the "living" room with a fireplace, where Biruta baked her delicious sourdough bread and dried her apples and herbal teas. There were a couple of beds in the living room for guests and two round, antique storage bins (*tīnes*), the kind you could find at the Latvian Ethnographic Open-Air Museum. An old, free-standing closet was jampacked with clothes and linens. Some of Juris' black and white photographs decorated the dark timber walls.

A narrow staircase in one corner led up to a trap door, which opened to the second floor, which was used mostly for storage. A long shelf contained a variety of antiques, including some old hand mills and antique photographs discovered in forsaken homes. Who had abandoned their ancestors? Portraits of strangers, couples with frozen gazes from a distant era, hinted at the drama of the 20th century. A large window provided a lovely view of the sunset. The second floor was rarely used, although one summer I worked there to complete my drawings for *Indian Tales.* The trap door nearly killed me, falling on my head once as I was edging myself down the stairs. Luckily I was wearing my Qaraqul hat.

Both Juris and Andris possessed an eye for beauty and charm. Thus Juris had commissioned an old friend, Mārtiņš Zaurs, to decorate the ends of a couple of crossbeams by carving faces into them. Zaurs (1915–1998) was a "leftover" from the old times (the First Republic) who had studied sculpture at the Latvian Academy of Art and was affiliated with *Zaļā vārna* ("Green Crow," 1925–1939), a group of artists, writers, actors, and musicians who exhibited, performed, and hung out together. Out of this camaraderie of creative personalities emerged some of Latvia's most famous artists and writers of the pre-war era: writers Austra Skujiņa, Aleksandrs Čaks, Ēriks Ādamsons, Jānis Kadilis; and artists Kārlis Baltgailis, Pēteris Upītis (my kindly mentor at the Art Academy), Francisks Varslavāns, Kārlis Štrāls, Valdis Kalnroze, Frīdrichs Milts, Ansis Cīrulis, and others. Juris had a knack for meeting and befriending remarkable people.

Mārtiņš Zaurs was a real character. His famous assembly of wooden sculptures, "Vagara trejača dzimta" ("The Dynasty of Foreman Three-Eyes"), was on permanent view at the Ethnographic Open-Air Museum. Zaurs had studied sculpture under Kārlis Zāle and had worked in porcelain and printmaking. In the 1980s he lived in Mežotne, Zemgale in a fairytale-like "castle" he built for himself as a studio, called Stūrīši. Apparently Stūrīši was a popular destination for young couples on their wedding day. Zaurs was an avid collector of porcelain, artists' self-portraits, bells, mortars, musical instruments, books, and antiques.

It was said that our granary sat on top of a 12th century gravesite. Information on the Internet ("Paulēnu senkapi"—Paulēni gravesite) corroborates this, but whether the burial ground is directly beneath the granary is not clear. What did these people look like? What did they wear? What did their language sound like? I often wished I could step into a time machine.

The shed was used for storing firewood and garden tools and as a garage for Juris' car. A ladder led up to a second floor, where guests could spend the night in a pile of sweet hay. Lake Inesis was visible through the window. In 1983 Andris and I painted some bird houses for thrushes with designs that included a Latvian flag and mounted them on the outside of the shed, giggling when the *ciema vecene* ("village hag"—chief of the village council) showed up a couple of times to check up on us.

The old cellar next to the cottage was in excellent condition. Long and dark and illuminated by a single lightbulb, it provided a cool storage area for our annual harvests of potatoes, carrots, beets, cabbage, and other vegetables, as well as the fruit of our labor—our preserves, including pickles, canned vegetables, jams, and juices. The roof of the cellar was covered with a layer of sod. Small bats slept in the cellar, hanging from the ceiling.

In 1983 Juris and Andris were just beginning work on a *pirts* (sauna), which they had positioned right next to the pond for immediate access to water. Once the woodstove and chimney were completed by a local mason who worked for a *polšs* (bottle of vodka), the *pirts* was ready for use. Oh heavenly invention! I could give up my ghost in a *pirts*! The experience of lounging naked in candlelight in its tremendous heat, feeling grimy sweat and bad feelings ooze away, is unforgettable.

It took about two hours to get the *pirts* ready. The stove, its mouth full of crackling firewood and dancing flames, heated up a large cauldron of water and a metal drum filled with rocks. When the firewood had burned up, you could shut the damper, open the door to the drum, and throw water over the super-hot rocks. A tongue of steam shot out through the door like the breath of a hissing dragon, filling the *pirts* with a hot mist that drew beads of sweat from our bodies. That scorching mist licked our naked skin, scraping it clean. Then it was time to get up on the *lāva* (bunk) to lie down and have someone spank you with a freshly cut birch switch (a *slota*). This massage felt amazing, and the birch leaves smelled of sweet tea.

Then it was time to take the plunge. Out through the door, down to the footbridge, and into the spring-fed cold pond we hurtled, sinking down and bobbing back up, reborn each time. Our incandescent bodies throbbed in the shock wave of iciness. The starry sky over Piebalga twinkled the way it had for millennia. Exhilaration! Over and over again you could run into and out of the *pirts*, cleansing your body, spirit, and mind. The experience of a Latvian *pirts* is the closest I have been to a sense of utter bliss. It was practically orgasmic.

After these breathtaking plunges, it was time to soap up, rinse off with the pond's soft water, and then dress to go home. Biruta had prepared a pot of hot tea, and it felt fabulous to settle into bed like a newborn babe. It was said that in the old days many a child was born in the *pirts*, and the deceased were washed there before being laid to rest. The *pirts* was heaven on earth, a physical connection between this life and some other realm, yes, indeed.

Strangely, it was the Rigans who built saunas on the properties they bought and renovated. Were the locals too busy, too tired, too drunk, or too indifferent to the thought of building their own wash house? Our milk providers came to our sauna to wash once in a while. At any rate, no daily showers for anyone, including me. The *pirts* was a once-a-week pleasure. For daily hygiene, we washed our feet and other unmentionable parts with cold pond water in the *pirts*.

Plum trees and black and red currant bushes grew near the pond. Juris added a strawberry bed there and planted a small orchard of apple trees, which began bearing fruit a few years later. A large vegetable garden on the west side of the cottage guaranteed tiresome weeding work all summer long, but the harvest was a joy. From the garden we reaped potatoes, carrots, yams, beets, turnips, rutabagas, cabbages, cauliflower, cucumbers, peas, beans, onions, lettuce, radishes, dill, etc. Juris built a simple greenhouse with a primitive frame and plastic siding for tomatoes.

Biruta had a small rose garden, and purple clematis opened its gorgeous blooms in June against the cottage's gray wall. Peonies flourished along the vegetable garden, as did a row of yellow *kaukāza* (Caucasian) plum trees. Juris kept the yard's grass neatly trimmed with a scythe. He and Biruta were very hard workers.

It was my summers at Paulēni that opened my eyes to the subtle beauty of the Latvian countryside. Sitting on the bench on the southwest side of the cottage, my gaze took off like a swallow from the top of Paulēnkalns and soared across the undulating tapestry of Vidzeme's highlands, a patchwork of evergreen trees and verdant meadows that changed colors with the wind, clouds, and sunlight. A crumbling windmill near the winding Ogre River added just the right touch of romanticism to burn this vista into my heart like a tattoo. Leaning against the round, upright millstones, one could gaze upon the shimmering waters of Lake Inesis and its seven islands. For Juris and Andris this was their way of preserving our cultural past, through restoration and beauty.

Left: Count Boris Sheremetev in a portrait by Ivan Argunov from 1768. Source: Wikimedia Commons https://commons.wikimedia.org/wiki/File:Boris_Sheremetyev_by _I.Argunov_%281768,_Kuskovo%29.jpg (© Public Domain)

The town of Ineši and its vicinity, including the land surrounding Paulēni, was part of the "Communism Road" kolhoz. The bad state of the roads and the depressed appearance of the area, despite its natural beauty, resulted in many jokes about the name of the kolhoz: in other words, the road to communism was going to hell. The village council was located in an old, run-down manor from 1786 that had once belonged to Russian Field Marshall Boris Sheremetev (1652–1719), *left*, who captured Rīga in 1710 in the Great Northern War. Sheremetev never actually lived on the remote estate that was presented to him by Peter the Great for his military accomplishments. The manor was burned down during civil unrest in 1905 but promptly rebuilt. The manor belonged to the Sheremetev family until 1920. To someone like Count Sheremetev, Piebalga might have seemed like the end of the world. He died in St. Petersburg. (Source: Celotajs.lv.)

Not far from the manor a road snaked off through an area called "Blood Valley," where writer Vizma Belševica (1931–2005) had a summer house. (Belševica was nominated for the Nobel Prize in Literature several times.) Blood Valley allegedly got its name when the army of Russia's Ivan the Terrible (1530–1584) swept through it in the 16th century Livonian War (1558–1583), killing every inhabitant in its path. Victims' heads were impaled on stakes. Or so the story goes. Piebalga was a place with a rich history that a few local enthusiasts and patriots were trying to preserve. The average lout on a tractor was more interested in booze than history, books, or artifacts. According to Juris, many old Piebalgans were gone forever on account of the war, and those who had moved in from other areas and worked for the kolhoz had no roots in or awareness of Piebalga's history. The loss of collective memory had taken a toll on Piebalga and other places in Latvia.

In Vecpiebalga's old cemetery we visited the graves of Atis Kronvalds (1837–1875) and the brothers Reinis (1839–1920) and Matīss Kaudzīte (1848–1926) to commemmorate the Latvian National Awakening period of the late 19th century. Kronvalds—a writer, teacher, linguist, and advocate for the rights of Latvians, their language, and culture—was a man whose portrait and importance I knew well from Latvian school in the United States. The two brothers Kaudzīte's most famous book, *Mērnieku laiki* ("The Era of the Surveyors"), I had read parts of; its colorful main characters were familiar to most Latvians. In the mid-1980s this famous book was drama-tized and performed next to Piebalga's Lake Alauksts with a huge cast, props, and real horses and wagons. My history lessons were coming to life in Piebalga. Kārlis Skalbe's lovely home, Saulrieti ("Sunsets"), was nearby. Our "King of Fairy Tales" was forced to flee in 1944 and died in exile in Sweden a year later.

What else was there in Ineši, the tiny village just past Vecpiebalga, besides an old manor and some ugly apartment buildings? Not much. A small stream called Orisāre that dried up in the summer. A store that offered little. A bus stop to get you to Cēsis, a bigger town down the road, and to Rīga, the magnet of rural youth. The road to communism was full of ruts and potholes. Yet the surrounding countryside was wild and beautiful.

Driving out from Vecpiebalga toward the village of Ineši and the domain of Communism Road, a substantial pile of rubble could be seen in the distance in the middle of a large meadow. That pile of stones was all that was left of the Rīga Archbishop's castle, built between 1340 and 1365. The castle was destroyed in 1577 in the the Livonian War*. For an American like me, the antiquity of such a site was positively thrilling. I had to think of my older brother Arvils, a history buff: he would have a blast exploring those ruins. *www.vecpiebalga.lv

For most of Piebalga's inhabitants, life was all about working the land and looking down at the soil—tilling, seeding, planting, weeding, harvesting. Feeding, milking, slaughtering livestock and stocking Soviet warehouses and freezers and one's own cellar with food for the long winter. This was farm country and always had been, although Piebalga's terrain was hilly and rocky. This paucity of large arable lands had spawned the emergence of artisans, weavers, and potters in the past. Those traditions had barely survived.

Not that much had changed since the olden days. People lived in houses heated by wood stoves (no central heating or cooling except in the Soviet era apartment buildings). Nor did most of these homes have running water; everyone had a well nearby, as well as an outhouse. Some old farm houses, such as my great-grandfather's, had a "dry toilet" inside of the house, which func-tioned perfectly (never any leaks or plumbing problems). Many women still washed and rinsed their laundry in a tub. There were no Laundromats in the area. You could still see people plough-ing their gardens with a horse; horse carts on the road were not uncommon. Under the Soviets, Latvia experienced a profound economic and technological regression. In the summer and fall Latvians went into the woods in search of berries and mushrooms to preserve, because straw-berry, raspberry, and blueberry jams, a labor intensive product, were not for sale in stores any-where. In addition, there was an enormous quality gap between the preserves sold in stores and those made at home.

Left: Incēni, the childhood home of Kārlis Skalbe, Latvia's "King of Fairy Tales," in Piebalga. Image courtesy of the National Library of Latvia collection "In Search of Lost Latvia."

Under the communists, besides working for the local kolhoz many people also had their own gardens and chickens, cows, and pigs. The unreliable kolhoz system simply did not produce enough food for local consumption. Fresh meat was not available at the Ineši store. Ironically, the Soviet kolhoz system reminded me of feudalism, in which serfs first had to attend to the needs and of their (German) master and his estate and only then to their own needs, as time permitted. I heard that most of what Latvia's kolhozes produced was shipped off, much of it for foreign (Russian) consumption. Moscow especially was a gigantic, hungry mouth. Sure, Latvia had its "super" kolhozes, such as Ādaži and Lāčplēsis; some of these had their own stores and market stands in Rīga. The Lāčplēsis store on Suvorova iela was a rather nice destination; I sometimes purchased delicious dill pickles and fresh eggs there.

In their spare time people watched TV and read print media. Newspaper and magazine subscriptions were cheap, subsidized by the state. Life in the countryside, however, was characterized by constant, steady work. To keep your house warm, you had to chop wood and feed the stoves. Water, heat, and food required active physical labor.

Left: Vecpiebalga Church as it looked in the 1980s. Image courtesy of the National Library of Latvia collection "In Search of Lost Latvia."

Piebalga, too, had been emptied during the war, and many old farmsteads further from the center remained abandoned, ownerless, falling apart, and vandalized. Vestiges of the distant past were everywhere: in the the the old farm buildings; cemeteries; the rubble of romantic old windmills and watermills; and the old furniture and crockery lying about in the old, abandoned farmhouses. I worried about the future of the abandoned farmhouses, churches, and manor houses. Once the roof caved in, the building, if it was made of wood, was all but lost. The historic wooden Cepļi building burned down soon after my arrival. I saw it for the first and last time in 1983 or '84. Built in 1817, it had once served as a gathering place for the Brethren's Congregation from Herrnhut, which enlightened Latvian peasants in the 18th century. Only walls remained of Vecpiebalga Church, completed in 1845 and then bombed and destroyed by the retreating German Army in 1944. Under the communist atheist regime there could be no talk of rebuilding the church.

It was up to the local patriots to keep Latvia's history alive. My father-in-law was such a person. Although not a native Piebalgan, he certainly acted like one. He befriended people who cared about what was going on around them. It was local activists who held the key to the preservation of Latvia's history and a distinct Latvian identity, which had evolved over centuries and was totally unlike Homo Sovieticus. Aware of the dangers of neglect, these patriots rushed to document all that could still be saved or preserved through the lens of a camera, the stroke of a pen, or a call to action—a *talka* (a voluntary group effort towards a specific cause).

Spring in Latvia unfolded slowly. After the snow and ice melted, the round, butter-yellow heads of globeflowers (*Trollius*) and marsh marigolds opened their happy faces to the sunshine, brightening the soggy, waking meadows. A bouquet of *sviestabumbas* ("butterballs," the local name for Trollius) in a simple ceramic pot was a sight fit for a king and queen. Style guru Martha Stewart would have said, "It's a good thing!" Andris ventured down into the low, wet areas in search of these sunny blooms. We had plenty of rubber boots lying around for such excursions.

With each day the light in the sky spread; sunlight flooded Piebalga's dales and caressed its rounded hills. In the springtime the Baltic sky was dotted with *cīruļi* or skylarks (*Alauda arvensis*), my grandmother Mimmī's favorite bird, which rose up into the heavens trilling cheerfully. I remember how thrilled and moved I felt hearing for the first time the voice of the *cīrulis*, the *dzeguze* (cuckoo, *Cuculus canorus*), the *grieze* (corncrake, *Crex crex*), and the *lakstīgala* (nightingale, *Luscinia luscinia*), birds I knew from Latvian folk songs. They were an indelible part of Latvia's rural "soundscape." Who would have thought that such subtle phenomena—the sounds of Latvia's birds—could move me to tears many years later, when I listened to soundbytes of their voices far away from the fatherland.

Springtime dandelions in Piebalga. With my son Krišjānis and my goddaughter Elīna in 1985. Photo: Andris Krieviņš.

As soon as it was warm enough and someone had been by to till the vegetable garden, Biruta got down to the business of sowing seeds and planting potatoes. Legumes and carrots were sown early; she rejoiced in plunging her hands into the spring soil. In 1983 I was granted permission to go to Piebalga as often as I wished. I quickly learned the chores and helped look after baby Elīna, who was often left in the care of her grandmother. Springtime was for *rumulēšanās*, an old tradition: when the cows were first let out of the barn in spring, they went crazy, dancing and kicking up their feet; that's when everyone was allowed to dump a bucket of water on someone else's head.

Then the Latvian midsummer descended upon Piebalga, sprinkling the colors of wildflowers throughout the lush meadows, where cows lazily grazed. Wild strawberries peeked from the roadside and in clearings. In 1983 I celebrated my first *Jāņi* or summer solstice in Piebalga. The ancient celebration of the longest day, fertility, light, and life started on June 23, name day of Līga, with women and girls wading through the lush meadows in search of wildflowers for wreaths. In the meantime men went out to fetch branches of oak and *meijas*—green, leafy branches and saplings—for decorating the house. Not only was it Līga's day, but all of this gathering of flowers, grasses, and branches was done in preparation for *Līgo* evening, also sometimes referred to as *Zāļu vakars* ("Eve of Grasses"). Anything that grew was considered good enough for weaving into a wreath, and over the years I have seen some fantastic Jāņi wreaths!

At Paulēni we chopped up *kalmes* (calamus or sweet flag), a perennial marsh plant, and scattered the aromatic pieces throughout the house. All day Biruta toiled in the kitchen baking traditional bacon buns—*pīrāgi*, cinnamon rolls, and Farmer's Cheese bread. She also made "wheels" of traditional solstice cheese. Juris brewed his own beer, which we began to sip as the clouds of mosquitoes descended on us at dusk. The scent of hops made me think about all the people who had come before me, who had brewed their Jāņi beer and worn their wreaths, and stared into the flames...

I spent my first Jāņi in the company of a bunch of young Latvians who showed up at Paulēni. They wanted try out the new *pirts*, and we joined them (me nervously). We all quickly shed our clothes and packed our bodies into the little "steamhouse": a boisterous bunch of young men and women. I wasn't exactly a prude, but in the close proximity of naked men I didn't know I felt squeamish and out of place. At a deeper level, however, there was something wonderful and exciting about the freedom of such behavior, which reminded me of the American hippie era and Woodstock. "We are stardust, we are golden, and we've got to get ourselves back to the garden." (Joni Mitchell) I imagined naked pagan couplings among the ferns of Latvia's lovely woods, devoid of poison ivy. I was quite certain that my pagan ancestors had fornicated freely at this time of the year, unfettered by Christian morality. The mixture of hot flesh and the aroma of moist birch leaves made me think of Dutch painter Hieronymus Bosch's masterpiece "The Garden of Earthly Delights," which titillated me as a young girl on the brink of puberty.

Instead of chanting traditional solstice songs that night, I sat by the bonfire listening to our guests singing their modern-day Latvian "folk" songs by our neighbor Imants Kalniņš and other popular composers. When I asked them if we could sing a Latvian folk song, they admitted that they did not know any folk songs. I was shocked. I had assumed that Latvians in Latvia knew the same Latvian folk songs we had been taught in America, but that clearly was not the case.

That Jāņi I was also shocked to see some of my countrymen burning rubber tires in bonfires. Driving around to gage people's participation in the ancient celebration, outlawed at the time, I saw such a bonfire near the town of Ērgļi. The toxic fire had created a plume of black, acrid smoke that like dirty claws scratched the crystal-pure air. How could anyone possibly enjoy it? It was disgusting and alien. Despite the official ban, Latvians celebrated Midsummer, and the

Soviets pretended not to see what was going on. (I suspect some of the Latvian apparachiks secretly ingested beer and caraway cheese while lounging at their dachas.)

Paulēni at Midsummer, bathed in morning light. (Photo: Andris Krieviņš)

The word "līgo" is the common refrain in all summer solstice songs, calling on "the chil-

259

dren of Jānis" (a Latvian pagan deity) to rejoice in the bounty of the earth. The Midsummer solstice is said to erase the borders between the real and the supernatural; one almost had to believe this sitting beneath the starry sky and gazing into the glowing embers of the Jāņi bonfire or jumping over it like a carefree spirit. Strange shapes and figures seemed to emerge from the glowing flames; they danced, cavorted, and melted away. From then on, the days would grow shorter.

By the 1980s many Latvians had forgotten the deeper meaning of Jāņi, yet like their ancestors they felt the need to preserve its external manifestations. At Jāņi one wore the meadow on one's head, drank beer, ate a lot of homemade food, walked from house to house, and jumped over the bonfire, staying up all night long to see the sun to rise. Some people sang. Walking home tired and happy from our neighbor's house, I saw a linden tree rising up out of the early morning mist. Its pyramidal form stood out in the wisps of damp air, which smelled of the earth. Right there we were in the midst of so many forms of life, breathing them in, deeply at one with them. Somewhere in the distance a corncrake rattled its song. My motherland lay in the unfolding dawn like a resplendent goddess possessed by the night sky, the mist rising from her gently heaving body. T

In 1983 Jāņi was not an official holiday, but it sure felt like one. Although nobody dared hoist a burning barrel into the air (an old Jāņi tradition), we huddled around our bonfire on the hill, and I thought about the communists' bizarre ban and its effect on my people. A couple more decades, and even these symbolic motions, an homage to our rich past, would cease to exist, because traditions demand continuity. I was lucky, because my parents-in-law were not "Sovietized.".

That first summer while Biruta toiled in her vegetable garden, I often put Elīna in the baby carriage, and we went for a walk down the winding gravel road, which was so pretty and quiet with hardly a car passing all day long. The meadows rustled in the warm summer wind, buzzing with insect life. Latvia's clouds were so bright and fluffy, the summer sky so clear and blue, unlike New Jersey, where it turned an ugly, muggy, blinding white in the hot weather. On one such walk, as my gaze wandered into the woods, I suddenly realized that I was looking at an enormous moose. It was standing behind a tree, its formidable horns sticking out on either side of the trunk. Instinctively, I turned the carriage around and slowly walked back, hoping the moose was not interested in charging. Until then my encounters with wild animals had been at the zoo, where I was separated from them by a tall fence. The moose, a huge, gangly herbivore, is considered dangerous only in the fall during mating season. A Piebalga neighbor told us the story of a moose chasing a man into Lake Inesis in the fall. Seeing this magnificent animal in its raw, natural setting was breathtaking, literally.

I saw moose several times during my time in Piebalga. Once in the early fall when the hunting season had started, an enormous, visibly distraught moose came hurtling over Paulēnkalns; lumbering across our vegetable garden, he galloped over the hill, crossed the road, and headed straight for the cover of the woods. We could hear gunshots in the distance. Beautiful, magnificent creatures they are, and Latvia's heavy blanket of forest is a wonderful refuge for them.

Playwright and Piebalgan Pauls Putniņš had a house down the road in a cluster of old homes, all occupied. His brother-in-law Ģirts Jakovļevs was a rakishly handsome actor; I once had a big crush on him, when I saw him in a Latvian movie in New York. An architect couple purchased the old granary near the lake. Another architect, Jānis Pipurs, bought an old house for his elderly mother near the Ogre River. In the 1970s and 1980s more and more Latvians from Rīga were looking to buy a summer house in the countryside. Piebalga with its beautiful landscape was very attractive.

For fresh milk we walked across the hill to a neighbor's house. Milda lived with her partner Aivars and had two sons and a daughter from a previous relationship; she kept cows, pigs, sheep, and chickens in her large barn. Her house and property could have used some remodeling, but few of the locals had money for home improvements. Milda's daughter had run away from home, become pregnant, and given birth to a girl she promptly abandoned. The little girl Alīda with her wide-set eyes and cheerful smile lived with Milda and called her mom; who knew where the daughter was. Handsome Milda with her dark hair and light blue eyes had her hands full minding her granddaughter and looking after the livestock and household. Her world was close to the ground and the dog bones and chicken feathers scattered across it, the laundry flapping in the wind, and the smell of manure wafting from the barn. On a hillside her cows called to her. Sometimes Milda, Aivars, and their sons came over to use our sauna. They never stayed to chat though; there seemed to be an invisible wall between most of the locals and the Rigans who arrived with their money, fresh ideas, and sense of beauty. This wall was called envy, and envy was a nasty trait mentioned in many Latvian dainas.

The gravel road near Paulēni was surrounded by patches of forest, meadows, and arable fields and snaked westward until it reached the Pipurs house, where it split, blocked by the Ogre River. The old wooden houses tucked away in this remote pocket sparked a strange, poetic, visceral sense of recognition in me; for the first time I was seeing, in their original setting, the types of buildings described by Pauls Kundziņš in his beautiful 1974 homage to traditional Latvian architecture, *Latvju sēta* ("The Latvian Farmstead"). I had leafed through this book from time to time in New Jersey.

Right: An old house in Piebalga near the Ogre River, a tributary of the Daugava River. The building in the distance is an old granary. This photograph is from 1975. Image courtesy of the National Library of Latvia collection "In Search of Lost Latvia."

We took many walks down that way to visit a farmstead called Kalna Antēni on the other side of the Ogre River. To get there, you had to pass an old house called Vītiņi. In 2013 I came across an old photograph of Vītiņi and its description on a website called *Zudusī Latvija* ("Lost Latvia"), an online compendium devoted to Latvian history and lost or endangered historical and cultural monuments. According to one Leonīds Stankēvičs who spent his childhood at Vītiņi, his grandfather Artūrs Breikšs had attributed the source of the word "Vītiņi" to Vikings, who had allegedly traveled up the Ogre River from the Daugava River in their wooden longships. Grandfather Breikšs recalled that the original house was down near the river, surrounded by an enormous, dense, primeval forest. In Stankēvičs' childhood the location of the old hearth was still discernible, mapped by fragments of clay pottery. Stankēvičs described the men and women in his family's old photographs as tall, with Scandinavian features and slightly slanted eyes. Online maps of Viking routes and settlements include this area of Latvia, so this story isn't far-fetched. (Source: Stankēvičs, Leonīds. "Inešu pagasts, Vītiņu mājas. 1975." Zudusī Latvija. Retrieved March 3, 2013. <http://www.zudusilatvija.lv/objects/object/21697>)

An elderly couple who had lost both sons to drowning lived just past Vītiņi at the very end of the road. We seldom saw them; their tragedy had sealed them off from the outside world. Crossing a rickety footbridge across the slow-moving Ogre River, we passed a shimmering pond where yellow *skalbes* (Siberian iris) bloomed in the spring, and a cluster of abandoned buildings that comprised the remains of an abandoned farmstead. A spectacular 300-year-old *rija* or threshing barn came into view. Kalna Antēni was run by an industrious woman who wove gorgeous traditional Piebalga wool blankets in her spare time. She lived together with her blind but nimble husband, her elderly mother, and her youngest son, Jānis. An older son, Māris, lived in Rīga, where he built custom-made bars for wealthy clients. Life at Kalna Antēni seemed frozen in time.

In 1983 the magnificent threshing barn's future was unclear: its old roof needed mending. It was a general rule that once the roof went, so did the rest of the building. Again, I must underscore how much I feared for the fate of Latvia's architectural legacy. Soviet communism and the collective farming system had no need for old houses or history, which the communists were busy rewriting. So many beautiful old farmsteads and other unique buildings had been abandoned and were buckling under the ravages of time and the elements. (*Photograph: The old threshing barn at Kalna Antēni. Photo: Vecpiebalga.lv*)

In Piebalga the noise of the city was faraway, and I listened to the birds, the wind, and the rustling foliage. It was peaceful. The air was wonderful. For the most part, Latvia's lakes and streams were relatively clean and full of healthy fish and other aquatic lifeforms. Gunārs Lūsis had spent time shooting fish underwater and fishing not only in Latvia but deep within Russia; he could vouch for it. Latvia's countryside was not stressed by an enormous population that taxed the land and natural resources. Of course, there were problems with agricultural runoff, but overall in Piebalga the countryside looked almost pristine. Nevertheless, I knew there were problems with the inefficient, sloppy kolhozes and lack of accountability. Somewhere out there were Russian Army bases; toxic military industrial waste was pooling somewhere. For me, Piebalga was everything I had pictured my fatherland to be: pretty, picturesque, and full of historical landmarks.

We swam naked in the pond and even in the lake. Only the sound of a solitary car passing by from time to time reminded us that there were other people about. The stars at night shone brilliantly; there was no light pollution. In my first summer at Paulēni I learned to start a fire in the woodstove and to cook a hot meal on it. I spent hours hunched over in the garden, helping Biruta pull out weeds. I pulled water from the well and carried it home. We washed, rinsed, air-dried, and ironed mountains of clothes. There was so much to do. We did not have a telephone, which contributed to the sense of isolation from modern life. No electronics. The wind was a permanent guest on our hilltop.

We picked wild strawberries in late June, a sweet, organic, divine delicacy I had never experienced, and drove to clearings to pick wild raspberries, which we preserved for the winter in the form of jam. Life in the countryside was mostly about work and lots of it; everyone wanted and needed a garden, a piece of the good Earth. Rigans with a place in the countryside also gardened, not only for fun but for practical reasons, thinking about the long winter ahead. My mother-in-law loved country life; she was a born farmer who saw the task of growing things not as a chore but as a pleasure. I saw how happy she was when her seeds turned into tender green shoots. A sense of accomplishment and a sense of wonder.

Life in the countryside revealed the absurdities, waste, and negative impact of the Soviet kolhoz system. Because the state owned the land, no one felt a sense of ownership. Communism with its top-down approach to everything had a destructive effect on Latvian mentality: deprived of ownership, many Latvians sank into a state of chronic depression, which they nursed with alchohol. The state-controlled economy spawned decades of theft, graft, fraud, and embezzlement: the state "stole" from itself; the state stole from the people; the people stole from the state. With no sense of a personal stake, people lost interest in preservation efforts, lost an interest in what was going on around them. They succumbed to apathy.

The waste was heartbreaking. Just down the road from us an old orchard on a pretty hillside beckoned in late summer with fruit-laden apple trees planted before the Soviet occupation. But there were no takers, no harvesters; no one cared. Ripe apples fell to the ground and rotted, even though the store had no fruit to sell. Ripe pea pods dangled within reach, off limits; they, too, would wither away. Many haystacks were never brought in for winter: all that hard work went to waste, even though people sometimes complained about hay shortages. Communism Road obviously had no interest in harvesting the apples and the peas. Thus nature's bounty provided a feast for insects, rodents, and roaming deer, yet the humans living nearby could only admire the tempting harvest. To sneak into the orchard to pick a basket full of ripe, delicious, organic apples would have been theft from the Soviet state. Lousy morale sometimes resulted harvests being tilled back into the ground.

I summered with my in-laws until 1990. Those summers were a school in co-habitation, family dynamics, yard and garden work, and patience for me. I tried to make myself as useful as possible while enjoying the surrounding beauty. I looked up to my mother-in-law as a genius of cooking, baking, cleaning, planting, harvesting, and preserving, and I watched, followed, and learned. She was the embodiment of practicality and old-fashioned homemaking. Nothing gave her more pleasure than to see her garden turn into an autumn harvest, which was then transported to her tidy root cellar for winter consumption.

She even seemed to enjoy washing the laundry, which was an enormous undertaking in the countryside. As the sheets and towels dried in the sun and the wind, she walked past them with pleasure, stroking everything to check if anything was ready for ironing. That boring task fell to me, ironing all that laundry with neat, crisp folds according to Biruta's wishes. Of course, it did feel great to lie down on sparkling clean, aromatic sheets washed in soft pond water and dried in the sun and Piebalga's breezes!

One day in the summer of 1985 we explored a forgotten part of Piebalga called Burkāni ("Carrots"), a string of abandoned farmsteads that were falling apart as the forest occupied former fields and meadows. The kolhoz had abandoned this area for some reason. What had become of the original inhabitants? Peonies, those hardy, steadfast perennials, bloomed and scented the air for no one. This was typical of Latvia's countryside. Forsaken farmsteads, some vandalized, some untouched, overgown gardens, the sigh of the forest nearby... There were incidents of people falling into old wells concealed by tall grass. These farmsteads faced ruin, which went hand in hand with amnesia. (Left: Exploring the Burkāni houses in Piebalga: my son Krišjānis rattling the door handle of an empty house.

Photo: Andris Krieviņš.)

I greatly enjoyed all excursions. It took the KGB about two years to realize that I was pretty harmless, and beginning in 1985 I was permitted to return to Piebalga and stay there for lengthy periods to help out with chores and enjoy our son's development in the fresh air and soothing pond and lake waters. Juris was a marvelous guide who showed me many beautiful places of cultural significance in the Piebalga area: the childhood and summer homes of writer Kārlis Skalbe (1879–1945), Incēni and Saulrieti ("Sunsets"); Vēveri ("Weavers"), an assortment of homes and buildings from the 19th century once populated by Piebalga artisans who specialized in weaving and other crafts; etc. The That decade was one of urgency; there was a sense of "clear and present" danger, of losing our historical and cultural legacy if things did not change. The purchase and restoration of old farm houses was for many Latvians a labor of love and patriotism.

A great local example of the backwardness of the Soviet era and the socio-economic regression caused by communism was nearby Cirstu Muiža ("Manor," Zirstenhoff in German), a beautiful, red brick, Gothic Revival manor near the Ineši-Ērgļi road, which was built in 1886 by Baron Magnus von Strandmann. Nearly a hundred years later it was being vandalized by demoralized Homo Sovieticus.

Coat of arms of Strandmann family. Source: Wikimedia Commons. https://commons.wikimedia.org/wiki/File:Strandmann_BWB.png (© Public Domain)

In the 1980s the von Strandmann coat of arms, *right*, designed by German heraldist Adolf Matthias Hildebrandt (1844–1918), was still visible above the main entrance of the manor house. Baron Magnus von Strandmann's own name stood out on a white plaque further up above the two Gothic arch windows. These details were reminders of a dif-

von Strandmann.

ferent era, which was based on private property and ownership. The hint of former grandeur and of purpose and order stood out clearly beneath the grimy squalor of Sovietization and collective "ownership," which really meant collective apathy.The Strandmann dynasty could be traced back to 17th century Rīga, but Zirstenhoff's name goes back to the 16th century.

An old photograph of Cirstu Manor in 1900 reveals a neat, well-maintained building. Eighty years later the scene had changed dramatically. During one of our excursions with our friends from Smiltene, we decided to get out of the car and take a closer look at the old manor, which was obviously in dire straits, open to anyone, welcoming to nobody. Some of the windows were cracked or broken. We lingered inside the barren vestibule for a moment before withdrawing, wishing to avoid an encounter with the tenants. One never knew.

The sturdy construction of the manor with its solid red bricks, evidence of fine craftsmanship, the marvelous roof tiles, and the building's unique decorative elements, such as the fancy weather vane, were in stark contrast to the pitiful reality of Soviet life. This building had already withstood the test of the time, whereas Soviet buildings came with a "limited warranty." Life under the Soviets was pushing Latvia back in time, hurting its development, hurting its chances.

At the time of our visit the manor was being used to house an assortment of people who obviously didn't care about anything around them. They had set up an outdoor toilet right next to the manor on the bank of the Ogre River: no screen; no privacy; no sense of decency. The "toilet" was, in fact, a horizontal wooden plank nailed to two posts driven into the ground. The idea was simple, based on gravity. One sat down on the bench with one's derriere pointing towards the Ogre, pooped, and *presto!*— A Soviet era stool rolled down the steep bank toward the scenic river. What ingenuity! All that was missing was a peg for shreds of *Cīņa* ("Battle"), the official Communist Party newspaper/toilet paper.

Left: Cirstu Manor circa 1900.

According to the website Pilis.lv, Cirstu Manor was burned down in 1905, presumably by angry revolutionaries, and then rebuilt. It was used as a school during the First Republic. An interesting, hexagon-shaped gothic tower to the left of the manor attracted our attention. There were other old buildings in various stages of decay, including an old chapel and brewery. However, after inspecting the poop propellant bench, we decided to cut our excursion short. Our friend Ilze, a doctor, looked pale. An intelligent, refined lady, she was an aesthete who liked to talk about the old days and the Baltic landed gentry.

Were and are Latvia's old Baltic German manor buildings worth saving? I thought so then and still do. Some Latvians think we shouldn't spend a dime on them, because they embody the history of the cruel rule of the German landed gentry over Latvians. As a fan of architecture, I disagree. If we approach our cultural legacy in that manner, then thousands of old castles and churches in all of Europe should be torn down. Europe's history is one of cruelty and enslavement. Once these manors stood for a way of life to which my ancestors were bound. Why willfully destroy these vestiges of our history? In addition, the old manors are worth saving as examples of masterful construction, carpentry, and artistry.

I became deeply attached to Piebalga's rolling hills, splendid vistas, and history. It was a special place and attracted interesting people. Piebalga and much of the Latvian countryside, with the exception of Latgale and areas along the Belarusian border, would remain largely Russian-free: that is, you did not hear the Russian language there, nor did many ethnic Russians choose to live in the countryside. Those who did had largely integrated. By the 1980s, due to a steady influx from Russia and other Soviet republics, Russian speakers had become the majority in Latvia's capital. And so it was that in Latvia's countryside I felt most at home; it was there that I felt my grandparents' Latvia. (Ironically, now that I live in the United States, when I hear Russian, it makes me think of Latvia.)

Estophile and Lettophile Garlieb Merkel (1769–1850) had spent his childhood in Vecpiebalga's parsonage. More than hundred and thirty years had passed since his death, but Piebalga had forgotten about him. No markers commemorated his time there. Merkel's work *Die Letten* (1796) described the dire circumstances of Latvian serfs in the 18th century. It caused an uproar, and its author was forced into exile in Gemrnay. The uncaring wind swept over Piebalga's hills, as it had for ages. Merkel's voice had been swept away; a new darkness had enveloped my fatherland.

My time in Latvia's countryside brought me closer to the the soil and all living things. I lost my fear of the dark and of insects, spiders, and snakes. I learned to appreciate the hard work of the farmer and thank the earth for its bounty. In the countryside there was a different sense of time, and being out in nature made me appreciate the cycle of the year, from dormancy to harvest time. Being close to the places where so many famous people in our history had lived was very special to me. Garlieb Merkel, Atis Kronvalds, the Kaudzīte brothers, Kārlis Skalbe, Antons Austriņš: all had left a lasting imprint on my nation's heritage, and I prayed for the times to change.

Ghosts

"Queen of the Latvian Press" in the 1930s: Emīlija Benjamiņš in the prime of life. Source: Wikipedia Commons
https://commons.wikimedia.org/wiki/File:BenjaminaEmilija_-_1920-30-LABR-Iz218-10.jpg (© Public Domain)

As winter turned into spring, with longer days, melting snow, blue shadows, and fresh breezes from the southwest, I was completely acclimatized, settled in, and enjoying my life in Rīga despite food shortages, long lines in stores, financial difficulty, and other annoying, "trivial" matters. Life in communist Latvia was all still new to me; it was all bearable. We were young and in love; we subsisted "on each other and not on food products" (Viktors Kalniņš, "Mēs pārtiekam viens no otra"). We tried to make our apartment more cheery and comfortable, framing artwork

and adding houseplants. Our vases were filled with flowers from the market. Andris attended to that. I often walked through the park to Raiņa bulvāris to peek into my relatives' mailbox to see if any mail had arrived from the United States. The mailbox in our stairwell was broken, and I was sure anything from abroad would be stolen. Letters from the outside world cheered me up greatly; after all, we were living inside a very large prison.

I had succeeded in establishing more contacts and continued to pick up translating work. Latvia had very few English speakers, and the translations I had read were far from perfect. Often they

were atrocious. Rīga almost seemed like a small town, where it was easy to bump into acquaintances on the street. Word got around about my existence, and people became more aware of
my potential to help out with translating. The first book I translated into English in Latvia was
Zīļuks or *Little Acorn* by Margarita Stāraste (1914–2014), a prolific author and illustrator of children's books, born in Vladimir in Tsarist Russia. *Little Acorn* was published in 1985 by Liesma in
a hard cover edition. It was quite a thrill to see my name in print.

More work followed when I was introduced to the
so-called Translation Board of the Latvian Writers'
Union. An Indian publishing firm was interested in
the works of Rūdolfs Blaumanis, our famous short
story author and playwright. As I undertook a literal
translation of Blaumanis' famous play *Ugunī* ("In
Fire") about a washerwoman's daughter, Kristīne,
and her lust and love for Edgars, a hot-headed bad
boy struggling to assert himself in Livonia's rigid, Ger-
man-run rural society, I found myself sniggering. In English the play, a classic of Latvian theater,
sounded like a melodramatic soap opera. The gist of Blaumanis' genius was in his language,
which beautifully conveyed a sense of time and place (a Baltic German manor in the 19th century). In English the play just didn't sound right. So much could be lost in translation, especially
the feeling of a culture. "In Fire" might have been good for a Bollywood production. I became a
frequent visitor to the Translation Board, where people sat at crowded desks, smoked, and rustled paperwork looking utterly bored. (Photo: Latvian actors Vija Artmane and Uldis Pūcītis in a
marvelous film, "Purva bridējs," an adaptation of the play.)

The Translation Board and the Latvian Writers' Union, as well as the professional associations of Latvia's artists and composers, were located in an imposing villa of grand proportions,
reminiscent of an Italian palazzo, which took up half a block on Barona iela opposite Vērmanes
Dārzs, a beautiful park. The villa was once known as *Benjamiņu nams* ("Benjamiņš House"), but
no one mentioned those bourgeois nationalists and capitalists – the Benjamiņš couple—in public. It was as if they had never existed. Slipping through the gigantic double doors of the main
entrance, visitors ascended a beautiful, curved wooden staircase to a set of polished glass doors
that opened to the offices of the Latvian Writers' Union. The grand staircase continued to wind
up to the offices of the Artists' Union and the Composers' Union. These professional associations
were typical of the Soviet Union and Eastern Europe's communist bloc.

The building's high ceilings, thick walls, enormous windows, ornate lighting fixtures, thick
wallpaper, and other fine architectural details hinted at the glory of the Benjamiņš era and "the
old (capitalist) days," which sharply contrasted with the shabbiness of the Soviet communist
world. The stories of Latvia's media moguls, who were once at the center of the Latvian Republic's high society, petered out with Emīlija Benjamiņa's deportation to and death in a Siberian
prison camp. Antons Benjamiņš died in time to avoid his wife's tragic fate.

In addition to attending events organized and sponsored by the Writers' Union, I sometimes
visited the so-called Writers' Polyclinic when I was sick, which was located in the basement of
the building. The services provided by the clinic's physicians were excellent, and everyone spoke

Latvian. To this day I remember the doctors, nurses, and employees of this clinic with gratitude and admiration. They were thorough, professional, and kind, unlike the personnel at most of the other medical facilities I had the bad luck of experiencing in Soviet-occupied Latvia.

Left: German architect Wilhelm Böckmann.

The grand villa (at 12 Barona iela), built for Rīga's wealthy Pfab family, was completed in 1876. It was designed by Böckmann and Ende, a notable German architectural firm established in 1860 and based in Berlin (Hermann Ende, 1829–1907, and Wilhelm Böckmann, 1832–1902). (Böckmann and Ende, incidentally, designed Japan's ornate Ministry of Justice in Tokyo.) Summoned from Germany to add sculptural ornaments to the mansion, sculptor August Franz Volz (1821–1926) established his famous studio in Rīga. The Pfab family's holdings at this time included the warehouses of Rīga Central Market, as well as the famous Dannenstern building in Old Rīga. The Pfab family's fortunes, mostly based on the flax market, dwindled over time; in 1928 they sold their mansion. In 1939, following Hitler's orders, the Pfabs repatriated to Germany along with other German Latvians.

The new owners of the palazzo were Latvia's media magnates, Antons (b. 1860) and Emīlija (b. 1881) Benjamiņš, the Latvian Republic's most influential couple. Eižens Laube (1880–1967), a notable Latvian architect who designed more than 200 buildings in Rīga, including many Art Nouveau masterpieces, was put in charge of remodeling and upgrading the Benjamiņš house. The work was completed in 1930. (Architect Laube left Latvia in 1944 and resettled in Portland, Oregon.—RL)

Left: Antons and Emīlija Benjamiņš on the front cover of their magazine *Atpūta* ["Relaxation"], photographed in their villa on Barona iela in Rīga, circa 1930.

The Benjamiņš couple had beautiful stained windows by Kārlis Brencēns installed in their villa, which became a repository of art. It was there that they hosted salons for Rīga's high society, which included artists, writers, musicians, and journalists.

Antons Benjamiņš died in 1939, a year before the Soviet occupation of Latvia. Under the Soviet communists the Benjamiņš couple's days of glory came to a tragic end: everything they owned was nationalized. Emīlija Benjamiņš was deported to Siberia in 1941; she died in Solikamsk of starvation that same year. It was reputed that her ignoble death on "on bare wooden boards" had been predicted by Eiž(enks) Finks, Rīga's famous soothsayer. The Benjamiņš's adopted son, Juris, was able to escape to Germany. The Benjamiņš House was turned over to Soviet Latvia's writers, composers, and artists in 1945.

In the 1980s I passed through the Benjamiņš House's front doors many times to pick up translation work, mingle with writers, or to see a doctor. The story of Antons and Emīlija Benjamiņš deserves to be told in a well-researched book: the lives of Antons and Emīlija Benjamiņš mirrored the rise and fall of the first Republic of Latvia. From humble beginnings, this couple worked hard for their wealth and power, achieving astonishing results in a short time, only to have everything destroyed by a foreign occupying power. In the Soviet era they were forgotten ghosts in their own country, apparitions from a different era. Nobody mentioned them. And Rīga was full of ghosts and fascinating, often tragic stories about all sorts of interesting people. Latvians, Germans, Jews, Poles, Russians… Rīga was a big, fat, leatherbound book waiting to be opened again and read.

Chapter sources:

(1) "Benjamiņu nams 12 K. Barona iela." Ambermarks.com. Retrieved on 3/5/2013. <http://www.amber-marks.com/_Pieminekli/IsieApraksti/Riga/Centrs/KBarona12_Benjam.htm>
(2) "Hermann Ende." Wikipedia. Retrieved on 3/5/2013. < http://en.wikipedia.org/wiki/Hermann_Ende>
(3) "Eižens Laube." Wikipedia. Retrieved on 3/5/2013. <http://en.wikipedia.org/wiki/Ei%C5%BEens_Laube>
(4) "Emīlija Benjamiņa." Wikipedia. Retrieved on 3/20/2013. <http://en.wikipedia.org/wiki/Em%C4%ABlija_Ben-jami%C5%86a>

Judenfrei: Tamāra and the Jews of Latvia

A Nazi era sign, "Judenfrei," indicating that a Nazi-occupied area has been "cleared" of Jews.

"Kārļonkuls (Uncle Karl) lived near Biķernieku Forest, and I remember him telling us how badly it smelled of burning flesh. The Nazis were apparently burning their Jewish victims' corpses. At the time nobody dared complain or speak openly about it."—A memory of my father, presumably from the spring of 1944, when the Germans were trying to cover up their crimes in advance of their departure.

"Everywhere, the Holocaust left a terrible legacy of guilt and hatred, among Jews and non-Jews alike."—Anne Applebaum, Iron Curtain (1)

"Regrettably, after more than six decades and a changeover of two to three generations, in numerous areas in Latvia, where Jews once comprised from 20 to 30 to 50% of the local population, today the local residents have not encountered a single Jew in their hometown, nor do they know much about Jews. Doctors, pharmacists, teachers, artisans, small Jewish shops: Jews were once part and parcel of many populated areas in (Latvia) before the war."—Meijers Melers (2)

It was strange to realize that practically nobody around me in occupied Latvia spoke English. In the 1980s the part of me that belonged to the English-speaking world felt linguistically isolated. Of course, I relished diving into my mother tongue, reading it, speaking it, seeing it around me, where it wasn't overshadowed by the Russian alphabet. Beneath the harsh and alien sound of Russian I picked up the muted melody of Latvian, my mother tongue. The English language—the wider cultural space of my youth—was forced to retreat to the back of my mind.

Right: A collector's item nowadays—a Soviet era pin. Family heirloom.

English was so uncommon in Latvia in the 1980s that, when artist Džemma Skulme displayed a collection of souvenir pins from the US on TV, no one except me noticed the camera zoom in on a pin emblazoned with a "Fuck you" sign. Boy oh boy, did I laugh then while feeling very much alone in my amusement; there really wasn't anyone with whom to share my mirth. Latvia's "head," so to speak, had been forcibly twisted by the Soviets to face east towards Moscow, Russia, and Siberia. Historically, Latvia had once been part of the Russian Empire; for more than a century, in fact, up until full independence in 1920 from the fledgeling Soviet Union. The many pretty Russian Orthodox churches in Latvia are reminders of my people's times under the Russian tsars. During the tsarist era Rīga and Latvia's population were never fully cut off from the West, however. Commerce and contacts with the West flourished. Under the Soviets it was different. All contacts with the Western world that lay beyond the Iron Curtain were brutally disrupted, and for the majority of Latvians even the Warsaw Pact countries were hard to reach. By the 1980s, Rīga had dwarfed to the status of a provincial town. The Kremlin largely saw it as a military outpost of the Soviet Baltic Military District and a place to dump Russians to dilute the native population.

At some social gathering at the Latvian Writers' Union in early 1983, I was introduced to an "English speaker" named Tamāra Zālīte (*left in a photograph from her youth*), a translator who had compiled an anthology of American poetry (1980). Tamāra came to visit me at our apartment. It was strange and compelling to hear her speak the language I had left behind, which by then had begun to feel bizarrely foreign. English made me think of the Free World and a culture that almost nobody in Rīga could relate to. By the time late winter rolled around, I hadn't been speaking English for several months.

I came to realize the enormously important role that language played in personal identity. If American English for me spoke of freedom, George Washington and Abraham Lincoln, the Civil War and the abolishment of slavery, the civil rights movement and its champions Woodie Guthrie, Bob Dylan, and Pete Seeger, rock 'n roll, blues, jazz, and wide-open spaces, then Latvian whispered to me of family, lineage, and our European heritage. English for me was the modern world, the New World, but Latvian represented the Old World and my roots. If American English felt big, like "amber waves of grain and purple mountains' majesty," then the Latvian language felt threatened, fragile, and precious, like the folk song about "the skylark sleeping by the side of the road" ("Cīrulīti, mazputniņ', negul ceļa maliņā"), whose nest and very existence are endangered by "the masters of war." The suppression of a language and an identity is a slow asphyxiation. Latvians were being asphyxiated, slowly but with increasing pressure, as the Russian population swelled.

But who was Tamāra, this charming lady with whom I chatted, as we sipped Liepāja Instant Coffee and munched on cookies? At the time I did not know that Tamāra was Jewish. There certainly weren't very many Jews or traces of Jewish life left in Rīga, nor was I looking for them. I was focused almost obsessively on my Latvian ethnicity. I knew very little about Latvia's Jews before the war, although they had been briefly mentioned at Latvian school in a paragraph about Latvia's ethnic minorities. In 1983 Tamāra Zālīte was simply "the lady who spoke English" in a country where the Latvian language struggled to coexist with the ever increasing din of Russian. For a decade I saw Soviet-occupied Latvia as black and white: Russian and Latvian. But there were shades of gray on both sides of the ethno-political divide, other cultures, languages, and identities. I only found out many years later that Tamāra was Jewish, and that her life story was also worthy of a book.

Unlike New York, a city known for its large Jewish population and its prominent synagogues, with Hasidic Jews highly visible on the streets of Manhattan, especially in the so-called Diamond

District and on the subway trains going out to Brooklyn, Rīga's Jewish history had virtually vanished by the 1980s. I had grown up in the New York metropolitan area where Jews, observant or not, were part and parcel of American society and a well known and respected minority with a strong presence. Jews were prominent doctors, academicians, bankers, attorneys, publishers, scientists, actors, artists, writers, musicians, and generous benefactors of the arts. One of my closest friends at Parsons, Janet, was Jewish, and she told me of her experience on a kibbutz in Israel; she could relate to my Latvian side. My brothers' best friends Roy and Andy, also brothers, were Jewish. Their mother and my mother had become friends through a shared love for poetry.

My wonderful, gentle childhood pediatrician Dr. Bernard Statman was Jewish. I had Jewish classmates and friends in Glen Ridge. Red-haired neighbor Heidi Braffman and I spent a lot of time playing together when I was little. In middle school we were exposed to the atrocities of the Nazi- perpetrated Holocaust, watching horrific documentary film footage and reading *The Diary of Anne Frank* and *Night* by Eli Wiesel, which deeply touched me. Yet I failed to make a connection between the subject and my fatherland, mainly because my parents never brought it up, nor was it discussed in Latvian school.

Life in the United States without Jews is unimaginable. (In no particular order) the Marx Brothers, the Three Stooges, Woody Allen, Rodney Dangerfield, Bob Dylan, Barbara Streisand, Carole King, Barry Manilow, Bette Midler, Kirk and Michael Douglas, Dustin Hoffman, Mark Rothko (born in Daugavpils, Latvia), Saul Steinberg, Maurice Sendak (*Where the Wild Things Are*), Elaine de Kooning, Helen Frankenthaler, Alex Katz, Sol LeWitt, Jim Dine, my idol of the 1970s sculptor Louise Nevelson, Steve Reich, Leonard Bernstein, Philip Glass, Saul Bellow, Stephen Spielberg, Peter Max (whose psychedelic colors lit up my bedroom one year in the form of a calendar), and so many other American Jews (not all of whom chose to advertise their roots) sparkled in the tapestry of American culture. Composer Aaron Copland's "Rodeo" and "Appalachian Spring" for me were love songs to America, capturing my birth country's vastness and greatness. Like many East Europeans, Jews had found a safe refuge in the United States. Many Jews, like Woody Allen and the Marx Brothers, had a zany type of humor that appealed to me. When I was growing up, caricaturist Al Hirschfeld of *The New York Times* brightened up my Sunday mornings with his portraits of the stars of the American entertainment world and his hidden "Ninas."

Nobel Prize laureates in science and medicine, I have always marveled at how brainy many Jews were; I admired their deep connection and commitment to the arts and humanities and other important fields. Surely these remarkable talents and gifts might have been a result of their historical status as a persecuted people, which fostered a keen ability to recognize the meaning of education and culture in a person's development. World War II scattered Latvia's people in all four directions; so many of them lost their homes and their homeland. Those born in Latvia would mourn this loss for decades to come. Yet Latvia's Jewish population was annihilated in the span of a couple of years, and few survived to remember their people's place in Latvian history.

A book I read shortly before leaving for Latvia, *Man's Search for Meaning* by Viktor Frankl, a Holocaust survivor, remains one of the most memorable books I have read. "For the first time in my life I saw the truth as it is set into song by so many poets, proclaimed as the final wisdom by so many thinkers. The truth that Love is the ultimate and highest goal to which man can aspire. Then I grasped the meaning of the greatest secret that human poetry and human thought and belief have to impart: The salvation of man is through love and in love." Frankl's moving message of spiritual reconciliation has stayed with me. The lives of Latvians and Jews had crossed paths many times in history, as evidenced in books and folk songs, yet by the end of the 20th century we had almost forgotten this. The Holocaust in Latvia left deep scars that few people wanted to remember or discuss. The Soviet occupation and the Soviet authorities' closed archives made it difficult to move this painful subject forward.

Rīga's once-famous Marijas iela, known before the war for its Jewish merchants and their "mom and pop" shops, went by the name of Suvorov under the Soviets. In the 1980s it was just a gray, grimy street with little of interest to the hungry Soviet shopper: a movie theater called Palladium, a couple of *komisijas* or consignment shops filled with antique furniture and knick knacks, and a kolhoz store. Synagogues that had not been destroyed by the Nazis during the German occupation had been converted by the Soviets for secular use, just like many Christian churches. Yet today a visit to the headquarters of the Rīga Jewish community on Skolas iela reveals the richness of Jewish life in Latvia before the war.

In the 1970s many Jews emigrated from the religiously intolerant, anti-Semitic Soviet Union to Israel and other countries, as described in Rīgan David Bezmozgis' hilarious and poignant book *The Free World*. I met one such Latvian Jewish émigré, artist Simon Shegelman, in Jersey City after my first trip to Latvia. A friend of his from the Latvian Art Academy, Georgs Smelters, whom I befriended in 1980, had urged me to look him up. Shegelman picked me up at my home in Glen Ridge, and I visited him in his studio in Jersey City in 1981. Latvia lost many fine and talented people to this wave of emigration. The historical plight of the Jews resonated with me deeply; like the Jews, Latvians, too, had suffered under the Soviets and Nazis and had become displaced. Living in exile, Latvians longed for a way back to their homeland, their "promised land" Latvia.

Besides Tamāra Zālīte, several notable Latvian Jews came to my attention during the 1980s; unlike ethnic Russians, Latvia's Jews were for the most part well integrated. Most of them were bilingual and seemed deeply attached to Latvia. People like Tamāra Zālīte and her brother, scientist Jāzeps Eiduss, the filmmaker Herz Frank (who moved to Israel), journalist, professor, and TV political commentator Mavriks Vulfsons, artist Aleksandrs Dembo, film expert Ābrams Kleckins (I can still hear him speaking with traces of Yiddish), movie critic and film expert Valentīna Freimane, and other Latvian Jews were living reminders of the historical minority that had once thrived in Rīga and other Latvian cities, contributing to Latvia's economic growth, cultural diversity, and unique charac-

ter. Freimane's autobiography *Ardievu, Atlantīda* (2010) is one of the best and saddest memoirs I've read: Freimane lost her parents, fiancé, and friends and relatives in the Holocaust in Latvia. Latvia's Jewish community was well represented in the Latvian Saeima (parliament) of the First Republic up until the (Kārlis) Ulmanis putsch in 1934.

Photographer Philippe Halsman, painter Mark Rothko, social and political theorist Sir Isaiah Berlin, violinst Gidon Kremer, and cellist Mischa Maisky were just some of the Latvian Jews who ended up outside of Latvia, for one reason or another.. Marģers Vestermanis, founder of the "Jews in Latvia" Museum and Documentation Centre, is one of the people deeply involved in the research on the Holocaust in Latvia. Vestermanis (1925) barely escaped with his life from a German concentration camp in Dundaga. The story of the Holocaust in Latvia has come to light, thanks to the tireless efforts of historians and survivors.

I began to read about the Holocaust in Latvia while writing this book. Bit by bit I came to understand the horrific events that transpired in Latvia during the Nazi occupation (1941–1945): that 90% of Latvia's Jewish population (around 75,000 Jews) was annihilated, with about 15,000 Jews from Germany and other occupied territories being massacred there as well. Most of Latvia's approximately 200 synagogues and Jewish houses of worship were destroyed or closed under the Nazis. Today Peitav-Shul is Rīga's only active synagogue. Many Jewish cemeteries were desecrated. Before the war Rīga had 14 active synagogues. After the war many of the Jews who had fled to the interior of the Soviet Union to escape Nazi persecution trickled back into Latvia, only to emigrate later when the opportunity arose.

Right – "A happy future together": A Nazi era propaganda poster showing the Germans as liberators of Latvia from the Soviets.

Jelgava; Rumbula; Biķernieku *mežs* ("forest"); Liepāja's Šķēdes dunes; the old Daugavpils Citadel; Rēzekne: in addition to the Rīga Ghetto, the Holocaust happened all over Latvia, with many "little ghettos" and mass graves scattered across the country. The Nazis enlisted the help of some deranged locals, too, during their occupation: namely the Arājs Commando, which participated in the mass murder of Latvia's Jews. The events as described by historians Andrievs Ezergailis, Meijers Melers, Kaspars Zellis, and others are chilling to read and raise questions about local involvement. The Holocaust is not only about the victims but also a complicated subject about terror, survival, emotional distancing, the workings of memory, and the post-traumatic stress disorder of the people who witnessed or knew about these atrocities but were incapable of preventing them. Not everyone had it in them to be a Jānis ("Žanis") Lipke (1900–1987), a "righteous among nations" Latvian who saved the lives of over 50 Latvian Jews. Traumatic memories surely cause lingering, disturbing feelings of guiltless guilt. What was it like to see or know that your neighbors and fellow citizens were being degraded, humiliated, ostracized, locked up, and then... murdered?

As an adult I found out that one of my parents' friends, "Ted," whom I remember well, had penned anti-Semitic propaganda articles during the Nazi occupation of Latvia. Ted, born at the outset of World War I, was considerably older than my parent. I was shocked to read that Ted had actively collaborated with the Nazis and was a "Nazi propagandist."* I read about this in Andrievs (Andrew) Ezergailis'groundbreaking book, *The Holocaust in Latvia 1941–1944* (1996). I recall Ezergailis and his wife Inta being among the guests at our house at least once in my youth. But Ted: he was a regular guest at our house. (* Andrew Ezergailis. *The Holocaust in Latvia: 1941–1944*. Rīga: The Historical Institute of Lativa in association with the United States Holocaust Memorial Museum, 1996, pp. 29, 73.)

Left: An anti-Semitic poster from the Nazi German occupation: "The Jew doesn't belong with you. Throw him out!"

When I asked my mother about Ted, she said that "rumors about his collaboration surfaced from time to time." Hard evidence would come later with Ezergailis' book and the emergence of a field of study devoted to the Holocaust in Latvia. My mother was disturbed by our conversation, to say the least; the few American friends she had were Jewish. A liberal by nature, she had always condemned anti-Semitism, xenophobia, bigotry, and homophobia. My discovery about a man whom I remembered as a constant presence in the social life of my parents led me to believe that there were many more "skeletons in the closet" of Latvian society.

An old postcard of the synagogue in Jelgava (Mitau in German). It was burned to the ground using hand grenades and gasoline shortly after the Germans captured the city in July of 1941.

Jews had also suffered under the Soviet occupation (1940–1941) prior to the Nazi invasion, with thousands being arrested and deported to Siberia. Before World War II Jews were a prominent segment of Rīga's moneyed class, involved in commerce, banking, manufacturing, and retail. They had their own newspapers, synagogues, and schools. A permanent exhibition installed at the Jewish Community of Latvia reveals their once vibrant presence in my fatherland.

In July 1941 the Nazis advanced into Latvia, bringing with them their efficient killing machine. Swift, methodical, and brutal, they swept across Latvia, which was still reeling from the terror of the Soviet occupation. The Nazis continued to cull Latvia's population by rooting out Jews, communists, Nazi opponents, Roma, and the mentally disabled. For example, on July 1, 1941 the Nazis entered Jelgava, a city about 50 kilometers south of Rīga and once the seat of the duchy of Kurland. Just one month later some 2,000 Jelgava Jews were driven into a ghetto and then shot and buried in sand pits outside of the city. This is how the beautiful, old city of Jelgava, once home to a flourishing Jewish community, came to be *Judenfrei*. The Nazis blamed Soviet atrocities on the Jews, playing on the raw emotions of Latvians who had just experienced the terror of communist rule.

Left: Jelgava Castle after the war.

In the 1970s I read Jerzy Kosinski's creepy novel *The Painted Bird* (1965), never realizing that the kind of human darkness the author described might have been possible in my fatherland. I grew up not knowing about the Holocaust in Latvia, and it was precisely this "not knowing" that later bothered me. It was a subject that was not discussed openly in Latvian society.

I was 53 when I read Ezergailis' book and envisioned the Jewish ghetto in Rīga, how all of its Jewish inmates—men, women, and children (about 25,000 in all)—were marched to Rumbula, ordered to take off their clothes and set aside any personal items, and shot over enormous pits. In the 1980s I sometimes drove past Rumbula, known then only for its car parts market. During the Soviet occupation I had no idea that Rumbula was linked to one of Latvia's biggest massacres. How could I? Ezergailis' book would be published a decade later; it would shed more light on the staggering tragedy of World War II in Latvia and "the Bloodlands" (Timothy Snyder) of the Nazis and Soviets. Latvians as a nation have sometimes been tragically lumped under the label of "Jew killers," partly due to misinformation, disinformation, and years of Soviet propaganda. Ezergailis' invaluable book has helped illuminate the Nazi years in Latvia while helping us, Latvians, see ourselves and our history in a new light. Ezergailis writes in his book that under the Soviets many historical archives were closed to researchers like him. This type of spotlight on our country's dark history is absolutely fundamental in setting the record straight about what happened in Latvia beginning in 1939, when the Molotov-Ribbentrop pact was signed in Moscow.

And Tamāra, a Latvian Jew, what was her story? Tamāra Zālīte and her brother, Jāzeps Eiduss, happened to be abroad when the Nazis invaded. Jāzeps Eiduss would end up fighting on the Soviet side of the war at the Battle of Moscow in 1941–1942. Because Tamāra was Jewish, for me her recollection of pre-war Latvia would have been particularly interesting to hear or read about—a different perspective, perhaps, on that era.

Jāzeps (Joseph) Eiduss (1916–2004), *right*, a scientist and professor at the University of Latvia, penned a tribute to his sister, Tamāra Zālīte, for an online publication called *Latvijas ļaudis* ("Latvia's People") in 1999. I had no idea that Tamāra Zālīte's life had been so interesting, although everyone of her generation seemed to have some fascinating personal story to tell. How could they not, when they had survived a war that blew up everything? I have taken the liberty of reprinting Professor Eiduss' eulogy to his sister (with a few grammatical tweaks) to provide a more accurate portrait of my charming guest in 1983.

World War I inflicted enormous losses on Latvia's population and economy. Masses of people abandoned their farmsteads and homes towns and cities, fleeing east. Thousands of soldiers mobilized by the Russian Army were killed in the first year of the war. Latvian riflemen fought and died in battles in Latvia and in the Russian civil war. Image courtesy of the National Library of Latvia collection "In Search of Lost Latvia."

(Reminder: The Republic of Latvia was founded in 1918. Following the Latvian Declaration of Independence on November 18, 1918, a few days after the end of World War I, Latvia plunged into further chaos and bloodshed until 1920, when it signed a peace treaty with the Soviet Union. World War I caused many of Latvia's inhabitants to abandon their homes and take refuge deeper in Russia. World War I and the Latvian War of Independence left the new republic in shambles. Latvia's dramatic recovery from that war and its economic renaissance prior to the Soviet invasion in 1940 remains a miracle to this day. Latvia's Jewish community was a big part of that resurgence.)

Tamāra Zālīte (b. Eiduss) was born into a (Latvian) Jewish family on February 14, 1918 in the town of Vologda, Russia. Her parents had fled to Russia, as German troops advanced into Kurzeme during World War I. Tamāra had one sibling, an older brother named Jāzeps who was born in 1916.

In 1920 Latvia's scattered refugees, including the Eiduss family, were able to return home. Although Tamāra's family was originally from Daugavpils, a town on the Daugava River in eastern Latvia with a large Jewish population before World War II, her father Aron Eiduss had moved the family to the port city of Liepāja in 1912, where he opened a small business. The men of the family worked at a lumber mill and received their education at Jewish religious schools or yeshivas.

In the early 1920s the Eiduss family moved to Rīga, where Tamāra attended the city's 16th Elementary School (the German Lutherschule). After 1934, when Kārlis Ulmanis seized power in a coup d'etat, minority children could only attend schools of their own nationality or Latvian schools. Tamāra started attending a Jewish school in Rīga. Her brother Jāzeps was attracted to the ideas of communism; he was a member of an underground communist youth organization, and his views influenced his sister.

In his autobiographical notes Jāzeps Eiduss wrote that as a secondary school student I became involved in the communist underground. In 1934 he was arrested together with a number of other boys, chiefly Germans. He was found guilty of being the ringleader and was sentenced to four years in prison, which he served at Rīga Central Prison and by digging peat at various bogs. He was expelled from the University of Latvia for 99 years.

Tamāra organized a student strike at her Jewish school, which demanded that the school introduce Soviet teaching methods; she was promptly expelled. She graduated from Rīga's so-called Society School in 1936. Jāzeps was already serving his prison term. That same year Tamāra became a student of chemistry at the University of Latvia. Befriending a communist named Raimonds Bočs, she joined the communist underground. She was arrested along with Bočs (who later ran a kolhoz in Soviet Latvia—RL). Due to insufficient evidence, Tamāra was released from jail. However, she did not complete her studies. Working as a children's tutor, Tamāra saved up some money and traveled to Great Britain in 1938 to improve her English. She studied at the London Polytechnic and graduated from the London Institute of Linguists. She enrolled in the English Department of Birkbeck College, London University. Jāzeps Eiduss was released from prison and joined Tamāra in London to go to school. Tamāra also worked at a meeting house of the Quakers as a secretary. (...)

Because of her leftist political affiliation, Tamāra was able to get a job at the Soviet TASS news agency in London in late June 1941; she recorded news from the radio and transmitted it further to (Soviet) press agencies. She worked there until the summer of 1946. Her life in London was exciting and fulfilling. Working for a press agency, she was always in the thick of things. With her decent wage she could afford a nice flat and was surrounded by friends and admirers. Tamāra was able to travel around the country despite the dangers of war and German air strikes. In London she resumed dancing ballet, a pursuit she had loved since childhood. She took part in performances at London's Unity Theater, a troupe dedicated to social and political issues. (Their performances were also directed against Nazism and fascism.—RL) Tamāra was also able to dance in the performances of Madame Marie Rambert (1888–1982), a Polish Jew who left a lasting impression on British ballet as a dancer and teacher.

Tamāra had a love affair with her brother's math professor, a descendant of Hungarian aristocracy. Tamāra's left-wing convictions introduced her to interesting members of London's Left, which included fighters of the Spanish Civil War, journalists, and literary people.

World War II ended in 1945 with Nazi Germany's defeat, and Tamāra longed to go back to Latvia. She believed her homeland had been set free from the Nazis by the Soviets and was now a workers' paradise. She longed to see her brother Joseph who by this time was back in Rīga after his own escapades both in London and the Soviet Union.

And so in 1946 idealistic Tamāra gave up her interesting, happy life in London to return to Latvia, now a part of the USSR. The realities of Soviet post-war life in her native country were a rude awakening for her, a person used to a comfortable existence. She had problems finding work, a place to live, and taking care of normal everyday matters. She was thrust into a bureaucratic labyrinth and encountered mounting hostility and suspicion from the Soviet authorities; they procrastinated on issuing a Soviet passport to her. The reality of life under the Soviets was dawning on her, as her communist convictions crumbled. Once employed by TASS in London, Tamāra decided to seek work in Moscow at the agency's headquarters. However, Moscow's terrible living conditions and starvation drove her back to Rīga.

Tamāra was fighting for her very existence. Her old friend Eduards Berklāvs from the days of the underground came to her aid. (Berklāvs would rise to great heights in the Latvian Communist Party but would be booted for being a "nationalist."—RL) Working her way up from lab assistant at the Rīga Pedagogical Institute to a lecturer at the University of Latvia's Department of Foreign Languages, Tamāra achieved a position of authority among her peers and students. She began working on her Ph.D. candidate thesis while translating Latvian literature into English. She married Varaidotis Zālītis, a singer at the National Opera, and joined the Latvian Writers Union. Things were looking up for her.

Left: Jāzeps or Joseph Eiduss in the Gulag's far north in 1955. Source: LatvijasĻaudis.lv.

In the early 1950s Tamāra and her brother Joseph were arrested separately and tried as British spies. Joseph was sentenced and shipped off to Vorkuta to work in the coal mines north of the Arctic Circle. Tamāra was packed off to work in the forests of Siberia's Archangelsk region. A former ballerina, she survived excruciating cold, hard labor, humiliation, and hunger, subsisting on 300 grams of bread a day. Without notifying her, Tamāra's husband divorced her. (Soviet law permitted this.) Following Stalin's death, in 1956 brother and sister were pardoned, and they returned to Latvia. (3) (Photo: LatvijasĻaudis.lv.)

Tamāra returned to the Rīga Pedagogical Institute and spent the rest of her life translating Latvian literature into English, penning literary criticism, and researching literature. A big Shakespeare fan, she joined the German Shakespeare Society in Weimar, Germany. Tamāra was also a member of the Latvian Writers Union. Not only did Tamāra translate Latvian literature into English (Rūdolfs Blaumanis, Andrejs Upīts, Alberts Bels, Regīna Ezera, and others), but she also authored several books for students about Graham Greene, T.S. Eliot, Muriel Spark, John Fowles, and other famous writers, as well as numerous essays. Her book *My Shakespeare* (1989) is devoted to one of her favorite writers.

Tamāra's brother Jāzeps Eiduss was a lecturer, scientific researcher, translator of scientific works, and beloved mentor at the University of Latvia. He specialized in spectroscopy and studied yellow phosphorus and solid state physics. He penned numerous papers and books, including a translation of Lucretius' *De Rerum Natura* ("On the Nature of Things") from Latin into Latvian. Joseph Eiduss was nominated as a fellow of Birkbeck, London University in 1996 together with Sir Aaron Klug, Nobel Prize recipient (Chemistry) in 1982 and President of the Royal Society of London. Jāzeps Eiduss' life motto was: "Don't let those bastards grind you down!" In his free time Eiduss enjoyed traveling along Siberia's mountain rivers, collected books, and loved Latvia's countryside. (4)

The Eiduss siblings were a couple of remarkable Latvian Jews who were lucky to avoid the Holocaust in Latvia; as staunch "lefties" they believed in the ideals of communism, experienced the Soviet Gulag but survived, and enriched the lives of their peers, friends, students, and Latvian community. I grieve for the terrible loss of life that Latvia's Jews suffered under the Soviet and Nazi occupations. During my time in Latvia I would get a general sense of the toll of the events of the 20th century on our human population. However, it was only later, after I had already left Latvia, that I would start piecing together those events with the help of some marvelous books about Latvia's history and the events of World War II.

Today, thanks to independence and the work of Latvian and Jewish historians, the Holocaust in Latvia and other crimes against humanity committed under the Soviet and Nazi occupations are being actively researched. Latvia's Jewish community, although small in comparison to what it once was, is again present in Latvia and well integrated. There are markers throughout Latvia to commemorate those who perished.

I now realize that I was missing stories about multicultural Rīga and Latvia's ethnic minorities. Jews, Old-Believers, Russians, Gypsies or Roma, Germans, Poles, Swedes, the English: they live in our dainas and were part of Latvia's historical population. Jews and Gypsies were mentioned in books, novels, and even in beloved plays, such as "Skroderdienas Silmačos" by Rūdolfs Blaumanis. In the First Republic Latvia's Jews fueled the country's economy with their business know-how. A journal from 1928 in my possession, *The Latvian Economist*, is full of advertisements for companies owned by Jews. In fact, up until the Holocaust wealthy Jews owned a percentage of prime Rīga real estate. Yet for many years, thanks to my upbringing, I was focused only on the Latvian aspect of Latvia.

I hope that today's Latvia's Jewish community is on the mend. In 1983 kindly and gracious Tamāra Zālīte was like a kindred spirit. It was delightful to speak English again; the language itself seemed to transport us beyond the Iron Curtain to the West and the freedom it symbolized. The ageing ballerina who loved Shakespeare was a living embodiment of the crazy history of Latvia in the 20th century. By spending some time researching the biographies of Tamāra Zālīte and her accomplished brother, Professor Jāzeps Eiduss, I was able to reflect on a chapter in Latvia's history that for many years remained in the dark: that is, what happened to Latvia's Jews. I wish to pay homage to a people who had lived side by side with Latvians for centuries. Their contribution to Latvia's historical and cultural landscape, as well as their suffering, cannot be forgotten.

It is possible to visit the former site of the Great Choral Synagogue on Gogoļa iela in Rīga, constructed between 1868 and 1871. The synagogue was burned down on July 4, 1941, allegedly with Jews locked inside. The Germans had entered Rīga just three days prior to torching this and other Jewish houses of worship in Rīga. The remains of the synagogue and a monument are just up the street from the Rīga Central Market. In July 2014 I bought some red gladiolas and walked over to take a look at what was left of this sanctuary: just a shell.

Rīga's oldest synagogue, Alt-Nay- Shul ("Old-New Synagogue) at 57 Maskavas iela nearby, which dated back to 1780, had also been torched in 1941. After the war it was converted into an apartment building. In the Soviet era, many aspects of World War II history were under wraps. The Latvian expatriate community had not come to terms with the Holocaust either. There are many other places in Latvia where one can leave flowers for the named and unnamed victims of the Holocaust in Latvia.

השלום עליהם

Chapter sources:

(1) Applebaum, Anne. *Iron Curtain: The Crushing of Eastern Europe.* New York: Doubleday, 2012. Page 118.

(2) Melers, Meijers. *Latvijas ebreju kopienas vēsture un holokausta piemiņas vietas.* Rīga: Rīgas Ebreju kopienas muzejs "Ebreji Latvijā" / LU Filozofijas un socioloģijas institūts, 2013. Page 1.

(3) Jāzeps Eiduss. "Tamāra Zālīte: Literary Critic, Translator of Latvian Into English, Member of Shakespear Society. In Memoriam." Latvijas ļaudis: Virtuālā enciklopēdija. January 19, 1999. Retrieved March 7, 2014. <http://latvijaslaudis.lv/userseng/zalite_tamara_eng?language=ru>

(4) Jāzeps Eiduss. "Jāzeps Eiduss: Physical Chemist, Professor at the University of Latvia, Honorary Member, Birkbeck, University of London." Retrieved March 7, 2013. <http://www.latvijaslaudis.lv/users/eiduss_jazeps>

Roosters and Cats in Old Rīga

Early spring 1983. Paulēni in all its glory: the old granary; the cellar to the right; the stately ash trees; the old mill stones. My mother-in-law and I are enjoying the new Siamese-mix kitten Ansis who rode on the train to Ērgļi. Photo: Andris Krieviņš

April 13, 1983, Letter to My Family

Ciao!

Bad weather has arrived; this morning we gazed out the window at flurries of wet snow. Winter here has been relentless and rotten. Yet spring's presence is tangible. It's out there, hiding behind the clouds; it just can't pluck up the courage to make the descent. (...) Our rooster Mārtiņš crows so often, that we think maybe he's a bit crazy. And he's driving us crazy. This morning he started his concert at 7:00. Andris got so mad, that he fetched a pail and put it over poor Mārtiņš. Sweet silence. But then our kitten Ansis climbed into bed and started playing with us, attacking our fingers and toes, our hair and our noses, so it was time to wake up. My hands and feet are covered in scratches, and my beloved purple tights have been torn to shreds! Our kitten likes to climb up my legs, and his nails are exceptionally sharp. Right now he's lying in my lap and purring. It's hard not to laugh as the little ball of fur jumps about stiffly on all four feet, hides in a boot, attacks a slipper, and stalks the rooster! Kitty's only bad Siamese trait is his relentless meowing (or rather squeaking). The rooster's frequent pooping is very annoying, but he'll soon be leaving us for Piebalga.

My husband was crazy about animals. He had spent his childhood summers in the countryside, surrounded by farm animals, learned to ride a horse, seen country life up close. We purchased our kitten Ansis at the market in Čiekurkalns, Rīga. Andris picked up Mārtiņš at a poultry show; the feisty brown rooster was destined to be king of the hill at Paulēni and wake up the sun. (In fact, he looked just like Bill Peet's Cock-a-doodle Dudley.) In 1984 or '85 we brought a gray cockatiel with orange cheeks back from the Vilnius market. We named him Čipa, and he was a wonderful pet, until one day he flew away from us in Piebalga. When we finally purchased our own house in the countryside, Andris wanted to stock the barn with cows and pigs. He bought a horse. But now I am getting ahead of myself.

283

Every Rīgan knew the famous "Cat Building" in Old Rīga (right). Apparently the cats were placed on top of the building to taunt a Rīga city official. The beautiful Art Nouveau building, completed in 1909, was designed by architect Friedrich Scheffel. Roosters perched on most of Rīga's church steeples. Photo: Una Šneidere (http://valoda.ailab.lv)

There were many stray cats in Rīga that were adored and fed by little old ladies. Latvia's dogs were aggressive. Big, scary guard dogs like the Caucasian Shepherd Dog ("Ovcharkas") were popular. But in downtown Rīga there were no dogs; at least I never saw any. The parks were clean. Only rats scampered along the banks of the canal. The sounds of jackdaws and seagulls filled the air. And just like everywhere in the world, there were pigeons.

The roosters, symbols of Apostle Peter, symbolized dawn, sunlight, and hope for me. According to St.PaulOnline.org, "The Biblical words for 'wind' and 'spirit' are the same in both the Hebrew of the Old Testament and the Greek of the New Testament. The rooster is an advent symbol calling people to 'arise, awake, and get ready' to join God where his 'Spirit' is at work in the world, as indicated by the direction of the 'wind' pointed out by the weather vane." In the last decade of oppressive Soviet rule in Latvia I often raised my eyes to the old church steeples and their golden roosters, knowing that nothing lasted forever, that all empires were doomed to collapse sooner or later.

Jūrmala

The famous "Jūras pērle" ("Sea Pearl") restaurant. Image courtesy of the National Library of Latvia collection "In Search of Lost Latvia."

Summer of '83. One day in late June or early July a significantly "Latvian" red-and-white-striped bikini arrived in the mail from the US, sent by my mother. With Andris at work and the heat rising, I decided to "take the plunge" and head out to Jūrmala, Latvia's famous seaside resort, for a day of sunbathing, reading, and swimming. Jūrmala is a 32-kilometer (20 mile) strip of land wedged between the Gulf of Rīga and the Lielupe River. It is a string of beach towns stretching from Lielupe to Ķemeri, known before the war for its famous spa with healing mud baths and curative springs. Jūrmala had grown from a bunch of rustic fishermen's villages into a fashionable summer resort for Rigans who built beautiful cottages and villas there. Once populated by Germans and Latvians, it now attracted hordes of Russians and other vacationers from all over the USSR. In the Soviet era it was decidedly Russian, as I would soon discover.

If I had known about serial rapist and killer Staņislavs Rogaļevs, I probably would not have ventured out to Jūrmala on my own. In the early 1980s, while working at the Soviet Latvian Ministry of the Interior, Rogaļevs committed a series of grisly rapes and murders, some in Jūrmala. Oblivious to local crime, which the Soviet press and mass media chose not to mention or gloss over, I lived in blissful ignorance. For a moment I hesitated: I was going alone; was it safe? Paradoxically, in a political system with little freedom the crime level was low (or so it seemed), and I never felt afraid of walking around alone, unlike in New Jersey, where I had been assaulted by a rapist on my street in Glen Ridge. (I kicked the jerk in the ski mask in the balls with my cowboy boot, and that scared him away.) However, by the mid-1980s in Rīga, I had heard some rather horrible stories, which were circulated by word of mouth: a jeweler and his family were murdered in their house in Jūrmala by criminals from Russia, etc. In that decade, however, mugshots of and warnings about dangerous criminals on the loose would sound off on the airwaves and TV, chilling viewers. I can still hear in my head a man's voice announcing: "Milicija meklē..." ("The police are looking for...") The only problem was, you never found out why law enforcement officials were looking for these people.

Left: An old photograph of the Bulduri Hotel— Hotel Bilderlingshof as it was once known—in Jūrmala.

I packed a book, a towel, and an apple into my American back-pack, put my bathing suit on be-neath a dress, and headed to Rīga Central Station to board one of the numerous trains departing for Jūrmala. In the summer the trains to Jūrmala were very crowded, and as you hauled yourself up into the train, you could get a good glimpse of hairy armpits (men's and women's) and be squashed against other sweaty bodies. People in Latvia did not wash as often as in the United States for many reasons: lack of a steady source of hot water; no bath or shower at home (showers were non-existent); or ignorance of or lack of interest in personal hygiene. Perhaps daily showers were just an American thing. Cheesy socks, sweaty armpits: it was the smell of humanity. It did not bother me much; I was breathing in a whole new lifestyle.

Jūrmala was a short 30 minute train ride to the west of Rīga. The windows were open, ad-mitting the warm summer air, and I managed to find a spot on a bench to look out at the passing scenery. The train rattled across the Daugava River and proceeded to make numerous stops, picking up and letting off passengers. I was immediately overwhelmed by a sense of delightful laziness. The heat, the sound of the train's clacking wheels, the tolerable scent of perspiration, and the murmur of passengers had a soothing effect on me. People in the Soviet Union were in no real hurry to get anywhere. After all, where could you go? Living in a prison state where the economy and media were controlled from "above," one got the sense that time stood still, or rather that one existed outside of time.

Latvians and Russian speakers were all packed into the train as one giant mass of flesh; some heading home from Rīga Central Market with cloth sacks stuffed with produce, some going to Jūrmala or maybe to their *mazdārziņi* ("gardens"), which were popular. This was vacation time, after all.

As we pulled into the Torņakalns train station on the other side of the river, I was reminded of what I had read about June 14, 1941, when thousands of innocent people—men, women, children, and the elderly—were rounded up by the Soviet NKVD and deported in cattlecars from that and other stations to far outposts and prison camps in Russia's Siberian wilderness. Was this where Uncle Eduards and Aunt Velta began their last journey? Many people died along the way, as described in Anne Applebaum's *Gulag*, Lithuanian Ruta Sepetys' *Between Shades of*

Gray, and other books and memoirs. A second wave of deportations from this station took place on March 25, 1949.

On that warm summer day in 1983 the station looked deserted; the late morning sun beat down on the shimmering tracks. *Not a care in the world.* People were thinking about their gardens, strawberries, the beach… There was nothing at the station to inform anyone about those sad days in Latvia's history. But older Latvians remembered; many of them passed their tragic memories and stories on to their children. The Balts knew what had happened, whereas the Russian colonists knew nothing. Torņakalns was a pretty area with lovely houses built before the war, old trees, and quiet streets. My mother remembered it from her childhood. Famous poet Ojārs Vācietis and his wife Ludmila Azarova lived there. My father-in-law knew Vācietis and had taken many wonderful photographs of him.

The train chugged on, passing old houses with fenced in yards, where clean laundry swayed in the lazy breeze. It rumbled past a new housing project going up in an area called Zolitūde (Solitude). Apartments in these drab, "cookie-cutter" "block" buildings were sought by many who languished in run-down buildings with no central plumbing and heating. The Russian military needed a place to live, as did Russian immigrants.

Once we rolled over the Lielupe River, I got out at the Lielupe station and started walking toward the beach, which I calculated to be nearby. The delightful, aromatic, soothing scent of pine trees baking in the summer sun enveloped me. It was peaceful and quiet. A few other people were headed in the same direction; not a car was in sight. After a 15–20 minute walk, I was descending down a sandy path to the beach, which stretched to the left (west) and right (east) toward Rīga. Warm, gravely sand sucked in my bare feet and tickled my toes. Directly in front of me lay the blue-gray waters of the Gulf of Rīga, lapping at the shoreline with gentle waves. This was no ocean.

I walked westward and then plopped down in the sand, looking around. It felt strange to be surrounded by what seemed to be only Russian speakers. This was Latvia, right? Off came my dress; I lay down on my towel in my bikini in Latvia's national colors and closed my eyes. In the distance the water murmured; overhead the gulls cried, as they do everywhere in the world. What a gorgeous place! The beach was not that crowded. Soon enough a Russian man in tiny swim trunks sauntered by, then slowed down and addressed me, but I blew him off with my eternal "Ya ne govoryu po russki!" ("I don't speak Russian!") That did the trick each time. He would be the only annoying fly on an otherwise lovely day.

I opened Hans Selye's (1907–1982) popular book *The Stress of Life*, which I had picked up at a Rīga bookstore, and struggled to read it in the blinding sunshine. I did not have sunglasses, nor had I seen sunglasses for sale anywhere, although I assumed they were sold somewhere. But where exactly? Averse to shopping in Rīga's overcrowded stores, I had decided that "less" was better. No point in reading and being "blinded by the light" ("…revved up like a deuce…").Lie back, relax, let the sun caress your pale Baltic skin… How many cities in the world offered a beautiful beach and refreshing seawater 30 minutes from downtown? Lying in the sun in the warm sand was a great way to lose one's sense of time, to dream of the past or consider the future…

Right: The Edinburg Sea Pavilion in Jūrmala in the early 1900s.

Right: The Edinburg Sea Pavilion in Jūrmala in the early 1900s.

Even in the 1980s Jūrmala had retained its charm; it was a lovely mix of sand, dunes, pines, heather, and pretty "gingerbread" cottages from the old days. Here and there Soviet era poured-concrete monstrosities marked the triumph of the proletariat. Once Baltic Germans had vacationed in fashionable Jūrmala. Old photographs from the beginning of the 20th century show the same pretty beach but with women with parasols and men in "onesies," tanned brown and grinning. By the 1980s Jūrmala's look wasn't quite so polished anymore, but it was still appealing. It was wildly popular with people from other Soviet republics, especially Russia, who rented cottages or rooms and flocked to the beach in the thousands. Several sanatoriums offered therapeutic procedures for the Soviet working man and woman.

High-ranking Moscow officials had their own luxury retreats in Jūrmala, like Rīgas Līcis ("Gulf of Rīga"), a Soviet era hotel with a large indoor pool, saunas, exercise rooms and equipment, and beautiful grounds leading up to the beach. Jūrmala was a favorite destination for Soviet hotshots, including Alexei Kosygin (1904–1980), a well known Soviet Russian statesman in the Cold War era. Andrei Gromyko (1909–1989), the Soviet Foreign Minister from 1957 until 1985, was charmed by Jūrmala, too. Later somebody told me that "Leonid Brezhnev had preferred the 'Soviet south' to the Baltics, which he instinctively disliked." The Balts were not fond of Brezhnev either.

Because of the influx of so many Russian speakers to Jūrmala in the summer months, ethnic Latvians tended to avoid it. They preferred the quiet and solitude of the Latvian countryside or the villages further out. I had spent my early childhood summers at the Jersey shore and loved sand, sun, and water. I was drawn to Jūrmala. There was talk of the water being rather polluted; the Sloka paper factory, located at the far end of Jūrmala, pumped its wastewater directly into the gulf. Although this worried me, it didn't prevent me from enjoying Jūrmala. After all, many people summered there and swam. And Rīga really was hot and smelly. I needed to get away from the city.

As I lay basking in the sun, I thought about the fact that Jūrmala was so close to Rīga and how wonderful Latvia's trains and public transportation were. There was a new highway that connected the outskirts of Rīga with Jūrmala, built at the request of Augusts Voss, the former First Secretary of the Central Committee of the Latvian Communist Party. Voss had wanted a fast track to his beloved Jūrmala, and he got it. Voss and other high-ranking Soviet officials could get to Jūrmala quickly in their Volgas and Chaikas, while the average Soviet citizen took the train.

That day I discovered that, at least where I had camped out, there were no decent public rest rooms, and people relieved themselves in the dunes or in the water, which is what I did.

The public rest room was a small building with just holes in the floor; it was so disgustingly filthy, that I avoided it.

Jūrmala had been a popular summer destination for more than a century. Its pretty old buildings still stood as a testimonial to better days: that is, the pre-war era of private property. Many structures showed signs of wear, tear, and neglect. Jūrmala was a popular place for several Soviet Pioneer camps; the Pioneers were a communist youth organization. The communists loved to lambaste the bourgeoisie and the capitalists of the pre-war era while enjoying the accomodations that the ""capitalist pigs" had built. The Soviet legacy of architecture in Jūrmala was an ugly intrusion on Jūrmala's delicate aesthetics; several massive-looking sanatoriums and hotels, as well as the famous Jūras Pērle ("Sea Pearl"), a restaurant and bar that jutted like a giant ship onto the beach, did not sit well in historical Jūrmala, a treasure trove of Victorian architecture.

> The average Soviet citizen could gain access to Sea Pearl with relative ease only in winter, because (from late spring until early fall) all the tables with views of the gulf were reserved for Intourist groups. In the summer only half of the restaurant was open to the Soviet public, and eager customers began to stand in line in the morning to gain entrance. When the doors opened, they rushed in to order broth with a pīrāgs ("bacon bun") and an entrée. The eager crowd was divided into two groups: the first knew that the tables at the one end of the restaurant were already reserved, and therefore they sat down off to the side and waited to be seated; the other group knew nothing about the Intourist reservations and rushed forward to the exclusive end of the restaurant, only to be rudely pushed back... This happened every day. The majority of clients were tourists from other Soviet republics or locals renting summer cottages in Jūrmala. However, there were no double-standards regarding how locals and foreigners were served: neither the dishes nor the cloth serviettes (napkins) differed. In the evenings tables sold out in a matter of ten to 20 minutes. (* Photo: Spoki.net. Text: Ivars Kleins. „Jūras Pērlē uzdzīvo elite." TVNet.lv. Published May 21, 2009. Retrieved March 10, 2013. <www.tvnet.lv/sievietem/persona/66283-juras_perle_uzdzivo_elite> Tr. RL)

Of course, to get into Sea Pearl without standing in line you needed *blats*—a connection. Reservations weren't free. Blats came with a price. And Sea Pearl was famous. According to Ivars Kleins, Sea Pearl also catered to some of Jūrmala's famous vacationers, like Soviet Foreign Minister Andrei Gromyko, Soviet statesman Nikolai Podgorny (1903–1983), and Aleksei Kosygin. For Soviet nostalgists those were "the good old days" in Latvia...

Because Jūrmala was such a popular destination for people from other Soviet republics, it was completely Russified in the summer. In spite of the Pioneer camps and crowds of Slavs, Jūrmala was also home to Latvians who lived in small but comfortable houses and kept pretty gardens. How I wished for a garden! When the summer rolled around, our small apartment seemed even smaller; I had gotten used to it, but with the advent of heat I longed for trees, flowers, and fresh air. I ventured into the water and splashed, floated, and swam. I missed the company of my husband; unlike me, he was no fan of Jūrmala. I kept my mouth tightly shut in case of any foul bacteria floating around. Despite this concern, the experience was turning out to be quite nice. It was so pretty! I pictured Estonia's islands, Saaremaa, Hiiumaa, Kihnu, Muhu, Vormsi, and Ruhnu, and enviously regretted that Latvia didn't have *any* islands in the Baltic Sea.

The Gulf of Rīga stretched out like a shimmering canvas. I floated on my back and watched fluffy clouds gliding above me in a serene procession. More than 700 years ago German ships had sailed this way, driven by Baltic gales and curiosity; they discovered the estuary of the Daugava River and new lands inhabited by the Livs and other tribes. My native land was full of surprises, beauty, and historical treasures hidden from sight from much of the world.

But an invisible, impermeable "curtain" stretched to the west of this lovely gulf, separating the Baltic States from the rest of Europe. Attempting to breach that curtain would be to risk one's life. As far as I knew, no one had succeeded. I fantasized about what would happen if I got on a motorboat and sped west across the gulf. At what point would I be intercepted, arrested, or shot at? For a country "on the water" like Latvia, there were very few motorboats. Unlike the Jersey shore, which teemed with private sailboats and yachts, Latvia was totally devoid of such signs of personal wealth.

Latvia's Baltic Sea shoreline to the west was off-limits to a "free bird" like me; much of it was off-limits even to Soviet citizens, as were the Estonian islands. It was a military zone, the Soviet Union's westernmost border, patrolled by the Soviet border army. After the war Latvian fishermen living by the Baltic Sea were no longer permitted to go out to sea to fish. Jūrmala was one of only a few places that westerners like me were allowed to venture to without special permission. So I was enjoying a deceptive sense of freedom by paddling around in the gulf's lazy waves. The people around me looked happy. In a country as far north as Latvia, the sun had a calming effect on everyone.

Yet once it had been different. Latvia had been free and inextricably linked to the West through trade. Private proprietors in Jūrmala had maintained beautiful hotels, inns, and spas for their summer clientele, and everything had been manicured to perfection. I base my assertion on photographs from the pre-war era. I was convinced that proper outhouses were part of the "old Jūrmala." In the "good old days" there were fines for spitting in public, a bad habit that many of our "liberators" engaged in along with chewing sunflower seeds and spitting the hulls on the ground. In the Soviet era one had to tread through the heather of Jūrmala's dunes with caution, assuming that one's feet could land in some fecal matter or pee. It was hard to believe that in the capitalist era of refinement there had been no restrooms for Jūrmala's vacationers.

Jūrmala had its own intriguing story about the doomed Latvian millionairess Emīlija Benjamiņa. Her famous summer villa, located at the western end of Jūrmala in the village of Majori, remained veiled in mystery, rumors, and hearsay. There was talk of the villa having sliding glass walls that apparently still worked after all these years. The idea of sliding glass walls seemed completely "back to the future" in the era of primitive Soviet architecture, which relied on poured concrete blocks and was completely lacking in finesse and aesthetic appeal. Sea Pearl was one of the most successful examples of Soviet-era architecture.

Upon its completion in 1939, the Emīlija Benjamiņa House, as it is known, was considered the most spectacular villa on the Baltic Sea's eastern shore. Once Emīlija was conveniently shipped off to Siberia in 1941, the brand-new luxury house and its immaculate grounds were claimed consecutively by the Soviets and the Nazis. In the Soviet era the house was a coveted retreat for high-ranking Soviet government officials from Moscow, as well as Latvia's top communists.

I noticed the villa for the first time in the early 1980s, when I happened to stroll past it on the beach; at the time I had no idea that it had belonged to Emīlija Benjamiņa, the famous publisher whose magazines my mother read as a girl. The villa at 13 Jūras iela, located on a bluff above the beach, was beautiful, elegant, and imposing. It was clear to anyone that someone of great wealth had lived there. It was also apparent that someone of great power was maintaining the building and its grounds. That someone was the Communist Party. A lavish cast-iron fence manufactured in Paris ensured privacy. The villa reposed on a grass-covered lawn seeded in soil imported from Germany, its large windows facing the Gulf of Rīga. The villa's construction had commenced in 1938 and ended in 1939, a year fateful for Latvia and Emīlija Benjamiņa, when the notorious Molotov-Ribbentrop Pact was signed on August 23 in Moscow.

So many years had passed since the end of the war and the ignoble death of proud Emīlija Benjamiņa in faraway Solikamsk, Russia in September of 1941, yet her initials, E.B., were still affixed to the villa's remarkable, hand-crafted gate. I remember slowing down to look at the initials, which aroused my interest. So personal, the letters were a vestige of the days of private ownership. They provided a tantalizing hint at the original owner's life of grandeur. A guard booth near the street signaled the importance of the building and its grounds as property of the Soviet state. At the time, I had no idea who "E.B." was.

One of Emīlija Benjamiņa's descendants and heirs, Peter Aicher, has written about the history of her summer villa. While I was writing my memoir, he was living in the house and was unsure of its future. When we spoke on the phone in 2014, we agreed that ideally the house should eventually be purchased by the Latvian state and preserved as a national monument.

> The whole history of the 20th century is wrapped up inside this house. Emilija Benjamin was quite conscious of the status that she had achieved as the most successful and wealthy person in Latvia and in many ways the final determinant of high style and culture in the country, and she chose her homes to reflect this fact. By the 1930s, in addition to owning the fabulously successful publishing business, she had considerable real estate holdings, including several apartment and commercial buildings in Rīga, among them those housing her printing plant, a factory complex in Kekava (a town close to the south edge of Rīga), and for personal use an impressive city residence located in the center of Rīga that in those days was still sometimes known by the name of its original owners as the Pfab Palace. (She also owned) a country estate called Waldeck and a summer house on land directly adjacent to the beach in the resort city of Jūrmala. The

summer house had been one of her first houses and was a late 19th century wooden building typical of the area. But by the mid 1930s Emilija was ready to upgrade her summer residence.

Her first concrete step in the plan was to purchase the neighbouring lot directly adjacent (to the east) of her existing lot, effectively doubling the land available to her.

As with everything she did, Emilija determined that the new beach residence would be second to none; in fact it would be the most exclusive house in Latvia. To draw up the plans, she commissioned the famous German architect Lange and then personally worked with him on the design.

The transformation of the property started with a transformation of the landscape itself. Unlike all the other (wooden) houses on the street at that time, which nestled behind the dunes for protection from the wind, this building would sit on the crest of a bluff specially created for it. Local residents who still remember the house being built recall half a dozen workers hauling sand in wheelbarrows for two years to make the hill. Then it was covered with topsoil brought in from Germany. Special German topsoil had been bought as premium potting soil by the bag, in Latvia, for years. But Emilija Benjamin brought in a trainload. The standard customs duties (over 100 000 lats) on such a quantity turned out to be a shock even for Mrs. Benjamin, and she ended up negotiating a settlement on the matter with the Latvian government.

In 1938 construction was ready to begin and lasted over a year. The design and layout of the house was thoroughly modern, with, for that era, huge windows. Architect Lange was famous for his use of natural light, and here he used his talents to the fullest. The windows were carefully sited to provide optimal views to the outside and (the interior). Seaward was a three-piece curved window running the full width of the dining room, but to the landward side was a glass wall running the full width of the central hall, which in the summer could be lowered into the floor by electric motors, opening the house wide to fresh breezes and the warmth of the sun, as this was also the south side of the building.

The motorized glass wall was not the only ultra-modern feature of the house. There were fixtures of aluminum, a metal as precious as gold at the time, and of Bakelite, the just developed forerunner of modern plastics.

At the same time, the design and overall look of the house, set far back from the road, was neo-classical and unmistakably declared that this owner had no need to show off.

Along the roadside the property was delineated by a wrought iron fence, designed separately by architect A. Antonov and especially handmade in Paris with the monogram "EB" hammered into the design of the front gate. The monogram was also repeated in the wrought iron railing of the front balcony on the house.

On the other side the house also featured a private, lockable entrance to the beach. The turn of the century (19th to 20th) teahouse right on the top of the sea wall was also retained.

But however grand was Emilija's dream, fate cut it cruelly short. Her husband Anton died just before the Benjamin House, for that was what the place came to be known as, was finished, and Emilija ended up moving in alone. And she herself was to live there for only a couple of months. For in 1939 the great dictators had decided a "future" for Eastern Europe and for the millions living there.

In 1940 Latvia was occupied, its government overthrown, and its society "socialized" by the Soviet Union. Emilija was summarily moved out of all her homes, initially "given" a small flat, but as a prime, in fact the prime, example of the (Latvian) "bourgeoisie," soon arrested, shipped by cattle car to a labor camp, and allowed to die.

The grandest home in her former country would now be the residence of the new determinant of order there, the commander of the Red Army occupation forces, Colonel-General Aleksandr Loktionov. He got to live in the house a few months longer than Emilija. Then the Germans came along and swiftly put the Red Army to flight; so swiftly that a scapegoat had to be found and heads had to roll. Just as he was leaving the area, General Loktionov was arrested by the NKVD and soon enough shot without a trial. He died less than five weeks after Emilija did.

With the advance of the Wehrmacht, the next new order had arrived. While the survivors of the Benjamin family received some of the properties the communists had confiscated ("nationalized") back from the German government, this grand house was not among them. After all, the next ruler of Latvia (and Lithuania, Estonia and Belorussia—the new National Socialist "Ostland") needed a residence befitting him. Gauleiter Hinrich Lohse, the Reichskommissar of Ostland, moved in. He actually got to live in the house for several years. While there his most famous visitor was Alfred Rosenberg, the Russian educated chief of ideology of the National Socialist German Workers (Nazi) Party, who apparently only stayed a few hours.

Lohse, too, had grand plans. Rumor had it that he had intended to raze the smaller neighbouring buildings and create a large park, but he never got to that. However, during this period the street in front of the house, Jūras Street, was paved for the first time with the work being done by the R.A.D. ("Reichsarbeitsdienst"—the Reich's Labor Service).

As the war gradually turned against Germany, Hinrich Lohse became increasingly concerned about his personal safety. The consequences of that are still visible today. The house, which had originally been finished in beautiful white marble stucco that shimmered in the sun, was repainted with camouflage stripes to make it less visible to enemy aircraft. The greenish and brownish stripes, while faded, are still visible today. Just across the little side street a bunker / air-raid shelter was built, and the street was closed to all traffic. The bunker still exists, and the street is still closed today.

During Lohse's time there, protection for the house and its occupant was provided by a platoon of security troops. The security detachment, however, was billeted down the street in the house at Juras Street 6, and the Benjamin House itself was routinely guarded by a three man shift. Gauleiter Lohse himself moved around in a closed car, which was always preceded by a military-type vehicle with a mounted machine-gun.

By autumn 1944 Lohse was gone. Just before leaving, he ordered removal vans and had the specially-made furniture, fine cutlery, and other valuable items packed and taken to Germany. He took everything except for some essential items he would require for the remainder of his stay. After the war Alfred Rosenberg was tried and hanged in Nuremberg; but however the Allied Powers decided these things, Hinrich Lohse was not executed and passed away of natural causes in his native Muhlenbarbek in Northern Germany in 1964.

With the return of the Red Army, the house again became the residence of the "most equal of the equal" Soviet citizens; that is—the highest ranking Communist Party members. Immediately after the war, then Chairman of the Latvian Communist Party Vilis Lācis, former employee and protégé of Emilija Benjamin and the man who actually signed the order sending her to her death, was reported to have enjoyed spending time there. The authorities in the Kremlin never actually allowed him to move in, however, instead officially giving him a smaller house nearby (at the end of Undīnes Street), where he lived in 1945–46. From 1946 onward he had a residence in the Marienbad Hotel building at the far end of Jūras Street.

Little is known about the specifics of who and what were in the Benjamin House during the period immediately after the war, as the Soviet regime pulled its customary thick curtain of secrecy around everything. Now instead of the area being turned into a park, as Lohse had dreamed, the entire neighbourhood was turned into a closed Soviet government zone, and gradually various other government buildings for mixed official and official leisure use were put up nearby. The Benjamin House, however, remained the jewel in the crown, to be used as an official guesthouse for the highest of guests.

Nikita Khrushchev, Mikhail Gorbachev, Richard Nixon, and Boris Yeltsin were among them. The longtime chairman of the French Communist Party, Georges Marchais, stayed there repeatedly; "to relax," he said, presumably from the strain of being "the most equal" of proletariats in France.

Due to the importance of the persons present, the house received progressively more elaborate communications equipment during this era, and the staff boasted that any Soviet Embassy anywhere in the world could be contacted directly from there any time of day or night. Vestiges of the switchboard setup are still present and visible today.

During the 1970s a major reconstruction project was undertaken in the basement level: an imitation log-cabin sauna was built in, complete with a small dipping pool. The well known Latvian artist Uldis Zemzaris created a background painting for the sauna.

For a time the new chairman of the Latvian Communist Party, August Voss, did manage to get the house as his personal residence, and as he was an avid film fan, his contribution to the house was a complete movie theater with a full size (twin 35mm film projectors) projection booth installed in the basement. All the equipment is still there today as a silent witness to history.

In 1986 architect Māris Gundars made minor additional changes to the interior, creating a new cloakroom setup, new railings for the stairs, as well as renewing the interior paint job. To maintain the unity of the appearance of the house, he researched 1930s styles for inspiration. (...) (Peter Aicher. "The History of the Emilija Benjamin House." The Emilija Benjamin House. 2009. Retrieved March 3, 2013. <www.theemilijabenjaminhouse.com>)

Pēteris Blūms, an architect and special adviser to the Latvian Culture, Monuments, and Heritage Bureau, penned his thoughts about the Emīlija Benjamiņš House, which symbolized the complete turnaround of Latvia from the ravages of World War I, as well as Latvia's tragic fate during and after World War II.

Many wonderful castles and manor houses of the Baltic German aristocracy can be found in Latvia, but none of these was created by Latvians as their property. What developed here after the collapse of the empire at the end of World War I is almost unbelievable, for Latvia only had some ten good years before the onset of World War II, and the Benjamin villa was one of its most exotic fruits.

With the benefit of hindsight it can surely be said that the possibility of another family villa equal to this one being created in Latvia, or for that matter anywhere in the Baltics, in this era was near zero, for no one else came close to the Benjamin family in financial resources. And if they had decided to build a new residence in Jūrmala, the rest would be determined solely by the personalities, ambitions, and tastes of the persons involved. Mrs. Benjamin wanted to live regally but not in an ancient Latvian style; rather more as a European aristocrat.

Special attention was paid to the windows, doors, and floors. The window and door fittings were manufactured in the famous Yale factory according to Bauhaus design drawings and are all still original and in working condition. Each door is a collector's piece, as each is made of the highest quality walnut, while the inlaid designs of the natural wood parquet floors never repeat themselves from one room to the next.

It is surprising to see how much of the original condition of the house has survived, though given the chronic poverty of the Soviet state that is in some ways understandable. This house, with only minor changes, functions with its original equipment and technology in heating, ventilation, electrical wiring, and motors. The furnace for the central heating system has been replaced, but all the bathroom fixtures and decorations are original Art Deco rarities. The fantastic garden must be mentioned: it has retained its original historic layout, structures, and details.

There is no private residence in the Baltic States that has so directly witnessed the radical, in fact grotesque changes of its era. Before Emilija Benjamin's bed had even cooled, her bedroom was taken over by the Commanding General of the Soviet Occupation Forces who himself was abruptly replaced by the highest ranking Nazi official in the Baltic area, who in turn was replaced for half a century by Soviet Communist Party bosses and their prominent guests from all over the world.

As the Soviet Union (imploded), its "gravedigger" Gorbachev and (and his wife) Raisa tarried here, as did Boris Yeltsin, Richard Nixon, the Swedish Royal Couple, and many, many others. It is understandable that this mysterious place is not particularly popular in Latvia, for none of its residents or guests yearned for popularity; in fact, quite the opposite, this house has always guaranteed its occupants absolute incognito status. Legends surround this house; it has an aura. (Source: Peter Blum. "Commentary by Peter Blum, Special Adviser to the Latvian Culture, Monuments and Heritage Bureau." TheEmilijaBenjaminHouse. Retrieved March 11, 2013. <www.theemilijabenjaminhouse.com>)

Having grown up in the United States, a capitalist country where private property was sacred, where it was proof of a person's success, talents, and skills, I saw the Soviet Union as a gigantic thiefdom, a system of burglary of epic proportions achieved by murder, deportation, and the forced flight of hundreds of thousands of terrified Latvian citizens. Nationalization was state-sanctioned, organized, and executed theft of Latvia's private and state property. Emīlija Benja-miņa's house was a brilliant case in point. While she faded away from hunger and cold in the Gulag, an occupant of her country drank from her cup and slept in her bed, as Pēteris Blūms so aptly put it.

The villa at 13 Jūras iela now rightfully belongs to Emīlija's descendants. If they were to sell the place, how would they calculate the historical value of the famous house? But there were hundreds of architectural gems nestled among the dunes of Jūrmala: Victorian wonders with elegant latticework, stained glass windows, towers, and porches, such as Latvian architect and philanthropist Kristaps Morbergs' (1844–1928) summer "cottage" from 1883 in Dzintari, now property of the University of Latvia. These buildings were state-owned in the Soviet era, which was incapable of ensuring their maintenance.

There were other once-famous places associated with the Jūrmala area, like the famous Latvian state-owned sanatorium and spa at Ķemeri, designed by architect Eižens Laube, which in its heyday had been a marvel of modernity, luxury, and comfort. As the children of nostalgic exiles, we had heard about the wonders of Ķemeri, its mud baths and sulphur springs. In the 1980s the sanatorium was still in use, but its shine and sparkle were gone. Ugly Soviet era buildings had gone up in the area to accommodate thousands of Soviet workers seeking rest and cures. Photographs from the early 1900s show the town of Ķemeri to be in tip top shape, with trams transporting guests, concerts in the parks, and a fantastic looking restaurant called "Jautrais ods" ("The Merry Mosquito"). That lifestyle, those fashions, that sense of beauty and refinement that could only be achieved in a system of private ownership, had vanished forever, it seemed.

On my first day in summer in famous Jūrmala, I ventured into the water several times, all the while keeping an eye on my belongings, afraid that someone might steal them. The walk back to the train station was lovely, the scent of pines intoxicating, as the shadows of late afternoon grew longer. The air was crisply dry; it was perfect. I had always hated New Jersey's humid summers; Latvia's summer temperature and low humidity felt fantastic. I breathed deeply, trying to stash Jūrmala's fresh, sweet air into the deep recesses of my lungs, preparing them for the tainted air of Rīga, where Soviet cars and buses spewed their heavy exhaust.

The train with its tired, sun-stewed passengers picked up speed, rolling over the shimmering Lielupe River towards Rīga. The northern Baltic sun had seared my skin. Back home, I peered at my flushed face in the mirror; my body had burned pink, and the pale white triangles of skin beneath my "Latvian flag" bikini looked funny. I hurt all over. That night my husband and I resumed our violent battle with the Old Town's hordes of merciless mosquitoes, which gained easy access through our open window. By morning the walls were spattered with the squashed and bloodied corpses of these horrible creatures. In late August we installed screens, which my parents rolled up and sent to us by mail. In 1983 our windows were probably the only screened windows in all of Latvia, if not the entire Soviet Union.

While I lived in Latvia, I went out to Jūrmala from time to time and always enjoyed it, regardless of the crowds of Russian speakers. In fact, I got used to them and didn't mind their presence so much anymore. The Baltic Sea and the beautiful Gulf of Rīga had shaped my fatherland's fate.

For centuries ships bearing friends and foes had sailed past these sunny beaches; it was all a wonderful story unfolding.

(Left) Majori, Jūrmala, circa 1990. This is where I usually hung out when I went to Jūrmala in the 1980s. Very little had changed in this scene since this photograph was taken: the wooden building and the wall with the arches were still there. Only the people, the way they dressed, and the language they spoke had changed. Image courtesy of the National Library of Latvia collection "In Search of Lost Latvia."

New Life

Left: A drawing of mine from August 23, 1983. Forty-four years had passed since the signing of the Molotov-Ribbentrop Pact...

Mushrooms

My first summer in Latvia introduced me to the pleasures of mushroom hunting and the skill of orientation—that is, figuring out which way to ramble about and get out of the woods. It was easy to get lost: Latvia's forests were big and home to wolves, moose, lynx, and other animals. Finding edible mushrooms was one of my countrymen's favorite practical pastimes. If in the United States I saw all mushrooms as poisonous (my mother was always warning me about *suṇasēnes*— "dog mushrooms"), then Latvia's forests were host to an amazing variety of edible, delicious, and nutritious "shrooms." There were also toxic mushrooms, but my mother-in-law was very careful; she always said that she picked only mushrooms that she knew and never anything she wasn't sure about. As I walked around in the forest, I learned to "read" the sky and the light for direction, even though cloudy days could cause problems.

A lot of work had gone into preparing for the long, cold months that lay ahead. I worked side by side with Biruta, watching and helping her cut, layer, and marinate vegetables in glass jars, which were placed in a vat of simmering hot water and then sealed with lids and stored in the wonderful root cellar. Making fruit and berry preserves and compotes filled the little cottage at Paulēni with delicious aromas. In the fall we used a juice press to make delicious apple cider. By late fall our well-stocked and locked cellar was proof of our hard work; it was a labor of love and necessity.

Up until the fall of 1983 I clung to my dream of resuming my art studies at the Latvian Art Academy. Then I was curtly informed that, if I wanted to enroll as a full-time student, I would have to revoke my American citizenship. That settled the matter. I had no intention of letting go of my blue passport, my ticket to freedom. Nevertheless, it was an enormous disappointment for me. For a while I felt completely crushed and disoriented.

This was not the first letdown in my attempts to fit into this very different society. Encouraged by my father-in-law, I had happily decided to participate in the "Young Writers'" seminar at the Latvian Writers' Union. After all, there were writers in my family, I wanted to write, and I knew Rimants Ziedonis and his famous father. Here I would meet people of my age; I could offer my translating skills. It would be an interesting, fun, and valuable experience for me. With my typical American optimism, I opened the great, heavy doors of the Writers' Union and stepped into the vestibule, proceeded upstairs, hung out for a while, introduced myself to a few people who were present, and went home feeling rather happy and pleased with myself (I am actually a rather shy person). So it was with a sense of shock that I heard my father-in-law tell me the next morning that he had received a telephone call from writer Māra Zālīte who kindly asked me to stay away from the seminar. No logical explanations were provided. What an awkward situation for Ms. Zālīte, a writer I admired! Juris was upset, too. I swallowed my pride and beat down my feeling of utter humiliation. This was the bitter reality: I was like an ant whose path would be blocked by an enormous, alien paw. My freedoms here in the fatherland were limited indeed.

Ojārs Vācietis

Go on and tell me
where the west lies.
I'll shutter that side,
because I don't want
the sun to set today.

And I don't want
the clocks to tick today.

Because my pulse beats
so righteously, so sharply,
that there is no time
in hours,
calendars,
or moments.

Time is in the blood.

("Pasaki man priekšā..." Tr. RL)

The Gift

In September 1983 I came down with a bad stomach ailment. Violent nausea, diarrhea, a strong aversion to pungent aromas and smells, fatigue, and, of course, a missed period spelled pregnancy, which was confirmed by a urine test at the doctor's office. After our initial excitement I faced a new dilemma: where to have the baby? I had heard horror stories about Rīga's hospitals and medical care; at the the same time, everyone around me appeared to have healthy children. For a while I considered the possibility of returning to the United States, but that idea quickly dissipated, as I did not want to be separated from my husband. The idea of leaving him to give birth on my own thousands of miles away seemed sad, and for both of us to travel to the United States was financially impossible. I could not ask my father to help us with that. Travel to and from Latvia was unpleasant and complicated in those days; America was far away. Sullen Soviet customs officers working the gateways of the Soviet Union were part of my bad memories about travel in this part of the world. I quickly decided that I would give birth in Latvia. After all, other women could do it; why couldn't I? The decision was also a financial one. By this time I had lost my American health insurance.

I felt I was in good hands with Dr. Viduleja, a respected gynecologist who was courteous and thorough. An obstetrician was also quickly engaged, thanks to my relatives who had friends in high places: in fact, Dr. Anita Andrejeva was a distant relative of mine on my father's side. She was married to a charming anesthesiologist, Dr. Georgs Andrejevs. I checked in with Dr. Andrejeva a couple of times at Rīga's First Hospital, an old, gloomy compound of buildings encircled by a tall wall between Ļeņina and Gorkija streets. The hospital had been one of Mayor George Armitstead's great projects at the turn of the 20th century. I looked around with worry: the place was creepy, dark, and seemed filthy. On the bright side, everything was going fine with my pregnancy, Dr. Andrejeva assured me. I skedaddled out of there.

My pregnancy filled me with immense joy. I was ready for a child, even though I was only 23. My childhood had been wonderful; I had enjoyed a particularly close relationship with my mother. In late fall, as I began to feel the baby's movements fluttering like a butterfly, I was overwhelmed by conflicting emotions—joy and hope, as well as fear for the baby's health and well-being in a land overrun by a foreign army. The baby would be born into a world full of lies and oppression. For the future, I put my trust in my blue passport. I also prayed.

That fall the US Vice Consul in Leningrad, Mr. Ronald Harms, telephoned to let us know in advance that he would coming to Rīga and would enjoy seeing us again to find out how we were faring. We had met him in Leningrad on our first trip there to seek advice at the consulate. Mr. Harms was trailed to our building in Old Rīga by a couple of shadowy figures; anticipating these "rats," we stood watching from Juris' window, which faced Jauniela. I hummed the theme music to "Mission Impossible." A veritable James Bond scene! A black figure huddled in the telephone booth near the restaurant Pūt, vējiņi, while a couple of other snoops vanished down Krāmu iela. One guy took the back stairs. We giggled. It seemed so stupid. Maybe the KGB suspected me of espionage?

Mr. Harms, in his mid-thirties at the time, was a most pleasant, gracious visitor; he was friendly, inquisitive, and concerned about our well-being. I was an object of curiosity for the American Consulate because of my choice to reside in the Soviet Union. The following spring in April, Mr. Harms was assaulted and beaten up in Leningrad while out with his Russian friends. I only learned of this incident years later, when I was writing this book.

A snippet from *The Miami News*, Wednesday, May 30, 1984.

U.S. diplomat assaulted in Russia

Vice Consul Ronald Harms, a U.S. diplomat serving in Leningrad, was assaulted and kicked by two Soviets outside a Leningrad restaurant, a U.S. Embassy spokesman said today. U.S. authorities made a "very strong protest" to Soviet officials in Moscow, Leningrad and Washington about the April 17 incident, said the spokesman, who requested that he not be identified. The embassy spokesman declined to comment on reports that Harms was meeting Soviet contacts, possibly dissidents, in the restaurant.

Mr. Harms, my fellow American, went back to Leningrad to report on our status. He was pleasantly surprised by Old Rīga and where we lived; my father-in-law's studio left an impression on him. His visit probably aroused the KGB's ire and suspicions. But by this time I was becoming rounder, fuller, and looking less and less like a CIA operative.

A couple we knew, Uģis and Mārīte, were also expecting a baby. At the end of 1983 Mārīte, a Soviet Latvian citizen, was preparing to leave occupied Latvia to join Uģis in West Germany, where he worked for Siemens. I felt conflicted. I was always agonizing over my decision to stay in Latvia and looked at other "mixed marriages" (Soviet/non-Soviet) for signals: in most cases, everyone chose to emigrate to the West. My husband did not want to leave Latvia; I did not want to leave. We went to say goodbye to our friends who were departing for a country flush with possibilities, affluent and free. But Uģis had a good job there; their situation was different than ours.

That winter I ate a lot of apples, carrots, cabbage, honey, cranberries, and nuts, anything I could get my hands on that provided our baby and me with vitamins and nourishment. I ate garlic to ward away germs but became sick anyway in the winter of 1984 with bronchitis. Andris taught me to stick garlic cloves into my nostrils; that tickled my nose delightfully and made me sneeze, relieving the pressure in my sinuses. To relieve headaches, Andris introduced me to an aromatic, soothing Vietnamese vapor rub sold in a tiny tin emblazoned with a yellow star; it was similar to Tiger Balm and Vick's Vapor Rub. Stuck inside, I watched the Sarajevo Winter Olympics, the snow blanketing the Dinaric Alps. Who could have predicted that a decade later Sarajevo would be torn apart in Yugoslavia's horrible civil war?

Various freelance jobs kept me busy, as my body, a wondrous, expanding vessel, prepared for childbirth. Artist Silvija Auere invited me to come and pose for her in the nude, while Andris took photographs; I can no longer find those beautiful, intimate images of my first pregnancy. Silvija's husband Edžus, an electrician/bibliophile, served us tea and pastries and kept us laughing with his funny Soviet jokes. Laughter, too, was medicine against the darkness and evil beyond our windows.

Ad Astra per Aspera:
Gunārs Astra, Our Bright Star

"They tried to bury us. They didn't know we were seeds."—Mexican proverb

Fireflies hint at light in the darkness. If there is only darkness without any light, then we are not aware of the presence of light. It is the same with dissidents. Dissidents are meant to remind us that not everything is as we are told; that there is no such thing as a single-minded Soviet people's viewpoint.

It is good for children to go to Čakste's* monument, because each teardrop that eats away at the prison bars is sacred. (*Jānis Čakste, 1859–1927, first President of the Republic of Latvia.)

"Tell me now, what kind of state is this where it isn't even possible to purchase lemons and oranges?!"—Astra uttered this caustic remark to a KGB officer in 1976, when he was allowed to meet his brother for the first time after spending 15 years in prison.

It hurts me and I feel humiliated when I realize that my native language is forced to retreat to reservations, such as the Ethnographic Open Air Museum, the stages of some theaters, and mass media outlets.

Gunārs Astra (1)

Left: Celebrating Christmas in Rīga in Demember 1983 with the in-laws.

In December 1983 I was five months pregnant. It was the darkest time of the year in Latvia, with short days and long nights. Rīga was cold and damp. As the darkness of late afternoon enveloped our neighborhood's slippery cobblestone streets, Old Rīga's lamps glowed in dull orbs of light. We hoped for snow and the sparkle and light it offered. The sky seemed eternally overcast, the cloud cover impenetrable. My first real Christmas in Rīga was fast approaching, and my thoughts focused on gifts, a Christmas tree, and the possibility of attending church.

While many Latvians prepared to quietly celebrate Christmas in their homes, a man by the name of Gunārs Astra was entering yet another dramatic phase in his life. Not too far from where we lived, Astra was being held behind bars and awaiting his trial. I had never heard of Gunārs Astra and would not know anything about this extraordinary person for several more years. My awareness of the significance of his actions and his sacrifice, as well as deep respect for his character and personal integrity, would solidify much later after Astra, our star, had returned to the earth as dust.

"Through adversity to the stars": the narrative of Latvia's nearly half-century of Soviet occupation and oppression includes the stories of its brightest protagonists, Latvia's dissidents and prisoners of conscience: people like Gunārs Astra, Viktors Kalniņš, Helēna Celmiņa, Lidija Doroņina-Lasmane, Žanis Skudra, Gunārs Rode, Juris Ziemelis, and others who quietly, inconspicuously, but steadfastly resisted Soviet indoctrination. Despite the ever present danger, these brave individuals pressed back by sharing banned literature, information, documentation of belligerent Soviet actions and policies, news from the Free World, and anti-Soviet views. They rigged their radios to listen to foreign news broadcasts and read secretly obtained copies of books from the other side of the Iron Curtain. These peaceful resisters knew Latvia's history and persistently objected to the Soviet version of the history of the Baltic States in the 20th century. They were aware of Soviet human rights abuses and discussed these in private. They nervously observed their country being flooded with more and more Russian colonists.

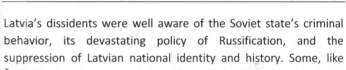

Left: Imprisoned for documenting the destruction of his country—Žanis Skudra (1924–1994).

Latvia's dissidents were well aware of the Soviet state's criminal behavior, its devastating policy of Russification, and the suppression of Latvian national identity and history. Some, like Žanis Skudra, documented the effects of the Soviet occupation in photographs. When their voices got too loud or their "criminal" actions (especially forbidden literature) were discovered, they were arrested, tried, and sent deep into Russia's interior, far away from Latvia and out of sight.

In late 1983 when Gunārs Astra was tried, Skudra was already serving his sentence in a prison camp in Chusovaya, Perm Oblast in the Ural Mountains. In 1978 he was arrested in Tallinn and sentenced to a 12 year prison term for espionage. Skudra had tirelessly documented life in Soviet Latvia in photographs and notes, taking pictures of abandoned farmsteads, churches, historical buildings, taverns, mills, and nature. His damning testimonial, *Okupētās Latvijas dienasgrāmata* ("The Diary of Occupied Latvia"), was smuggled out of Latvia by his friend and former schoolmate Laimonis Niedra, a Swedish citizen, and published under the pseudonym of Jānis Dzintars in Sweden. Skudra had paid special attention to the destruction of Latvia's Lutheran churches. (2)

"Skudra was deeply pained by the destruction of (Latvia's) cultural and historical monuments and the pollution of its rivers and other natural resources. Today we can speak of these problems openly, but (the people) who protested (in the Soviet era) could end up spending te years of their life in prison." (3)

Soviet society was deeply infiltrated by KGB agents and informants, allies of the "thought police" whose job it was to expose non-conformists. The biographies of Gunārs Astra and other Soviet dissidents are the age-old story of oppression versus freedom, the state versus the individual, censorship, resistance, crime and punishment, the choice between good and evil, trust versus betrayal, as well as human dignity, decency, faith, and hope. Their stories underscore the fact that there were people in Soviet-occupied Latvia with a strong moral compass, and that we have a responsibility to remember their bravery and honor them.

News about the arrests, trials, and sentences of Latvia's prisoners of conscience barely seeped out to the Latvian community in the Free World. Because of the Soviet Union's hard clampdown on the media and on its citizens' contacts with people living abroad, information about life in the Soviet Union remained murky. For exiled Balts it was very difficult to get a clear picture of the situation in their native countries for many years after the war. *Rīga retour*, a book about Andris Kadeģis' and Valda Dreimane's trip to Latvia in 1960, was one of the first accounts to provide a sobering description of the troubling changes that were taking place in Latvia under the Soviets.

In 1970 the story of Simas Kudirka, the Lithuanian who attempted to jump ship to freedom, had hit the Baltic American news circuit. (The US Coast Guard handed him back to the Russians, and Kudirka served a ten year sentence.) In my late teens I read about how the Soviets were confining dissidents to psychiatric wards and torturing them with drugs and electroshock. But mostly the USSR did a pretty good job of keeping its repressive measures against its citizens under tight wraps.

In the late 1970s we attended an event at the Latvian Daugavas Vanagi building in the Bronx. A couple of special guests, Soviet Latvian dissidents Viktors Kalniņš and Helēna Celmiņa, a married couple, had arrived to meet with the New York Latvian community. They were expelled from the Soviet Union in 1976. While living in exile in the US, Celmiņa penned a book about what she experienced while in prison: *Sievietes PSRS cietumos* ("Women in Soviet Prisons," 1980), *right*. The book was translated into English and published by Paragon House Publishers in 1985. Viktors Celmiņš testified at the US Congress and the Australian Parliament about Soviet human rights abuses. (4, 5)

The names of Russians Alexander Solzhenitsyn (1918–2008) and Andrei Sakharov (1921–1989) speak for themselves. These famous Russians exposed the dark side of the Soviet Union, especially its human rights abuses, suffered the consequences (Solzhenitsyn was expelled from the USSR, Sakharov was isolated), but achieved world-wide recognition. Solzhenitsyn received the Nobel Prize in Literature in 1970; Sakharov received the Nobel Peace Prize in 1975. What the West – infatuated with Russia at the expense of this hungry giant's occupied states and oppressed peoples – needs to realize is that there were millions of people of other nationalities and religious groups besides the Russians who suffered under Soviet (synonymous with Russian) occupation and tyranny. For non-Russian former independent states Russification was an additional grievance. In fact, the Balts would often refer to the Soviet years as *krievu laiki* ("the Russian era"), when the Russian language was synonymous with Soviet rule and used to oppress other languages, cultures, and identities.

Gunārs Astra was born on October 22, 1931 in Rīga to Larions and Elza Astra. He was the couple's second child. In 1940 Astra began school at Rīga's P.S. 48; he graduated in 1947. That same year he enrolled in Rīga's Electro-Mechanical Technical School. He also began to work at VEF (Valsts Elektrotehniskā fabrika -"State Electrotechnical Factory"), Latvia's leading manufacturer of communication technology, including telephones and radios. Upon graduating from school in 1952, Astra was promoted to the position of engineer-technologist at VEF. From 1954–1956 he completed his mandatory military service in the Soviet Army. He returned to his job in 1966 and was promoted again, becoming head of one of the factory's departments. A year later he received another promotion at the factory. It was during this time that Astra became closely acquainted with what he would later refer to as the factory's "administrative and ideological 'kitchen'" at his second trial in 1983: "I am pained, and I feel humiliated, when I see that behind the large, bright letters of the Staume, VEF, and RER plants it is just one big Russian conglomerate: instructions, orders, signs, slogans, technical documents—everything is in Russian." Alongside total political indoctrination, the Russification of Latvia was in full swing. (6)

In autumn of 1958, Astra left VEF to enroll at the Rīga Pedagogical Institute. From March until October 1959 he worked at the (A. Popov) Rīga Radio Factory as an engineer-constructor; he left that job to work at a sound and lighting laboratory at the the University of Latvia. By the late 1950s, Gunārs Astra was corresponding with some Latvian expatriates, listening to "Voice of America" on his radio, and sometimes failed to suppress his national sentiments. It was at this time that the KGB began taking an interest in him. While employed at the University, Astra took English correspondence courses. (7, 8)

Astra's biographer Māris Ruks has described Astra's 1958 meeting with US diplomats from Moscow as a chance encounter, which started at Rīga's busy department store Universālveikals and led to an evening of friendly talks at Astra's apartment. One of the diplomats promised to send Astra some English language instruction books and American technical magazines; he also gave Astra a copy of *Newsweek* magazine. Did the American diplomats have any inkling about the dire consequences of their meeting for their young, friendly, and inquisitive Latvian host? (9)

Once successfully employed, with a promising future, Astra's fall from grace was swift, when the Latvian KGB zeroed in on him. He was arrested in February 1961 and kept in a KGB isolation cell until the fall. The criminal investigation was lengthy. Astra's "crimes" included contacts with American diplomats ("espionage") and anti-Soviet agitation and propaganda. The 1961 trial, closed to the public, took place in a historical building on Palasta iela in Old Rīga, which had once served as the Rīga residence of Russian Tsar Peter the Great. The trial was conducted in Russian. The increasing dominance of the Russian language was, of course, one of Astra's life-long grievances concerning the Soviet occupation.

On October 26, 1961, the Baltic Military District tribunal in Rīga sentenced Gunārs Astra, 30 years old, on charges of betrayal of the homeland, anti-Soviet agitation and propaganda, and espionage. Pronounced guilty, he was given a 15 year sentence and sent to a prison camp in the Mordovian Autonomous Soviet Republic. The camps in Potma, Russia, where Soviet political prisoners were concentrated in the 1960s and 70s, would later be recalled by many of their former Baltic inmates: (Latvians) Vitolds Baikovs, Ints Cālītis, Gunārs Freimanis, Viktors Kalniņš, Arnis Pūpols, Dailis Rijnieks, Gunārs Rode, Knuts Skujenieks, Voldemārs Zariņš, Modris Zichmanis, Juris Ziemelis; (Estonians) Enn Tarto and Mart Niklus; and (Lithuanians) Viktoras Petkus and Balys Gajauskas ("Iron Balys," *above*), among others. Some prisoners like Gajauskas spent over 35 years in various Soviet prison camps. (10A, 10B)

For Americans it would seem shocking that chatting with foreign diplomats, reading certain books, and quietly voicing one's opinions could land you in jail as a felon. The most basic freedoms—the freedom of religion, the freedom of speech, the freedom of the press, the freedom of assembly—in the Soviet Union were judged as criminal actions, the perpetrators labeled "anti-Soviet" criminals, arrested, and deported. The mighty Russian superpower was paranoid about free thought. So paranoid, that Astra's trial and sentence went unpublicized.

High walls, barbed wire, and armed guards cannot suppress human thought. In Mordovia Astra could actually talk with his fellow Balts without fear. "(In camp) they were thrown together—(a bunch of political prisoners) with similar thoughts and views. There they could finally talk freely. They no longer had to worry about being arrested or losing their jobs… They were free to debate, argue, and assess. The Balts banded together, as did the Ukrainians, Moldovans, Georgians, and others. All nationalities were represented in the camps… Russian dissidents had difficulty understanding the other prisoners' ethnic problems. (The Russians') main cause was standing up to the authoritarian communist regime. They, too, spent long years in the camps." On top of everything else, non-Russian inmates grappled with the issue of Russification in their homelands. (11)

"Towards communism!" In 1962 Latvian architect Ivars Strautmanis came up with a sketch for the new Intourist Hotel to be built at the intersection of Ļeņina and Kirova streets. Fifteen years later, in 1976, the hotel's construction commenced. Gunārs Astra was released in 1976 and came home. Rīga's chekists were surprised to discover that the Soviet penal system hadn't changed him much. The Mordovian prison camp authorities called him unrepentant. They were astounded to learn that Astra had turned down the Solzhenitsyn Foundation prize, worth 5,000 Soviet roubles. It was clear to them that Astra's contacts and activities would have to be monitored. (12)

Things back home were both the same and different. Sadly, Astra's mother and father had died while he was away, and his first wife had divorced him. An emotional Astra listened to his mother's farewell in a tape recording. Latvia was even more Russified than when he had left it. Astra's stance had not changed. If anything, it had hardened. While Astra was gone, Latvia was undergoing a transformation that endangered the very existence of its native Latvian population. According to Astra's biographer Māris Ruks, statisticians have estimated that during the Soviet occupation about five million Soviet migrants moved through the territory of Latvia. (13)

With open borders between Latvia, Belarus, and Russia, such movement was extremely easy, and many Soviet citizens were drawn to the Baltic States, where the standard of living was higher than elsewhere in the Soviet Union. There was the promise of work in a factory and an apartment in a new highrise. Slowly but surely, Latvia was being colonized by Russians and Russian speakers. New work places and apartment buildings were absorbing the influx. By the 1980s Latvians had become a minority in their own capital. Belarusians were buying up abandoned farms on Latvia's side of the border.

In 1976 Gunārs Astra remarried. He moved into his parents' old house on Lucavsala, a pretty, quiet island on the Daugava River near Rīga. He got a job at the Straume factory. His wife Līvija (b. Valgale) gave birth to a son, Kaspars. The Astras started growing flowers for a living. Gunārs' friends, including former camp inmates, came to call. They refused to speak Russian to each other, finding other ways to communicate. They agreed that Alexander Solzhenitsyn's *Gulag Archipelago* was a good book, but that the author had little understanding of nations other than the Russians. To play it safe, Gunārs and Lidija Doroņina-Lasmane messaged each other on an Etch-A-Sketch someone had sent Lidija from Sweden. (14)

Astra was a warm, hospitable host, and people enjoyed his company. He was witty, well read, and perceptive, with a great sense of humor. He was also nervous about Soviet Latvia's new Russian reality. The "corruption" of the Latvian language irritated him to no end. Russian slang and Russian words had seeped into Latvian, "tainting" it. Astra was quick to correct anyone who used Russicisms when speaking Latvian. "Russians are guests who will have to go home sooner or later. If they've forgotten this, we'll remind them," Astra said. No doubt the KGB was aware of the "criminal" guests who visited the Astra house. (15)

In 1979 the Soviet Union invaded Afghanistan; Latvian conscripts were dispatched to Afghanistan to fight. Many were destined to return to Latvia in zinc coffins. Astra and his allies worried about Pļavnieki, a new housing "massive" going up in Rīga. The influx of Russians had to be stopped before it was too late. But how? They felt strongly that they must let the world know what was happening to their country, even though memories of their time in prison were still fresh and painful. While Astra and his friends discussed Latvia's dire situation, Latvia's KGB worried that "despite great achievements in building communism, there were still manifestations of nationalism and hostility (towards Soviet authority) in Latvia, and anti-Russian sentiment had not subsided in part of the population." (16)

"On August 23, 1979, more than 40 Baltic dissidents signed a manifesto, the Baltic Charter, in honor of Charter 77. As representatives of occupied nations, the signatories also included political demands in the charter. They demanded the right for the Baltic peoples to decide their own fate, and they also demanded statehood. The Baltic Charter was an appeal to the USSR,

West Germany, East Germany, the signatories of the Atlantic Charter, and the UN Secretary-General to annul the Molotov-Ribbentrop Pact of August 23, 1939 and to do away with its consequences. Later the Baltic Charter became known as the Baltic Memorandum." Gunārs Astra penned its Latvian translation (the memorandum was drafted in Russian). Despite applying all sorts of repressive measures, it was apparently impossible to completely muzzle these Balts. (17)

In 1980, as I was preparing to travel to Latvia for the first time, more Latvians were being arrested to appease Moscow's displeasure. According to the Communist Party bosses in Moscow, Soviet Latvia was not doing enough to build new factories and import workers from the wide expanses of the USSR. The KGB in Rīga nervously reported that they were still controlling and interrogating Gunārs Astra and other "recividists," promising to make arrests as soon as they had a lead. (18)

"In 1983 the (Latvian) KGB organized its last campaign of persecution in the history of Soviet Latvia against people it considered dangerous to the Soviet state. Numerous suspects were arrested, criminal investigations and proceedings were initiated; many households were searched, including Astra's. The KGB summoned Astra to talks; he refused to testify against his friends." One by one, his friends and family were summoned to exhausting talks with the KGB. Finally, in September of 1983, Gunārs Astra was arrested. (19)

I was already well settled in Rīga and pregnant at this time. Did my father-in-law know Astra? Juris got around; he knew a lot of people. We had our own nagging problems with the KGB. My presence in Soviet Latvia was probably unnerving for them. If I had known about Astra, I would have been very excited and very afraid for him.

Once more Astra found himself in the notorious *Stūra māja* ("Corner House") on Ļeņina iela (*left in an old photograph*), which the Soviet NKVD had used in 1940–1941 and later to hold, interrogate, torture, and even kill prisoners. During the Soviet occupation the sprawling building housed the headquarters of Latvia's KGB organization. I was questioned there by Comrade Šteinbriks in 1981. It was there that Gunārs Astra and his friends and family were subjected to relentless, demeaning interrogations.

At the time of Astra's sentencing I was holed up in our nest, with no knowledge of the man, his past, his principles, the trial, or its outcome. If his sentencing had been reported in the news, Astra would have been depicted as a dangerous, subversive enemy of the Soviet state, a spy, and a traitor. I had left the realm of factual, objective news on the other side of the Iron Curtain.

In communist Latvia we were living in a vacuum, separated from reality by the Berlin Wall, oblivious. Censored news. No Internet, no social media. Phones tapped and international calls monitored. Letters filtered. Facts detrimental to the Party whitewashed. Soviet censors had to earn their money. We remained in the dark about human rights abuses being committed in our own "backyard." Only at the end of the decade would I start learning about the extent of these abuses, read about about Gunārs Astra's martyrdom, and mourn his passing. In a sense, ignorance was bliss.

I lived quietly and lay low; I knew it could take just one wrong move to be kicked out of the Soviet Union. Seeking out dissidents would have guaranteed a one-way ticket back to the US. People with similar viewpoints fraternized, but organized resistance, if you could call it that, was limited. It was simply too dangerous. "Cells" could be easily infiltrated and exposed. There were enough people who were willing to slip over to "the dark side" for personal gain. Public displays of national dissent—such as hoisting the Latvian flag somewhere—were quickly quelled, their reckless perpetrators severely punished. Years later some people would ask: why did so few resist Soviet rule?

I decided not to blame anyone in Latvia, under the circumstances, for not speaking out forcefully about the crimes of the occupation; it took great, rare bravery, and who was I to judge? "Both the memory of recent violence and the threat of future violence hovered constantly in the background. If one person in a group of twenty acquaintances was arrested, that might suffice to keep the other nineteen afraid. The secret police's informer network was ever present, and even when it wasn't people thought it might be. The unavoidable, repetitive propaganda in schools, in the media, on the streets, and at all kinds of 'apolitical' meetings and events also made the slogans seem inevitable and the system unavoidable. What was the point of objecting? (...) Meanwhile the systematic destruction of alternative sources of authority and of civil society (...) meant that those who questioned the system and its values felt isolated and alone."—Anne Applebaum, *Iron Curtain* (p. 388)

As I trundled past *Stūra māja* with its opaque windows, I had no idea what was going on behind its walls, even though I knew of its sinister history and function. Its notoriety had been passed down to the children of expatriates in faraway lands. I was more focused on not slipping on the snow-covered, icy sidewalks. There were several shops on that block between Marksa (Marx) and Engelsa (Engels) streets that attracted my attention. Mid-December marked my fifth month of pregnancy.

Christmas of '83: new life moved in my belly, but a Latvian compatriot, Gunārs Astra, had just been sentenced and was deported from the fatherland to a prison camp in Russia, a country that had brought Latvia so much misery. Before being lead away, Astra would look his prosecutors in the eye and voice his grievances. *Our grievances.* His "Last Word," spoken at the end of his trial, would express everything that was wrong with the Soviet Russian occupation of Latvia. It would reach the Free World and circulate at the highest levels. President Ronald Reagan would mention Gunārs Astra three times during his presidency, according to Astra's widow, Līvija Astra. (20)

In 1982, a year prior to Astra's sentencing, President Reagan had declared June 14 Baltic Freedom Day in his Proclamation 4948, inviting Americans to commemorate the Baltic victims of the Soviet deportations of June 14, 1941. During his tenure Reagan continued to support the release of Baltic prisoners of conscience. From Gunārs Astra's perspective in his prison cell, the Free World might just as well been in another galaxy. Yet he believed. It seemed terribly faraway to me. (21)

Crippling Humility

(...) The indictment read to Astra in 1983 included the following: "In 1981 at his home in Rīga Astra gave to Gunārs Freimanis a Xerox copy of Edmunds Zirnītis' book Andrejs Eglītis, in which the Soviet state and Soviet society were cynically described as 'a terrible tyranny,' 'the communists' absurd system,' 'a Russian colonial prison,' 'the world's most brutal power' that 'grinds into the mud and blood and desecrates ... the nation's soul'; (the book) alleges that the Soviet Union utilizes 'slave labor,' that nations are smothered 'in Soviet colonialism's fumes and destruction of the soul,' (...); Marxism-Leninism (and) the Soviet state's foreign and domestic policy are maligned; renewal of Soviet power and the reality of life in Latvia in 1940–1941 and after the war are described from an anti-Soviet position, which mendaciously calls Soviet rule 'captivity and slavery,' 'a tragedy,' and 'the enemy regime'; (the author) alleges that the country is ruled by the 'most savage, most brutal Eastern power,' that communism is 'an enemy of any nation and civilization'; at the same time (the book's author) urges action to begin the war against Soviet power to defeat it."

The indictment rambled on, charging Gunārs Astra with making photo negatives of Anšlāvs Eglītis' anti-Soviet book Laimīgie ("The Fortunate"). "The text on the negatives contains mendacious fabrications, which discredit the Soviet state and its society, and in the spirit of anti-Soviet lies demeans Soviet power in Latvia, which is portrayed as treating its own people with aggression; (the text) designates Soviet authority representatives as 'lickspittles, traitors, professional liars, thieves, and murderers,' and alleges that Soviet Army soldiers, when liberating Soviet Latvia from the German fascists in 1944, tortured and killed unarmed civilians; (the text) slanders in an anti-Soviet manner the Russian people and argues that Soviet Latvia was 'occupied' after the war; (the text) emphasizes that the Russian nation has provided 'millions of obedient, brutally insensitive prison camp guards, millions of overseers in the occupied satellite states'; (the text) compares Soviet authority in Latvia to a 'Soviet prison.'" The indictment also charged Gunārs Astra with making "20 tape recordings with his own tape recorder and recording and storing mendacious, anti-Soviet foreign radio stations broadcasts, conversations, poems, and texts, all of which expressed hatred for Soviet authority and the socialist state, which was compared to fascism, and maintained that in the Baltic republics today oppression exists, that they have been 'occupied by the Russians'; (these recordings) expressed sharp criticism of the Communist Party, which allegedly pursues an aggressive foreign policy."

In those years of deepest Soviet stagnation, the early 1980s, such publications (if found on a person or in their home—RL) were fatal transgressions, and only a person of great courage could utter such (accusations against the Soviets—RL) and share them with others with conviction. Because of his personality, Gunārs Astra did not stand silently on the sidelines as was customary for most Latvians. He had formulated firm principles about a national, Latvian-strong Latvia; he nurtured those principles based on his personal integrity and what he knew about Latvia's history. Astra's allies said that Astra frequently used the word "self-esteem," urging his fellow Latvians to resist humility, which cripples human beings.

On December 19, 1983, the Criminal Court Panel of the Latvian SSR Supreme Court found "Astra, Gunārs, son of Larion, guilty of all charges" and sentenced "him to deprivation of liberty for a period of seven years followed by five years of exile (from Latvia)." (Four years later) in 1987 the Latvian SSR Writers Union board met to review a letter submitted to it by a committee established to free Gunārs Astra, as well as a copy of Astra's Last Word. Board Chairman Jānis Peters submitted a letter of inquiry to Assistant General Prosecutor Jānis Batarags, asking if the verdict contained every crime that Astra had been convicted of and sentenced for, and if any crime had been omitted. (Batarags' response confirmed that) Astra's only "crimes" had been the possession (and distribution) of copies of books by Latvian writers in exile, such as Veronika Strēlerte, Gunārs Freimanis, and Andrejs Eglītis, as well as Alexander Solzhenitsyn's Gulag Archipelago, George Orwell's 1984, and (other Soviet-banned works).

Everyone knew that to ascribe the word "criminal" to the possession of such books was an excuse to try to destroy individuals who had learned to think independently, courageously, and express themselves in a righteous manner to inspire those around them. Astra's courage, intelligence, and moral integrity were eloquently captured in his Last Word before his sentencing at the Latvian SSR Supreme Court in 1983. Russian dissident Andrei Sinyavsky (1925–1997; a fellow inmate of Astra's who later emigrated from the USSR and settled in Paris—RL) wrote in his magazine, Sintaksis, published in Paris, that "the KGB saw Gunārs Astra as a non-standard opponent. Having spent several years in incarceration, in a Russian language environment on top of that, Astra continued to simply and naturally represent (the essence of) the European man. Astra's Europeanism was evident in his Last Word, which was characterized by honesty, dignity, and a steadfast calmness, which is typical of very strong and masculine men; calm and composed, this was a person who knew that his rights and his responsibility to be honest stood on firm ground."

Gunārs Astra's Last Word, which he spoke in (December) 1983, is the memorandum of a confident Latvian patriot and an honest man addressed to to those who were still only learning to love their country Latvia. A fragment from Astra's Last Word: "'A shto takoye Ojārs Vācietis?' ['And who is Ojārs Vācietis?'] This is what my cellmate asked me on the evening of my first day in court when I returned to Cell No. 24, where I was incarcerated and had just finished reading in (the newspaper) Cīņa about (Latvian poet) Ojārs Vācietis' death, which I reported to my cellmate. (My cellmate) is 24 years old. Born and raised in Latvia. A Latvian? A maximally improved Latvian. Bound to this country only by the border guards. The border guards caught him on a beach in Kurzeme—on his way to Sweden. That wasn't the only incident of its kind on the sea coast of Latvia in these past nine months.'" Astra ploughed through his absurd indictment, absolving himself while "nailing" his prosecutors to the wall of shame. (22)

Astra's Last Word listed his grievances and summarized, point by point, the many injustices that Latvians suffered under the Soviet Russian communist occupation. Excerpts:

I am pained and feel humiliated when I am forced to recognize that the majority of Russians born and raised in Latvia are not learning, nor do they want to learn, Latvian; for a (Russian) secondary school graduate the Latvian language is an object of ridicule, and none of his teachers expect him to learn Latvian, whereas every Latvian is expected to learn Russian.

I am pained and feel humiliated when Latvian students compensate their difficulty in expressing themselves in their native language with the help of Russian swear words.

I am sad that Latvian children have to watch their evening program from Moscow (in Russian) because (actor) Harijs Misiņš can only make it to the Radio Building, that our kindergartens do not teach Latvian children folk songs from our golden folklore repository, that Rīga's streets—Nameja and Aspazijas, Valdemāra and Vaidavas—have been renamed after (Vladimir) Mayakovsky, (...), (Maxim) Gorky, Yermolenko, (Yakov) Sverdlov, (Sergei) Lulin, and other Russian historical figures, that Rīga's main streets so precisely and submissively reflect the events of history—Alexander (Alexander III—the second to last Russian tsar—RL), Freedom, Adolf Hitler, Lenin. (Note: Up until the late 1980s the only TV program available to Latvian children in the evening, "Spokoynoy Nochi, Malyshi," was in Russian. Latvian children tuned into a children's radio program hosted by Harijs Misiņš. – RL)

I feel deeply offended and humiliated when in any public space—be it a store, an office, an institution, public transportation, on the street anywhere in Latvia—I am forced to witness an arrogant, chauvinistic attitude toward my language. At best I have to hear "Чего, Чего? По Руски!" („What, what? Speak Russian!") At worst I have to look at the person I addressed stare through me as though I were a glass pane, and afterwards I can admire the back of their head. (23)

Some Latvians now know Astra's words by heart: "I believe that this era will vanish like an evil nightmare. My belief gives me the strength to stand here and breathe. Our nation has suffered immensely and learned to and will survive these dark times." Astra went on to say: "I thank my wife and my daughter, my loved ones, my friends and benefactors for their loyalty, my attorney Beljanis for his good intentions; I thank the state prosecutor who honored me by calling Andrei Sakharov my confederate and thus brilliantly demonstrated his impotence. Thank you for your attention." The court room must have been silent. It is also safe to say that the trial itself was a mere formality; Astra's verdict and sentence had already been determined beforehand.

On December 19, 1983, the "gentle giant" Gunārs Astra, a Latvian who embodied the essence of peaceful resistance, was sentenced and thendeported to Perm-36 in Chusovaya, Perm Oblast, the harshest political camp of the Soviet Union, which is now *the only* preserved prison camp in the entire former Soviet territory. In 1988 it was the last Gulag camp to be shut down. (Note: As this book goes to the press, I sadly report that under the Putin regime this museum has been closed.)

Prior to my departure for Latvia, I corresponded with Anšlavs Eglītis (1906–1993), one of the authors the Soviets despised and whose name was mentioned in Astra's indictment. Anšlavs Eglītis left Latvia in 1944, a refugee like my grandparents and countless other Balts. He eventually ended up in California and rubbed shoulders with Hollywood's stars, writing a column about them for the Latvian newspaper *Laiks*, published in Brooklyn, NY. Eglītis was a talented and pro-lific writer. Several of his novels incurred the wrath of the Soviets: *Laimīgie* ("The Lucky Ones"); *Piecas dienas* ("Five Days"); *Vai te var dabūt alu?* ("Do You Sell Beer Here?"); and *Es nebiju va-ronis* ("I Wasn't a Hero"). The subject of these books was the war and the Soviet occupation. His father Viktors Eglītis (b. 1877), a writer who would partly sully his reputation by penning anti-Semitic articles under the Nazis, was killed by the Soviets in prison in 1945. The books of Uldis Ģērmanis (1915–1997), an expatriate in Sweden, were also blacklisted by the Soviets. His Lat-vian history book, *Latviešu tautas piedzīvojumi* ("The Adventures of the Latvian People"), first published in 1959, was used also used as "evidence" against Astra. It remains a wonderful read for young Latvians interested in their country's history.

Left: Astra, Latvia's bright star, in a photograph taken by his wife Līvija at Perm-36. located 1,400 kilometers east of Moscow in the Perm region, a camp reserved for the Soviet Union's most "dangerous" political prisoners: opponents of the communist government; authors and distributors of anti-Soviet literature; the USSR's most prominent dissidents; anti-government organisation leaders; advocates for human rights; and other "enemies of the state.". (24)

As we stepped across the threshold into the New Year, 1984, Gunārs Astra arrived at Perm-32, one of the Soviet Union's most no-torious prison camps. His old friends from Mordovia, Lithuanians Balys Gajauskas and Viktoras Petkus and Estonians Mart Nikluss and Enn Tarto, were already there to welcome him. The con-ditions at Perm-36 were worse than at prison camps for real criminals. The Soviet Union consid-ered dissidents more dangerous than murderers and rapists. There were frequent detentions in the so-called punishment cell for the slightest transgressions. (25)

According to a letter written by Balys Gajauskas, which was smuggled out and circulated in the Free World in 1984, "the daily regimen of the camp is like that of a KGB isolation cell. The camp authorities try to keep us prisoners apart to limit social interaction. Right now we are two to five people in a cell. We do not encounter inmates from other cells... The walking cells are set up in such a way that it's impossible to exchange notes (with other prisoners). To discourage talking, a guard watches us from above. If we strike up a conversation, our walk is terminated.

"The toilets are in our cells and work rooms... Because there is no ventilation, the cells always stink... The work rooms are poorly lit; the lights have to be kept on even during the day. It's especially bad in the fall and winter, when we spent 24 hours a day in the light of electricity. Even at night the lights are kept on. Many prisoners complain of eye discomfort; their eyesight is deteriorating... There are no breaks for the sick, the infirm, and the disabled. You work until you die. The meals are bad. The groat and meat (tendons and bones) are often rancid. There are almost no fresh vegetables... Bibles are immediately confiscated... It is forbidden to keep notes, which are confiscated. (...) The water tastes foul; most of the time it is drawn from the bog and boiled for consumption." According to Gajauskas, the inmates called their exercise areas "bar-rels:" round, narrow, sunless enclosures topped by a mesh of barbed wire guarded from above. (26)

313

Astra disappeared from occupied Latvia. *No person, no problem.* The economic stagnation of the Brezhnev era continued. The days became longer as winter waned. I continued my long walks in Rīga with an expanding belly. I was getting used to hearing the Russian language dominate the public space. I continued (and would so for all my years under Soviet rule) to address and respond to Russians in Latvian, oblivious to their insults aimed at my mother tongue. "Ya ne govoryu po russki!" "I don't speak Russian!"—I continued to repeat, obstinately and angrily. I was conveniently armed with the shield of ignorance coupled with deep indignation and spite. Insults hurled at me by Russians, Russian women being the biggest culprits, bounced off of me like drops of water from a duck.

It was a matter of principle for me. Astra was a man of principle. Many Latvians were not. Time and time again I saw and heard them slip subserviently into the Russian language, as they stood in long queues in stores or rode mashed together with their homeland's colonists in public transportation. I wasn't against the Russian language itself, but against its usurpation of Latvian in my fatherland. There is only one Latvia, only one historical homeland for my people. It wasn't right; it isn't right; it was a crime against identity.

It was a known habit, often bemoaned and yet endlessly perpetuated, that if there was only one Russian in the room, all the Latvians present, even when they outnumbered that person six to one, would switch to Russian to accommodate the Russian. I gazed at my people's curved backs, their obsequious gestures. It was said that Latvians had "soft, flexible backbones" due to their long history of multiple occupations by foreign powers. What had happened to my countrymen's self-esteem? Had the Soviet occupation wiped it out? Were we a nation of "bootlickers"? No, Gunārs Astra proved that there were heroes among us, people who did not bend in the face of tyranny.

Refusing to yield to this linguistic bullying, one day in the winter of '84 I rode the trolleybus with my husband and cursed the living daylights out of a Russian woman who insulted me, big belly and all, for not getting out of her way and refusing to answer her in Russian. That day a handful of Russian *mat* swear words, taught to me by my husband early on ("You'll need them!"), flew out of my mouth with such vigor that my attacker grew pale, blinked her beady eyes in surprise, backed off, and scurried out of the trolleybus, as soon as the doors flew open at the next exit. All chatter ceased. My husband had an enormous, proud grin on his face. More than once I was subjected to this ultimate insult, a Russian barking "fascist!" at me, a Latvian in my fatherland, when I professed my ignorance of Russian. Interestingly, in all cases the aggressor was female.

Was I proud of my response? No, it depressed me. That belittling, insulting attitude of superiority that I personally experienced would resurface years later in the tragic events in Ukraine and Crimea. As I watched a 2014 video of Russian women screaming at a Ukrainian woman and her toddler daughter for bringing food to Ukrainian soldiers locked up at their base in Crimea, I recognized those looks, that hatred, that lack of respect and compassion...

In response to Latvia's Russification, we jokingly planned on naming our firstborn (if a son) Krievplēsis ("Russian-slayer") in an homage to our nation's famous mythical hero, *Lāčplēsis* ("Bearslayer"), the main character in Andrejs Pumpurs' epic tale of gods and men, black magic, love, betrayal, and good versus evil. That is how angry we were at the Russian bullies who had moved into our country. Just a few months into my new life in Latvia, I was already tired of being called a fascist bitch.

While Astra was locked up in Perm, politics in the Soviet Union would begin to change under its new leader Mikhail Gorbachev. The peoples of the Baltic States would begin to band together and participate in mass demonstrations, exhibiting a growing rock-solid solidarity. Under mounting pressure from foreign governments and various organizations Gunārs Astra would be released in February of 1988, five years into his sentence. Yet he would not be out of danger. His remarkable leadership qualities would remain of great concern to Latvia's Communist Party and its security apparatus, the KGB. Astra and other Baltic human rights activists would attract international attention...

Astra was released on February 1, 1988. In March Astra and his wife Līvija traveled by train to Leningrad, where he suddenly became very ill. Astra was transported to Botkin Hospital. The doctors' consilium could (or would) not divulge a diagnosis. At first they said it was the flu. A week later the doctors announced that sepsis had set in. On March 19 Astra was moved to Leningrad's Military Hospital, where it was announced that he had a heart valve infection. An operation was performed on March 25. Astra's situation did not improve. On April 6 Gunārs Astra was pronounced dead.

Those who knew Gunārs Astra were convinced that he had been murdered. In an interview for Radio Free Europe Vitaly Kalinichenko, a member of Ukraine's Helsinki group, said: "The tragic death of Gunārs Astra is the result of a policy adopted by the KGB. This was a policy of targeting and destroying a nation's top representatives." Latvian dissident Jānis Rožkalns held the same opinion, emphasizing that Astra would surely have become involved in building Latvia's fledgeling democracy, and that he would have been a leader in steering Latvia clear of the problems that it faces today. This is why Jānis Rožkalns remains convinced that the Soviet Cheka killed Gunārs Astra. In his opinion, the murder was carried out with the finest precision to resemble a natural death. It was not possible to check if Astra's death was of natural causes: all of his internal organs, which could have helped determine the cause of death, had been removed.

(...) "For standing tall (Gunārs Astra) paid dearly, or, according to the Gospel, he was not destined to walk in soft clothing. (...) Which is why he could stand, calmly and resolutely, and look any person in the eye, for though humiliated from the outside, he remained free and unbroken within." Those were the words spoken by Reverend Modris Plāte next to Latvian freedom fighter Gunārs Astra's grave on April 19, 1988. Astra's grave was covered by the Latvian red-white-red flag, openly displayed for the first time in the territory of Soviet-occupied Latvia. Hundreds of chekists mingled with the mourners who numbered in the thousands, which is probably why no one tried to prevent them from singing (the Latvian national anthem) "Dievs, svētī Latviju!" ("God, Bless Latvia!"), nor did anyone try to confiscate the flag. Astra's mourners filled in the grave with their bare hands. (27)

Gunārs Astra's death in early spring of 1988 would coincide with the blossoming of Latvia's "awakening." His spirit energized those who knew him or who knew about him. What nobody at his funeral, friend and foe alike, could imagine was how close the Soviet Union, "the Evil Empire," was to disintegration.

A plaque (left) that commemorates Astra's 1983 trial and Last Word adorns the façade of the courthouse where he was sentenced in December 1983. ("I believe that this era will vanish like an evil nightmare. (My faith) gives me the strength to stand here and breathe.")

Astra's life was based on dignity, righteousness, and unwavering hope. His spirit remained uncrushed by his long years in prison. He was a giant among his fellow Latvians. I regret not having met Astra, not having known more about him when he was alive, and not having attended his funeral. If ever there was a Latvian hero in my life, it was Gunārs Astra.

Čekas maisi—"the Cheka's (KGB) 'bags' (lists of names of KGB officers, agents, and snitches)" is the subject of collaboration with the Soviet authorities and the Soviet secret police. It is a subject that remains murky in Latvia today. Those who committed crimes against others in the name of the state and its harsh, unforgiving ideology remain unpunished. Because the Soviet communist authorities punished anyone who stepped out of line so ruthlessly, people like Gunārs Astra, Lidija Doroņina-Lasmane, and others were all the more remarkable and admirable, although their simple form of resistance, the reading and sharing of 'Soviet-forbidden' literature, did not constitute a crime from the Free World perspective.

Chapter sources:

(1) "Gunārs Astra." Wikipedia. <http://lv.wikipedia.org/wiki/Gun%C4%81rs_Astra>)

(2) "Iznākusi grāmata par Astras līdzgaitnieku." www.ir.lv 11/23/2011; 3/20/2014. <http://www.ir.lv/20 11/11/23/iznakusi-gramata-par-astras-lidzgaitnieku>

(3) Sandra Gintere. "Dzelzs aizkara abās pusēs: Cīņa pret kristiešu vajāšanām Latvijā padomju laikā." Svētdienasrīts.lv July 6, 2012.; 3/19/2014. <http://www.svetdienasrits.lv/2012/07/06/dzelzs-aizkara-abas-puses-cina-pret-kristies u-vajasanam-latvija-padomju-laika>

(4) Imants Balodis. "Brīvības cīnītājus pieminot." Laikraksts latvietis. 9/20/2010; 3/19/2014. <http://www.laik raksts.com/raksti/raksts.php?KursRaksts=618>

(5) Dāvis Baltkājs, Ingūna Štulberga. "Helēna Celmiņa." Latvijas ļaudis. 04/05/2012. <http://www.latvijaslaudis.lv/us ers/helena-celmina-0?language=en>

(6) "Par Gunāru Astru." www.archiv.lv.org <http://www.archiv.org.lv/astra/index.php?id=102>

(7) Ibid 6

(8) Ibid 6

(9) Māris Ruks. ""20. gadsimta latvietis Gunārs Astra." Rīga: Antava, 2012. P. 27–28

(10) [A] "Gunārs Astra." Wikipedia. 01/14/2014; 3/20/2014. http://lv.wikipedia.org/wiki/Gun%C4%81rs_Astra [B] Ibid 9, p. 40

(11) Ibid 9, pp. 69–70

(12) Ibid 9, p. 80

(13) Ibid 9, p. 88

(14) Ibid 9, p. 91

(15) Ibid 9, p. 96

(16) Ibid 9, p. 99

(17) "Charter 77—The Inspiration for the Baltic Charter" www.itl.rtu.lv <http://www.itl.rtu.lv/LVA/Praga68/in dex.php?id=1040>

(18) Ibid 9, p. 97

(19) Ibid 6

(20) Ineta Lipše. "Astras atraitne šajā valstī jūtas labi." Vakar avīze, Vakara ziņas. 11/17/2000. <http://news.lv/Vakara_Avize_Vakara_Zinas/2000/11/17/astras-atraitne-saja-valsti-jutas-labi>

(21) Ronald Reagan. "Proclamation 4948—Baltic Freedom Day." June 14, 1982. Online by Gerhard Peters and John T. Woolley. The American Presidency Project. <http://www.presidency.ucsb.edu/ws/?pid=42652>

(22) Elita Veidemane. "Leģendārajam latviešu disidentam Astram 22. oktobrī būtu 80 gadu." NRA.lv. October 21, 2011. http://nra.lv/latvija/58302-legendarajam-latviesu-disidentam-astram-22-oktobri-butu-80-gadu.htm>

(23) Gunārs Astra. "Last Word." "Gunārs Astra." Wikipedia. <http://lv.wikipedia.org/wiki/Gun%C4%81rs_Astra> ; Gunārs Astra. "Last Word." Historia.lv 09/04/2002 / 03/24.2013 http://www.historia.lv/alfabets/A/AS/astra_g/dok/1983.12.15..htm

(24) "'Perm 36' Soviet Political Repression Camp (GULAG) and Chusovaya History Museum." Ultratourism.com <www.uraltourism.com/perm36.php>

(25) Ibid 9, p. 154

(26) Ibid 9, pp. 156–157

(27) Ibid 22

All texts translated by the author (Rita Laima)

"Traitors": Remnants of Bourgeois Nationalism

A meeting of "bourgeois nationalist" Latvians, including my maternal grandfather Jānis Bičolis (second row, third from right), at a Displaced Persons (DP) camp in Traunstein, Germany in 1949. Anticipating another Soviet wave of terror, over 150,000 Latvians escaped from Latvia in 1944. (Family photo)

Left: Poet Veronika Strēlerte.

"The Rotten West," "decadent," "degenerate," "capitalist pigs," "bourgeois nationalists": these were some of the epithets that the communists in Soviet-occupied Latvia used to describe Latvians in exile; that is, the "losers" who had "abandoned" the fatherland at the end of the war. Who were these "enemies" of socialism and "progress" whose works Gunārs Astra had read, cherished, and shared with his friends? To us, the Latvian diaspora, they were well known, beloved writers. Margita Gūtmane's 1982 book about poet and translator Veronika Strēlerte (born Rudīte Strēlerte, 1912–1995) had apparently displeased someone in Rīga, because it referred to Soviet Latvia as "occupied" and "the liberation of Soviet Latvia from German fascist aggressors in 1944" as "the introduction of Red Terror (in Latvia)" (from Gunārs Astra's indictment). Strēlerte left Latvia as a refugee in 1944, settled in Sweden, and married Latvian writer and literary critic Andrejs Johansons (1922–1983). Strēlerte's son Pāvils Johansons was in a Latvian Swedish rock and roll band called Dundurs ("Horsefly") that we loved to listen to in the 1970s. Our compatriots Strēlerte, Johansons, and other "émigrés" were personae non gratae in communist Latvia, because they were "remnants" of the "bourgeois nationalist" era in Latvia.

As children we had heard the patriotic poetry of Andrejs Eglītis (1912–2006) and other Latvian poets recited at Latvian Independence Day gatherings. Many of us even had to learn such poems by heart for such venues. But to the Soviet communists, any expatriate Latvian was a worthless Latvian, to be discredited or struck from the annals of Latvian history. The names of many notable Latvians—historians, writers, artists, musicians, scientists, politicians, and representatives of the pre-war government of the Republic of Latvia who succeeded in escaping at the end of the war—were excluded from Soviet Latvian reference books, causing occupied Latvia's population to experience a kind of historical and cultural "amnesia." The decades-long occupation would cause a schism in Latvian memory. Some people born and raised in occupied Latvia would even absorb and perpetuate the false Soviet narrative and negative attitudes towards *trimda*, the exile community.

Latvju Enciklopēdija ("The Latvian Encyclopedia"), edited by Latvian historian Arveds Švābe (1888–1959), was first published in Sweden in 1952–1953, less than a decade after the dramatic flight of Balts from their homelands. It remains a marvelous compendium of facts and figures and includes many biographical entries about Latvia's military, which was purged in the communist-occupied fatherland. The marvelous encyclopedia published abroad would serve as a "who's who" guide to Latvia's cream of society before the war, an illustration of a nation that was shredded to pieces by military conflict.

Gunārs Astra's interest in the writer Andrejs Eglītis was one of his many "crimes." Before World War II Andrejs Eglītis tried his hand at sports, a military career, journalism, and theology, before he turned to writing. He is best known for the haunting words to Latvian composer Lūcija Garūta's (1902–1977) dramatic 1943 cantata "Dievs, Tava zeme deg" ("God, Your Land is Burning"), which evokes Latvia's tragic losses during World War II and its impending occupation. In 1943 Eglītis was called up for military duty in the Latvian Legion. In 1945 he left Latvia as a refugee, reaching Sweden by boat. Eglītis remained in Sweden, where he was active in the exile community. In 1947 he helped found the Latvian National Foundation and remained at its helm until 2000. To the Soviets he was anathema for his fierce nationalism and vocal anti-Soviet stance. (1)

Eglītis' poetry, like that of many other exiled Latvian writers, spoke of the painful experiences that Latvians endured during and after World War II; it spoke of loss and love for the fatherland. His poetry remained optimistic: just like his compatriot Gunārs Astra in occupied Latvia, he believed that the nightmare of Soviet communist rule would one day end. In exile Eglītis remained an unwavering voice of protest; in Soviet Latvia he was derided and "buried" under a litany of false accusations and lies. Lūcija Garūta's cantata was banned under the Soviets. (2)

The tide of refugees, which flowed away from Latvia like lifeblood to Germany, Sweden, and beyond, included many of Latvia's brightest minds. These people were traitors by virtue of their status in pre-war Latvia or their hasty, panicky escape in advance of the Soviet Red Army. The Latvian exile community produced many notable published works in Latvian, including invaluable encyclopedias, dictionaries, and compendiums. These treasure troves of information about Latvia's history and culture were banned in Soviet Latvia. The memory of life in Latvia before the Soviet occupation was perceived by the communists as a threat to their authority.

"Like all of the thrice-occupied (Soviet, then German, then Soviet) lands east of the Molotov-Ribbentrop line, the Baltic States entered the USSR in 1945 having lost much of their elite, and indeed a significant share of the total population." (Timothy Snyder, *Bloodlands*, p. 329). As the Iron Curtain fell, separating Latvia, Lithuania, and Estonia from the West and the Free World, contacts between Latvia and its expatriates were ruptured and hampered for decades. Once well known names in Latvian culture faded into obscurity in Soviet Latvia, censored, repressed. My own grandfathers were examples of this exclusion. Information about the Supreme Court of the Republic of Latvia was scrubbed. Jānis Bičolis—philologist, editor, writer—no longer existed. They were lucky to get out of Latvia alive.

In his old age my maternal grandfather Jānis Bičolis suffered from angst, questioning his decision to leave Latvia in 1944. The fear of deportation was a thing of the past; now only regret remained. He felt cut off from the country, nation, culture, and language that were the focus of his work and passion. As someone who had studied Baltic philology and whose life was devoted to the Latvian language and Latvian literature, he felt painfully isolated and excluded despite his efforts and work in exile. "Maybe we would have survived; I would have a found a way back into the academic world in Latvia": these were his deep, lasting regrets. It was not nostalgia. It was a searing sense of cultural deprivation, displacement, and the diminishment of one's identity—so closely tied to the fatherland and the mother tongue. My grandparents in America felt like strangers in a strange land.

The notable poet Edvarts Virza (1883–1940), favored by the last Latvian President Kārlis Ulmanis; Virza's wife poet Elza Stērste (1885–1976), *right*, arrested in 1951 and deported to Siberia for "betrayal of the homeland"; poet Leonīds Breikšs (1908–1942), arrested in April 1941 and deported to the USSR, where he died the same year; Aleksandrs Grīns (1895–1941), a beloved writer from my grandfather's native Sēlija whose work was devoted to Latvian history—he was arrested, deported, and shot in a prison in Astrakhan: the list of Latvians who did not fit into communist society and Soviet memory was long. But there were Latvians in occupied Latvia who clung to the memory of their lost, banished, repressed compatriots with a deep, secret reverence. The books of banned writers were stashed away like precious jewels. My father-in-law had his own stash of Soviet-banned literature squirreled away somewhere in his rooftop studio. Latvians in exile kept the memory of these writers alive by publishing their works; some smuggled those books into Latvia.

As soon as they could after the war, Latvian refugees around the world worked like tireless ants to restore and preserve the history and culture of their war-torn nation. They knew that under the Soviet communists Latvia's history would be revised and rewritten. These two great generations, the Latvians who left Latvia as adults, and their children, felt compelled to devote their free time and capital to the preservation of historical truth, justice, and Latvian identity. It was precisely these efforts, aimed at preserving and reminding the world of the truthful version of Latvia's history, which the Soviets feared and attacked in their press and by other means from behind the Iron Curtain. The Soviets also sowed seeds of wicked incrimination among Nazi crimes investigators in the West, as documented in Andrievs Ezergailis' book *Nazi Soviet Disinformation about the Holocaust in Nazi-Occupied Latvia* (2005). Ezergailis exposed the way in which the Latvian KGB orchestrated a campaign of lies against some of the Latvian exile community's most prominent leaders, dragging their reputations through the mud.

Thus the outcome of World War II split Latvians into several groups or sub-cultures and mentalities. There was *trimda* to which I belonged: the Latvian diaspora obsessed with the loss of their native land and their past and the "recreation" of Latvia in the countries that took them in as refugees. There were the "comrades" and chameleons in Latvia who imbibed Soviet propaganda and its version of history and played by communist rules, thus contributing to the corruption of Latvian society and its mentality. There were people like most of my relatives and friends who simply tried to survive outside of the ideological dictates of Soviet rule, trying to preserve their integrity. There were some individuals who hinted at the truth, such as poets Vizma Belševica and Ojārs Vācietis. There were the "foolhardy" dissidents and human rights activists, a tiny minority who risked everything to stand up to the Soviets. They were the most remarkable Latvians of all. And then there were those who were stuck in Siberia on account of the Soviet deportations of 1941 and 1949; sadly, most of them never made it back and were lost to their fatherland. Their tragic stories have been documented by Dzintra Geka in her film *Sibirijas bērni* ("Siberia's Children") and emerging literature.

As an innocent bystander, a skylark in its nest, Latvia was swept into the vortex of World War II and emerged disjointed, disoriented, and broken. Living in Latvia in the fourth decade of the Soviet occupation, the gravity of Latvia's situation hit me full force. Time was running out, as Russians kept moving in.

Chapter sources:

(1) "Andrejs Eglītis." Wikipedia. 10/25/2013 ; 3/24/2014. <http://lv.wikipedia.org/wiki/Andrejs_Egl%C4%ABtis>
(2) "Lūcija Garūta." Wikipedia 02/05/2014 ; 03/24/2013. < http://lv.wikipedia.org/wiki/L%C5%ABcija_Gar%C5%ABta>

Russian Boots on the Ground

"What does a boot know of pain? It doesn't think but steps on you..."
(Guntars Godiņš, "A Song about (Army) Boots")

Rīga, Latvia, USSR, November 1984. Waiting for the Soviet Army tanks to roll by on Padomju ("Soviet") bulvāris, as Latvia's communists prepare to celebrate the anniversary of the October Revolution. Our son is six months old, forced to breathe in the Russian tanks' fumes as they rumble by, shaking his tiny body. Photo: Andris Krieviņš.

Although I was not aware of Gunārs Astra, his trial, or his fate, the man had just voiced the pain and anger I felt living in my nation's capital, which had come to be dominated by the Russian language, the Russian military, arrogant Russian officers' wives in mink and Qaraqul coats and hats, and Russophiles from all walks of life. They were our "liberators" who expected us to be grateful and grovel before them forever. To be sure, not all of the Russian speakers were ethnic Russians: there were Belarusians and Ukrainians in Latvia too, but they were better behaved. The highly visible presence of the Soviet military coupled with the Russian alphabet and the sound of Russian everywhere induced a state of angst in me. This was... my grandparents' Rīga? The *Latvian* capital? Forty plus years after the war this beautiful European city had been reduced to a Russian military outpost. Didn't liberators usually leave after liberating a country? Not these Russian bastards...

For more than 40 years the Baltic States were the USSR's western border, an area where the Soviet military placed their latest weapons aimed at the West. "According to the Baltic Military District, 3,009 Soviet Army units were stationed in 24 of Latvia's 26 regions between 1944 and 1990. This list does not include the units of the Soviet Baltic Fleet, stationed in all of Latvia's ports. The presence of the Soviet Armed Forces in Latvia for more than 50 years (...) would impact Latvia's national economy for many years to come. (1)

Latvia, with tens of thousands of Soviet military personnel stationed there, was part of the wider so-called Baltic Military District, which included the three Baltic States and Kaliningrad. On my daily walks I saw Russian military personnel walking around or riding in their transport vehicles. I often saw Russian Army trucks with soldiers inside. I walked past the buildings that the Soviet (read Russian) military had occupied in Rīga, and I was dimly aware of the fact that there were bases and firing ranges all over Latvia. Friends of mine had served in the Soviet Army. There were whispered talks of brutal *dedovshchina* or hazing incidents with lethal outcomes in training camps in faraway Soviet republics, where the Balts were vulnerable. Their "fascist" reputation" put them at high risk: because the Latvian Legion fought alongside the Germans against the Red Army, Latvians would be permanently branded as fascists. Pregnant, I worried about the future of my child...

The various offices and facilities of the Baltic Military District were located in numerous charming, pre-war buildings, including the Latvian *Māmuļa* ("Mother" or "Mommy") building at Merķeļa iela 13, which had played such an important role in the Latvian National Awakening in the late 19th century. It had been the seat of the once famous Rīga Latvian Society, the oldest Latvian organization, and served as a central meeting place for Latvians under German rule in Tsarist Russia. A beautiful frieze by Latvian painter Janis Rozentāls decorated the top of its façade. In 1940 Latvians were rudely thrown out of the magnificent building by the communists who then handed it over to the Soviet Red Army. The building remained a Soviet (Russian) officers' club until 1989. An insult on a grand scale!

From January 26 until February 3, 1946, the Soviet Baltic Military District held a public war tribunal in the Māmuļa building. Seven Nazi German generals of Reichskommissariat Ostland (1941–1944), which included the territory of Latvia, were sentenced to death, among them Higher SS and Police Leader Friedrich Jeckeln who oversaw the massacre of some 24,000 Jews at Rumbula at the end of 1941. In 1944 Jeckeln had also issued the order to shoot eight Latvian officers who served under Latvian General Jānis Kurelis (1882–1954, Chicago). Jeckeln had also given the order for the massacre of about 160 Latvian civilians at Zlēkas in Kurzeme, punished for supporting Latvian partisans. However, these latter two incidents were not mentioned at the trial. (2)

Friedrich Jeckeln, standing on the left, being tried by a Soviet war tribunal in the building known to Latvians as Māmuļa. Source: Wikimedia Commons. https://commons. wikimedia.org/wiki/File:Friedrich_Jeckeln_on_trial.jpg (© Public Domain)

The Nazis were hanged on February 3, 1946 on the other side of the Daugava River at the future site of the Soviets' Victory Monument in front of about 4,000 spectators, most of them Russian military personnel. According to a witness, as soon as the officers were pronounced dead, the people in the front rows rushed over to pull off the Germans' high-quality leather boots. (2, 3)

Walking past the famous building and remembering its central role in the Latvian "awakening" period, any self-respecting Latvian probably seethed the way I did. Latvia was overrun by the Soviet military, which really meant the *Russian* military, because the Soviet Union was essentially a union of "forced marriages" between Russia and much smaller, thoroughly bullied republics and nations. In the Soviet era Rīga was home to the Bryusov Military School, the Alksnis Aviation School, and the Civil Aviation School, which also attracted students from African countries with friendly ties to the USSR. (Black students in Rīga were a source of fascination for Latvians and Russians alike.)

Russian officers lived with their families in apartments next to the people whose country they had occupied; they were oblivious to "our" version of history and had no regard for or interest in our language and traditions. People complained that many Russian officers' wives were employed in the corrupt housing authority, where Russian was spoken as though it were the official language of Latvia (de facto it was). Russian military families were mostly privileged and took their status for granted. I suspected they looked down upon us as a worthless people.

Latvians complained that Russians bragged about introducing culture to Latvia. Latvians were insulted by such ethnocentric contempt. Older Latvians remembered Russian women parading about in Rīga dressed up in nightgowns, which they mistook for ball gowns. Latvians recalled how Russian soldiers did not know what a fork and knife were for, how they drank water from toilets, how Russian soldiers defecated in the homes they had occupied, and so on. The cultural divide between the European inhabitants of Rīga and the Red Army and the hordes that followed it into occupied Latvia must have been staggering.

Many East Europeans shared similar memories of their Russian "liberators": the theft of watches; the rape of women... When the Soviets invaded Poland in 1939, the cultural gap between the occupier and the occupied became apparent: "Collectivization and industrialization had modernized the Soviet Union, but without the attention to the population, or rather to consumers, that characterized the capitalist West. The Soviet citizens who ruled eastern Poland were falling off bicycles, eating toothpaste, using toilets as sinks, wearing multiple watches, or bras as earmuffs, or lingerie as evening gowns." (Timothy Snyder, *Bloodlands*, p. 139)

One of the reasons why foreign tourist travel was so limited in Latvia was due to the presence of Soviet Army bases and strategic military installations. Even "the locals"—Soviet Latvian citizens—weren't permitted to get close to them. For nearly a decade I dreamed of going out to the Kurzeme coast to experience the open Baltic Sea, which I knew from photographs and folk songs. My first time there was in 1995, after independence.

In his heartfelt tribute to Latvia from 1988, *Īkšķojot pa Latviju* ("Hitchhiking through Latvia"), Alfrēds Stinkulis, a long-haired hippie type whom I met briefly before he emigrated, traveled around Latvia documenting the effects of several decades of Soviet rule on Latvia's historical and cultural monuments. He describes his nasty encounter with a grouchy Russian Army *chinovnik* (official) on a quiet road in Kurzeme, as well as Soviet restrictions on public access to the Baltic Sea. Stinkulis paid attention to places of historical and cultural significance to Latvians that were being neglected or even purposefully destroyed by the Soviets, such as churches, chapels, cemeteries, war memorials, ancient castle hills, and so on. These landmarks were part of our national memory, important to our knowledge of Latvia's history, culture, our national identity, and our dignity. Stinkulis was allowed to leave the Soviet Union in 1986.

Left: Alfrēds Stinkulis and his Inguna in 1986. Photo: Helēna Hofmane

Kurzeme: Strazde—Spāre—Pope—Ventspils—Ēdole—Alsunga—Kuldīga

The trip back to Ventspils seemed shorter this time. We flagged down a car, which took us to the next church in Spāre. All of the churches in this area are very old, and this one is no exception: its construction was commenced in 1658. The brick and mortar church is small and lacks a steeple. An ancient wrought iron weather vane resembling a flag is perched on the roof. The church's walls were once covered with plaster that is now crumbling, revealing red bricks here and there. Many window frames are broken, their glass panes smashed. Here and there old wooden scaffolding leans against the walls.

Right: The church in Spāre in a photograph from 1980. "How many years has the scaffolding been there? Ten? Fifteen? From what I've heard, a few years back the church was used as an outbuilding or warehouse. The trees planted around the church in a circle are still verdant. Compared to the church in Strazde, this one leaves a sorrowful impression." – A. Stinkulis. Source: Zudusī Latvija, National Library of Latvia

Making our way back towards Ventspils, Loretta and I stood for a while at the roadside, where we could see Gulbja ezers (lake) shimmering. It was late afternoon, and the road was empty. A passenger car bounced towards us and stopped. The fellow at the wheel was completely soused. We turned down his offer to take us to Ugāle; we didn't want to risk any new adventures...

We were able to stop an army truck. The driver was willing to accomodate us, but his master—a Red Army lieutenant or sergeant—was categorically opposed. Nyet! He was obviously turned off by our Baltic language and appearance. This pompous fool was a typical representative of the occupying power—a mindless, arrogant marionette. Go fuck yourself! Ventspils isn't going anywhere.

(...) A bit later we squeezed into a passenger car with three friendly and talkative Latvian fellows. They offered us a drink from their bottle and were willing to stop for us and go and see the Pope castle hill. (...) An old folk tale mentions a cat that was tied to a rope and lowered into a hole at the top of the castle hill. When the rope was pulled up, the cat had vanished. Pope is mentioned in documents as far back as 1231.

We made it into Ventspils shortly before sunset, and our driver and his companions drove us around, showing us the city. We walked down to the Baltic Sea, which is different than near Rīga: more expressive; grander; harsher. We are allowed to loiter there only during certain hours; that is, until dusk. Each night the beach is ploughed into two lanes to make it easier for the guards to see if someone has tried to reach the water. In the darkness patrols make their rounds on foot and by car. This stretch of public beach is fenced off at either end. The beaches beyond are separated from the rest of the world by barbed wire. Along the waterfront fully armed Red Army soldiers sit in their guard towers equipped with searchlights.

From the beach we can see ships waiting their turn to head out to sea. The Venta estuary with its lighthouses and pier is well visible but unreachable, distant...

"Latvian, this land does not belong to you; it was taken away from you by force in front of your very eyes; you are being tormented; they are laughing about your love for your homeland." Baiting us behind a loaded gun.

Of Latvia's 495 coastline kilometers (about 300 miles—RL) the average Soviet citizen has access to only 200: that is, the stretch from Rīga to Mērsrags (the village itself lies within the Soviets' restricted territory) and from Rīga to the Estonian border, just beyond the village of Ainaži. For a Latvian to be able to visit the seaside in his own country, he has to submit a special request or have a relative or friend who lives in one of the few remaining fishing villages file an invitation for a visit with the authorities. The restricted zone extends up to 25 kilometers inland; for instance, it begins right outside the town of Dundaga. Checkpoints are set up along all of the roads leading into the restricted border zone. Roads are blocked. The cūkcepures ("pighats") aren't always around though, and if you're cautious, it's possible to circumvent these roadblocks and checkpoints and continue on down the road. This is harder to accomplish in the more populated places, where the local "activists" and busybodies will sound the alarm if they spot a stranger. The scene is even sadder near the coast in Estonia and Lithuania, because the open sea is especially dangerous to the Soviet citizen. We hear the popular and optimistic Soviet song from the 1930s: "Широка страна моя родная, Много в ней лесов, полей и рек. Я другой такой страны не знаю, Где так вольно дышит человек!" ... "Mighty wide is my native land / with many forests, fields, and rivers. / I don't know of any other (country) / where a person can breathe so freely."

Of course, if you're locked away in a dark cellar, then it's not possible to see other countries.

"Oh, Ventspils, Ventspils, you provoke obscene thoughts! It's all a provocation!"

Having gazed with amazement at the open Baltic Sea and the giant ships, we found our lodging for the night. Turns out it was right in the center of town in a gloomy, nondescript place: a neighborhood of once white, now sooty-gray three-to-five-story brick buildings, the architectural wonderwork of the 50s and 60s.

My friend was there to greet us. He introduced us to our inebriated host. The situation looked bleak, because our Ventspils man was muttering something about informants, his innocence, and kept embellishing his slurred speech with a string of Russian swear words. Since I knew him well, I wasn't too worried, but it was unpleasant due to the presence of our lady friend. We managed to calm him down and even got around to listening to music. (...) It was a hard night, literally, because I slept on the floor on an old coat, using something like a blanket to keep warm. I am used to sleeping on hard surfaces and on the floor, because I don't use beds, but even this experience was rough on my bones. During the night it rained, and it was cold. A gray working man's everyday dawned in this city by the Baltic Sea, 176 kilometers from Rīga and even closer to Gotland.

The next morning J. was more coherent, but his Russian linguistic additives hadn't settled down. I wanted to see the wreck of an oil tanker that had exploded and burned. We were able to take some good photographs from a rooftop nearby. Four sailors died in this tragedy. It was reported on Western broadcasting stations. We took a look at the new buildings of the Ventspils Executive Committee and the KGB. (...)

Ventspils still has the appearance of a very old city because of the many old buildings that remain standing, such as the walls of the (Livonian) Order's castle fortress and its massive four-sided tower. In Latvia the only castles from the 13th century that have survived are in Venstpils and Rīga. Records from as far back as 1341 describe large foreign vessels sailing into the Venta River, which lies next to the castle. The port has been deepened. Opposite the castle on the other side of the river lies the so-called Export Harbor, where ships from many countries are loaded and unloaded. This part of the river is under special surveillance: guard towers; fences; barbed wire; warning signs; border guards; weapons; searchlights. This comes as no surprise, because the ships are but a short swim away, and someone just might desire to leave the workers' paradise.

The ancient castle's surroundings have been heavily ravaged. A border patrol base was set up in its vicinity upon the return of the Red Army in 1944. The damage, which includes widespread filth, litter, and a pervasive awful stench, is grim and difficult to understand. Some of the walls are "decorated" with socialist realist graffiti: the art of military patriotism and inculcation. The dominant color is bright blue with red, of course. A wall approximately 10 meters high and four meters wide is decorated with the following: on the left is our blue planet Earth and the bright red contours of the Soviet Union; from the contours of this superpower a ship—the icebreaker "Lenin"—emerges; above the globe—the red hammer and sickle flag. At the center of the mural are socialist and communist superstructures and achievements—apartment buildings, parks, factory smokestacks. An idyllic scene. On the right a brave Soviet border guard clutches a Kalashnikov, a faithful guard dog at his side.

Wonderful! The area near this wall is like a city after an aerial bombing. Luckily the roof of the castle and the tower seem adequately covered with tiles. Scaffolding has been placed here and there next to the walls. A Soviet border post in bright green and red colors marks the corner of a building. The entry gate has been fashioned from piping to look like a five-pointed star. (4)

In 1988 my favorite Latvian rock and roll band Līvi (the Livs) came out with a raucous song called "Zābaki" ("Boots") with music by Ainārs Virga and words by Guntars Godiņš, which became a big hit: "Many boots are tramping across my country, / And it hurts. / But what does a boot know of pain, / It can't think but only tramples. / The heavy boots step on our shadows, our shadows that fall away from us. / I wish the dogs would take a bite out of those boots, / I wish the boots would get tangled up in their conscience. / I wish lightning would strike their soles,/ These boots are our destruction." Their grandfathers shot, killed, deported, terrorized, or humiliated, Latvian men could only dream or fantasize about driving the Russian forces out. In the 1980s it looked like the Soviet Army would never leave.

An occupation regime change took place in 1944: the boots of the soldiers of the Red Army began to trample Latvia once again. This time the Soviet leadership made it clear there would be no talks of formal independence. Latvia was now one of 15 "full-fledged" Soviet republics with "equal rights"; it was not a "protectorate" with limited rights like Poland, Czechoslovakia, and the other Eastern Bloc countries. A vast number of Soviet Armed Forces units were permanently deployed in the territory of Latvia immediately after World War II. Their distribution and the necessary space and facilities for stationing them was entirely up to the Soviet military authorities, which resulted in Latvia's local government authorities having no right to appeal or protest. The territories controlled by the Soviet military were actually like a state within a state, because the local authorities had no say (in military matters). The Soviet military did as it pleased wherever it set up its bases. Many people still remember that the entire Kurzeme coastline was declared a border zone and access to it was limited. The inhabitants of the coastal area were driven into several fishermen's kolhoz villages (Kolka, Roja, etc.), but the rest of the territory was handed over to Soviet border troops. The domestic passports of all of the people living in this area were stamped with a special note: Житель приграничного („Border Area Resident").

Even Latvia's highest hill Gaiziņš was for many years off-limits to the average Soviet Latvian citizen. In 1955 the Soviet Army began setting up long and mid-range nuclear missile sites in Alūksne, Bārta, and Vaiņode (western Kurzeme—RL). In 1957 construction of a missile launch pad was commenced in Mārciena near Madona, a town in Vidzeme. An area of 47.2 hectares of land near Gaiziņš was handed over to the Russian military for the construction of a missile launch pad. Work on a cement roadway was initiated to accomodate the first nuclear missiles, which were very heavy and could only be transported by train or on specially constructed roads. The cloak of secrecy surrounding these endeavors was lifted when Oleg Penkovsky, a senior Soviet Army intelligence officer who spied for the United States and the United Kingdom, passed this information on to his employers. The projects were no longer secret. The missiles in Mārciena were removed, and the construction work at Gaiziņš was stopped. The unfinished cement road in Bērzaune and the many fir trees planted on Gaiziņš remain as a reminder of the Soviets' military strategy at that time.

After the Soviet Union fell apart, several large-scale Soviet military objects remained unfinished: a three-story underground anti-aircraft defense command bunker at Zaķumuiža near Rīga; a long-distance early warning radar facility—the Daryal-UM—in Skrunda (demolished in a controlled explosion in May 1995—RL); a space communication center named Kristāls („Crystal") in Irbene near Ventspils (popularly referred to as Zvaigznīte or Star, it is now the Ventspils International Radio Astronomy Center); Soviet long-range communication towers at Upīškalns near Tukums to keep in touch with the Soviet Baltic Fleet and nuclear submarines around the world; and many other smaller projects.

These weren't the only 'gashes' in Latvia's face. Soviet Army units were deployed near just about every populated area. It is not possible to say exactly how many Soviet troops were stationed in Soviet Latvia. In the mid-1980s the Baltic Military District was comprised of about 350,000 men, not including the Soviet Border Troops and Interior Ministry forces. Thus one can reasonably conclude that a couple of decades ago the number of Soviet military personnel in Latvia,

Lithuania, and Estonia was close to half a million. There were military and aviation bases and aviation bombing landfills near Ādaži, Zvārde, Pape, Vaiņode, and Tukums, a tankodrom, anti-missile radar installations, and countless other military compounds, facilities, and testing areas. According to records that the Baltic Military District submitted to the Latvian Cabinet of Ministers in 1994, it was possible to conclude that between 1944 and 1994 more than 3,000 military units were stationed in Latvia; they were distributed over 700 sites in 24 out of Latvia's 26 regions. The territory occupied by Soviet military units and their infrastructure took up more than 120,000 hectares. Latvia was like an unsinkable Soviet military base.

The Soviet military apparatus (in Latvia) was supported by technical repair bases such as in Liepāja. Tanks, armored vehicles, explosives, airplanes, and naval ships were not manufactured in Latvia. Soviet doctrine was based on a war of aggression (from the West—RL), and therefore Latvia, because of its proximity to what the Soviets said was a potential war zone, was unsuitable for manufacturing military equipment. The biggest maintenance and repair center for the Soviet Baltic Fleet was in Tosmare. (During the Soviet occupation) the aquatorium at Liepāja's military port had become the biggest Soviet naval ship and submarine cemetery in the Baltic Sea, which created major headaches during the Soviet Army withdrawal from Latvia in the 1990s (after Latvia regained independence). (5)

No wonder the Soviet authorities in Latvia were paranoid about foreign tourists. Soviet military installations—army bases, naval ports, radio towers, and nuclear launch pads—were every-where, which meant that Western spies might be lurking behind each and every bush.

"The last of the Soviet occupying forces would withdraw from Latvia in August of 1994, leaving in their wake destroyed buildings, empty missile silos, dangerous explosive materials, and toxic waste and debris that still litters and poisons some areas today. In 1988 the Soviet Baltic Fleet (…) detonated 440 World War II era aviation bombs filled with phosphorus in the Baltic Sea. Such bombs are normally dismantled, and the phosphorus is either melted or burned. The result was the spread of phosphorus parts over large areas of the Baltic Sea. In water phosphorus comes to resemble amber. People looking for amber can mistake phosphorus for the attractive resin; phosphorus can cause deep, severe burns. Only recently have studies emerged about the Soviet Union's legacy of toxic chemical pollution in the Baltic Sea area. Lastly, despite Russian troop withdrawal, many retired Russian military personnel were permitted to stay on in Latvia and Estonia as civilians, where they continue to receive Russian pensions; they, too, are a legacy of the Soviet era." (6)

Chapter sources:

(1) Upmalis, Ilgonis. „PSRS (Krievijas) armijas un militāri rūpnieciskā kompleksa nodarīto zaudējumu aprēķins Latvijas tautsaimniecībai." Padomju Savienības nodarītie zaudējumi Baltijā. 2012: Zelta Rudens, Rīga

(2) Ērglis, Dzintars. "Paraugprāva Rīgā. 'Mazajai Nirbergai' 60." Apollo.lv. 02/05/2006. ; 03/25/2014. <http://www.apollo.lv/zinas/paraugprava-riga-mazajai-nirnbergai-60/325475>

(3) "Friedrich Jekeln." 6 Feb 2014 <http://en.wikipedia.org/wiki/Friedrich_Jeckeln>

(4) Stinkulis, Alfrēds. Īkšķojot pa Latviju. Stockholm: LNF (Latviešu Nacionālais Fonds), 1987.

(5) Ciganovs, Juris. "Latvija—Padomju Savienības karabāze." TVNet 17/07/2006 ; 3/25/2014. < http://www.tvnet.lv/zinas/latvija/211821-latvija-padomju-savienibas-karabaze>

(6) Upmalis, Ilgonis. "Latvia—Soviet War Bases 1944–1994."Latvianhistory.wordpress.com 03/01/2013 ; 03/25/2014. <http://latvianhistory.wordpress.com/2013/03/01/latvia-soviet-war-base-1944-1994>

Vot, vot, Comrade Ilmarovna!

In beautiful Sigulda in the winter of 1983.. Sigulda was one of the few places outside of Rīga that foreigners were permitted to visit. Photo: Andris Krieviņš.

Was she an American spy? Was she a KGB agent?—These questions might have swirled in the minds of some of my compatriots in Latvia in the early 1980s. "Why on earth would you want to live here?" some people would ask me, adding, "This ship is sinking!" Excellent, I thought; let's stick around! There were those who seemed afraid to speak to me, who looked at me askance, ducked their heads, and hurried past me. Latvians with drooping shoulders and furtive stares: their probing stares scurried over my face and clothes. An alien, an American. What is she doing here?

I wanted "in." I loved Latvia and respected and admired many of the people I was introduced to. I wanted to live in Latvia to see what life there was really like, to get to know my fatherland better despite the occupation, which had damaged it. There was more to Latvia than the occupation itself. There was its history to be seen, touched, explored, and grasped, and its culture to be enjoyed. Everything I had learned from my years in Latvian school in the United States was coming to life. There was the land itself—the countryside beckoning with its landscape, old farm houses, and nature. And there were my fellow Latvians with oh so many interesting, sad, and funny stories and wickedly dark humor. Of course, the language itself, my mother tongue, was reason enough for me to stay. I was relishing plunging into it. Practical life in communist Latvia was miserable and caused us all anxiety, but I was looking beyond that.

Naturally, my good and innocent intentions weren't that apparent to the shadowy people who kept the "show" running smoothly for the Communist Party in the USSR and Soviet Latvia— that is, the KGB. When I made the decision to stay and try life in Latvia, I was sure I was going to have encounters with them, directly or indirectly. I knew several people who were directly linked to the KGB but operated behind a façade (that is, the Cultural Liaison Committee); instinctively I did not trust any of them despite their smiles and handshakes. My encounters with them had been brief and cordial and ended when I took up residency in Latvia.

My encounters with the KGB, the Soviet Union's feared secret police organization, took place sporadically from the time of my arrival in late 1982 until 1987. On those occasions I would nervously make my way to the foreign visa office on Anrija Barbisa (Henri Barbusse) iela to chat with a fellow who called himself Comrade Jānis Ruciņš, an agent assigned to my "file." I met Comrade Ruciņš for the first time in 1981; as I've already mentioned, I was asked to explain certain statements in my article about my first trip to Latvia in 1980. Ruciņš would remain "attached" to me until the end of the decade, when it became clear that the KGB had no future as an organization in Latvia. My husband met with KGB operatives at a different location. His meetings with the KGB had already started prior to my arrival in the winter of 1982. The Latvian KGB was aware of our year-long correspondence and had questions for him.

What the KGB wanted from us was not all that apparent. Perhaps my youth, looks, friendly demeanor, and evasive answers were hard for Comrade Ruciņš to deal with. I managed to keep myself "slippery" and out of reach. His scariness quickly faded, and I found the man to be somewhat of a simpleton. The word that came to mind was *divpirkstpiere* ("dimwit"). He lacked substance. I never felt he was getting the best of me. He did not give the impression of a shrewd, hardened *nagumaucējs* ("nail ripper"), which was the sadistic image of the KGB's predecessor, the NKVD. Comrade Ruciņš spoke with a heavy Russian accent, peppering his sentences with "vot, vot." With a round face, Slavic features, and "piggy" eyes, I thought he may have been born in Russia. I never asked. It helped to maintain an air of humor in our conversations. I professed complete ignorance of politics and politicians, always stressing that I was an art student, an artist. In fact, I think I made Ruciņš nervous, maybe because he did not know how to "handle" me.

In my husband's case, the KGB "comrades" could not "crack" him either: his spine was as rigid as an iron rod. He was a fierce Latvian patriot and would remain one all his life. It was one of the reasons I fell in love with him and married him. He had no intention of abandoning Latvia, and he had no intention of becoming a traitor. He was extremely stubborn, confident, and even cocksure in all situations. Like a wild, impossible to tame stallion.

My chats with Comrade Ruciņš always took place in the same drab office in the eerily quiet foreign visa office that I had been summoned to in the fall of 1981. Lenin was always there on the wall looking down on me. The red telephone on Comrade Ruciņš's desk was cute: "revolution red." Yet the bright color signaled danger. Later a friend told me that red telephones were special: they were connected directly to the Central Committee of the Latvian Communist Party for emergencies. And the Interior Ministry, too, probably.The office was small and austere: white walls; a bulky Soviet-style desk; a barred window that looked out onto a walled courtyard. What a crazy history! The lifetime of Mr. Karl von Strike, a German beer manufacturer and original proprietor of this manor, seemed eons ago.

Luckily for me, there was never any offer or threat to come over to "the Dark Side." I am not sure how I would have reacted in such a case and what the consequences of a refusal to cooperate would have been. I theorized that it was also convenient for the Soviet Latvian authorities to let me live there for the sake of publicity, as well as to see what exactly I was up to and with whom I met.

I was grateful that I only had Comrade Ruciņš to deal with. After my brief and uncomfortable meeting in the fall of 1981 with high-ranking KGB officer Bruno Šteinbriks, when I had to explain the shenanigans of a couple of inebriated, long-haired Latvians at Sheremetyevo Airport, I never met this comrade again and was glad of that. He was of a different caliber than his subordinate Ruciņš. Meeting with someone of his rank made me squirm. That time he made me feel guilty of a crime I had not committed. His colleagues in Moscow must have been furious over the silly incident. When I was introduced to Comrade Šteinbriks, he was in charge of the Latvian KGB's counter-intelligence unit and would swiftly move up the ranks. I am sure that after seeing me, a blushing, stammering young lady of 23, Comrade Šteinbriks realized there were bigger fish to fry. Despite being an American, I was an inconsequential speck compared to someone like Gunārs Astra.

Our phone was a funny thing. Once in a while when it rang and I picked up the receiver, a distant-sounding woman's voice could be heard saying, "Andris, please." When I asked who was calling, the voice repeated the phrase. If Andris was home and came to the phone, the caller hung up. This went on for about two or three years, while we lived in Old Rīga; I believe it was the KGB annoying us.

A couple of silly episodes regarding the Latvian KGB stand out. Twice when my mother visited, in May of 1983 and 1984, we were granted permission to go to Piebalga. No doubt this was "a big risk" for the authorities, granting permission for a trip to an area closed to foreigners. To make sure we didn't stray from the path and take photographs of military objects, we were personally chauffeured by Comrade Ruciņš, who on both occasions was accompanied by women, a different one each time. We suspected they were also affiliated with the KGB, assigned to keep a careful eye on my mother, the dangerous "bourgeois nationalist" poet from the imperialist USA.

During our drive up to Piebalga, Ruciņš and his mysterious female companion -his "cousin" he claimed—were a great source of merriment for my husband, my mother, and me, all scrunched together in the back seat. At Paulēni we were welcomed by Biruta and treated to a delicious meal. The conversation was pleasant enough—superficial chit-chat. Ruciņš's companion kept her eyes glued on my mother as if she were seeing a Martian. It was weird. My mother and I were enjoying the beautiful Latvian countryside, the awareness of Piebalga's history and culture, and each other's company. We were being ourselves—positive, happy, innocent, and open to new impressions. But what were Comrade Ruciņš and his "sister" thinking? Did he and his superiors seriously think we were spies? The "sister" never uttered a word, never smiled, never engaged in conversation. She was as cold and creepy as a corpse.

While I remained at Paulēni, Ruciņš invited Andris and my mother to come see the hunting lodge where they were staying. The Soviet nomenklatura or ruling class maintained exclusive hunting lodges and areas in the Latvian countryside, and I had heard some sad stories of how they "hunted" animals.

"The lodge was empty, of course, and felt creepy, given the circumstances," my mother recalled. She and my husband got a tour of the building and the grounds and then ended up in

Ruciņš's room for a chat. Ruciņš tried, without success, to ply Andris and my mother with champagne, as the talks dragged on. My mother could sense her son-in-law's temper heating up.

At one point the subject of the 1980 Moscow Summer Olympics came up. The success of Soviet-occupied Latvia's athletes at the games (they won a total of 13 medals) had been muted, with no international resonance. The games were boycotted by the US and other countries on account of the Soviet Union's invasion of Afghanistan. For Latvian athletes their success must have been bittersweet, as part of the world shunned the event. According to my mother, this subject was the breaking point for Andris. Hothead that he was, he jumped into the taboo subject of the Latvian athletes' status: that they were forced to compete under the Soviet flag. The conversation ended on a sour note. "The night sky was full of brilliant stars, the landscape bathed in the moon's bright light. Driving back to Paulēni, I remember how the dust picked up behind our car as Andris drove the gas pedal into the floor. He was furious. It was surreal," my mother remembered.

One year later in May 1984, Comrade Ruciņš again drove us to Paulēni, this time with a different female companion. This "lady friend" turned out to be a relentless stalker, following my mother everywhere she went, even as she carried our baby around the small house and outside in the garden. She even stood next to the outhouse, where my mother was attending to nature's call. A delusional paranoiac? Didn't that describe the KGB apparatus and the Soviet state as a whole?

For my husband, my mother, and me these were bizarre experiences. We all pretended not to know why Ruciņš and his companions, all complete strangers, had accompanied us. In our conversations we pretended that we liked and had respect for each other. My mother and I pretended that we weren't afraid of the KGB. They pretended to trust us.

The fruitless talks with Comrade Ruciņš continued until 1987, when big events began to shake up the Soviet Union. The KGB would lose all interest in me. When I went on my last visit to Barbisa iela at the end of the decade, a short, chubby chekist with a shock of curly hair was waiting for me in "our"room. Ruciņš had vanished. "Tautmīlis Fatz-Katz," he curtly introduced himself. I immediately sensed that this would not be a pleasant conversation. Comrade Fatz-Katz (whose true name I have chosen not to divulge) proved to be far more menacing than his colleagues. After a short and forgettable conversation, he gave me a withering look and asked if I knew anyone from Helsinki-86, a small group of Latvian dissidents from Liepāja. As I shook my head, he proceeded to threaten me and my family, saying that if the KGB found out that we had anything to do with "those criminals," we would be very sorry. That was all. I slunk out of the building with a sick feeling in my stomach. I felt like a beaten dog, and I shed some tears, as I hobbled towards Gorkija iela. What a slime!

Today's Internet search brings up the name of Mr. Fatz-Katz on the list of employees of the Latvian KGB's "central apparatus" in 1989. Comrade Ruciņš's name does not appear on the list, so I assume that "Ruciņš" was an alias. *Afanasyev, Aksyonov, Alexeyev, Amelkovich, Andrusov, Antonov, Babykov, Bakanov, Baranov, Baskova, Batygin, Blinova, Buryhin, Cherkasov, Chervynsky, Dubrovin, Fateyev, Gavrilenko, Generalov...* The list suggests that the vast majority of KGB "central apparatus" employees in Soviet Latvia were of Russian descent; most of the surnames are Russian. The fact that there are Latvian names on the list angers me, of course: Ābeltiņš;

Ancāns; Bērziņš; Bitenieks; Gailis; Graudiņš: all traitors. Obviously, there was more to the KGB than its "central apparatus." To this day the names of informants have not been made public, but we know that without informants chekists would have had a harder time doing their job.

What happened to Jānis Ruciņš? Where is he today? The last time I saw him was in the late 1980s on Ļeņina iela near the Russian Orthodox Cathedral. He had arranged a meeting with me there. He got to the point right away: would I be interested in becoming a go-between for business transactions between "his colleagues" and Western companies by helping import electronics for lucrative pay? "Think it over, Comrade Ilmarovna," he said with a smile. I politely declined. That was the last I saw of him. Google suggests Mr. Fatz-Katz now lives in Jelgava and is involved in some sort of business affairs. (1)

The Latvian KGB would break up after independence, diving into business and engagaging in lucrative deals and money-making schemes in the murky post-Soviet world, where there was so much state property to seize, embezzle, and sell. I have no idea what became of all of the people of the Latvian KGB's central apparatus or its countless "eyes and ears"; they continue to live in independent Latvia with impunity. The dead are dead, and some of my compatriots who were tormented and punished under the Soviets have found it in themselves to forgive those who wronged them. But I am disappointed in Latvia for not undergoing full lustration; it feels like an unpaid debt.

Today in photographs the building that once housed the foreign visa office looks abandoned. Prompted by my Facebook post in 2014, which included a photograph of the dreary building, several Latvian Americans and Canadians shared their memories of unpleasant encounters there with Soviet chekists.

Chapter sources:

(1) "VDK/KGB darbinieku saraksts 1989. gadā / Latvijas PSR VDK Centrālais aparāts" Latvijas Republikas Tautas tribunāls <http://tautastribunals.eu/?p=364>

Entertainment

"Long live the USSR": A garishly decorated Latvian National Theater in the Stalinist Soviet era, when it was called the Drama Theater. Photograph courtesy of the Museum of Occupation 1940–1991.

Free time and lots of it. As I struggled to understand what to do with myself in this new environment, we visited a lot with relatives and friends. Our frequent visits to Raiņa bulvāris made me feel like I had a family away from my family in the United States. Latvians have a great sense of humor, and we laughed a lot at jokes and anecdotes while savoring some delicious homemade alcoholic concoction, like a berry liquer, or the popular Armenian cognac, a favorite of Latvians at the time. The only wine I remember from the Soviet years was *Lāča asinis* ("Bear's Blood") from Bulgaria. In the Soviet era most Latvians had forgotten the pleasures of wine. Communists prefered vodka. There was always something delicious to be tasted, when you were a guest in the home of Latvians; they knew how to whip up treats out of nothing and nowhere. I was discovering my fellow countrymen's wonderful hospitality.

Tickets to the theater were cheap or easy to come by for me through my cousin Māra; I had established my *blats* in the theater world. We enjoyed many a wonderful production at the beautiful Latvian Drama (later National) Theater, where Latvia's independence had been declared on November 18, 1918. We also frequented the Daile Theater—a massive poured concrete structure on Ļeņina iela. Sometimes we went to plays at the Latvian SSR Lenin Komsomol State Theater, which was headed by Ādolfs Šapiro (b. 1939); already by the mid-1980s this theater was known for its novel productions. Rīga's Russian Drama Theater in the Old Town served the city's large Russian speaking community. Many bilingual Latvians enjoyed its productions, too.

Latvians loved theater both in Latvia and in exile. Not only was theater a form of artistic expression and communication, it was also a form of escapism in the Orwellian state of communist Latvia. I especially loved the Drama Theater, which was just a few blocks away from where we lived. Knowing the theater's role in Latvia's history was thrilling for me, as was the old building's beautiful, ornate interior. On my daily walks I often ventured into the vestibile of the Drama Theater to scour the calendar for upcoming shows that were of interest to me. A

335

knock on a small shuttered window brought it to life. A face appeared, roubles were pushed in, out came tickets! Excitement! A thrill that I can't describe!

We had a portable cassette player (made in Latvia), so at home I sometimes listened to popular Latvian groups. Yet it was very hard to be cut off from American and British rock, punk, and pop. Sometimes I picked up strains of European pop music on a radio station in Warsaw, Poland. Nor were there music-only stations in communist Latvia or the Soviet Union. Latvian bands had great lyrics, but their music was too slick, their vocals too smooth. I loved raspy, raw-sounding voices (Janis Joplin, The Band, Tom Waits, etc.), which is why I fell in love with the Liepāja band Līvi.

The music of our Piebalga neighbor Imants Kalniņš (b. 1941) was catchy and seductive. An accomplished composer in the classical genre, Kalniņš was versatile enough to delve into popular music with success and was idolized by Latvia's youth. His oeuvre includes symphonies, operas, including the Soviet Union's very first rock opera *Ej, jūs tur* ("Hey, You There!"), oratorios, and music for theater and film. He set Imants Ziedonis' poem "Ļeņinam" ("To Lenin") to music; it remains a great example of the Soviet state's demands on its artists. (Today no one has the nerve or stomach to sing it anymore.) Kalniņš's sound is unmistakable. His symphonies are full of passion. For years he was involved in rock music, too, which Latvian critics have called "intellectual rock" for his choice of lyrics—poems by Latvia's finest poets.

Raimonds Pauls (b. 1936), a Soviet superstar of popular music, composed catchy pop tunes that were belted out by Latvian pop stars like Viktors Lapčenoks, Nora Bumbiere, Mirdza Zīvere, Aija Kukule, and the beautiful, husky-voiced Laima Vaikule. Pauls was famous throughout the Soviet Union and also composed songs for Russia's pop megastar Alla Pugacheva and other Russian singers. Now a lot of this music is available on YouTube, and when I listen to it, I remember the 1980s in communist Latvia. I still enjoy listening to the music of Imants Kalniņš and Raimonds Pauls, whose talents are undeniable. Soviet pop music's most recognizable star in the US might be the "Trololo" guy Eduard Khil (1934–2012), a famous Russian singer. His unforgettable song "I am Glad Because I am Coming Home" was recorded in 1976. The popular American TV show "Family Guy" raised the "Trololo" song from the dead in one of its hilarious episodes, and in 2013 it was a big hit at my son's middle school in Ohio.

We watched cheesy "varieté" programs on TV, especially on New Year's Eve. I took it all in stride as a taste of a different culture and mentality. The music got better each year, it seemed. By the end of the decade there were new groups that I really liked, like Jumprava, Jauns Mēness, Zodiaks, Remix, and Līvi, of course. After independence, the sounds of Western rock and popular music would come crashing into Latvia like an enormous tidal wave, sweeping Soviet Latvia's *estrādes* (popular) music away.

Raised on art, I greatly enjoyed my visits to the Latvian State Art Museum, which featured a permanent collection of works by famous Latvian painters and sculptors, as well as a lovely exhibit of Russian art, which I knew nothing about when I lived in the US. The imagery of Russian painters like Kuzma Petrov-Vodkin (1878–1939), Zinaida Serebriakova (1884–1967), and Filipp Malyavin (1869–1940) in books and at the museum has stayed with me. I recall a lovely painting by Malyavin of two rosy-cheeked Russian peasant girls wrapped in bright shawls in a snowy field with a wooden monastery in the background: the pretty scene contrasted sharply with Soviet reality, so gray and *oh so drab*. What had happened to those bright and happy Russian colors? Had the revolution and communism wiped them out? I enjoyed looking at the works of Russian masters Ilya Repin (1844–1930) and Ivan Shiskin (1832–1898) in books and at the Hermitage Museum in Leningrad; these were famous painters whose work was well known to people born in this part of Europe, especially Latvians who had studied in St. Petersburg. I knew very little about Russia, Latvia's enormous neighbor that had impacted my fatherland's history time and time again.

I returned to the quiet museum time and time again to gaze upon the paintings of Nicholas Roerich (1874–1947), a "Russian painter, writer, archaeologist, theosophist, (…) enlightener, philosopher, and public figure" (Wikipedia) whose small, mystical paintings of lonely figures and shrines against the backdrop of Asia's towering mountains seemed truly "other-worldly" when compared to the Soviet reality just outside. These paintings spoke to me and pulled me in: I could meditate by gazing at their bright hues of blue and purple. The small Roerich collection at the art museum was one of my spiritual sanctuaries in the last dark decade of Soviet rule. These brilliant discoveries of art illuminated an otherwise dark and dreary era.

1984: A Ruckus at St. Peter's

Winter ebbed, spring murmured. The baby was due in mid-April, possibly on my birthday. Another Aries! I felt wonderful and continued to take my long walks through the city, sauntering for miles at a time sucking on glucose tablets. My first baby was light and easy to carry. Like most Latvians before us, we were superstitious and purchased nothing for our baby during the pregnancy. "All in due time," Biruta would gently remind me. Too pregnant to sit comfortably at my desk, I entered a meditative stage, absorbing the city's sights or lying down at home and reading or simply thinking.

My due date coincided with a week-long festival devoted to art, *Mākslas dienas* ("Art Days"). This was one of several rather delightful festivals organized throughout the year to keep the working people entertained. In the fall Latvians flocked to *Dzejas dienas* ("Poetry Days"), a popular event that showcased Latvia's literary talents. Some of Latvia's poets like Imants Ziedonis and Ojārs Vācietis attracted a cult-like following. Soviet-occupied Latvia also celebrated International Theater Day on March 27, which featured charming actors engaged in all sorts of antics in Old Rīga. In summer the Ethnographic Open Air Museum drew large crowds to its delightful crafts fair, where a Latvian American like me could feel most at home. I don't think I ever heard any Russian at these events; the relationship between Latvia's Latvian and Russian communities was tenuous at best.

The weather had warmed in April, and there were rumors that some of the art exhibits were going to be special and unusual, especially at St. Peter's just around the corner. I was determined to see as much as possible. On April 13, in my long American coat and a pair of comfortable, navy blue walking shoes purchased at the *valūtas* store, I waddled over to the Art Foundation in Old Rīga to attend the opening of Aija Zariņa's (b. 1954) first solo show. Zariņa's paintings were unlike anything I'd seen before in Rīga. Her large canvases were covered with crudely painted simple figures, forms, and bright colors that created arresting compositions. The handsome, petite artist looked sublimely cool; an enormous black and white portrait of Zariņa by Jānis Deināts had been mounted on the wall. Her partner Ivars Runkovskis, and her young daughter were there, as was a flock of her attractive artist friends. They were emerging as a powerhouse of Latvian painting at this time.

With Aija Zariņa's wildly colorful paintings still on my mind, I trundled to St. Peter's. My husband was out taking pictures; we would meet up later in the day. My cautious gait was a bit too slow for him. Once I'd stepped through the enormous wooden portal of St. Peter's, I threw back my head to look up at the church's magnificent arches and the soft, diffused light playing on the high walls. Then I looked around, surprised and delighted by what I saw. Numerous installations had been set up in and near St. Peter's as part of an exhibition called *Daba, Vide, Cilvēks* ("Nature, Environment, Man"), inspired by the artist Ojārs Ābols (b. 1922) who had died of cancer in 1983. This was the first exhibit ever of installation art in Soviet-occupied Latvia. Young artists eager to explore new concepts and materials had put in a huge, concerted effort to "break the mold," so to speak. It worked. Crowds of people were surging towards and into the cathedral; they had never seen anything like it. Their surprise, excitement, and even shock were palpable.

In the altar section of the church a group of young painters (Aija Zariņa, Ieva Iltnere, Sandra Krastiņa, Jānis Mitrēvics, Edgars Vērpe, Ģirts Muižnieks, and others) had set up an interpretation of Leonardo da Vinci's "Last Supper." Plaster casts of the artists' faces served as depictions of Jesus' disciples. Religion was not a subject that was actively explored by artists in the atheistic communist era for obvious reasons. And Christianity had been banned from St. Peter's for decades; under the Soviets it served as a secular space reserved for various exhibitions.

Andris Breže, Andra Neiburga, and Valdis Ošiņš had installed a rusty, chipped car in the church. It was padded with sod and occupied by plaster human figures reminiscent of George Segal's work. The installation was called "A Trip to the Countryside." Nearby Juris and Zaiga Putrāms and their friend Mārtiņš Bikše had built a pyramid with several entrances/exits ("Object with Five Designated Exits") and an opening at the top, drawing one's gaze upwards toward the vaulted ceiling of the church.

These young artists, recent graduates of the Latvian Art Academy, were the same age as me, and they were obviously eager to explore new concepts, ideas, directions, and materials in art. The installations were refreshing, unconventional, and daring against the backdrop of rigid Soviet communist ideology, which had held Latvian society in a stranglehold for too long. That day the Kremlin in Moscow seemed very far away. *Rīga dimd! Rīga dimd!* ("Rīga is ringing!")

Just outside the church curious onlookers were milling around, gawking at a replica of a helicopter created by artists Ivars and Inese Mailītis. Everyone was waiting for something spectacular to happen. The orange helicopter event was one of the most viewed performances ever in the history of Latvian art, according to Ivars Mailītis: "Our group (of artists) was a kind of 'radar' (back then). Inese and I were expecting the birth of our son Austris, and we were engaged in various positive yet ambiguous 'campaigns.' (…) With our performance we wanted to show that we were headed for a high-impact collision (in a handbuilt flying contraption) with the Soviet nomenklatura, KGB informants, and chekists, which included some of our 'friends.'" The Mailītis performance was about the dangers of conformity. The young artists wished to remind the public that it was impossible to ignore the subject of betrayal and traitors.

"St. Peter's Square was filled with curious onlookers. People were packed together so tightly, that it took Inese an hour to squeeze through to get into the helicopter. Filmmakers Juris Podnieks and Andris Slapiņš had been raised above the crowd with the help of a construction crane. Because of the immensity and density of the crowd, we were afraid to use the explosives provided by the Rīga Film Studio. As we scrambled to come up with an alternative denouement, our friend Aigars Grauba (who later fronted one of Latvia's all-time best rock bands, Jumprava— RL) picked up a megaphone and announced that this was the first performance art event *ever* in Soviet Latvia. Then our 'flight' commenced: two objects destined to collide sped toward each other along a cable. In our orchestrated battle above the crowd 'we' won, but the 'evil' object, which symbolized conformity and collaboration, crashed down on top of the filmmakers and their cameras! As far as I know, the Podnieks Studio has saved a few frames of the event leading up to the collision." Unfortunately, I was not there to witness the event; clasping my belly, I was walking away from the crowd, which made me uncomfortable.

According to Mailītis, some Latvians, including some artists, sided with the authorities in their disparagement of the show at St. Peter's and the helicopter performance. "I can tell you that today some of those 'chameleons' are writing our country's 'art history.' Their conscience hasn't prevented them from organizing exhibitions, in which they do not hesitate to call themselves 'non-conformists.' I know you know some of these people. The more honest folks have come clean and regretted their mistakes," Ivars added.

Ivars Mailītis: "My mother's brother was conducting the (Latvian) Home Guard orchestra on the Daugavpils Bridge, when the Red Army invaded Latvia. He was arrested on the spot and deported to Karaganda in Kazakhstan. When I was little, we lived in the forest, because the Russians had blown up my mother's house near Gaiziņkalns. They thought the wind generator and radio antenna were transmitters. My mother managed to hide, but her relatives were rounded up and deported to Siberia. We grew up in the forest. My father quit his studies to become a forest ranger. All of our neighbors were highly educated people, but after the war they worked for my father as simple lumberjacks. Many of them had done time in Siberia.

"In April 1984 we were hoping that a lot of children would see our performance. We wanted kids to grow up knowing that it was important to resist (evil) and to be aware of the difference between right and wrong. Inese was carrying Austris in her belly at the time. I've never shied away from speaking my mind, and it's easy to see for whom this causes discomfort." Ivars Mailītis shared his memories of April 1984 with me in an e-mail dated 6/12/2012.

That spring a gentle wind of change was stirring up the dust and soot of Old Rīga, as well as many repressed emotions and thoughts. For a few days our medieval town was transformed into a happy carnival of art. There was a wonderful sense of buoyancy in the air. Happy, laughing people filled the cobblestone streets of Old Rīga. If the KGB was out and about, nobody felt or cared about their presence. The sun rose higher, piercing the old town's shady winding streets with its warming rays.

How did the Latvian communist authorities react to the St. Peter's show and events? Jānis Borgs, a friend of Ojārs Ābols (the man behind the concept of the show), recalls: "The show was shut down early because of a visit by a delegation of hardline East German communists, more orthodox than the Pope in Rome, who expressed their outrage: 'What's going on here?! A manifestation of bourgeois ideology?! We're going to complain to Moscow!' Aivars Goris, the Latvian Communist Party's ideological secretary, announced that if the planned TV feature about the show wasn't critical, then it could not be broadcast. A whole bunch of us—instructors from the Academy, art historians, etc.—met up at St. Peter's to discuss the situation. Nobody found much to criticize." Nevertheless, the show was closed to minimize damage to the Soviet Latvian authorities. (1)

Borgs: "Because the organizers, including myself, refused to criticize the exhibit, the event received zero news coverage, with the exception of one particularly nasty review by a well know art critic." He added: "I remember the ridiculous reaction of some communists: how dare those artists set up their 'Last Supper' exhibit in the altar of a church, a holy place! The sanctity of the church was used as an argument (by the communists) in support of their official ideology! (...)" Even though the show closed early, it generated a lasting effect on those lucky enough to have witnessed it. (2)

The St. Peter's exhibit was a watershed moment for Latvia's art scene. Nothing was quite the same from April 13, 1984 on. Young Latvian artists jumped right into new forms of expression, taking on conceptual art and building installations to convey ideas. Video and sound were gradually introduced as new media, often replacing the traditional "old school" media of oil paint, watercolors, pastels, pencil, and stone. Subsequent art exhibits revealed new elements of surprise. The old, rusty car parked in the church had roared back to life, whisking its surprised passengers down the road of no return.

Chapter source

(2) Laima Slava. "Cietuma sidraba maliņa: Saruna ar Jāni Borgu." Studija <http://www.studija.lv/?parent=1526>
(3) Ibid 1

The Water Breaks

With sculptor Ojārs Feldbergs and his wife, afternoon of April 13, 1984, "Latvija" Exhibition Hall. Photo: Andris Krieviņš.

April 13. Morning turned into afternoon. Tired and hungry, at about five o'clock Andris and I left the large art show near Hotel Latvija and headed back to Old Rīga, walking at a leisurely pace. It had been a wonderful, uplifting day of unusual events. I began my ascent up the many flights of stairs, gripping the railing. As I stepped onto our landing, a torrent of warm, clear placenta water suddenly burst forth, streaming down my legs, puddling, and expanding in a warm rivulet. This was it! Like a moving waterfall, I pushed into our apartment, as Andris ran to the phone to summon a taxi. Stunned and awkward was how I felt. The moment I had been both dreading and anticipating had finally arrived!

Soon enough the dispatcher phoned to let us know a taxi was waiting for us on Krāmu iela. I began my descent, as the water continued to flow, leaving a trail of amniotic fluid behind me. Our kind Russian neighbor mopped up the mess. Embarrassed, I slid into the taxi murmuring apologies. I clutched my husband's hand. Our ride lasted about ten minutes, as the taxi sped up Ļeņina iela toward Rīga's gloomy First Hospital. Buildings, parks, and pedestrians flashed by as if in a dream. The day's events—bright canvases, milling crowds, and St. Peter's heavenly arches—suddenly seemed like a long time ago. I was drifting into another dimension.

We were deposited within the complex of the hospital, the oldest civilian hospital in Latvia, founded in 1803 as a hospital for the poor. In 1984 it looked positively scary, a large assembly of yellow-gray brick buildings, dusty paths, elusive staff, and patients in saggy pajamas. I was scared, my legs still moist, my heart racing. I had no idea what I was in for. The fact that my mother was so far away, and that my husband would not be permitted to stay with me, heightened my sense of dread and loneliness. To give birth was still a mystery to me; it was uncharted territory. I felt unprepared for what lay ahead.

So young and nervous as first-time parents, we walked up to a black iron door with a small, shuttered window, and Andris pressed the red doorbell. There was a sign next to the door that said "Pregnant Women Only" or something like that. The window popped open, revealing a pair of beady eyes. *"Chto vy hotite?"* ("What do you want?"): a sharp, annoyed voice barked through the crack. "My wife's water broke!" my husband replied, the anger in his voice rising quickly. Clink, clank! The heavy door swung open like the gates to hell, and I was ushered inside. The attendant immediately told Andris that he would have to leave after I undressed. No men allowed.

I was ordered into a curtained cubicle, told to take off my clothes, and handed a used (!) shaver with which to denude my private parts of pubic hair in the nearby grimy shower, which had only cold water. Andris bundled up my clothes, planted a kiss on my forehead, wished me good luck, and left. And there I remained, a stranger in an alien, cold setting, naked, vulnerable, my heart pounding, my belly pulsating. Another attendant gave me a thin cotton robe to put on. My vital signs were registered, and then I was ushered into a large room with high windows and row upon row of maternity beds. I was the only woman there.

I lay down in the clearly old, uncomfortable iron bed, feeling its coils sagging, and wondered what would happen next. The bed looked like an antique. At least the sheets were clean. I hardly knew what to expect. My doctor had never coached me, nor had I asked any questions. As dusk fell, I felt terribly alone, like the only human woman in the universe about to go through what is one of the most agonizing physical experiences imaginable. Anyone's presence would have comforted me, yet nobody came to see me for what seemed like hours. As I lay there, I thought about my mother and grandmother, about what was to come, and watched daylight on the wall fade. It felt good to cry. But my body had its own plans. It was shifting into another gear to work its magical ways, gently extinguishing my thoughts.

Dull overhead lights came on, as my labor commenced. Slowly at first but building gradually, waves of pain washed over me, pushing me into a state of hazy semi-consciousness. At one point a nurse came in, jabbed a large needle into my taut thigh muscle "to speed up the delivery," and vanished. Apparently most of my amniotic fluid was gone. The baby had to come out soon. By this time in early evening several other women had been admitted. I barely took notice of their arrival. At one point I realized we were all moaning together in our worn-out, sweat-soaked beds. Someone cursed. Another woman whimpered and then screamed. I clung to the image of my mother like an icon. My baby was pushing against muscle, against a wall in darkness. I grabbed onto the iron bars of the headboard for relief, moaning, twisting, and turning. Pain had enveloped all of us, women from different backgrounds, dragging us into another realm.

It might have been around 23:00 (11 o'clock), when Dr. A. arrived to examine me. "Not yet," she said and left. My lonely agony continued. By this time I was only vaguely *there*. Intense, sharp pain dulls the senses. *Mammiṇa, mammiṇa*—I whispered. New life seemed to be tearing me apart. Yet just beyond the confines of my body an aura of wonder and deep joy was glimmering. I struggled to contain my noisy agony, hoping to see a light—my baby—at the end of the tunnel soon.

It is past midnight. Dr. A. appears in her white uniform like an angel, gently prodding me to get up and out of my bed. I gratefully rise and follow her, limping into the delivery room next door, which is lined with birthing tables. I sense that the end of this torture is near. Someone helps push me up onto the table; my legs are placed into a pair of ice-cold stirrups. I feel cold and clammy. The orders to push begin. "Keep your eyes open!" the doctor yells at me. And I do, looking up at the lights and then down at my belly and the doctor and nurse between my legs. Heave! Ho!

At 1:10 in the morning my body, a pod, expels a beautifully formed seed, as all pain subsides. The sound of an infant's first cries in the world resounds, piercing the quiet of the room. The doctor and the nurse sound relieved, but I am crying and laughing and feeling an incredible sense of release, freedom, and weightlessness.

A baby—a boy—is handed to me. My son! A set of enormous blue eyes interlock with mine. A tiny human being, my very own flesh and blood! Precious life! I hold my baby and kiss him and look at him intently, absorbing his features, and then the nurse wraps him up and takes him away "for observation." The doctor hovers nearby, waiting for my body to expel the afterbirth. I am cleaned up and ushered through a dim corridor into a dark room with two beds, where I can finally lie down without pain and rest. The rectangle of the curtainless window admits a soft glow from an outdoor lamp. The shadows of nearby trees move on the darkened walls. But I can't sleep. My whole being is wide awake, alert, and longing to hold the baby. Where is he? When will I see him again? I hope soon. Only towards morning do I finally fall asleep.

Daylight: a new day had dawned. April 14. My birthday! Our son was born on my birthday! What a precious gift! Someone brought me my breakfast: tea and some sort of porridge, actually quite palatable. Another young mother joined me in my room; she had given birth to a daughter. We chatted. She named her baby Elīna, a very popular name in Latvia at the time. Andris and I had decided on a solid, old-fashioned Latvian name for our son—Krišjānis. Preparations were underway to celebrate Krišjānis Barons' 150th anniversary. "The father of the Latvian daina" was someone near and dear to us. I was not a fan of the names that many of my compatriots in Latvia were choosing for their babies, like Elvis or Santa.

Morning turned into afternoon. Still no sign of our baby. I was becoming anxious. I was impatient to see and hold him. I waited for Andris to come, for someone to show up and talk to me and let me know what was going on. The hospital wing seemed deserted. I needed to go to the bathroom. I wanted to take a shower. A nurse pointed down the hallway. Hobbling along with bloody sanitary rags squeezed between my thighs, I found it: a room of such filth and squalor, that it has continued to haunt me in my dreams. The toilet had no seat. Smears of feces in the toilet bowl and on the wall told me that no one cleaned up here, that no one cared. Apparently even the doctors. No toilet paper, just a few ripped pieces of newspaper. The floor looks like it had never been washed. I averted my gaze. No soap to wash one's hands. A horrible stench of human waste invaded my throat, making me gag: the smell of urine, feces, and blood. The shower was even more disgusting, its filthy floor splotched with the slimy clumps of other women's blood clots. I dared not step into it, feeling nauseated by the sight and stench. All this in the ward where new life comes into the world!

"For God's sake, doesn't anyone clean this hospital?!"—my brain screamed, as I returned to my room feeling revolted and very unclean. It was unpleasant to look around. Later I hear Dr. A. complain that it was very hard to find any decent *sanitāri* or orderlies. The pay was low, the work dirty and unpleasant. The orderlies were mostly alcoholics, she said, and as such unfit for this or any type of work. The medical doctors of the workers' paradise had become inured to the filthy conditions in which they worked.

Getting back into bed, I began to worry about what I have just seen and remembered the rumors about staph infections at the hospital. Oh God, please don't expose our baby to such horrors, I shuddered. He is so tiny and so fragile. How could such disgusting conditions be tolerated? How could the doctors tolerate it? Dr. A. worked in these conditions all the time. Her demeanor was steely. No wonder.

Finally, Andris came to visit and tossed me a bag of fruit and pastries through the open window: such was the custom! The day waned. Night fell. I was still recuperating, and I trusted that everything was as it should be. During the night my breasts became engorged with milk. Pain was now a thing of the past; only joy and hope remained.

A day and a half after giving birth, a nurse brought our baby to me. No one had said a word to me since the delivery; nobody has bothered to come and talk to me, not even Dr. A. I was elated taking my newborn child into my arms and putting my lips to his sweet, soft skin. I coddled my little boy and gaze at him; I touched him and pried at the tight swaddling, hoping to see his tiny body. He lay peacefully in my arms, and I nursed him a bit. We snuggled and dozed together. We are together again, mother and child, pod and pea, and all is well in the world. We will be leaving the hospital together in two days, they say.

Leaving First Hospital on April 17, from the left: me (very glad it's all over); Gita; Biruta and Elīna; Andris and Krišjānis. Photo: Juris Krieviņš.

The spring air was still cool in the morning. Krišjānis was bundled up, our papers in order, and we were ready to leave the hospital. My young husband stood proudly holding his son. My in-laws had brought flowers. My father-in-law was there with the car and his camera. I was still a bit shaky and anxious. No one has taught me anything about babies; it was up to me to learn by doing. Still, it was a joyful moment—going home with our first child, our blue-eyed spring *vizbulīte* (Hepatica nobilis)!

We owed the hospital nothing. Nor do we officially, technically owe our doctor and the nurses anything but gratitude. Our child had been delivered by their practiced hands into the Soviet state's embrace, and the state had paid for the service. However, the Latvians have a great proverb: *Ko lēti pērk, tas dārgi maksā* ("What you buy cheap will cost you dearly"). I didn't take anything for granted. I was happy to leave the dirty, germ-infested facility. Our baby appeared healthy, thanks be to God! I myself was looking forward to a warm bath. I feltl very dirty. Of course, we planned on thanking the obstetrician personally at a later date, in some nice way. This was the Soviet way. Flowers, money, chocolates, deficit consumer goods, such as good coffee, a cut of lean meat, hard-to-find imports: the doctors' real pay, and these professionals livedcomfortably despite their relatively low wages. Our doctor asked us if my mother, who was planning on visiting in a month, could get her grandson a pair of toddler's boots..

Our son was wrapped up in a bright blue bow—as blue as the spring sky above us. The skylarks were returning from the south to nest. Krišjānis—welcome to your fatherland Latvia! You are a full-fledged Soviet citizen, born to suffer the "rights" and restrictions bestowed upon you by the Union of Soviet Socialist Republics. Already that morning, I was thinking ahead about how to get to Leningrad to register my son's birth and secure him American citizenship. I had no intention of relinquishing my son to the Evil Empire then or ever.

Baby Blues

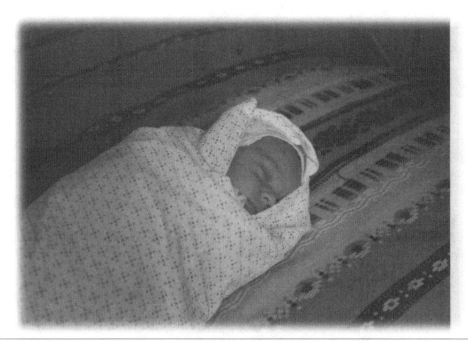

First hour at home: a tightly and expertly swaddled firstborn baby. Photo: Andris Krieviņš.

Our Baltic baby's first hours in his new home in the old town of Rīga... Perfectly formed, with soft, peachy skin, blue sky eyes, and a tiny rosebud mouth, he lay before me in all his naked glory making baby grimaces and soft, gurgling noises. Biruta had left after demonstrating with her expert hands how to swaddle him. As soon as she had closed the door behind her, I had forgotten everything she showed me. I panicked. Andris was at work. The baby peed, and I sat on the divan and wept, because I couldn't remember how to wrap him up. No self-seal diapers in Soviet-occupied Latvia. The gauze diaper and flannel wrapping kept falling off, as the baby flailed his tiny legs. At 24, I felt like a helpless teenage mother.

Pilna Māras istabiņa / Sīku mazu šūpulīšu: / Vienu Māra kustināja, / Visi līdzi līgojās. "Mara's room is filled / With tiny cradles: / When Māra rocked a cradle, / The others rocked along." (Latvian daina)

A young mother's learning curve... I managed to figure out the swaddling technique. Caring for our baby was a new education, and my supplies were limited. There were no infant care supplies in our nearby department store, so I had to do with what I had stocked up on, which was very little. I could not wait to see my mother who would be arriving in May. She was sure to pack something of practical value.

In the distance a train clattered across the Daugava River. I dozed next to my baby who slept in his hundred-year-old cradle hung from a flexible pole, a lovely contraption installed by his father. As the baby moved, the cradle moved, rocking him. My hunger for sleep was enormous and aching. I was always hungry, increasingly exhausted. The nights seemed unbearably long, and breast-feeding had turned into physical agony. My nipples were beginning to crack, and each feeding was like torture. Applications of honey and aloe didn't help. I felt helpless and guilt-ridden. Breast-feeding was sacred, in my mind. And I was failing at it; failing to execute the most basic responsibility of a mother. Guilt piled on top of fatigue. Putting our son up to my swollen breasts made me cringe from the anticipation of the excruciating pain. And yet I went through with it again and again, because I had no one to turn to for advice. I was ashamed. It was turning into a rough experience.

When we brought Krišjānis home from the hospital, I kept saying enthusiastically that he looked like an Indian baby: he was so nice and bronzed. But the pediatrician who came to see him explained that he had neonatal jaundice, and that we would have to use the *kalna saulīte* ("mountain sun"), a quartz iodine lamp, on him. The phototherapy sessions and exposure to natural sunlight worked, even though they added to my postpartum stress. Indian baby in sun-glasses turned back into a fair-skinned Balt. The lamp also supposedly helped disinfect our living space. (In the Soviet era these valuable lamps were manufactured by a small factory in the town of Madona called "Darba spars"—"Power of Work.")

As soon as I felt strong enough and the temperature outside had climbed, I began my long walks with the baby, happy to breathe in the spring air and expose our cheeks to sunshine, which rarely showed itself in winter in this part of the world. Gita lent me her East European pram, a wonderful vehicle with large, rubberized wheels that glided over Old Rīga's stubborn cobblestones effortlessly, gently rocking my child. It was great for shopping, too, with ample room for bottles of milk, bread, and other purchases. With envy I looked down at the sleeping baby; how I wished I could curl up in there with him and sleep and sleep and sleep. Instead of doing the smart thing and catching up on sleep at home, I forced myself to push the baby around in a stupor.

My first visit with the baby to the nearby children's "polyclinic" was humiliating. The doctor spoke only Russian and continued to speak to me in Russian, even when I told her that I didn't speak Russian. She made no attempt to make arrangements to find a Latvian doctor. I sat in her office listening to a stream of comments and instructions, none of which I understood. Apparently she refused to believe that someone in Latvia did *not, could not* speak Russian. This charade was repeated several times over the next few months, despite my husband's protests. Russian rules here, Comrade Ilmarovna. Get used to it. The callous doctor was not the first Russian to express her disbelief when I said I did not speak Russian.

A month later a pediatrician from Philadelphia, Dr. Zvārgulis, paid a surprise visit. Apparently my mother had told him about us and our baby, and he wanted to see the infant with his own two eyes. What an angel! Gently taking Krišjānis from me, he undressed him and examined his spine and muscles and dangled him upside down like a doll. "Perfect! And don't worry! Babies are resilient!" he said, handing our boy back to me. His visit was a vivid reminder of the life I'd chosen for myself and my child and of the differences in *attitudes.* A Russian doctor who didn't care that a young, inexperienced mother didn't understand a word of what she was saying, and an American doctor (albeit Latvian) who came to see us and examined our son with tenderness and care and discussed our baby and his development with me. Life in Soviet-occupied Latvia was often unnecessarily complicated, thanks to the ridiculous political system.

Hunger and fatigue. Hunger because I was too tired to feed myself properly, and there was little in the fridge to subsist on. My young husband was also inexperienced, too busy to notice, I guess. I took to eating bread, porridge, and cottage cheese. My milk supply was low because I was weak. Because there was no formula to be had in the USSR in 1984, I was forced to supplement the baby's feedings with oatmeal *tume*, its simple but time-consuming recipe spelled out to me by Biruta. Several times a day I prepared it by boiling and straining oatmeal through a small sieve. The gelatinous stuff was rich in nutrients and tasty; combined with warm milk, it was my Latvian baby formula. I poured the *tume* into a glass baby bottle, popped a nipple on, and the baby sucked on it ravenously. I drank liters of hot caraway tea with milk and honey, hoping to improve my milk production. In fact, I did not give myself any breaks, nor did anyone else think of cutting me some slack. In the first month of our baby's life, his mother was turning into a walking zombie.

Our tender feeding times. As I looked at the baby, my eyes closed. The sandman was always hovering nearby, ready to knock me over. I was always afraid that if I fell asleep in the chair, the baby would tumble out of my arms and hit the floor.

No diapers, no steady, dependable stream of running water for me. All day long the empty pipes rattled and whined, taunting me when I turned the faucet. The baby's soiled gauze diapers, swaddling cloths, and other washables sat in a pail until late evening. Washing these items close to midnight was exhausting. Despite my careful rinsing, the gauze became stiffer and acquired a yellowish tinge. Sometimes I boiled these shreds and hung them in our tiny bathroom to dry. Pampers were thousands of miles away, in another country, in another reality.

Apparently my spouse was oblivious to the fact that I needed *more* food, healthier food—fruits, nuts, and vegetables, meat and protein, and a bit of help in the kitchen. We were both young and new at parenting. He was out running around and didn't handle the baby much, although I could see how delighted he was with his son. In my lifetime I would often think about women and their strength to go the extra mile.

Getting out of the house to go for a walk with the baby was an arduous task. The pram was large and cumbersome. First, I had to get it down many flights of stairs, hoping its construction would remain intact after all the bumps and jolts. Then I had to climb back up to get baby Krišjānis and my purse. Usually I headed to Kronvalda Park with its winding paths, old trees, and quiet corners. I liked to stop at a café called Ainava ("Landscape") on the canal to buy a fresh pastry or an ice cream "cocktail." I strolled through the park for a couple of hours, sunning my baby. I noted that Rīga's pretty parks lacked playgrounds. The swing set behind the café was old

and rusted. An old water fountain nearby from the 1930s with whimsical sculptures by Richards Maurs had no water. Where would our little boy romp and frolic when he got older?

Kronvalda Park in Rīga in late April 1984. Photo: Andris Krieviņš.

On my way home I often stopped in a couple of stores to make purchases. Then it was time to get the carriage, the baby, and my purchases, which often include heavy glass containers, up the stairs. Because the door's entry lock was usually broken, I was always nervous about leaving the carriage downstairs, while I labored up the stairs with my precious burden and my purchases. Gita's pram was very attractive. By the time I had hauled everything upstairs, my hands were trembling from the strain. I was quickly losing weight.

Right: My joyful reunion with my mother at Rīga Aiport swarming with chekists. We wrapped our son in the traditional red-white-red Lielvārde belt as a symbol of resistance.

My mother's visit in May did wonders for my spirits. Finally I had someone to talk to, heart to heart. Like all Latvian tourists from the Free World, my mother arrived in Rīga with several enormous suitcases, which her enthusiastic son-in-law carried up the stairs with ease. They were packed with gifts, clothes, and the fresh scent of American stores. Andris sniffed appreciatively. Nestlé's chocolate *Quik*! Peanut butter! Real toothpaste, not like the foul stuff they used in Latvia. A scraper for carrots and potatoes. New shoes for me! Snazzy baby clothes! Soft and cuddly stuffed animals. Hair elastics. Liquid multi-vitamins for the baby. Plastic diaper pants. Dr. Benjamin Spock's book *Baby and Child* Care, which was an invaluable reference for me. But the biggest gift of all was a collapsible stroller, meant to help me get around with greater ease. And a Baby Björn baby carrier. The wonders of capitalism!

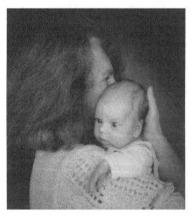

We spent our two short weeks catching up and walking around showing my mother the city she had left as a young girl and of which she remembered very little. She met my relatives from my father's side. In the evenings we sat in our apartment talking by candlelight. My mother was angry that we were being bothered by the KGB; we laughed it off. They tagged after us, even venturing up the other staircase to try to spy on us through the window. It was more amusing than annoying for us. My mother and my father-in-law took these efforts at intimidation more seriously. Juris told us angrily to put a pillow on the phone. We obliged, giggling.

My mother went back to the United States full of mostly happy feelings and interesting stories. I hated to see her go. This was one of the hardest aspects of my choice to live in Latvia: being separated from my family. My parents' involvement in my children's lives remained minimal due to geography.

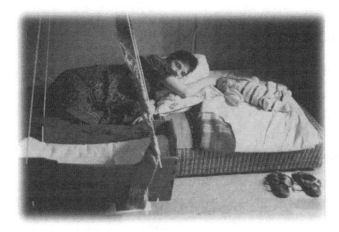

A sleepy baby and his exhausted mother: sleepless nights taking their toll. Photo: Andris Krieviņš.

Nosy Russian babushkas started coming up to me on the street, in the park, and in public transportation to get a better look at the Baby Björn carrier in which Krišjānis snuggled. They blinked, cracked a sly smile, and proceeded to berate me, warning me that the carrier would deform the baby's spine. *Da*, always willing to contribute their "two kopecks" of worthless advice. I hustled away. *Leave me alone!* At other times I got offers to buy the fancy stroller, which looked almost like an alien spaceship in communism-depressed Rīga. Always the offers came from Russian women and in Russian. Not one of these busybodies tried to speak to me in Latvian. "Devushka, devushka..." ("Girl, girl...")

By summer our little boy had plumpened up. His eyes were bright and shining. By July he was kicking his feet, making his cradle bounce. Wisps of hair covered his head like soft fuz. He loved being picked up and sung to. He lay in his little bed looking at the rectangle of light that was our window. The jackdaws on the rooftop congregated and cawed: "Kra! Kra! Kra!" As summer heat found its way into our nest, I found out that I was no longer permitted to go to Piebalga, baby or not. My request to spend the summer there had been rejected.

I was crushed thinking about spending the summer "on the rocks" with our baby. Rīga was a lovely city but also polluted by smelly Ikarus buses, cars, and trucks. Its beautiful buildings were covered in a layer of soot and grime. Our windowsills had to be wiped twice a week. Fresh air! Peace! Quiet! The pond! The lake! The sauna! The woods and rolling hills! Meadows of flowers! All of these simple, healthy pleasures were now forbidden. The KGB was displeased with me? One year ago I could go to Piebalga as often as I pleased.

The summer of 1984 was one of devotion to our baby, cooking and cleaning, walking, bathing, shopping at the market, when possible—napping, and cuddling. We were out a lot, sunning our cheeks, always hunting for something fresh and bringing home summer's flowers to perfume and light up the room. The market became one of my favorite destinations together with my baby: it was there that I gleefully searched for healthy foods, snapping up anything that looked fresh, green, and nutritious. I began making him porridge from rye and wheat flour. By August Krišjānis had tasted wild strawberries, raspberries, red and black currants, blueberries, apples, pears, plums, tomatoes, baby carrots, baby potatoes, peas, as well as fresh meat, minced and mashed into a soft consistency in my Soviet food processor. The meat at the market was so expensive, that I could only afford a tiny piece for the baby. I made him cottage cheese with calcium lactate tablets: dropped into warm milk, the tablet curdled it into soft, tasty clumps. Our boy's cheeks were round and glowing; he was a happy, alert baby.

Still, it was a summer tinged with sadness. I spent a lot of time by myself, when Andris went to Paulēni to help with the chores. I let him go, thinking it selfish not to. Little Elīna was there, lucky girl, spending the summer with her grandmother in the fresh air. I tried hard not to think of beautiful Piebalga, its delightful pond, and the shimmering lake where one could swim and cool down. Rīga felt like a prison. Going out to Jūrmala with the baby seemed like an arduous task: getting the stroller up those horrible steps into the train; the crowds of Russians... I was forced to accept my situation and make the best of it. My sense of loneliness would never truly fade in the years to come. My life as an outsider had only just begun.

I quickly realized how lucky people with extended families were, with parents, siblings, and relatives to rely on for help. My mother-in-law was babysitting her granddaughter and taking care of her garden in the countryside; my father-in-law was busy with his work and helping out at Paulēni. As a transplant, my roots were struggling to adjust to the limits of my new life in Soviet-occupied Latvia. I had been transplanted into a small, tight pot. I was embarrassed to ask for help or companionship from the people I knew; this was a bad trait of mind that deepened my sense of having to deal with many issues and obstacles on my own. In August I was refused permission to travel to Leimaņi in the region of Sēlija in the eastern part of Latvia to be present at the internment of my grandfather Jānis Bičolis' urn. Andris went in my place. Again, I swallowed the bitter pill of exclusion.

The famous stroller in a whimsical drawing I made in the summer of 1984.

Maskačka's Edžus

Old 19th century wooden houses: A typical street view of Maskačka or Moscow Suburb, once known as Lastadia (from the German word "die Last" or cargo).

Was it easy to make friends in Latvia? Despite their hospitality, Latvians were an insular folk. I had already experienced Latvian cliques, a kind of tribalism, in the United States. In communist Latvia people were understandably shy and even reticent. After all, who was I and what did I want in their world? The fact that I was Latvian was apparently secondary. I was a westerner, free to come and go as I chose, or so it appeared. And Americans had the bad reputation of being imperial capitalists: that is, if you believed what the Soviets told you. Some Latvians liked to believe that. Obviously, there was a certain cultural gap between my origins in the Free World and the experiences of my compatriots behind the Iron Curtain. I was quickly doused with ice cold water: the Latvian Art Academy closed its doors to me; the Young Writers' Seminar booted me. Stay away from us. Later motherhood proved to be another isolating factor, especially when we moved to the outskirts of Rīga.

Despite various contacts through my freelance work, I felt quite lonely in Latvia. My husband was often away on assignments, and I spent most of my time on my own with our firstborn. I had no backup, no grandparents who could babysit, and few true friends to lean on. In addition, everyone was very busy. A shy stoic by nature, I did not complain. In fact, I felt I had no right to complain about anything. As a mother I did not have much time left over for myself, for creative pursuits, or for a social life; the struggle between parenting and the urge to create caused me considerable angst for several decades. Ultimately, in Rīga I felt happiest visiting my relatives on Raiņa bulvāris.

One of the nicest people we met in in the early 1980s was a man by the name of Edmunds ("Edžus") Auers. Our friendship would be tragically brief, but our times spent together were unforgettable, like a warm bonfire in the middle of the Siberian tundra in winter. Edžus *was* that crackling fire in the darkness and cold: he was warm and fuzzy and funny. And humor warms the soul. We became fast friends with Edžus in the winter of 1983. He was an electrician by day, a bibliophile by night, and a rare book hunter on the weekends. Like Juris Krieviņš, Edžus frequented the black book market in search of bibliographic treasures.

I don't exactly recall how we met Edžus. I believe Juris introduced him at his studio, and then Edžus invited us over for tea. Our friendship blossomed. A tall fellow with black hair, a black mustache and beard, and friendly, sparkling, onyx black eyes, he made me think of American tall tale hero Paul Bunyan. He lived with his artist wife Silvija, his mother, and a black cat in an old apartment in what most Rigans said was the bad part of town—*Maskačka* or Moscow (now Latgales) Suburb, located on the right side of the Daugava River behind the Central Market.

From what I saw of Maskačka in the last Soviet decade, it looked pretty grim and seedy; its depressed appearance belied its colorful history.

Maskačka dated back to the 14th century or even earlier and was once known as Lastadia, a word derived from the German *die Last,* meaning "cargo." Historically Maskačka was settled by people of different ethnic and religious backgrounds—Russians, Latvian Catholics from Latgale, Lithuanians, Poles, and Jews. The underside of Rīga's society—thieves, crooks, and cheap tavern clientele—also inhabited the old wooden houses along Maskačka's cobblestone streets. In the old days many of these people were not permitted inside Rīga's ramparts. Old Believers persecuted in Russia had settled here, as had Russian barge haulers. Maskačka's street names were derived from Latgale, Latvia's easternmost region, and Russia. The famous Kuznecov porcelain factory had been located here. All in all, Maskačka was kind of a magical place for a storyteller. And it was very photogenic. (1)

Moscow Suburb is unique, because the churches of five different confessions can be found there. The Lutheran *Svētā Jēzus* or Church of St. Jesus, *left* in a photograph from 1875, is a wooden church in the style of classicism. It is the biggest historical wooden building in Latvia. Its foundation stone was laid in 1635. The building was destroyed and rebuilt several times. (2)

The Grebenshchikov Old-Believers' House of Prayer and attached cloister (*right*) on Mazā Krasta iela dates back to 1760. In 1826 the expanded church was named after Russian merchant Alexander P. Grebenshchikov. In the 19th century the Grebenshchikov Old Believers' community of Rīga had a school, library, choir, and club devoted to Russian history. The congregation cared for the old and opened an orphanage in 1900. According to *Cita Rīga*, a website devoted to Rīga's attractions, Rīga's Grebenshchikov congregation is the biggest Old Believers' congregation in the world, with about 25,000 members. (3)

Other notable churches in Moscow Suburb include: (Roman Catholic) *Sv. Franciska katoļu baznīca* (St. Francis Church) on Katoļu (Catholic) iela; (Russian Orthodox) *Vissvētās Dievmātes pasludināšanas baznīca, Svētā Nikolaja Brīnumdara baznīca* (Annunciation of Our Most Holy Lady Church), first mentioned in the 15th century, on Gogoļa iela; (Eastern Orthodox) *Visu svēto pareizticīgo baznīca* (All Saints Church) on Katoļu (Catholic) iela; (Russian Orthodox) *Svētā Jāņa Priekšteča pareizticīgo katedrāle* (St. John the Baptist Orthodox Cathedral) (*above*), on Lielā Kalna iela (its construction was funded by Sidor Kuznecov, owner of Rīga's famous Kuznecov Porcelain and Faience Factory); and the

Great Choral Synagogue on Gogoļa iela, which was burned down in July 1941 by the Nazi Germans. (Image: www.Riga.lv) (4)

Moscow Suburb was also where the Nazi occupation authorities chose to establish Rīga's Jewish ghetto in 1941; its inhabitants were murdered that same year. Afterwards, Jews from Germany and Czechoslovakia were sent to Rīga and filled the ghetto. They, too, were killed. When we visited Edžus, I had no idea he lived in the area that was once part of the former ghetto. The site of the former Old Jewish Cemetery was just a few blocks away.

The war, the German Nazi occupation, and decades of Soviet communism and Russification dramatically decimated and altered Latvia's multicultural community. Rīga's civic society, which had evolved over centuries, was torn to shreds and ethnically "doctored." A myriad of cultures and traditions and historical continuity in Latvia were almost permanently destroyed. And then a new "breed" of people, Homo Sovieticus, poured into Latvia with no regard for its history and society. The disregard for the preservation of cemeteries, the dead, and memory in Latvia was appalling. The Nazis were cold-blooded exterminators, the Soviet communists were barbarians.

By the 1980s Maskačka had morphed into a mostly Slavic area where Latvian was seldom heard. Nearly all traces of Maskačka's Jews and Jewish life were gone. Many of the old wooden houses, so unique to Rīga, looked like they hadn't been touched in decades. People said Maskavas Suburb was crime-ridden; Latvians grumbled about its large Slavic population. Much of Maskačka's architectural legacy was intact but in desperate need of capital investment. So close to downtown, with money this area could have been turned into a yuppie neighborhood. But in the 1980s there were no yuppies or hipsters in Latvia, only young artists with a vision but few resources.

Some of Maskačka's old graveyards had been turned into parks: Miera ("Peace") Park, established in 1908, had once been a cemetery where the city's paupers were buried from 1773–1872. St. Francis Catholic Church is located on the grounds of this park. Klusais ("Quiet") dārzs ("Garden"), called Kiev Park under the Soviets, was created in 1960 on top of All Saints' Cemetery. All Saints' Orthodox Church, designed by first Latvian architect Jānis Baumanis and consecrated in 1891, is located in that park. That same year another park, Komunistisko brigāžu parks ("Communist Brigades' Park"), was created on top of Rīga's Old Jewish Cemetery. (4, 5)

The Old Jewish Cemetery was the very first piece of land that Jews obtained in Rīga. Up until the beginning of the 17th century, Rīga's Jews had to transport their deceased to Poland and later to the Duchy of Courland to the Jewish cemetery near Jelgava. In 1725 Rīga's municipal authorities set aside an area in Kojusala for the creation of a Jewish cemetery. Usually the Jewish funeral processions went up Maskavas iela and then turned into a steep road that lead to the cemetery. Already in the 19th century this road was associated with Jewish funeral processions. At the end of the 19th century this road would officially become known as Žīdu ("Jewish") iela. It is the only street in Rīga to attest to the Jews' long historical presence in Rīga. (...) Twice in 1868 and 1896 the Jewish cemetery was expanded. The entrance to the Old Jewish Cemetery was located on the corner of Līksnas and Žīdu. Several wooden houses were clustered near the entrance, occupied by guards and the Chevra Kadisha burial society. In 1883 an entry gate was erected, but in 1884 a brick wall was put up around the

cemetery; part of that wall still stands. In 1903 a beautiful chapel designed by (Rīga's first) Jewish architect Paul Mandelshtam (1872–1941), *right*, was completed. Until then the design of Jewish cultural buildings (in Latvia) had been in the hands of German architects. (6)

According to *Nekropole.lv*, Paul Mandelshtam, who designed more than 70 buildings in downtown Rīga, was shot near his house in August 1941, because he had stepped onto the sidewalk, which was forbidden to Jews by the Nazis. RL(7)

During World War I the Old Jewish Cemetery became too small. A new Jewish cemetery was created at Šmerlis in the 1920s; the original cemetery became known as Rīga's Old Jewish Cemetery. In the fall of 1941 the Old Jewish Cemetery became part of the Jewish ghetto. On November 29–30, 1941, when most of the ghetto's inhabitants were marched off to Rumbula to be shot, more than 800 Jews were killed in the ghetto itself. An opening was made in the cemetery's wall near Viļānu iela to move the victims out of the ghetto and into an enormous pit in the cemetery. Later more pits were dug to bury the ghetto's resistance fighters and other Jews who succumbed to the inhumane conditions. (8)

After the war Rīga's Old Jewish Cemetery languished: the brick walls crumbled; gravestones were carted away. Finally in 1960 the cemetery was leveled. The Soviet authorities refused to preserve the cemetery as a unique monument, even the wall that showed traces of bullets. Its territory was turned into Communist Brigades' Park (9)

As we disembarked from the tram and hurried up the street toward Edžus and Silvija's apartment building, I always glanced back to see if anyone was trailing us. Edžus with his interest in pre-war Latvian history and literature certainly wasn't the type of person to be looked upon kindly by the KGB. He had devoted his life to old books; their preservation was his mission. Books were his passion, and he handled them like dainty Kuznecov porcelain. I was delighted to discover how well he knew the writers of Latvia's pre-war era. He had a cosy sitting room in his apartment with shelves of books, but he kept his more "incriminating" finds, which dealt with history and the remarkable accomplishments of the First Republic, hidden away. I remember how proud he was to share with me his books by Aleksandrs Grīns and Leonīds Breikšs; both Latvian writers were repressed by the Soviets, as I've already mentioned. Edžus' books from the pre-war era were in excellent shape; their quality was a glaring contrast to most Soviet era books printed on cheap, low-grade paper.

Our visits became a monthly tradition. Each time we visited, Edžus' mother had baked some delicious pastry, which she served with hot tea and black currant jam. Neither she nor Silvija ever participated in our chats, but they certainly made us feel welcome. After tea the interesting talks and merriment commenced. Andris and Edžus shared a great sense of humor and a knack for remembering and telling jokes, and thus we sat in our comfortable chairs for a couple of hours laughing until our sides ached. Edžus knew all sorts of jokes about the failings of communism, the Soviet Union's inept leaders, and the absurdities of Soviet reality. This black humor had a wonderful way of lifting one's spirits in the prevailing gloom and hopelessness of those times. Humor, especially the blackest kind, was like a stress valve. It helped people deal with the headaches of the Soviet economy and daily life and the utopian promises of the Communist Party.

Edžus told his jokes with relish and enjoyed watching us shake with laughter. He chuckled along with delight. The jokes really were very funny and clever. Nobody was spared. There were jokes about Russians, the Politburo, Stalin, Khrushchev, Brezhnev, Andropov, Chernenko, the KGB, important Soviet Russian military figures, Jews, Poles, the French, Americans, Armenians, and so on. There were cruel but hilarious jokes about the Chuchkas, a people similar to the American Eskimos: they were ruthlessly portrayed as backwards nincompoops. World leaders were brought together in absurd situations. I wished there were jokes about Latvians: I felt we needed to laugh about ourselves more.

> Question: How does every Russian (Soviet) joke start?
> Answer: By looking over your shoulder.

> Q: What's meant by an exchange of opinions in the Soviet Communist Party?
> A: It's when I come to a party meeting with my own opinion, and I leave with the party's.

> Q: What is 150 yards long and eats potatoes?
> A: A Moscow queue waiting to buy meat.

> Q: What is communism?
> A: The Poles say it's the longest and most painful road to capitalism.

> Q: What did the Russians (or Latvians) light their houses with before they started using candles?
> A: Electricity.

> (A sampler of Soviet era jokes from Jokes4us.com)

In late summer of 1984 Edžus took a walk with me in the park, gently pushing my son in the stroller. Our usually jolly friend was strangely quiet and withdrawn and had lost weight. Edžus died in late autumn, defeated by cancer. He died much too young. He was laid to rest in the "Ivanovskaya" Russian Cemetery near his house. Perhaps his mother was Russian; unfortunately, I no longer remember. In late November we went to visit his grave; I took note of the plastic flowers near Russian graves, something you never saw in Latvian cemeteries. Russians had an interesting, appealing tradition of going to the cemetery to eat and drink near their loved ones' graves. The tall, leafless trees cast long shadows over the Russian graveyard and the Orthodox crosses. Poor Edžus! And poor us! We really missed him. Latvia had lost another good son. Life was a gift yet could be cruel and unkind. The stress of life in Latvia killed people in various ways.

A joke about Rīga's monuments.

In memory of Edmunds ("Edžus") Auers

Rainis: "Where the hell do they come from?!"

Lenin: "From the East!"

Milda: "Where can we dump them?"

Stučka: "Into the Daugava!"

Photo credits from the top: Jānis Rainis monument—LU Fotoarhīvs (University of Latvia); Lenin Monument—National History Museum of Latvia; Latvian Freedom Monument ("Milda")—Evija Trifanova, LETA; Communist Pēteris Stučka—Google Images.

Chapter sources:

(1) "Maskavas forštate" Wikipedia Retrieved 4/2/2013 <http://lv.wikipedia.org/wiki/Maskavas_for%C5%A1tate>
(2) Ibid 1
(3) "Grebenščikova vecticībnieku lūgšanas nams" Cita Rīga <http://www.citariga.lv/lat/maskavas-forstate/baznicas/grebenscikova-lugsanas-nams>
(4) Ibid 1
(5) "Miera dārzs" Wikipedia <http http://lv.wikipedia.org/wiki/Miera_d%C4%81rzs>
(6) "Vecā Ebreju kapsēta" Cita Rīga Retrieved 4/3/2014 <http://www.citariga.lv/lat/maskavas-forstate/parki/veca-ebreju-kapseta>
(7) "Pauls Mandelštams" Nekropole Retrieved 4/3/2103 <http://nekropole.info/lv/Pauls-Mandelstams>
(8) Ibid 6
(9) Ibid 6

1985–1986 / Squeezed

Late winter 1985: Family growing, space shrinking. Photo: Andris Krieviņš.

By spring of 1985 our son had grown into a healthy, inquisitive toddler, and I was beginning to realize with a mounting sense of urgency, that our living conditions were not suitable for family life. My letters from those early years reflect my growing discomfort, as I struggled to accept our physical confines. Our tiny apartment began to feel almost claustrophobic. I no longer enjoyed the view through our windows. If you looked straight out, all you could see was a wall. There was no privacy for me, no corner to crawl into, out of sight.

What stressed me was the thought that our situation truly could not and would not change. In other words, hope was just a four letter word. The Soviet Union was a command economy, and just about everything was controlled by the state. We "small people" had no say, no leeway, and apparently no real options with our meager income. The limited availability of apartments and modern housing in Rīga and elsewhere was a huge problem in the Soviet era. Like in just about every sector of the Soviet economy, the corrupt system of *blats* ("connections") prevailed. We did not have the resources to build a house (a very remote but theoretically pleasant possibility) or purchase a "cooperative" apartment. My parents in America were not millionaires.

As I have already mentioned, many people were stuck in communal apartments for years waiting "in line" to get a new apartment, their own apartment, and some privacy. Luckily, we were in our own little space. But it was small and getting smaller. Looking at our son, I remembered my own childhood in Glen Ridge with fondness: the large backyard; my own bedroom; lots of space to run around in; trees to climb; a real playground nearby.

Now that I was a parent, I was looking at my surroundings in a different way, with a critical eye. I was sniffing the air, eyeing the streets, wondering how our situation and the environment would affect our child's development. Krišjānis was a very active, inquisitive child who wore me down. His little hands reached for everything; he ran around in circles in the limited space that was ours. We spent a lot of time outdoors in the parks, circling, walking, and feeding the ducks. And I was grasping at the empty air for solutions. I considered the idea of returning to the United States. Then I banished the thought. There was no pot of gold at the end of that rainbow. Surely there was some other solution. But what?

Right: With Gints Grīnbergs, a Latvian American friend, and Krišjānis in his fancy stroller in 1985 in Dome Square.

Cat Stevens once sang: "Where do the children play?" I wondered where the children of Rīga played. Apparently many of them interacted in the gloomy courtyards behind the city's old buildings, sealing friendships or settling scores. This was how many Latvian children learned Russian: by playing with Russian kids. Our apartment building did not have such a courtyard. Old Rīga seemed devoid of children. Sometimes we climbed to the top of Bastejkalns, the hill in the park near Freedom Monument, and Krišjānis made his way down along the rocky ledge, pretending he was an alpinist. At the bottom he wanted to go sit on *zizī* ("horsey"), the lovely 1970 bronze sculpture of a frisky foal by Gaida Grundberga. I knew I shouldn't permit this, but I couldn't resist. Zizī was the only attraction in sight for my little boy other than the ducks. And probably thousands of other little Rigans' butts had straddled the horsey's back, hoping it would whinny and trot away.

We made the best of it, walking up and down park paths, picking up acorns and looking at pigeons. When it snowed, I dressed our boy in a warm snowsuit and pulled him in a sled to Bastejkalns. Almost two years into my life in Rīga, I was growing increasingly frustrated. But I kept my frustration to myself, bottling it. The pressure was mounting. Exhausted by our long walks, we crawled up the staircase to our "nest." I simmered at the injustice and stupidity of the system that was causing Latvia to regress and was shortening people's lives from stress. Playgrounds seemed like such a simple amenity to add to downtown Rīga's lovely parks. The old swing set behind the Central Committee of the Latvian Communist Party looked like it hadn't been fixed in decades. The Soviet Union set aside plenty of money for tanks, missiles, and guns but very little for its children, health care, environmental protection, and other crucial matters.

In 1984 we submitted paperwork to petition the Rīga housing authority for an apartment and then settled down to wait. We hoped my unusual status would work in our favor. After our son was born, my husband realized that our living conditions had to be quickly improved. He crawled up into the attic space above his father's studio and discovered a large area directly beneath the roof: it had the potential to be turned into a loft. He filed another petition requesting studio space there and then decided to remodel our apartment. We hoped that eventually our apartment and the loft space could be connected. The idea was fantastic, pending approval.

Late summer 1984: With my cousin Videmārs, his wife Maija and their firstborn, Oskars, and Andris and Krišjānis on the roof of our apartment building. From this perch it was obvious how dilapidated historic Old Rīga's buildings were.

In June 1985 I was allowed to celebrate the summer solstice at Paulēni; we spent a couple of weeks there to soak up the sun, breathe in the fresh air, and help Biruta. Apparently the KGB was pleased with me (or rather, I hadn't done anything to displease them). It was to be a long summer "on the rocks" in Rīga: Andris was getting ready to remodel our apartment, and arrangements were made with my ever-helpful relatives for Krišjānis and me to stay with them on Raiņa bulvāris, while the work was completed. Also, my father was coming for a visit in July, his first time back in Latvia after a 40 year absence. The city was gearing up for another Latvian song festival, a popular historical tradition, yet one that had been partially ruined by Soviet ideology and communist pomp and circumstance.

The last time my father saw his mother was in September 1944; my father was 15 then. Autumn of '44 broke my father's family into two equal halves. In July 1985 the reunion between my grandmother and her oldest sons, Ilmārs and Visvaldis, was bittersweet. Forty years had passed. Omamma was getting old; I wondered what thoughts went through her head, when she was brought face to face with her long-lost children. As an onlooker I found the encounter very sad. Their separation had been long, almost too long. It had left scars on everyone.

July 1985, from the left: Uncle Andrismy son and I; Omamma; my father Ilmārs; my cousin Videmārs (standing); Uncle Ģirts; and Uncle Jāzeps.

I was stuck that summer in a room at Rīga's First Hospital for about three days with a pain in my side. What an experience! No doctors around, flies on the wall, flies sipping from a pool of blood under a bed in the hallway. On the fifth day I simply walked out, disgusted and outraged that the puddle was still there, that nobody inquired after me, that nobody seemed to care about anything. No one even bothered to follow up to find out where I'd gone. Socialized medicine had hardened many healthcare workers.

While I whiled away my time with our son in the park and at Raiņa bulvāris, feeling more and more like an intruder, Andris tore out the dividing wall that separated our "living room" from our "kitchen." The old ceiling was also torn out, lifted higher, and replaced with new planks. Years of leaking had caused extensive damage. Our pinkish walls were painted white. A green linoleum floor was installed. The old black cupboard was placed in the middle of the open space for a very small measure of privacy. Andris hung his photographs on the walls; yes, the impression was lovely, artistic, and quaint.

Although we had not yet received permission to create a studio space above our apartment, Andris went ahead and installed a window and a skylight in the loft. He was bubbling with hope and enthusiasm, as was I. Sadly, he never got further than installing the windows. In some photographs of the Jauniela building one of the windows is clearly visible. It is all that remains of our dream from that era to build our "nest" upwards. At the end of the summer permission was denied. And now two rooms had become one.

Andris took photographs at that summer's Latvian Song and Dance Festival, which he called *Padomju uzvaras svētki* ("Soviet Victory Fest"). He came home fully disgusted, telling me I hadn't missed anything. The Latvian song festival tradition had been turned into a perverse display of Soviet military might sprinkled with liberal doses of Russian language and culture. Of course, 1985 marked the 40th anniversary of the Soviet Union's annexation of the Baltic States.

A clip from the 1985 Latvian SSR Song and Dance Festival video: Latvian dancers are marching back and forth creating words like "Uzvara" ("Victory") to "celebrate" 40 years of Soviet Russian occupation.

In fact, the 1985 Latvian SSR Song and Dance Festival was more like a Soviet military lovefest, with red communist flags, men in military uniforms, mass dancer formations spelling out words like *Uzvara* ("Victory"), *Darbs* ("Work"), *Miers* ("Peace"), and the number "40" for the number of years Latvia had been squashed by Russian Army boots. A video recording of the 1985 festival* starts out showing Soviet (read Russian) Navy men marching down the steps of the amphitheater through the crowd of Latvian singers. A slogan—"Padomju dziesma dzimtenei lai skan" ("Soviet Song Shall Resound for the Native Land")—is splashed along the top edge of the amphitheater. A Soviet brass band parades onto the stage with more red flags waving. In the video Latvians can be heard singing *in Russian* the Russian song "*Den Pobedy*," which commemorates May 9, 1945 or Victory Day. Unlike Russians, Latvians, Lithuanians, and Estonians would always associate May 9 with the Soviet occupation of their countries.

The *real* Latvian Song and Dance Festival of '85 took place on Folklore Day at the Ethnographic Open-Air Museum, which was dedicated to Latvian folk music, folk traditions, crafts, and, of course, to the 150th birthday of Krišjānis Barons (b. 1835), "Father of the (Latvian) Daina." No Russian military tunes or communist propaganda there! Latvian folk music ensembles from all over Latvia had gathered together in their beautiful traditional folk costumes to sing old Latvian folk songs and perform folk dances. Artisans demonstrated their skills while selling beautiful handmade baskets, wooden toys, wool blankets, linen towels, jewelry, and ceramics, which attracted crowds of happy people. All I could hear was the Latvian language. An old wooden church from 1704, Usmas *baznīca* ("Usma Church"), towered above us like a kindly matron in stately simplicity. Years later my cousin Videmārs would serve as pastor of this church's congregation!

Nestled among pine-covered dunes that seemed to ripple outward from nearby Juglas ezers ("lake") were examples of Latvia's historical rural architecture. These were lovingly preserved beautiful wooden structures: an old tavern; residential houses; granaries; threshing and cattle barns; an old warehouse; a windmill; old beehives; etc. Their windows open to the summer breeze, the warm sunshine, and buzzing bumblebees, the old homes from the various regions of Latvia were outfitted with old tools and implements used in country life —beautiful *sprēslīcas* ("distaffs"), old spoons, *muldas* (troughs), as well as an array of antique furniture. There were simple wooden beds covered in traditional blankets with dutifully hand-stitched pillowcases, antique cradles, old wooden wardrobes, dowry chests with painted flowers and birds, looms and spinning wheels, rickety chairs made from tree roots and quaint hand-carved stools, old clocks with their hands frozen in time, a *vienkocis* (a boat made from a single log), and other household items from the distant past. The beauty of this place was its simplicity and evidence of hard work.

With Krišjānis at the Open-Air Museum in 1985.

These simple, thatched and wood shingle covered buildings and their humble furnishings spoke of my nation's past, of our existence before the 20th century's terrible wars and the foreign occupations that nearly wiped us out. For me, the old tools and home accessories, handwrought and timeworn, were more precious than gold for me; they spoke of the passage of time and of human perseverance. Beautiful perennials bloomed near the old buildings. Bees were gathered honey, as they had since the beginning of time. It was peaceful. Soviet lalaland, its empty rhetoric, blood-stained communist ideology, and the harsh sounds of the Russian language seemed far away...

I walked around with Krišjānis experiencing a sense of joyful relaxation and hope. I would

probably have suffered a nervous breakdown if I had gone to "Soviet Victory Fest." What the communists had done to our song and dance festival was blasphemous. The perverted 1985 festival would be the last of its kind.

A photograph by Jānis Rieksts of the VI Latvian Song Festival in June 1926 in downtown Rīga. Image courtesy of the National Library of Latvia collection "In Search of Lost Latvia."

In 2008 UNESCO added the Baltic song and dance festivals to its "Representative List of the Intangible Cultural Heritage of Humanity." The Latvian Song and Dance Festival has been an integral part of Latvian identity since 1873. Organized once every five years, it brings together Latvian singers and dancers from all around the country and the world. Among the participants are thousands of choirs, dance ensembles, brass bands, and folk music ensembles, not to mention the viewers. It is a wonderful celebration of Latvian culture and a special time, when our nation feels as one.

I credit Latvia's "folklore" movement for helping restore Latvians' pride in their ethnic culture and history. In the 1980s it was the folklore movement in which I felt at home, safe and among my own kind. These people, folks like Dainist† and Helmī Stalts, and their fantastic ensemble Skandinieki, Ojārs Rode and his group of feisty singers, Budēļi ("Mummers"), Ilga Reizniece, and others, were among the many steadfast guardians of Latvian ethnic culture. Latvian folk music resonated deeply with me; it had been part of my musical upbringing in the United States. The gentle sounds of the Latvian kokle and the fiddle playing an old folk tune were like a balm for the soul in a state that touted military might over everything else. Our unique ethnic heritage was endangered and had to be preserved. These people, the pioneers of Latvia's folk movement in the Soviet era, were doing just that.

In late August we christened Krišjānis at Saules baznīca, a small Lutheran church in Mežaparks. In order to accomplish this, Andris also had to be christened. He obliged but stood near the altar like a rigid telephone pole, while our son ran around the church wearing his new American toddler boots making a lot of noise and causing us considerable grief and amusement. One of the Latvian Lutheran Church's young firebrand ministers threatened my poor husband with eternal damnation in hell, if he didn't agree to his own christening. My husband was christened but never truly converted. The pagan fire of spite burned brightly within him.

Autumn arrived. Despite my husband's enormous efforts to make our apartment look nicer, I began to suffer, although I did not realize it at the time. The end result did not add any space whatsoever, which is what we needed most; although it made the apartment look bigger, we had lost more privacy with the removal of the kitchen wall. We purchased a China-red convertible couch at the *Mēbeļu nams* ("Furniture House") store. Unfolded at night, it took up half of

our living space. The old cupboard was all that separated us from my father-in-law's innocent intrusions, which happened several times a day. We still shared our tiny refrigerator with him. Sex and physical intimacy went out the window. Although I did not realize it at the time, the lack of personal space was applying steely, unrelenting pressure on my nerves. In fact, it was sickening me. Until then, I never knew how important personal space was to mental health.

At Siļķes: Kārlis Jansons, seated, his grandson Matiass Jansons who also grew up to be a sculptor, and Krišjānis cuddling with the Jansons' dog. Photo: Andris Krieviņš.

In the fall we took a trip up to Cēsis: Andris was scheduled to photograph the old sculptor Kārlis Jansons (1896–1986) who lived in a lovely old house called "Siļķes" ("Herring") near the Gauja River with his extended family. Going out into the yard and looking around, I was filled with an aching longing for a yard with trees and room to roam and plant. Jansons' house and studio were filled with art and history. A marvelous place! I vividly recall returning to our tiny apartment in Old Rīga and feeling like I was stepping back into a cage.

In 2014 I had the pleasure of reading the memoir of Kārlis Jansons' son Juris who grew up in Siļķes, apparently first mentioned in the 14th century. The house, property, and family came with many wonderful stories and funny anecdotes about people, places, and incidents in the town of Cēsis and elsewhere: an angry swarm of bees trying to get into the house; an Estonian sculptor whose pants were stolen at the seaside; the famous sculptor's rattling, steam-powered contraption that hauled enormous boulders to the house... Juris Jansons' memoir is storytelling at its best: a bit of everything, including side-splitting humor and dark tragedy. The author's paternal grandparents were deported by the Soviet communists in June 1941; only his grandmother returned after Stalin's death.

There was a great possibility that sculptor Kārlis Jansons' brother Artūrs Jansons (b. 1893), a decorated Latvian veteran and recipient of the Order of Lāčplēsis (3/244), had known Eduards Rapss, my great-uncle. They were both involved in the Home Guard in the 1930s; they both shared the same fate. After World War I, Artūrs Jansons wanted to become a farmer. Siļķes was "easy on the eyes and good for the soul but not for the wallet," he had said to his brother Kārlis. Artūrs cut down his part of the woods; his wife Anna chipped in her dowry money, and they bought 80 hectares of land. They developed a successful dairy farm called Peltes near Sigulda and sold their products in Rīga. Their blissful life was short-lived.

Left: Lieutenant Colonel Artūrs Jansons.

When the Russians occupied Latvia and the Cheka began searching for my uncle, he hid in the forest. One winter's eve in 1941 he showed up at Siļķes to get some food and clothing. Our neighbor, that Judas Šics—I don't even know his first name—saw and reported him. My uncle made a fatal mistake, basically. He may have survived until the outbreak of the war, and then the story would have been different.

(The NKVD) arrested him and took him away; he was shot on June 22 near Baltezers. Afterwards, everyone who had lost a relative was invited to come and identify the dead. All of the men who had been shot were Latvian military personnel. Their hands had been bound behind their backs with barbed wire—a classic Cheka touch... Papa recognized his brother, Lieutenant Colonel Artūrs Jansons.

Papa decided to design a memorial for the victims. During the German occupation he made a plaster model. He envisioned a large, monolithic, rough-hewn cross placed on top of a mound, with the burial plots descending from it in a series of terraces (...), with figural groups, people with bound hands—the victims—who had fallen on top of each other... The model is still in the attic of Siļķes.

But who would finance such a large project in wartime, especially in Ostland! It's good he never completed the project: otherwise our family would have been liquidated in 1945 or 1946, at the latest. After the war the Russians ordered the town council to create a new burial site on top of the (mass grave) to conceal the (crime) and erase memory. Somebody was buried on top of Uncle Artūrs. Now you can find memorial plaques there. I worked with Šics at the television studio. When I started talking to him, he confessed. Yet the traitor received his punishment: for several years he suffered terribly from cancer in his Rīga apartment...

What I don't understand is why an experienced, high-ranking military official (like Uncle Artūrs) who had fought against the Bolsheviks didn't choose a better hideout. A lot of the members of the Home Guard, army officers, and policemen vanished into the forests and were able to save themselves. Artūrs hid in the woods near our house. Maybe he was worried about his wife and daughter, what would happen to them, that he could somehow help them? I don't know. Some men offered to help hide him in the forest, but he refused.

I remember how Papa said that when Stalin forced (Latvian President) Ulmanis to accommodate Soviet military bases and the Red Army in Latvia in 1939, Uncle Artūrs said, "Brother, as an officer I can tell you, a foreign army in our country won't lead to anything good!" (2)

Artūrs Jansons was shot along with 112 other Latvian officers on June 22, 1941 at Baltezers, just outside of Rīga. Artūrs and Anna Jansons' dairy farm was destroyed under the Soviets. His wife Anna and daughter Marīte fled the country at the end of the war. They ended up in Canada.

Jelgava. Brīvības piemineklis.

In 1932 a monument by Kārlis Jansons to those who liberated Jelgava from the (Pavel) Bermondt-Avalov Army in 1919 was unveiled near the city's train station. Hewn from Finnish granite, the monument depicted our Latvian hero Lāčplēsis ("Bearslayer") standing over the body of the (German) Black Knight. During the Nazi occupation of Latvia the Germans removed the figure of the Black Knight. Under the Soviets the monument was replaced by a statue of Lenin. Today a replica of Kārlis Jansons' monument made by his son Andrejs Jansons stands in this spot. Image courtesy of the National Library of Latvia collection "In Search of Lost Latvia." (3)

Chapter sources

(1) Juris Jansons (aka A II Pozitīvs) *Jansonu nerrīgie stāsti* 2013: Rīga, Izdevniecība Drukātava. Tr. RL
(2) Ibid 1
(3) National Library of Latvia <http://data.lnb.lv/digitala_biblioteka/atklatnes/Skatu/Latviski/773.htm>

Visual:

(4) ***1985 Latvian SSR Song and Dance Festival**: http://www.youtube.com/watch?v=smCYS3uEzzk
(5) **„День Победы" Russian original**: http://www.youtube.com/watch?v=0QrUZqNt07E

1985: The Red Spot

Mikhail Gorbachev did not have nor could he have had anyone present at that moment (in Rīga) to provide a basic outline of Latvia's history, which is why he said: "And isn't it wonderful that the grandchildren of (Latvian) shepherds and artisans have risen to the level of important scientists, builders of the most complicated radio-electronic devices, agricultural specialists, and outstanding writers and artists." There was nobody there to tell him that the "shepherd and artisan" nation had once risen to those heights, but the totalitarian system, which Gorbachev himself was destined to destroy, had taken all of that away (from Latvia) and would not permit Gorbachev to listen to the people's voice and hear its soul. (1)

USSR General Secretary Mikhail Gorbachev arrives in Rīga in February 1987. Source: National Archives of Latvia

The robotic Leonid Brezhnev (b. 1906), General Secretary of the Communist Party of the Soviet Union for nearly 20 years and the butt of many Soviet jokes at home and abroad, died in November 1982. He was replaced by KGB strongman Yuri Andropov (b. 1914) who died in February 1984, a couple of months before the birth of our son. Andropov's successor, the geriatric Konstantin Chernenko (b. 1911), passed away in March 1985. The new man to rise to to the apex of the Soviet Communist Party was Mikhail Gorbachev (b. 1931), a fellow with a big red spot on his bald head. Compared to his Politburo colleagues, he was a youngster: "He was the only general secretary in the history of the Soviet Union to have been born after the October Revolution." That fact caused some excitement in Latvia. (2)

Comrade Gorbachev's red spot had Latvia's mystics and soothsayers whispering and conjecturing. Wild rumors spread that our own famous oracle Eižens Finks (1885–1958) and even Nostradamus had predicted the rise of a man with a red mark on his head, and in his time great changes would occur... Gorbachev was an unknown, a dark horse in the Kremlin, it seemed. But for us average folks talk of change seemed like more of the "same old same old." We continued to trudge to our meagerly stocked stores with our cloth sacks, hoping things would improve.

By the 1980s the entire country—the massive, seemingly monolithic USSR—appeared to be grinding to a halt; its central economy was stagnating, and shortages of just about everything were widespread. Decades of diverting massive funds to the buildup of the Soviet military, as well as the Soviet Union's laborious, wasteful, inefficient centralized economy, which suffered from a lack of competition and innovation, had taken a toll. Shops were poorly stocked, lines were long, a vibrant private sector virtually non-existent. As the youngest member of the Politburo (which reminded us of an "old boys'" club), where the need to maintain the status quo affected each and every decision, Gorbachev sought to turn things around. He wanted to shake things up by calling for increased productivity, modernization of the Soviet economy, and a more efficient state bureaucracy.

When his calls for change remained unheeded, in 1987 Gorbachev announced the urgent need for deeper reforms. He called for *glasnost* or "openness" and *perestroika* ("restructuring"). In Latvian the word for perestroika was *pārkārtošanās*, and we heard it a lot. The introduction of these two magical words and new Soviet public policies would serve as electrifying triggers in Soviet society while alarming the grumpy fuddy-duddies of the centralized apparatus of the Communist Party in Moscow. While they, the "more equal of the equals," grumbled and fidgeted, listening to their younger colleague Comrade Gorbachev espouse change, outside the walls of the Kremlin on the Soviet Union's westernmost periphery the disgruntled, impatient Baltic peoples would grow increasingly agitated. I believe that nowhere in the Soviet Union did these "triggers" produce more astounding results than in the three Baltic States of Latvia, Estonia, and Lithuania.

With Gorbachev's blessing from Moscow, so to speak, Latvians, Estonians, and Lithuanians of the most progressive Soviet republics, with their historic ties to the West, stirred. They really only needed a very little push to get buzzing, bubbling, and voicing their discontent with nearly everything. The effect of Gorbachev's new policies would be similar to a cautious but unwitting skier triggering an enormous avalanche. Or, Mr. Gorbachev accidently touched the first domino. Or, unknowingly dropping a smoldering match in a parched, dying forest that was the Union of Soviet Socialist Republics.

"Gorby" was a pretty good *muldoņa* ("babbler"), I thought; he was sharper than his predecessors and willing to address some key issues that were affecting the Soviet economy and future development. He had a talent for talking a lot and dropping key words, yet I still suspected that little of that was of real substance, and I doubted that any of his promises would amount to much. His visit to Latvia in 1987 proved that he had no idea where he was or what Latvia was like before the Soviet occupation. Comrade Gorbachev would, of course, remain the best thing that happened to the Baltic States in the Soviet era.

I like to picture Mr. Gorbachev as a "reject" cog that malfunctioned at just the right time and in the right spot, causing the enormous machine, the Soviet Empire, to break down permanently. Decades later Russian President Vladimir Putin angrily rejected Gorbachev's legacy: in 2005 he called the breakup of the Soviet Union "the greatest geopolitical tragedy of the 20th century." (Mr. Putin refrained from asking the Baltic States for their opinion on the matter.)

Would the Balts owe Mikhail Gorbachev gratitude? No, in my opinion the Balts would owe no one in Moscow any thanks for all they had endured under the Soviets: murder; deportation; exodus; the theft and destruction of their national economies and property; the ravaging of a way of life in the Baltic countryside; the lies; the threats and intimidation; the prison state; Russification... In fact, Russia owes Latvia, Lithuania, and Estonia billions of dollars in restitution money for the damage the Soviet Union (read Russia) inflicted on the Baltic States in its 50 year totalitarian rule. Moscow owed and continues to owe the Baltic States *an enormous apology.* I'll eat my shoe the day Moscow and its current leaders apologize to the Baltic States for all the wrongs the Soviet Union inflicted on the Baltic peoples.

According to *New York Times* correspondent Bill Keller, Gorbachev saw the Baltic States as "impatient little children": "Moscow, and Gorbachev in particular, seemed to have a very complicated relationship with the Baltics and with Lithuania. I think there was a part of him that quietly admired the Lithuanians, for their determination and for their culture, but he got extremely impatient with the fact that people in the Baltics rightly wanted their freedom. Sometimes when he would talk about the Baltics, there was a special quality of irritation in his voice— 'why can't these children wait until the time is right.' He wanted to be regarded as a savior by people in the Baltics, and that was not going to happen." (3)

In 1985 few of us read the official Communist Party newspaper *Cīṇa* or paid special attention to General Secretary Gorbachev's speeches on TV, which were long-winded, boring, and lacked substance. I remember attempting to read a translation of one of them and giving up. I disliked pointless babbling. Soviet apparatchiks had a real talent for empty rhetoric. However, Gorbachev's *glasnost* and *perestroika* would stick, like a lethal harpoon in a whale's back.

By the late 1980s people in Latvia were setting up cooperatives, the first step towards establishing a private sector and competing with state-owned and operated manufacturing plants and service providers. By the late 1980s names and events in Latvian history that had been repressed for decades resurfaced, as did the colors of the Latvian national flag. But I'm getting ahead of myself. In 1985 Comrade Gorbachev was just a smooth-talking head with a big red spot on his forehead that excited Latvia's mystics. But I was hoping these mystics were right. The unreal Soviet reality was wearing me down quickly.

Chapter source:

(1) Artūrs Žvinklis "Latvijas valsts Kinofotofonodokumentu arhīva kinohroniku un fotodokumentu kolekcijas: Mihaila Gorbačova vizīte Rīgā 1987. gada 17.-19. februārī" arhivi.lv 4/8/2014 <http://www.arhivi.lv/sitedata/ZUR-NALS/zurnalu_raksti/157-163-FotoArhivs-Gorbacovs.pdf> Tr. RL
(2) "Mikhail Gorbachev" Wikipedia 04/07/2014 ; 04/07/2014 <http://en.wikipedia.org/wiki/Mikhail_Gorbachev>
(3) "The New York Times Reporter Bill Keller: Gorbachev quietly admired Lithuanians but was irritated by them." 15min.lt. August 22, 2012 // 04/13/2014 <http://www.15min.lt/en/article/culture-society/the-new-york-times-re-porter-bill-keller-gorbachev-quietly-admired-lithuanians-but-was-irritated-by-them-528-243260>

1986: Our Rage against the Machine: Chernobyl

The Chernobyl sarcophagus, November 17, 1986. Photo: Latvijas sabiedrība "Černobiļa."

April 26, 1986. A gray spring day in Rīga, Latvia. A day like so many others. Or was it? A few days later on May 3, I penned a frantic letter to my family in the United States. A helpful Latvian Swede mailed it from Stockholm.

Hello! I'm writing from Paulēni. We're going to be here for a while. In August we will go back to Rīga for the opening of Valdis Kupris' art exhibit. As you probably already know, a terrible calamity took place near Kyiv: a nuclear power plant exploded, and now a radioactive cloud is traveling northwest dispersing radioactivity. The cloud allegedly passed over Rīga but NOBODY KNEW, because there were NO WARNINGS. I don't think we have to be too worried; still, the idea that the government is hiding something from us is excruciatingly unpleasant. In fact, it's criminal! Please send us a dosimeter! Send two, if they're not expensive! We don't want to be eating radioactive products! We're hoping nothing is brought in from Ukraine, but there's no shortage of jerks here capable of doing such a thing just to make a couple of roubles. We heard that the radiation level in the Baltic Sea is dangerously high, which would mean an end to all the fisheries. If you know of anyone coming to Latvia, please send us some newspaper articles about the disaster, so that we know what's really going on. I am completely shocked! Somebody screwed up big time.

On April 26, 1986 a powerful explosion at reactor Number Four and the ensuing graphite fire at the Chernobyl Nuclear Power Plant near Pripyat in the Ukrainian SSR shot large quantities of radioactive particles into the Earth's atmosphere. The Level 7 disaster occurred during a botched systems test of the poorly designed nuclear reactor. The blast was so powerful, that it propelled the reactor's 2,000 ton upper plate through the roof of the reactor building. A second explosion dispersed the damaged core. As the radioactive plume spread over a large area of the western rim of the Soviet Union and parts of Europe, including the Scandinavian countries, Moscow kept mum. For several days the Soviet public was kept in the dark, as the Kremlin struggled to assess the situation and implement damage control. I was 26 at the time, our son was two.

News of the ugly, terrifying event seeped out, as radiation levels in the atmosphere set off alarms at the Forsmark Nuclear Power Plant in Sweden. Latvians who were often in tune with the West through relatives living abroad, visiting tourists, and shortwave radio knew quickly that something was amiss. As the rest of the world clamored for an explanation, Moscow was forced to admit that there had been an accident, even as it downplayed the severity of the calamity, which threatened to spin out of control.

As the news spread, the uncertainty of the situation at Chernobyl spawned speculation, rumors, and fear. The absence of real, factual news in a calamity of this nature creates a vacuum that humans feel compelled to fill. Lots of half-truths, hearsay, exaggerations, and even nightmare scenarios were floating around. What food was safe? Did we know where our food came from? Was food coming into Latvia from Ukraine across our porous border with Belarus? If so, were the products contaminated? Who could or would check our products for radiation? Would the Soviet authorities sell contaminated meat and produce to the public? We all suspected the answer was yes; the Balts never believed Moscow. It had lost its credibility prior to Chernobyl.

Had we all been exposed to nuclear fallout? If so, to what degree? Would Latvia's pregnant women give birth to mutants? None of us knew what had really happened, so hard facts were replaced by conjecture, hypotheses, and wild guesses. We ruminated about the size and direction of the radioactive cloud, the possible need to use iodine, the extent of the contamination, a future with cancer, etc. We raged against the machine—the Soviet Politburo, which resembled an evil octopus holding us in its poisonous grip. I cursed the Soviet state and its system of lies ten times a day for trying to cover up the disaster. As a mother, a nuclear disaster was one of my worst fears. The Three Mile Island disaster in the US in 1979 had already spooked me. But this was a lot worse, apparently. The Rīga Central Market was a frequent destination for vendors from other Soviet republics, including Belarus and Ukraine. Now nobody trusted anyone and least of all the omnipotent, highly secretive Soviet government and Communist Party. Its secrecy would prove to be its fallibility.

Worst of all, the people of the city of Pripyat near the reactor were not immediately informed of what had transpired. It didn't take long to realize something was terribly wrong, as dozens of people became violently ill. An evacuation of the city was launched on April 27. Inhabitants were forced to leave with a minimum amount of personal possessions; they were never allowed to return. To this day Pripyat remains an eerie ghost town, the setting for crime novels, horror movies, and creepy video games. The reactor's crew, which made the crucial first mistakes, and first responders died within a few weeks of the disaster. The emergency workers who were involved in the initial mitigation efforts were neither adequately prepared nor properly shielded from the deadly radiation. Eventually about 500,000 people would be involved in various furious efforts to stem the calamity. Over time many of them would succumb to cancer or suffer from debilitating ailments, including post-traumatic stress disorder. (1)

Latvian reservists near Pripyat's Ferris wheel in 1986. Source: Latvijas savienība Černobiļa.

On April 28, 1986, two days after the explosion, a short announcement was read on the Moscow nightly news program "Vremya" at 21:00: "There has been an accident at the Chernobyl Nuclear Power Plant. One of the nuclear reactors was damaged. The effects of the accident are being remedied. Assistance has been provided for any affected people. An investigative committee has been established." (2)

Great. That told us a lot. To live in a state of *not knowing the facts* was truly frightening. I knew that somebody knew something but wasn't saying what it was. For the Soviet Communist Party, it was absolutely essential to preserve the veneer that hid the rotted wood beneath. The Soviet Union was essentially one big Potemkin village, where many things were not what they seemed.

What really happened at Chernobyl would remain unclear for many years to come to many people, including scientists and physicians. After Latvia's independence, Chernobyl and other Soviet era disasters and unpleasantries quickly faded from memory. Nobody wanted to remember them or the victims. Yet thousands of men from Latvia and other parts of the Soviet Union, heroes all, died or continue to suffer from the long-term effects of being sent to Chernobyl to contain the disaster, which could have spun completely out of control. According to Marina Kosteņecka (b. 1945), a Russian Latvian journalist, in the days following the blast about 6,000 men (reservists and others) were recruited from Latvia as "liquidators" to deal with the clean-up work at Chernobyl. Her account, one of the rare stories to emerge from Latvia about Chernobyl, is worth recalling.

"The trip to Chernobyl was not an excursion for me. Women were not invited to go there. But I bumped into (writer) Uldis Bērziņš at the bus stop, and he had volunteered to go. He was the only (Latvian writer) to volunteer. And then I knew that it was also important for me to go." This is how writer Marina Kosteņecka recalls autumn of 1986, sixth months after the Chernobyl catastrophe. (Photo: Uldis Bērziņš and Marina Kosteņecka in the tent city near Chernobyl in 1986. Source: www.Latvijas ļaudis.lv.)

Marina Kosteņecka:

> On the back of a photograph you can see the autographs of the first three helicopter pilots who were ordered to fly up above the reactor to take photographs to provide first responders and, most importantly, the Soviet Politburo with a better picture of what had happened. Gorbachev saw this photograph in the first hours of the disaster but subsequently claimed that he knew nothing about its magnitude...
>
> How did I obtain this photograph? After a feature on Chernobyl in which I spoke to Dr. Andris Jungs, I received a telephone call from a radio listener who said she was a nuclear physicist. She ended up working in Chernobyl for four years after the disaster. After our conversation, we met several times both on the air and in my office. Her name was Lidiya Zhuravlova. She had graduated from the University of Latvia as a nuclear physicist in 1963 and then worked for 22 years at the Soviet nuclear physics research center in Dubna, a city near Moscow. When Chernobyl exploded, she was "forced to volunteer" and relocate to Chernobyl to work. She complied.
>
> Lidiya showed me many unique documents, which revealed how the truth about the magnitude of the disaster was concealed. But this photograph remains the most precious souvenir that she gave me. When the reactor exploded, reservists were called up all from over the Soviet Union to liquidate the disaster's aftermath. Three regiments and several battalions of reservists were drawn up from the

Baltic Military District (...), which included Latvia, Lithuania, Estonia, and Kaliningrad. Latvia constituted a separate regiment.

About 6,000 liquidators from Latvia passed through the hell of Chernobyl. Right now about 50% or 3000 men are disabled; 600 are partly incapacitated; but 500 of these or every 12th man are no longer among the living. Conscripts were between 20 and 35 years old. The oldest of them is now nearing the age of 50. Many of the men received their summonses at work. I have heard many different stories about that, like about the doctor beginning his rounds at the hospital who was whisked away from his job to the recruitment center. Mobilization commenced on May 8; by May 12 a separate regiment had been created. "Our" regiment, the so-called tent city, was about 30 kilometers from the reactor. These men were involved in the dirty clean-up work called deactivation. Even on the third day after the accident, on April 29, Soviet television was claiming that there was no destruction, no victims, and no radiation. But an hour after the accident a helicopter had been dispatched from Kyiv; it flew over the reactor and took photographs, and these photographs were sent to the Politburo (...).Everyone knew what had happened. Gorbachev should stop telling his fairytales. We were told that everything was fine, and a song called "Chernobyl, the entire country stands by you!" was broadcast on the radio.

It's the beginning of October (1986—RL). I am standing near the Matīsa tirgus ("market") trolleybus stop at 11:00 in the evening, when suddenly I see poet Uldis Bērziņš approaching me. It was a Saturday. And he suddenly says to me, "Marīna, would you like to fly to Chernobyl with me on Monday?" And I'm thinking to myself—either I'm drunk or he's drunk... But then Uldis starts telling me that the reservists in the Estonian regiment have rebelled. The Estonians have always been radical. But when they were called up for duty, they were assured that they would be in Chernobyl for a maximum of two months. Five months had passed, and no one had replaced them. They were cynically told, "You guys are already ruined; we're not going to ruin any new guys; you can't have kids anyway;" and so on. The Estonians rebelled; they beat up their commanders, lined up, and set off for the train station.

But what was happening at the Latvian regiment? A soldier had just hanged himself. A couple of days later a doctor committed suicide. They found a note in his shirt pocket. He had understood the effects of the radiation on his health and how painful his death would be. (The Latvian Communist Party) Central Committee sounded the alarm after these two deaths. It was time to boost morale; otherwise, we could expect a spate of suicides. It was fall, the season of depression. They ordered the Writers' Union to put together a collection of books by Latvia's most popular writers and have them autographed; the union was also told to organize a delegation of three Latvian writers to visit the Latvian regiment to let them know that "Chernobyl, the entire country stands by you!" Volunteers. Everyone signed the books, but only Uldis Bērziņš took that extra big step. Andris Sproģis, editor of Literatūra un Māksla (...), offered to go, too. He was forced pa partijas līniju ("according to Party guidelines"). They failed to find a third volunteer, but the flight was scheduled for the upcoming Monday.

And so Bērziņš bumps into Kosteņecka at the trolleybus stop (although women were not invited to go). Back then I was a popular writer, and I realized that if a woman showed up in that bog, that would help boost the soldiers' morale. Bērziņš said to me: "I have two children, I don't need anymore." And I said, "I don't have any and won't." Although I got a bad grade in physics, I had an inkling of what lay ahead. We did not believe the radio broadcasts, but what we did know was that these men were saving the planet. (...) I knew exactly where I was going. It would not be an excursion. I would be there for three days. There were about a thousand men in that regiment.

(Later in Ukraine) in the evening, as we were drinking tea, I asked, "I suppose I'm the only woman here?" And they replied, "No, there are two. There is a female dog here, too." I felt so proud! There we were, two ladies, and they were treating us as if we were the last two bearers of life on the planet. We slept in the medical sanitary battalion, and it was cold; it was fall. The little stove burned all night long, and the soldier on duty came by every now and then to add firewood. Of course, I couldn't sleep, I was agitated. We were sleeping in our coats covered with some sort of flannel blankets. In the morning when it was very cold, I saw the orderly take off his coat and put it over me. At that moment I felt like (Countess) Natasha Rostova (from Leo Tolstoy's War and Peace—RL). Never in my life had I felt more like a woman as in that tent. (...)

Of course, I needed to see everything, not just the regiment. The authorities were not forthcoming, until I made the point that I had already been irradiated in the 30 kilometer zone. What moral right did I have to write about any of it, if I didn't see the actual site of the disaster? We climbed into a "bobik" (a Soviet Jeep-type vehicle—RL) and were ordered to duck behind the seats each time we neared one of checkpoints leading up to the power plant. Our vehicle had a general access permit. And thus ducking every 100 meters or so, we drove right up to the Chernobyl AES.

I knew that volunteers from our regiment as well as from other regiments were brought in to pick up and toss the melted pieces of graphite off the roof of Block (Reactor) Three. There were six volunteers from our medical unit, all with Russian surnames. They are no longer among the living. After that no more volunteers; everyone had to go whether they wanted to or not. That same day (those guys) were brought down from the roof vomiting like crazy. They were sent to the hospital in Kyiv; a day later they were sent back to the regiment with orders to be demobilized and sent home. Who would save them in Latvia and how, nobody knew. Kyiv was inundated with victims.

We then drove to Pripyat. A city in the moonlight. Not a single light. Not a single streetlight. Only uncut grass, two meters high. The city was cordoned off with an electric barbed wire fence to ward away burglars. Of course, they had descended upon the town in droves, but that's another story. Suddenly I heard a cat meowing. My first reaction was to reach for it, pick it up, and bring it home. But the colonel slapped my hand: that's forbidden! It means death! The female dog I mentioned: she too walked around, radioactive. But no one could pull the trigger. These small incidents speak volumes.

If the IAEA is now claiming that Chernobyl wasn't that dangerous, then they are delusional. In Latvia alone: there are 3000 disabled and 500 young men in the grave. They were all liquidators. The IAEA has to sanitize nuclear energy, to lull Europe and the world into thinking it's safe. Nuclear energy is cheaper, there's an energy crisis on hand, and it's necessary to forget about Chernobyl. I remember... how when we returned, they washed and washed the tires of our car with laundry detergent. But where did the water run off? Into a ditch lined with plastic. And down the ditch into the well. Those stations were a joke!

When the regiment returned to Latvia, they were ordered to take everything with them. Every last syringe. Nothing was allowed to remain in Chernobyl. All that stuff was disposed of in Baldone in cement-lined pits. All the vehicles went back to Latvia and were placed in a hangar. One day later the hangar was emitting high doses of radiation. The vehicles' technical papers were changed, and the vehicles were distributed to kolhozes. A few years later a tractor driver who had never been to Chernobyl died. From what? Why? Well, that was criminal. My article was sanitized by Glavlit (the Soviet censors' office) and the military censors. I was not permitted to say everything I wanted to. For example, why I went to Chernobyl. They just wanted the word "heroic" repeated. I am somewhat ashamed to read that piece today. Still, it was important to say between the lines that not everything the official press told us was right Only later in the glasnost era did the truth spill out. In 1989–1990 I served on the Saeima (parliament) Committee for Veterans and the Disabled. We drafted a law on the Chernobyl men. (...)

The (Soviet) state tried to cover up the extent of the tragedy by all means possible. Back then in 1989–1990, right after Chernobyl, a lot of measures could have been taken. The world offered its help; the world was prepared to do something, not only out of compassion but for selfish reasons too, to protect itself, to build the sarcophagus as quickly as possible. But our people convinced them to back off by saying nothing terrible happened, that we didn't need anything; we could take care of it ourselves. I remember how the Soviet Union almost refused to admit an American doctor who later did bone marrow transplants on firefighters. But then the USSR ran out of money. I often meet with the veterans of Chernobyl. They say, "Let bygones be bygones. We won't get our health back. We just want people to know what happened and tell us quietly 'Thank you.'" (3)

Some young reservists like Mārtiņš G. went into hiding after the disaster; he was relentlessly pursued and eventually caught in Liepāja by the Soviet Latvian *Kara komisariāts* (Soviet Military Registration and Enlistment Office).

Mārtiņš: "In the 'Russian times' men had to serve (in the Soviet military) for two years. After completing military service you were considered a reservist and you could be called up for active duty at any time, let's say for a month, to attend additional military training. The Soviet military took advantage of this rule to dispatch reservists to do the work that nobody else in the Soviet Union wanted to do. For example, you could spend three months harvesting (wheat) in the Russian steppes. Nobody volunteered to go to Chernobyl, which is why this 'mechanism' was engaged. If you refused to attend this additional training, called *sbory* in Russian, then you were criminally liable, which is why it was very important to avoid receiving the actual summons. Once you signed the summons paper, then there were only two options—*sbory*, which could mean Chernobyl or something equally horrible, or prison time, which nobody considered a viable option."

Ultimately, Mārtiņš was one of the lucky ones. In the end no one sent him to Chernobyl, even though he sat around all day drinking and waiting for the phone call that never came. In his blog about his frightening 1986 cat and mouse adventure he quotes Jimi Hendrix: "I'm goin' way down south / Way down where I can be free / Ain't no one gonna find me / Ain't no hangman gonna / He ain't gonna put a rope around me..." In the case of Chernobyl, the *Kara komisariāts* put a rope around thousands of young men's necks.

My husband's cousin Viesturs Lorencis, born in 1960 like me, was one such unlucky fellow. He was sent to Chernobyl in 1986 to take part in the clean-up work. We laid him to rest in May of 1990 in a beautiful cemetery in the village of Aumeisteri. According to his mother, Viesturs lost all strength and faded away. He was 26 years old when he was deployed, 30 when he died.

The grave of Viesturs Lorencis, one of the victims of the Chernobyl clean-up efforts. He died in 1990 at the age of 30. Photo: Andris Krieviņš.

Chernobyl exposed the cruel nature of the Soviet regime, in which the individual (in the case of Chernobyl a healthy young man) was regarded as a tool, nut, bolt, or cogwheel in the empire's machine, with no say in his fate. A very Stalinist approach. When Anne Applebaum writes sbout the economic reasoning behind the Soviet Gulag system, one can easily substitute certain words to describe the Soviet state's approach to the nuclear disaster in Chernobyl:

> Within the Gulag (*or Soviet*) system, prisoners (*or reservists*) were treated as cattle, or rather as lumps of iron ore. Guards (*or Soviet Army officials*) shuttled them around at will, loading and unloading them into cattle (*or Chernobyl-bound train*) cars, weighing and measuring them. (...) They were, to use Marxist language, exploited, reified, and commodified. Unless they were productive, their lives were useless to their masters." (4)

The Soviet state's lack of transparency, its unwillingness to divulge the severity of the Chernobyl disaster and share critical information, and its callous disregard for human safety and life remain among the greatest tragedies of Chernobyl. Instead of alerting its citizens to what had transpired and warning them to take precautions, the Soviet Politburo remained virtually mum about the situation. People in nearby Kyiv marched in the May Day parade, exposing themselves to radiation. Chernobyl and the Soviet Union's war in Afghanistan (1979–1989) would take an additional toll on Latvia's manpower, already tragically diminished in World War II.

Latvia's veterans of Chernobyl eventually formed an NGO called *Latvijas savienība "Černobiļa"* ("Latvian Union Chernobyl") to raise awareness about their experiences and their unique problems in the aftermath of the disaster. Soviet Army reserve officer 1st Lieutenant Gunārs Opmanis, a WMD (Weapons of Mass Destruction) expert, was sent to Chernobyl in May 1986 and has written a book about his experience, yet to be translated into a more widely accessible language.

Gunārs Opmanis, born in 1943, was involved in and is knowledgeable about the Soviet military's chemical industry and dosimetry. Opmanis was called up from the reserve and sent to the

Suži 257th Civilian Defense Regiment on May 8, 1986 (about a week and a half after the explosion). He recalls first being alerted to the gravity of the disaster, as he was riding on the train towards Kyiv. "During the night of May 11 a train hauling cisterns full of gasoline passed us headed northwest: its radioactive contamination was 50 mR/h or 0.5 mSv/h."

Opmanis and his men were stationed in a field camp about 1.5 km to the northwest of a village called Buda-Varovychi, 38 kilometers directly to the west of Chernobyl AES Reactor #4 and Prypyat. "I served in a chemical-radiological company. We were there to map radioactive contamination and levels of radioactivity and conduct decontamination and radiation control experiments. We provided dosimetry services within the camp and in its surroundings. On May 15 we dispatched our first shift to Dibrova's 30 km zone control point to decontaminate transport vehicles.

"When I was there (in Chernobyl), only volunteers were working at the reactor. They were drivers. The (reactor's) territory was littered with debris from the exploded reactor, all very dangerous. They were trying to haul it away. There our guys wore special rubberized, hermetically sealed protective gear, which provided minimal protection (up to 50 Sv/h). The work was physically grueling and very dangerous in an environment with fluctuating, often high levels of radiation.

"The rest of the men wore their regular field uniforms and respirators. Nobody wore any special protective gear (...); they did wear very primitive respirators. The rest of our regiment worked in Sector 3, as well as at the control point in Dibrova, which is about 100 kilometers to the west of Prypyat. The officers and some warrant officers worked like slaves—for unlimited periods of time. They got no time off. It was very hot during the day; 30 degrees Celsius (86 degrees Fahrenheit) was the average, and I remember it went up to 39 (102° F) with no wind. That was horrible. The camp conditions were alright—a sauna, clean water, and food."

When I asked Opmanis how many men from Latvia were deployed to Chernobyl, he replied, "I don't have a precise number. I have registered the men from our regiment, the ones we know about, but some names are missing, because they had died before the register was set up, as in your case (Viesturs Lorencis), or had left Latvia. The number of reservists was about 5,200. But there were soldiers who were already serving, officers, and warrant officers. That brings the number to over 6,000."

"There were 29 men in my company. By 2006 five of them had died. How many men from the regiment have died by now, I can't say. The register was only set up in 1994, which is why two of our fatalities who passed away in 1988 were not even included. What is clear is that just about everyone on the register is severely disabled. Most of the men from the chemical company who were the first to start washing down vehicles in Dibrovo, which constituted the 30 km zone, have died.

"Nobody told us anything about the situation. (Our superiors) appealed to our honor, sense of duty, and our political bearing. The various inspectors were the worst: they had something to prove; they criticized and cursed us. Higher level superiors were more supportive. Sadly, later they informed us that we would have to be there for another half year. So we assumed they had been lying to us all along. A lot of men started protesting.

"After a few weeks our eyes became infected from radioactive contaminants. Later we started experiencing problems with our digestive system. In late June many of us started experiencing neurological disorders, problems with coordination of movements. Our central nervous systems were being attacked. All of this is typical of the effects of radiation on the human body. Our white blood cell counts were checked; they were much lower than before. Despite this, most of us were still able to work."

In his e-mail from June 2013, Gunārs Opmanis wrote that about 90% of Latvia's surviving Chernobyl veterans were disabled. Most of them suffered from diseases of the central nervous system, problems with immunity, and joint problems. "I have about ten different physical ailments, all of them related to the first stages of oncological disease. I hope to make it to 2016 to celebrate my 50th wedding anniversary and maybe to mark 30 years since Chernobyl with the publication of my memoir in three languages. But I doubt that I'll make it."

When I asked Opmanis how he felt about the Soviet government's response to the disaster, he wrote: "At any rate it was a crime against the Soviet Union's population and the inhabitants of Earth. The Soviet leaders did not receive precise information right away, and then it was too late. In an ideal situation in which everything was known, would they have been motivated enough to evacuate a million people, cease all industrial and agricultural production, and disrupt transportation? The real situation kept changing, becoming worse and worse. Even the Japanese (to whom we sent our recommendations) couldn't deal with the situation (at Fukushima) properly because of financial issues." Latvian Army Major Gunārs Opmanis, Retired, is still alive today (4/11/2014). He has four children.

Questionable technology, professional mistakes, and a lethargic government response in the case of Chernobyl made the Soviet Union look really bad. Everyone was boiling mad. According to the World Nuclear Organization, "the Chernobyl accident in 1986 was the result of a flawed reactor design that was operated with inadequately trained personnel. (...) It was a direct consequence of Cold War isolation and the resulting lack of any safety culture." (5)

The accident triggered permanent fears over nuclear safety. After Chernobyl Latvians became jittery about Ignalina, the nuclear power station in nearby Lithuania, which was of the same design as the flawed Chernobyl reactor. Ignalina was shut down in 2009 due to safety concerns.

Areas most affected by the radioactive fallout were Ukraine, Belarus, and western Russia. The exact number of victims directly linked to the disaster is impossible to calculate. Despite the initial and appalling incredulity of Western experts, the presumption that the high incidence of thyroid cancer among children in the areas of Belarus closest to Chernobyl is gaining ground and support. Even today parts of Europe, especially Germany, are dealing with contamination in the form of radioactive wild boar and mushrooms. The most contaminated areas resulted in mutant animals and insects, children born with terrible deformities, and a high incidence of cancer. The ruptured reactor's toxic plume spewed radioactive contaminants across large swathes of Europe.

Because of Chernobyl, I came to believe that Soviet cover-ups were rampant. Later when I was back in the US, the tragedy of the Kursk nuclear submarine in the summer of 2000 reminded me of Chernobyl and the Moscow cover-up. The men on the Kursk died apparently needlessly.

Chernobyl was the worst of all of my worries and concerns in the 1980s. Yet other "little" horror stories floated around: untreated wastewater from the Sloka paper factory flowing into the Gulf of Rīga; laundry detergent added to milk at dairy farms as a preservative; bovine leukemia; rat infestations and rat-borne diseases; staph epidemics at the hospitals; toxic air and ground pollution from the Olaine pharmaceutical plant and other factories and military installations; salmonella outbreaks... For a long time most of these stories were not official news items; they were rumors that instilled me with worry.

Chernobyl, the world's worst nuclear reactor disaster, helped expand Mikhail Gorbachev's policy of government transparency, *glasnost*. Ecology and the environment became one of Latvia's central issues in public calls for change. The presence of the top-secret Soviet "military-industrial complex" in Latvia made many Latvians nervous about what went on within it.

Today numerous excellent documentary films provide a harrowing depiction of the tragic events that unfolded in April 1986 in Soviet Ukraine. For me, Chernobyl underscored the need for government transparency, accountability, and checks and balances, as well as the importance of a free and independent press.

Freedom. Freedom of speech. The right to uncensored information about matters affecting public health and safety. Living in that dark barrel of ignorance was frightening, to say the least. If anything, Chernobyl heightened our "rage against the machine"—the communist bureaucrats in Moscow's Kremlin. It was a machine that wanted to control everything, everybody, our thoughts, our movements, our lives, and even our deaths. And hide the truth from us. Power corrupts; unchecked power breeds a sense of inviolability. But a state that covers up its rot is doomed to fail, ultimately.

Chapter sources:

(1)   IAEA Staff Reporters "Chernobyl's 700,000 'Liquidators' Struggle with Psychological and Social Consequences IAEA August 2005 <http://www.iaea.org/newscenter/features/chernobyl-15/liquidators.shtml>
(2)   "Chernobyl Disaster" Wikipedia Updated 04/08/2014 ; retrieved 04/03/2013 http://en.wikipedia.org/wiki/Chernobyl_disaster
(3)   "Černobiļa—tas jāzin katram!" Notepad.lv 4/9/2013 <http://www.notepad.lv/cernobila-tas-jazin-katram-t4269.html> Tr. RL
(4)   Ibid 2
(5)   Anne Applebaum. *Gulag: A History.* 2003: Anchor Books, New York. Introduction, xxxix)
(6)   "Chernobyl Accident 1986" World Nuclear Association Updated April 2014 <http://www.world-nuclear.org/info/Safety-and-Security/Safety-of-Plants/Chernobyl-Accident/#.Ua9wodfD_3g>
(7)   "FOTO: Rīgā atklāts piemineklis Afganistānā kritušajiem Latvijas dēliem" LETA 04/12/2014 ; 04/14/2012 <http://www.diena.lv/latvija/zinas/foto-riga-atklats-piemineklis-afganistanas-kara-kritusajiem-latvijas-deliem-14052058>

Is It Easy to be Young?
Latvian Youth Behind the Iron Curtain

In 1986 a documentary film called *Vai viegli būt jaunam?* ("Is It Easy to be Young?"), directed by Juris Podnieks (1950–1992), made its debut; it quickly became hugely popular in and outside of Latvia. We went to the Rīga Film Studio to see it in a special preview. Podnieks was there to introduce it. I cried when I first saw it; I cried watching it again in 2013. Podnieks' delicate, gently probing questions addressed to various Latvian teenagers tugged at the veil of lies, a veil that the movie's main characters, teenagers in the early 1980s, had grown up entangled in. This veil was the promise of a bright future in communism, which by then had lost all meaning and validity. Podnieks circumvented politically touchy subjects; his teenage subjects groped for words. The youth that Podnieks filmed was the youth I could have belonged to but didn't because of fate. Despite our differences, we shared some of the same questions and uncertainties.

Kids like us when we were teenagers. We American-born Latvian kids rocked to the Rolling Stones' "Brown Sugar" and "Taking Care of Business" by Bachman Turner Overdrive. "I'll be takin' care of business every day! Takin' care of business every way!" Girls clung to boys and boys clung to girls swaying to "Stairway to Heaven" by Led Zeppelin. In Latvia kids rocked to the serious poetry of Pērkons and its founder Juris Kulakovs who once gave me a ride through a dark park on his bike. American lyrics were easy on the mind; Latvian lyrics lingered. Ached. Klāvs Elsbergs, Māris Melgalvs, Vizma Belševica, Imants Ziedonis…

Beginning with footage filmed at a Pērkons concert in the town of Ogre, the film introduces us to some of the teenagers going crazy at the performance of their beloved band. Among the gyrating, screaming, ecstatic, breakdancing youngsters we also get glimpses of their adult counterparts, grim, condescending, and bewildered by the youthful antics of the next generation. The Soviet *militsiya* (police) stand around, watching, waiting …

One of the things that unnerved me in the 1980s was the fact that most of the policemen (Soviet/Russian *militsiya*) in Rīga were ethnic Russians. That automatically created a barrier of mistrust that I could not overcome. *They* were Russians; I was sure *they* didn't like us Latvians— "fascist remnants." *They* had guns and cars; they wielded authority. I remembered the friendly Glen Ridge police officers of my youth; in contrast the Russian police looked mean. Stupid mean. Juris Jansons, the son of sculptor Kārlis Jansons, worked as a traffic policeman in Rīga for a while and reminisces about his experiences in his autobiography…

> When I went to work for the State Autoinspection, the (Soviet) militsiya were not considered a prestigious employer; unfortunately, that reputation (in independent Latvia) has persisted. (Latvian) Lieutenant Colonel Ruzgass tried to attract more ethnic Latvians to the militsiya. Some of the senior investigators who had graduated as jurists hailed from the regions of Vidzeme and Kurzeme, but the vast majority of the militsiya in Latvia—about 90%—were Russians or guys from (Latvia's eastern region) Latgale.
>
> How did I end up there? Ruzgass was hiring Latvians with a higher education. He was upset that so few Latvians wanted to join; unfortunately, he was unsuccessful in attracting "national cadres." (…)

> A lot of the militsiya officers had served in the (Soviet/Russian) Army as drivers or had experience driving tractors. Everyone with some knowledge of mechanics was discharged in 1945 and placed in the auto-inspection service. So a sergeant with little between his ears could easily be promoted to the rank of a lieutenant-colonel. No real education was required, only tractor driving courses, completion of his village elementary school, and a bit of experience! The IQ level of these guys... (1)

In his film Podnieks drew a clear line between generations. Some of his endearing real life characters were Latvia's young punks, who reminded me of immature, wild animals. Boys, not men. The babies of Latvia's women. "When they arrested us..." "I feel like an animal..." "A *purns* (muzzle) in a uniform..." "Emotions 5,000 people strong..." "There's nothing to look forward to..." "There's nothing to fight for..." "What could hold us back from doing something..." "We should topple something..." "Punks without ideas..." "Material things have little value..." "Don't be a burden to others..." This is a sampling of the fuzzy emotions that some of the film's teenagers confide to Podnieks.

Episodes shift between close-up cameos of the teenagers and their antics at the concert in Ogre. Then things become serious. The camera has been placed in a court room, where seven teenagers are on trial for vandalizing a train car on their way back to Rīga. The damages are assessed at about 5,000 roubles. One of the teenagers is sentenced to *three* years in a corrective labor colony; others receive a two-year sentence. It becomes clear that many participated in the trashing of the train but only seven were "caught." Some were betrayed by their peers. Podnieks listens to a teenager providing incriminating testimony. The seven become scapegoats for the actions of a train car full of young animals—the future of Latvia. Claws unsheathed. Babies who grew up behind the Iron Curtain. How long could a people exist in captivity?

An interesting comment beneath the film's YouTube post: "The prosecutors forgot to mention that the riots on the train back to Rīga started in Salaspils, where around ten representatives of our 'brotherly nation' (Russians) got on board and started belittling and insulting us, calling us 'gansi,' swearing at us, and so on." "Gans" was a common epithet Russians used to describe Latvians; it is derived from the German name Hans. "Fascist" is a synonym for "gans." Was this allegation true?

The film's main characters are a motley crew: from brazen punks with dark "goth" make-up and crazy hairdos, leather jackets, and chains to kids looking forward to careers, making lots of money, having their own place to live, a car, a wife, who want to be the square pegs in their society's square holes. Podnieks spends time with each and every one of them, gently prodding and listening attentively.

Later film critic Ābrams Kļeckins would say that Podnieks was the first (in Latvia) to tune in to what Latvia's youth had to say, what they were thinking, what their concerns and attitudes were. We are introduced to a breakdancing kid with a long shaft of hair falling over his eyes in a rebellious fashion. Then there's the fellow who chose to sit it out at the wild concert; he dons a military uniform each day to participate in the high-stepping, militarized honor guard at the monument to the Red Riflemen near the Daugava River. He clearly draws a line between himself and "the punks who lack ideas." There's the true punk in seach of a girl and love to stave off loneliness. A girl who was at the concert, became pregnant, and gave birth to a baby girl: suddenly she is afraid, thinking about Chernobyl. She has matured into an adult. A young man working as a mortician reflects on death.

There's a young fellow who works as a mailman; he is a practicing Hindu who wanted to study architecture but quickly realized that it would lead to nowhere: "So what would I design—another type of Līvāni house kit?" He is referring to the ugly, prefabricated houses manufactured in Līvāni, Latvia. The camera pans over a Russian language newspaper with a black and white photograph of a party official on the front page. I could relate to all of it, all the wordless inferences. In the background from time to time we hear the Russian language—the de facto official language of Soviet-occupied Latvia. Russian: the sound of Rīga in the 1980s.

The aspiring filmmaker Igors Linga struggles to make sense of his world through the camera: "Life is like a set of winding corridors; you never know what you'll encounter around the next bend. Maybe death." Linga dwells on the fact that so many of his friends have succumbed to drug addiction. Podnieks visits a facility for drug addicts and attempts to speak to kids who are clearly under the influence. The nurse in white giggles and expresses amazement at all the new substances they're experimenting with to get high.

Then there's Gennady, a smiling, shy young man who lost his father to cancer; he plans on studying medicine and oncology. When Podnieks goes back to visit him, he is shocked to find out from a heatbroken mother that Gennady himself has died of cancer.

There's the fellow who looks forward to military duty to toughen him up. And the young Latvians who were deployed to Afghanistan to fight in a war they didn't believe in. They've come back from the war zone forever changed, some of them disabled and even limbless, others suffering from post-traumatic stress disorder, struggling to make sense of what they've been through. "Our mothers, our loved ones, our friends understand us. But the fallen, the crippled: nobody wants to talk about them."

"War ages a person," says a sad-eyed young veteran who has become a firefighter. He hints at the events of World War II. Young men longing for compassion. So much remains unsaid yet implied. In a totalitarian state people find a way to hint at ugly truths.

Duplicity, deceit, lies, the confines of social norms, and an ideology enforced by force: these are the themes that lie beneath the surface of the film, which these young kids struggle to express in a system that wields so much power and influence over their futures. "We've hidden so many historical truths," someone musters up the courage to say. *Is It Easy to Be Young* ends with a tender, melancholy song about loneliness by Juris Kulakovs and poet Māris Melgalvs, "Pie baltas lapas" ("By a White Page"). Melgalvs was one of the first young poets I met in Soviet-occupied Latvia in 1982 in the building from which poet Klāvs Elsbergs would plunge to his death. *Is It Easy to Be Young*? garnered several awards, was wildly popular, and remains a sensitive portrait of a generation growing up in communist Latvia. It came out shortly before the Soviet Union would begin changing in ways nobody could imagine. No, it was not easy to be Latvian in Latvia in the second half of the 20th century. At the same time, I met enough extraordinary Latvians in occupied Latvia to understand that humanity was everywhere, and that "fireflies hint at light in the darkness" (Gunārs Astra).

Pie baltas lapas

Pie baltas lapas apsēžos / Kā pie baltas domas kapa / Un kas pažēlos reiz tos, / Kas viens otru nesastapa. / Un kas būs tik drosmīgs pateikt, / Ka nav vainojams neviens, / Kas būs tik drosmīgs pateikt, / Ka nav vainojams neviens. / Šodien mums visvairāk stāsta / Lietus lāses pieskāriens / Un man pietrūkst viena glāsta, / Vai tev nepietrūkst neviena?

By a White Page

I sit down by a white page / Like the grave of a white thought / And who will take pity on those / Who never met each other. / And who will be brave enough to say / That no one is to blame, / Who will be brave enough to say / That no one is to blame. / Today the caress of a raindrops/ Tells us the most / And I need someone's caress, / Don't you miss someone? (Māris Melgalvs. Tr. RL)

Chapter sources:

(1) Jansons, Juris (A II Pozitīvs). Jansonu nerrīgie stāsti. Rīga: Izdevniecība Drukātava, 2013, pp. 115, 137. Tr. RL

1986: Hoping for Change

In the summer of 1986 or thereabouts we were informed that we had been assigned a two-room apartment in Zolitūde ("Solitude"), a new apartment complex going up between Jūrmala Highway and the Rīga-Jūrmala-Tukums train line. The official order was signed by none other than Comrade Alfrēds Rubiks (b. 1935), the last communist mayor of Rīga (his official title was Chairman of the Rīga City Executive Committee). At the end of the decade Rubiks, a staunch communist, achieved notoriety for his fierce opposition to Latvia's secession from the Soviet Union. After independence Rubiks was tried and sentenced in 1995 to eight years in prison for treason. He was granted an early release in 1997. In 2009 he was elected to the European Parliament. Rubiks still clings to and defends communism. In 1986 I was quite sure that our request for an apartment was accommodated in the self-interests of the Soviet authorities to appear benevolent and interested in our family's well-being.

Living in such close proximity to my father-in-law and vacationing together in the summertime with my in-laws at Paulēni had made me nervous and depressed. They were good people, for sure, but I longed for independence and privacy. My husband didn't appear to be bothered by these arrangements; then again, that was his nuclear family, and he was very fond of Paulēni. I looked forward to seeing the new apartment, and I longed for a place of our own in the countryside, too. Paulēni was a beautiful property but too small for all of us. Paulēni was not *my place*; it would always be Juris and Biruta's.

My new friend Renāte from the small town of Smiltene came out to visit me from time to time at Paulēni, which cheered me up greatly. She was studying English at the University of Latvia, played the violin, and was great fun. Yet I never felt like I could fully relax at Paulēni and plan my own time or be myself. Biruta needed help; even though she never asked for it, I felt compelled to lend a hand where I could with the never-ending chores.

At the end of the summer a face-to-face meeting between US and Soviet officials under the auspices of the Chautaqua Institution took place in Jūrmala. Word of the Chautaqua Conference perked Latvians' interest. "Wow! There are American government officials in our seaside town!"—was my own feeling. The Soviet-maligned USA seemed like a faraway, unreachable alien planet to people in Latvia, and from the Soviet perspective Americans were evil aliens. A delegation of Latvians from the exile community also participated. Unbeknownst to us, "two of the American delegates who were to take prominent positions in the Jūrmala conference (...), Jack Matlock, special assistant to the (US) president for national security, and (Mark) Palmer, at the time ambassador designate to the Hungarian People's Republic, (...) spoke about the non-recognition policy of the US government toward Soviet rule in Latvia. Matlock gave a detailed background description of Latvia, describing the 1940 elections (...) as a 'farce.' 'This is not a conference in the USSR,' he insisted. 'This is a conference in Latvia among Americans, Soviets, and Latvians.'"* Apparently Mr. Matlock had read his statement in Latvian. If I had been able to participate in the conference, I would have been terribly excited by Mr. Matlock's speech. Busy with our son and house duties, I was not paying much attention to Soviet news at the time; by then I was too jaded. And anyway, the conference guest list had been carefully screened: the Soviets would not let things get out of control. (1)

"Chautaqua" came and went with no change in sight. Autumn turned into winter; the cold weather and the snow arrived. In December we bundled up and headed out to Zolitūde to see what our new apartment looked like. My spouse showed little enthusiasm for the outing. I realized how relatively privileged we were to receive this apartment in an economy in which the housing sector was ridden by corruption. I felt almost guilty. Because of me, someone else who had been waiting in line for years did not get an apartment and would continue to suffer in communal misery or in some sorry dwelling.

We disembarked from bus No. 53, surveying the construction site that lay ahead of us. The frame of the nine-story building at Ruses Street 24/I-19 was up. We trudged toward our promised communist cubbyhole in the whirling snow in the twilight of a wintry day. There was a lot of work going on inside: workers in *zaķenes* (winter hats with ear flaps) and batted jackets or *pufaikas* moved in and out of the shadows. Projector lights illuminated the ground-floor corridor and the stairwell. Our apartment on the fifth floor was far from ready, contrary to our expectations.

Bottling up our respective thoughts and feelings could not have been good for our marriage. A small two-room apartment was no house with a white picket fence and rose garden, but where I saw a dim beam of hope for some privacy and our own space, my dejected spouse saw failure. A product of the Soviet era "box," he must have loathed the idea of moving into such a building.

The snow continued to fall softly with a faint hiss, as we made our way back to the bus stop. Perhaps it was the wonderful white stuff shimmering in the evening lights, icy and refreshing, which filled me with a sense of hope and peace as I looked back at our building in Zolitūde. The new apartment appeared to be my only exit from our crowded situation in Old Rīga. I saw our glass of fortune as half-full. Anyway, we could now be officially "registered" at this address. A *pieraksts* ("registration") was required of all Soviet citizens: that is, they had to be registered at a specific address. However, this did not mean that everyone lived at the address where they were registered. Towards spring we would be back to inspect the workers' final result.

Right: Krišjānis perched on the windowsill of his grandfather's studio in Old Rīga looking down at the rooftops and pigeons. Photo: Andris Krieviņš.

From a letter dated December 21, 1986: *We didn't even get into our building. We were able to take a look at the two and three-room apartments in the building next door. There is no way I'm going to live there, for several reasons. I just hope we can find someone in downtown Rīga who is willing to exchange their apartment for this one. We would really need a three-room apartment. The two-room apartment that has been assigned to us is barely bigger than our space in Old Rīga. [...]*

Encouraged by our good friends Andris and Dace, in the fall of 1986 I joined Budēļi, a "folk tradition" ensemble led by Ojārs Rode, a fellow who worked at the Latvian Institute of Solid State Physics (Cietvielu fizikas Institūts) of the University of Latvia. The rehearsals took place twice a week at the Institute. I was learning lots of new old songs. More and more ensembles interested in traditional Latvian folk music were emerging and converging, thanks to the groundbreaking efforts of the Skandinieki ensemble, as well as Ilga Reizniece, Zane Šmite, Biruta Ozoliņa, and other notable folk song singers who were drawing attention to our ethnic heritage. In late fall of '86 I also began attending preparatory courses at the Latvian Art Academy, with the idea of taking entrance exams the following summer. Getting out of the house to sing and draw gave me a sense of purpose. Our apartment by this time felt claustrophobic.

In November Dace and Andris invited me to become their baby daughter Lība's godmother; I would be sharing my godparenting with Ojārs Rode. We christened the baby in the church and then came home to perform a traditional Latvian ritual that possibly pre-dated the Christian era in Latvia. Of course, it was largely improvised. It was a solemn yet joyful occasion, and I was able to wear a traditional Piebalga folk costume, which filled me with pride. I took our preparations for this wonderful ceremony seriously, memorizing the words of songs passed down from previous centuries.

I was proud to take part in a ceremony that included old rituals and words, and beautiful songs to celebrate the beginning of this Latvian baby's life. Under the Soviets many Latvians had lost touch with their ethnic heritage due to Soviet indoctrination. I was grateful to and inspired by the people involved in Latvia's folklore movement in the 1980s: they were the keepers of our identity. I'm happy to say, my goddaughter Lība grew up to be a beautiful, multi-talented woman.

A painting from the 1980s: Art as preservation. My red Dala horse given to me by my grandmother; Paika, an old doll that my husband inherited from his aunt; pūpoli or pussywillow branches (a symbol of Easter); and the antique peacock vase I purchased at one of Rīga's consignment shops on Sverdlova (Marijas today) iela..

In the winter of '86 I enjoyed my solitary walks through the streets of Old Rīga and the park near Bastejkalns, illuminated by warmly glowing lanterns, to the Art Academy. It was so good to sit in a classroom again and immerse myself in drawing. I knew it was an uphill battle to convince the authorities to permit me to go back to school. I wanted it so bad. I looked at my younger fellow students enviously; some of them would surely be admitted to this prestigious institution. I concentrated on the immediate task of doing well at the courses. In that venerable old building I could be myself, by myself. It was there, seated among other hopefuls, that I felt at peace with myself, happy, and free. I was out of my cage there, able to breathe...

One evening I bumped into one of my old artist buddies from 1980 on my way to my courses. We walked together for a while. When he heard that I had joined a folk ensemble, he threw out a snide comment belittling Latvia's folklorists. That was the first time that I realized that Latvians had been beaten down so badly, that they did not recognize the beauty of their own unique cultural legacy anymore. It was an awkward encounter. We had drifted apart. My "friend" was becoming famous in those years with his gigantic prints. Apparently many Latvians did not want to look back; the past was too painful or perhaps too narrow for them. The world beckoned with neon lights.

In December I heard that my younger brother would be studying in Denmark in the first half of 1987. I wrote to Artis, urging him to come and visit us. I longed for my family. The year 1986 ended on the notes of a haunting song that portended events to come. A song called "Dzimtā valoda" ("Native Language") by my favorite Latvian band Līvi was voted the number one song of 1986 in the so-called Mikrofons *Aptauja* ("Survey") of the year's most popular songs in Latvia. Līvi hailed from the port city of Liepāja and represented the hard rock side of Latvian popular music in the 1980s.

The Latvian Communist Party pressured the Mikrofons Survey people, complaining that the song's text was nationalistic, despite the fact that its author was Moldovan; they also criticized lead singer Jānis Grodums' loud, scratchy voice. The Communist Party ordered a new recording of the song to make it sound less harsh, but because of a technical mistake, the original version was aired on television. (2)

What lead singer Jānis Grodums belted out was a hymn for those times. The words to the song were based on a poem by Moldovan poet Grigore Vieru (1935–2009), "În limba ta" ("In Your [Native] Language"), which had been translated by Imants Ziedonis and set to music by the band's guitarist Ainārs Virga. The song riveted Latvians. Just a few months later, in 1987, Latvia's national "awakening" would begin with the actions of a small but very courageous group of people, also from Liepāja, who called themselves Helsinki-86. The Līvi song still resonates with Latvians today.

"Dzimtā valoda" and Vieru's original poem are about one's native language as the key component of personal identity. Latvians have traditionally referred to their native language as *tēva valoda* ("father tongue"). By the 1980s Latvia and the Latvian language were in danger of being overrun by Russian immigration. The situation had become critical!

"Soviet Latvia" (July 21, 1990): the newspaper of the Central Committee of the Communist Party of Latvia.

Many years later in 2012, I reviewed a Latvian translation of an article by Russ Rymer called "Vanishing Voices," which was published in *National Geographic Magazine*. Rymer wrote: "A last speaker with no one to talk to exists in unspeakable solitude." He also wrote: "One language dies every 14 days. By the next century nearly half of the roughly 7,000 languages spoken on Earth will likely disappear, as communities abandon native tongues in favor of English, Mandarin, or Spanish. What is lost when a language goes silent?" This reminded me of the

Latvian language's precarious situation during the Soviet occupation, which was a period of methodical Russification of my fatherland. (3)

By the 1980s my mother tongue, Latvian, was being crowded out by swarms of Russian immigrants; Russian kindergartens and schools outnumbered Latvian schools in Rīga, and Russian billboards, street signs, and Russian policemen made Rīga feel like a Russian city. Another 50 years of Russian domination and we, Latvians, would vanish from our native country, taking our language with us to the grave or into exile. Of this I am convinced.

Vienā valodā raud visi ļaudis, / Vienā valodā, valodā tie smej. / Tikai dzimtā valoda dzēš sāpes, / Prieku dziesmas dod, atdod pasaulei. // Kad nespēsi ne dziedāt, ne raudāt, / Kad tu nespēsi vairs it nekā—ar debesīm, / Zemi tu klusēsi, tas būs tavā dzimtā valodā. // **Chorus:** *Dzimtā valodā ir māte, māte, dzimtā valodā / Vīns vēl saldāks, / Dzimtā valodā pasmejies / Par sevi pats. (The words to the Līvi song "Dzimtā valoda")*

Translation: In one tongue all people weep, / In one tongue all people laugh. / Only one's mother tongue erases pain, / And gives songs of joy back to the world. // When you can no longer sing nor weep, / When you can no longer do anything—Together with the sky, / The earth you will remain silent, in your mother tongue. // Chorus: Your mother is your native tongue, / Wine is sweeter in your mother tongue, / In your mother tongue you can laugh about yourself. (Translation of "Dzimtā valoda"—RL)

Paul Abucean's full translation of Vieru's poem, "În limba ta" ("In Your Language"), from Moldovan into English:

Everybody giggles / In the same old language, / Everybody whimpers / In the same old tongue. Yet only in your language / Are words that give you comfort, / And only in your language / Is joy the path to song. / You feel you miss your mother / In only it—your language. / And dinner's like no other / In only it—your language. / It's only in your language / That you can laugh alone. / And only it, your language / Can stop your sobbing moan. / And when the weeping ceases, / And even laughter ends, / When nothing's left that eases, / No singing, no amends, / With endless skies before you / And ending earth behind, / You learn the words of silence / Your tongue is sure to find.

The song "Dzimtā valoda" was produced as a music video. It opens with lead singer Jānis Grodums and his bandmates standing in the Ethnographic Open-Air Museum, a bastion of Latvian tradition and culture against the intrusive, pervasive, ever encroaching Russian world around us. No wonder Gunārs Astra mentioned it in his Last Word. Then the video shifts to the Brothers' Cemetery, where many of our heroes from the Latvian War of Independence (1918–1920) are interred. The figure of Mother Latvia is visible behind the band, as they sing near the Eternal Flame. Ainārs Virga moves his fingers over his electric guitar, eliciting a haunting wail. Gritty, raw, and deeply moving... Every time I hear it, I am compelled to think about what Latvia and its people had to endure in the 20th century.

Chapter sources:

(1) Mackenzie, Ross. When Stars and Stripes Met Hammer and Sickle: The Chautaqua Conferences on US-Soviet Relations 1985–1989. The University of South Carolina Press, 2006. P. 53

(2) "Mikrofona aptauja 1986." Wikipedia. 12/03/2013 ; 4/15/2014 <http://lv.wikipedia.org/wiki/Mikrofona_aptauja_1986>

(3) Rymer, Russ. "Vanishing Voices." *National Geographic Magazine*. July 2012

 Visual:

(4) **Līvi song "Dzimtā valoda" ("Native Language")** <http://www.youtube.com/watch?v=Osrj-Q-pkKA>

PART FIVE:
The Thaw

Spring clouds in Piebalga. Photograph by Juris Krieviņš.

Springtime in Latvia's countryside: the sun grows brighter and rises higher each day, melting away the snow and ice. The wet soil rises like dough and oozes moisture, and an incredible freshness in the air lifts your spirit. You feel like a weightless bird, a skylark dancing to Vivaldi's "Spring," as if the mantle of Baltic ice has fallen from your very own shoulders. The sky is a pure blue tabula rasa. When the bright yellow *purenes* (marsh marigolds) burst into bloom, they make you happy like a child. You are full of hope and anticipation, waiting for the moment to plant a seed.

Klāvs

A voice of his generation: Klāvs Elsbergs, 1959–1987. Photograph by Mārtiņš Zelmenis.

Neatvadīsimies
rūgts ir ne tikai analgīns
bet arī dzīve ziniet
nevajag zaķi nesteigsimies
neatvadīsimies

asara zirnekļa tīklā
tāds ir mans liktenis ziniet
bet nevajag notraukt vienalga
neatvadīsimies

(Translation: **Let's Not Say Goodbye** / Not only Analgin is bitter / but life too you know / let's not bunny* let's not hurry / let's not say goodbye // a teardrop in a spider's web / such is my fate you know / but don't brush it aside whatever / let's not say goodbye)

(Tr. RL)

* "Bunny" is a term of endearment in Latvian

On February 6, 1987 we woke up to the shocking news that Klāvs Elsbergs was dead. Born one year ahead of me in 1959, Elsbergs was just 28 years old at the time. He had already achieved widespread popularity as a young poet, writer, literary critic, and translator of French poetry. He had just joined the staff of the new magazine, *Avots* ("Wellspring"), published from 1987 until 1992 and destined to become Soviet Latvia's most famous publication. Several of Elsbergs' poems had been set to music by our Latvian rock star Juris Kulakovs and his group Pērkons, and tens of thousands of young Latvians knew his lyrics by heart.

Vizma Belševica in a 1976 portrait by Juris Krieviņš.

Although I did not know Klāvs personally, I knew about him, had read and enjoyed his poetry, and was well aware of his stature among his peers. His mother Vizma Belševica (1931–2005), *right*, was a revered poet, writer, and translator whose poetry had been suppressed in the early 1970s by the communist censors. Her book *Gadu gredzeni* ("The Years' Rings") from 1969 caused a sensation, as it explored historical motifs and drew parallels between the Holy Roman Empire's Northern Crusades (against the Baltic heathens) and Soviet oppression. It provoked the ire of the Communist Party, and for a while Belševica was ostracized. Many Latvians perceived Belševica and her writing as Latvia's conscience in the Soviet era. Belševica was nominated several times for the Nobel Prize in Literature. That awful morning my thoughts flew to her—Klāvs' mother. There was a time when I had cried reading her poetry in Michigan in autumn of 1981: it had moved me deeply. *And now this.* What had transpired in Jūrmala?

Klāvs' death, which Belševica claimed (and many Latvians still claim) was a murder, took place at the Writers' House in Dubulti, Jūrmala, a seaside retreat for writers not only from Latvia but the entire Soviet Union. I was there in 1980 during my first trip to Latvia. Klāvs had allegedly been pushed through the ninth story hallway window and had fallen to his death. He had been socializing with some Russian writers from Moscow. His violent death and the subsequent murky investigation cranked up the rumor mill. Drinking and/or suicide (the convenient explanations) or assault and murder (as we suspected)? Impunity, the ugly face of the society of "the more equal than the equals," loomed over the investigation.

Vizma Belševica was convinced that it was a premeditated political murder. In an emotional tribute to her son published in *Jaunā Gaita*, an expat journal, in 1990, one year before Latvia's independence from the Soviet Union, she spelled out her accusation clearly...

> The spider's fine strand snapped when the poet was 28. His murderers tossed him through the ninth story glass.
> A trembling child's voice on the telephone: "Grandma, dad died. Some guy pushed dad so hard that he died."
> (...)
> There is a line in a poem by Klāvs—"the linden that died from my tears." The linden died, but (Klāvs) never showed his tears. I could remember only one time. The first time our apartment was searched. Klāvs was in the other room with his grandmother and didn't see or hear anything; it all took place quietly. When they were taking me away, noiselessly, Klāvs ran out of the room screaming: "Mommy, don't go with them! Don't! Don't go!"
> Did he feel betrayed that time: useless to cry; useless to yell; mother is blind and deaf to his pain? Klāvs was four. What can one say to a four-year-old about the KGB?
> He was old enough to understand the second search. He sat in his room, his teeth clenched, staring, unseeing, at his algebra book. For the entire 16 hours.
> This incident was followed by years of disgrace, when the press hounded me, my friends retreated, and acquaintances crossed the street to avoid greeting me. At

school and at kindergarten the teachers persecuted Klāvs and (his little brother) Jānis as best they could. I don't think someone ordered them to act that way: they were trying to attract notice and approval.

Disgrace means dire poverty—when Klāvs was an adolescent and wanted to be like everyone else, but he had to be poorer than everyone. Shabby and ostracized. Klāvs had buddies in school, our courtyard, on his basketball team. But only one real childhood friend. And the love of his life was also just one girl whom he grew up playing with outside, went to school with, and married after his first year at the University.

Klāvs started writing when he was 14. He didn't tell me, nor did he ask for advice or my appraisal. I knew, because his room was littered with the rough drafts of poems. But because he said nothing, I was able to know nothing and could hope that he would grow out of it, because no parent wants to wish such a hard life on their child. And what is more difficult than being an honest poet in the Soviet Union? Klāvs was honest.

(...)

Klāvs Elsbergs left us three books of poetry, some stories, and translations from French, English, and Russian.

He left us a small, Latvian style grave marker made of oak among the monuments to other Latvian writers near the fence in Raiņa Cemetery. There is a memorial stone in Staicele, a small town where Klāvs spent his summers at basketball camp. The students of Staicele placed the stone there despite efforts by our Culture Foundation and the authorities to derail their efforts.

He left us songs with his words. Flowers on his grave. The love of his people. The authorities' hatred and betrayal. His murderers have not been and won't be tried. After Klāvs' death the parents of many murdered Latvian youths whose assailants went unpunished called and wrote to me of how they had sought justice in the Soviet courts in vain. The father of a young scientist wrote to me: "They always die when they're 28. That is the age when a person's potential and stance are clear."

(...)

Klāvs spent a lot of time developing Avots magazine. Avots—an angry, avant-garde youth magazine—appeared at the very outset of the transparency era; it was the most courageous, most scathing publication in the entire Soviet Union. Avots and Klāvs, in particular, were the recipients of material that could not be published elsewhere.

Based on news published in the Russian exile journal Posev, Colonel Krasnov gave Klāvs Elsbergs material about our (Communist Party) Central Committee's mafia-type activities. That sealed Klāvs' fate. He had to die.

(...) Everything seemed alright. Klāvs was issued a voucher for a stay at Dubulti— at a building where writers could work for a month, all expenses paid.

Klāvs was writing poems, translating Victor Hugo's Ninety-Three; he came home from time to time to visit his family or to go to his office at Avots. The fact that he'd been beset by a bunch of writers from Moscow also didn't seem unusual. Avots not only published bold material; it also paid its contributors well. (Perhaps) the Muscovites were looking for an introduction to the new magazine. After all, they were staying right next to an Avots staff member.

"They're interesting people, but they drink too much," Klāvs told us.

Klāvs' voucher was valid until February 7. Writers there usually used the time to their advantage. Klāvs called us on the 3rd and asked us to come and pick him up on the 5th (that is, two days before the voucher was set to expire). He wanted to avoid the traditional farewell drinking ritual; after all, he was a parent.

We were notified of his death on the morning of the 5th. "Wine and women" were mentioned as part of the circumstances.

(...)

The desk he had worked at looked neat and orderly; his poems and translations were stacked in neat piles. The kind of piles you see in writers' memorial museums or rooms... Not for one second has Klāvs' desk ever looked like that. Klāvs' desk always looked like the aftermath of a house search, but those who were looking for dangerous material did not know that. They did not dare leave the table ransacked. They stacked everything properly. This small but significant fact confirms the Posev version that it was a political murder.

A post-mortem was skipped. As well as an investigation of his clothes. His clothes were evidence of what had happened before he was hurled through the glass; his clothes were destroyed and are not even mentioned in the case material. Witnesses nearby who heard something and only later understood what had happened were not summoned to testify. The employees of the Dubulti Writers' House have been ordered to keep silent about the event. (...)

You are reading all of this and thinking that this is a traumatized mother's distraught imagination at work. It wasn't possible for a bunch of writers to band together and murder their colleague.

Yet it was possible. In the Soviet Union it is possible to be not only a writer and a KGB informant, but an assassin as well. This is a unique aspect of the Soviet Union even in this era of transparency, hailed by a humanity fooled yet again by lovely words and promises.

The name of Klāvs Elsbergs is only one on the list of bloody victims of the Gorbachev era. The list grows longer day by day, because there are no political trials or official incarcerations or death sentences by shooting. There are accidents—more and more of them. (...) (1)

Our dark suspicions were enhanced by rumors of the shoddy, secretive investigation and its inconclusive findings. After Klāvs' death Belševica stopped writing poetry. She withdrew her nomination for Soviet Latvia's annual prize in literature, stating that, "Until my son's murderers are tried, I cannot accept any prize from this state. That would be blood money." (2)

Belševica's accusations are haunting; her claim that the Communist Party's leaders had mor-phed into a mafia-type organization, which continued to mutate and penetrate Latvian society and the Latvian economy, made sense to me. No doubt the Soviet Communist Party's core was criminal, if you thought about all the people that their underlings, the KGB, had harassed, intim-idated, arrested, and imprisoned. Gunārs Astra died in mysterious circumstances one year after Klāvs Elsbergs. Under the guise of perestroika, massive embezzlement took place throughout the Soviet Union, enriching those with direct access to funds, property, and commodities; this toxic corruption continued after the collapse of the Soviet Union both in Russia and Latvia, as well as other former Soviet republics. The system's toxicity had penetrated Soviet society to the bone. Belševica was also right when she sneered about "humanity being fooled again" by Moscow's "pretty words and promises." Moscow did not believe in tears.

The white morning light of February 6, 1987 seemed so cold and piercing, like daggers, as I trudged past Vērmanes Garden. The cracked ice made me think of Klāvs' cracked glasses. Where I was headed, I don't recall, but I know I was thinking of Klāvs' family and what they must be going through. Vizma Belševica's life under the Soviets hadn't been easy, but her son's death was like a last straw. The murder was never solved; Klāvs' "companions" from Moscow were never investigated or tried. By now most of them are dead, I believe.

Young, brilliant, sensitive. Dead. Klāvs' murder, never proved but never in doubt, shook us up, shook us to our core. The idea that someone could get away with murder was bitterly unpalatable, yet injustice lay at the very heart of the Soviet system. In fact, the Soviet Empire was built on terror, death, and bullet-ruptured brains. When Klāvs' limp body thudded against the hard, frozen ground in Jūrmala, it sent deep tremors through the ice that was smothering the fatherland.

("Wellspring")

The masthead for *Avots*, a magazine that shook up Latvia.

Poet and translator Guntars Godiņš's (b. 1958) recollections of his time at *Avots*, following the death of Klāvs Elsbergs, provide a sense of what this extraordinary magazine was all about and what role it played in galvanizing its readers. It is important to note that *Avots* had a "Russian twin," the magazine *Rodnik*; it was one of the rare times when Latvians and Russians worked together on a joint literary product.

> If one could believe in the existence of an elixir of youth, one might presume it had touched Avots magazine. Avots expressed the freedom of ideas at a time when the "freedom of speech" was an incomprehensible notion; the power of the magazine's visual appearance has not diminished over time. (Anda Boluža)
> It was in February of 1987 that I met with Avots' chief editor Aivars Kļavis. He asked me if I wanted to take over from Klāvs Elsbergs who had died so suddenly and mysteriously. Avots' first issue had just been published. The month of February was gloomy; Klāvs' death hung over our heads like a curse damning the writers of our generation. The efforts of the Soviet minions to conceal the facts of the tragic event and suppress the truth were detestable. At the time I was working in the literary broadcast department of Latvian Radio. I was in the crosshairs of our station's managers, because the politics of my broadcasts were wrong. It was in February of '87 that a feature that I had prepared, "Vārda spēks un vājums" ("The Power and the Weakness of the Word"), in which I hinted at (our political) system's duplicitous nature, was scandalously banned. The sudden disappearance of a highly anticipated special feature alerted our listeners to the censors' wakeful

eye and sharp ear. In the radio building's main studio we were subjected to a tirade of accusations and threats: this feature would harm Soviet Latvia, and I was a borderline dissident. Latvia's "awakening" hadn't really started yet.

Avots was like a breath of fresh air in the oppressive, stifling Soviet atmosphere of that time. I was offered a job there and left the radio building, letting the doors fall shut behind me with a loud bang.

(Note from the author: This last comment is hilarious to me. The Soviets had not invented or discovered the door mechanism known as a dashpot, which allows a door to close gently and safely. The State Radio building's door always slammed shut with a loud bang.)

Avots in Latvia and Vikerkaar ("Rainbow") in Estonia were the official publications of the Komsomol of the Latvian and Estonian Soviet Socialist Republics and their respective writers' unions. Discourse about perestroika had already started in Russia, which caused the Latvian and Estonian communists and their Komsomol organizations to shift and try to change things around them. If Moscow insists! It is ironic that the communists' proposal to publish a new magazine would eventually turn on them, initiating a very real and permanent perestroika in social thought and perception.

The editorial staff of Avots was a group of young, creative, like-minded people with unusual ideas and a sense of style, who understood that the magazine was a great vehicle for expressing the unspoken and uncovering cover-ups. These were our guidelines for each and every issue. We did not adhere to the standard boring magazine and newspaper model; we featured interviews; articles about art; stuff about music...

Work on Avots and its Russian counterpart Rodnik *was a very creative process. For example, (theater and movie critic) Normunds Naumanis would say, "Hey, I have a great article about such and such a film!" (Writer) Rudīte Kalpiņa would jump in to offer a feature; I would offer a good story, a bunch of poems, an essay that would fit into the common thread and stylistic landscape. Aivars Kļavis was there to bridge the gap between us, the generators of new and audacious ideas, and the censor. Artist Sarmīte Māliņa was always thinking ahead about illustrative material for the next issue. Vladis Spāre and Andrejs Ļevkins (Andrey Levkin) would fill us in on what was going into the next issue of Rodnik. If any of the department editors had good and topical material to offer, everyone was very supportive.*

I remember how Laima Žihare had translated a small book from Hungarian about (astronaut) Yuri Gagarin, in which the author claimed that Gagarin had never been to outerspace, and his achievement was just another socialist lie. We decided to publish the entire book in one issue. We had more than enough sensational material for that time: George Orwell's Animal Farm*; Samuel Beckett's* Waiting for Godot*; Viktor Suvorov's* The Icebreaker*; an interview with (poet) Knuts Skujenieks, in which he opened up for the first time about the Gulag; Ojārs Vācietis' previously unpublished poem „Resurrection of the Vadonis" ('Leader')," etc.*

Right after (the Latvian children's magazine) Zīlīte *published its famous „erotic" (meaning sex ed) issue, Avots put out its erotic issue. In contrast to* Zīlīte's *physiological content, Avots published erotic poetry, prose, and articles about erotic films along with visual material. Another big event was our issue devoted to the literature of Latvians in exile, an unprecedented event.*

In 1988 Rodnik *published a drawing of Lenin's head caught in a rat trap, his brains ruptured and scattered. That caused a huge uproar. The chief ideologist of the (Latvian Communist Party's) Central Committee, Ivars Ķezbers, was summoned to Moscow to explain. (Our chief editor) Aivars Kļavis got in trouble, too, of course. Outraged proletariats from Latvia and Russia were telephoning us. At the time our editorial office was located on the last floor of the Press Building. I remember being there one evening to do some editing after everyone had left. The telephone rang non-stop. The question was always the same: „Is that really Lenin on the cover?" Because the calls were annoying, I took to receiver off the hook, set it on my desk, and continued to read. Suddenly I was very surprised to hear the phone, which was off the hook, ring. I put the receiver to my ear and heard the telephone operator say to me in an angry voice: „Why have you taken the receiver off the hook? People keep calling, and they're complaining to our telephone central!" Then the operator connected me to a woman who announced in Russian that she was calling on behalf of the entire workforce of the VEF factory to complain and express their indignation and condemnation of how we had insulted our great leader Lenin. This sort of stuff happened on a regular basis. Life was exciting and interesting.*

(Author's note: The Soviet Union did not publish erotic or pornographic magazines. Western tourists often placed porn or girlie magazines near the top of their packed suitcases to draw attention away from other more serious literature that they were attempting to smuggle into the Soviet Union, such as history books.)

Of course, the publication of forbidden or previously unknown material was the magazine's primary source of popularity, but beyond that a magazine that featured a completely new type of content and style had appeared in Latvia; it provided the beginning of a new way of thinking. The magazine attracted artists, writers, musicians, journalists, and scholars and promoted active discussions and debates. Compared to today's numbers, the magazine's circulation was enormous: 140,000 copies. I know that many people waited impatiently for each new issue, and I know that there are many people who have saved all of their issues.

The putsch in 1991 changed things considerably. When the OMON forces took over the Press Building, we were forced to print two issues in Estonia. I remember how during the barricades we stood in the streets passing out the latest issue, fresh off of an Estonian press. The air was filled with the smoke of bonfires and big questions about Latvia's future.

By 1992 our staff had been cut back to just a few people. Due to financial constraints we were forced to put out double issues. In June of that year the magazine folded. When I look at the March-April 1992 issue, I am still very happy about its content, which included: the French modernist playwright Alfred Jarry's play Ubu Roi *with original illustrations; poems by the French poets Jacques Prévert and Paul Éluard; a conversation with the French film director Claude Lelouch; an essay called „The Secret of Zen" by Scottish American poet, professor of philology, and Buddhism scholar Gilbert Hyatt; an essay by Estonian poet Jaan Kaplinski called „New Worlds"; a travelogue by the German poet Hans Magnus Enzensberger; and more. All of this material is fresh even after 18 years.*

Looking at the situation in Latvia today (2010) in regard to magazines and newspapers devoted to culture, I often recall the Avots *era and remain convinced that a magazine like it would find its reader today. I also understand that nothing can be repeated nor should it.* Avots *was and remains a phenomenon, a legend in Latvia's cultural history. (...) (3)*

No Latvian magazine since *Avots* has been able to match its youthful exuberance, creativity, and passion. The (literally) bleak Soviet landscape of the late 1980s provided an ideal backdrop for the colorful, bold, and devilishly impudent nature of *Avots* magazine; that landscape changed after Latvia's independence. With the advent of fax machines and the Internet in the 1990s, the notion of forbidden literature and the experience of state censorship faded into obscurity in the Baltic States.

While *Avots* absorbed my husband, I floated on the periphery, a full-time mother trying to balance parenting with freelance work and living in Zolitūde, a Soviet style suburb, in solitude. I was an outsider, partly because of the restrictions of motherhood and because I was unsure of myself and what I could contribute. Even as my knowledge of the Latvian language deepened, my confidence in my written Latvian faltered. I had stopped writing poetry; my Latvian peers' brilliance, as I saw it, eclipsed anything I thought I could say or write. I was struggling with a bad case of low self-esteem. I realized how difficult it was to belong to two distinct cultures, one of which (American, in this case) was unfamiliar to the people around me. Unlike my compatriots in occupied Latvia, who specialized in double entendre, I was direct to a fault.

Like a thirsty sponge, I read a lot and absorbed what was going on; I greatly admired my husband's new colleagues but also envied them, ironically, for sharing a common past and cultural identity. Yes, we were all Latvians, but growing up under communism was an experience they probably thought I could not understand. But maybe, just maybe there was some value in "looking in" with an outsider's set of eyes.

Chapter sources:

(1) Belševica, Vizma. „Asara zirnekļa tīklā—tāds ir mans liktenis, ziniet..." Jaunā Gaita No. 176. February 1990 ; Retrieved 04/15/2014. <http://zagarins.net/jg/jg176/JG176_Belsevica.htm>

(2) „Vizmas Belševicas daiļrade" Gudrinieks.lv <http://www.gudrinieks.lv/referati/referats/vizmas-belsevicas-dailrade-puslapis1.html>

(3) Godiņš, Guntars. „Daži atmiņu avoti par Avotu un kas ar mums notiek." Dizaina studija / Delfi Kultūra 03/19/2010 ; 4/17/2013 <http://www.delfi.lv/kultura/archive/guntars-godins-dazi-atminu-avoti-par-avotu-un-kas-ar-mums-notiek.d?id=30707751>

1987: Depression

My brother Artis had grown up. I barely recognized him when he stepped off the train in Rīga in April 1987. When I left for Latvia in 1982, he was 18 and in his last year of high school. Back then I hadn't seen him much; he had spent most of his weekends hanging out with his Latvian American buddies. Now he was in Denmark studying for a semester. We did some touristy things and went out to Zolitūde to show him our new apartment, which by then was ready but stood empty, because Andris had no interest in moving there. When my brother went to take a piss in the toilet, his pee puddled out onto the floor. More problems! We were shocked at the shoddiness of the construction. We were still hoping to do an apartment swap and stay in downtown Rīga. This was the easiest way to move into a new place: by swapping. Maybe some Russians were interested in exchanging their pre-war apartment for our proletariat's paradise nest?

It was good to see my brother, yet I sensed that Latvia would not be part of his future. His impressions of Rīga revolted, depressed, and angered him, the masses of Russians in particular. Reflecting on his choice and mine later in life, I was reminded of the 1998 movie "Sliding Doors" with Gwyneth Paltrow about a young woman's two divergent paths in life based on whether or not she succeeds in boarding a subway in London. Was this Fate?

Left: The tower of dreams.

In early summer we decided to approach our Russian neighbors in Old Rīga with an offer to swap apartments. How we hoped that they would agree to it! All Russians dreamed of living in a Soviet high-rise with a loggia, right? And I couldn't stop thinking about the tower that they had access to. What delightful possibilities that conjured up! A reading space with a chair and pillows. Flowering plants and stained glass windows. A tea table for three. We happily gave them the key to our cubby of Soviet bliss in Zolitūde and then sat back and waited. At the end of the day came a knock; a brief conversation ensued. My husband shut the door. By his expression I could tell it was a big *nyet*. Zolitūde remained ours, unwanted, unoccupied. We were devastated.

By late summer of 1987, after almost five years in communist Latvia without a break, I knew something was wrong. We had run into a dead-end. Our lives were permeated by a subtle tension, a lurking sense of frustration, of the premise of no solution for years to come. I had slowly begun to crack, having internalized stress for too long, and it was wreaking havoc on my stamina. We had run out of space, literally and figuratively speaking.

With my husband out on shooting assignments, I remained in Rīga to work on a translation of Andrejs Pumpurs' *Lāčplēsis* ("Bearslayer") while trying to entertain a very bored little boy. My mother-in-law had told me she couldn't handle two young children in the countryside, so I had to work things out, as I always did. On my own. I remember standing by the window of our apartment in July gazing out towards the Daugava River, struggling to contain a torrent of tears in order not to upset our little boy.

As I read through the manuscript, transcribing Pumpurs' lines, I began experiencing panic attacks. The stress of working while parenting, as well as other problems, had taken a toll on me. There seemed to be no one around in whom to confide. My husband was distracted by other things. I was overwhelmed by physical and mental fatigue, but when I lay down, I could not fall asleep. Nor could I afford to sleep during the day, with our son being so active and inquisitive.

Years later I would read that depression could be caused by trying to be too strong for too long. So many of the obstacles I had battled through I had taken to be normal aspects of life, when in fact they were not. The Soviet communist system was not healthy for humans. The perpetual shortage of goods, the constant, repetitive thud of Soviet propaganda and blatant lies, unpleasant rendez-vous with the secret police, and a lack of privacy were some of the aspects of life in communist Latvia that had finally hit a raw nerve. Unlike me, however, Soviet citizens did not have a way out. I had always reminded myself of this, of how privileged I was. There was very little leeway for squirming one's way out of uncomfortable or even downright stressful circumstances. People drank, smoked, ate poorly, and engaged in casual sex, which often ended in unwanted pregnancies.

> Perhaps no other index of the role of Sovietization is as indicative as the gap in life expectancy between Latvia and Finland, the Baltic States' northern neighbor. In 1988 Finland registered life span rates of 70.7 years for males and 78.7 for females, which were 6.5 and 4.1 years higher than the respective rates in Latvia. By 1994 life expectancy in Latvia (would increase) only marginally: 64.4 years for males and 74.8 years for females, compared with Finland's rates of 72.1 years for males and 79.9 years for females. During the 1930s (prior to World War II—RL), Latvia's rates had been higher than those in Finland and on par with those of Austria, Belgium, France, and Scotland.
>
> The infant mortality rate would rise to 17.4 deaths per 1,000 live births in 1992, after a steady decline beginning in 1970 and an estimated eleven deaths per 1,000 live births in 1988. Its rate was higher than that of Estonia and Lithuania and almost three times the rate of infant mortality in Finland. In 1994 there (would be) 16.3 deaths per 1,000 population in Latvia. The primary causes of infant deaths in Latvia are perinatal diseases; congenital anomalies; infectious, parasitic, or intestinal diseases; respiratory diseases; and accidents and poisonings. Environmental factors and alcoholism and drug abuse also contribute to infant mortality.
>
> Latvia outpaced most of the other republics in the Soviet Union in deaths from accidents, poisonings, and traumas. In 1989 some 16 percent of males and 5.6 percent of females (would die) from these causes. The suicide rate of 25.9 per 100,000 in 1990, or a total of 695, (would be) more than twice that of the United States. In 1992 the number of suicides (would increase) to 883. Other major causes of death include cancer, respiratory conditions, and such stress-related afflictions as heart disease and stroke. (Walter R. Iwaskiw, ed. Latvia: A Country Study. Washington: GPO for the Library of Congress, 1995. <http://countrystudies.us/latvia/13.htm>)

There was daily shopping to be done with a rambunctious child in tow, and our staircase took on a formidable appearance, as I climbed it each day. Our running water appeared and disappeared. Everything was erratic and unpredictable. I was dragging myself to work (the typewriter), looking after our child, and doing daily chores. With no washing machine or dryer, soiled clothes were a permanent headache. I also realized that as a family we did not plan things, such as getaways. The family feuds at Paulēni had lost their novelty and appeal. I wasn't cut out for communal living.

One hot afternoon a panic attack so severe made me pick up the phone and call my doctor friends Jānis and Ilze Krūmals in Smiltene. I needed help, and I needed a way out. They immediately responded, inviting me to come for an extended stay and a check-up. I was overwhelmed by a sense of relief. I managed to get in touch with Andris to let him know we were going away, packed a small travel bag, and we walked to the bus station and left Rīga behind. My poor child who snuggled against me... Mamma was a mess.

I came to realize that I had expected too much of myself. I had thrown myself into an alien world at a young and impressionable age; my experiences there had gradually robbed me of my vitality and hope. The shock of seeing our fatherland so humiliated and abused had depressed me. My initial enthusiasm was replaced by a wide range of worries and practical hurdles. I tried to balance my work, which was important for my self-esteem, with being a full-time, hands-on mother. My husband's career often took him away from us, and in his free time he mainly wanted to go to his parents' place in the countryside, while I longed for a place of our own. Our interests diverged early on. After all, we were so young when we got married, and we scarcely knew each other. The pressure of living together in close confines also took its toll on me. Personal space, as it turned out, was a crucial aspect in the health of a relationship. At least a Latvian one. I also felt like I was the one always left behind, as my partner pursued a career that took him to interesting people, places, and events. I didn't blame him; I blamed myself for not speaking out to seek a remedy.

My week in Smiltene under the kind and gentle care of Dr. Ilze Krūmala, a physical therapist, worked wonders. Andris came by to pick up Krišjānis and took him to Paulēni, so that I could devote myself entirely to getting better. Each morning Ilze and I had breakfast together and talked; she was an interesting conversation partner. She was interested in Smiltene's local history and proudly showed me the neat hospital that she and Jānis, a surgeon, lovingly maintained. It was spotless. She listened to me attentively and prescribed some soothing procedures. For the first time in a long time, I felt like someone really cared about me. Nobody until then had ever asked me how I was coping with the strange and harsh world of the proletariat. *I had felt voiceless: not allowed to and incapable of expressing my anger at what was happening around me.* My life in 1987 felt like a cage within a cage.

I admired the Krūmals' beautifully maintained garden and its profusion of flowers. I took walks in the pretty little town in northern Latvia, where no Russian could be heard. It had been a long time since I had been on my own. In the evenings before going to bed in my kind hosts' cosy living room, I read on the couch. It was quiet. I had time to think. "You should take a break from Latvia," Ilze suggested. Go home to the United States. And that was exactly what I planned on doing.

Sandy*

*This chapter is a tribute to my home state, New Jersey. "Sandy" is a reference to one of my favorite songs by Bruce Springsteen, a musician I listened to prior to going to Latvia.

Fall of 1987: preparing to board the Rīga-Moscow train. Krišjānis helping out, while Grandpa Juris looks on. Photo: Andris Krieviņš.

And so it was settled. I was going back to the United States for a much needed rest. Our son Krišjānis was coming with me. I would visit with my family and patch up my nerves. Not that my departure, trip, and absence would change anything in our circumstances in Rīga. I needed to forget about all of that for a while. Andris would join us later at Christmas time. My general constitution was still strong, but aspects of Soviet life had chipped away at it, leaving me feeling brittle and weak. My rose-tinted glasses about the fatherland had shattered.

Our little man was three, with no idea of what lay ahead of him: a ride on a train; a trip on a plane; a Richard Scarry storybook trip. He was excited, and his enthusiasm buoyed me. As I packed, I already felt better. *There was something to look forward to*. This in and of itself was one of life's keys to happiness, I realized. On a September afternoon Andris, Krišjānis, and I boarded the Rīga-Moscow train, waving goodbye to our friends, who had come to wish us a safe journey. Renāte Krūmala, Andris Kapusts, and Māris Jansons serenaded our departure on the fiddle, accordion, and tambourine: they were all involved in Latvia's folk music renaissance to a greater or lesser degree. Grandpa "Pacītis" was there, too, to bid farewell, as was Gita and her latest beau, Juris. Strangers nearby seemed to enjoy the merry sounds, as they looked on with curiosity. Latvia! I needed to leave you to love you again!

We bid farewell to Andris ("Tita") at Sheremetyevo Airport. I could not wait to get on that "big ol' jet airliner," which would take us far away from the USSR. With my little man next to me, I was now in adventure mode. We had obtained an American passport for him, which provided me with a measure of comfort. Up in the sky, we gazed through the window at the clouds and Russia's landmass below; already I felt myself shedding the weight of the last five years.

Everything about the plane was a wonder for Krišjānis. The seats, the buttons, the sounds, the stewardesses! And the clouds outside! No snoozing for me either!

Many hours later we touched down in Newfoundland for refueling. We were permitted to disembark and ventured into a small shop at the airport. Krišjānis had stumbled onto Treasure Island; his eyes grew big, as he absorbed all the bright and attractively packaged Western goods—candy, trinkets, small toys, and other colorful merchandise. Every little item with its happy, shiny colors was like a magic bauble for him, a child used to seeing everything in dull Soviet hues. It was almost painful to see his enthusiasm. I could barely pull him out of there.

As we flew in over the New York metropolitan area, I was overwhelmed by an array of emotions: joy; love; gratitude; and American patriotism. I loved New York City more than I did Rīga, I thought at that moment, and I was amazed by what I was seeing, even if I had seen it countless times before in my previous life, in my pre-Soviet youth. That life felt like decades ago! Life in the Free World! The New York area was jampacked with urban development and life! Every square inch as seen from the plane was covered with houses, buildings, and streets, whereas most of Latvia was covered by dark green forests, meadows, and fields. New York was an enormous hub of human activity. Busy. Fast. Moving. Tiny cars racing along a jumble of traffic arteries. Non-stop, fantastic New York, which never slept! Rīga seemed tiny by comparison. And Moscow, from which we had departed from the Union of Soviet Socialist Republics, was cold and forbidding. I tried to stem the flood of hot tears...

We were met at the airport by Valdis Kupris, my Latvian American friend and Krišjānis' godfather who had become a frequent visitor to Latvia, shooting videos and taking photographs, drawing, and helping orphans and sick children. That good man had a big bunch of bananas with him, which Krišjānis proceeded to devour one after the other like Curious George, as if bananas were the most delicious food in the world. It had been five years since I'd tasted a banana. By the time we hit the New Jersey Turnpike, all the bananas were in my son's bulging belly!

As we drove across the magnificent Verrazano Narrows Bridge, I gazed upon the wonder that was the island of Manhattan, caressing with my eyes its mesh of skyscrapers, the stately Twin Towers of the World Trade Center, and the shimmering Hudson River way below us. Far off in the distance was Ellis Island, symbol of the United States of America's immigrant culture and a new life in the New World, and the Statue of Liberty, which symbolized freedom and hope. How I loved all of it! My familiar world that I had abandoned! This land had nurtured my spirit and taught me the meaning of freedom, real freedom. Because of it, I cherished freedom most of all.

Coming back "home" to Glen Ridge was strange and delightful. I was seeing my old world through the eyes of a deeply changed person. I felt ten years older and 20 years more experienced. Only five years had passed since I left the comfort of this old house? As Valdis' car pulled into the driveway, the gravel crunched in the familiar way: the sound of my father returning from work each day. The old dogwoods were turning red. As my mother opened the door for us, I sniffed appreciatively: the scent of childhood and home! My father's painting "Midnight Procession" was still on the wall in the veranda, delighting me. Used to being confined to our tiny apartment in Old Rīga, Krišjānis commenced exploring the house like a cat, climbing up and down the two staircases looking positively elated. *So much space!* Yes, it was as if twenty years had passed.

Seeing my old bedroom again was an emotional moment. My photographs and artwork were still on the wall: a photograph by Latvian American photographer Daina Vipule; Andris Breže's black and white self-portrait with a poem about the Latvian language; Ojārs Pētersons in a Soviet Army uniform; my pre-war map of Latvia; my green and orange Indian blanket above my bed; my books; my orange cupboard; the desk where I had done my homework and written letters to Latvia. Not much had changed. What was different was me. I had changed. Immensely. I had grown up. I had given birth to a child. I was now a responsible adult. And I had seen a different, darker side of humanity.

I turned on the radio. On my first day back in the USA I listened hungrily to the sound of American English. It was a sound I had forgotten: laid-back, chatty, natural. For once commercial radio didn't bother me. And songs I'd missed! As some Neil Young tune took hold of me, I gazed through the windows at the falling twilight. I could see my old elementary school, Linden, through the trees. Linden had a playground! The sun had dipped behind the horizon in the west. California...

Oh it gets so lonely / When you're walking / And the streets are full of strangers / All the news of home you read / Just gives you the blues... (Joni Mitchell, "California")

Five years had passed since I had set out for the East and the rising sun. I continued to believe that one day the sun would also rise for Latvia, just like the men and boys who fought for Latvia's freedom in the War of Independence believed it would rise over their fatherland: many of their banners depicted a rising sun. The best was yet to come, they had believed. They had laid down their lives for that hope, that sweet dream.

My parents had purchased a mattress for Krišjānis. It took up all the free space in my tiny bedroom. In the evening of my first day back "home" I happily drew the shades; my little boy laid his tired head on a pillow sheathed in a Peanuts pillowcase, surrounded by stuffed animals that my excited family had purchased in anticipation of our arrival. So fluffy and soft. Even a stuffed animal was too hard for the Soviet communists to figure out how to make. We drifted off into a deep sleep, mamma and son, overwhelmed by jet lag and happy emotions. And so it began—my healing.

Right: First night back home in the States in 1987. Krišjānis is playing with his new "friends."

As I re-accustomed myself to my old sur-roundings, I delighted in so many things that most Americans took for granted. Clean tap water, which I drank with relish, thinking of the fluoride it contained that would strengthen our teeth. (The teeth of the fatherland's Latvians were mostly bad.) Regular mail delivery to an unbroken mailbox. The weekly trash collection, so regular, so predictable, so convenient. And friendly neighbors and strangers.

I took long, hot showers, singing an old song by Miķelis Akerbergs: "Ūdens, ūdens, lūk, kā ūdens plūst, dzejojot, dejojot..." ("Water, water, see the water flow, writing poems and dancing...") It was washing away my blues. I loved giving Krišjānis bubblebaths. His skin and hair began to glow in just a few days. It must have been the fresh air. We raked leaves, and he fell into them. One of the joys of having a yard of your own. The scent of autumn invigorated me. My panic attacks subsided.

I could listen to real news on the radio instead of some kind of crazy fake stuff about how much the milk production had increased in some backwards kolhoz. The Soviet concept of reality had really unnerved me. I could sit on our back porch and watch Krišjānis run around in the yard and climb trees like a little monkey. The sounds of the bluejays filled me with glee.. No sound of the Russian language, which in Latvia symbolized imperialism coupled with arrogance, ethnocentrism, and bigotry. No pushy, rude people. It was still warm in late autumn, and I enjoyed that. Our house had a thermostat, so I knew we could turn on the heat when it got colder.

With delight I washed our clothes in the basement and folded them in neat piles: Americans were spoiled rotten with their appliances and gadgets! My parents' refrigerator seemed enormous after what we were used to cramming food into in Rīga. In the mornings I sat in my old spot in the kitchen and watched the sunshine bathe the old geraniums in a gentle light; how was it that one's sense of time could be so altered by moving to another place? For my entire childhood the morning sunlight had fallen on those red geraniums, but now it felt like I had crossed an abyss and nothing would ever be the same. My parents' old straw-wrapped wine bottles hung above the kitchen windows, reminding me of our dinners together, when I was young and naïve.

Once settled in, we began taking walks, encountering pleasant people who smiled or nodded and said hello. Krišjānis' little face brightened. Police cruisers passed by; the policemen waved to us, making me feel safe and welcome. A firetruck drove by; the firemen also waved, as my son practically jumped from joy. These were small gestures that I picked up on right away: the manifestations of a civil society.

In nearby Bloomfield I reacquainted myself with American stores that competed for our attention with sales, bargains, and a huge selection. I never once saw a sale sign in a Soviet store. Polite, friendly, helpful salespeople approached me, offering their assistance and politely moving away when I declined. Inexpensive, attractive clothes and shoes beckoned. I never was a shopaholic, but I enjoyed the relaxed atmosphere of American stores, where there were no double lines (order and pay and pick-up), where you could actually try on clothes easily, because you were more or less trusted, etc. And why was everything in Rīga so expensive?!

How wonderful it was to explore our old Glen Ridge Public Library on Ridgewood Avenue with Krišjānis. Unlike in Rīga, the books were accessible to anyone. Krišjānis was delighted to find more Richard Scarry picture books on the shelves with "Kozo" (Goldbug), his favorite book character. We obtained a card right away and lugged home a backpack full of wonderful picture books. My hometown streets were quiet and clean, with tidy gardens and many old trees. I now marveled at the old gas lanterns, realizing what a unique aspect of Glen Ridge they were.

I visited a doctor who told me I was suffering from a form of depression. I saw him only once, because I kept feeling better and better with each passing day. I slept well and ate with relish. And then I began thinking about the future and choices. Did I really want to go back to Latvia? I enrolled Krišjānis in a daycare program twice a week at Congregational Church to expose him to English. He loved it. Our walks home along quiet, pretty Hillside Avenue were a natural anti-depressant. Absorbing my old surroundings with a newfound delight, I kept telling myself that there was no way I was going back to communist Latvia. I took to looking for jobs in the news-paper. Andris would be arriving in December. I would get a job, and we should stay in the United States. But I also realized that this sense of peace would not last. My brothers were still in the house, and once my husband arrived, it would get crowded.

There were so many tiny sensations that soothed my frayed nerves. That autumn my body and mind were like a sponge, absorbing calming phenomena. We visited several parks, where nobody approached me to ask in Russian if I'd like to sell them my clothes, my stroller, my dig-nity. I felt inconspicuous and at peace. I absorbed the brilliant fall foliage, savoring it like sweet marzipan for the eyes: yellow; gold; orange; red. The colors of autumn maple leaves had been burned into my memory in childhood; now I was feasting on them.

Classic rock songs on the radio delighted me. It was good to be back and hear the music of my fellow New Jerseyans Bruce Springsteen, Patti Smith, Debbie Harry, John Bon Jovi, Al Di Me-ola... Packed though it was, New Jersey had a great vibe that maybe only someone born there could feel. I was regaining my "Jersey bounce" (Ella Fitzgerald). And so was my son! I put on Bruce Springsteen's album "The Wild, the Innocent, and the E-Street Shuffle," the first record I'd ever bought, and listened to "Fourth of July, Asbury Park" (*Sandy) over and over again. The last time I listened to that album, I was still in my age of innocence. The rosy cocoon of a safe childhood had slipped away, and the world looked harsher than before.

My parents delighted in conversing with their first grandchild; my father liked to lie in bed with him and tell him stories about World War II. We visited my maternal grandmother Līvija at her apartment in Montclair. What happy meetings those were, as she listened in wonder to her great grandson Krišjānis speak to her in perfect Latvian!

By December I felt great. I began looking forward to welcoming my husband in the US. How-ever, by then my sense of tranquility had dissipated. I was nervous. Just as I had predicted, things tensed up right away, when he arrived. Our house was old, the rooms were small. The three of us in my narrow bedroom was no longer a comfortable arrangement. My husband had come over primarily to do a stretch of photo shows in America and Canada to make some money. The preparation for these exhibits was stressful, as it involved buying materials, matting, and fram-ing, all of which required time, travel, and money, which we had little of. I hated asking my father favors. My general discomfort in living in a communal dwelling (which is what our house had become) caused me to quickly change my mind and begin thinking of going back to Latvia. My husband had no intention of staying in America. By January I felt ready for departure.

Nevertheless, it was good to be back together again. We took some trips, saw some places: Amish country in Pennsylvania; the Catskill Mountains; Philadelphia; Chicago; Toronto; Boston... We met some wonderful people. Home... Yes, home was where the heart was, and it was Latvia, I told myself. I was only a visitor in Glen Ridge, New Jersey. I needed space and my own place.

March 1988: Krišjānis and Old Glory in an old cemetery in the Catskill Mountains.. Photo: Aina Balgalvis.

In March I buzzed my hair down to a butch, probably to spite Soviet customs officials, and we flew out of New York's JFK, bound for West Germany. My husband had made a bundle of cash selling his photographs and wanted to buy a car. We would stay at a friend's place and shop around in Münster.

All the way to Europe Krišjānis and I giggled at a book of Gary Larson's "Far Side" cartoons, a present from our friends, Sondors and Anna Abens, who had also sold us their old Peugeot for a dollar. (It broke down a month later, and we left it in the Glen Ridge driveway.) Laughter was medicine, they said. I was preparing myself mentally for the return to the "Evil Empire."

1988: "Rīga Retour"

Dr. Andris Kadeģis (1933–2012), our good friend and host in West Germany.

In West Germany we stayed with our friend Dr. Andris Kadeģis at his lovely home outside of Münster in the neatly manicured German countryside, which, compared to Latvia, looked almost too tidy. Oh, those Germans! They even planted forests in rows. My parents knew Andris; over the years he had shown up from time to time at some of the Latvian gatherings in the New York City area. In 1983 I had bumped into him in Old Rīga. He came to visit us at our apartment, and the rest was history. We had a blast that time: Kadeģis was inquisitive, and my husband loved to tell stories. When our son was born, he had supplied us with infant multivitamin drops.

Born in Liepāja, Kadeģis was one of the hundreds of thousands of Latvians who left Latvia in 1944 to escape an impending second Soviet occupation; the Germans were retreating, but the Russian tanks were rolling in. Kadeģis studied medicine at Rutgers University in New Jersey and at Ludwig Maximilian University in Munich, West Germany, and became a pathologist. He was very involved in Latvian life in exile, especially that of the Latvian secondary school in Münster. Well-read, cultured, and with a great sense of humor and a deep understanding of the wrongs inflicted on the Baltic States in the 20th century, Andris Kadeģis was a good friend who helped us in our time of need.

My husband wasted no time looking for a used car. Flush with cash from his successful exhibitions in North America, he knew it was our only chance to get our hands on a motor vehicle, albeit a used one. Quickly he tracked down an old red Opel. Although no beauty, the car seemed sturdy, comfortable, and dependable. In the meantime I enjoyed searching for simple household items in West German stores. The simplest items—a hanging storage basket, a colorful soap dish, kitchen sponges, *the most mundane stuff*—filled me with pleasure. Cheap thrills!

And then one sunny day we loaded up the Opel, our first family car, bid farewell to our good friend the pathologist in Münster, and began our long drive east, headed for Brest, Belarus, the border crossing point into the Soviet Union, with Krišjānis bouncing around in the back seat (no car seats or restraints back then). Driving into East Germany, we immediately sensed a change. The effects of communism were palpable: the cold demeanor of the border guards; the stark

East German landscape; the sense that the great, unsheathed paw of Russia was casting a cold shadow over this part of Europe. I couldn't shake the icy feeling. We had left the Free World behind. The countryside in East Germany looked less appealing than its counterpart on the other side of the Iron Curtain. There private farmlands owned by West German farmers were manicured to perfection, and West Germany's small towns offered rest and relaxation in cosy privately owned inns, restaurants, cafés, and pubs.

Years later, watching the riveting film "The Lives of Others" (2006) about the East German Stasi (secret police) and life under their pervasive surveillance, I was reminded of our own lives in Soviet-occupied Latvia, lived in the crosshairs of strangers. I had heard that the Stasi were even nastier than the Russian KGB. The murders of East Germans trying to cross the Berlin Wall seemed to confirm this. I nervously glanced at the speedometer. A long, uncertain drive lay ahead of us, and Andris was determined not to stop anywhere, except to heed the call of nature or for emergencies. A Soviet citizen and an American citizen in one car: it looked peculiar, even though our travel papers were in order.

"Welcome to your life / There's no turning back / Even while we sleep / We will find you..." (Tears for Fears "Everybody Wants to Rule the World")

We estimated that it was a 12 hour trip to the border. Although the sun shines above you, the countryside around you is alien; no one speaks your language; no one cares about you; Americans are the devil; and you hope your car's motor and tires won't fail. This was communist Europe, where cold, cynical behavior on the part of bureaucrats was the norm. People could be unpredictable and mean. The Polish countryside looked deserted and endless.

The trip seems even longer, when you're driving all that distance *back* after arrival at the Soviet border, having endured the humiliating, corrupt attitude of Soviet customs, being extorted by official thugs for a sum ten times the value of your beat-up old car, with an American wife as a liability seated next to you (who doesn't know what the hell is going on), and a squirmy, antsy son who has spent too many hours in the backseat bored out of his mind... It was then in the spring of 1988, as we idled on the threshold of the Soviet empire, berated, belittled, and made to look like fools, that the horrible horridness of Soviet life really hit me. We had just been in the United States, where the government bureaucracy was relatively transparent, and bureaucrats were paid to make your life easier, not more difficult and frustrating. In the USSR the Soviet authorities with their shiny buttons were the cruel cat that played with its mice—its citizens. What kind of state makes one feel so tiny, helpless, unwanted, useless, and expendable?!

Our failure to get by Soviet customs (that is, pay them off) to travel on to "our" own country now reminds me of *Rīga retour* (1961), Dr. Andris Kadeģis' marvelous travelogue about his return to Soviet-occupied Latvia in 1960 via Moscow. The mere fact that for decades expatriate Latvians had to travel to Latvia via Moscow, the seat of their oppressors, was humiliating. Before the war Rīga had once been an international hub of travel, linked directly with Western Europe. In 1988 we were required to make a huge detour through Brest to get to Latvia, which was extremely irritating, to put it mildly.

So there we were: an innocent couple with a small child prevented by a dirty Soviet customs boot from entering the door to get back home. Realizing we were in a helpless situation, unable to cough up the outrageous sum the comrades in caps and epaulets salivated for, we retreated back into Poland. We drove back to Münster in stony silence, grappling with our angry thoughts, humiliation, and physical and mental exhaustion. Neither Andris nor I had slept a wink since leaving Münster the morning of the previous day. Our money was running out, too. It felt surreal to be retracing our route, hitting the West German roadways, nearing Münster again some 25 hours later. The Brest experience was traumatic.

Was Andris Kadeģis surprised? Only slightly. He took us miserable travelers in, fed and pampered us, listened to our story, and drove us to West Berlin a couple of days later. We would go home by train, leaving the Opel in Münster for future pickup. By then we were too exhausted and depleted to wait around any longer. We wanted to go home.

We spent the night in a bed and breakfast. The next day we strolled around town and visited the Berlin Zoo. Berlin had been heavily bombed during the war, and I didn't find its modern architecture particularly appealing, although I did find Kaiser William Memorial Church a moving reminder of "the war to end all wars." In the evening we set off for the train station. In East Berlin we waited to board the train that would take us further east to Rīga. Struggling to keep an eye on our mountain of luggage, we stationed Krišjānis near it as a sentry as we began loading our belongings on the train. We weren't watchful enough. Some creep managed to steal a large bag full of our little man's stuffed animals. Childhood innocence lost! Hell, we didn't even want to think of the car we were forced to leave in Münster. It would wait for us; we would be back.

East Germany, Poland, the Soviet border, Belarus, Lithuania, Latvia, Rīga, home... The train's soothing rhythm helped us forget our unsuccessful car trip; we were slipping in and out of consciousness. In another more light-hearted world Bobby McFerrin was singing "Don't worry, be happy." Happiness in the Soviet Union was a prescribed concept, an artificial construct, an order from above, a daisy beneath the heel of a Russian Army boot.

1987: Helsinki-86; "Queen Latvia is Awakening"

A nation divided: East Germany's Erich Honecker (left) and West Germany's Helmut Schmidt in Helsinki in 1975 at the Conference on Security and Cooperation, which was an attempt to improve relations between the West (the "Free World") and the Communist Bloc. The communist East would ignore the Decalogue (the ten principles) of the non-binding Helsinki Accords. This conference served as a reference point for Baltic freedom fighters. Source: Wikimedia Commons. https://commons.wikimedia.org/wiki/File:Bun desarchiv_Bild_146-1990-009-13,_Helsinki,_KSZE-Konferenz.jpg (© Bundesarchiv, B 145 Bild-F046227-0058 / Engelbert Reineke / CC BY-SA 3.0 https://creativecommons.org/licenses/by-sa/3.0/de/deed.en)

*"(The) Declaration on Principles Guiding Relations between Participating States" ("The Decalogue") of the Helsinki Accords was signed in Helsinki, Finland on August 1, 1975 by Austria, Belgium, **Bulgaria**, Canada, Cyprus, **Czechoslovakia**, Denmark, Finland, France, the **German Democratic Republic**, the Federal Republic of Germany, Greece, the Holy See, **Hungary**, Iceland, Ireland, Italy, Liechtenstein, Luxembourg, Malta, Monaco, the Netherlands, Norway, **Poland**, Portugal, **Romania**, San Marino, Spain, Sweden, Switzerland, Turkey, the **Soviet Union**, the United Kingdom, the USA and **Yugoslavia**. (Countries under the Soviet sphere of influence in bold.—RL)*

The non-binding principles: (1) Sovereign equality, respect for the rights inherent in sovereignty; (2) Refraining from the threat or use of force; (3) Inviolability of frontiers; (4) Territorial integrity of States; (5) Peaceful settlement of disputes; (6) Non-intervention in internal affairs; (7) Respect for human rights and fundamental freedoms, including the freedom of thought, conscience, religion or belief; (8) Equal rights and self-determination of people; (9) Co-operation among States; (10) Fulfilment in good faith of obligations under international law (Source: OSCE.org)

In the summer of 1987, when I was struggling with severe depression, a storm of historic proportions was brewing in Latvia. "After the rain comes the rainbow." Responding to perestroika, the "ungrateful" Balts were beginning to test the patience of Moscow. Because Latvia's press and media were still muzzled, people went about their daily lives without realizing that a few unforeseen events would set off a chain reaction with a spectacular outcome. A serious book about the late 1980s in Latvia is waiting to be written; many brave individuals deserve to be mentioned. Their biographies serve as a grim reminder of Latvia under the Soviet Russian boot of occupation.

In 1986 a Latvian trio from Liepāja, a port city by then was heavily militarized by the Soviets, had founded a human rights group by the name of "Helsinki-86." Linards Grantiņš, Raimonds Bitenieks, and Mārtiņš Bariss chose this name to refer to the Helsinki Accords, which had been agreed upon and signed in Finland in 1975 (*see introduction to this chapter*). The non-binding agreement had spelled out important principles that the signatories, including the Soviet Union and the communist bloc countries, promised to honor. These principles included "equal rights and self-determination of people." I was a silent witness to the Soviets' daily non-observance of the accord's principles.

Latvians have a saying: *Solīts makā nekrīt* ("Promises don't fill the wallet"). Eleven years had passed since the Helsinki Accords, yet the situation for ethnic Latvians in Latvia continued to deteriorate under Soviet communist rule. My people were on the verge of becoming a minority in their ancient fatherland. Given the chance, Balts could have easily testified how the Soviet Union brazenly disregarded the so-called Decalogue. Helsinki-86 was able to smuggle a letter of protest out of the country: it was an indictment of the Central Committee of the Communist Party of the Soviet Union and the Central Committee of the Communist Party of Soviet Latvia.

As Midsummer drew near, we heard a rumor that some sort of unsanctioned gathering was going to take place on June 14 at the Freedom Monument. This rumor was electrifying, of course, because every single Latvian knew about the tragic historical events associated with that date: on June 14, 1941 the Soviets deported about 15,000 Latvian citizens of all ages to Soviet death camps and forced settlements in Siberia. In the Soviet Cheka's sweep of the country not one segment of Latvia's demographic had been spared, as men, pregnant women, infants, young children, and frail, old people were locked into cattlecars and sent east across the Soviet border, my great aunt and uncle included.

As it turned out, Helsinki-86, a group of people that almost nobody in Latvia knew about, was inviting people to gather near the Freedom Monument for the first time in Latvia's history since the Soviet occupation to openly commemorate the victims of the June 14, 1941 deportations. With the appearance of restructuring and glasnost underway, apparently they felt the time was right.

The subject of "Helsinki-86" would surface in my last "official" meeting with the Latvian KGB in 1987. The chubby chekist who warned me to stay away from Helsinki-86 basically alerted me to the nature of the group. If the KGB didn't like them, it meant they were people with a good cause.

On June 14, 1987 an extraordinary convergence of hearts, minds, and physical bodies took place at the foot of Mother Latvia, our Freedom Monument, in the center of Rīga. A small group of people showed up near the monument bearing flowers and commemorative banners emblazoned with words like "For Fatherland and Freedom," the inscription at the base of the Freedom Monument, and "God, Bless Latvia," the title of the Latvian national anthem. Just a short while ago such a public manifestation of Latvian nationalism and "anti-Soviet propaganda" would have guaranteed immediate arrest, a hasty trial, and a lengthy prison term in the Russian heartland. At the time Gunārs Astra was still locked up in Perm-36, a brutal forced labor camp.

Contrary to everyone's nervous expectations, instead of being immediately rounded up and whisked away by Soviet law enforcement, these recklessly brave individuals were quietly standing around having their photographs taken. They placed their flowers, wreaths, and banners by the monument, as an ever surging crowd closed in, looking on with curiosity, admiration, and rising emotion. It was a "moment" of electrifying suspense. A tiny white mouse, a "Miss Bianca," waving its tail under the whiskers of Mamelouk, the ferocious cat (*The Rescuers* by Marjorie Sharp).

Apparently, Helsinki -86 had spread the word about the gathering through Voice of America and Radio Free Europe/Radio Liberty, shortwave radio programs that some Latvians secretly tuned into for news from the Free World. The call on Latvians to meet at the monument on June 14 was an audacious move, to say the least. By doing so, the participants risked severe reprisal. (To put this in perspective, by the end of the year, pressured by the West, Gorbachev would dissolve the Gulag system, which had broken the lives of millions of people.) For those bystanders who had survived the Gulag or whose loved ones had perished, their hearts must have been breaking from positive emotion.

Who exactly were these "dangerous" people whom I was explicitly warned about? The parents and grandparents of Linards Grantiņš, a jewelry maker, had been deported to Siberia on March 25, 1949 in a wave of mass arrests that took place in the Baltics. Linards Grantiņš was born in Siberia. The family returned to Latvia in 1956. In an interview with Latvian journalist Anita Bormane, Grantiņš says that he woke up one night in 1987 and "heard a voice" ordering him to organize the June 14, 1987 gathering at the Freedom Monument. (1)

Linards Grantiņš, Raimonds Bitenieks, and Mārtiņš Bariss, the founders of Helsinki-86, were not on hand at the June 14 gathering. On August 21, 1986 Grantiņš had been arrested and thrown into jail; he was convinced that he would not come out alive. However, thanks to his friend Elvīra Pujēna, photocopies of Helsinki-86 petitions and documents would soon be circulated abroad thanks to Western broadcast channels; this probably saved his life. After five months in prison, Grantiņš was released. To deter him from future political activities, the authorities re-arrested Grantiņš on June 9, 1987, falsely accusing him of shirking military duty. This time he was incarcerated with hardcore criminals; they beat him so badly, that they broke his rib cage. "These are my worst memories: (the KGB) locked me up with criminals, hoping the thugs would kill me. When they broke my rib cage, I passed out every time I coughed: the pain was so bad." (2)

Grantiņš was forced to emigrate: the KGB said they could not guarantee his safety in Latvia. He was separated from his children—his daughters who remained in Latvia. He ended up in West Germany and eventually became a truck driver. (3)

Raimonds Bitenieks was first alerted to the nature of the Soviet regime, when people started vanishing from the streets of Liepāja on March 25, 1949. He was six years old at the time. In September of 1983 he and a friend and their teenage children made an attempt to escape to Sweden from Liepāja with a specially equipped motorboat. They were intercepted by the Soviets and returned to Latvia, and the men were sentenced to two years in prison. (4)

When Bitenieks was released, the KGB took to following him around. "The only things that changed were the license numbers and the drivers," he recalled. In 1986 Bitenieks did not hesitate to join Helsinki-86. He trusted Linards Grantiņš instinctively and signed the founding documents without really reading them.

On August 22, 1987, one day prior to mass demonstrations near the Freedom Monument in Rīga, Bitenieks would be arrested and would spend the next five months in an isolation cell at the "Corner House" on Ļeņina iela. Eventually the KGB forced Bitenieks to make a choice: leave the Soviet Union permanently or end up in "sunny" Magadan, one of its primary destinations for political activists (in spite of Gorbachev's promises to the West). (5)

"If I had stayed in the Soviet Union, I would have faced a seven-year prison term and a five-year resettlement in a Siberian kolhoz" (Bitenieks). After his experience in prison and in an isolation cell, and sick of the contant presence of the KGB, by the end of 1987 Bitenieks chose to emigrate from the Soviet Union, thinking he could eventually settle in the United States. He ended up in West Germany, too, because "from Münster you can walk to Latvia..." Bitenieks credited his "fighting spirit" for the courage to do what he did in the late era of Soviet communist rule in Latvia. In 1989 Bitenieks' daughters Eva and Jana were reunited with their father in West Germany. Eva was the famous young woman in a Latvian folk costume who took part in the June 14, 1986 event near the Freedom Monument. (6)

Mārtiņš Bariss never left Latvia. He joined Helsinki-86 because he believed that it was "now or never." He was able to withstand the KGB's psychological pressure tactics and efforts at intimidation. He would lose touch with Grantiņš and Bitenieks, bitter at them for leaving Latvia. (7)

The presence of Eva Biteniece in her folk costume, a manifestation of Latvian pride and patriotism, and Rolands Silaraups, the handsome young man in an attractive, light-colored suit, was surprising and refreshing for many of the curious onlookers: these were young people who were risking state pressure and persecution. In a 1997 interview in the daily *Diena*, Biteniece said she remembered feeling absolutely no fear on that day. She had already experienced some sizzling excitement during her father Raimonds' attempted escape to Sweden in a motorboat. She and 15-year-old Agris Vansovičs were on that boat, when they were caught by the Soviet border patrol and sent back to Liepāja. (8)

It was precisely this sort of manifestation that Comrade Fatz-Katz and his cohorts were worried about. There were lots and lots of people milling around in the vicinity of the monument and the Soviet militsiya and undercover chekists standing by on high alert. My husband and I lingered on the periphery as a precaution. We went home feeling ecstatic. It was one of the most thrilling days of my life. We seemed to be waking up from a nightmare. The full story of that day and what happened to the founders of Helsinki-86 emerged many years later, when most Latvians had already forgotten about their heroes.

A couple of months later in August, while I was battling full-blown depression, Helsinki-86 managed to attract another large gathering at the Freedom Monument on the 23rd to remind Latvians of the infamous Molotov-Ribbentrop Pact signed in 1939, which sealed the fates of the Baltic States for decades to come. As an enormous crowd of Latvians of all ages, including young children clinging to their mothers, gathered near the monument chanting "Demokrātiju!" ("Democracy!"), "Brīvību!" ("Freedom!"), "Tēvzemei un brīvibai!" ("For Fatherland and Freedom!"), and "Dievs, svētī Latviju!" ("God, bless Latvia!"), the Soviet (read Russian) militsiya attempted to cordon off the area around the monument, pushing back the chanting masses. It was still open to public transporation vehicles, and the crowds weren't letting them through.

Mother Latvia was struck speechless by her children's behavior. For decades they had shunned her, barely looking up at her downcast face, as they hurried by. On August 23, 1987 Latvians broke into spontaneous singing, whistling at the line of policemen—the ignorant, mostly Russian-speaking militsiya who were on edge and positively clueless as to what was going on. In a video recording of the historic event, a Russian policewoman with a megaphone can be heard barking warnings to the surging crowd. This was a marvelous example of the ethnic aspect of the Soviet occupation: the oppressors (Russians) versus the oppressed (ethnic Latvians). The Russian policemen probably thought that the monument was a depiction of *Mat' Rossiya* (Mother Russia). In addition, most of them probably did not understand the *sobaka* ("dog") language of the multitude of Latvian "fascists" that had gathered there to cause trouble. It is important to understand that if many Latvians could still remember their free and independent state, then the ethnic Russians of Soviet Latvia, the vast majority of them post-war immigrants and de facto colonists, had no memory or concept of freedom. They knew nothing of Latvia's history, Latvian culture, what transpired in Latvia between 1939 and 1945, the Soviet deportations, Soviet terror, and so on. Nor did these immigrants even know the brutal history of their own country, Soviet Russia, it seemed, yet they claimed Latvia for themselves.

Old Latvians, the generation that had suffered the most, stood by quietly with flowers in their hands. And then the militsiya and chekists started grabbing people, mostly young men, and hauling them off to waiting cars, as the outraged crowd screamed, whistled, and jeered. Other bystanders were assaulted. Fire trucks were dispatched to the scene to disperse protesters with water. Scores of people were arrested; members of Helsinki-86 were nowhere to be found. Apparently they had been arrested and isolated in a building near the monument. It was clear that the Soviet Latvian authorities were very nervous and unsure of how to deal with the situation.

"Demokrātiju! Demokrātiju!" ("Democracy! Democracy!") The dramatic scenes of that day have been preserved in raw footage that can be viewed on YouTube ("1987. g. 23. augusts Rīgā"). As a Latvian and a Balt, I remain very proud of how Latvians behaved at that dramatic time, when Rīga was surrounded and permeated by Soviet (read Russian) military forces and legions of cynical chekists. From day one of "the Singing Revolution," the Latvian, Lithuanian, and Estonian nations' peaceful rebellion against Soviet tyranny, the Balts demonstrated remarkable composure and self-restraint, which was enhanced by their propensity to face danger and misfortune with song.

 Visual: <http://www.youtube.com/watch?v=-_emGdT40ro>

While I was away in the United States, people gathered again at the Latvian Freedom Monument to observe Latvian Independence Day on November 18, 1987. The pressure cooker was heating up.

One of Helsinki-86's most trusted members, Juris Ziemelis (b. 1941), a dissident who had spent most of his adult life in various Soviet prison camps, would die mysteriously the following year (1988). In 1987 he gave an impassioned speech at the foot of the Freedom Monument, arguing that "the ideologues, historians, and writers from 'the Ministry of Truth' tried to whitewash the crime of August 23, 1939 RLby saying that war is peace, ignorance is power, and slavery is freedom." Not everyone in these every-growing crowds was an enthusiastic listener. (9)

"Es izvēlējos pārāk ērkšķainu ceļu, pa kuru ne visiem tīk staigāt." ("I chose a thorny path for myself, one that not everyone is prepared to take." (Juris Ziemelis)

Juris Ziemelis was a hardened *politzeks* (political convict) whose entire family was arrested in Vecmuiža on March 25, 1949 and deported to Omsk. His family returned to Latvia in 1957. Ziemelis' "freedom" was short-lived. Forced to attend a Russian language school in Bauska, he was arrested for storing an illegal weapon and spent two years in a juvenile prison colony near Cēsis. Upon reaching adulthood, he was sent to a prison camp in Mordovia. It was there that Ziemelis decided to devote his life to restoring Latvia's freedom. In 1960 he was arrested again for avoiding military service. Ziemelis told his chekist interrogators that he was a citizen of the Republic of Latvia. His 10 year prison sentence was extended to 15 years, which he served in prison camps near Vladimir, in Mordovia, Perm, and elsewhere. To his family he wrote: "I will never support this regime—so says my mind. *Against* until the very end! No matter what sort of end!" (10)

Ziemelis returned to Latvia in 1975 and lived and worked in Bārbele, a small town near Bauska, where the KGB kept a close watch on him. He was incarcerated from time to time, even as he kept in touch with former political inmates. Ziemelis was one of the first brave Balts to sign the Baltic Appeal (in Latvian "45 baltiešu memorands," in Estonian "Balti apell," in Lithuanian "45 memorandumas"), an address to the General Secretary of the United Nations, the Soviet Union, East Germany and West Germany, and the signatories of the Atlantic Charter (1941). The appeal, which was sent out on August 23, 1979 to mark the 40th anniversary of the Molotov-Ribbentrop Pact, demanded public disclosure of the agreement between Moscow and Berlin and its secret protocols, an annulment of the pact *ab initio*, and restoration of the independence of the Baltic States. "The appeal was published in the foreign press and constituted the basis for the European Parliament's decision of January 13, 1983 in support of its demands. In Soviet-controlled territory, it was circulated through forbidden literature." It is difficult to overestimate the courage of the Balts who signed the appeal. (11)

The signatories of the 1979 Baltic Appeal: Romas Andrijauskas; Stase Andrijauskiene; Alfonsas Andriukaitis; Vytautas Bastys; Vytautas Bogušis; Vladas Bobinas; Romas Vitkevičius; Jonas Volungevičius; Jonas Dambrauskas; Romas Eišvydas; Rimas Žukovskas; Ivars Žukovskis; Alfrēds Zaideks; Juris Ziemelis; Liutauras Kazakevičius; Leonas Laurinskas; Valdis Larius; Algirdas Mocius; Mart-Olav Niklus; Napoleonas Norkūnas; Uldis Ofkants; Sigitas Paulavičius; Angele Paškauskiene; Jonas Pratusevičius; Jadvyga Petkevičiene; Jonas Petkevičius; Fēlikss Nikmanis; Sigitas Randys; Endel Ratas; Henrikas Sambora; Julius Sasnauskas; Leonora Sasnauskaite; Algis Statkevičius; Kestutis Subačius; Enn Tarto; Antanas Terleckas; Erik Udam; Ints Cālītis; Petras Cidzikas; Arvydas Čekanavičius; Vladas Šakalys; Jonas Šerkšnas; Zigmas Širvinskas; Mečislovas Jurevičius; Virgilijus Jaugelis. (12)

Ziemelis joined Helsinki-86 in the spring of 1987 and headed its Rīga chapter. He became one of the group's informal leaders. He was active in the founding committee of the Latvian People's Front, the grassroots movement that won a majority of seats in Soviet-occupied Latvia's first free Supreme Soviet elections in 1989. Ziemelis was present at all of the main events of Latvia's Awakening leading up to his death. He was laid to rest on January 3, 1989. Thousands of Latvians filled in his grave with their bare hands. According to Konstantīns Pupurs, a Helsinki-86 activist from 1988, Ziemelis was one of the organization's most trusted members. He was eloquent, persuasive, and carried a lot of weight, mainly his long years in the Gulag. He remained "unrepentant." Like many, Konstantīns Pupurs remains convinced that Ziemelis was murdered by the KGB. (13)

The summer of 1987 was the beginning of an extraordinary chain of events and growing possibilities that Latvians had only dreamed about for decades both inside and outside of Latvia. By the end of the decade, as unrest spread and freedom of speech expanded, I began attending the thousands-strong demonstrations, which remain among the most thrilling events of my life. By the end of 1987 the Baltic "pot" was bubbling, hissing, and rattling its lid. And so it was born, our fantastic National Awakening, out of the courage of a few recklessly brave and determined individuals. The response of the Latvian people, hungry for freedom and dignity, would gradually build to a thundering crescendo, as a cascade of events followed, ultimately resulting in the break-up of the Soviet Union.

Among the many people advocating for truth and justice at that time, but in his own artistic way, was composer Zigmārs Liepiņš (b. 1952), whose song "Sena kalpu dziesma" ("Ancient Servant Song") was a huge hit at the end of 1987. The song's words by Kaspars Dimiters were a rallying call for Latvians to wake up and take a stand against their oppressors.

Ancient Servant Song

Call the servants; call them out from the dark forests onto the road! Blow your horns in the markets and on street corners with all your might!

Chorus: Tomorrow or the day after tomorrow our Lady Ruler will rise from her sleep.

Arrogant masters, abandon your fame and fortune! Ask your wives to commit your children into her service.

On the shore of the sea she sleeps through seven hundred years of sorrow. Call the servants, call them out from the dark forests onto the road!

Tomorrow our queen will awake and listen for her servants' songs. We will sing to our Lady Ruler, Queen Latvia, forever!

Silly thought the words might sound in English, there was a commanding force to them in Latvian. With Liepiņš pounding on his synthesizer, his wife Mirdza Zīvere and lead singers Imants Vanzovičs and Zigfrīds Muktupāvels belted out the song with emotion and evident pride: "Soon Queen Latvia will wake!" The "wind of change" was picking up!

 Visual: "Ancient Servant Song" <http://www.youtube.com/watch?v=nLQzYoKS2is>

As the fifth decade of Soviet communist rule drew to a close, some visual artists were exploring the subject of the "Rape of Europa" as well as experimenting with installations and video as alternative means of expression. Conceptual art was appearing in Rīga, attracting crowds of happy young people and inquisitive onlookers. The names of Latvian writers and artists who had been pressed into obscurity by Soviet censors were making a comeback. Our memory was being restored, as our gaze looked westward towards the Free World.

In 1987 a much talked about retrospective exhibition devoted to the artist Zenta Logina (b. Zenta Knope, 1908–1983) was unveiled at St. Peter's Cathedral. Logina's work was unknown to many of her compatriots. Before the war Logina had participated in many of Rīga's art exhibits. During the Soviet occupation in 1941 her husband was arrested by the NKVD and vanished. After the war Logina worked on her art in a communal apartment; her unusual abstract drawings and designs were woven into tapestries by her devoted sister Elīze Atāre. What was permitted in the applied arts during the era of socialist realism was forbidden in the fine arts. In 1950 Logina was thrown out of the Latvian SSR Artists' Union, because her "formalist" work did not conform to socialist realism. The association would later take her back, but with the stipulation that she work only in textile art. She was harassed by the KGB. Logina remained true to herself, exploring existential and philosophical themes and the universe. (14)

Today photographs of the June 14, 1986 commemorative event at the Latvian Freedom Monument remind us of the courage of a handful of individuals who put their lives in danger to send a signal to their compatriots *to remember and to resist*. Many Latvians have forgotten Helsinki-86 and the significance of that day, which forced opened the floodgates, allowing Latvia's national "Awakening" to sweep over Latvia and dissolve the Soviet Russian occupation and totalitarian rule once and for all.

The year 1987 started with a tragedy: the unsolved death of Klāvs Elsbergs. It ended on a note of resolve: to stand together side by side, shoulder to shoulder, and look the enemy, the

Evil (Soviet) Empire, squarely in the eye. There was no going back to the ways of the past, the status quo and stagnation, the darkness of lies and repression, the hopelessness, and the downward spiral. Russian occupants and Latvian traitors, move aside! It was time for change!

Chapter sources:

(1) Bormane, Anita. "Viņi bija sākumā." Mājas Viesis / Lauku Avīze / TVNet. July 7, 2006 / April 23, 2013. <http://www.tvnet.lv/zinas/latvija/208637-helsinkiesi_vini_bija_sakuma>
(2) Ibid 1
(3) Ibid 1
(4) Ibid 1
(5) Ibid 1
(6) Ibid 1
(7) Ibid 1
(8) Štāls, Aigars. "Eva neparakstījās un aizejot aizcirta čekas durvis." Diena. April 4, 1997 / April 25, 2013. < http://www.diena.lv/arhivs/eva-neparakstijas-un-aizejot-aizcirta-cekas-durvis-10005954>
(9) "Juris Ziemelis." <http://nekropole.info/lv/Juris-ZIEMELIS>
(10) "The Baltic Appeal." <http://en.wikipedia.org/wiki/Baltic_Appeal>
(11) Ibid 11
(12) Ibid 10
(13) "Zenta Logina." <www.zentalogina.lv>

1988: Life in an Approximation

The old Imanta train station (1894) near Zolitūde. Source: Wikimedia Commons
https://commons.wikimedia.org/wiki/File:Imantas_stacija_6.JPG (© CC BY-SA 3.0 https://creativecommons.org/licenses/by-sa/3.0/deed.en)

(he) came home / turned on the light / hung up (his) coat / looked around the room / as though seeing it for the first time / or maybe to take note / of the placement of objects / the falling shadows / and the reflections of lights / then (he) lay down on the floor / and remained lying like that / staring at the lightbulb / the coat in the hallway / lifted its sleeve / and switched off the light

one floor below / in the neighbors' flat / the electrician Gosha / knocked out Sveta, his wife, / with a well-aimed punch to her jaw

and so one by one / with metaphysical / or physical force / the lights went out / in all of the microdistrict's windows

(Andris Žebers, *Blaknes* ["Side Effects"], 2007. Translated by RL.)

I am back home in Latvia. I am very happy to be home. I knew then, in 1988, that Latvia would always be my real home, no matter what, no matter where life would take me. My mind felt clear. I was full of energy, hope, and good expectations. The Free World had nursed me back to life. To hell with the car in Germany; we would figure things out, go back and try again. On a warm and balmy early summer day Krišjānis and I boarded the train to Jūrmala to inspect our apartment in Zolitūde. The toilet that hadn't worked in 1987 had been fixed, and the apartment, brand new and uninhabited, was waiting for someone. Toward the end of our travels I had made up my mind that I, or rather we—Krišjānis and I, needed a change. I knew we had to get away from the confines of Krāmu iela and give Zolitūde a chance.

The train picked up speed over the Daugava River, and we sat back to relax and look out at the green scenes of Pārdaugava flashing by. We disembarked at the old Imanta station, a charming wooden building that was nearly a century old, and crossed the tracks to the Zolitūde side. A labyrinthian canyon of newly constructed Soviet style highrises interspersed by poorly manicured grassy areas lay ahead of us. We noticed the new grocery store called Venta covered in chocolate brown tiles, the main "design feature" of this "microraion."

A lovely breeze from the west caressed us, as we breathed in the fresh air. It smelled of mowed grass, one of my favorite scents. The air seemed to sparkle. It was one of those beautiful Latvian summer days with low humidity and lazy cumulus clouds drifting peacefully across the blue sky. The wind was blowing in from the southwest and the great forests of Kurzeme. Vendors near the station were selling flowers and strawberries. I couldn't believe it: I was actually relishing the idea of moving to this Soviet monstrosity! Was it the bright sun or the fresh, sweet air? Or simply hope that it would work out? I was excited looking at Krišjānis running ahead of me gleefully.

We walked past the supermarket and proceeded down the main artery of the neighborhood, Ruses iela. I vaguely remembered the location of our building: 24 Ruses iela, Korpuss I. What a drab address. It rang no bells. Ruses... This name meant nothing to me. In fact, it was a "friendly" homage to Bulgaria's fifth largest city, Ruse, on the Danube River, a "brotherly city" of Rīga.

Ambling along at a leisurely pace, I examined our future surroundings. Everything looked the same. We had wandered into a typical Soviet cityscape of concrete boxes, like giant, colorless

Legos. I noticed that many first floor apartment owners had installed a variety of security bars on their balconies and loggias to dissuade burglars from attempting entry; this was a typical sight in all Soviet "hoods." The visual variety of these security bars resulted in a messy, jumbled look. Our own family "nest" was slotted into the fifth floor, though I had heard stories of burglars scaling balconies like monkeys to reach higher apartments. Nevertheless, I was in a hopeful mood.

Soviet era apartments ranged from tiny one-room flats to comfortable four-room apartments. You could only find large apartments with more than four rooms in pre-war buildings; most of those apartments were still communal. The communists imposed size restrictions on the living space of Soviet citizens: that is, each person was entitled to only a certain number of square meters. This is why the private homes built in the Soviet era were so small. However, the "more equal than others" comrades, including favored artists, writers, and composers, were granted bigger and better apartments. Unlike the beautiful, unique apartment buildings of pre-war Rīga, Soviet "block" buildings, as they were called, were just giant crates of poured concrete. The Russian cities of Moscow and Leningrad were also surrounded by this architectural drudgery, as were many urban centers in communist Eastern Europe.

Whereas many pre-war apartments still had ornately tiled woodstoves (that worked) and plaster wall and ceiling decorations, Soviet era apartments were the epitome of simplicity: four walls; a floor; a ceiling; and windows. Nothing extraneous, no frills such as stained glass or molded wood. The Soviet nomenklatura—"the more equals"—lived in their own special apartment buildings with quality flooring and neatly tiled kitchens and bathrooms. Average folks like us lived in glorified boxes with the barest of essentials. Of course, people who could afford it made changes to their new apartments, improving and beautifying them as best they could.

Left: Krišjānis in his bedroom in Zolitūde in the summer of 1988. We replaced the tacky wallpaper, still visible here, that summer. Photo: Andris Krieviņš.

As we neared our building, I noticed it was next to a Russian school. I hoped our son would not have to deal with Russian bullies. A Latvian school was still under construction nearby. It was rather apparent that the education of Russian youth in communist Latvia came before the needs of ethnic Latvian youth. In the USSR, Russians were "more equal than others" in the "friendly" Soviet family of nations. Later I found out that the Russian school had a pool, and Krišjānis went there from time to time to swim.

There was a big open area with a decent running track behind our building. Some old trees had been saved from destruction, and a few private homes filled in the gaps between the highrises or were encircled by them.

We rode the brand new elevator to the fifth floor of our building and slipped the key into the lock of apartment No. 19. I tingled with excitement. The door swung open, revealing a bright scene on account of the big windows. As we began our enthusiastic inspection, quickly I noticed that workmanship was lacking. The workers had taken a minimalist, slapdash approach to the finishing touches. Basically, the quality was good enough for nearsighted people. That is, if I took off my glasses, it looked perfectly fine. The Soviet construction sector was notoriously inefficient, its workers careless, lazy, and irresponsible. Our new apartment would need some sort of facelift...

The "French" doors had been pieced together from damp plywood and painted white; the fresh paint was already cracking. I would have to settle for an "approximation" of quality. After all, other people did too. We would have to make our own improvements, add our own touch. Zolitūde was perhaps just a slightly nicer version of other Soviet highrise "hoods." While once visiting Leningrad, we spent the night at a Russian couple's apartment in a neighborhood of inhuman proportions, with tall apartment towers in a bare landscape: no trees or other plantings for aesthetic and ecological cushioning. That time, with the snow coming down with Siberian intensity, the place looked desolate and positively alien. I noticed that in Zolitūde, too, no one had thought of planting new trees or ornamental bushes to create a homier look. Perhaps I could install some flower boxes on our balcony and loggia, I mused, noting that the apartment faced south. The bare minimum is how I would describe the communists' approach to the needs of its people. Many things were free, such as education and health care. Or were they? "Free" came at a cost: a lesson I had learned at Rīga's First Hospital. Investments and real advances in design and technology were reserved for only one sector, and that was the military-industrial complex. Guns over people, Comrade Ilmarovna!

We bought new wallpaper and hired a handyman to redo the walls. And then we moved to Zolitūde at the end of the summer, exactly one year after my nervous breakdown. Our beautiful oak cupboard with its exquisite pink and green stained glass windows and our other antiques didn't look quite right in the new setting. The ceiling was too low. We didn't have the money to install carpets or better linoleum, not to mention a parquet floor, so I had to try to get used to the painted linoleum, which was quickly abraded; our socks bore traces of paint powder. Did it contain lead? Many Soviet household items, appliances, and materials were quite expensive in relation to the average wage; we would have to wait for new flooring. Once the wallpaper was replaced, the apartment looked somewhat presentable.

Andris could barely drill any holes into the concrete walls to hang artwork. He fussed and fumed, as the drill whined and spat and the rock-hard wall refused to give. The floors of the WC and the bathroom were covered with scuffed up tiles that still bore splotches of hardened cement, which were impossible to remove. The workers hadn't bothered to install tiles beneath the bathtub, which was simply rough cement, impossible to clean. Sandpaper rough, it tore up any washcloth or sponge. A ventilation hole above the bathtub was just that: a hole in the wall between two concrete panels. If you were stupid or lazy, you could toss stuff down the hole. Perhaps that explains how a family of mice got into our apartment one autumn; it took us a week to kill the mice with mousetraps, one mouse at a time.

But hell, it wasn't so bad. Friends of ours gave us a bunk bed for Krišjānis. We purchased a shelf and desk unit for him, made in Latvia by a company called Zunda. Simple lace curtains, his Richard Scarry, Tintin, and other favorite American books, his toys, "tootsies" (cars), and a green, leafy fern made his room look bright and cheery. There was space on the loggia for his little bike.

(A neighbor would steal it from him shortly after we moved in, painting it black to conceal its original appearance.)

The kitchen was small, with just enough room for a small refrigerator, a table for three, and a sideboard, in which I stored all of our dishes and non-perishables. We finally had a nice gas stove with a working oven and a functional sink, which usually dispensed water; that is, water that had to be thoroughly boiled before use. Zolitūde's water was sourced from the Daugava River.

Neither Zolitūde nor any of the other Soviet-era "massives" were completely Russian despite the overall impression and jokes. Latvians were a minority in these symbols of Russification efforts, but they were there, on the first and last floors. You just didn't *hear* them as much; they were more inconspicuous. The Latvian film director and cameraman Andris Slapiņš lived in Zolitūde with his Russian wife. So did my friends, computer programmer Valdis Supe and his wife Inese, a model, and their young son. The King of Latvian Rock, composer and pianist Juris Kulakovs, lived there with his wife and daughter. Like the Supes, they lived in a tiny one-room apartment. My husband's friend Artūrs, an obstetrician, and his lovely wife Ilona and their two daughters lived in a two-room apartment just like ours. However, theirs was a cooperative flat and therefore nicer, with parquet floors, a hot item in Soviet real estate.

Like everywhere in Rīga, there were a lot of Russians or Russian speakers in Zolitūde. Many Russian military families lived there. Obviously, I did not relish having them as neighbors. However, our immediate neighbors—all Russian—were quiet and polite. As far as I could tell, no drunks, no wife beaters, no rabid "anti-fascist" Russian nationalists. I suspected there were very few ethnic Latvians in our building. I was very surprised to see groups of Vietnamese in Zolitūde; they were quartered in one of the highrises and worked in the Soviet Latvian textile industry. They kept to themselves, apparently shipped in for the short term. Neither Latvians nor Russians seemed to appreciate their presence there. Latvians worried that the ethnic Latvian population was being increasingly diluted. There were rumors of a plan to build a new subway system in Rīga, which would require the influx of thousands of workers from other Soviet republics. By now, people were grumbling without reservation.

And so, with many thoughts on our minds, it began: our new life in Zolitūde. I adjusted quickly, even though it was difficult to live without a telephone for about half a year. It took about 25 minutes to get from our bus stop to downtown Rīga. I still went downtown to retrieve translations and other freelance work. Sometimes I got out at the Press Building to meet someone or pick up a job or a payment. We usually rode the yellow Ikarus bus No. 53, which zigzagged along the quaint and shady Pārdaugava streets lined on both sides by tall privacy fences concealing old wooden houses. The public transportation from Zolitūde, the bus and the train, was quite good, even though I preferred trolleybuses and trams.

We were delighted to discover that the Venta supermarket provided shopping carts. Progress! Eventually checkout lines with cash registers were also installed. I paid our rent and utility bills at the nearby post office.

More apartment highrises were going up nearby, and you had to wonder who they were for. By the late 1980s the "sensitive" issues of housing and apartment shortages and the ethnic bias in favor of Russian immigrants were being openly discussed. A TV reporter named Brigita Zelt-kalne latched on to this topic, producing a series of exposés about the corruption and inequality in the Rīga housing "market." As in all societies, there were the haves and the have-nots. Besides privileged Communist Party members, the Soviet nomenklatura, chekists, factory bosses, Russian Army officers and "Great Patriotic" war veterans, the "connected," store managers, car mechanics, those in charge of and access to goods and services (they had money and bartering power), etc., there were also *Mātes Varones* or "Mother Heroines" (women with ten or more children) who were entitled to some kind of preferential treatment. Personally, I did not know a single Latvian with a family that big. If anything, Latvian families were shrinking. At the bottom of the communist heap were people who refused to join the Party, average workers, many ethnic Latvians, people who had survived the Gulag, the old, infirm, disabled, etc.

The Soviet *Mat' Geroinya* ("Mother Heroine") award. Photo: Wikimedia Commons https://commons.wikimedia.org/wiki/File:MotherHeroine.jpg (© Public Domain)

In December 1988 northern Soviet Armenia was rocked by a massive 6.9 earthquake, dubbed the Spitak or Leninakan earthquake, which leveled countless buildings, including highrises like our own, killing more than 45,000 people. Experts deemed the Armenian highrise apartment buildings, similar to those in Zolitūde and other Soviet microdistricts, substandard. The Armenian earthquake and its enormous death toll frightened me. With glasnost in full swing, we would begin hearing all sorts of scary things. From time to time I imagined the buildings around us shaking and then imploding, crumbling, flattening like giant accordions. So I prayed. Everything about our microdistrict spoke of poor, cheap, hasty construction. Luckily, Rīga wasn't prone to earthquakes, but still...

Despite all of my immediate and long-term concerns, I was happy for the change in scenery. It was the view from our new apartment that appealed to me the most: the big patch of sky towards Rīga Airport; the afternoon sunlight; and the large, open area behind our our building. During our inspection Krišjānis squealed with delight, stepping outside onto his loggia. God, I hope it doesn't collapse, I caught myself thinking.

There wasn't much happening in this "sleeping" neighborhood of the capital. In the summer I could keep the doors open to let in the fresh air. In the winter many parents bundled up their babies and put them outside on a balcony to sleep in a baby carriage. These basic apartments were home for millions in the Soviet Union, and tenants did their best to insulate and improve them. I continued to pare down my needs and expectations.

As we settled in, I began walking around with Krišjānis to get a better sense of the neighborhood. Once in a while we wandered into the private home neighborhood nearby. Enviously I looked at the houses with their privacy fences, yards, and flowers! It was so quiet and pretty there. Occasionally, when the water main broke, some people headed over with buckets to the nearest houses to ask for water. What an annoyance that was for the owners! I still remember looking down from my balcony at my Zolitūde neighbors lugging pails of water to their apartment buildings... Trés charmante, la Solitude...

More on Approximation

Hardijs Lediņš (1955–2004), one of Latvia's cultural icons of the 1980s and "the father of Latvian avant-garde music" (Daiga Mazvērsīte), coined a phrase that got stuck in my mind and persists today as a reference to the Soviet era microdistricts or "massives": he brilliantly dubbed our new neighborhood "Approximate Zolitūde."

Lediņš was a musician, poet, and performance artist, as well as a popular DJ. He lived by another microdistrict called Imanta on the other side of the train tracks from us and saw our "canyon" of poured concrete going up. Lediņš pursued interests very different from what the Communist Party expected of Soviet citizens. Educated as a construction specialist, in his spare time he played New Wave music to ecstatic disco crowds and engaged in weird, funky, very creative endeavors. An artist and a cultural rebel, if there ever was one in communist Latvia.

Stout with shortly cropped hair and a long straggly beard, Lediņš and his cohorts created an unusual body of work—videos, music, and performances that had nothing to do with Marxism-Leninism and communist ideology. This loosely knit group founded by Lediņš and his pal Juris Boiko went by the name "Nebijušu sajūtu restaurēšanas darbnīca" ("Workshop for the Restoration of Never Experienced Sensations") or NSRD for short. For devotees in the 1980s, this "workshop" added a splash of color, a dash of irony, and a spritz of absurdity to a culture rapidly shedding the constraints of a corrupt political ideology. NSRD believed in "art for art's sake," as opposed to "art belongs to the people," a tenet promulgated by the Communist Party of the Soviet Union. I translated Daiga Mazvērsīte's article about Hardijs Lediņš to learn more about my neighbor who I never met. Mazvērsīte is one of Latvia's leading musicologists, a DJ, and writer..

> According to his mother, translator Ruta Lediņa, Hardijs was very bright and did well in school; however, he was often bored, and his teachers sent a lot of notes home about his behavior and mischief. (...) Lediņš's buddy at Rīga Secondary School No. 5, Juris Boiko, would become his life-long creative collaborator in NSRD, exploring and creating multi-media art and music. When Lediņš and Boiko were in 11th grade, they published an "underground" magazine called Zirgābols ("Horse Poop"). It was a single copy publication, but its ten issues were so far out of the Soviet world, that some chekists showed up at school and scared the daylights out of them and their parents. Juris and Hardijs shared a love for poetry, theater, art, and music. (1)
>
> Lediņš studied construction at the Department of Architecture at Rīga Polytechnical Institute. He did well in math and physics and learned a decent amount of German. He was an avid music collector and created one of the first discotheques in Latvia at the Anglican Church in Old Rīga. In 1977 he organized an avant-garde music festival in Rīga with musicologists Ingrīda Zemzare and Guntars Pupa. Several famous musicians took part, including the now world famous Estonian composer Arvo Pärt, Russian pianist Alexei Lubimov, Estonia's Hortus Musicus ensemble, and the Vilnius String Quartet. After the festival the institute's rector sent Lediņš an angry letter forbidding any such festivals in the future. (2)
>
> Lediņš graduated and worked for ten years at the Building Construction Institute in Rīga. In his free time he oversaw the Kosmoss discotheque at the so-called October Culture House. In the summers Lediņš DJ'd at Asari Park in Jūrmala. One

of his noisy discos was even written up in Zvaigzne ("Star"), a popular Soviet Latvian magazine. While in school, he cut off his long hair, opting for a long, shaggy beard that he was very proud of. (3)

His friends and contemporaries would remember him as a person who was quick to notice anything new from the West and introduce it in some way to Latvia, which is why he was passionate about his discotheques; he was discriminate in his choice of music, drawing a big artsy crowd to his events. Lediņš introduced New Wave music to his fans: he played the music of groups like Ultravox, Soft Cell, Trio, and the Police at his discos. Lediņš wrote the words to the song "Milžu cīņa" ("Battle of the Giants"), which was made famous by the group Dzeltenie Pastnieki ("Yellow Postmen"), an alternative electronic music band that enjoyed a widespread following in Latvia. The song was written expressly for the Kosmoss disco for a Radio Luxembourg competition. Initially all of the Dzeltenie Pastnieki songs were by Lediņš and Juris Boiko, and the group (headed by Ingus Baušķenieks, the son of artist Auseklis Baušķenieks—RL) continued to collaborate with Lediņš, viewing him as their mentor. In 1983 Kosmoss was shut down. The Soviet authorities claimed it was a hotbed for nationalists, drug addicts, and prostitutes. (4)

(In the 1980s) NSRD took up most of Hardijs Lediņš's free time. NSRD's first concert performance took place at Kosmoss, with the performers emerging on stage from a closet. Their minimalist songs like "Ciku caku caurā tumba" ("Ciku caku Broken Speaker"), "Kabinets" ("The Cabinet"—1985), and "Salauztā kafejnīca" ("Broken Café") were created expressly for the disco, and NSRD called them the first Latvian examples of New Wave. In fact, these songs were the first examples of Latvian minimalism. (Available on YouTube.—RL) Lediņš's piano skills were those of a third-grader but sufficient for the minimalist tunes. "Broken Café" became a big hit for Dzeltenie Pastnieki. (5)

Besides alternative music, NSRD dabbled in other forms of self- expression; multi-media conceptual art, philosophy, literature and poetry, the visual arts, video, theater, happenings, and performance were all equally important pursuitss. They described their activities as "approximate art" and postmodernism. Lediņš even translated and published a book on postmodernism. Ingūna Rubene, NSRD's long-time member, vocalist, and flutist, recalls: "We gathered information for our projects. We went to Piebalga for three days and walked up and down its roads using maps from pre-war Latvia. We stopped at houses; some had already caved in, but each house had its own unique aura. One could still feel the people who had once lived there. We came up with a story about each house, about the people and the place, and we wrote the stories down. And so various texts came into existence; they were gathered at special, mystical places in Latvia. In Rīga we used some of these as texts for songs (…)." (6)

Kuncendorfs un Osendovskis

NSRD's conceptual "albums"— "Kuncendorfs un Osendovskis" ("Kuntzendorf and Osendovsky"— 1984), (...), "Invalīdu tramvajs" ("Tram for the Disabled"—1983), "Medicīna un māksla" ("Medicine and Art"—1985), "Vējš vītolos" ("The Wind in the Willows"—1986), "Faktu vispār nav" ("There are no facts"—1987), "Dr. Enesera binokulāro deju kursi" ("Dr. Eneser's Binocular Dance Courses"— 1987), "30/15" (1988), "Neskaties" ("Don't Look"—1988), "Sarkanie Rakordi" ("The Red Raccords"— 1989)—are some of NSRD's musical projects released on tape that epitomized the group's unfettered imagination. The recordings were done at Boiko's house in the country, at a summer cottage in Jūrmala, at Lediņš's house in Imanta, etc. (7)

"I remember how Hardijs was shoveling snow by his house while listening to one of his favorite musicians, Brian Eno, on a tape recorder. His shoveling movements corresponded to the music, almost as if he were dancing. This was what was so charming: our music reflected small episodes from our daily lives. Often music offers only variations of the theme 'I love you, you love me.' But NSRD could turn any practical situation, like shoveling snow, into art. This was what was so important for Latvia—this liveliness and movement. And this music still has value, because it encompasses human values and a world view," according to Ingūna Rubene. (8)

NSRD's music is its most memorable legacy. There are also numerous video films, like "Transwelt/Transzeit" (1986), "Aisberga ilgas/Vulkāna sapņi" ("The Iceberg's Longings/The Volcano's Dreams"—1987), "Pavasara tecila" ("Springtime Whetstone"—1987), "Garie acumirkļi" ("Long Moments"—1989), and "Ābeļziedi" ("Apple Blossoms"—1989), in which the group utilized the latest in Western technology to achieve the effect they wanted. The films documented their artistic endeavors and hikes, the most famous one being to Bolderāja on the periphery of Rīga, an area that had seen better days. By the 1980s it was heavily Russified by Russian proletariats. (9)

"Our goal was to walk until we saw the sun come up. We walked along the railroad line with the aim of reaching Bolderāja, but stuff happened along the way. Someone walked past us and then for no reason set a suitcase down and walked away. We passed wooden shacks, a kind of Harlem inhabited by people; this triggered new feelings and ideas that we later turned into performances." (NSRD member) The long, brown coat that Lediņš wore on his Bolderāja walk would become part of all of his and NSRD's future performances. The coat was from the First Republic, and Lediņš wore it when he later went to West Germany on concert tours. (10)

Hardijs Lediņš died on June 21, 2004 at the age of 49. A life-long chain smoker, he epitomized the words in Neil Young's song "It's better to burn out than it is to rust." Lediņš was probably

Latvia's greatest avant-garde artist in the Soviet era. NSRD's creative endeavors have been collected and documented on a website called Pietura.lv. ("Pietura" means "stop" as in "bus stop,"
"tram stop," or "train station.") Freethinker Hardijs Lediņš's reflections on the scourge of Soviet
microdistricts were published in an article called "Approximate Loneliness in Zolitūde" in 1987
in the newspaper *Literatūra un Māksla*. Witty, funny, full of irony and melancholy, it was accompanied by black and white photographs that included a shot of our playground, which our son
had enthusiastically dubbed "Indian Village." The article resonated with a lot of people who
despised the Soviet construction monstrosities, which were absorbing thousands of Russians.

> What color do you think loneliness is?
> Blue? Or violet?
> The tone of this color should, at least, be cool.
> Of course, we don't always have to accept these emotional stereotypes. See,
> here's a new myth about loneliness. In the 1950s the parents of a little girl decided
> to spend part of their vacation in Sochi. Because the trains were overcrowded and
> hot, they decided that their daughter should stay home in their Rīga apartment.
> To make her happy, they bought her lots of chocolate and waffles. Still the little
> girl felt very lonely, and later in life she always pictured loneliness as being the
> color of chocolate and waffles. While taking the train to Jūrmala in May 1987, she
> was surprised to see on the left side of the tracks near the Imanta station that
> someone had captured her sense of loneliness in spatial form. "You're exactly
> right," said someone sitting next to her. "Solitude in French (and English) means
> loneliness."
> Zolitūde used to be called Solitūde and was (located) in Rīga's western suburbs.
> (Its appearance) corresponded to the meaning of its name of French origin; it was
> a lonely spot, where houses were tucked in here and there between trees and
> bushes in the flat fields. (…) Possibly we could dig up some myths, legends, and
> historical tales, which would provide an emotional connection to this area.
> But the people who designed Zolitūde were not swayed by nostalgia. And let's be
> blunt: the apartment shortage problem and the construction sector's mishaps
> have denied us this pleasure. Designers have offered us yet another industrial
> revolution myth from a series that was launched 30 years ago. We've already
> gotten used to not believing ZTR's* myths, which tell us that cars and technology
> will rapidly improve our lives, that the sun, the universe, and standard-form
> aesthetics are better than our historical heritage and other remnants of our past,
> that life in these new buildings is free of all social ills, that something new and big
> is better than something old and small, etc. The manifestations of these modernist
> utopias have been compromised, which is why it's no surprise that you'll be
> reading some skeptical comments about Zolitūde. (*ZTR: Zinātniski tehniskā
> revolūcija or the "Scientific-Technological Revolution" is a term translated from
> the Russian language, which in the Soviet area referred to technological progress
> [not only in the construction sector], including industrialization and
> automatization as a forerunner to the computer era."—Mārtiņš Mintaurs)
> The Zolitūde microdistrict has been ruined by the boring routine of modernism,
> which designers are having a problem getting away from. (Unfortunately, it's not
> up to the designers to ditch that routine.) First of all, atmosphere as a component
> has been completely ignored. With no respect for the old infrastructure and the

old layout, a completely new network with new angles has been created. Some of the old streets, like Rikšotāju, have been destroyed, yet others barricaded. Any old infrastructure that was left intact has been enclosed by the enormous 119-series buildings like giant parentheses. (...)

Another manifestation of modernism's hackneyed routine is visible on the facades of the apartment buildings. They are interesting as a single unit, yet overall the finished parts of Zolitūde are dominated by a grid of buildings/diagrams or buildings/microcircuits; the overall appearance is electronic, but unconvincing when it comes to human comfort. The same can be said about the chocolate and waffle colors. This color combination is fine only in small doses: indulgence is fine, but not all the time. (In Zolitūde) it looks like a process of prolonged overeating. (...)

Some of Zolitūde's positive qualities are ambiguous. The diagonal pedestrian street, which commences at the Imanta Station, looks like a Broadway moved to Piltene or Smiltene (small Latvian towns—RL). On one hand, the people who live along it feel like they're living in the countryside: minimal traffic; fresh air. And so they take up a rural kind of life, speaking loudly and boisterously, while the sounds of their radios, televisions, and tape recorders surge from the windows and loggias, bouncing off of the walls of the buildings nearby, gaining amplitude. People's telephone conversations resonate particularly well. The street (...) seems to correspond to an urban boulevard but then does not. Some of the individually designed service points seem to exhibit the diverse characteristics of a city's "historical center," but the (surrounding) apartment buildings clearly present themselves as a "new" and homogenous area. (...)

The shiny tiles that cover the surface of the various service points seem to indicate a touch of modernity, and the bricks give one the impression that someone has put some thought into creating atmosphere. In my opinion, the design of the supermarket demonstrates the potential of our architects, and it is even pleasant to hang out at the storefront. The newspaper kiosk's pillars and the glass recycling point's mysterious niche seem to hint at a mythical presence, although that may have been completely unintentional.

Zolitūde's biggest surprise is its old, tree-lined alleys or rather fragments of alleys that correspond to the placement of the apartment buildings. It seems like a fantastic gift, that you can walk home to your nine-story building along a tree-shaded alley. The apartments in these buildings (with nearby old-growth trees) should be distributed through a special lottery.

I'm tired of talking about the poor quality of construction work, which is why I would like to introduce a kind of positive twist to this story. Perhaps our worries about straight and even seams, perfectly vertical walls, and quality exterior materials were topical in the triumphant "total design" period, when people thought that an entire city or even region could be encompassed under one enormous design project—from the buildings down to the kitchen cabinets and even spoons. Over time the implementation of these ideas in various parts of the world did not provide positive results. These places looked sterile, rational, and inhuman. After all, humans really are only very approximate, like everything in nature, which is why straight angles should not be the main criterion for our living space. And we can be happy that nothing like that is evident in Zolitūde. Individual examples of these buildings' exteriors, as well as the exteriors in general, are indicative of the level of 1980s construction technology and the organization of the work process. In fact, we can even detect coded signs of the construction workers' personal lives and experiences, the quality of their health, the weather conditions, the genetic codes of various nationalities, nostalgia for one's native republic, region, or district, successes and failures in their sex lives, payday sentiments, etc.

Which is why the not so straight and perfect slab of cement is much cosier and more human than high tech. Just as approximate as the human being itself and its loneliness in Zolitūde (...) No architect could describe solitude any better. (11)

I am still chuckling over what Hardijs Lediņš wrote about "Approximate Zolitūde." The adjective stuck. Indeed, the highrises of Zolitūde and other Soviet-era constructions seemed like *approximations*: not quite right; not quite straight; a bit off. The walls and floors of our apartment were

hard, massive slabs of reinforced concrete; the ugly linoleum's painted surface faded quickly; the windows did not open and were improperly sealed; and the plastic piping, which broke time and time again, flooded our newly wallpapered kitchen.

A Soviet microdistrict in Latvia: Approximations like Zolitūde were one of the "accomplishments" of the Soviet Union's "Scientific-Technological Revolution." Photograph courtesy of Mārtiņš Mintaurs.

What Hardijs Lediņš described so eloquently and with a note of resignation was in fact Soviet urban blight, which was rippling outwards from the center of Rīga like a toxic fungus. Uniform in appearance, Soviet "hoods" were neither conducive to building communities nor aesthetically pleasing. Their "microcircuit" appearance was anything but organic. They were proletariat "plopdoms," haphazard mazes of reinforced concrete thrown down on top of a pretty field or meadow or previously quiet wooded area. These concrete monstrosities looked the same everywhere in the USSR. They reminded my of America's highrise ghettos.

What then was Zolitūde like in the old days? "Due to sandy soil and marshlands, Rīga's countryside was sparsely populated. In the 15th and 16th centuries Rīga's city council members and wealthy proprietors were granted plots of land to build their manors, which were then named after them. When Rīga's Patrimonial Region (*Rigisches Stadt Patrimonialgebiet*—RL) was divided into three sections in 1604, (the Zolitūde) area became part of Piņķu (Pinkenhof) Parish. A map from 1683 includes Prastingshof and Ludendorfshof Manor and Skudru ("Ant") Tavern. At the beginning of the 18th century the manor belonged to Hermann Friedrich von Vietinghoff (1670–1746) and then to his son, Otto Hermann von Vietinghoff. At this time Johann (III) Bernulli (1744–1807), *right*, Berlin's chief astronomer, visited the manor and later described it in his memoir published in 1788: "... It is a fine estate whose proprietor, the secret counsel to the city, supplies (Rīga)

with vegetables, milk, and cream. He has created a wonderful guest house, where he organizes picnics for his visitors. The manor has a lovely park (...) with shady lanes, ponds, and green lawns. There are three recreational buildings in the park; one of them features two orangeries on either side. The orangeries are decorated with marble statues and busts. One of the statues is of Venus. There are also paintings in the pavilions, although these are of little value." (12)

"Beginning in 1782, the manor belonged to Anna Ulrika von Vietinghoff who renamed it Champêtre (from the French words *les champs*—'fields') and Solitude. The two names described the property's remote location in the countryside; there was only one tavern on the estate (...)." In 1988 not a trace of this history remained, as far as I could see, save for the name of Šampētera iela, derived from Champêtre. (13)

Ironically, I appreciated the little touches of creativity that Hardijs Lediņš had taken note of in Zolitūde, like the "Grecian" columns near the kiosk, where one could purchase newspapers, soap, and other small items. I doubt that anyone sensed the presence of anything "mythical" in the "niche" of the glass recycling point; the dour faces of its employees and the pungent odor of empty beer bottles brought us, lost in reverie, back down to earth. The attempt at aesthetics was so feeble that it was laughable. But Hardijs Lediņš's laughter was not mean. It was sad.

The Beginning and End of Indian Village

While my husband avoided Zolitūde as much as he could, Krišjānis and I warmed to it, if only for the fresh air and open space it afforded. For a couple of years my little boy's "Indian village" playground remained appealing, but it didn't take long for the local hooligans to dismantle it piece by piece, as they carved their Cyrillic initials into the logs, scattered cigarette butts, and kicked and dislodged what they could. I was very sad to see it go to pieces so quickly, and explaining such behavior to my son made me even sadder. I began avoiding the place, looking for other spots for him to play. There really were no playgrounds in our vicinity other than the log village. I did not understand the wish or need to destroy what was constructed for the benefit of society and especially children. I felt sorry for the workers who had taken the time and effort to design and construct the wonderful log playground. It seemed like every time something new and nice was installed, some idiots had to go and wreck it. Latvians blamed vandalism on rootless Russian immigrants. What did Latvia mean to someone without a historical memory whose parents hailed from a poor village in Russia?

A particularly nasty form of vandalism was the burning of elevator control buttons. By our second year in Zolitūde most of our new elevator's buttons were already singed and partially melted. In addition, nobody used plastic bags for disposing garbage; meat bones, scraps of old food, bloody napkins, dirty diapers, and all sorts of disgusting, smelly garbage was dumped down the garbage chutes that ran from the top floor to the garbage container on the first. It didn't take long for the chute to stink badly.

A couple of years into our occupancy, our Russian neighbor installed a privacy door without consulting with us, effectively creating a double entrance to our apartment. I appreciated the effort: it increased our security in the event of an attempted robbery, and we could leave our shoes outside the door. But what about a fire? People were constructing things in and near their apartments that surely were violations of the fire code, if there even was one. But nobody cared, nobody made inspections. At some point some people even installed wood stoves in their Soviet apartments, when the heat didn't come on. Pipes sticking out of poured concrete walls...

Once or twice a year our building's plastic nine-story kitchen sewage main would back up, causing flooding that quickly ruined the pretty wallpaper near the kitchen sink. I was appalled by how primitive the sewage system was. The plastic drain pipe beneath our kitchen sink was simply stuck into the building's main drain pipe through a shoddy opening: no fancy welding or tight fittings; no neatly curved metal piping. With no sink sieves available, all sorts of gook ended up in that scarily thin nine-story pipe. The plumbing of a population that loved bacon eventually resembled a blocked artery. So every once in a while we all had a mess on our hands. Thank goodness we never experienced a toilet backup.

In the winter from our vantage point on the fifth floor we could clearly see where the hot water main was: the snow right above it had melted. People grumbled about the incredible waste of energy and the stupidity of "the System." Stupid and wasteful it was. Our building was heated by hot water carried a long distance from some central heating source. Apartment build-ings in the Soviet Union did not have individualized heating systems, boilers, or furnaces. No-body had a thermostat in their apartment that could control the inside temperature, so in the fall everyone was at the mercy of Rīgas Siltums, the state heating company. The heat usually came on in late October, when the ground was already freezing and the cold winds were rattling our windows. Every autumn we would wait for the heat, hoping, praying...

My life in Zolitūde or "loneliness" had commenced. For a short while I enjoyed the experi-ence, but it was the beginning of the end of an era for me. Decades later, when I was living in the United States, the name Zolitūde came to stand for corruption, one of the toxic legacies of the Soviet era.

Chapter sources:

(1) Mazvērsīte, Daiga. "Hardijs. Latviešu avangarda mūzikas tēvs." Una. November 30, 2004 ; 4/28/2013 <http://w ww.apollo.lv/zinas/hardijs-latviesu-avangarda-muzikas-tevs/295471>
(2) Ibid 1
(3) Ibid 1
(4) Ibid 1
(5) Ibid 1
(6) Ibid 1
(7) Ibid 1
(8) Ibid 1
(9) Ibid 1
(10) Ibid 1
(11) Lediņš, Hardijs. *Literatūra un Māksla.* July 17, 1987, No. 28, P. 8 "Zolitūde." Wikipedia. January 24, 2014 / April 29, 2014 <http://lv.wikipedia.org/wiki/Zolit%C5%ABde>
(12) Ibid 12

In memoriam: Hardijs Lediņš, 1955–2004

Milžu cīņa ("The Battle of the Giants")

Battle of the giants, battle of the giants
These giants have only one option left
They have to take part in the Battle of the Giants
To be aired on the radio and TV
The world will find out all about it
Whosoever wins this battle
Will be invited to a banquet
And applauded and cheered
So happy everyone will scream
Battle of the giants, battle of the giants
But behind the scenes they'll whisper
You know, he's such a giant giant
And they'll talk and say
He's the unhappy giant
(Because he's a giant)
These hungry giants, they have nothing to eat
They can't just go into the woods to kill bears
They have intellectual potential
They're not from the province
Every morning they read the newspapers
They watch all the latest theater shows
But what to do, they're hungry
So hungry
So hungry that they'll pull their hair out
Battle of the giants, battle of the giants (...)

(13)   Visual Source: "Battle of the Giants" http://www.youtube.com/watch?v=SuLxMDgGS4I

1988: The Latvian Flag

In early June, as I set my sights on a new life on the periphery of the capital, Latvia's so-called "creative" unions, including writers, artists, architects, cinematographers, composers, theater workers, journalists, as well as experts from other fields, gathered in a plenary session at the so-called Political Education Building in downtown Rīga. There they proceeded to unleash a torrent of grievances aimed at the (Soviet) system and, in essence, "the top" (that is, the Communist Party). My husband was busy taking photographs there, while I tuned in from Paulēni via our transistor radio, carrying it with me everywhere I went.

Methodically pulling stubborn weeds out of the strawberry patch in the warm sunshine, I could not believe what I was hearing: my fellow Latvians were speaking their minds instead of lip-synching communist lies. My heart was beating faster and faster. *Something enormous was happening!* Environmental issues, particularly pollution, emerged as a dominant theme. Following Dainis Īvāns' and Artūrs Snips' October 17, 1986 article "Considering the Fate of the Daugava River" in *Literatūra un Māksla*, the popular newspaper, Latvians had succeeded in halting the Soviets' plans for building another hydroelectric power station on the Daugava River near Daugavpils. The project, if it had gone through, would have caused irreversible damage to the river's natural beauty and history. The Soviets had already ruined part of the river with the Pļaviņas HES, which submerged one of Latvia's most scenic areas near Koknese, including Staburags, the famous cliff. The Soviets were known for their crazy ideas, such as reversing the flow of rivers. Other sensitive and crucial issues, such as the worsening situation of the Latvian language, uncontrolled immigration, and demographic problems, bubbled up from the depths' of my fellow Latvians' despair. Astonishingly, historical grievances were also vented. Mavriks Vulfsons (1918–2004), a Latvian Jewish journalist, professor, and popular political commentator, had the audacity to bring up the Secret Protocols of the Molotov-Ribbentrop Pact, thereby confirming that there had been no socialist revolution in Latvia. Our country had been unlawfully annexed by the Soviet Union. For decades the existence of these protocols, which had slated the Baltic States for occupation, had been denied by Moscow.

Gorbachev's policies of glasnost and perestroika provided the gathering with a legal framework, a cushion against reprisal from the Latvian Communist Party bosses. First Secretary Boriss Pugo, a communist hardliner and member of the meeting's presidium, sat near the podium looking glum. Or grim. One could only imagine what was going on inside his head.

The talks and debates were like a collective stream of consciousness: repressed anger, once bottled up, was now overflowing. Probably every Latvian radio was tuned into the meeting, everyone was listening with bated breath. We were all worried about the plans for a new subway system to be built in Rīga; construction was due to commence in 1990. The influx of thousands of Russian workers could prove catastrophic to Rīga's ethnic Latvian population, which had already been reduced to a minority under years of Russification efforts by Moscow. Given the historic opportunity to voice these concerns, Latvians and friends of Latvians simply could not stop talking. The fate of the Daugava River became a rallying cause and a symbol for Latvian resistance and insubordination; after all, it was our "river of fate." We felt like Latvia was being smothered.

The two-day meeting culminated in the drafting of a diplomatically worded resolution calling for immediate changes in many aspects of life in Soviet Latvia. It remains an invaluable document that sums up the severe losses, damage, and long-term problems incurred by Latvia and its people under the 40-year Soviet occupation. Published on June 6, 1988 in the newspaper *Padomju Jaunatne* ("Soviet Youth"), the plenary meeting's resolution was a watershed moment: all grievances were out in the open. Some excerpts from the resolution include: supporting efforts to promote individuals not affiliated with the (Communist) Party to executive positions; demanding that Stalinist interpretations of history be revoked (...), "which continue to cripple the Soviet people and the Latvian nation and Latvia's history"; concluding that Latvia's membership and purpose of existence in the USSR was compromised under Stalinism; complaining that the Latvian SSR's participation in the economic and social development of the USSR does not comply with the principle of parity of an equal, sovereign state within a union of free states, which has led to Latvia's indigenous nation—the Latvians—becoming a minority in their ethnographic territory; etc. (2)

Aired publicly, the electrifying meeting jolted Latvians into action. A grassroots organization, Latvia's Popular Front, would emerge in the wake of the meeting as a force to be reckoned with; the quickly established itself as a clear alternative to the Communist Party.

June 14, 1988

Exactly a year had passed since Helsinki-86 triggered unrest and change in Latvia with their historic demonstration near the Freedom Monument. The founders had more or less vanished; others, however, had taken up their cause. Andrejs Cīrulis, editor of *Padomju Jaunatne*, recalled what followed in the wake of the June plenary meeting:

> The next important event was the rally at the (Political Education Building) on June 14, 1988, which I was in charge of. A sea of radically inclined people had gathered there, but what the crowd was not aware of was that the large auditorium of the Political Education Building of the Central Committee of the Latvian Communist Party was full of 'movie watchers'—armed Soviet Army soldiers, and that the Baltic Military District's garnizone had been placed on full alert, its troops ready for action. Among the many speakers was Jānis Rukšāns, whom nobody really knew; he stirred up the crowd with his speech, completely unaware of what was lurking within the nearby building. (Rukšāns is a world renowned crocus expert.— RL) And Valdis Turins was threatening to incite the crowd to break the windows of the nearby Central Committee, if I didn't let Eduards Berklavs speak. Foreign news broadcasts had informed us that recent similar protests in Kazakhstan had ended in a bloodbath. I personally did not know Eduards Berklavs, but First Secretary (of the Central Committee) Boriss Pugo had called me a few days ago to warn me that if I let Berklavs speak, I would be sorry. However, at that moment I was more afraid of Valdis Turins' threats, so I let Berklavs speak... (3)

Konstantīns Pupurs (b. 1964), a youthful member of Helsinki-86 since 1988, was also on hand at the rally. By the end of the day he would achieve lasting fame, but a month later the Soviet authorities would kick him out of the Soviet Union.

> About 100,000 people had gathered for the rally. As if to test our endurance, we were soaked by a sudden rain shower. We were surprised to see Andris Zukovskis and Uģis Šulcs, two guys from VAK (the Environmental Protection Club, a Latvian NGO founded in 1987—RL), standing on the steps of the Political Education Building holding two large black flags with horizontal white stripes in the middle. What did the flags look like on the black and white television sets of that era? No need to answer. It was a brilliant move! There were 17 speakers in all, representing various segments of society. Eduards Berklavs' speech was well-argumented, full of facts, and scathing in its criticism of the current authorities. (...) Standing close to the microphone, I could see the frightened expressions of many of the officials and Komsomol representatives who were present, (...) as if Berklavs had been put in charge of their fates. (...) After the speech the huge crowd roared "Berklavs! Berklavs! Berklavs!" I can imagine how scared of the crowd and angry at Berklavs Boriss Pugo and the KGB were: they were too scared to leave the Political Education Building during the rally, although they were protected by hundreds of policemen and chekists. (Konstantīns Pupurs) (4)

A sea of people had scared the Soviet Latvian authorities into inaction. What could they do or say at that point? Eduards Berklavs (1914–2004) had once been a staunch communist and had worked for them, had once been one of *them*. In the late 1950s he was sacked by the Latvian Communist Party as a "national communist" for trying to defend Latvia's national interests and curb Russian immigration. He was deported to Vladimir, Russia. When he returned, he became a dissident and remained a persona non grata in the Soviets' eyes. Pugo didn't want Berklavs around, yet there he was, the feisty old man, addressing the surging crowd. Anti-Soviet posters and banners held by people expressed their emotions and demands:

> *Pieprasām Latvijas neatkarību!* ("We demand Latvia's independence!")
> *Nost ar Latvijas kangariem!* ("Down with Latvia's traitors!")
> *Brīvību Latvijai!* ("Freedom for Latvia!")
> *Pārtraukt migrāciju Latvijas PSR!* ("Stop the migration into the Latvian SSR!")
> *Latviešu tauta un tās kultūra atrodas uz izzušanas robežas!* ("The Latvian nation and its culture are on the brink of extinction!")
> *Vai mūs vairs neskars represijas?* ("Will we be repressed again?")
> *Nost 1940. gada staļinisko okupācijas režīmu!* ("Down with the 1940 Stalinist occupation regime!")
> *Arī mazas tautas grib dzīvot!* ("Small nations want to exist too!")
> *Brīvu Latviju vienotā Eiropā!* ("A free Latvia in a united Europe!")

The demonstrators were blunt: they wanted OUT of the Soviet Union. Mavriks Vulfsons and theologian Juris Rubenis, whose popularity was soaring at this time, also addressed the enormous crowd that stood listening attentively, as if the end of the world were near. Vulfsons would spearhead Latvia's efforts to set the record straight on what happened in Latvia from 1939 onward (following the signing of the Molotov-Ribbentrop Pact). Rubenis (b. 1961) was a member of an informal, anti-communist group of several prominent Lutheran ministers called

Atdzimšana un atjaunošana ("Rebirth and Renewal"), including Reverend Modris Plāte who had presided over dissident and freedom fighter Gunārs Astra's funeral in April. The youthful Rubenis would become a kind of spiritual guide or guru for Latvians thirsting for truth, stability, hope, and harmony.

That same day, following the massive rally, 24-year-old Konstantīns Pupurs carried the Latvian national flag from the Freedom Monument all the way to the Cemetery of the Brothers. A huge crowd of people accompanied him, as chekists looked on in rage. Their hands were tied by Gorbachev's new policies of appeasement.

Pupurs has described his audacious James Bond-like maneuvers to outwit and evade the KGB on June 14, 1988 in a pamphlet called *Karogs sarkanbalts* ("The Red-White Flag," Rīga, 2011). His personal odyssey is also described in Igors Vārpa's 2012 book *Atmodas eiforija un atmošanās paģiras* ("The Awakening's Euphoria and Hangover"). A few translated excerpts:

> Konstantīns Pupurs was born on March 5, 1964 in Rīga. After mandatory Soviet military service, in 1983 he began studying philology at the Moscow History and Archive Institute (part of the Russian State University for the Humanities—RL), focusing on ancient Russian and Slavic languages and archival recordkeeping. Pupurs became involved in activities that opposed the communist regime, starting a " History Exploration Club" for his fellow students.
>
> In March 1986 Pupurs was arrested at school. Chekists escorted him back to his dormitory room, where they seized his "illegal" possessions, including books by Alexander Solzhenitsyn and other authors, a collection of antique uniform pins and badges, leaflets, and a Bible with a cross. A series of interrogations followed. For the next three months Pupurs was essentially under house arrest: every morning he was required to report his arrival at school. He was permitted to attend classes but was required to return to his dorm room as soon as they ended. In July he was expelled from school.
>
> Pupurs returned to Rīga and was allowed to resume his studies at the Department of History and Philosophy of the University of Latvia. Although he knew that the Latvian KGB was monitoring him, he did not cease his political activities. In January 1988 he joined the ranks of Helsinki-86. (He pinned a small red-white-red badge to his jacket and wore it to school every day, inciting the wrath of his instructors and the contempt of some of his fellow students.—RL) His department tried to "repress" Pupurs by forcing his fellow students to take a vote on his expulsion. (Much to Pupurs' pleasant surprise) only two girls voted to expel him. All the other students saw nothing wrong in what he had done.
>
> On March 25, 1988 (to commemorate the 39th anniversary of the 1949 mass deportations of Latvians to Siberia—RL) Pupurs planned to place flowers and red-white-red ribbons at the Freedom Monument. However, he was grabbed at the Laima clock, shoved into a waiting Volga, and taken to the October District militsiya station in Sarkandaugava. He was interrogated and threatened with bodily harm and worse. He was also warned that if he didn't cease his activities, he would be thrown out of the country. His friends, however, made it to the monument to place flowers and ribbons.
>
> On June 14, 1988 members of Helsinki-86 were in the large crowd that had gathered near the Freedom Monument to commemorate the victims of the 1941

Soviet deportations. It was at this time that Konstantīns Pupurs unfurled the Latvian flag and began his historic procession through Rīga from the monument to the Cemetery of the Brothers with Anta Bergmane at his side and hundreds of people walking with him.

"We succeeded in carrying the flag all the way through Rīga to the Cemetery of the Brothers. That procession was like Russian roulette. We never dreamed that we would make it all the way through the city. We were expecting a confrontation at any moment, especially when we saw Soviet Army troops and the militsiya near Hotel Latvija. At the cemetery I was close to an emotional breakdown; people were falling on their knees and kissing the flag. Many were weeping. They could not believe that they were seeing our flag again."

This manifestation resonated within Latvia and beyond its borders. According to the Soviet laws of the time, Pupurs could have been charged with anti-Soviet propaganda. Prior to that moment, he could have been sentenced to five years in a Mordovian political prison camp, but he was spared by perestroika, glasnost, and Mikhail Gorbachev, who had told the world that dissidents in the Soviet Union would no longer be arrested. Under the new terms of democratic change, the KGB did not dare use its previous tactics against the members of Helsinki-86. Instead, they resorted to forcing their victims to give up Soviet citizenship and leave the USSR. When it came to Konstantīns Pupurs, the flag procession was the last straw for the KGB.

One month later the KGB stripped Pupurs of Soviet citizenship and forced him to emigrate. Pupurs told them he would not leave his mother behind. Together they took the train to Moscow, from which they departed on July 11, 1988, bound for Austria. In Vienna they were met by Pāvils Brūveris and Rolfs Ekmanis of Radio Free Europe. (Ekmanis was editor of the magazine *Latvija šodien* ["Latvia Today"], a publication devoted to the late Soviet period in Latvia.—RL) Pupurs and his mother settled in Münster, Germany, where they were both hired by the expat newspapers *Laiks* and *Brīvā Latvija*. (5)

Konstantīns Pupurs: "A person can be pressured into leaving his homeland, his family, friends, and all that he has acquired. Repeat summonses to the prosecutor's office, constant shadowing, having your telephone disconnected, being arrested, receiving veiled or open threats... (In 1988) we thought we were leaving for good... I was an idealist and a maximalist. But (in exile) I was painfully aware of the alien mentality around me, the alien surroundings, the alien language. Although I was relieved that I was no longer in danger of being sent to Soviet prison, for a long time I would continue to look back over my shoulder, when I was walking down the street..." (6)

For those of us lucky to be born in a free and democratic society, state intimidation of individuals is an alien concept. Yet it was Latvia's reality for decades after World War II. Today Konstantīns Pupurs lives quietly outside of Rīga and has no interest in participating in politics. Yet nearly 30 years ago he risked everything for the hopes and ideals that united Latvians and Balts at home and around the world. The famous flag that he carried on that day is now part of a collection called "100 Relics of Latvian History."

Chapter sources:

(1) Bluķe, Dace. "Radošo Savienību plēnuma 25. gadadiena." Diena. June 1, 2103. <https://www.ir.lv/2013/6/1/ra doso-savienibu-plenuma-25-gadadiena>

(2)   Barikadopēdija. < http://www.barikadopedija.lv/raksti/536999>

(3)   "Andrejs Cīrulis." Latvijas ļaudis. 09/23/2011. / 4/30/2013. < http://www.latvijaslaudis.lv/users/andrejs-cirulis>

(4)   Pupurs, Konstantīns. "1988. gada 14. Jūnijs, mītiņš pie politiskās izglītības nama." Karogs sarkanbalts. Rīga, 2011.

(5)   Vārpa, Igors. Atmodas eiforija un atmošanās paģiras. Rīga: Zvaigzne, 2012.

(6)   Bormane, Anita. "Viņi bija sākumā." Mājas Viesis / Lauku Avīze / TVNet. July 7, 2006 / April 23, 2013. http://www.tvnet.lv/zinas/latvija/208637-helsinkiesi_vini_bija_sakuma

Labvakar! ("Good Evening, Latvia!")

In my Zolitūde kitchen in the late 1980s, trying to make the best of things in Soviet-occupied communist Latvia.

As Latvia simmered, I began to watch TV, especially the news. Prior to 1988 I had little interest in what Latvian communist TV had to offer. Propaganda and bland "varieté" programs were not my cup of tea. But by now the content of Latvian news programs had become unpredictable and almost sensational compared to the recent past. Perestroika and glasnost were propelling us forward like a Zaporozhets fitted with a jet engine. No more censor-approved gibberish about American imperialism and overinflated economic statistics that were contradicted by the scene in stores around the country. The Soviet economy was dangerously stagnant. Each and every newscast offered some new revelation.

Gorbachev and his cronies in Moscow were probably nervous by now: those Balts just won't shut up! The seeds of investigative journalism had been sewn in Latvia, and new stories were capturing everyone's attention, mainly because they no longer adhered to a flunked ideological precept. Crime, housing shortages, corruption, pollution: these once taboo subjects were now on the table. I could imagine Latvians all around me watching TV, nodding their heads and mumbling, "Damn right!"

In January 1988 a new Sunday talk show called "Labvakar!" ("Good Evening!") was launched, anchored by reporters Ojārs Rubenis (who lived in Zolitūde), Edvīns Inkens, and Jānis Šipkēvics. "Labvakar!" became so popular, that just about every Latvian dropped what they were doing to watch the show. It opened with an uplifting theme song composed by Jānis Lūsēns, "Labvakar, Latvija!" sung by his wife Maija Lūsēna. The words "Labvakar, Latvija, labvakar, tēvuzeme" ("Good evening, Latvia, good evening, fatherland") had a wonderful, warm, undeniably patriotic feel to them. Although I wasn't friends with Lūsēns, on whose behalf I got into trouble in 1981, I was happy for him, and his music made me happy.

By the end of 1988 Latvians could openly wear their national colors without fearing reprisal and a visit to the Corner House for questioning and harassment. The Latvian flag had been raised from its tomb, and many Latvians were walking around with the sign of the morning star, Auseklis, a traditional ornament, proudly pinned to their breast.

"Labvakar!" was pivotal in accelerating the thrust of the so-called National Awakening; its popularity would remain unmatched for years to come in Latvia. The show's threesome, Rubenis, Inkēns, and Šipkēvics, sat around chatting (a novel approach for Soviet television format) about the constantly changing course of events that we were experiencing. Like *Avots* magazine, they were testing the boundaries of the Soviet state by introducing increasing amounts of Western clips and sensitive topics. How could we not like it?!

Sometimes the "Labvakar" guys made blunders in their choice of material. One Sunday they ended the show with a snippet of pornography that made me jump up out of my chair and chase Krišjānis out of the room. For many Soviet citizens unused to erotica, it was a titillating thrill. Yet there was no introduction to the clip, no warning, nor did any comments follow; just a flash of the Western world's garden of earthly delights, which probably elicited all sorts of reactions in Latvian households. In the USSR the subject of sex was not openly discussed, and the only pornography stashed away somewhere had originated in "rotten" Western countries. *Playboy* and *Hustler* were good for bribing Soviet customs officers.

My friend Mārtiņš Zelmenis recalled an awkward "Labvakar!" episode, in which Edvīns Inkēns attempted to interview Cindy Lauper: "(Inkens) neither knew English, nor did he really know who Cindy Lauper was and what her accomplishments were, but the poor gal tried her best to assist him in doing his job." Latvians had been forced to *dzīvot mucā* ("live in a barrel"), so to speak.

Another friend remembered an episode devoted to the serious subject of Russian immigration: "There was a clip about how Russian migrants arrived in Rīga by train, were welcomed, and then handed a key to a new apartment. (Our) Russians were very upset and demanded that the show apologize. The following week the show's hosts announced on air that they were removing the clip; then they proceeded to play it in reverse. The migrant hands over his key, goes to the station, gets on the train, and leaves. That caused a real furor among Russians." Latvians were sick and tired of being bullied by Russians.

Ēvalds Krieviņš, a retired Latvian military officer: "'Labvakar' was an integral part of the perestroika-glasnost plan. Our 'boys' were given an opportunity to prove their worth, and their efforts were later crowned with the All-Union Lenin Komsomol's top prize. The show was an

effort to maneuver between the anvil and the hammer, and they succeeded. The show was intended as a 'pressure-release valve.' However, our national 'awakening' was a force that blew out all the 'pressure-relief valves,' and the show became superfluous."

Krišjānis celebrating Jāņi in Piebalga in the summer of 1988. Photograph by Andris Krieviņš.

In 1988 the Latvians' age-old Midsummer celebration, Jāņi, was legalized after decades of being outlawed; June 24 was deemed a national holiday. And so that June we raised our first Līgo pole with a burning barrel on top of the hill at Paulēni and saw with great joy other fires flickering in the distance like in ancient times.

1988: Baltica

The Cēsis Castle ruins in an illustration from 1793 by Johann Christoph Brotze. Image: Wikimedia Commons https://commons.wikimedia.org/wiki/File:Bm05119am.jpg (© Public Domain)

Aside from the strange and mysterious episode at the Rīga Bourse in the winter of 1983, I personally would not see Latvia's national colors out in the open until the summer of 1988. After more than 40 years of banishment, it would make a spectacular and emotional comeback. And from then on, I would always associate our flag with the joyful sounds of Latvian folk music, which had survived centuries of wars, bloodshed, and oppression by foreign masters. Despite the efforts of the Soviet state, there were still Latvians in Latvia singing the songs and playing the melodies of our ancestors. Our old songs were making a real comeback in the 1980s, thanks to many folk music ensembles.

In July 1988 hundreds of folk ensembles from Latvia, Lithuania, Estonia, Bulgaria, Spain, Norway, Poland, Finland, Russia, Sweden, West Germany, and even the United States descended on Rīga to take part in the joyful "Baltica 88" festival, a celebration of traditional music, dance, and culture. Latvians were proud to host so many guests from the Free World. Rīga was full of music and laughter and people dressed in a bright array of ethnic costumes from all over the world. A group of Americans performed square dances, eliciting a buzz of delight and excitement mong onlookers. Americans!

The ensembles from the Free World brought with them a breath of fresh air, normalcy, and a fleeting sense of serenity at a time of suspense, unease, and unrest. In the festival's opening parade through Rīga, the multitude of merry musicians followed one mighty man, Dainis Stalts in his straw hat, who carried the Latvian national flag. It was an unforgettable sight! And there were more flags behind Stalts, hovering above Latvians and others dressed in their traditional finest: the women *kā liepiņas* ("like lindens") in long woolen skirts of beautiful hues and pristine white blouses embroidered with traditional Latvian ornaments; married women with traditional head wraps, *aubes*; the men *kā ozoli* ("like oaks") wearing traditional hats, their long coats fastened by beautiful woven belts, their feet clad in sturdy leather boots, some pierced with jingles for a rhythmic sound. How fine we all felt, how elated, how proud in front of our guests from the Free World beyond the Iron Curtain! We felt free!

Dainis Stalts leading the opening parade of Baltica 88. Photograph: Andris Krieviņš.

Dainis Stalts and his wife Helmi, who counted themselves among Latvia's last native Livs, were founders of the famous folk music ensemble Skandinieki, which had been reviving and performing traditional Latvian, Liv, and Latgalian songs since its inception in 1976. The Skandinieki wanted to instill Latvians with pride in their ancient culture. It wasn't easy. Their ambitions did not conform to Soviet ideology, and some Latvians had been sovietized. When my mother and I visited Dainis and Helmi at their house in Pārdaugava in the mid-1980s, they told us about their experiences with the KGB: the rude house searches; the confiscation of books and personal possessions; the threats... Even traditional folk music was perceived as threat by the Soviet state.

Baltica 88's most memorable venue was in Cēsis, Latvia's fourth oldest town founded in 1206. It was said that the Latvian red-white-red flag originated in Cēsis. I was present at the top of the old castle tower with many other happy participants, when Dainis Stalts raised the Latvian flag above the grizzled old town, which at the moment felt like the heart of Latvia. The outcome of *Cēsu kaujas* or the so-called Battle of Cēsis (also known as the Battle of Wenden) in June 1919 played an important role in securing the independence of Latvia and Estonia from German and Russian Bolshevik rule. And there we were, standing on top of the castle ruins nearly 70 years later, gazing at our beautiful flag with unspeakable joy. "How many years can a people exist before they're allowed to be free?" sang Bob Dylan in my youth. That time was coming; of this we were sure. How could it not? The power of song would defeat tanks and guns.

While many people savored Baltica's joyful atmosphere in Rīga and Cēsis, others were reminded of who was still in charge. In June Konstantīns Pupurs and his friends had been enjoying another folk festival in Cēsis. "During the concert no one gave any trite speeches glorifying the (Soviet) regime, and I didn't see any militsiya nearby or signs reminding us of Moscow's power and the communist system."* Pupurs was even invited to the stage to speak, and he delivered an impromptu speech about "unity and patriotism," reminding everyone in attendance about the efforts of the communist authorities to intimidate Helsinki-86. Last but not least, he promised "to raise the Latvian flag on June 14." The public responded with an ovation. That night Konstantīns' mother received several scary phone calls, including a death threat against her son, if he dared exhibit the Latvian flag on June 14. Their telephone was disconnected until late evening of the 14th. Outwardly, the unprecedented changes in Latvia seemed to be moving forward without a hitch. Yet those Latvians who stuck their necks out for the good of all of us were still in danger. Beneath Mikhail Gorbachev's flowery words the Soviet Union was still its old self, and Russia would never really change. As I enjoyed Baltica and the vibe of patriotism, Pupurs was experiencing the wrath of the KGB. * (Konstantīns Pupurs. "Karogs sarkanbalts." Rīga, 2011)

1988: Bearslayer

LETTISCHE AVANTGARDE

RIGA

LATVIEŠU AVANGARDS

Neue Gesellschaft für bildende Kunst (Hrsg.)   ELEFANTEN PRESS

The catalogue for a Latvian avant-garde exhibition in Berlin in 1988. Elefanten Press.

From a letter to my grandmother dated August 9, 1988: … *Andris' vacation just started. He's leaving shortly to attend the Liepāja Music Festival, which will feature many of Latvia's best rock bands. Just recently a group of our young Latvian artists returned from West Berlin, where their show was well received. A young Latvian American, Andris Rūtiņš, is getting married here to a Latvian girl! …*

The Liepāja music festival of the summer of 1988 is best remembered for singer Ieva Akurātera's emotional rendition of a song called "Manai tautai" ("To My Nation"), composed by Latvian American Lolita Ritmanis with lyrics by her father Dr. Andris Ritmanis. The song, which became the unofficial anthem of Latvia's National Awakening, was about the longing of many Latvians for freedom and for our nation's two divided halves, one in Latvia, the other in exile, to be reunited:

My thoughts are running every which way, forward, sideways, sometimes in circles. My roots, I can feel, don't grow as they should; even in fertile soil they bend and wither. My nation grows weak all over the world. Without its own soil, it struggles and splinters. Even in its own land it fails to flourish. Help us, God, help the Latvian nation! Bring us together again on the banks of the Daugava River! Help the Latvian nation take root in the soil of a free Latvia! Every day is painful for the Latvian nation; divided, separated, its song is sad. Its flame is dying. Help us, God! Help the Latvian nation take root in the soil of a free Latvia!

Latvia's music scene had changed since 1982, when I arrived, and it had definitely improved. There were groups that I really liked, like Jumprava; they were wildly popular with songs like "Vēlreiz" ("One More Time," 1988), a tender love song, and "Ziemeļmeita" ("Northern Girl") with a music video featuring the artwork of our friend Anita Kreituse. The group Dzeltenie Pastnieki ("The Yellow Postmen") was popular with its electronic sound and nonsensical lyrics. The "smooth jazz" group Remix, fronted by popular singer Igo (Rodrigo Fomins), could have done well in the United States. Their song "Vienīgai" ("The Only One") about their hometown Liepāja still sounds great today. Liepāja was badly battered in World War II and by the Soviets, who

447

turned it into a military port and closed it to outsiders. Its nickname, "the City where the Wind is Born," is derived from a popular Imants Kalniņš song.

Increasingly, people were traveling outside of the Soviet Union (with official permission from the Soviet authorities), slipping through the rigid Iron Curtain that separated the West and the Free World from Soviet communist reality. Exposed to the western way of life, its affluent market economies, and freedom of speech, they were returning with powerful impressions and messages. A group show, "Lettische Avantgarde" ("Latvian Avantgarde"), opened at the Staatliche Kunsthalle in West Berlin to critical acclaim. Not only were Latvians "importing" Western ideas at a rapid rate, they were also beginning to "export" Latvian culture through art and music. "The dark side of the Moon" was slowly swiveling into view. The fame of my former buddies Andris Breže, Ojārs Pētersons, and Juris Putrāms was growing. They had attracted interest with their *supergrafika* ("super graphics" or large prints) and were experimenting in installation art.

Bearslayer

From a letter dated August 24, 1988 to my family in the USA: *"Yesterday we went to Zigmārs Liepiņš's and Māra Zālīte's rock opera "Lāčplēsis" ("Bearslayer"). It was unforgettable. And everyone knew who the real antagonist was: Dietrich was wearing a fantastic helmet → (see illustration), which (the authorities) had forbidden, but he wore it anyway."*

In August we joined hundreds if not thousands of Latvians at beautiful, mysterious Lake Burtnieks in Vidzeme for a rehearsal of composer Zigmārs Liepiņš's rock opera "Lāčplēsis" ("Bearslayer"). Andris was there to take photographs, and I enjoyed the lovely setting and exciting atmosphere. It was clear that "Lāčplēsis" would be an enormous event in Latvian popular culture. As I listened to the singers belting out their lyrics, my skin tingled from goosebumps. Was the sunken castle in the nearby lake finally going to rise, and would Latvia shake off its chains? On that day anything seemed possible. "A small child plays at the crossroads beneath the wheels, hooves, and ironclad feet. A small child at the crossroads: like time, the sand slips between his fingers—our freedom, our life..." The lyrics by Māra Zālīte spoke of our dire situation, of time running out for us.

"Lāčplēsis" premiered on August 23, 1988 (exactly 49 years after the Molotov-Ribbentrop Pact was signed in Moscow) at Rīga's *Sporta manēža* (Sports Arena) to an audience of about 4,000 people. It went on to become a blockbuster hit for Liepiņš, libretto author Māra Zālīte, and the opera's main stars Rodrigo Fomins, Maija Lūsēna, Niks Matvejevs, Zigfrīds Muktupāvels, and others with some 43 shows, each with a huge turnout. *Lāčplēsis* the rock opera was based on Andrejs Pumpurs' 1888 epic poem of the same name, which I had been translating into English in 1987 before my breakdown.

Lake Burtnieks, one of Latvia's biggest lakes, is the setting in Pumpurs' epic tale for the castle of Burtnieks, a fictional Latvian chieftain from the 13th century. On August 23 gusts of wind scurried over the lake and played with our hair; our National Awakening was in full swing, and everyone was in an "ain't no stopping us now" mood. There are many legends and tales about the lake, including how it once fell out of the sky, submerging an old church and a castle... Its name, first mentioned in 1366, is derived from an old castle that once stood nearby. That day we could sense the depth and beauty of our history on the wings of the wind.

In Pumpurs' epic, our Latvian superhero Bearslayer descends down a mysterious staircase and enters a cavernous tunnel that leads him to the center of the lake. There he comes upon a strange and mysterious castle submerged in the watery gloom. Much to his surprise, he encounters his true love Laimdota reading old scrolls in candlelight. Laimdota informs her unexpected visitor that whoever could survive one night in the castle would raise the spellbound castle from its watery tomb. Of course, Bearslayer proclaims that he is the man for the task and begins waiting for something to happen. Who or what would he encounter?

In all the rooms a sudden whirlwind ran, / And seven demon fiends rushed through the door. / They bore a coffin with an ancient man, / Like scythes his teeth, like knives the nails he bore. / Although at first it seemed that he was dead, / He moved himself and uttered ghastly groans, / With opened eyes, 'How cold I am!' he said.—/ An unwished shudder gripped Bearslayer's bones. ("Bearslayer Conquers Demons and Raises the Sunken Castle": *Bearslayer* by Andrejs Pumpurs, translated by Arthur Cropley, 2005)

Lāčplēsis proceeds to defeat the horde of horrible demons and the evil Spīdala, and the castle with its ancient treasures and secrets rises to the surface. Legend also has it that when the time was right, a castle ("of light and freedom") would rise up out of some lake's murky depths, signifying our nation's rebirth. Our famous choir song "Gaismas pils" ("Castle of Light") by Latvian composer Jāzeps Vītols (1863–1948) remains a staple of all Latvian song festivals. The atmosphere near shimmering Lake Burtnieks on August 23, 1988 was pure magic. I fully expected an ancient castle encrusted with shells and covered in algae and sludge to bubble up and pierce the surface of the lake during the performance.

"Bearslayer" the rock opera was one of the most memorable visual and musical expressions of our National Awakening. Liepiņš and Zālīte made it clear who the bad guys were: the people who ruled under communism's red star. "Lāčplēsis" was another manifestation of hope and courage, a reminder that we could and should believe the unbelievable: *that things would change. Soon.*

In my letter from August 24 I also wrote: "Yesterday thousands of people gathered at the Freedom Monument; it was a sea of red-white-red flags and flowers. They say that ethnic Latvians comprise less than 50% of Latvia's population today, while Russian immigrants keep pouring in. Latvians have finally decided to rise up against this terrible injustice. May God grant us a positive outcome!"

On September 17 Krišjānis and I drove up to Viļķene in Vidzeme with my father-in-law to participate in the consecration of a monument dedicated to Kārlis Baumanis (1835–1905), composer of the Latvian national anthem "Dievs, svētī Latviju!" ("God, Bless Latvia!"). We stood beside hundreds of Latvians clutching miniature Latvian flags and wearing Latvian ribbons and

Auseklis ("Morning Star") pins to commemorate our beloved hymn's composer. Like everything associated with Latvian independence and statehood, "God, Bless Latvia" had been repressed for nearly 50 years. We also visited the cemetery in Limbaži and laid flowers at Baumanis' beautifully maintained gravesite. The white sand had been lovingly raked into a tidy pattern, and people had laid fresh flowers along the edges.

Krišjānis n Viļķene on September 17, 1988 at the consecration of a monument to Kārlis Baumanis, composer of the Latvian national anthem. The monument was designed by sculptor Vilnis Titāns. Photograph: Juris Krieviņš

I had sung "Dievs, svētī Latviju!" growing up in the United States, whereas my nation in Latvia had to hold its tongue for decades. In 1981, when I was still just a tourist in Latvia, a the friend of a friend in Jūrmala produced a music box from the pre-war era to show me: as he opened the lid, the notes of our anthem began chiming. And then just like, Agris whisked it away, as if a bunch of chekists were lurking nearby, ready to pounce on us. For just that small gesture he could have gotten into very big trouble with the Soviet authorities. It had been a solemn, somber, surreal moment. Seven years later in 1988, Latvians were reclaiming their flag, their anthem, their history and culture, their heroes, and their very identity, as their "liberators," the Russian and Latvian communists, the Soviet military, as well as Latvian turncoats, chekists, enforcers, and informants seethed. *Those Latvian fascists!* And there were plenty of "Kangars" ("traitor") types in our midst. (Kangars is a dark character in Pumpurs' epic.)

A Stronghold in the Fatherland

Dreaming of a place of our own while working on illustrations for a children's book (left) in Zolitūde.

As we adjusted to our new surroundings in the canyons of Zolitūde, I began buying *Lauku Avīze*, a new Latvian language newspaper that had appeared in January of that year. It was devoted expressly to rural life, which appealed to me: I had gotten a good taste of it in Piebalga. If anything, life in Latvia taught me to appreciate the hard work of farmers and the joys of gardening. Hunched over my desk in Zolitūde, I combed through the Want Ad section of the newspaper looking at listings of houses for sale in the Vidzeme countryside. I had decided that we had to buy our own place in the countryside; I was tired of communal living. It was hard to play second fiddle, to not be involved in decision-making, to be a permanent guest, even if I was a full-fledged member of the family. I was nurturing a romantic vision of planting a flower garden, creating an orchard, harvesting homegrown berries, and tending to our very own vegetables. Just like at Paulēni, we would have a pond full of fish and a Latvian sauna for rejuvenating our bodies, minds, and souls. Hopefully, we would have more children, a dog and a cat, perhaps a rooster and a flock of hens. Our house would be my permanent stronghold in the fatherland. There I could finally unfurl my roots and plant them in Latvia's soil. Oh my, I was so idealistic, so full of hope and love!

Our farm would have to be in Vidzeme, with which I was somewhat familiar. Ideally, we would find a house in Piebalga, an area that I had come to love deeply for its beauty and history.. I also liked the fact that Piebalga was attracting writers, artists, architects, and actors who were buying up old houses to restore. A community was forming.

After some hesitation and questioning looks from his parents, Andris went along with the idea. We began driving around Piebalga in search of a house to buy. I became obsessed. Every house along the dusty roads attracted my attention. At that time house prices in the countryside were relatively affordable. For about 10,000 roubles—less than the Soviet market value of a Sony boom box—you could purchase a relatively nice fixer-upper. No wonder a couple of chekists thought I might be interested in going into the import business with them.

We logged many gravelly kilometers, scrambling out of the car whenever something caught our eye. Many old, abandoned houses were surrounded by deep grass. It was heartbreaking. The war and the Soviet deportations of 1941 and 1949, as well as the centralized kolhoz system, had emptied many homes permanently.

That summer we stumbled upon an old house near Gaiziņš, Latvia's highest point. Its price: 500 roubles (!). Set far back from the road, the old house felt remote and lonely. It belonged to an old woman who no longer lived there. I didn't like the fact that we had only one set of neighbors within view: who knew what they were like, if they were friendly or helpful. What if they drank? After much talk and consideration, we abandoned that idea. We circled back towards the Cēsis-Madona "highway," plunging into the scenic Liezere landscape. A house in a dreamy setting where a neighbor claimed the well water was bad... Another house in Jaunpiebalga where the owner was on his deathbed, dying of cancer... A lovely, decaying house on top of a hill in Jaunpiebalga encircled by oaks and lindens, which we would have bought if only the legal owner were willing. She lived at the bottom of the hill in a roadside house, had survived the Gulag, lost her loved ones there, and just couldn't or wouldn't sell. *Ne pašam, ne Sašam!* ("Not for me, not for Sasha!")

As talks of denationalization loomed, many people found it hard to sell off their family homes, which reminded them of their family's losses, pain, and suffering. We could only drive away feeling disappointed, wondering what would ultimately happen to these properties, which were in desperate need of repair. Leaking roofs, paneless windows, smashed stoves, rotting floors... We encountered this mentality several times, and it was discouraging.

And then we found Lieljānēni in Jaunpiebalga. We had been in the area before, but this time we wanted to take a look at Ansis Epners' (1937–2003) place in the woods, which he was offering to sell. Again, this locale was not only beautiful; it was rich with cultural history. We drove past Jāņa skola ("Jāņa School"), a pretty red brick building near the Vecpiebalga-Jaunpiebalga road, where composer Emīls Dārziņš (1875–1910) was born. Writer Jānis Sudrabkalns (1894–1975) had attended Jāņa skola. His own childhood home nearby, Zelta krogs ("Gold Tavern"), was by the late 1980s just a dusty, overgrown shell with no markers. If Juris Krieviņš hadn't said something, I would never have known it had something to do with Sudrabkalns, who was touted by the communists as one of Latvia's great writers when, in fact, his accomplishments were rather mediocre.

Not that I really knew anything about Sudrabkalns, a communist who lived "well" under the Soviets; he is remembered for having sung his praises to Stalin and the communists. Our Latvian school curriculum in the US contained few references to Latvian Bolsheviks and communists like Sudrabkalns; he was a traitor in the eyes of the expats. Zelta krogs once had a *stadula*—a building for horses, carts, and carriages, and within that stadula there had been a stone inscribed with the number 1813, according to the website "Zudusī Latvija." Was the marker still there? Few locals were interested in exploring these wrecks.

Sudrabkalns' father and the father of Emīls Dārziņš had worked at Zelta krogs as innkeepers. Dārziņš's "Melancholy Waltz" still fills me with longing for a place that perhaps does not exist for me. Dārziņš died at the age of 35. His waltz, so hauntingly beautiful, remains his greatest legacy. I was drawn to traces of the distant past, as I longed for a place that had been lost. And who knew if it could be restored?

A 1967 photograph of Zelta krogs ("Gold Tavern") in Jaunpiebalga. By the mid-1980s the roof had caved in, and not much was left of its original appearance. Photograph: Jānis Kučers. Image courtesy of the National Library of Latvia collection "In Search of Lost Latvia."

We slowed down before Jāņa skola, turning into a road that descended into a pretty valley. This was the way to Epners' digs. The road ended in a cluster of homes called Jānēni. We soon discovered that Epners' house sat way back in the woods with no road for easy access, and there was no electricity. Those two factors, as well as the appearance of the house itself, crossed the option off our list. As we made our way back to where we had parked the car, we noticed that the very last house in Jānēni looked uninhabited. Cables leading to the house indicated that it had electricity. It looked like the house came with a large, solid hay shed, a barn in need of repair, a fine granary, an orchard, and several berry bushes, all of which heightened our excitement.

A small stream, nearly dry at the time, separated the buildings from the meadows beyond. We took in the wonderful view of the valley and the nearby woods. My heart was racing. Back then a real estate tour in the Latvian countryside consisted of prying open a window or door. We hoisted ourselves in through a weakly hinged window and took a tour of the empty rooms. The old kitchen had a pump with a basin and drain mounted in the floor, a delightful asset that we had never seen before.

I could already picture the house with crisply painted walls decorated with my husband's beautiful photographs and my drawings and paintings. We would find some antique beds, chairs, and cupboards. The rooms were bright and spacious with lots of potential. We went back outside to peer through the cracks of the shuttered barn, which looked dry and sound. The house was shaded by old trees. It was perfect! Just 25 minutes from Paulēni! Despite not wanting to live with my in-laws, I still liked them well enough to want to be close to them. Before getting back in the car, we ask a pleasant neighbor about the house, who owned it, how we could get in touch with that person. My adrenaline level was high. The hunt was on.

Our attempts to persuade the owner to sell, our competition with others to buy the house: sadly, by late fall it became clear the deal had fallen through. Sensing there were bidders, the owner raised his price. We let go, and I was bitterly disappointed.

In the fall of 1988 Latvia's first international film festival "Arsenāls" ("Arsenal") made its debut, thanks to the ongoing efforts of a bunch of film enthusiasts, including Augusts Sukuts, Māris Gailis, and others. Arsenāls was built on the memorable *Kino dienas* ("Film Days") of 1986 in Rīga, an unusual event for its time. According to Kristīne Matīsa, one of the organizers, "In 1986 the Awakening was just on the horizon, and most people were too afraid of the regime to try something new. *Kino dienas,* an initiative of a handful of people, was a surprising manifestation of freedom, a weeklong festival of culture with all sorts of events at various venues in Rīga. The *Arsenāls* part of the 1986 festival was devoted to banned Soviet film. After its success and the buzz it generated, the organizers decided to turn this event into a regular event." It was yet another example of Latvians thinking "outside of the box" at a time when it wasn't particularly safe to do so. Featuring an impressive program of hundreds of foreign films, the 1988 Arsenāls festival attracted local and international attention and exposed Rigans to new names in film and novel approaches to cinematography. The festival was devoted to art film and would become a staple of the Rīga culture scene for some time to come. There was so much activity going on behind the heavy Iron Curtain that few in the Free World knew about.

The Latvian Popular Front

From a letter dated October 4, 1988 to my family in the US: *... We hope to get a telephone line soon. I'm sick and tired of running to the phone booth to make calls, especially in the evening. Krišjānis finally has a bike and enjoys pedaling around everywhere. We have a new First Secretary (of the Latvian Communist Party). His name is Jānis Vagris. I don't know anything about him; is he just another robot? A lot of people were hoping Anatolijs Gorbunovs would get the job. Instead, Gorbunovs is now Chairman of the Supreme Soviet. That's good, too.*

On October 6, 1988 the Latvian Supreme Soviet, the precursor to the Latvian Saeima (Parliament), proclaimed Latvian as the official state language of Latvia. This was an enormous, emotional victory for Latvians, who had experienced their mother tongue being diminished, trivialized, and squeezed out of use.

"For a Judicial State in Latvia!": A depiction of the Latvian Freedom Monument as a focal point at the October 7, 1988 demonstration in Rīga. Photograph: Andris Krieviņš.

On October 7, thousands of people gathered at the Mežaparks Ampitheater for a "people's manifestation" calling for a "judicial state in Latvia." A sea of Latvian flags... Latvia's sovereignty no longer seemed implausible, when so many people stood shoulder to shoulder.

The Latvian Popular Front (LPF), which was attracting some of Latvia's brightest minds, held its founding congress at the Political Education Building on October 8–9. Journalist Dainis Īvāns, who had campaigned tirelessly to save the Daugava River from another HES, was elected Chairman of the LPF. Old actor and veteran Latvian Rifleman Ēvalds Valters (1894–1994) addressed the assembly, which included representatives of the Western media:

"My beloved, my courageous nation of *arāji* ('plowmen' [a reference to our history as an agrarian nation – RL])! My courageous, tenacious, hardy nation, of which a Latvian daina says: 'My fatherland and all its fallow lands belong to me; I will be master and plowman here.' Several hundred years later one of our finest poets (Vilis Plūdons—RL) expressed the same courageous words: 'We want to be masters of our native land; we want to decide our laws for ourselves. This land is ours, these cities are ours; we don't want to ask for what is ours but take it.' Inspired by these words, Latvian riflemen once assembled for battle. We shed our blood for a free Latvia. Lenin understood this. Latvia became a sovereign state. I believe that after this long night day will come."

The old actor could finally speak what was on his mind and in his heart, like all Latvians, without fear of reprisal. Whether Comrade Lenin understood the Latvians' longing for freedom and independence from Russia was debatable. Valters was treading softly. (1)

A letter to my parents dated November 10, 1988: *It's a beautiful day, cold and sunny! I am so happy with our sun-filled rooms. The renovations are complete, and our new wallpaper looks lovely. We are finally getting a television antenna, so that I don't have to look at a blurry image. Were we ever excited to find a message in our mailbox that your package had arrived! We went downtown to the central post office to pick up it up. Krišjānis is thrilled about everything, especially his "pilot" jacket. We had to pay a 30 rouble customs tariff. Winter came early. We spent the October Revolution celebration in the countryside, where it had snowed.*

Time to think about Christmas. People are saying that maybe, after such a long time, there might be a Christmas mass at St. Mary's Cathedral. Tomorrow is Lāčplēsis Day, and many events are planned. (On Lāčplēsis Day, November 11, Latvians commemorate all those who fought and died for Latvia's freedom.—RL) A monument to Colonel Oskars Kalpaks (1882–1919) will be revealed in Airītes. The Latvian flag and the flag of the city of Rīga will be raised for the first time since the war on top of Rīga Castle. I can't decide where we should go—to Airītes or stay in Rīga. It's all so wonderful! I have to see the exhibit "Latvia between Two World Wars" at the Museum of History and Navigation. The uniforms of the Latvian Army, military decorations, our pre-war currency, etc. are on view. Despite these fantastic, positive changes, the atmosphere here is tense. Our so-called Interfront (the International Front of the Working People of the Latvian SSR) is creating a rift in Latvian society. What a bunch of Neanderthals! I can't believe that Gorbachev would side with these people! I would love to know how the world is reacting to the events in Latvia, Lithuania, and Estonia!

On November 11, 1988, Ēvalds Valters and Latvian writer Alberts Bels raised the Latvian flag at the top of Rīga Castle's Tower of the Holy Spirit, which once held the castle's treasures. My father-in-law Juris Krieviņš had invited me along, and with Krišjānis in tow, I was lucky to be on hand to witness the historic event. Ascending the stairs of the ancient tower, looking out over our "river of fate" shimmering below, and seeing the Latvian flag raised are priceless memories.

The Latvian Popular Front was Latvia's largest popular movement in history, uniting about 230,000 Latvians and representatives of the country's ethnic minorities. It was a movement characterized by *broad consensus* and *peaceful resistance*. Its main goals were the democratization and spiritual renewal of society, as well as the restoration of Latvia's sovereignty. In December 1988 the LTF began publishing its own newspaper, *Atmoda* ("Awakening"), in Latvian, Russian, and English. (2)

Chapter sources:

(1) "Latvijas Tautas fronts dibināšanas congress." Latinform/Barikadopēdija. October 11, 1988; 5/6/2013. <http://www.barikadopedija.lv/raksti/925828>
(2) "Latvijas Tautas fronte." Letonika. <http://www.letonika.lv/groups/default.aspx?cid=31864>

Litene

Camp Litene in the 1930s. Image courtesy of the National Library of Latvia collection "In Search of Lost Latvia."

As a result of glasnost and the Latvians' push for historical truth and justice, in October 1988 the Latvian SSR Prosecutor's Office launched an investigation into the 1941 arrests, murders, and/or deportations of officers of the Latvian Army from their summer training camp in Litene. For years this tragedy had been silenced, but now its skeletons were knocking on the door, gasping to be let out. For Latvians the name Litene stood for Soviet atrocities and crimes against humanity. In 1987 poet Uldis Bērziņš referred to Litene's tragic events in his poem "Litene: An Attempt at Memorization." Litene symbolized the Soviet Union's methodical destruction of the Latvian Army officer corps. Some Latvian military men were able to survive the first Soviet occupation because they went into hiding.

The story of how the Soviet Union destroyed the Latvian military with brutal methods is a long one. In the Soviet era it remained under wraps. When I was growing up in the United States, the General Kārlis Goppers Foundation in Canada stood for philanthropy: it supported various cultural and educational projects of the Latvian diaspora. But its namesake, General Kārlis Goppers, was one of the countless victims of Soviet terror in my fatherland; his story and the fate of Latvia's military during World War II was not well known in the West in the Soviet era. Silencing these crimes was an egregious insult to injury. It was closure that many Latvians and Balts longed for.

Latvian General Kārlis Goppers (April 2, 1876—March 25, 1941) and at the time of his arrest in 1940 (below). (Photos: Wikipedia)

Latvian General Kārlis Goppers did not die at Litene, nor was he deported to Siberia; he was murdered in just one of the many Soviet NKVD's special gruesome tasks aimed at decapitating Latvian society. A recipient of Latvia's highest military decoration, the Order of Lāčplēsis, General Goppers could look back to a truly distinguished military career, which included service in the Russian Army, active participation in Latvia's War of Independence, as well as fighting against the Bolsheviks in Yaroslavl and Samara. These facts would be used against him by the Soviets. General Goppers was an active, revered, and distinguished member of Latvian society. He presided over the Latvian Scout Organization, which he helped found. He was arrested in September 1940, tortured by the NKVD in captivity, and then shot on March 25, 1941 in a forest in Ulbroka. He was buried in a mass grave with other Latvians. In 1944 his remains were exhumed and interred at the Brothers' Cemetery in Rīga. His heart was buried in his native Trikāte. (1)

To provide my reader with a sense of what transpired at Camp Litene and nearby Camp Ostrovieši in the early summer of 1941, I have translated the following description of the events as summarized on a website called "Sargs.lv," which is devoted to the Latvian military. Historian Ēriks Jēkabsons says that it has been nearly impossible for Latvian historians to gain access to some of the most sensitive archives in Russia that could shed light on the arrests, trials, and sentences of Latvia's senior officers who were sent to Moscow under the pretext of training courses. This speaks volumes about the transparency of the Russian government and its institutions today, as well as about Russia's approach towards Soviet history.

The Latvian Army established Camp Litene in 1935 as a summer training camp for its Latgale Division. The army created roads and paths, dug wells, built cabins and kitchens, and constructed a sturdy wooden bridge over the Pededze River. A modern firing range was located close by. From May until autumn thousands of Latvian soldiers received tactical training outdoors. They were drilled in marksmanship and hardened physically and mentally.

After Latvia was annexed by the Soviet Union, the Latvian War Ministry was shuttered on September 27, 1940. The Soviets created the Soviet Red Army's 24th Territorial Corps with the remnants of the Latvian Army. Prior to this move, about 10,037 Latvian soldiers were decommissioned. Those who were retained were pressured to join the Soviet youth organization, the Komsomol. Soldiers who were considered disloyal or whose actions in the past made them suspect were quickly expelled from the 24th Territorial Corps.

By June 1941 more than 300 Latvian officers, instructors, and soldiers had been arrested for mass deportation or already executed.

At the beginning of June 1941 the Latvian commanding officers of the 24th Territorial Corpus were replaced, so that they could attend special "courses" in Moscow. Almost all of these senior officers were arrested later that month, tried (on trumped up charges— RL), and executed or deported to Soviet prison camps, where they perished.

Latvian General Roberts Kļaviņš (1885–1941), commander of the 24th Territorial Corpus, was a highly decorated Latvian officer with a lifetime career of active military duty and experience. Kļaviņš fought in Latvia's War of Independence (1918–1920). In June 1941 he was sent to "courses" in Moscow along with other senior Latvian officers. He was arrested on June 22. He was tried on July 29, executed on October 16, 1941, his body dumped into a mass grave in Kommunarka near Moscow. (Wikipedia: "Roberts Kļaviņš")

The Red Army's commanders wanted to deploy Latvian soldiers to Litene as early as May 15, 1941, but because of the severe winter and cold spring Major General Roberts Kļaviņš of the 24th Corpus was able to postpone their deployment to Litene until June 1st and to Ostrovieši until June 10th. After the record cold winter the air temperature was still below normal, and frost covered the ground after the sun went down. The Latvian troops were cold in their tents at night.

Soon after their arrival in Litene, Latvian soldiers from the 1939 draft were released from military duty. They were replaced by conscripts from the Soviet Union who did not speak Latvian; this reduced the percentage of Latvians in the 24th Territorial Corpus by half. The Russian soldiers were distributed among the Latvian units in proportion to the number of Latvians.

The Latvian soldiers no longer had access to the news; newspaper delivery was erratic, their personal mail was controlled, and they were only allowed to listen to local news (...).

The camp was guarded by soldiers from other Soviet republics (who did not speak Latvian—RL). The Latvian soldiers were not allowed to leave the camp without the permission of the camp's (...) commander and politruk (political commissar—RL). They were forbidden to go to the nearby town of Gulbene.

Upon their arrival the Latvian soldiers were vaccinated against tetanus; afterwards many of them felt sick and tired. Those who tried to shirk the innoculations were punished. (...)

On June 11 the last remaining Latvian regiment commanders relinquished their duties to their Red Army counterparts. On June 12 the Latvian division commanders relinquished their duties.

On June 12 and 13 more than twenty senior Latvian Army officers were sent to "qualification improvement courses" in Moscow. Some of them were tried and executed in Moscow, others were deported to slave camps in Siberia.

On June 13 the Latvian officers in Litene received orders not to leave the camp's territory. Subordinate Latvian units were ordered to turn in their firearms at the camp's warehouse. The camp commanders were told to issue weapons to the new conscripts from other Soviet republics. Some of the units were told to prepare for "training."

On the morning of June 14 (Russian) officers were placed on duty to guard the camp at strategic points. Special Red Army units and patrols were placed throughout the camp. Latvian officers were divested of their pistols' cartridges and ordered to sleep together in the commanders' tents. The other units were informed of the impending "training."

What happened next on June 14 has been described by an eyewitness, Kārlis Bergs, a Latvian cavalry captain: "...Right after breakfast a list of officers to be sent to field training exercises near Gulbene was read out loud; these men would bring with them maps, binoculars, and raincoats. Everyone would meet up in an hour by a certain cabin to board waiting transport vehicles. I wasn't surprised (by this announcement), because this sort of officer training happened all the time. Usually only a certain number of officers of a certain rank were assigned to field training depending on the subject of the training and the scope of the planned activities.

"After the announcement, events unfolded quickly. The officers climbed into the waiting trucks and were driven out toward Litene Manor, where they were joined by other trucks carrying (Latvian) officers from the corpus' headquarters and other units. Following the new camp chief Major Tkachyov's orders, all the vehicles turned into a narrow country lane. After a couple of kilometers the lane narrowed even more, where it was surrounded on both sides by thick bushes. Suddenly the convoy was ordered to a halt, and everyone was told to get out and line up on the road. Then Major Tkachov came forward and screamed, "This is how we do field training... Hands up!" At that moment the thickets on both sides of the road parted to reveal two long chains of Red Army soldiers with their guns trained at the Latvian officers. Anyone who showed the slightest resistance was shot on the spot. Even a Russian officer was shot. The (Latvian) officers were forced back into the transport vehicles and were driven to the train station in Gulbene, accompanied by a convoy of armored vehicles. There they were locked into cattle cars."

During their arrest the Latvian officers were divested of their personal weapons and possessions; their military insignia was ripped off of their uniforms.

At around 23 hours (11:00 pm) on the evening of June 14 a train pulling 17–20 cattle cars filled with about 430 Latvian officers (from Camp Litene and nearby Camp Ostrovieši—RL) departed from the train station in Gulbene. On June 15 the train idled in Rīga, where about 130–135 more Latvian officers, either infirm or who had been away on a mission or on vacation, were added to this ("cargo"). On June 16–17 the train began its long trip eastward to Siberia. (At this same time officers of the Lithuanian 29th and Estonian 22nd territorial corpuses were also arrested.)

Most of the deported Latvian officers were sentenced in absentia between autumn of 1941 and spring of 1942 (that is, they were already dead or in Soviet prison camps—RL); they were convicted of high treason. Only about 80 Latvian soldiers survived their ordeal to make it back to Latvia.

A memorial called the "Wall of Pain" by artists Ivars Feldbergs and Sandra Gribanovska was unveiled on June 14, 2001 at the cemetery in Litene. It commemorates Litene's deported and murdered Latvian Army officers. The Latvian Army summer camp at Litene is on Latvia's register of cultural and historical heritage monuments; it is a place of national historical significance. (2)

First Lieutenant of Aizpute's 10th Infantry Frīdrichs Feldmanis (1911—1941) was one of two Latvian Army officers who tried to resist arrest in the forest near Litene. The other was heavy artillery regiment Lieutenant Commander Arveds Teodors Lulla. First Lieutenant Feldmanis shot and killed Soviet Army politruk Doroshchenko at the time of his arrest. According to Nekropole.lv, after Feldmanis shot the commissar, he was attacked, beaten and stabbed, and died on the spot. (3)

Latvian War Museum historian Kārlis Dambītis: "The biggest tragedy took place at the end of June 1941, when the Red Army evacuated Litene, retreating from the advancing German Army. The Latvian soldiers were demobilized, and then they were shot as they were leaving the camp's territory. They are buried at the cemetery in Litene, but there may be many more graves in the forest." In fact, "the end of June for the 24th Territorial Corpus was, simply put, a nightmare," according to Dambītis. "Part of the 24th Corpus was moved to Carnikava. On its way there the soldiers were turned back. They were attacked by national partisans, German saboteurs, and the German Luftwaffe. The column of Latvian soldiers was also intercepted near Liepna by Germans in motorized vehicles. Many Latvians deserted from their units. No one trusted the Latvian soldiers. Before and after the march many men were demobilized. How many left voluntarily, how many were shot along the way? Only

14 remains have been found. According to the local people, there should be more graves, because only a small area of the woods near Litene was combed. I think the number is well over 100, but how many died in and near Litene, how many along the way, how many deserted? How many were shot as deserters? How many as politically suspect? How many during friendly fire? I have no idea. Almost all of the Latvian officers from the Litene and Ostrovieši camps ended up in Norilsk in a huge, intricate system of slave labor camps."

The truth about Litene finally ruptured under the policy of glasnost, like a deep abcess, allowing Latvians and the families of the victims to grieve openly and opening up the possibility for Latvian historians to shed light on other Soviet crimes. For years the story of Litene was talked about only in the Latvian exile community. Memoirs published outside of Latvia would remain an invaluable source of information for historians.

A BBC map with Norilsk, Russia, the final destination of many Latvian Army officers.

"After the war the subject of Litene was approached through the tight demands that governed Soviet historiography, with one of its most essential principles being the complete silencing of any facts or their sum, which were 'inconvenient' to Soviet doctrine. Undoubtedly, such inconvenient truths were so many as to comprise a majority. In the event that it was impossible to cover up something, another principle of Soviet historiography was the method of telling blatant lies and changing facts. Thus, Soviet historians spoke only of 'socialist changes in the army' and of (the absolute majority of) simple soldiers' enthusiasm for the transformation and their opportunity to serve in the RKK (*Raboche-Krestyanskaya Krasnaya Armiya* or the Worker-Peasantry's Red Army) while mentioning the expulsion of 'reactionary' Latvian officers from the army only in passing. (Soviet historians) do not mention these repressions; the fact that they occurred was simply silenced, just as the mass repressions in (Soviet-occupied) Latvia were never mentioned." (Ēriks Jēkabsons, *Latvijas armijas iznīcināšana un Sarkanās armijas 24. Teritoriālais strēlnieku korpuss 1940.-1941. gadā: Izpētes stāvoklis un iespējas.* [The Destruction of the Latvian Army and the 24th Territorial Riflemen's Corpus in 1940–1941: The Status of Research and Possibilities]. Tr. RL)

"The Soviets succeeded in completely destroying the Latvian Army in 1940–1941. Of 2193 former Latvian Army officers, 299 had been arrested prior to June 14, 1941; on one date alone, June 14, 1941, 562 officers were arrested and deported; 247 had gone missing. Between June 17, 1940 and June 14, 1941 the Soviets repressed 1,100 Latvian officers. The number of officers murdered in Litene remains unknown (...)." (4)

Being denied their history for such a long time was traumatic for Latvians, Lithuanians, and Estonians. Litene's story was every Latvian's personal story. Like Poland's Katyn, Litene was a symbol of Soviet savagery.

Chapter sources:

(1) "Kārlis Goppers." Wikipedia. September 12, 2013; May 9, 2014. <http://lv.wikipedia.org/wiki/K%C4%8 1rlis_Goppers>

(2) "Litene: Latvijas armijas Katiņa." Sargs.lv. May 30, 2011; 5/7/2013 <http://www.sargs.lv/Vesture/Vesture/2011/05/30-02.aspx#lastcomment>

(3) Dzērve, Astra. "Atklās izstādi par 10. Aizputes kājnieku pulka virsleitnanta Fridriha Feldmaņa traģisko likteni." Laiki.lv. <http://www.laiki.lv/_Liepaja/default.aspx?pg=ad632e9d-d28d-4bf8-b9e9-9d0cf612ee4b>

(4) "Litene—The Latvian Katyn." Latvian History. February 15, 2013; May 12, 2013. <http://latvianhistory.wordpress.com/2013/02/15/litene-the-latvian-katyn>

Light in Darkness

Insubordination simmered in *Pribaltika* (the Russian term for the area of the three Baltic States), as the cold season arrived. What a year it had been! Vadim Medvedev, a member of Moscow's Politburo, arrived for a visit on November 13 to discuss the situation in Latvia with his Latvian Communist Party counterparts. Who knows what plans the comrades discussed. A few days later, on November 18, Latvians gathered at the Freedom Monument to commemorate Independence Day. The chekists had evaporated, it seemed.

Mikhail Gorbachev had unwittingly opened a Pandora's Box in his attempt to improve the Soviet economy and social climate. The Latvian nation would converge time and time again in the months to come at "people's manifestations" to demand change and freedom. Similar processes were taking place in our neighboring countries, Estonia and Lithuania. We were brothers (and sisters) in arms. The possibility of finally breaking free from the grip of the Soviet Union loomed.

On November 19, the Latvian Olympic Committee was revived. Latvian athletes had competed for years under the Soviet flag; it was high time for change. We had all dreamed of the day when they would march under the red-white-red flag in the Olympic Games' opening ceremony and compete for their country, Latvia!

The Latvian Olympic team at the 1924 Winter Olympics in Chamonix, France.

We rejoiced when the heat finally came on. Our apartment fell warm and cosy. I loved looking out through the window, as daylight faded and thousands of lights came on in the apartment buildings in the distance. Zolitūde could also be charming, when one squinted. Those lights were like the hopes and dreams that we, the oppressed Balts, had felt in the darkness that had enveloped the Baltics for too long.

Winter arrived with soft, shimmering snowflakes whirling about and piling up on our balcony. Snow blanketed Zolitūde in white tranquility. A remarkable year was drawing to a close, and we waited in suspense for what would come next.

1989: "Come out, justice, from your metal coffin"

A photograph by Boriss Koļesņikovs of one of the many Latvian mass demonstrations in the late 1980s.

Come out of your metal coffin, / Come out, justice, come out! / Everything is draped in beads of tears / And covered with roses of blood... (Words from a poem called "Taisnība" ["Justice"] by Edvarts Trei-manis-Zvārgulis [1866–1950], which was set to music by Jānis Lūsēns. It was a big hit in 1989.)

The Interfont (short for the Latvian SSR Workers' International Front), comprised of diehard communists and staunch advocates for the preservation of the Soviet Union, was officially founded in a meeting at (again) the Political Education Building of the Central Committee of the Communist Party in Rīga on January 7, 1989. As noted, the Interfront and the Latvian Popular Front represented two diametrically opposed ideologies and directions, and echoes of that schism can be felt today, as Soviet nostalgists (albeit in decreasing numbers) and Russian language advocates clash with Latvian nationalists. Latvians were putting all their weight into pulling the rope westward into the Free World's embrace and out of the Soviet sphere of influence for good. Their antagonists—the communists and Soviet Russian imperialists—were pulling the rope eastward towards Moscow. And poor Mother Latvia was that taut, frayed rope. As Latvia's progressive forces were putting their heads together to map a way forward and out of Moscow's grasp, so were supporters of the Soviet status quo, the Interfront, a movement established to counter the Latvian Popular Front. The Interfront was comprised mostly of Russians and the bosses of Soviet Latvia's big industrial plants, retired Russian military officers, and hard-core communists who had enjoyed power and privilege in the Soviet political system. People like Alfrēds Rubiks, Anatolijs Aleksejevs, Anatolijs Belaičuks, Igors Lopatins, Sergejs Dīmanis, and Tat-jana Ždanoka actively opposed the Latvians' move towards independence.

By 1989 the Latvian Communist Party and its bosses in Moscow were very nervous. Insubor-dinance pointing towards independence had overwhelmed Latvia's quislings; they no longer knew what to do or how to act. Their hands were tied by Gorbachev's policies and promises to the West. In October 1988 Jānis Vagris had replaced communist hardliner Boris Pugo as First Secretary of the Central Committee of the Latvian Communist Party. Shortly after his appoint-ment at one of the large gatherings at Mežaparks, Vagris addressed the huge crowd, awkwardly saying that "he'd never done anything to harm the Latvian people." Vagris gave the impression of a deer caught in headlights, unsure of how to handle the situation in Latvia and how to im-press the thousands of angry Latvians staring at him.

Augusts Voss, Boris Pugo, Jānis Vagris, Anatolijs Gorbunovs, Alfrēds Rubiks, Nikolajs Neilands, Ivars Ķezbers: these were some of the Latvian communist honchos of the 1980s, "my time" in occupied Latvia. That decade was drawing to a close. Voss was slowly expiring in Moscow, but there was no lack of "friends of Moscow" in Latvia. And these people were very anxious.

In the spring of 1989 we headed back to West Germany to fetch our car and visit friends in Münster and Munich. We stayed with our friend Dr. Andris Kadeģis in his lovely house in the German countryside, savoring his breakfast spreads of soft, freshly baked white bread, German cold cuts, and lively conversations. We visited the Münster Latvian Gymnasium, where wonderful Inga Grīnberga, a dear friend from Boston, Massachussetts was working; she let us use her little VW Golf, as the Red Opel was being readied for departure. We drove down to Munich to stay with the Ziemelis family; Uģis, originally from Canada, was now working for Siemens in West Germany, and his wife Mārīte was from Latvia.

We were able to explore the Bavarian Alps and get a look at some exquisite churches and a couple of the castles constructed for Bavarian King Ludwig II (1845–1886), Neuschwanstein and Schloss Linderhof. Bavaria itself was captivating, magnificent, and unforgettable; we rode the train up the side of Zugspitze, Germany's highest mountain peak. As deprived Ostländers we looked with envy at the content Germans lounging in their ski suits sipping beer and wine on a deck with an amazing view; an invisible wall seemed to separate us from them. The trip back to Münster through the Rhine Valley was also magical for us gray Soviet people used to nothing but drabness and bitter faces. We stopped to explore some of the old castles along the Rhine, enjoying the sunshine and splendid views. I thought of Latvia's German legacy, the crumbling manors and churches in need of renovation.

With close to a decade of life under Soviet communism behind me, my eyes had become "sovietized." In West Germany I was staring at people's clothes, shoes, complexions, and teeth (not that I had bad teeth, but many Latvians had really bad teeth, which ruined their smiles). I was peering at the quality of construction, at home "details" like sinks, ovens, refrigerators, appliances, the way windows fit so snugly and neatly into walls, how they opened and closed so easily, the perfect smoothness and transparency of the window glass, the quality of the floors, the safe-looking electrical outlets... Our new flat in Zolitūde was so crappy, that picturing it in my head as we sat in our friends' sleek, comfortable West German apartment with its magnificent view of the mountains made me cringe inwardly. I peered at our son's face with worry, imagining that the very paleness of his skin reflected our gray, sparkle-less Soviet world.

My husband was probably ogling the gorgeous, shiny German BMWs, Mercedes Benzes, and Porsches zipping around everywhere. We shopped for clothes in a vast second-hand store and visited a wholesale store that offered wild game for sale: fully intact wild boar and stags were on view in huge freezers, reminding me of the marvelous dioramas of New York's Museum of Natural History. We could sense the pride of the local Bavarians for their mountains, prettily painted chalets, beer, lederhosen, and traditional hats; our own Latvian pride had been nearly stamped into the ground by Russian tanks and decades of overwhelming, greedy Russian masses. Beautiful Bavaria was such a painfully sharp contrast to our reality back home. Clean, efficient, beautiful, orderly West Germany: its stores were glutted with high quality goods; its people with their self-assured manners, healthy complexions, and bicycle culture made us envious. The contrasts between our respective lifestyles were jarring.

It was time to hit the road. The Opel was ready. Our minds had processed delightful scenes; our bodies had enjoyed many wonderful meals and lots of fruit. Already Krišjānis appeared to look healthier; he'd lost that pasty Soviet complexion. It was hard to leave West Germany, the Free World, democracy, and "civilization" behind and head back to the backwards, corrupt, scary Soviet Union. We were nervous recalling our disastrous outcome from the year before. We drove into East Germany full of apprehension. Freedom, western values, modernity, colors, lights, and smiles receded, as the old Opel hurtled east through the lands stuck behind barbed wire with their mean, distrustful customs officers, guns, and zombie propaganda. Deeper and deeper we drove into Eastern Europe's shadowy territories ("Woman in Chains" [Tears for Fears]), which continued to exist under the Soviet sphere of influence.

A friend in Münster, Jānis Liepiņš, had provided us with a pile of music tapes that helped us pass the time: Kate Bush; Tears for Fears ("I spy tears in their eyes / They look to the skies for some kind of divine intervention"); Sting; Sinead O'Connor; Peter Gabriel... Any of the tracks from those recordings now floods me with memories of Poland in particular and its endless fields of yellow rapeseed ("fields of gold")—a sense of endlessness. Poland really did seem like forever to us, tired, fearful Latvian travelers. We were like abused dogs approaching their master's house, anticipating his hard fist and stinging whip. As the sun followed its arc in the sky, shifting shadows until they raced ahead of us, dusk fell over Polish fields and meadows and small patches of woods, villages with huge Catholic churches, and the Poles themselves who had seen hell in the war, like the Balts. The distance between West Germany's border and our car kept growing and now felt like the expanse of the universe itself. I prayed that the Opel, which had seen better days, wouldn't break down.

We were in Warsaw by nightfall, passing shabby houses, block buildings, dreary looking bars, the thought of "let's keep moving" hammering at our brains. Krišjānis was up, then asleep, and then up again, pressing his little nose against the glass. Because I didn't have a driver's license at the time, the pressure of driving was on my husband alone. I struggled to stay awake for his sake, humming, chewing gum, chatting. Our steady, relentless march across Poland, a country that was part of World War II's "Bloodlands," was taking us in a northeasterly direction past towns with names with soft Slavic sounds—zh, sh... The Opel chugged on, eating up the road to Lazdynai and the Lithuanian frontier, the "almost home."

We arrived at the border in the morning. But much to our horror, we were turned away. At "fault" was my American passport. Americans were not allowed to enter the Soviet Union at Lazdynai. I remember standing at one end of the road looking towards Lithuania and struggling to contain my rage, humiliation, and disappointment. *So close and yet so far*. There was *Baltija* (the Baltics) and home, clearly visible. We could see the border posts and the Lithuanian checkpoint. But we were locked out. It was a terrible moment after the long drive: we hadn't slept the previous night, intent on covering as much ground as possible. It was late morning, and some not unkind border guard advised us to head south to the Brest, Belarus border crossing. Not that place again! The drive south felt like a very long time, maybe five hours, through what seemed like the middle of nowhere. Our nerves were throbbing. We were at the threshold of the Evil Empire; we could feel its icy presence.

Finally, the sign to Brest and the border crossing appeared. Welcome to the netherworld. Cold, rude, unhelpful border guards and customs officers with piggy eyes: why did the Soviet Union treat its citizens like scum? My husband and our son were Soviet citizens. As we slowly proceeded forward through the bureaucratic tunnel and its booby traps, we discovered there was no place to pee or defecate. The public restrooms were the epitome of filth. Shit and piss everywhere, turds and smeared newspapers on the floor, clogged toilets, no privacy, a horrible stench. Yet we had managed to come out on the other side and were told to wait...

Years later I would read about a similar experience in Omsk, Russia as described by Ian Frazier in his epic *Travels in Siberia* (2010): "The men's room at the Omsk airport was unbelievably disgusting. (...) No surface inside the men's room, including the ceiling was clean. There were troughs and stools, but no partitions, stalls, or doors. (...) The floor was strewn with filth of a wide and eye-catching variety." Okay, that was Omsk, deep in the heartland of Russia in Siberia. Nor was Brest in Russia. It was the western person's first glimpse of the mighty, invincible Soviet Union. Footprints on the rim of the toilet?! If it's one thing I remember from the Soviet era with a shudder, it's the shit-smear handwipe: the three-digit foul, brown smears on the restroom walls. We were forced to tread carefully in the neaby woods to relieve ourselves; everywhere you looked, other humans had left their mark. What I saw at the Brest customs point literally took my breath away.

I struggled to contain a sense of impending doom, perhaps induced by the sight of human waste and the fact that it didn't seem to bother any of the people who worked there. Perhaps we would be murdered in the woods beyond the border control, if we ever made it past these shitheads? By 1989 Latvians were making trips to Poland and West Germany, bringing back goods, hard currency, and used cars. There were stories of wayside attacks, even brutal murders. Our West German kitchen knife—a potential weapon of self-defense—was confiscated along with our bananas and oranges by a smug female customs officer. Again the customs officials were trying to extort money from us. If I remember correctly, we had to get in touch with Rīga to have my father-in-law wire the money. However, this time the amount was less than a year ago. To be honest, I don't fully recall how we spent those 36 hours on the Belarusian border. Andris' patience was stretched to the limit, and there was nothing I could do to help. It was a living nightmare.

When the green light to proceed was eventually given to the pale, traumatized family of Baltic fascists, including an American imperialist, the angry driver Comrade Andris Jurisovich Krieviņš could barely keep his foot from slamming down on the gas pedal. When we were safely out of range, he increased the Opel's speed on the highway, shifted into fourth gear, and floored it. As we hurtled through the Belarusian woods, we kept looking around and back to see if anyone was following us. Nobody. No Belarusian highwaymen, criminals, thugs, the mafia, the *militsiya*, the KGB, the army. I murmured my prayers to God and tried to wipe my mind clean of all thoughts other than our final destination, Latvia.

God, how happy we were to cross into Lithuania! It felt like home! The rest of the trip was one of steady, deep breaths, counting our blessings, caressing the Baltic landscape with our eyes, laughing, and pushing away our fatigue. "I never made promises lightly / And there have been some that I've broken / But I swear in the days still left / We'll walk in fields of gold." (Sting, "Fields of Gold")

We were so happy and relieved to be back on terra cognita. Zemgale, my grandmother Līvija's origins! Never had I loved Latvia so much as at that moment, when the tires of our car touched its surface. My memory of that long, unpleasant trip blacked out for decades to come. From Zugspitze's gold-tanned, relaxed German ski bums to Brest's incomprehensible filth, the contrast between the Free World and the Soviet Union was staggering. But Latvia looked beautiful to us.

"Sex scandal"

Although Latvia was not yet officially out of the Soviet Union in 1989, the Latvian flag and other symbols of Latvian independence had entered mainstream media. Left, illustrator Māris Putniņš's cover for the "scandalous" reproductive health issue of *Zīlīte*, the popular children's magazine.

In March of '89 Latvia was rocked by a "sex scandal" in the form of a children's magazine, *Zīlīte* ("Chickadee"), which had put out a special issue about "the birds and the bees." Charmingly illustrated by Māris Putniņš, the special issue was designed as a comic strip that explained sex and reproductive health to young children (and anyone else, for that matter). Personal hygiene, sex, and childbirth: all of these seemed to be taboo subjects in communist Latvia. My overall impression was that young people knew very little about the science of human reproduction, and sadly, abortions were the norm, when it came to birth control in the USSR.

When the magazine hit the newsstands and subscribers' mailboxes, the editors began receiving letters and phone calls expressing outrage and condemnation. "How dare you corrupt minors? ... This is appalling! ... We are canceling our subscription!" Shocked parents—mostly mothers—viewed the whimsical illustrations as pornographic, which was absurd and sad, of course, as they were meant to enlighten young people in a gentle way about their bodies' potential. I realized then that a majority of Latvian society was conservative to the point of being backward, especially in the countryside, where young people knew little about health or the consequences of their actions. Latvia's already fragile demographic situation in regard to ethnic Latvians suffered from too many unwanted pregnancies and too many abortions.

Latvians really were a conservative bunch. When I showed up for a confirmation party in New Jersey in 1978 or 1979 with my long hair let down, wearing a pretty floor-length dress made in India, one of my old Latvian school teachers verbally attacked me for my appearance, especially my long hair, calling it messy. There were some subjects one simply did not write about or mention in Latvian American society, like crime or failure. Sex was a seldom explored subject in Latvian literature, which is why *Sex Songs of the Ancient Letts* perked my interest, when I first read it in my early teens in the US. Published in 1969, it was a glamorous book with a sleek black cover, the title emblazoned in gold letters. Nobody knew who Bud Berzing was, but the book was a big hit in our family and amongst friends.

Berzing had put together a collection of naughty (erotic) Latvian *dainas* describing fornication and human reproductive organs in mostly hilarious ways. These *dainas* gave me the sense that my ancestors had viewed sex in a healthy, natural way, as a wonderful gift from Nature to be celebrated and engaged in, be it outside in the meadow, in the forest, or even *sūdu vešanas talkā* ("during transportation of manure from the barn to the fields"), according to famous Latvian painter Kārlis Miesnieks. Those who read Latvian poetry called my mother "the erotic poetess" on account of some of her sensual poems. Rumors circulated in the mostly conservative Latvian exile community that she danced the can can in black stockings on a piano.

X-Rated

Although I no longer have *Sex Songs of the Ancient Letts* in my possession, I do own a copy of *Latviešu nerātnās tautas dziesmas, mīklas, sakāmvārdi un parunas* ("Latvian Naughty Folk Songs, Riddles, Proverbs, and Sayings," published by Imanta in Copenhagen, MCMLVII). I have translated some of these dirty ditties to provide you with a sampling of my Latvian ancestors' down-to-earth take on sex:

> *Ai āzīti murmulīti, / Nepis kazu vakarā, / Pis rīta saulītē, / Tad būs balti kazlēniņi!* ("Hey, billy-goat, silly billy, / Don't fuck the goat at night, / Screw her in the morning, / Then you'll have white kids!")
>
> *Vai vai Brencīti, / Tavu asu (lielu) rīku! / No zirga lēkdams, / Nodūra sivēnu.* "Holy, moly, Brencītis, / You've got one big dick! / Jumping off your horse / You impaled a little pig.)
>
> *Ai Dieviņ, ai Dieviņ, / Nekaunīga vedekliņa: / No ratiem izkāpdama, / Mīza, kāju pacēlusi, / Par slieksnīti pārkāpdama, / Laida garu bezdieniņu, / Dūmi vien nokūpēja / Skursteniša galiņā.* ("Oh my goodness, oh my Lord, / My daughter-in-law's a tramp: / Getting out of the cart, / She took a piss, lifting her leg; / Stepping over the threshold, / She let out a long fart; / The smoke rose through the chimney.")
>
> *Ai, manu Pēcīti, / Kā tu mani mīlēji! / Kur es tevi glabāšu / Mīlēdama? / Kad liku plauktā, / Tad grauza žurkas, / Kad aizkrāsnē, / Tad circenīši. / Tīruma vidū / Akmeņu starpā, // Tur mīžu virsū, / Ganīdama.* ("Oh my dear Peter, / How you did love me! / Where shall I keep you / While I love you? / When I put you on the shelf, / The rats gnawed you, / When behind the stove, / The crickets nibbled you. / In the middle of the field, / Between the stones, / That's where I piss on you, / While I herd the cows.")
>
> *Ņemat mani, ciema puiši, / Es bagāta mātes meita: / Man pupiņi sudraboti, / Kūsīts zelta lapiņām.* ("Take me, take me, village lads, / I'm a rich woman's daughter: / My boobs are clad in silver, / My bush with golden leaves.")
>
> *Tu, Jānīti, smuks puisītis / Par visiem puisīšiem: /Tu ik rīta mazgājies / Jaunas meitas mīzelos.* ("Hey, Johnny, you're a handsome lad, / Handsomer than the rest: / Every morning you washed yourself / In a young lass' piss.")
>
> *Aiz upītes kalniņā / Sarkankūša mamzelīte; / Tai vajaga zīda pautu, / Sudrabiņa pipelītes.* ("Beyond the river on the hill /There's a red cunt girl; /She needs silken balls / And silver wankers.")
>
> *Ak tu traka tautu meita, / Iemīzuse pļaviņā; / Man cēlās pipelīte, / Izkaptiņu strīķējot.* ("Oh you crazy girl / Pissing in the field; / My dick did rise, / As I sharpened my scythe.")
>
> *Apdomā, līgaviņa, / Kā mēs mīļi runājām; / Visu cauru garu nakti /Viens uz otru gulējām.* ("Just think, my bride, / How lovingly we talked; / All night long / On top of each other.")

The uproar over the *Zīlīte* issue was both funny and lamentable, considering that there were young girls in Latvia who didn't recognize the basic signs of pregnancy. Had life under the communists, who had tried to stamp out my nation's *joie de vivre*, ruined their libido? Was it really possible to make love the Alex Comfort way (*The Joy of Sex*) with your parents listening? A rhetorical question. By the late 1980s Latvians were extremely concerned about their eroding demographic situation.

A Death in Piebalga

On June 3, 1989, when the Latvian summer was nearing its zenith, Midsummer, Andris showed up at Paulēni with his boss Fēlikss Zvaigznons, editor-in-chief of *Skolotāju Avīze* ("Teachers' Newspaper"), a publication devoted to education. Andris had been hired by the newspaper as a photographer, and I knew that he admired and respected Zvaigznons. I was there to welcome them. They had come to take part in the nearby Kaudzīšu School's 120th anniversary celebration. Shortly after their arrival, as I was busying myself in the kitchen to heat up some water for coffee and prepare some refreshments, I heard a strange thump followed by some commotion. As I opened the kitchen door to look outside, I saw Zvaigznons, whom I had just seen sitting on our stairs and gazing at the lake in the distance, slumped over in Andris' lap. My husband appeared to be struggling to revive his colleague. What had happened?!

With no telephone for kilometers to call an emergency service, there were very few options. Andris dragged Zvaignons' limp body to his father's car, jumped in behind the wheel, and sped off in search of help. People in the Latvian countryside were almost helpless in this sort of situation. Not only were their lives at risk, their homes were too, in the event of a fire. Telephone lines in rural areas were viewed as an unnecessary luxury by the Communist Party, apparently. According to Juris, before the war almost every house in the countryside had a telephone. But this was a different era, when those in charge pumped the Party's money into armaments.

A telephone in the countryside was a real luxury that had ended with Latvia's "liberation" by the Russian communists and the introduction of the Soviet *bardaks*, a Latvian slang word for "a complete mess." Soviet "order" ignored or purposefully destroyed remarkable pre-war achievements in the countryside, such as private water and windmills. When I broke my foot at Paulēni, I had to send my son and my niece to my neighbors down the road for help, because there was no way to call an ambulance. That time our neighbor, a dentist, drove the children and me all the way to Rīga (a two hour drive), as it would have been impossible for me to stay in the countryside with a broken foot.

On that fateful day, Andris set off on a desperate trek, transporting his friend's corpse halfway across Vidzeme. My poor husband drove around for several hours, frantically trying to find help, tossed from one point to the next by medical workers. From Vecpiebalga he traveled to Cēsis and then finally on to Rīga with the body of his colleague. On June 8 Fēlikss Zaigznons was laid to rest in Cēsis.

With Fēlikss Zvaigznons' death Latvia lost yet another of its good sons. Just 39 years old at the time of his death, by the late 1980s Zvaigznons was a rising star in Latvia's drive for independence. (The word "zvaigzne" means "star.") Born in 1950 in Jaunpiebalga, Zvaigznons went to school in Sigulda, studied philology at the University of Latvia, worked in the Soviet Latvian education system and in journalism, and joined the Latvian Communist Party. When he became editor of *Skolotāju Avīze* in September 1987, Zvaigznons was an idealist. Under his leadership the newspaper became an important outlet for Latvians' disenchantment with the Soviet system and a venue for implementing change. According to his then colleague Inta Lehmuse, "(under Zvaigznons) *Skolotāju Avīze* ceased to be a timid, boring leaflet and became a newspaper, helping restore (Latvian) teachers' self-esteem; it was a newspaper that not only teachers but everyone wanted to read." Zvaigznons' death left a void. We assumed that an autopsy was conducted, yet to this day I do not know why he died suddenly at the age of 39. (1)

Another very famous and important figure of the Latvian Awakening, Mavriks Vulfsons (1918–2004), penned a tribute to Zvaigznons in a 1991 issue of *Izglītība*, the successor to *Skolotāju Avīze*. One of the highlights of the Latvian Awakening was the illumination of the Molotov-Ribbentrop Pact's secret protocols. Vulfsons' speech at the historic plenary meeting of Latvia's so-called creative unions, in which he mentioned the notorious protocols, which divided Poland, Romania, the Baltic States, and Finland into Nazi and Soviet "spheres of influence," spooked the Soviets.

Vulfsons: "After my June 2, 1988 speech (at the plenary meeting) it became clear that a war would be launched against those protocols. A few days later I came under pressure on account of my speech. In those difficult days I received a phone call from Fēlikss Zvaigznons. He said to me, 'Comrade Vulfsons, here at *Skolotāju Avīze* we plan on printing your speech. Please come to our office to read the transcription.' Fēlikss was calm and smiling, when I met him and his devoted staff. From what I've heard, the (Soviet) censors and the (Latvian SSR) Ministry of Education tried to pressure Zvaigznons into withdrawing my speech, but he didn't back down. 'We're printing it,' he said. And the next day the speech was right there in *Skolotāju Avīze*. In my opinion, this was a truly heroic move for those times. A bit later I penned an article for the newspaper, in which I supported my views about the Molotov-Ribbentrop Pact. And again Zvaigznons signed off on the paper. (...) He was brave both in words and deeds." (2)

In March 1989, just a few months before his untimely death, Zvaigznons gave an eloquent speech at a meeting of Latvia's creative unions. He demanded freedom for Latvia's education system. "We need the freedom to create our own national school. We need to align the principles, levels, and content of our education system with world standards and to ensure a free exchange of pedagogical information (with our counterparts in the world). (...) We need to radically improve our foreign language instruction through such cooperation. We need to promote Latvian education abroad. (...)" (From Zvaigznons' speech published in *Literatūra un Māksla* on April 15, 1989.) Fēlikss Zvaigznons' premature death was a shock to everyone, especially to us: we saw him struck down by our doorstep by some invisible hand. And we were helpless to save him. As a nation of only about 2.5 million people, we felt this loss deeply. (3)

Chapter sources:

(1) "Felikss Zvaigznons." Latvijaslaudis. November 2009; May 14, 2013. http://latvijaslaudis.lv/users/zvaigznons_felikss
(2) Ibid 1
(3) Ibid 1

1989: The Human Chain

"Brīvību Baltijai!" ("Freedom for the Baltics!"): *Baltijas ceļš* ("The Baltic Way") in Latvia on August 23, 1989. Photograph: Juris Krieviņš.

Summer began to simmer, and we stewed, too, in a state of nervous anticipation. The Latvian Popular Front was openly discussing Latvia's full independence from the Soviet Union. On August 23 at least two million Latvians, Lithuanians, and Estonians joined hands in a human chain that stretched for more than 600 kilometers across the three Baltic States. "The Baltic Way" (*Balti kett* in Estonian, *Baltijas ceļš* in Latvian, *Baltijos kelias* in Lithuanian) was a remarkable, peaceful demonstration of solidarity to protest the 1939 Molotov-Ribbentrop Pact, which had fated these three countries to years of brutal oppression and tragedy. I watched it on TV from Piebalga, where I was helping Biruta and minding the children, Elīna, Krišjānis, and Alise.

The Baltic Way became "a historical symbol, which proved that three small countries can create a spiritual unity, destroying a totalitarian regime without resorting to violence, and overcoming the consequences of World War II." (UNESCO) In 2009 "the Baltic Way" was added to UNESCO's "Memory of the World" register as an event of "world significance and outstanding universal value." The event attracted international attention, much to the dismay of the Soviet Politburo in Moscow, which was not ready to give up an inch of annexed soil.

The "living chain" proved that under extreme duress we Balts were capable of joining hands in solidarity across our friendly borders. Photographs from the historic and unforgettable event epitomize the peaceful, non-violent resistance and restraint that the Balts displayed as they pursued their ultimate aim—freedom. They faced great danger yet stood strong.

Too Good to Be True?

A labor of love: autumn 1989 at Vecpaulēni. hawse have invited some friends over to help clear space for a pond. Pictured from the left: Vecpiebalga neighbor Pēteris Cimdiņš, Renāte Krūmale of Smiltene, and I. Photograph: Andris Krieviņš.

In late summer or early autumn of 1989 our neighbor in Vecpiebalga offered to sell us his house. A famous composer, he was a recluse, and we barely saw him, although his property was a stone's throw away on the other side of our beautiful pond. The composer lived in Rīga and came out to Piebalga to rest and relax. The offer took us by a big surprise; in fact, it blew both of us away.

I knew little about the composer other than his popular music and the fact that he had had several wives and had sired a bunch of kids. We mostly saw his son and his stepkids running around. I often cut through his property on my way across the hill to fetch a can of milk from our neighbor Māra. I had chatted with the composer's mother, an old woman with remarkable Finno-Ugric features who hobbled around with a cane.

When Andris broke the good news to me, it was like lightning out of a blue sky. I was dumfounded and overjoyed, even ecstatic. After all of our unsuccessful searches, I had given up hope that we would ever find ourselves a house in the countryside. This surprise announcement filled me with a tremendous rush of energy and joy. It was just fantastic! We would be next to Juris and Biruta, yet in our own little world! And it was a beautiful one at the top of the hill with some splendid views.

We paid up, and the composer handed us the house keys, assuring us that as soon as he had a free moment, we would meet to sign the final paperwork. He and his brood retreated, and we moved in, breathlessly excited to start major clean-up work right away. The house was old and in pretty bad shape. I had heard that it was infested by rats, but I never saw any signs of rodents. It was strange: the composer had left a lot of his furniture there, so we ended up sleeping in his beds. The kitchen was small, dark, and primitive, but who cared? We would fix it up. It was ours... Or was it? I was uneasy, as I swept, scrubbed, washed, and organized. I fried pancakes, potatoes, and bacon on the old stove, envisioning new windows to let in sunshine. Geraniums on the sills...

We decided to start with landscaping and dig a pond. We invited friends over to help clean out the brush. Laboring in the cool fall air invigorated me; I felt I could move mountains. I was overjoyed to be the proprietress of such a beautiful piece of Latvia! It was wonderful to be so close to my parents-in-law and yet apart from them. They were helpful and lent good, practical advice.

The property came with an old barn and a small tool shed. Everything was run-down and in need of repair. But there were berry bushes and lots of sunny corners for vegetables and flowers. The place was loaded with potential. Our brains buzzed with ideas. Most of all there was the splendid view of the beautiful Piebalga landscape. Tiny, delicate roots were unfurling from the palms of my hands, grasping at the soil of the land that I loved.

We celebrated the arrival of the New Year in our new home, surrounded by deep, white snow. The year 1990 descended on us in the shape of Bohemian Waxwings (*Bombycilla garrulous*), beautiful birds with crested heads. They were perched in the old cherry trees like Christmas ornaments, and we gazed at them in wonder through the window. The fatherland was a winter wonderland. Firewood crackled in the old stove; the house was warm and cosy. Who had lived here before the war? What happened to the owners? How big had their property been? I would never find out the answers to these questions, because I never had the chance to.

By the time spring and planting season rolled around, it became painfully clear that the "sale" was off, and that the composer had simply used us, taking our money to buy a car in West Germany. We felt humiliated and embarrassed to be taken in like that. Back at my in-laws' cottage, I felt angry whenever I saw the composer drive by in his new car. We got our money back a year later along with an awkward apology. *Vīrs un vārds* ("A man of his word"): was this a dying breed in Latvia?

The Fall of the Berlin Wall

"Lai dzīvo Latvija!" "Long live Latvia!" Latvian Americans at the Berlin Wall in 1986. From the left: Andris Levenšteins; Gints Grīnbergs; my younger brother Artis Rumpēters; and Nils Melngailis.

(Spokesman for the East German Communist Party Politburo) Günter Schabowski's press conference on November 9, 1989 was a fairly dull affair for most of its duration, according to those present. But a question by an Italian journalist right at the end turned it into one of European history's most memorable events.

Schabowski was asked just before 7 pm about when a new law permitting GDR citizens more freedom of travel would go into effect. Schabowski famously told the journalist: "As far as I know, that goes into effect now, immediately."

Since television viewers in both East and West Germany were following the live press conference, his comments electrified East Germans and eventually led to a redrawing of the European map.

Immediately following the remark, GDR citizens rushed to the border separating East and West Berlin, wanting to visit the western part of the city. The GDR border guards were unaware of the press conference, and, taken aback by the crowds gathering in front of them, made repeated calls to their superiors asking for guidance. They successfully prevented citizens from crossing the border for three hours. But later in the evening, the guards relented and opened the borders. People were able to cross freely from East to West for the first time since the wall was erected on August 21, 1961. (1)

The Iron Curtain appeared to be fraying. As East Germans scrambled over "the Wall of Shame," embracing their western compatriots in joyful celebration, the world looked on in disbelief. I watched coverage of these events on Latvian television: it was breathtaking, amazing, unbelievable, and infinitely moving! Germany would be reunited a year later on October 3, 1990. Infuriated Germans chipped away at the despised wall, which was eventually bulldozed. A piece of the wall would end up in Rīga.

"Death to tyrants!" My brother (right) and his friend Gints at the despised Berlin Wall.

Just recently we had seen the wall with our own eyes during our travels and understood its grim symbolism. The Berlin Wall and the Iron Curtain had divided and alienated countries and peoples. Constructed by communist East Germany in the 1960s, my childhood, the *Antifaschistischer*

Schutzwall ("Anti-Fascist Protection Rampart") divided Berlin and its population, turned West Berlin into an enclave surrounded by a hostile East Germany, and became a deadly trap for East Germans attempting to escape to West Berlin and the Free World. On the West German side the wall was covered in graffiti, including art and slogans calling for freedom and democracy in the communist lands on the other side.

Nothing evokes the excitement of that time and the dramatic, joyful end of the Berlin Wall more than the Scorpions' song "Wind of Change." Inspired by a trip to Moscow, the band's frontman Klaus Meine wrote the words that still resonate with me today.

The song remains a hymn to the collapse of communism in Eastern Europe. For Latvians, Lithuanians, and Estonians, the fall of the Berlin Wall was like an enormous push toward freedom and reunification with Europe, out of Mother Russia's suffocating embrace.

Chapter sources:

(1)   Von Hellfeld, Matthias. Editor Kyle James. "November 9, 1989—The day that changed European history." Deutsche Welle. August 11, 2009; May 15, 2014. <http://www.dw.de/november-9-1989-the-day-that-changed-european-history/a-4867139>

1990: A New Beginning

Pedraudzes in 1990.
Photo by Andris Krieviņš.

A decade had gone by since I had first set foot on Latvian soil in 1980, stepping off of the Tallinn train bearing a heavy backpack full of love, hope, expectations, and questions on my young shoulders. In 1980 I could not imagine that I would eventually end up living in Latvia for almost two decades, witnessing enormous historical changes in my fatherland. I had been raised with the idealistic promise of a free and independent Latvia, and now, almost unbelievably, it looked like that promise just might come true. What would *this* new decade—the 1990s—bring?

According to *Barikadopēdija*, a website devoted to Latvia's "Third Awakening," the first official currency exchange store in the entire Soviet Union opened at Rīga's Central Railway Station on January 30, 1990. It would quickly grow into a powerful bank called Parex. Such exchange points would appear all over Rīga, sprouting like slimy mushrooms in dingy basements and at the end of poorly lit hallways. There was a sordid quality to all of them: money changed hands in dim light; the faces of the people handling and doling out the money were obscured. Mostly these shadowy figures spoke Russian. The new decade would bring new questions and problems, typical for dramatic periods of change. (1)

In January 1990 the Latvian Supreme Soviet adopted amendments to the LSSR Constitution, permitting citizens to form political parties and social organizations. These amendments considerably diminished the status and clout of the Latvian Communist Party. Its days of glory and omnipotence were effectively coming to an end. Nobody except for the Interfront and the ignorant believed in the party anymore. Latvia's progressive people had had enough of the Party's heavy-handed bullying and ideological absurdities. On January 13 the Green Party was officially founded on the basis of Latvia's Environmental Protection Club (*Vides aizsardzības klubs* or VAK), an NGO that had drawn attention to serious environmental concerns. Pollution of Latvia's soil and waters had continued unabated for decades in a state obsessed with military prowess. (2)

VAK was founded on February 22, 1987 and was affiliated with the *Tramvaju un trolejbusu pārvalde* (Tram and Trolleybus Administration), which oversaw Rīga's public transportation sector. VAK was a political organization disguised as a club. Under Gorbachev's almost revolutionary policies, which permitted increasingly democratic thought and speech, VAK was able to take advantage of the situation to push its agenda. VAK grew out of a semi-official group of enthusiasts who called themselves the *Pieminekļu aizsardzības centrs* ("Monument Protection Center," est. 1984), which devoted itself to the restoration of Latvia's rundown churches. (3)

VAK's first public protest over clean air took place at the so-called VEF Culture Palace on Ļeņina iela in 1987. The protesters were quickly dispersed by the *militsiya*; Alfrēds Rubiks, the "mayor" of Rīga at the time, was a Communist Party hardliner who did not tolerate deviation from Soviet norms. On April 27, 1988 VAK drew an enormous crowd of 30,000 people to Arkādijas Park to protest plans for building a subway system in Rīga. That same year they organized a demonstration called "Prayer by the Sea" to draw attention to water pollution; a line of about 300,000 people extended along the Baltic Sea coast. VAK also organized a protest against the public transportation hub near the Freedom Monument. (4)

The Environmental Protection Club began in 1986, when a bunch of people concerned about Latvia's deteriorating environment and cultural and historical legacy were cleaning up the 16th century Zemīte Lutheran church in Kandava. Arveds Ulme, one of the club's founders, remembered: "I was sorting some boards from a collapsed shed near the church. I sat down to rest and looked out at the enormous field of dandelions, but I couldn't see any bees. And then I spoke to a local tractor driver who said he hadn't seen bees there for several years; apparently they had all been poisoned. And then I thought to myself: we're trying to save bits and pieces here, but the Earth is dying!" (5)

By the late 1980s VAK's members numbered in the tens of thousands. It was a solid organization with numerous branches. The mass demonstrations organized by VAK, Helsinki-86, and the Latvian National Independence Movement were aimed at renewing independence: this was their ultimate political goal, coupled with a focus on environmental and even existential issues. VAK's organized protest against the construction of a subway system in Rīga that would have flooded thousands of Russian-speaking laborers into Latvia helped put an end to the plan. (6)

Visual: Video footage of the 1988 VAK anti-metro (subway) demonstration and other public protests: <https://www.youtube.com/watch?v=rllTZJCeFZk>

Jānis Rukšāns, a world famous crocus specialist, and Haralds Sīmanis, an expert roofer, organist, and popular musician, whose scratchy, soulful vocals and guitar strumming evoked his Gypsy roots, were involved in the Environmental Protection Club; Sīmanis was its "bard."

Visual: Haralds Sīmanis singing a song called "Ezers" ("Lake"): <https://www.youtube.com/watch?v=snSVQxmR3uo>

On February 15 the Latvian Supreme Soviet adopted a declaration regarding Latvia's independence, which deemed the Latvian Saeima's (Parliament's) June 21, 1940 declaration on joining the USSR illegitimate from the moment of its adoption. Based on the declaration on Latvia's sovereignty of July 28, 1989, the Latvian Supreme Soviet declared that henceforth all its work would be devoted to reshaping the Latvian Soviet Socialist Republic into a free and independent country in a union of countries that would follow a humane and democratic path of socialism and establish its relationships with other countries on the basis of treaties. The Supreme Soviet also adopted amendments to the Latvian SSR Constitution, which reinstated Latvia's national flag, coat of arms, and the anthem "Dievs, svētī Latviju!" ("God, Bless Latvia!"). On February 27, 1990 the Latvian national flag was raised at the Supreme Soviet and other important government buildings. The righting of wrongs, new possibilities, Baltic camaraderie and solidarity, a better future, truth and justice: 1990 would be a year of "new beginnings." I had just turned 30 years old and was infinitely grateful to be in the fatherland at such a fantastic time. (7)

My grandfather Senator Augusts Rumpēters must have been smiling down from heaven. The grievances of the tractate he had penned in exile, *Soviet Aggression against the Baltic States*, were resurfacing at this time. Latvia was standing up to the Russian bear!

On March 2 the Supreme Soviet recognized the need to establish a central bank in Latvia, Latvijas Banka. Each and every one of the Supreme Soviet's actions essentially snipped yet another string tying Rīga to Moscow. The March 18 Supreme Soviet elections handed the Latvian Popular Front a solid majority. The stately building in Old Rīga, originally built for the German Livonian Noble Corporation, had been transformed into a beehive buzzing with excitement; you could no longer hear the Russian language in its vicinity. Latvian had made a comeback. Gone were the robotic communist bureaucrats who raised their hands and chimed "da" in chorus with Moscow. Our elected representatives convened to work on a new declaration of independence to be based on Latvia's historic declaration of independence from November 18, 1918. (8)

In March Supreme Soviet Chairman Anatolijs Gorbunovs, the handsome, perfectly coiffed and groomed communist-turned-independence-advocate traveled with a group of delegates to Moscow to meet with Mr. Gorbachev and other high-ranking Soviet Russian officials to discuss Latvia's economic and political independence. Gorbunovs' popularity with Latvians was spiking; he was respected for his calm demeanor and new stance in regard to Latvia's drive towards independence. I can still hear Gorbunovs' soft and steady voice moderating the lively debates at the Supreme Soviet. He was especially popular with older women. He gave the impression of being the perfect public servant. (9)

As the feisty Balts—Latvians, Lithuanians, and Estonians—were making it increasingly obvious that they would settle for nothing less than full independence, Mr. Gorbachev and his conservative colleagues, including Latvian hardliner Boris Pugo, who by now was in Moscow, were struggling to plot their next move. I don't believe that Mr. Gorbachev ever fully understood the Baltic peoples, nor was he ever interested in historical truth and justice.

In early spring Andris and his friend Artūrs planned to go to the Warsaw market to make a few "bucks." They had heard stories of Latvians selling all sorts of stuff from Latvia and the Soviet Union in the Polish capital and coming back with lots of *valūta* (hard currency). A very nice Oriental-looking rug wrapped in plastic, which I had just hauled home on our son's old stroller from the Central Market, was never even unpacked; it was set aside as an item for sale. It would have looked so nice in our new apartment! Who knows what else these two intrepid Latvians had packed up for sale? I was never informed. Off they went, while Krišjānis and I stayed home to await their return, entertaining stories (my husband was a very good storyteller), and riches.

They were back in two days, exhausted and elated. As I eagerly awaited stories of Warsaw's conquest, my husband drew several 50 dollar bills from his wallet and proudly handed them to me. As I glanced at them, I cringed. Born and raised in the USA, I could smell a real dollar bill, and I knew right away that my poor husband and his friend had been swindled. My carpet! Their efforts! The time! Lousy Polacks! My husband was completely "deflated." His anger and shame gave way to sheepish snickering. It was too funny, really. How many more stupid, greedy Soviet people had been cheated this way?

Some of the unconfirmed stories we had heard about this new form of "international" commerce weren't that funny: Latvians traveling to Poland with "get rich" schemes getting waylaid on lonely Polish roads... Sinister stories were countered with humor. I recall a story in some popular magazine, possibly *Liesma*, about a freezer truck full of bulls' testicles and penises, which either crashed or was flagged down by the police somewhere in Lithuania: apparently the entrepreneurs thought there was good market for their exotic delicacies on the other side of the Soviet border. I cannot date or verify the story, but I remember it along with a black and white photograph of the strange cargo. The Baltic fringe Homo Sovieticus was desperate to cross borders and get his hands on some hard currency. One can only imagine the shenanigans and murky wheelings and dealings that went on in both directions on both sides of the border, as the Iron Curtain began crumbling.

Cooperatives, the first step towards private enterprise and a market economy, were flourishing. In 1989 or so I watched a television interview with a man named Tālis Freimanis about establishing a private banking system in Latvia. Until then everyone kept their meager savings in "a sock" or at the state-run Krājbanka ("Savings Bank"). Just a few years later Freimanis and his partner Aleksandrs Lavents would be sitting at the top of Latvia's first and the Baltic States' biggest private bank, Banka Baltija.

In April Andris and I traveled by train to West Germany. By the end of the year West and East Germany would be officially united. Biruta came to Zolitūde to stay with Krišjānis. We were going to a Latvian teachers' conference in Münster and had a travel companion, a gay Latvian film critic who flirted with my husband unabashedly, while I stared out the window at the scenes passing by. I pretended not to notice his awkward advances. It was hard and even illegal to be gay in the Soviet Union.

While Andris ignored the conference for the most part, thoroughly engaged in the search for a new used car, I suddenly realized that I was pregnant, as I struggled with morning sickness and nausea. The smell of German *Würstchen* (sausages), cigarettes, and other odors and aromas floating around made me gag. Despite my queasy feeling and fatigue, I was overjoyed. A sibling for Krišjānis! Another Latvian for a nation that was sadly depleted: yes, my pregnancy was patriotic.

In a letter sent to my parents from Münster, Germany in April 1990: *Hi, Mamma! It's morning, around 10:30 am. I'm sitting in our little room here at the dormitory and listening to the music of Mikis Theodorakis, which reminds me of my childhood! I'm waiting for the laundry to be done washing and drying. (...) We really want to go home. We talked to Andris' parents yesterday on the phone. Apparently today the Interfront is organizing a large demonstration; the atmosphere in Rīga is tense. Our car, a small used BMW, is almost good to go. We just need to insure it and change the tires. Thanks for all your help! We're down to our last kapeikas ("kopeks"). We hope that we can leave soon. (...) Will God be merciful? Latvia would not survive another purge, another bloodbath. I'm both concerned and hopeful.*

In April the Bureau of the Communist Party Committee of the City of Rīga halted the publication of the evening newspaper *Rīgas Balss* ("Voice of Rīga"), because "it openly confronted the ideological and political stance of the USSR." On April 7 communist hardliner Alfrēds Rubiks replaced Jānis Vagris as First Secretary of the Communist Party of Latvia. Despite all the recent uplifting events, we realized that the Latvian Communist Party was still largely in control and backed up by the predominantly Russian-speaking militsiya, the KGB, and the Soviet Army with its troops, guns, and tanks. While trouble appeared to be brewing, wonderful things continued to happen. The Russian Orthodox Cathedral got its crosses back, donated by Voldemārs and Mirdza Feldmanis of West Germany. Religion was no longer banned. (11)

On May 4, 1990 the Supreme Soviet, henceforth called the Supreme *Council* of the Latvian SSR, adopted the "Declaration on the Renewal of the Republic of Latvia." We believed this was the beginning of the end of the Soviet occupation. We seemed to be moving closer and closer to the brink of something, an open door or a precipice...

We took the train back to Rīga. Our pistachio-green BMW would be rolling to Latvia in the near future. As my pregnancy symptoms subsided, my life went back to its usual rhythm. I worked on illustrations for a book about the Latvian ABCs. Hunched over my desk in our sunny living room, my art work helped me while away my boredom. Stay-at-home mothers lead a rather isolated life; my choice to live at home to care for my child was based on my mother's experience, my ability to find freelance work, and my possibly unfair perception of Latvia's day-care centers. I found it hard to let go of Krišjānis, although a daycare setting might have been a good fit for our energetic, inquisitive son. Because most women worked, daycare facilities were full, and it was hard to get in.

With a ravenous appetite, I followed the daily news on radio and television; I couldn't get enough of it! It was so interesting to be in Latvia at this time! Economically not much had changed; we were still short of just about everything. In fact, that year ordinary products like flour, pasta, and grain products could only be purchased with special state-issued *taloni* (coupons). That's how bad the Soviet economic situation was. I gave my coupons to my practical mother-in-law; I had no intention of hoarding products. (10)

Now with a second child on the way, I was just happy to be at home as a nurturer. I began experimenting with our new stove, cooking and baking, took long walks, and let Krišjānis run around the "canyons" of Zolitūde with his new friend Dāvis, who lived with his parents and his twin sisters just across the street. The two boys had their share of adventures, including peeing on the radiator in our building while singing "Strauja, strauja upe tecēj'" ("Swiftly, swiftly the river did run"). They were both caught by a Russian neighbor and paraded to our door in a walk of shame. Zolitūde seemed like a relatively safe neighborhood for the youngsters. I wanted Krišjānis to play outside, the way I had in the New Jersey suburbs. Andris was away much of the time on various work assignments.

On May 12 leaders from the three Baltic States, Anatolijs Gorbunovs, Vytautas Landsbergis (Lithuania), and Arnold Ruutel (Estonia) met in Tallinn to sign a declaration of cooperation and to announce their countries' intent to join the OSCE (Organization for Security and Cooperation in Europe). In their efforts to shake off the Soviet yoke, the three Baltic States were united as one. I always felt that the hopes and aspirations of Latvia's first Foreign Minister Zigfrīds Anna

Meierovics to achieve long-lasting cooperation between the Baltic States never went far enough. It gave me great strength and hope at that time to know that Estonians, Lithuanians, and Latvians had formed a united front against Soviet Russia. (12)

Latvia was crawling with hostile forces too numerous to count. In fact, a peaceful insurgency would not stand a chance, if the Soviet Army was ordered to quash resistance. RLOn May 15 thousands of Interfront activists tried to attack the Supreme Council building. They were repelled by OMON (*Otryad Mobilniy Osobogo Naznacheniya*—Special Purpose Mobile Unit or Soviet Special Forces), also known as the "Black Berets" (for their signature hats). A serious clash between the old and new order seemed inevitable.

At the end of May, the Central Committee of the Latvian Communist Party shut down its newspaper *Cīņa*, because the editorial staff refused to follow party guidelines. Instead, the Communist Party aligned itself with the Russian language *Sovetskaya Latvija*, translating the newspaper into Latvian. The fired *Cīņa* employees founded their own paper, *Neatkarīgā cīņa* ("Independent Battle"). On May 30 Latvia's Supreme Council decided that subjecting Latvia's newspapers and magazines to Latvian Communist Party control was illegal. Latvia's recently established Council of Ministers took over management of the Press Building, a strategic hub for journalistic activity and the exchange of information. (13)

In June the Supreme Council confirmed Aloizs Vaznis (b. 1934) as the country's new Interior Minister. Vaznis had studied law at the University of Latvia and had 35 years of experience in Soviet law enforcement, specializing in criminal investigation. He was a decorated veteran policeman; however, neither the Soviet Union's last KGB boss Vadim Bakatin, nor high-ranking Latvian chekist Bruno Šteinbriks (who preceded Vaznis), supported his appointment. (Šteinbriks had lectured me in 1981 following my synthesizer debacle at Moscow's Sheremetyevo Airport.) Latvia's newly elected Supreme Council was enjoying the support of all of Latvia's law enforcement departments. In Rīga, however, only half of the heavily Russified capital's mostly Russian law enforcement workers supported the legally elected authorities. (14)

In June a new newspaper called *Diena* appeared on the scene. As our view of the western horizon was expanding, dark clouds loomed to the east, across the border in Russia. Young Latvian expatriates, some of whom I knew, were arriving in Rīga at this time, excited by the recent events that seemed to point in one direction: freedom! Idealists like me, they wanted to lend a hand.

Together in Eternity

At my grandmother Omamma's funeral in June 1990, Vidriži. Photograph: Andris Krieviņš.

On June 5, 1990 my paternal grandmother Emma Rumpētere died in her sleep at Vīganti, her husband's family's farm, from which she had watched my father walk away and disappear in 1944. She was 94 when she died. Born in Aloja in northern Latvia in 1896, she was laid to rest at the nearby cemetery. An urn containing my grandfather Senator Augusts Rumpēters' ashes was placed on top of her simple casket; after 46 years apart, Omamma and Opaps were reunited. I was so happy that my grandfather's urn was interred in Latvia, the country he had loved and served faithfully all his life, even in exile. I felt at home in the cemetery, surrounded by the dust of those who had lived before my time.

The old graveyard was quiet and peaceful in the warm June sun. Summer flowers swayed near the headstones; colorful blooms filled an assortment of vases. The sun in the brilliant blue sky danced down throught the branches, and the evergreen plantings and tall trees cast a soft green light on this place of eternal rest. Deeper within the cemetery we found very old graves hidden in a tangle of brush and fallen branches. Faded headstones, rusted crosses, and neglected, overgrown plots whispered of faded lineages and Latvia's cruel history. The cemeteries of Latvia were like beautiful parks, where spirits or wood sprites seemed to flicker in the dappled shade. Or was it just a dragonfly's shimmering wings?

An old cross in Vidriži Cemetery that bears my maiden name, Rumpēters. The inscription reads: "For my beloved brothers Jānis and Pēteris Rumpēter(s). 1901." According to my cousin, Jānis and Pēters Rumpēters were my great-grandfather Augusts Rumpēters' cousins. Their brother, Kārlis Augusts Rumpēters, who died in the city of Blagoveschensk, Amur Oblast, Russia in 1912, erected this cross. According to my cousin, Kārlis Rumpēters was a minister in a Lutheran parish in Vladivostok who visited Lutherans, including soldiers, once a year in Amur and other parts of eastern Siberia. (Photo: Guntars Rumpēters)

Omamma's life wasn't easy. She lost her husband and two of her sons to the war and exile and had to raise two sons on her own. These days, when I find myself longing for my older sons in Latvia, I think about what my grandmother went through. The distance is painful; family is also about physical presence, talking, touching, embracing, and shared meals and holidays together, such as Christmas and Easter. She was a strong woman, my Omamma.

After the funeral we drove to a local cafeteria, talked, enjoyed simple but hearty food, drank a bit, and savored one of those scrumptious Latvian *biskvīttortes* made with lots and lots of eggs, butter, and homemade jam. I could feel the presence of Omamma and Opaps. They were sitting together in the corner holding hands ever so quietly. Lovingly. There is a lot to be said for living among your own people, going through life together with them, participating in their *godi* (the most important celebrations in life, baptisms, weddings, and funerals). World War II scattered too many Baltic families, ripping many apart for good. The war and the Soviet and Nazi occupations disrupted traditions and rituals and severed the links that had held old family chains together in one place, in one land, generation after generation.

Together in Song

In July Latvians congealed into one enormous mass for the 1990 Latvian Song and Dance Festival. It felt like all the Latvians in the world had come together in Rīga to rise up against Soviet oppression through song and dance. No wonder our National Awakening (by "our" I mean all three Baltic nations—Latvians, Lithuanians, and Estonians) is still remembered as "the Singing Revolution." Instead of rocks, bats, and Molotov cocktails, we stood up to our oppressors with our songs.

Čikāgas piecīšie ("The Chicago Five"), a popular Latvian American group from the "windy city," was a special guest; its youthful founder, composer, and singer Alberts Legzdiņš cracked jokes about pigs' heads and politics. The huge crowd roared with delight. As twilight bathed us in its gentle hues, the enormous choir stitched lovingly together from Latvians from all over the country sent many deeply cherished old songs washing over us, as the Latvian flag moved in the gentle breeze. Just five years ago the song festival had taken place under the hard Russian Army boot, so to speak; that time the tribute to the Red Army and Soviet might had made a mockery of our festival. What a shocking difference! The festival in 1990 was a celebration of the resilient spirit of the Latvian nation. Begone, you Russian Army boots and alien military culture!

Summer had arrived on the wings of a hundred-year-old song, "Gaismas pils" ("The Castle of Light" [1891–1900]) by composer Jāzeps Vītols (1863–1948) with words by Auseklis (the pen name of Latvian poet Miķelis Krogzemis [1850–1879]). Jāzeps Vītols, *right*, was a conductor at the Latvian National Opera and founder of the Latvian Conservatory of Music. Vītols also left Latvia in 1944, as his country fell to the Soviet Red Army; he died in Lübeck, Germany in 1948. Auseklis' words stirred up images of our country in ancient times, when  lakes could fly, and castles rose up from lakes... The song begins with a murmur and ends with a crescendo, going from slavery's despair to hope and freedom.

Kurzemīte, Dievzemīte, / Brīvas tautas auklētāj'! / Kur palika sirmie dievi, / Brīvas tautas dēliņi, / Jā, tautas dēliņi. / Tie līgoja vecos laikos / Gaismas kalna galotnē. / Visapkārt egļu meži, / Vidū gaiša tautas pils. / Asiņainas dienas ausa / Tēvu zemes ielejā; / Vergu valgā tauta nāca, / Nāvē krita varoņi. / Ātri grima, ātri zuda / Gaismas kalna staltā pils. / Tur guļ mūsu tēvu dievi, / Tautas gara greznumi. / Tas slēpj svētu piles vārdu / Dziļās siržu rētiņās, / Jā, siržu rētiņās. / Ja kas vārdu uzminētu, / Augšām celtos vecā pils, / Tālu laistu tautas slavu, / Gaismas starus margodam'! / Kurga laukā atskanētu / Sirmo garu dainojums. / Tautas dēli uzminēja / Sen aizmirstu svētumu: / Gaismu sauca, Gaisma ausa! / Augšām cēlās Gaismas pils!

Kurzemīte, God's own land, / Cradle of a nation free! / Where did the ancient gods go, / Sons of a nation free, / Yes, her sons. / They sang in the days of old / At the top of the Mountain of Light. / All around them forests of fir, / In the center the nation's Castle of Light. / Bloody days dawned / In the native land's dales; The nation was enslaved, / Its heroes died fighting. / Quickly it sank and vanished, / The castle of the Mountain of Light. / There lie our ancestors' gods, / The riches of our nation's soul. / The mountain hides the sacred castle's name / Within hearts' deep scars, / Yes, within hearts' deep scars. / If someone were to guess its name, / The old castle would rise again, / Spreading far the nation's fame, / With shimmering rays of light. / O'er the fields of Kurgis / The ancient gods' poetry would resound. / The sons of the nation guessed / A long forgotten sanctity: / They called for Light and Light did rise! / The Castle of Light did rise again! (Tr. RL)

The famous Latvian choir song "Gaismas pils" (2008, Conductor Imants Kokars): <http://www.youtube.com/watch?v=v8tJCv8hwb0>

Old faces like worn books, young, optimistic faces, the faces of children, innocent, sweet, tired faces forgetting sadness... Hopeful eyes, bright with joy... Survivors who had been to Siberia and back, fresh babes who'd just arrived in the world, born in the land of their ancestors. And Latvians from abroad, people like me, hoping to find a way home... *Dievs, svētī Latviju!* God, bless Latvia!

Summertime

I packed up our things, and Krišjānis and I went to Piebalga to rest and help Biruta with summer chores. Slowly ripening into a round plum, I perched on the steps of the old Paulēni granary looking at Lake Inesis in the distance and wondering why we couldn't find a house to buy. It was difficult to look at the composer's house on the other side of the pond without feeling bitter...

In July the Latvian Supreme Council set a course for establishing the Bank of Latvia, which would issue a national currency. I remembered how thrilling it was to hold an old silver five lat coin from the pre-war era in my hand: large, heavy, and solid, the coin was embellished with the profile of Mother Latvia and Latvia's coat of arms. The coin seemed to underscore the validity and success of the First Republic. In 1980 Uncle Ģirts showed me his prized collection of coins and bills from the Republic of Latvia, which must have belonged to his father—my Opaps, a numismatist. We had examined the beautiful money with amazement and sadness. The domestic Russian rouble had come to represent the disastrous Soviet economy: it would get you nowhere in "the real world," that is, beyond the Iron Curtain. Nobody wanted it in the "real world." The Soviet Union was like an alien planet. What would Latvian money eventually look like? We were moving toward establishing our own currency? Was I dreaming?! These were moments when I had to pinch myself. (15)

Left: A five lat coin designed by Rihards Zariņš and minted in 1931.

I took long naps but did as much as I could around the house and in the yard to lend a hand. Life in the countryside was all about work, but this work was a labor of love. Often I listened to the radio as I worked; I wanted to follow the news carefully. Our future was still veiled, and nothing was certain. Gasoline rations were increased that summer.The independent Latvian Association of Journalists was founded in Rīga in July. But in Russia there were ominous rumbles of disapproval, like distant thunder. (16)

It was a beautiful summer, full of expectation. A baby—the promise of new life—was growing inside of me. The wind rustled the leaves of the tall ash trees, and apples and pears ripened in the yard. Krišjānis and his cousin Elīna loved to swim, so we often walked to the lake to relax or splashed around in the pond. Piebalga was idyllic.

And then one day in August Andris arrived to tell me that he had found a house. No, it wasn't in Piebalga. It was way up north near Valka and Gaujiena, where Juris (and composer Jāzeps Vītols) were born. The property was located in the so-called Gauja meadows, which we had once explored. From the luxurious lap of these meadows sprang enormous oak trees. The meadows, covered in lush grasses and wildflowers, brushed up against the winding Gauja River. Yes, I remembered it as a beautiful area. But I was suddenly struck with doubt: did I want to live so far away from Piebalga? I had come to feel at home there in the pretty hills, valleys, clusters of homes, and recognizable people. But my father-in-law seemed excited, and his enthusiasm fired me up.

There was only one way to find out! We drove north on the Pskov (now Vidzemes) Highway, taking a detour through Smiltene, a wonderful small town that was over 90% ethnic Latvian. We drove into a huge forest, the kind that Latvians call *mūžamežs* ("eternal forest"). The old farmstead was off of a country road linking Valka with Gaujiena and was not immediately visible. A long driveway wound through the beautiful woods with their ruler-straight pine trees and soft clumps of lichen and moss.

So *this* would be my Paradise, this remote corner of Latvia with nobody in sight? The feeling of isolation would be hard to get used to, as I took in my new surroundings. No other homes were in view, although we did have neighbors; they simply weren't visible.

Black snakes with golden "crowns"—the magical *zalktis* from Latvian folk tales—slithered into the long grass and abandoned hay piles, as we approached. They made me jump. I would simply have to get used to them. It was adders that I was afraid of. Latvia's only venomous snake was a creature to be respected. I stared at the low threshold with worry: hopefully the snakes wouldn't get into the house.

The deal went through quickly. We bought the house from artist Biruta Delle for $1,000, kindly provided by my father. And immediately began making plans. I felt both excited and apprehensive. It would be very, very hard to leave Piebalga! It was so quiet at Pedraudzes. A timeless kind of quiet.

All of this—the forest, the meadows, this patch of green earth—was ours! My father-in-law could scarcely suppress his excitement. He had a soft spot for this area: his childhood home was down the road. There was a lot to take in: assorted buildings; the nearby forest; the meadows scintillating with life; and the strange dark ponds, Gauja's old branches, which were filled with still, dark waters that repelled rather than lured. It was a nature lover's dream. Hopefully, by the next summer we would be settled in with our new baby.

While Latvia's legislators engaged in talks with Moscow, pushing the independence envelope closer and closer to Mr. Gorbachev, the Latvian Communist Party and the KGB took a backseat. We all knew that these "comrades" were in a bad mood, upredictable, and dangerous.

In September the town of Stučka, named after reviled communist Pēteris Stučka, took back its old name, Aizkraukle. "In the 13th century Aizkraukle was one of the Liv nation's biggest centers on the right bank of the Daugava. The Livs' fortified wooden castle once stood on top of the Aizkraukle castle hill near a stream named Aškere: apparently this was the castle that Andrejs Pumpurs mentioned in *Bearslayer*. In 1205 the Livonian Brothers of the Sword burned down the castle, and a year later Aizkraukle was visited by preachers of Christianity who forced the indigenous people to adopt the Catholic faith. Aizkraukle's stone castle was hastily built in 1211 as a defense against marauding Lithuanians and occupied by the Sword Brethrens' komturs." By the late 20th century the Livs were all but gone, and my own Latvian nation faced an uncertain future. (17)

First day of school

September 1, 1990! First day of school for Latvia's children! And for Krišjānis! Was I nervous! I helped our little boy get dressed, as he yawned and fidgeted. The clean, white dress shirt looked marvelous on him. His hair had just been cut; he was cute as a button. Andris had purchased a large bouquet of red gladiolas for his new teacher.

Some of Rīga's Russian kids would be walking to the Lenin Monument on Ļeņina iela to lay flowers at its base. They lived in another world. By 1990 Latvians had ceased to engage in this charade; they could finally skip this humiliating ritual. No one would punish them anymore for turning their backs on the Father of the Russian Revolution. Lenin symbolized misery and oppression; Lenin had unleashed the beast within Russia's soul, and countries like Latvia, Lithuania, and Estonia had suffered at its hands...

Nevertheless, a huge portrait of Lenin wrought in metal was still hanging on the wall in the vestibule of Rīga's English Secondary School, one of the Latvian capital's "elite" schools. Was the school nervous about taking it down? I felt chilled looking at it.

September 1, 1990: Our little "Bearslayer" is getting ready for his first day of school. Photograph: Andris Krieviņš.

In 1990 our son's school was divided into morning and afternoon sessions due to crowding. As an afternoon pupil, Krišjānis was able to sleep in but would arrive home late, at around 7:00 pm. What were we thinking back then, I would later wonder, sending him to a school so far away? Initially, Andris helped him get to school, but later our little boy took the train by himself, getting out at the Central Railway Station, from which he walked to a tram that stopped by his school. It took him almost an hour to get there using two modes of public transportation. With a backpack on his back, he was a seven-year-old trooper who learned to get around Rīga at very early age.

At the end of each day when it got dark, I began worrying, pacing back and forth and waiting for him to ring at the door. By this time I was seven months pregnant. Subjecting our son to these commutes was wrong, I realized much later, when a new Latvian school devoted to the languages of the Nordic countries opened in Zolitūde. On the other hand, kids in Rīga were exceptionally streetwise. Very young children rode trains, trams, and buses on their own, and no one had a problem with it. There seemed to be no accidents and no abductions. Parental "helicoptering" did not exist in Latvia, as far as I could tell.

Our little "ram" in the back row, far right, on his first day of school, September 1, 1990. His posture hints at his stubborn nature and trouble to come. (Photo: Andris Krieviņš)

My oldest son's "adventures" in the Latvian school system would eventually cause the roots of my hair to turn silver. But that is a story I will keep to myself. It is a story that belongs to the 1990s in Latvia, a period of soul searching and confusion. Soviet Latvia's education system produced both brilliant minds and lots of cynics. To this day my son "suffers" from an "allergy" to school. His rambunctious spirit was never tamed, although his teachers tried hard by shaming him. On September 1, 1990 we sent him off with great expectations, yet I could not get the image of Lenin out of my mind.

By the end of September I was big and round and waddled around waiting for our baby's due date. We hoped the baby really would be born on November 18, Latvian Independence Day, as predicted. With Krišjānis away in the afternoon, I cleaned, baked, rested, and read. No longer comfortable sitting and drawing, I put my ABCs book on hold and kept myself physically busy.

Ten customs points opened on the borders with Russia and Belarus in September, paving the way for a manned physical border with our neighboring countries and filtered entry. The semblance of a real border was taking place. I would have liked a wall and a wide moat to go up between Latvia and Russia. In October a chunk of the Berlin Wall was brought back to Rīga and set down next to the Laima Clock near the Freedom Monument. Latvia accredited its first foreign diplomat (from Lithuania) since World War II. (18)

October arrived. I listened to the news nervously. The Latvian Supreme Council issued a protest concerning Soviet President Mikhail Gorbachev's decree permitting Soviet Army parades on November 7 in all the cities where Soviet military headquarters were located, including Rīga. The Latvian Supreme Soviet argued that such a display of Soviet military might would be in direct conflict with Latvia's sovereignty, would heighten political tensions, and would again remind the world that Latvia was forcibly annexed. We had all had enough of the loud Russian tank parades that rattled Rīga's graceful old boulevards. They were an ugly affront to our dignity. But the parade took place on November 7, as Latvians looked on in disgust. (19)

On November 2, OMON forces attacked the Press Building, shot at a militsiya car, and terrorized the Press Building's employees. I knew this building well, and it was frightening to imagine what those thugs could do if given a free hand. As the Soviet Army paraded, the OMON thugs raised the Soviet flag on the roof of the Press Building, stoking fear, anger, and outrage. We were quite sure Alfrēds Rubiks, the Latvian Communist Party, and the Interfront had something to do with this provocative gesture. (20)

Just a couple of weeks away from giving birth, I secluded myself in Zolitūde. I waited for my husband to come home and report on what he had seen and what he knew. Sometimes he stayed overnight in Old Rīga to be closer to the action. By now it was too late to consider leaving Latvia, nor did I want to. We had arranged that I would deliver the baby at the Stradiņš Hospital in Pārdaugava, not too far from where we lived. No bridges to cross, just in case...

Our plans changed dramatically, when we woke up one morning to the news that a large quantity of toxic chemicals had been "accidentally" spilled into the Daugava River by a Soviet military compound in Belarus, thereby contaminating the drinking water used by the people living on our side of the Daugava River. I was already always boiling the water out of fear of contracting a nasty stomach ailment. But this was different: these were hardcore toxins. What to do? There was only one option, we quickly realized: I had to evacuate to Pedraudzes. We called our friends, Drs. Jānis and Ilze Krūmals in Smiltene, and it was arranged that if things didn't get better quickly in Rīga, I would give birth at their hospital. And so I packed up my things and bid farewell to Rīga, which by now was experiencing growing hostilities between Latvian independence supporters and the Old Guard—Communist Party conservatives who had run out of patience. Although they denied it, we all knew they were responsible for OMON's scare tactics. Mr. Rubiks in particular seemed vigorously opposed to any changes to the old status quo.

On November 10, Latvia, Lithuania, and Estonia turned down the Soviet Council of Ministers' proposal to sign an agreement with the Soviet Union on its preservation. Moscow offered a proposal laced with overt threats: it promised to cut off the Baltic republics' hard currency supply for the purchase of commodities and a wide range of consumer goods and threatened to charge the Baltic States for energy resources in hard currency and saddle them with part of the

Soviet Union's foreign debt. The Politburo's white gloves were coming off, revealing a large, furry paw with unsheathed claws. (21)

On Lāčplēsis Day (November 11) a memorial to the Latvian Legion's fallen was revealed in Džūkste, a small town in Kurzeme. For decades the Soviets had tried to erase or falsify the history of the "fascist" soldiers of the Latvian Legion; now no more. The Latvian Legion's soldiers were victims of World War II and the Nazi occupation. The story of the Latvian Legion is truly tragic. It was time to set the record straight. (22)

On November 14, the Latvian Supreme Council adopted a resolution criminalizing any subversive actions that could be taken by Soviet Special Forces and the Soviet Armed Forces in Latvia. The supply of goods and services to the Soviet Army and Soviet Communist Party organizations stationed in the republic was to be suspended immediately, until Moscow agreed to begin talks about the status of the Soviet military in Latvia. Things were getting dicey. (23)

At a November 16 session of the Supreme Soviet in Moscow, Mikhail Gorbachev blasted the Latvian Supreme Council's resolution to suspend supply deliveries to the Soviet Army in Latvia. He said it was time to make several republics accountable for the mounting losses to the All-Union's food, cash, and consumer goods supply. According to Gorbachev, Latvia, Lithuania, and Estonia were the main culprits. Then he softened his stance, urging the disobedient Balts to return to the table and abide by the Soviet Constitution and Soviet law. Latvian Surpeme Council Chairman Anatolijs Gorbunovs refuted President Gorbachev's accusations. Latvia had reached a point of no return. (24)

It's a boy!

Our baby was due on Latvian Independence Day. About a week into my uneventful, boring stay at our "ranch," I became violently ill after a dinner of delicious smoked *reņģes* (pilchard) and withdrew to our bedroom to endure a night of physical agony. Was it a case of food poisoning? I spent the night on all fours, maneuvering between two buckets. I was terrified that my ungodly heaving and vomiting would push the baby out. Oh, what misery I endured, as everyone else slept. In the morning I fell into bed, shivering uncontrollably.

My husband called Smiltene Hospital, and it was arranged that I would be admitted for treatment and to rest and await the birth of our baby. That week of attentive care in Smiltene did wonders for my body and soul. I underwent a kind of "detoxification" process and began eating more. I slept a lot, walked about, talked to the doctors and nurses, and listened to the radio. There was talk of the movement of Soviet tanks, army vehicles, and troops near Rīga. To what end? What was being planned? What would happen to us? The answer seemed clear, punishment inevitable. Our farm was far from Rīga but close to a Soviet military base in Estonia. From time to time Soviet military planes and helicopters skimmed the treetops, reminding us of the presence of vast numbers of enemy troops and and deadly weapons in the Baltics. Would our wild endeavor to disengage from the Evil Empire end in bloodshed? We were all prepared to a degree, as we knew what kind of state we were dealing with.

My husband, who had hoped to avoid participating in the birth of our baby, became an unwilling partner in my ordeal: chastised by my midwife Valentīna, he hovered outside the birthing room, as I writhed and moaned. It all ended rather quickly this time with a happy song: our son

Jurģis came out bellowing. Born on the evening of November 15, he was a big, healthy, rose-pink baby. Valentīna placed him on my belly. Our second gift of life!

As we rejoiced over our newborn son, we worried about the future of Latvia. Photograph: Andris Krieviņš.

The baby and I spent about a week in the hospital under the doctors' supervision and the nurses' attentive care. I was astounded at the difference in the level of care and hygiene between this small hospital, which would soon regain its original name, the Smiltene Red Cross Hospital, and Rīga's First Hospital', where Krišjānis was born. The Krūmals took care of the beautiful old hospital and its tree-shaded grounds as if it were their personal property. The pretty hospital provided a good sense of what life had been like before the war. The hospital had been a gift to the town of Smiltene by Fürst (Prince) Paul Lieven, former proprietor of Smiltene Manor.

According to Wikipedia, the Lievens claimed that they were descended from Kaupo of Tu-raida, "the Livonian *quasi rex* who converted to Christianity in 1186, when Bishop Meinhard attempted to Christianize the region." According to *Henrici Chronicon Lyvoniae* (The Chronicle of Henry of Livonia), Kaupo traveled to Rome in the winter of 1203–1204 with Theodoric, a Cistercian monk, who founded the Livonian Brothers of the Sword (Schwertbrüderorden in German, Fratres militiæ Christi Livoniae in Latin) and become the first bishop of Estonia. "In Rome they were received by Pope Innocent III, who backed their plans to Christianize Livonia, as part of the territories of present-day Latvia and Estonia were known back then." Dr. Ilze Krūmala, my kind host in Smiltene, spoke often and fondly of the Lievens and their ties to the area. A gracious, almost aristocratic woman, she did not belong in the world of the proletariat. (25)

Fürst Paul Lieven's firstborn son died of an untreatable disease, and the prince decided to build a hospital where people could receive proper medical care. He drew up the architectural plan for the hospital, oversaw its construction, and paid for everything out of his own pocket. The hospital was designed for surgery, with modern equipment, 25 beds, and two wings, one for men and one for women. The park surrounding the hospital was designed at the same time. The hospital was inaugurated on September 14, 1903. After World War I Smiltene Manor was nationalized, and the Red Cross assumed ownership of the hospital. It was the prettiest hospital I had seen in Latvia. (26)

An old postcard of the Red Cross Hospital in Smiltene. It looks nearly the same today, with the exception of a new wing that was added during the Soviet era

While I spent happy days in the hospital nursing and cradling our son, whom we named Jurģis, Soviet President Mikhail Gorbachev ordered an economic blockade of Latvia. Smiltene and Latvia's far north seemed leagues away from Rīga, by now a hotspot. We bundled up the baby and drove home to Pedraudzes through the great forests of northern Vidzeme, where everything stood still, succumbing to late autumn's cold touch. Already on the ground there was a dusting of snow. The old house was warm and welcomed its new inhabitant. Biruta fussed over the baby, while grandpa Juris beamed and gloated. Big brother Krišjānis smiled and giggled and gently beeped the baby on his tiny nose. (27)

On November 21, the Latvian Supreme Council sent Pesident Gorbachev a request to cease Soviet military intervention in Latvia's internal affairs and demanded that the Soviet OMON forces stationed in Rīga be withdrawn. The Baltic republics refused to sign the Soviet Union agreement but expressed their willingness to sign agreements with individual Soviet republics to further political relations and economic cooperation. (28)

Our farm in winter.

The Latvian "Month of Wolves," December, arrived, and we returned to Rīga, where the water supply situation had stabilized. Pedraudzes was a wonderful transition from the hospital to the real world, but I felt stifled there and lonely, surrounded by the woods and wilderness. Rīga was where the action was, even though my hands were tied. With a baby on my hands, I was of no help to anyone.

Members of the three Baltic parliaments met in Vilnius, Lithuania on December 1; the chairmen of the three republics' supreme councils signed an appeal to the world's legislative bodies to exert pressure on the Soviet Union to persuade it to abstain from a policy of pressure, threats, and economic and political sanctions against Latvia, Lithuania, and Estonia, and to urge the Soviet Union to immediately commence talks with the Baltic States on recognizing their independence. The Balts also demanded that a precise timeframe be drawn up for the withdrawal of Soviet troops from their territories. (29)

On the night of December 5, several monuments dedicated to soldiers of the Latvian Legion were blown up in Budki Cemetery in Code, in Džūkste in the Tukums region, at Saulpils Hill in Jaunpils, and in More near Cēsis. These despicable acts could have been ordered by Soviet Defense Minister Dmitry Yazov; someone in Moscow was permitting the Soviet Armed Forces to interfere in other Soviet republics' domestic affairs, and local Soviet Army commanders held authority over military monuments in the republics. Again, Latvians were forced to witness a series of barbaric, inflammatory actions; there was little they could do short of standing by and guarding each and every historical monument. (30)

The following day, on December 5, the so-called *Vislatvijas glābšanas komiteja* ("Committee to Save the Society of All of Latvia"), headed by Comrade Alfrēds Rubiks, urged Soviet President Gorbachev to introduce a state of emergency and Soviet presidential rule in Latvia because of the absence of an effective mechanism to counter the "anti-constitutional" actions of Latvia's government institutions. Six days later a bomb went off at 5 Krišjāņa Valdemāra iela, a building affiliated with the Central Committee of the Latvian Communist Party, and at the Political Education Building, followed by a series of explosions throughout Rīga. The Latvian Popular Front warned all supporters of Latvia's independence that reactionary forces within the country were becoming increasingly active. (31)

On December 22, two days before Christmas, senior representatives of the Soviet Union's Baltic Military District convened behind closed doors to work out a plan on how and when to "neutralize" the Latvian parliament. On Christmas Eve Latvians went to church, lit the candles in their Christmas trees, exchanged small gifts, embraced each other, ate, and celebrated the birth of Christ and/or the winter solstice, which symbolized the end of darkness and the return of light. They spoke of the past and the future, united in hope. The bright star that twinkled above Old Rīga's ancient church spires—was it white or blood red? A time of reckoning was coming. We could all feel it. (32)

Chapter sources:

(1) "1990." Barikadopēdija. < http://www.barikadopedija.lv/raksti/1990>
(2) Ibid 1
(3) Leiškalne, Anda. "Vides aizsardzības klubs svin 25 gadu jubileju." Kasjauns. February 28, 2012; May 22, 2013. <http://www.kasjauns.lv/lv/zinas/73798/vides-aizsardzibas-klubs-svin-25-gadu-jubileju-foto>
(4) Ulme, Arvīds. "Meklējot Atmodas laika kino un video materiālus." Ir. January 8, 2014. <http://www.ir.lv/blogi/poli tika/meklejot-atmodas-laika-kino-un-videomaterialus>
(5) Ibid 3
(6) Ibid 3
(7) Ibid 1
(8) Ibid 7
(9) Ibid 7
(10) Ibid 7
(11) Ibid 7
(12) Ibid 7
(13) Ibid 7
(14) Ibid 7
(15) Ibid 7
(16) Ibid 7
(17) Aizkraukle.lv. <http://dev.aizkraukle.lv/tourism/tour>
(18) Ibid 7
(19) Ibid 7
(20) Ibid 7
(21) Ibid 7
(22) Ibid 7
(23) Ibid 7
(24) Ibid 7
(25) "Lieven." Wikipedia. January 27, 2014; May 21; 2013. <http://en.wikipedia.org/wiki/Lieven>
(26) "Smiltene. Sarkanā Krusta slimnīca." Zudusī Latvija. <http://www.zudusilatvija.lv/objects/object/596>
(27) Ibid 7
(28) Ibid 7
(29) Ibid 7
(30) Ibid 7
(31) Ibid 7
(32) Ibid 7

The Lenins Come Down

In the autumn of 1990 Latvia's Lenin statues started falling one after the other. Latvians looked on with glee and satisfaction. Begone, ogre!

The Lenin monument in downtown Valmiera being taken down on September 20, 1991

The Lenin monument in Limbaži being dismantled on September 26, 1990.
Both images courtesy of the National Library of Latvia collection "In Search of Lost Latvia."

1991: The Barricades, January 13–21

With my boys in northern Latvia on the first day of the New Year in 1991. Photograph: Andris Krieviņš.

Frigid and icy are Latvia's Januaries, but the light in the sky lingered longer each day, reminding us that nothing lasts forever. Winter wrapped its clammy, cold hands around our concrete apartment building in Zolitūde, tapping at the cheap glass and blowing through the seams around the windows. The lace curtains moved ever so slightly, hinting at a draft. I rolled up old shirts and stuffed them beneath the windows as primitive insulation. The baby slept in a crib next to me, his hands thrown back, and I watched him nervously, longing for the predictable, soft warmth of a woodstove. Those blasted, incompetent communists! The heat was on, but the building was "approximately" warm.

We had celebrated New Year's at our farm. Andris caught a fantastic amount of fish through a hole in the ice; the gleaming fish writhed in the metal pail like quicksilver. Was this a sign of fortune? We had eaten every single pea in the bowl for good luck, an old Latvian tradition. Latvia needed it.

Just two days into the New Year, apparently following the Latvian Communist Party's orders, OMON commandos stormed the Press Building, partially paralyzing the production of Latvia's democratic periodicals. This was a rude awakening; the Soviet authorities were finally reacting to the uncontrollable events of the past four years. (1)

Established on December 12, 1988 under Soviet Interior Minister Vadim Bakatin to guard state institutions, fight crime, and control crowds, Rīga's OMON unit, allegedly aided by other Soviet Special Forces, perpetrated dozens of vicious attacks on various Baltic state facilities, was behind a series of provocative explosions, and beat up hundreds of people. In these acts of terror six people in Latvia would die. As the New Year dawned, we suddenly realized that a bunch of heavily armed, out-of-control thugs were running around Rīga, terrorizing ordinary citizens, and hinting at things to come. (2)

The Press Building not only housed the editorial offices of scores of publications, it also housed Rīga's main printing press. Employees were being frisked, their I.D. cards confiscated, offices searched. Latvian Interior Minister Aloizs Vaznis, Deputy Chairman of the Latvian Council of Ministers Ilmārs Bišers, and Deputy Speaker of the Latvian Supreme Council Dainis Īvāns arrived to negotiate with the commandos but were turned away. (3)

I had been to the Press Building many times. It was an ugly Soviet-style building, but it hummed with life and communication. Cigarette smoke flowed freely in the hallways; offices were cluttered with papers, books, magazines, and stained coffee mugs and teacups. Both Latvian and Russian periodicals were published there, so you could hear both languages, as you stood in line for coffee or lunch. It was a very important hub of communication in the capital and as such was targeted for disruption.

Contrary to the OMON commandos' claims, Boris Pugo (then Soviet Minister of the Interior) and Soviet President Mikhail Gorbachev denied any involvement in or knowledge of the Black Berets' actions. On January 4 a group of senior representatives of the Soviet Interior Ministry arrived in Rīga to investigate the situation. A few days later, under orders from Gorbachev, Soviet Marshal Dmitry Yazov ordered (additional) special commando units deployed to Latvia, Estonia, and Lithuania to ensure proper conscription of Baltic men into the Soviet Armed Forces. In light of recent events, Balts perceived a Soviet military draft as especially insulting and unacceptable. (4)

The OMON forces made everyone nervous, because they seemed to answer to no one. Gun-toting, cocky, and mean-looking, no one wanted to mess with them. Everyone knew they were up to no good. Angered by the presence of OMON forces and Moscow's plan to send additional special forces to Latvia, on January 8 the Latvian Supreme Council adopted a resolution denouncing the plan and urged Latvia's citizens to refrain from any engagement with Soviet military formations and Soviet draft offices. At this time Deputy Soviet Defense Minister Colonel General Vladislav Achalov slipped into Latvia secretly to meet with General Lieutenant Fyodor Kuzmin, Commander of the Baltic Military District, and Alfrēds Rubiks, the rabid communist whose "Salvation Committee" stood by ready to wrench power from the legally elected pro-independence Latvian government authorities. Hard-core Soviet preservationists, these men would consider any means to squash the Baltics' efforts to break away from the Soviet Union. (5)

I listened to the radio and watched the evening news, as I took care of the boys, straining to understand what was unfolding on the other side of the Daugava River. My husband was away for long stretches of time. American baby formula and diapers were finally available for purchase here and there. No more plastic pants and gauze, the stuff of Krišjānis' childhood. With this second baby I felt more comfortable and in control. I had more to eat, which made a huge difference. The supermarket was close by. Ironically, surrounded by Russian military families, I felt secluded but safe. What were *they* thinking? Whose side were *they* on? The answer seemed obvious. Our building was quiet, the neighborhood was quiet. It was cold; there was snow on the ground. People—Latvians and Russians—bundled up up to go to work; they came home, watched TV... Latvians and Russians were watching and reading two different sources of news. Latvia was a largely segregated society.

On January 9 the United States issued a statement condemning Soviet plans to send additional military forces to the Baltic republics. For decades the United States had refused to recognize the Soviet annexation of the Baltic States, thanks in part to the intense lobbying efforts of Latvian Americans. Despite the miserable provisions of the Yalta Conference, the US would become a steadfast ally of these three countries in their efforts to break free from the Soviet claw.

An unsanctioned rally of thousands of Interfront activists took place at the Latvian Council of Ministers on Ļeņina iela on January 10; the protesters demanded that Prime Minister Ivars Godmanis' government step down. The demonstrators tried unsuccessfully to break into the building. Because I was sequestered in Zolitūde, the full effect of the dramatic escalation of the conflict was lost on me. But the drama was real. (6)

Dedovshchina: "Hazing"

Late 1980s: Latvian mothers by the Freedom Monument with portraits of their sons who died while serving in the Soviet military. Photo: Gunārs Birkerts.

On January 11 the Latvian Women's League gathered at Esplanāde (Communard Park in the Soviet era) in downtown Rīga to protest the Soviet draft. About 6,000 people were there to support them.

As the mother of two young boys born in the Soviet Union, stories of brutal hazing in the Soviet military were hard for me to stomach and made me nervous. How many of our Latvian boys had died or been mutilated or traumatized in these incidents? As a result of glasnost and Mikhail Gorbachev's aim to create socialism "with a human face," Latvia's women had also become active participants in the democratization process. (7)

Betija Ceļmale was an active member of the Latvian Women's League. The mother of three sons, she understood the fears and worries of other mothers and their resistance to the Soviet draft.

Betija Ceļmale:

It was only logical that Latvia's women activists decided to create an organization, the Latvian Women's League, to defend women's interests. Its goals were: (1) the 'humanization' of relations in all walks of life (in the family, at work, in schools, in the state apparatus, etc.); (2) the demilitarization and de-occupation of the Baltic States; (3) supervision of and control over the operations of military organizations (in cooperation with the Latvian Republic's Defense and Interior Ministries and the Customs Department beginning in 1990); (4) promoting a clean environment; (5) active involvement in humanitarian efforts and charity work; and (6) protection of the rights of women and children and strengthening the role of the family. Initially our organization's primary concerns were devoted to our sons' military service in the Soviet Armed Forces: we aimed to abolish the Soviet draft once and for all.

Everyone knew that in the Soviet Union everything related to the Soviet military was pure propaganda; (the Soviet Armed Forces were a massive organization) cloaked in secrecy, which led to unsanctioned, illegal activities within the military, from dedovischina or the hazing of young recruits to corruption and theft among officers and generals. Until 1986 none of these problems was open to public discussion. In Gorbachev's perestroika years all sorts of topics surfaced, and people began to actively protest what was going on in the Soviet Army, as well as the war in Afghanistan. People realized that the only way to fight these injustices and crimes was to band together. (8)

According to Betija Ceļmale, some of the most shocking stories to emerge and anger the Latvian public were of Latvian youths' experiences in the Soviet Army. When the majority of Latvians aligned themselves with the Latvian Popular Front, thereby demonstrating their hope for the restoration of Latvia's independence, the Soviet military allegedly began terrorizing young Latvian, Lithuanian, and Estonian men. There were brutal incidents of torture and even rape, which drove many young Baltic men to suicide and desertion. It was a tradition within the Soviet military to call Baltic youths "fascists" and "ganses" ("Hanses").

"The women who chose to join the Latvian Women's League were mothers whose sons were already serving or who were about to be drafted. These women fought to minimize the emotional and mental damage their sons sustained during their military service. Anyone who wanted to help draft dodgers and draftees joined our cause. Initially the Latvian Women's League tried to persuade the Soviet Armed Forces to let Latvian youths serve in Latvia. Although these women were fighting for their sons in their own country, they were also in touch with a similar association of mothers in Moscow; these problems were the same all over the Soviet Union. A mother's love and her worries know neither boundaries nor ethnic divisions." (Betija Ceļmale)

An enormous amount of patient work went into the Latvian Women's League, according to Ceļmale. "At the end of the 1980s the organization was involved in hiding deserters and draft dodgers; then it became involved in the legal defense of deserters. The women contacted lawyers and obtained medical summaries from doctors. There were cases when their efforts bore fruit, but up until independence (in 1991) many young men were still drafted despite their obvious physical ailments. As a result the mortality rate in the Soviet Army was unacceptably high. Young men with heart conditions were unable to withstand the pressures of military training and died. This fired up the women of the league to fight for their country's independence with doubled efforts."

Brutal hazing occured all over the Soviet Union and still plagues the Russian Army today, according to several sources, including RFERL.org ("Russia: Military Conscripts Caught in 'Deadly Cycle of Violence'"). There was also an ethnic component to *dedovshchina*, but ultimately it was a problem of the corrupt culture of the Soviet Army. Until Latvia's independence from the Soviet Union, military service in the Soviet Army remained an issue of great concern for me, and I had decided to leave Latvia before my sons got old enough to expect their summonses, in the event that nothing in Latvia changed.

While the Latvian Women's League and its large crowd of supporters rallied against the Soviet draft at Esplanāde, a closed meeting of senior commanders of the Baltic Military District was taking place at its headquarters just one block away on Gorkija iela, in which it was decided to issue automatic weapons to officers and military school cadets. I had passed this building numerous times over the years, noticing Russian officers coming and going. There was a noticeable increase in Russian Army vehicle movement in Rīga. (9)

Surprisingly for us, on January 12 the Presidium of the Supreme Soviet of the Russian Soviet Federative Socialist Republic passed a resolution urging the Soviet Union to withdraw any additional Soviet forces from the Baltic States. The idea that Russia itself appeare divided was hopeful. Meanwhile in Moscow, Latvia's representatives Ilmārs Bišers, Juris Dobelis, and Jānis Peters met with Soviet Defense Minister Dimitry Yazov and Soviet Army General Mikhail Moiseev, who promised not to send additional military forces to Latvia. Mikhail Gorbachev also promised Latvian Supreme Council Chairman Anatolijs Gorbunovs and Latvian Prime Minister Ivars Godmanis that military force would not be used in Latvia. Already saturated with the Russian military, additional troops would have ensured a complete stranglehold. (10)

After midnight on January 13, Soviet tanks and troops surrounded the Lithuanian Supreme Council building in Vilnius and occupied the Lithuanian Television Center, Lithuanian Radio, and the Lithuanian telegraph service. As peaceful Lithuanians broke into song, chanting "Lietuva! Lietuva!" ("Lithuania! Lithuania!") in hopes of stopping the advance of Russian tanks, 14 protesters were killed and 110 were wounded. The news spread like wildfire through the Baltics and the world. I watched dark, grainy footage of the events in Vilnius from our apartment in Zolitūde, shocked at the brutality of what I was seeing. Russian soldiers bashing Lithuanians in the head with their guns, tanks crushing peaceful protesters... These images encapsulated the meaning of Soviet Russian "friendship" with its "allied" republics. (11)

Visual: "Soviet Troops vs Unarmed Lithuanian Civilians, Vilnius, 1991": <https://www.youtube.com/watch?v=I2SvhDY23So>

On January 13, the Latvian Supreme Council immediately created a post for manning the defense of its building in Old Rīga; the post was to be run by Andrejs Krastiņš, a criminal investigator), Odisejs Kostanda, a history teacher, and Tālavs Jundzis, a criminologist and jurist. Krastiņš was "the face" of LNNK, the Latvian National Independence Movement, which, like the Latvian Popular Front, had been pushing for full independence from the Soviet Union under perestroika. The post was also responsible for the defense of Old Rīga. Our old apartment on Krāmu Street was just a couple of blocks away from the Supreme Council building. I could only guess what the situation there looked like, as I sat near our television set in Zolitūde. The tragic loss of human life in Vilnius had shocked everyone. It also revealed the true nature of Mr. Gorbachev: despite his pleasantries, calls for change, and promises to the West, he wanted things to stay the same. And he would continue to deny his involvement in the Vilnius bloodshed. (14)

In the wee morning hours of January 13, Dainis Īvāns surfaced on Latvian Radio to summon all people of Latvia to take part in a demonstration the next day at Dome Square in a show of solidarity with Lithuania. A journalist and father of four children, Īvāns was a gentle, soft-spoken idealist who had been thrust to the forefront of Latvia's dramatic political events in his campaign to save the Daugava River. (12)

Would the Soviets begin arresting and deporting people again? Shooting them on the spot? Anything seemed possible now, considering the 14 dead and hundreds wounded in Vilnius. Gorbachev's mask had fallen off. And there I was, "stuck" in Latvia with a seven-year-old and a baby, with little chance of getting out if all hell broke loose. But I didn't really want to go anywhere. To be in Latvia at such a tumultuous and historic time was a gift, no matter what the outcome, and I felt very strongly that it would be positive. Solidarity with one's nation in its time of need was more important than our personal safety, I thought.

Never for a moment did I doubt the course the Balts had undertaken in search of historical justice. Not fanatically religious, I nevertheless put my faith in God and the spirits of our ancestors; surely they were with us! I thought of Vilnius, a beautiful old city (1323) that we had visited, and of our sister nation, the Lithuanians, whose language was so similar to ours, who looked and sounded like Latvians, who were peaceful and friendly, and who were confronting their oppressors with songs and smiles. As the Soviet tanks had rolled in on that fateful night, I could recognize some of the words in their songs. There was no turning the clock back now. I was sure Latvians would stick together with their Lithuanian and Estonian neighbors till "death do us part."

On January 13, about 600,000 people gathered along the Daugava River to express solidarity with Lithuania. Latvian Popular Front Chairman Romualdas Ražukas (b. 1955), a doctor, addressed the crowd, stressing that it was time to begin building barricades to defend our fledgling state against Soviet military aggression. Drivers with access to log carriers and logs, trucks, and large agricultural and construction vehicles were urged to lose no time and get those vehicles and materials to Rīga. Overhead Soviet military helicopters buzzed like angry wasps, scattering leaflets with warnings over the protesters' heads.

After the demonstration, a wave of Latvian "rebels" flowed through the streets of Old Rīga toward the Freedom Monument and dispersed in all directions to begin building barricades and obstacles from anything they could lay their hands on to impede any advance of Soviet tanks and armored vehicles on strategic objects, which included the Supreme Council building in Old Rīga, the Council of Ministers on Ļeņina iela, the Latvian Radio and TV Center on Zaķusala Island, the Latvian Radio offices on Dome Square, the Rīga Telephone and Telegraph Central, and numerous important bridges. (13)

Romualdas Ražukas addressing a huge crowd of Latvian "rebels" on January 13, 1991 in Rīga, calling for the protection of strategic objects. Photo by Juris Krieviņš.

Latvia's patriots worked non-stop into the night and the following day, transporting large, heavy objects—logs, metal beams, concrete blocks, anything—and stacking them into piles as barricades against the Soviet Army. They patrolled the streets and camped out near strategic objects. Volunteers provided hot beverages and food for the defenders of Latvia's dignity, first tender shoots of freedom, and future. Barricades were also constructed in the cities of Liepāja and Kuldīga. The events of January 1991 show how dramatic and precarious this time was for Latvia and its "siblings," Lithuania and Estonia. It was "now or never," "do-or-die."

On January 14, NATO condemned the Soviet Union's use of force against the democratically elected Lithuanian government, calling this a scare tactic against the other two Baltic States. This was reassuring for me; most democratic Western countries probably could not imagine what we were up against. Meanwhile President Gorbachev repeated Soviet Interior Minister

Boris Pugo's statement that the Soviet Army had done the right thing in Vilnius, thereby destroying the last shred of credibility he possessed. Latvia's representative Jānis Peters met with President Gorbachev and Anatoly Lukyanov, chairman of the Supreme Soviet, in Moscow. The Russians deemed the situation in the Baltics dangerous and invited the Baltic States to the table to resolve the conflict. Back in Rīga Peters summed up the meeting by saying that there was little hope that the Soviet Union was prepared to grant Latvia independence. We already knew this. (15)

Defenders in good spirits staying warm near a bonfire by St. Mary's. Photo by Juris Krieviņš.

While Latvia's supporters of independence worked tirelessly like ants to build up their defenses, OMON commandos attacked the defenders of Vecmīlgrāvis Bridge on January 14, shot at their cars, assaulted and beat up people, and stole personal belongings. That same day the Black Berets attacked another group of people on Brasas Bridge, threw Molotov cocktails at cars, and started a fire. That day they set 17 cars on fire. The radio station "Svoboda" warned of an impending military coup in Latvia. (The OMON commandos' style of terrorist warfare would resurface decades later in the Ukrainian-Russian conflict.) (16)

During the night of January 15, OMON commandos stormed the Latvian Interior Ministry's Minsk Militsiya School at 8 Zeļļu iela, beat up students, trashed the school, and stole weapons. The so-called Latvian Salvation Committee announced at an Interfront rally at the ASK Stadium in Rīga that it was prepared to assume power. According to these people, it was imperative that Latvia remain part of the USSR. The Soviet Union was imploding economically; the country was a scary joke, a heavily militarized, nuclear state, but not much else. Yet these imperialists wanted to continue to live in the mess created by communism. Russians had never experienced anything better in their history, apparently. (17)

Barricades near the Latvian Council of Ministers on Ļeņina iela. Photograph by Juris Krieviņš.

On January 16, OMON commandos attacked the defenders of Vecmīlgrāvis Bridge again, this time shooting and killing Roberts Mūrnieks, a driver for the Ministry of Transportation. In the evening they attacked the defenders of Brasas Bridge, injuring several of them. It was a scary time of random violence meant to intimidate Latvia's peaceful resistance. (18)

All I could do was sit around in Zolitūde and wait in suspense for news and a telephone call. Jurģis was two months old, as fragile as Latvia's situation that moment. I wondered what my parents were thinking, if they even knew how serious things were. A strike committee formed by the Latvian Communist Party was claiming that Latvia was being run by a "fascist regime." When Moscow wanted to make someone look bad, it called them "fascist."

A delegation of representatives of the Soviet Union's Supreme Soviet, headed by a fellow named Anatoly Denisov, returned to Moscow after a visit to Rīga on January 17 to inform Mr. Gorbachev that Latvia supported the introduction of presidential rule in its territory. Later in February apparently this same fellow Denisov would refute Western criticism of Soviet intervention in the Baltics, claiming that their pro-independence governments were creating "a situation of lawlessness." Mr. Denisov defended Moscow at the 43 nation UN Human Rights Commission, alleging that "Lithuania, Latvia, and Estonia had disregarded central legislation, violated human rights, and discriminated against minorities." (For years to come, Moscow would continue to criticize the Baltic States for ethnic discrimination.) (19)

On January 20, some 100,000 demonstrators went out into the streets of Moscow to protest the Soviet crackdown in Vilnius; they demanded the resignation of President Gorbachev, Marshal Yazov, Latvian-born Interior Minister Boris Pugo, and KGB Chief Vladimir Kryuchkov. (20)

It was particularly exciting to feel the support of the Russians. I had been raised in an anti-Russian environment, absorbing stories of the cruelty of the Soviet occupation of Latvia. Expatriate Balts were not exactly fond of Russians for understandable reasons. And the behavior of many Russians in Latvia towards Latvians, including me, wasn't exactly friendly; many Russians' attitudes towards Latvians seemed to range from paternalistic to outright hostile. They were our "liberators," we were "thankless" "fascists." However, there were Russians and other "non-Latvians" who were on our side; that is, they supported Latvia's move towards independence. Philologist Ita Kozakēviča of Polish descent, Lithuanian-born Romualdas Ražukas, Ruta Marjaša (Latvian Jewish lawyer, activist, politician), Mavriks Vulfsons (Latvian Jewish professor, politician, journalist), Russian journalist, writer, and politician Vladlen Dozortsev, and writer Marina Kosteņecka: these were some of the better known representatives of Latvia's ethnic minorities who joined the Latvian/Baltic cause.

Shortly after 9:00 pm on January 20, OMON forces launched a 30-minute shooting spree at the Interior Ministry on Raiņa bulvāris, a few buildings down from where my relatives lived. Tracer bullets whined from the Ministry building into the park near Bastejkalns, whizzing over the canal into the darkness, where people hunkered down in fear. Later there were claims that shots also emanated from Bastejkalns. (21

When it was all over, two Latvian militsiya lieutenants—Sergey Kononenko and Vladimir Gomanovich—were dead, as was cameramen Andris Slapiņš (b. 1949), a close associate and friend of filmmaker Juris Podnieks, who huddled nearby. Their colleague and close friend, cameraman Gvido Zvaigzne (b. 1958), died a few days later from his wounds. Slapiņš and his young family also lived in Zolitūde; I had spoken to his Russian-born wife there a couple of times. A high school student named Edijs Riekstiņš was shot dead. Other people were wounded. The attackers retreated to the Latvian Communist Party headquarters a couple of blocks away.

Juris Podnieks had just been in Vilnius and filmed the Soviet crackdown that left 14 peaceful Lithuanian protesters dead. In 1987 Podnieks had started working on a five-part documentary film series called "Hello, Do You Hear Us?" in collaboration with British Television. The series documented the irreversible changes taking place in the Soviet Union in the late 1980s as a result of perestroika, as well as its final unraveling, captured in the final installment called "End of Empire." For the series, Podnieks and his crew visited Soviet "hot spots": the forbidden radioactive zone in Chernobyl; the earthquake ruins in Armenia; striking workers in Yaroslavl; etc. Juris Podnieks captured his friend Andris Slapiņš's last moments of life on film; these were incorporated into the film "End of Empire." (22)

I seem to recall watching much of this madness in real time on TV. Someone was filming tracer bullets being shot from the Latvian Radio Building on Dome Square. The dark footage gave the impression that bullets were flying toward our old building on Jauniela. I wondered where my husband was. The violence felt unreal.

On January 21, Anatolijs Gorbunovs headed to Moscow to meet with Soviet leader Gorbachev to discuss the situation in Latvia; the latter was coming under increasing pressure from the West to refrain from using violent force in dealing with the breakaway Baltic States. (23)

The unforgettable, dramatic, and fantastic "Barricades" period lasted from January 13 until the 21st. On January 21 a barricades volunteer named Ilgvars Grieziņš (b. 1938) was accidentally killed near the Supreme Council building, where he had gone to offer his English language skills to facilitate communication with westerners. As barricades volunteers went home, the future remained unclear, and we mourned the victims of Soviet terror. (24)

Fragile democracy, frail baby

In mid-January our baby began coughing. I woke up at night and listened to the strange noises coming from his tiny chest, turn on the light, and look at him anxiously, as he slept. A deepening sense of unease about the baby's health clawed at my peace of mind. Soon enough the baby was running a high temperature; I walked around with him in my arms, weeping. He was diagnosed with pneumonia, and we ended up at the children's hospital in Pārdaugava. We were assigned to a dark room with a dirty, old bed, and then the baby was taken away from me for treatment, which included head injections that made my skin crawl.

From this time I can only remember the terrible sense of being completely alone in the world with a sick baby, with no one there to comfort me, let me know what was going on, speak to me, put a friendly hand on my shoulder. As wonderful as his birth had been in Smiltene, our week in the hospital was a nightmare that reminded me that the "free" Soviet health care system was, in fact, dehumanizing and callous. Our son's physical struggle coincided with Latvia's struggle to break free of its diseased connection to the Soviet Union. Latvia was weak, too, and we did not know if our hopes and goals would survive.

Our son was saved by a heavy dose of antibiotics. We went home to wait for spring. When I could, I bundled up the boys, and we took long walks around Zolitūde and over the tracks into Imanta. We found a small café, where we ate pastries and sippled delicious ice cream "cocktails." We were always suffering from a shortage of cash; life in Latvia wasn't cheap. I gladly took on freelance translating and illustration work to supplement our income. Wages were low. I desperately wanted to make our apartment nicer and warmer by installing a wooden floor or rug, replacing the cheap doors, putting in new kitchen and bathroom fixtures, tiles, etc. But we never had enough cash for that, and my spouse didn't seem interested in investing any money into our apartment in Zolitūde.

Left: Jurģis in the spring of 1991 in the countryside, peeking out from his baby carriage. Photo: Andris Krieviņš.

In April, when the baby had recovered from another bout of bronchitis, I was so sick of antibiotics and superficial, overworked, desensitized doctors, that I packed up and had Andris drive us and our Cocker Spaniel Frīda to the farm. We had a couple of woodstoves there to keep us warm and the pine forest nearby. I was sure the fresh air would invigorate our son and clean out his lungs. Though the surroundings were beautiful and pristine, I lived there with a sense of dread, expecting robbers or an ax-wielding drunk to show up. Our neighbors were not directly visible, lending the farm a sense of isolation. In Piebalga we could see the smoking chimneys of other people's houses and the road, but our farm next to the great Valka forest was a different kind of world, more primordial, more remote, where wolves and mushroom seekers prowled.

It was sooo quiet. No cars, no people, no nothing, which made me jumpy. Stories of bandits breaking into the homes of old people in the countryside, tying them up and torturing them to extort money and valuables, had left their effect on me. I realized that we were completely helpless if a bunch of burglars or marauding sadists showed up. Frīda was a small dog with a mind of her own, not very obedient, not very fear-inspiring. The house could be broken into in a second, even if I locked the door. Having watched Soviet Latvia's militsiya announcements seeking help in tracking down dangerous criminals, which were always preceded by a creepy gong, my fears were heightened by my active imagination. I tried to bat away these stupid and exaggerated fears, happy to have a telephone, which I used every day to call home.

Every day the baby, Frīda, and I went on a walk in the forest or to some sunny, slowly waking corner of a meadow to gather lichen, pine buds, and oak bark: natural remedies for clearing up respiratory ailments that I had read about in a book. Pushing the pram with the dog tagging along, we made our way through and into the mysterious forest. I gathered, scraped, and snipped my ingredients, which I then soaked and boiled and strained into a nasty tea for my son. The lichen tea was horribly bitter, so I added honey (supposedly a no-no), and Jurģis happily guzzled down his cough medicine. The walks were lovely, of course. The spring sun was so bright and clear; I watched it brightening my baby's cheeks, as he looked around with inquisitive eyes.

I missed Krišjānis. As evening approached, we would come in, lock the door, and spend the evening in the warmth, playing and reading. If the dog barked, I twitched. I was angry at myself, thinking about the two old women who lived by the side of the road nearby. They didn't seem particularly afraid. It was not the forest and the wild animals I feared: it was human beings. And they had slaughtered each other ferociously at various points in history in my fatherland.

The two weeks dragged on. By the end I couldn't wait to get back to Rīga. I was tired of being afraid. Our young son's health, though improved, reflected our country's precarious future. One step at a time, we were moving forward and away from the oppressive past and sickness. And now, when independence seemed ready to land in our outstretched hands like a timid spring skylark, I had a permanent place in my fatherland: a farmstead and land for our children. There was much to plan and so much work to be done! We would do it, because we were young, strong, and determined. I knew I could overcome my fear of living alone in this glorious paradise.

Chapter sources:

(1) "1991." Barikadopēdija. <http://www.barikadopedija.lv/raksti/1991>
(2) "Rīgas OMON." Wikipedia. <http://lv.wikipedia.org/wiki/R%C4%ABgas_OMON>
(3) "1991. gads Latvijā." Wikipedia. <http://lv.wikipedia.org/wiki/1991._gads_Latvij%C4%81#Janv.C4.81ris>
(4) Ibid 3
(5) Ibid 1, 3
(6) Ibid 1, 3
(7) Ibid 1, 3
(8) "Betija Ceļmale: Trešās Atmodas dalībniece, Latvijas Sieviešu līgas sekretāre." Latvijaslaudis.lv. July 1, 2012; May 27, 2013. <http://www.latvijaslaudis.lv/users/betija-celmale>
(9) Ibid 1, 3
(10) Ibid 3
(11) Ibid 1, 3
(12) Ibid 3
(13) Ibid 1, 3
(14) Ibid 1, 3
(15) Ibid 3
(16) Ibid 1, 3
(17) Ibid 1, 3
(18) Ibid 1, 3
(19) "Supreme Soviet Member Rejects Criticism on Baltics with AM-Soviet-Baltics." Associated Press. February 11, 1991; May 30, 2014. <http://www.apnewsarchive.com/1991/Supreme-Soviet-Member-Rejects-Criticism-on-Baltics-With-AM-Soviet-Baltics/id-a734f11a6cc3221561cfba5f6cc77532>
(20) Ibid 1, 3
(21) Ibid 1, 3
(22) "Juris Podnieks." Latfilma. <http://www.latfilma.lv/cm/podnieks>
(23) Ibid 1, 3
(24) Ibid 1, 3

1991–1992: A Dream by the Gauja

Jurģis and his four-legged companions Frīda (left) and Duksis playing near the Gauja River, which runs past Pedraudzes, in the summer of '92. Photograph by Juris Krieviņš.

When we purchased Pedraudzes in the summer of 1990, I was too busy thinking about the future to begin researching the property's history. I could tell by the look of the old granary and threshing barn that Pedraudzes was a rather old farm. It was only many years later, when I had access to the Internet, that I discovered the names of the original owners, Aleksis and Karlīne Pedraudze, both born in the second half of the 19th century. The name of the farm was intriguing. Initially we thought the farmstead was called "Pēdraudzes," which roughly translates as "footprint seekers." A photograph of one Jānis Pedraudze, which I came across in the National Library's online archive, made me wonder if his property, "Gaujmalas," was nearby. "Gaujmalas" means "Near the Gauja." Was he related to the original proprietors of our farm? Pedraudze is an unusual, even rare name in Latvia.

Zvārtava Parish, *right*, stretches south of the town of Valka; its eastern edge, delineated by the Gauja River, lies along the border with Estonia. It is a heavily forested area. It is hard to imagine that the people who once farmed there in the open spaces between the woods acquired any great wealth. My father-in-law remembered seeing *plostnieki* (raftsmen) floating down the Gauja in his childhood. The forest next to Pedraudzes was a sea of tall, straight pine trees.

Pedraudze, Aleksis Aleksandrs, son of Jānis, born in 1865, Pedraudzes; deported on March 25, 1949; died en route, Poyma Station, April 23, 1949. File No. 6101. (2) (Source: Nekropole.lv)

Pedraudze, Karlīne, daughter of Fricis, born in 1870, Pedraudzes; deported on March 25, 1949; Tomsk Oblast, Asinovsky District; died on November 4, 1949. File Nr. 6101. (3) (Source: Nekropole.lv)

The names of the farmstead's original inhabitants are among those Latvians arrested and deported by the Soviets from the Valka area on March 25, 1949. Aleksis Pedraudze was 84 years old at the time, Karlīne was 79. They were among the 90,000 or so people to be deported from Latvia, Lithuania, and Estonia to Siberia in 1949 in a Soviet action that aimed to get rid of Baltic *kulaks* (wealthy farmers), "bandits" (national partisans) and their families, as well as the families of the "bandits" who had already been executed. The code name for this action was "Krasta banga" ("Coastal Surge"). More than a quarter of the deportees were under 16 years of age. To accomplish this task, about 9,000 Russian soldiers were sent into Latvia and Estonia along with an array of Soviet security forces: in all, over 75,000 people were sent into the Baltic republics from Russia to arrest and deport the Balts. (1)

About half of the Baltic deportees were from Latvia. Property left behind was confiscated or abandoned. Unlike in the 1941 deportations, families were allowed to stay together. The majority of deportees (25,834) were sent to Irkutsk. About 22,542 went to Omsk, 16,065 to Tomsk, 13,823 to Krasnoyarsk, 10,064 to Novosibirsk, and 5,451 to the very remote Amur region. The deportees were told they would remain there forever; they were put to work in kolhozes, sovhozes, gold mines, and the timber industry as slave laborers. Latvia lost 13,624 families in the action; Estonia 7,488; Lithuania 9,518. In all, about 44,191 of Latvia's inhabitants were deported to Siberia on March 25, 1949. After Stalin's death Nikita Kruschev condemned Stalinism, and the deportees who had survived were allowed to return home, where they faced further discrimination and ostracism. (2)

More than 130 online pages list the names of Latvians who lived in the Valka District and were arrested by the Soviets and deported in March 1949 (http://www.ar-chiv.org.lv/dep1941/saraksti/22_Valkas_apr.pdf). From old people to young children: nobody was spared. Two other people were arrested at Pedraudzes and deported: Alma Vilciņa (b. 1901) and Juris Vilciņš (b. 1940). As far as I can tell, Alma was Aleksis' and Karlīne's daughter. Alma and Juris survived. Where were they? So many questions... (3)

When we assumed ownership of Pedraudzes in 1990, all that was left of the Pedraudze couple were the original farm buildings. The scenery probably hadn't changed much. People vanished, strangers moved in. The personal mementos of the deported meant little to strangers. Antiques were not in vogue, and pre-war items were often cast out into the trash.

A view of the old threshing barn at Pedraudzes. Photograph by Aina Balgalvis.

This is my favorite photograph of the idyllic, quintessentially Latvian farmstead that we bought in 1990, when I was pregnant with our second son. Our sprawling "ranch" was located about 180 km to the northeast of Rīga. The Gauja River flowed past our land like a natural property line. On the other side of the river lay Estonia. The closest town, Valka, was linguistically split, with its twin counterpart Valga in Estonia.

The countryside around us was sparsely populated, but that was typical for much of Latvia. In late summer wild mushrooms sprouted from the forest floor, providing bountiful harvests. Morels popped up in the sandy road in the spring. Estonians also foraged in our woods for fungi and berries; sometimes we saw inquisitive mushroom gatherers peek over the dune at our house and then politely retreat. We could scoop up lingonberries and blueberries while taking a jaunt in the woods.

At the time of purchase $1,000 bought us about 35 hectares and a collection of relatively well-preserved buildings: a house; an old *rija* or threshing barn; a *klēts* (granary); a large hay shed; a solid cellar tucked into a dune; a small, snug barn; an outhouse; a well; and a generous chunk of pinelands spread over shady dunes, meadows, and seemingly bottomless ponds—the old "arms" of the Gauja.

The farmstead was adjacent to an old floodplain. Juris Krieviņš told me that in ancient times this area had once been covered by sea water. When the wind rustled in the pines, you could almost picture a shimmering sea beyond the dunes, which rose and fell away from us. One spring the waters of the Gauja rose so high, that they came close to lapping at the baseboards of the house.

The forest floor was so clean and pure and naturally sumptuous, that you could walk there with bare feet. No poison ivy! At night you could look up into the endless sky studded with blazing diamonds, a "blanket of stars," as the old Latvian song goes. Devoid of light pollution, the heavens seemed close and within reach. I hoped to see the northern lights in Latvia.

I was afraid of adders and ticks. My father-in-law was hospitalized for a month with meningitis after being bitten by a tick. I only saw an *odze* once, but I encountered a lot of golden *glodenes* (*Anguis fragilis* or slow worms) and black *zalkši* (*Natrix natrix* or grass snakes). In the summertime the meadows buzzed with insect life. Bees foraged in the old lindens, kindly sharing their blossoms with me. Those wonderful summers, when I could gather teas there! My mother-in-law had taught me well.

In the summer it was possible to wade across the Gauja River into Estonia. Our naked children frolicked on Estonian sandbars, running in and out of the moving water. Neither deep nor particularly swift in this portion, the river turned dangerous further downstream. There were stories of whirlpools and "double bottoms" that sucked in unwary swimmers. I could picture raftsmen floating by. For me, a Latvian born in the United States, a house on the Gauja was like "living the dream," as in the famous song "Pie Gaujas" ("By the Gauja") with words by the poet Rieteklis (1856–1940). It was a popular song that several generations of expatriate Latvians had sung far from home, scattered across Western Europe, the Americas, and Australia, by backyard barbecues and camp bonfires, in kitchens that smelled of *kāposti ar desiņām* ("stewed cabbage with sausages"), in hotel lobbies and smoky pubs, to express their longing for their fatherland.

To this place where pine forests sway I am dearly bound; / This is my fatherland, I was born a Gauja man. / I've heard it's nice in foreign lands, / Many lovely wonders: / High mountains, boundless meadows, / Decked with lovely flowers. / But what are foreign lands, islands with their beauty to me, / When here by the Gauja I hear the Latvian language? / I am Latvian, will be Latvian, I'll always remain Latvian, / And for my fatherland I'll sacrifice my life. / Only by the Gauja, by the Gauja, by the Gauja I wish to be. / And on a high cliff find myself a bride. / Hello, Gauja, flow swiftly to the sea! May the Latvian nation flourish for centuries to come! (Tr. RL)

In 1990 it was a dream that had come true for me: Pedraudzes would be my permanent connection to Latvia, a place to finally call my own. I would plant things and watch them grow, as our children played in the superbly fresh air. We would breathe new life into the old farm.

In June 1991 my mother came to visit in time for the summer solstice. Andris picked her up at the airport and drove straight to Pedraudzes. "You were waiting for us, standing inside by the window holding Jurģis in your arms"—she remembered. We spent almost a month together there. My poor mother: she had to endure mosquitoes and *miģeles*—tiny black flies that would attack in swarms, usually at sundown. With no one around, we went skinny dipping in the pond and sunbathed in the nude. I slowly organized my household; there were a zillion things to do.

Left: Winter fun in the Latvian countryside, December 1990. Krišjānis and his grandfather on the ice.

The work at Pedraudzes began in earnest as soon as the farm was ours. We dug a pond and built a Latvian *pirts* (sauna) in the summer of '91. (Our workers took a break each day to go inside the house to watch the popular Spanish soap opera "Dona Beija." Our workers watched the show religiously. I spent a lot of time at the stove cooking for everyone but did so with joy: the old farmstead was coming back to life!

In my desire to create a flower garden, which I knew was the pride and joy of all Latvian women, I hauled wheelbarrow after wheelbarrow of topsoil and manure to my chosen spot next to our house to fatten up the ground for primroses, peonies, roses, dahlias, and mums. The only flowers to grace the house at the time of purchase were purple *miķelīši* (perennial asters), and I wondered if they had been planted by Karlīne Pedraudze. The flower "cult" was definitely one of the most marvelous aspects of living in Latvia. For two summers, in 1991 and 1992, I toiled, watching the garden take shape, the rose and clematis climb up the wall, my first dahlias and hollyhocks bloom.

Work at Pedraudzes was endless. The men focused their attention on the old buildings. Our large shed opened its plank doors to swallows, bats, and owls. It was a marvelous place for storing equipment. The old threshing barn was a vision from a distant era; Juris and his workers replaced the lower logs, which had rotted. We quickly realized we would need all the hands we could find to manage this place. My mother-in-law moved in with us in the fall of 1991, and some cows, pigs, and poultry were acquired for the little barn. My father-in-law took over another corner of the house. The idea of independence and privacy, a driving force behind the search for our own home, evaporated. I cast my resentment aside, and we settled into a daily routine that required ceaseless physical labor and stamina. My father-in-law built a greenhouse for Biruta's tomatoes. The work of cleaning, clearing, and inhabiting was invigorating. While working in the kitchen cooking or rinsing dishes, I had one ear cocked toward the radio, which was broadcasting the great political changes taking place on a daily basis.

At the very end of July we were shocked to hear that during the night OMON forces had attacked the Lithuanian customs post in Medininkai on the Vilnius-Minsk highway, killing seven Lithuanian customs and police officers: Mindaugas Balavakas; Algimantas Juozakas; Juozas Janonis; Algirdas Kazlauskas; Antanas Musteikis; Stanislovas Orlavičius; Ričardas Rabavičius; and Tomas Šernas (who survived but suffered severe brain damage). They had been shot in the head. Their weapons were missing, the building a shambles. The brutality of the attack was stunning and reminded us of the Soviet and Nazi atrocities of World War II. The attacks on the Medininkai and Kybartai posts were the last of a series of OMON's attacks on Lithuanian and Latvian border posts, when border guards were beaten up, their stations ransacked. Soviet President Gorbachev denied Russia's involvement in these attacks. (3)

The summer clock ticked on; the shadows of the pine trees shifting across the grass. On the morning of August 19 we woke up to news that made me jump out of my bed. A coup d'état was underway in Moscow, and our very future was at stake. As I stumbled out of bed and got busy preparing breakfast, the radio buzzed, as we talked feverishly. What would happen now? If the conservative hardliners were able to wrest control from President Gorbachev and get the army and the KGB on their side (highly likely), then that spelled doom for us. These nostalgists had had enough of Gorbachev's reforms and decentralization; they had other plans for him, his family, the Soviet Russian communist empire, and those troublemakers in the Baltics. Already my mind was racing: could Estonia be an escape route to Finland? Madness! It was clear we would not be going to Rīga anytime soon.

On that fateful day seconds seemed like minutes, minutes like hours. As Soviet tanks milled near the Russian Parliament, surrounded on all sides by Russian protesters, our hearts beat quickly, painfully. The Baltic States' fate hinged on the outcome of events in Moscow. The Soviet Union was cracking, yet there were people trying to glue it back together, trying to hold on to the past the old way, with tanks, guns, and potentially widespread repressions.

The coup failed, thanks to the feisty leadership of Boris Yeltsin, President of the Russian Soviet Federative Socialist Republic, and his followers who had gathered to defend the White House (Russia's Parliament) from the putsch planners. The army, which was sent in to smash the resistance, withdrew. The Soviet Union was imploding. On August 22 Boris Pugo, the son of Latvian communists, and his wife allegedly commited suicide. The other coup organizers were arrested. While we were up at Pedraudzes, dramatic events were unfolding in Rīga in tandem with the attempted coup in Moscow.

On August 21, 1991 the Supreme Council of the Republic of Latvia adopted the constitutional law 'On the Statehood of the Republic of Latvia' with 111 members of the Council voting in favor and 13 against. August 21 is the date that brought our country real independence and international recognition, initiated the actual restoration of our country's independence, revived the Constitution, and disengaged Latvian law from USSR law.

The Supreme Council of the Republic of Latvia adopted the constitutional law at a (dramatic) time, when a coup d'état was attempted in the USSR. OMON forces had occupied the Latvian Television Center, the Latvian Radio Building, the Telephone and Telegraph Central, and the Interior Ministry; they had also vandalized the headquarters of the Latvian Popular Front. A state of emergency had been declared throughout the Soviet Union.

At this politically unclear and dangerous time members of the Latvian Supreme Council were able to assemble for a meeting to prepare and adopt the constitutional law. The August 21 debates about the content of the constitutional law were interrupted by an announcement that armed OMON transport vehicles were approaching the Supreme Council building (PHOTO). In spite of this, Members of the Council continued to discuss the content of the constitutional law and voted to adopt it. (5)

The Latvian Freedom Monument's figures of the oppressed pulling off their chains. Photo: Peters J. Vecrumba.

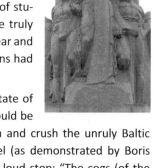

The Latvian Freedom Monument's figures of the oppressed pulling off their chains. Photo: Peters J. Vecrumba.

When the coup in Moscow failed, it was really the end of the Soviet Union, aka the Evil Empire. The OMON criminals left Latvia at the end of August. On August 21, 1991 the realization struck us like a bolt of stupendous, beautiful lightning: Latvia, Lithuania, and Estonia were truly free, once and for all, of the smothering embrace of the Russian bear and Soviet communist rule. Only then did we believe it, that our chains had been broken, that the Iron Curtain had lifted! (6)

For a brief moment during the putsch, we had existed in a state of semi-terror, fearing that the developments of the recent past would be upended, and that the dark forces in Moscow would rise again and crush the unruly Baltic peoples forever. The Soviet "machine's" primitive, rusted wheel (as demonstrated by Boris Yeltsin in Juris Podnieks' film "End of Empire") had ground to a loud stop: "The cogs (of the Soviet Union) had to be pushed inch by inch... Someone had to give the first push." Of course, that first push was initiated by Mikhail Gorbachev, who now stood in the smoking debris of the empire he had sought to remodel.

Iceland was the first country to recognize the independence of the Baltic States on August 22, 1991, followed by Denmark the following day. Fifty-two years after the signing of the Molotov-Ribbentrop Pact in Moscow, Latvian authorities assumed control of the headquarters of the Central Committee of the Latvian Communist Party in downtown Rīga and triumphantly raised the Latvian flag there on August 23. (Six years later in 1997 I began working working for the Delegation of the European Commission in that building.) It seemed almost impossible to assess the suffering and damage that the Soviet Communist Party and Soviet Russia had inflicted on the Baltic States during their decades-long rule. On August 21 thousands of Latvians gathered in downtown Rīga to remove the Lenin monument they loathed. The removal of Latvia's Lenins had already begun in 1990. What were Latvia's Russians thinking? Their hero was yanked off his pedestal, as crowds of jubilant Latvians jeered, whistled, and applauded. (7, 8)

Mr. Ints Silins, first American Ambassador to Latvia (1992–1995), reminisced about the precarious times leading up to Latvia's independence:

> The independence of the Baltic States was still up in the air. Even today, any person with knowledge of Baltic history realizes that nothing is for sure in that area. (In the late 1980s) Baltic residents felt that momentum toward independence was accelerating. But from the Soviet Union point of view... Gorbachev at this time apparently still believed that the Baltic States could be a sort of laboratory for testing ideas to rejuvenate the Soviet Union. I think that's how he thought of them, as a valuable part of the USSR. Because of their past history and ties with the West, because of their small size, because of their reputation for a high degree of education and industrial productivity, they could be used as a test bed to experiment with techniques that might then be expanded on a broader scale to rejuvenate the entire Soviet Union. He entirely missed, misunderstood, failed to grasp, the strength of national feeling in the Baltic States.

Maybe even today he is still puzzled about why the Balts show little gratitude for what the Soviets tried to do for them. That point of view is shared by a lot of Russians who, to this day, continue to regard the Balts as ungrateful pests who during the Soviet era enjoyed a standard of living higher than the average for the USSR. Many Russians apparently are convinced that the Balts benefited from their relationship with the Soviet Union. They cannot imagine that from the Baltic perspective their half century inside the USSR was a long, painful period when economic, political, and social development was smothered by the Russian occupation. Many Balts feel confident that if they had remained independent, their economies would have kept pace with, say, those of Denmark of Finland or Sweden. Instead, upon finally regaining their independence, they found themselves far poorer than any EU members. (...)

Many Russians were clearly reluctant to relinquish the Baltic States. They considered them to be a signature acquisition of Peter the Great. They considered that the territory had been bought with Russian blood, that this relationship went back hundreds of years. There is also in Russia a certain lack of appreciation and respect for small nations. Many Russians are disinclined to take them seriously. Some Russians even felt that way about the Swedes, I found. I remember when I told one of my Russian friends in Leningrad that my next diplomatic assignment was going to be in Sweden, he looked baffled and said, 'Why would you want to go to such a small country?' And he was an anti-authoritarian painter.

Then, too, Latvia became sort of a Palm Beach for retired KGB, Soviet military, and people with reactionary views about Russia and Russian history and what Russia ought to be doing in that region. And so, with the continuing presence of thousands of disgruntled and unpaid Soviet troops and the horrific economic collapse that followed Latvia's separation from the Soviet Union. (9)

Indeed, for several years to come the situation in Latvia would remain tentative, as Soviet troops lingered on their bases. The Russian historical perspective, which Mr. Silins describes, would continue to cause friction between ethnic Russians and Latvians.

On August 23, 1991 the Latvian Communist Party's First Secretary Alfrēds Rubiks was arrested and charged with organizing an attempted coup in Latvia. Dramatic! Just a few years prior to these dramatic events Rubiks had signed off on our apartment papers. That same day the Latvian and Estonian popular fronts and Lithuania's Sajūdis organized a pan-Baltic demonstration of solidarity against Soviet rule, the failed coup in Moscow, and to commemorate the Molotov-Ribbentrop Pact. (10, 11)

Our Zolitūde neighbors Jānis and Līga Graudiņš and their three children joined us at our farm, and we drove out from Pedraudzes to a bigger country road to build a bonfire. Other fires glimmered along the road, burning brightly in the summer twilight. Trucks and cars drove by, tooting and honking and tossing out extra firewood to the people who had converged there to celebrate. The Baltic nations—keepers of the flame of freedom...

As the sun sank beyond the western horizon, the stars emerged above our heads—*zvaigžņu sega, žvaigždžių antklodė, tähtede tekk*—shimmering and winking. I like to think that those stars were the souls of the millions of Baltic peoples who had come before us, who had existed here on this "lunar side" of Europe, their lights eclipsed for so long (Ivar Ivask, "Third Elegy"). I liked to think that the spirits of my grandparents, Jānis and Līvija and Augusts and Emma, as well as those of Aleksis and Karlīne Pedraudze and many others, were twinkling up there, too.

On August 25, 1991 Russian President Boris Yeltsin signed a decree recognizing the independence of the Baltic States. The United States under President George H. W. Bush formally recognized the independence of Latvia, Lithuania, and Estonia only on September 2, much to my embarrassment. The fact that Russia's Yeltsin outpaced President Bush bothered me. What was the US waiting for?! It was the end of the Evil Empire!

Seven years after submitting a manuscript and illustrations to Liesma, one of Latvia's main publishers, my book *Indiāņu teikas* ("Indian Tales") was finally published in 1991. Written by Jaime de Angulo (1887–1950)", *Indian Tales* was basically a compilation of California Pit River Indian myths. I had nearly forgotten about the book. Long waits were typical of the book publishing industry in communist Latvia. I had spent many hours working on the illustrations in the winter of 1983, poring over books about North American Indians that my mother had sent me for guidance and inspiration. At heart I had always felt like an Indian: displaced and driven from my home.

My husband and I walked over to the office of Sprīdītis, the actual publisher, to accept some copies. It was all very anti-climactic. I was pleased with the appearance of the book, although its binding looked dubious. No reception, no champagne. No reviews either. Disappointing. Thus it was delightful to later hear and read from time to time about people praising the book and mentioning it with fondness. 1991 was a year of uncertainty and enormous change. The book already belonged to another era, our "Junk Street" era, when we were living on top of Rīga's old history, and chekists were snooping around our doorstep. Focusing on American Indians had seemed like a good way to introduce something novel to the Latvian reader and stay creatively active at a time when I wasn't sure of my place in Latvia.

In late September Andris bought some geese and ducks in Blome for our pond at Pedraudzes. By now we had chickens, and there was talk of buying some sheep for wool. Andris harvested 12 large sacks of barley; we had our own potatoes, carrots, beans, peas, and other goodies. Autumn had bronzed the countryside, and we loved getting away from Rīga. Knowing that prices would rise, I tried to convince my father to invest more in Latvian real estate and urged my family to consider moving to Latvia. Wasn't this what everybody in exile was supposed to be doing? Wasn't a free Latvia our dream, our ideal, our promise to ourselves, and our responsibility? By 1991 a handful of Latvians from abroad had moved to Latvia, but many others apparently balked at the idea.

Our baby was growing stronger, and my life revolved around the boys. A bad thrush infection that autumn in Rīga caused Jurģis a great deal of discomfort; I worried incessantly about his health. Still, he was a very happy, smiling baby, my sunshine in the darkening days of early winter. Krišjānis commuted to school and ran around with his little friend Dāvis during his free time. I was glad that there was so much space in Zolitūde for those two rascals to explore.

Christmas of '91. Gingerbread cookies wait to be baked but never make it to the oven. A door slams; a person runs off into the night. Where? Why? I stand in our little kitchen looking out at Zolitūde's lights in the darkness and then place the untouched dough back into the refrigerator. I tuck the boys into bed, turn off the lights, and lie alone in bed gazing through the lace curtains into the darkness. Freedom has come at a steep price.

Chapter sources:

(1) "1949. gada marta deportācijas." Wikipedia. <http://lv.wikipedia.org/wiki/1949._gada_marta_deport%C4%81cijas

(2) Ibid 1

(3) "Latvijas iedzīvotāju 1949. gada 25. marta deportācija: Valkas apriņķis, Valka." Retrieved 6/2/2013. <http://www.itl.rtu.lv/LVA/dep1941/saraksti/22_Valkas_apr.pdf>

(4) "Soviet OMON assaults on Lithuanian border posts." Wikipedia. March 24, 2014; May 31, 2013. <http://en.wikipedia.org/wiki/Soviet_OMON_assaults_on_Lithuanian_border_posts>

(5) "1991 Soviet Coup d'Etat." Wikipedia. <http://en.wikipedia.org/wiki/1991_Soviet_coup_d%27%C3%A9tat_attempt>

(6) Rasnačs, Dzintars. "1991. Gada 21. Augusts—Konstitucionālā likuma 'Par Latvijas Republikas valstisko statusu' pieņemšanas diena." Retrieved June 6, 2013. <http://www.dzintarsrasnacs.lv/index.php?id=95%3A1991gada-21augusts-konstitucionl-likuma-par-latvijas-re&option=com_content&view=article>

(7) "Rīgas OMON." Wikipedia. January 12, 2014; June 2, 2014. <http://lv.wikipedia.org/wiki/R%C4%ABgas_OMON>

(8) "1991." Barikadopēdija. <http://www.barikadopedija.lv/raksti/1991>

(9) "1991. gads Latvijā." Wikipedia. April 17, 2014; June 2, 2014. <http://lv.wikipedia.org/wiki/1991._gads_Latvij%C4%81>

(10) Siliņš, Ints. "Latvia Country Reader." Association for Diplomatic Studies and Training. (Adst.org.) <http://www.adst.org/Readers/Latvia.pdf>

(11) Ibid 7,8

(12) Ibid 7,8

"And It's All Over Now, Baby Blue"

"Man vienalga, kuŗš ir vainīgs, es vai tu, jo viss ir tagad zudis, Baby Blue..." ("And I don't care who's to blame, you or me, 'cause it's all over now, Baby Blue.")—An adaptation of Bob Dylan's "Baby Blue" by the popular Latvian American folk rock group "Frikadeļu zupa" ("Meatball Soup")

My boys at Pedraudzes in the summer of 1992 with their cousins Elīna and Alise. Photograph by Valdis Kupris.

As the 1992 January cold stalked us in Rīga, I bundled up Jurģis, and we set off on long walks for fresh air and so that I could clear my head. A book by German alpinist Reinhold Messner's solo climb drew me into his thoughts on loneliness in life and on death. I read it in the evenings after the boys had fallen asleep. I lay in bed thinking. My husband was away a lot. I sought some sort of explanation in Messner's writing for my profound sense of solitude. Our son was sickly, and worries about his health consumed me. I felt very much alone in my worries.

Summer came, offering respite from health concerns and a chance to escape to the countryside with its fresh air and good food, thanks to my mother-in-law's talents. I loved working outside, especially in the flower garden, and the forest near our house was simply exquisite. The children played up in the dunes, building structures out of sticks, moss, and stones. My boys' cousins Elīna and Alise were frequent visitors. I learned a simple new cake recipe, which the children asked me to bake day after day. I baked for them and helped my parents-in-law, who worked tirelessly; they were typical Latvian workaholics. My mother-in-law loved taking care of her cows, pigs, and chickens. She loved all farm work, and we enjoyed the fruits of her labor: fresh milk; Farmer's Cheese; cream; and bread, which she still baked on a weekly basis in our bread oven.

A photograph of the old stove at Pedraudzes some 20 years after my departure: a pan of chanterelles gathered nearby is simmering. To the right is the hot water receptacle, which had to be filled with water every day and was indispensable for dishwashing. Photograph by Ieva Balgalvis.

I spent the entire summer at Pedraudzes with the children and my parents-in-law. It was all work and no play for us three adults. I did most of the cooking and washing; my mother-in-law toiled in the garden and looked after the farm animals. This was her world, the farm, and she was good at it—practical, clever, industrious. My father-in-law lived in his separate corner of the house and also helped with cutting the grass and other chores. He appeared to be in love with the farm and the locale.

Simple things like washing the dishes or clothes required a lot of time and patience. Washing the laundry was a three day affair. I did it all, because there was no alternative. Weeding the garden in a cloud of *miģeles*, the tiny pests of the north, was another dose of country living. I was living my dream, I thought. But there was one person missing from that idyllic setting, and I felt apprehensive and sad.

The summer solstice of '92 was marred by tragedy: our beloved filmmaker Juris Podnieks died in Zvirgzdu Lake in Kurzeme while scuba diving. The news stunned me; I could scarcely believe it. I was devastated. I had a crush on Mr. Podnieks; I liked his work; I liked the man. The news of his unusual death stunned all of Latvia. Many people assumed he had been done in by Russia's agents. This theory still prevails. After all, he filmed the Russian attack on the Vilnius Television Center, as well as the OMON rampage near Bastejkalns in Rīga. Other theories included robbery (Podnieks worked in the UK in the late '80's and early '90's), envy, a freak accident related to the dangers of diving, and a falling out with a Georgian "magician" and UFO specialist. I suspected the involvement of Russian agents. But perhaps it was just a terrible accident. Podnieks' death was a tremendous loss to Latvia, and I still mourn his passing. He had given so much and had so much to give. (1)

The summer went by without a single telephone call, it seemed. My relatives, including wonderful Uncle Jāzeps, and a friend from the US came out to visit; as I showed them around, my mind was elsewhere, and I think they could sense it. Latvia was free, but my joy had evaporated. They left, and I threw myself into work to ward away my worry. In the evenings I fell into bed exhausted.

From a letter to my family in the United States dated July 24, 1992: *"...Hot, dry, very dry. They're talking about a* bada gads *('famine year'). I am trying to stay calm. The forests are on fire somewhere not too far from here, and it feels like I am also burning up."*

Imminent danger seemed to manifest itself in the form of a snake that I nearly stumbled over near the granary in late July. A copper-colored adder slithered directly across my path, greatly startling me. When we first moved into the house, there were grass snakes everywhere. They vanished, as we began cleaning up the area, carting away old hay and mowing the lawn. But an adder! With small children around! I lost sight of the creature, but it left a chill in the air... Ice-cold eyes, a forked tongue...

By the end of August it became clear that my life as I knew it had burned up in the dry, hot summer: the radio was reporting stories about savage forest fires in Latvia, especially in Kurzeme. But somewhere not too far from us another fire had broken out, and there were moments when I wondered if we would have to escape across the Gauja into Estonia. My marriage was over. Letters to my family from that time reveal my state of mind: desperation; a longing for flight; the bitterness of betrayal; and a horrible sense of shame—the worst feeling of all. I was overwhelmed by a terrible sense of failure.

The first day of school was approaching; it was time to pack up and go back to Rīga. Juris and Biruta would remain at Pedraudzes; in fact, they would be living there as permanent caretakers of our property. We had a barn full of animals—Biruta's dominion. Suddenly I no longer cared about any of it. We climbed into Juris' car, and my father-in-law drove us to the Valka train station. I could not look back. The farm had lost all of its charm and meaning; in it there was no room for me anymore. I was suddenly displaced. Thrown overboard into a new, cold reality.

We boarded the Valka-Rīga train, and the father of my children and I sat down on opposite sides of the aisle. It was over; my dream was over. It was a late August day, and people were boarding the train carrying baskets full of mushrooms. I stared through them as if they were ghosts. I clung to my son, kissing his blond hair, and gazed out at the Latvian countryside sliding by in the lengthening shadows of the day. A painful sense of meaninglessness came over me. The open windows were admitting the sweet scent of the receding summer, the Vidzeme forests, and the meadows lush with hay. Only the warm weight of my younger son snuggling in my lap and my older son's chattering reminded me that I was alive, and that someone needed me. "Mazs bij' tēva novadiņis" ("Small was my father's land"): the words to a folk song that I loved came to me, cutting me like a knife.

Someone got off at Rīga's Central Railway Station and strode away without looking back, vanishing down the stairs, as three pairs of eyes looked on blankly. My boys and I remained seated. A jolt shook the train as it picked up speed, rumbling over the Daugava, river of souls, towards the lonely canyons of Zolitūde.

Chapter sources:

(1) "Četri iespējamie Podnieka nāves iemesli." Delfi/Mango.lv. December 14, 2010; June 4, 2014. <http://www.delfi.lv/izklaide/archive/cetri-iespejamie-podnieka-naves-iemesli.d?id=35726985>

PART SIX:
The 1990s; Freedom; Farewell.

With my boys in Rīga in 1996. Latvia is free and independent, and so am I. (Photo: Ilmārs Znotiņš, Diena)

In September 1992 my sister-in-law died. I was already grappling with the dissolution of my marriage and my new life as a single mother, when news of her death reached me. After her funeral I banished myself from Pedraudzes with an aching heart. Dazed, confused, and numb, I was unable to pick up the phone and reach out to relatives and friends for help and support. It was as if an iron curtain separated me from the rest of the world. For a while I wanted to crawl into some dark space and sleep away my pain.

The American Embassy had opened in Rīga in October of 1991 in a room at Hotel Rīdzene; Ints Silins, a Latvian American, arrived as Chargé d'Affaires to lay the groundwork for a permanent American presence in Rīga. At the time remnants of the barricades were still visible. "There were still, when I was living (in Hotel Rīdzene), bullet holes in the glass that lined the staircase leading up to the second floor from the lobby," Mr. Silins remembered. Those were souvenirs of the OMON attack on the Interior Ministry just across the street in January 1991. Mr. Silins' arrival in Rīga provided me with a sweet sense of victory: democracy had won! Tyranny had been toppled. In February 1992 President Bush appointed Mr. Silins as US Ambassador to Latvia. He held that post until 1995. Born in Latvia, Ambassador Silins lost his father, a soldier, to the Soviets. (1)

> The Germans were in control of Latvia at the time of my birth in 1942. But in 1944 Germany's defeat was looming, as was the likelihood that the Russians would be coming back to impose their brutal regime. So when I was just two, my mother and I joined thousands of other Latvians who fled the country as best they could, mostly to Sweden or Germany. We made our way to Germany and ended up spending five years there, in various displaced persons camps—DP camps, as they were called, eventually in the American zone. My father remained in Latvia with other soldiers holding out in the hope that the Allies would come to their aid. That help did not come. They were taken prisoner by Russian troops and sent to Siberia. A few years later, he died in a Soviet death camp. (2)

Sometime in the 1980s I had arranged to meet Mr. Silins at Hotel Latvija; for what reason, I cannot recall. A nasty little Russian concierge swooped towards me, talons unfurled, and refused to grant me entrance to the hotel, until Mr. Silins came to my rescue. The concierge refused to believe that I did not speak Russian. She refused to believe that I was an American. Many Soviet mannerisms, including Russian arrogance, would take years to fade away.

For a decade I had walked around Rīga fantasizing about the day when an American embassy would open in Latvia. Although provincial in many ways, Latvia was suddenly no longer a province. Foreign embassies began moving into lovely old buildings, re-establishing Latvia's historic ties with the West. Denmark, France, Great Britain, Germany, Sweden... Russia's presence was contracting dramatically, squeezed into an imposing embassy building near Kronvalda Park. Russia's "spy central" in Latvia.

Life went on, and I was forced to stay busy; the boys needed me, and that gave me immense strength. The ordinary rituals of life, cooking, shopping, paying bills, riding the bus to pick up a payment, making the children their bath, and reading books to them—stabilized me. Despite my personal loss, Latvia was free, and this gave me hope and resolve. Slowly, I began to pick up the pieces of my life.

In autumn of '92 I landed a full time job, thanks to a visiting Latvian American friend, Uldis Bluķis. I was hired as an assistant to the incoming United Nations Development Programme Resident Resident. With a good local wage, I felt stronger and in control of my life. My boss Lynn was very supportive, and we got along splendidly. It wasn't easy, however, combining full-time work with the responsibilities of a single mother. Dropping a crying, miserable son off at daycare and then rushing back at the end of the day strained my nervous system considerably. Krišjānis, our little commuter, was an amazing trooper, but I worried about how his parents' break-up would affect him. As Jurģis repeatedly fell ill at daycare, in November I was forced to pack him off to Pēdraudzes. Knowing that he was being cared by Biruta put my mind to rest, but my heart ached for him. We would be apart for long stretches of time for about a year, until I hired a nanny.

After my divorce in September 1993, I switched apartments, happy to leave Zolitūde, its leaking pipes, cockroaches, burned elevator buttons, Russian graffiti and vandalism, and the commute behind. We moved into a large, somewhat dilapidated five-room apartment on the fifth floor of a building on Ģertrūdes iela, one block from Old Ģertrūdes Church. Some very notable Latvians had once lived there, including my grandparents' mentor and colleague, famous linguist Jānis Endzelīns, and Latvian composer Jāzeps Vītols. The apartment exchange had involved bribes and dubious paperwork, which eventually came back to haunt me, but for a while we were happy there. Krišjānis' new school was just four blocks away, and I could walk to work.

The once magnificent building, still lovely from the outside, was in serious need of renovation, as so many of Latvia's old buildings were. The Soviets had a knack for running things into the ground. Despite windows on every other landing, the wide stairwell was gloomy and reeked of urine. Only a few lightbulbs worked; there were times when the entire stairwell was enveloped in darkness. Unbelievably, the ancient, vandalized, coffin-like elevator worked, but I rarely used it, dreading being wedged in between floors or, worse, plunging to my death. The staircase covered in oak parquet was so worn as to have indentations from all the feet that had tramped up and down it for more than 50 years. Those stairs had once been clad in carpet. That was before the war, when Latvia was run by "nationalist-fascist-capitalist pigs."

So many details revealed the quality of Latvia's architecture and construction before the Soviet occupation. The apartment's massive double doors made of oak could be locked from the inside with an enormous iron *krampis* (hook) that slipped into an equally impressive iron *cemme* (shackle). An intruder would have needed an ax to get through those doors, which also had a wonderful peephole for inspecting visitors. The apartment's ceilings were very high compared to our ceiling in Zolitūde, and most of them still had their original moldings.

In fact, nothing in the apartment had been upgraded since the war, with the exception of wallpaper (ghastly patterns and colors) and perhaps the kitchen sink. The kitchen itself was long and narrow, with a spacious pantry, as well as a *meitas istaba* (servant's room) that I hoped to clean out and remodel. Sturdy shelves had been built between the back exit doors, thus sealing off access to the back staircase that presumably led down to the building's basement. Windows facing north towards Valdemāra iela revealed a courtyard with trees. On the other side of the apartment I could look into the windows of a Soviet era office building on Skolas iela; I could observe people sitting, working, drinking coffee, reading, chatting, and moving about.

The bathtub was at least 50 years old. Large, clunky, its old porcelain faded and cracked, it rested on four lion's paws. The bathwater drained into a hole in the floor: you could actually see the water draining down into a big, black hole in the floor, which must have been an old pipe of a considerable size. A most curious sight for me: it was both fascinating and somehow freaky. Everything about the apartment was big: big rooms; big doors; big windows; wide windowsills; high ceilings; wide and solid wooden plank floors in a couple of the bedrooms and the kitchen; old, worn parquet in others; and plenty of space.

The WC was also antique: an ancient porcelain toilet of a unique design. One's poop fell onto a shelf and was then washed away over a "waterfall" by a torrent of water released from a tank up by the ceiling. My father got a big kick out of that toilet, marveling at how one could examine one's BM, before it was permanently swept away over "the falls" into Rīga's sewers. I kept a spare bucket of water there to keep things moving along.

The apartment was in need of repairs and modernization. All in due time, I told myself; I needed to save up money. I occupied a small room near the entrance and re-papered the walls. It looked lovely. The boys got their own big bedroom, and my goddaughter Elīna, who moved in with me for a while, got a room of her own. My antique furniture looked great in the apartment; however, all the clunky Soviet pieces looked out of place.

A reputed Gypsy healer lived on the third floor. Sometimes I saw his clients on the stairs. I even recognized some of the faces. Latvians, Russians, all sorts of people who believed in this stuff; I wondered what their complaints were. Maybe the guy really did possess magical powers? Latvia was obsessed with the occult. *Zilā kalna* ("Blue Mountain") Marta was Latvia's most famous healer at the time, but judging by the long lines, I guess our neighbor was famous, too. *Zilā kalna* Marta (1908–1992) was said to have possessed a golden aura, which one could detect at night; apparently she had cured around over 70,000 people from all over the Soviet Union of various ailments. There is no way I can confirm or deny this famous Latvian healer's powers. I attributed this obsession with paranormal activity, the occult, the supernatural, UFOs and aliens, and *dziednieki* (healers) to the absence of religion and spirituality in many people's lives, the low quality of Soviet medicine, and a general spiritual malaise. Interestingly, my mother said that my great-grandfather had been a healer. (3)

Most of the apartments in our building were communal. Right below me lived a Jewish scientist, his wife, and his brother. They were good neighbors: when I accidently flooded them a couple of times, they complained. But after my profuse apologies, they smiled kindly and forgave me and even invited me in for a chat. I wish I had gotten to know them better. Old Mrs. Šēnhofs, who lived a landing above me, would come down from time to time to ask for a bit of money; she was so old and so frail, that I obliged. Her son, a bum and an alcoholic, rang at my door, too, a couple of times. I learned to use the peephole on a regular basis.

I hired a nanny, and Jurģis came back to live with me in the fall of 1993. It was a joyful reunion; I had missed my little boy terribly. Later Elīna went to live with my ex and his girlfriend in her late mother's flat a few blocks away. The lives of our children went through great upheavals, as if being bounced up and down by the nervous tremors of Latvia, as it disentangled itself from Russia. Before the nanny's arrival, it had been very hard to go to work; I had to leave Krišjānis home alone in the morning for several hours, until it was time for him to go to school. Sometimes I let him come over and hang out at the UNDP office on Teātra iela in Old Rīga. But most of the time I called him every half-hour to see if he was alright and ask him what he was doing. I could never thank my boss Lynn Wallis enough for her patience. Krišjānis learned to fend off juvenile thugs and found his way around Rīga with ease.

The Russian Mafia

In the early 1990s my Latvian American friend Valdis Kupris, an artist from New York City, moved into the attic of an old wooden building a block away, next to Old St. Gertrude's Church. He set up his studio there, and I visited him occasionally, enjoying his company. His building was near a café called Sēnīte ("Mushroom") on Baznīcas iela, which had opened in the late 1980s, when Latvia's first cooperatives were founded. In the 1990s several people associated with the Russian mafia were shot to death there. Someone attempted to bomb the café/restaurant/deli, which apparently served as a front for Russian gang activities. I ate at the café once, but then decided it was too dangerous for my liking. Collateral damage didn't seem to bother this new breed of thugs who had crawled out of the rotted woodwork of communism.

When it was warm, accordion street music floated up and through the windows of our office on Teātra iela, grating on our nerves like a broken record. Every day we listened to the street musicians' same old songs. With songs like "Zilais lakatiņš" ("The Blue Kerchief") cranking in the background, from our office windows I caught sight of suspicious-looking guys coming and going at Hotel Rīga. BMWs and Mercedes Benzes with tinted windows pulled up, and swarthy, Slavic-looking guys in sunglasses, dark leather jackets, and thick gold chains stepped out, chatting on cell phones. Sometimes they stood around waiting for somebody, jumped into other cars that pulled up, or vanished into the hotel. I don't think they were up to anything good... Independence triggered a turf war in the 1990s and into the 21st century amongst various criminal factions, most of them Russian. In the early years of Latvia's independence, racketeering became a problem for many start-up companies.

According to Juris Rekšņa, former Latvian Chief of Police, the most brutal incidents of settling scores and contract murders took place from the early to mid-1990s, when Latvia's independence had just taken off, and everything was in flux: "If we compare 2006 with 1993, then the number of such murders has decreased by 50%. Criminals used to use explosives; now they use guns in most cases." According to Rekšņa, most of the victims were "people who weren't friends with the law. (…) (These murders) involved those who ordered them, who orchestrated them, and who actually committed them. Often the assassins became victims themselves (…)" Latvia felt like "the wild East" in those days. (4)

Dainis Peimanis, owner of a business called Jaunpagasts Plus, an alcohol manufacturer, was murdered on December 15, 2000 in his car on his way to Rīga. His attackers forced his car to the side of the road and then shot at him through the window. Soon after the murder the alleged killer, Normunds Rijkuris, was also murdered. Investigators were unable to track down the person(s) responsible for ordering the killing. (5)

"Many contract killers come in from Russia. That makes tracking them down even harder," said Rekšņa. In his words, the cost of a contract murder could vary "from $300 to $50,000, depending on the killer's professional status." Commenting on a case from January 2007, when criminals attacked a businessman, his wife, and two children with Kalashnikovs, Rekšņa said, "Strangely enough, criminals have their own code of conduct, which includes not shooting children and not shooting in public spaces where there are a lot of people. This attack was a mess— cheaply orchestrated." Such sordid stories were part of our country's "growing pains." (6)

A 2007 article with the headline "Pasūtījuma slepkavību var noorganizēt pat par $300" ("A Contract Killing Can Be Organized for a Mere $300") lists some of the more prominent turf war murders in Latvia after independence from the Soviet Union in 1991. (7)

1996
April 9. Yury S., director of Voleri, a firm specializing in transit commerce with Russia, was shot to death in front of his wife and friends at a café in Ilģuciems.

September 22. Mono Vice-President Valerijs Mačugins (b. 1958) and Natālija Meisāne (b. 1969), owner of the Natalie model agency, are shot dead in downtown Rīga.

December 17. Ivars Bīriņš (b. 1955), president of Thormann & Co., is shot dead in downtown Rīga.

1998
The body of Gundars Kņevinskis (b. 1969), owner of a firm named Terra-komerc that allegedly defrauded its investors, is discovered in the Ogre River. The victim's neck had been broken.

1999
September 29. Businessman Josifs Bermans (b. 1936) is murdered.

December 14. Businessman Arnis Šķesteris (b. 1957), involved in the alcohol business, is shot and killed in downtown Rīga.

2000
February 17. Latvian Privatization Agency official Ilona Skadiņa (b. 1949) is murdered.

February 29. Rīga Yacht Club President Egons Stieģelis is murdered.

April 30. Ļevs Krēmers (b. 1953), president of the bankrupt Olimpija Bank, is murdered.

December 15. Dainis Peimanis (b. 1951), owner of the firm Jaunpagasts Plus, is murdered.

2001

June 14. Vjašeclavs Liscovs, Chief of the Ludza District State Income Service, is murdered.

October 15. Rīga District Court Judge Jānis Laukroze is murdered. (8)

In 1996, when I was working in marketing for the Latvian daily *Diena*, a stunningly beautiful woman, Natālija Meisāne (b. 1969), came to my office to discuss our newspaper's possible interest in supporting a fashion show at the Latvian National Opera. Shortly after our meeting, she was gunned down in a courtyard in downtown Rīga on September 22 along with Mr. Mačugins, a Russian businessman. Corpses were found floating in rivers, businessmen vanished. The alchohol business figured in many of these brutal murders.

Many of Latvia's alleged contract murders remained unsolved. A well known Russian mobster's dacha was located next to my son's school in Jūrmala. Some of Latvia's criminal authorities were killed; others emigrated or legalized their businesses. In the vacuum created by the sudden collapse of the Soviet Union, there was a lot of room for embezzlement, fraud, racketeering, contraband, and other nefarious activities. Latvia's new business world was teeming with greedy novices, naïve idealists, thugs, and hardcore criminals. How little this world had to do with our dream of a free and independent Latvia! The news stories about these murders revealed a sordid, violent post-Soviet reality that I did not really want to know about.

I became a shareholder in a company that was to take over the former Soviet Army base in Ādaži. With the company's founder, a distant relative, we drove to the former firing range to check it out. I "invested" some Latvian roubles, and that was the end of that. I never heard back from my enthusiastic relation, a scientist who specialized in some sort of "luminescence." There were plenty of start-ups and many failures. Businessmen lived in fear of ruthless extortionists. Sometimes I remembered Comrade Ruciņš and the KGB's offer to participate in a business venture. I shuddered.

Suddenly Latvia was flooded with new technology. I remember the fax machine room and "tech hub" of the Latvian Ministry of Foreign Affairs in 1992, with faxes going out to and coming in from all over the world. Latvia was buzzing and beeping, reconnecting to the world it had been cut off from for nearly half a century. By 2015 the three Baltic States would be among the world's "IT-savviest" countries.

I never did get a cell phone in Latvia, but there were plenty of young men lounging around in Rīga's cafés yakking on their *mobīlie telefoni*. The Soviet era's dilapidated telephone booths quickly vanished (as they have elsewhere in the world). Latvians latched on to modern technology with great speed, earning praise in Tom Friedman's 1999 bestseller about globalization, *The Lexus and the Olive Tree.* Today Latvia's Internet is listed as one of the fastest in the world.

McDonald's opened on Aspazijas bulvāris ("Soviet Boulevard" in the Soviet era). Although I had little interest in its fast food menu, I discovered a clean public restroom on the second floor. Kellogg's opened a cereal manufacturing plant in Ādaži. For someone like me, the presence of these American brand names provided a wonderful sense of reassurance that the nightmarish communist era really was over, and that Latvia was reconnecting with the Western world to which it belonged.

Latvia's first private bank Banka Baltija, which survived from 1993 until 1995, grew at a dizzying rate and employed about 1,300 people at its peak. When it collapsed, it wiped out the savings accounts of hundreds of thousands of clients. In 2007, the bank's chairman Aleksandrs Lavents and its president Tālis Freimanis were convicted and sent to jail. Where did the money, the millions entrusted to the bank by Latvia's gullible post-Soviet people, vanish?

Other banks popped up and then went bust in independent Latvia. The Soviet era Latvijas Krājbanka ("Latvian Savings Bank"), which was actually a continuation of the pre-war Latvian Postal Savings Bank founded in 1924, was fine under the Soviets; I actually trusted it. But independent Latvia's new banks were too unsavory; I could not ditch the feeling that most of them were somehow linked to organized crime, and that they operated as a Laundromat for Russia's criminal world.

I thought it better to hide my money in a sock. My income was small anyway; it fit into a sock. I had enough to pay the rent, my bills, my nanny, and buy us food and clothes with just a bit to spare. As I carefully calculated my expenses, dividing my monthly wage into five envelopes, some of my compatriots were suddenly becoming *miljonāri* ("millionaires"). They drove luxury cars and feasted at new, expensive restaurants with their platinum blonde "arm candy." Many people had a "get rich" scheme; some plotted how to strip Latvia of its assets. Soviet era manufacturing plants were mysteriously privatized. Real estate companies proliferated, and the price of real estate and housing skyrocketed. Latvia's beautiful forests were thinned by whining chainsaws.

Banka Baltija also "bedded" the Latvian state electrical utility company, Latvenergo. This coupling spawned the sordid "Three Million Affair," in which three million Latvian lats (US $6 million) evaporated into thin air. Several key figures associated with Latvenergo died mysteriously. The rule of law was having a hard time establishing itself in my post-communist fatherland. (9)

To protect Latvia from the Russian rouble and to plug a growing Russian rouble deficit, in 1992 Latvia's Monetary Reform Committee issued the Latvian rouble. Designed by Kirils Šmelkovs, the Latvian rouble with its bright colors and gaudy patterns looked a lot like Monopoly money. Our national currency, the Lat, made its debut in 1993. Until 2014, when Latvia joined the Eurozone, the Lat's exchange rate remained virtually unchanged: one Lat was roughly equal to two US dollars. My wonderful relation Gunārs Lūsis designed some of Latvia's currency. What an accomplishment, and how far we had come!

New stores were cropping up everywhere, and they were expensive. To add insult to injury, many of these stores offered products and merchandise of dubious quality. When you calculated the price of goods into dollars, the prices were outrageous. "Humpala" (humanitarian aid) stores proliferated, offering decent used clothing for a fraction of the cost of new clothes. United Colors of Benetton opened on Brīvības iela; I went in a couple of time, looked around, and promptly left. The prices were ridiculous compared to our salaries.

With the influx of Western goods, hard currency, investment opportunities, and contacts, Latvia's society quickly splintered, again, into "the haves" and "have-nots." The economic rift between the moneyed and the poor in capitalist Latvia would deepen over time, as it has in many countries. While a Barbie-beautiful, expensively attired woman sporting a Gucci bag and sunglasses stepped out from the latest model BMW or Mercedes, just around the corner an old, poor woman offered tiny bouquets of wildflowers for sale, so she could purchase some bread. These Dickensian juxtapositions unnerved me. In Latvia the income gap quickly deepened, eventually leading to mass emigration.

Casinos spread through Rīga like a toxic fungus, making me wonder about their role in the laundering of dirty money. Those with money and clout continued to do the talking, the wheeling and dealing, the dicing, and the scheming. In other words, there was much that went on "behind the scenes" in the Republic of Latvia that most of us did not know about. One could only sense it, smell it: it was like getting a whiff of sewage next to a fancy restaurant. You couldn't see it, but you could smell it: corruption.

After independence, locally produced girlie magazines appeared, with names like *Melnā pantēra* ("Black Panther") and *Princese* ("Princess"). Latvian and Russian girls eagerly stripped for the camera, flaunting their enviable assets. Titty clubs and bars, nude revues, massage parlors, hostess bars, and brothels proliferated in downtown Rīga, attracting the attention of foreign male tourists and British "stag" parties. Rīga would go from being a drab, sooty factory girl to a platinum blond, plastic boob, thong-kinda gal; the lucrative sex industry ensnared young, naive, or desperate women. Baltic prostitutes were a subject of Swedish writer Stieg Larsson's bestselling *Millennium* series.

Privatization certificates were issued to citizens of Latvia; not knowing what to do with them, many people sold them off to buyers in dim, shabby offices in weird places around town. Coupons and cash were exchanged through small windows in the gloom. The dreary locations were just like the currency exchange points. The language spoken at these points was mostly Russian. Why?

In the 1990s security companies proliferated, presumably due to extortion. I wondered if these companies were involved at both ends: extorting *and* offering protection. There was a brashness about these guys that was unpleasant, as if they were above the law. In many ways they reminded me of the OMON thugs.

I had many questions about Latvia's privatization process, which was partly written up in the press in the 1990s. It produced new owners, new companies, and lots of questions about the legitimacy of the process, the origins of the "seed money," and how exactly these people got their hands on previously state-owned businesses. Manufacturing was discontinued, and people were laid off. Some factories like Laima, a producer of chocolate, managed to survive.

As manufacturing died off and factories and plants were shuttered, a growing service sector emerged. New, modern-looking hotels and excellent restaurants competed for customers, thereby promoting higher standards. New cafés and discotheques livened up the Rīga night scene. Coffee tasted like coffee, and overall the service was better. Stores remembered for their pyramid displays of stacked canned foods, limited choice of products, and jostling, angry masses now offered new and interesting products, shopping carts, and relatively courteous salespeople. The city looked brighter, as merchants spruced up their windows. Retail space underwent extensive remodeling, turning into modern, comfortable, pleasant places to frequent. It was exciting, to say the least. After all, Rīga was a beautiful city.

I still don't know how the majority of Latvia's large Russian minority felt, when Latvia regained independence. Despite Soviet troop withdrawal, retired Russian officers were permitted to stay in Latvia under an agreement between Latvia and Russia. The schism between these two ethnic groups persisted. When Russians gathered on May 9 at the so-called Victory Monument, which commemorates the defeat of Nazi Germany, Latvians seethed; the Soviet "liberation" (occupation) had been so destructive. Many Russians seemed to loathe the idea of learning the Latvian language. Another far more serious problem woud develop over time: Russians absorbing the propaganda of state-controlled Russian television beamed in from Moscow.

In the summer of 1994 I became involved with Cornelius, a foreigner whom I met through work. Our warm friendship lasted for four happy years. My lover was kind, sweet, and funny; he loved books and good music and told me lots of humorous stories about his time in Africa. Friendship, laughter, and intimacy helped me recover from my painful wounds.

Fed up with the dullness of administrative work, I left UNDP in the early summer of 1994 to work for the English language weekly. Although my salary decreased considerably, I craved for the freedom to write. My first feature was about a group of Iraqi refugees who had sought our help at the UNDP office. The story of their long and arduous flight from Iraq to Latvia was captivating. It was a sign of things to come. We helped find them temporary shelter in an old school outside of Rīga and provided food and clothing. Eventually, the group made it to Sweden. Theirs was but one of many compelling stories about Latvia.

My time working for *The Baltic Observer* and its successor, *The Baltic Times*, remains one of my happiest times in Latvia. I loved writing. I was free to choose my topics, and there was no shortage of fascinating subjects in post-Soviet Latvia. Every old building had a story to tell, and then there were the people.

As independence began to transform and brighten the face of our capital Rīga, people began to travel abroad, and the number of tourists visiting Latvia surged. Direct contacts with the West pushed development forward. Despite exciting changes, there were signs that something was amiss. Street urchins and beggars were reminders that not everyone was reaping the benefits of independence and capitalization. Economic transformation also included inflation and unemployment, which hurt a large percentage of the population.

Like the pink, horrible Blob (of the 1958 classic horror flick), Russian troops withdrew completely from Lithuania on August 31, 1993 and from Latvia and Estonia a year later, on August 31, 1994, leaving a trail of toxic residue. The Balts breathed a sigh of relief. Once the Soviet Army was gone, Latvians could assess the wreckage and poison left in the enemy's wake. Former Soviet Army firing ranges demanded careful inspection for any live artillery shells; extensive clean-up work lay ahead.

"After the collapse of the Soviet Union, the Soviet military suffered a huge 'breakdown' of sorts. Former military training areas and firing ranges were dotted with antiquated live ammo and toxic chemical compounds, as well as missile fuel dumps. A lot of Soviet military equipment was sold off to third countries or simply vanished," according to Ēvalds Krieviņš, a retired army officer. "Some places, like the high-precision, high-altitude bombing range in Zvārde, have not been cleaned up to this day. Usually after any live-firing exercises unexploded artillery shells were disposed of, but many of them still remain undetonated within the former range's security zone. At Ādaži the old firing ranges were burned in a controlled fire to 'weed out' live ammo."

Soviet era pollution would require years of clean-up and remediation. Among the many hot spots of concern were: sulphuric acid goudron ponds near Inčukalns; a toxic liquid dump in Olaine; the former Soviet Naval Port in Liepāja; a toxic chemical dump called "Kosmoss" near the city of Jelgava; etc. Pollution had continued for years unabated.

I obtained my driver's license and bought a car, a used Opel from Germany. Used cars were a lucrative business right after independence. It was wonderful to experience the freedom of the road. The 1990s made me realize how important my individual freedom was.

Modern fashion and better make-up did wonders in transforming Latvia's Cinderellas into drob-dead gorgeous women; many girls would make it to the fashion runways of Paris, Milan, London, and New York. New women's magazines emerged: colorful and printed on glossy paper, they put the shabby women's magazines of the Soviet era to shame. Women opened up about their personal, marital, and sexual problems.

In September 1996 we lost hot water in our building. As always, I hoped and assumed it was a temporary problem. I experienced an unpleasant encounter with the manager of the building, a mean fellow named Mr. Circenis ("Cricket"). He showed up at our door one day, introduced himself, and then barged in with a couple of stodgy women to look around, probably trying to assess the market value of what he was seeing. This was after our rents had been raised astronomically, and I had complained. Cricket barked at me, "You can move if you can't pay the rent. You shouldn't be here anyway. You were bamboozled." And part of me sensed he was right; the building had been denationalized prior to my move, someone had been bribed, and I was left with short end of the stick.

The rightful owners of the building lived in the United States and didn't seem to care about the tenants. As the outside temperature dipped and the rooms cooled, I was able to obtain an address and wrote to them, explaining who I was and complained about the tactics of "Cricket." I wrote about my neighbors, elderly and young children who were being treated like refuse. A young woman who lived below us told me she had asthma. It got colder. By November it was clear that the hot water was not coming back, and then suddenly we were all informed that the building would have no heat at all that winter because of an unpaid heating bill. Rīgas Siltums was the energy monster that terrorized Rīga's population each fall by not turning on the heat when it got cold. We weren't sure if the threat was real. Maybe Cricket really did plan on freezing most of us out of the building.

November 1996. Taking a cold bath with my cat Pūce ("Owl"). Photo: Normunds Mežiņš, AFI.

By late November the situation had deteriorated to the point where we went to bed in sweaters and pants, and my nanny Anna and I kept the kitchen's gas stove burning for most of the day, which produced an unpleasant odor. Anna, my wonderful Anna! That fall she boiled potatoes in the morning and put them under the blankets next to my boys to warm them. She was my rock, someone whom I could completely trust. I paid her generously, and she was absolutely dependable. I wrote up a story for our newspaper about our situation, and someone took a photograph of me sitting in my cold bath with frigid water trickling from the faucet. Our cat Pūce ("Owl") didn't seem to mind the cold, but that same fall she caught and ate our parrot, Tonton, which added to my sense of impending doom. My mind raced furiously: what to do? What to do?! I feared for our health and commiserated with everyone in the building, especially the old, frail, and weak.

One night something caused me to suddenly wake up; my heart was pounding like crazy. Something didn't seem right. What was that... rumbling? I got out of bed and went to the window to draw the curtains and look outside. My heart did a flip: a strange orange glow was flickering in the windows and on the walks of the building next to us. Suddenly I realized that a building was on fire! Our building! I raced to my sons' room to wake the boys, dressed them, and then we opened our front door, preparing to race down the stairs and out onto the street. Instead, we encountered a fireman rushing up the stairs past our door to the apartment on the top floor. A fat water hose snaked up the stairwell like a gigantic python. Another fireman told us that the blaze was under control and would be quickly extinguished. We spent the night at my friend's apartment. I was pretty shaken.

I found out that two old ladies in the apartment on the last floor had died of smoke inhalation. Their communal apartment looked horrible; the fire had gutted it. The walls were burned to a cinder; stuff lay on the floor in filthy piles. The sight chilled me. The old ladies were probably trying to stay warm with an electric heater. The building's electrical wiring was more than 45 years old. I cursed Cricket and his kind.

The situation at my newspaper seemed to be deteriorating. Some time in 1996–1997 the owner of our newspaper vanished along with his family. What happened? Later I heard rumors that he had incurred the wrath of the Russian mafia. Had they fled? Was there some sort of debt? Had our newspaper been purchased with dirty money? Gambling? I would never know. This story exemplified post-Soviet Latvia in the 1990s.

In 1997 my mother helped my buy an apartment in Pārdaugava: finally a place of my own! And I had a new job working for the European Commission. Latvia was planning on joining the

European Union and NATO. Slowly, Latvians were regaining their self-esteem after years of submission to their Russian "liberators." Still, they had a tendency to bow too much. Russification had left a long-term effect on my compatriots. Some grumbled that the European Union was the same old Soviet Union. After everything we had been through, I wasn't surprised by this attitude.

Cornelius and I discovered Rīgas Līcis, a Soviet era sanatorium in Jūrmala for Moscow's Communist Party elite. Neat paths through the pines lead down towards the beach. The property was well maintained. It was easy to imagine Soviet honchos there with their wives or girlfriends, strolling about, nodding to each other, gloating, looking out at the gray waters of the Gulf of Rīga: theirs, all theirs. Rīgas Līcis was probably among the best of the best Soviet resorts for the Soviet privileged, whose lives were different than those of the average Soviet citizen. In the mid-1990s Rīgas Līcis was still being guarded by a sentry in a guard booth, an electronic security gate, and a tall iron fence that kept the average proletariat out. What probably got Cornelius *in* was his red diplomatic license plate. At that time the future of the sanatorium was unclear. It was a marvelous facility.

As we swam in the beautiful pool and ate in the magnificent dining hall, I thought about the once privileged communist bosses who had enjoyed their own private hunting grounds, enviable apartments, good (Soviet) cars (the Volga was their Cadillac), their own stores, big salaries, and opportunities to rest, relax, and romp in exclusive resorts like Rīgas Līcis and other exclusive retreats throughout the Soviet Union. Surely someone was eyeing this sanatorium and salivating. Privatization was a process that triggered passions, complicated lawsuits, and ugly crimes. Everyone wanted a stake in something, and there was so much for the taking. Only once did we encounter a group of people entering the building: a few Latvian government officials who had arrived in their fancy cars. Since the place was so huge, we never saw where they vanished. The dining hall remained empty even then, and the whole place was eerily silent. The times were rapidly changing, and new feet were stepping into old shoes to enjoy power, privilege, and luxury.

Chapter sources:

(1) Siliņš, Ints. "Latvia Country Reader." Association for Diplomatic Studies and Training. (Adst.org.) <http://www.adst.org/Readers/Latvia.pdf>
(2) Ibid 1
(3) "Zilākalna Marta. Leģenda atmiņās." TVNET. June 18, 2012; June 3, 2013. < http://www.tvnet.lv/sievietem/attiecibas/425943-zilakalna_marta_legenda_atminas>
(4) Zvērs, Jānis. "Pasūtījuma slepkavību var noorganizēt pat par $300." NRA/TVNET. January 22, 2007; June 3, 2013. <http://www.tvnet.lv/zinas/kriminalzinas/287166-pasutijuma_slepkavibu_var_noorganizet_pat_par_300_dolaru>
(5) Ibid 4
(6) Ibid 4
(7) Ibid 4
(8) Ibid 4
(9) Slavenā 'Latvenergo' trīs miljonu lieta beigusies ar prokuratūras fiasco, Grūtups izsprucis sveikā." Pietiek.com. September 18, 2012; June 3, 2013. <http://www.pietiek.com/raksti/slavena_latvenergo_tris_miljonu_lieta_beigusies_ar_prokuraturas_fiasko,_grutups_izsprucis_sveika>

Latvia: The Most Beautiful Country in the World

In the summer of 1998 my older brother Arvils came to Latvia to visit me. For most of his life he had rebelled against his Latvian upbringing, but the two trips he took to the fatherland affected him profoundly. A lifelong history buff, he was ecstatic to see so much old stuff around him. Centuries-old churches, medieval buildings, castle ruins: it all thrilled him, and I shared his excitement. With Krišjānis in tow, we drove out to Kurzeme in my "new" old car, a little VW Golf bequeathed to me by my wonderful Dutch friend Lotte. Talking, laughing, blasting music, and looking around, we hurtled across our fatherland absorbing the luscious summer scenery. My bro'!

We stopped at beautiful Jaunmoku Castle to look around. It was hard to drive past the building; it was simply too inviting. The castle was designed by Wilhelm Ludwig Nikolai Bokslaff (1858–1945) and built in 1901 for Rīga's Mayor George Armitstead, who intended to use it as a hunting lodge. During World War II both the Russian and German armies occupied it. In the Soviet era the castle served multiple purposes: as office space; for social activities; as a store; and then for housing. By 1974 the castle was in ruins. It was handed over to the Ministry of Forestry, which commenced renovation work that lasted 20 years, typical of the Soviet era. We were glad to see that someone was fixing up the grand, old manor. (1)

We drove west through "Kurzeme's Switzerland," a scenic region of hills, valleys, and old towns. The Abava River flows through this area, which is also known as "Abavas senleja" ("Ancient Abava River Valley"). We slowed down in Sabile, a town first mentioned in 1253 and known for its old vineyard, which still holds the Guinness world record for being the world's most northerly vineyard. Wine had been produced in Sabile since the 16th century.

The old Sabile synagogue, built in 1890, stands as a memorial to the Jews of Sabile who were slaughtered during the Nazi occupation. In the Soviet era it was used as a gym. Sabile once had a large Gypsy or Roma community. In 2012 Latvian journalist Otto Ozols published a story about Mārtiņš Bērziņš, a savior and hero of Sabile's Roma community.

> Not far from Sabile, abour six kilometers in the direction of Kuldīga and about 20 paces from the road, one can visit a sobering reminder of (Latvia's) history: it is a large, gaping pit once dug to be used as a mass grave. This pit is associated with Mārtiņš Bērziņš and the local Roma community. During World War II Bērziņš is said to have saved about 300 Roma from execution. This mass grave was intended for them. After the war the Roma saved Bērziņš from communist repressions, and when he died, they erected a monument. (...) Today traces of the empty pit are vanishing beneath bushes. Next to it is another mass grave, which, tragically, did not remain empty. In it lie the remains of about 240 Sabile Jews, including women, old people, and children who were shot on August 6, 1941. A monument from the Soviet era marks this grave. (2)

We drove over the river and up the road leading to the Pedvāle Open-Air Art Museum, an art park established in 1991 by sculptor Ojārs Feldbergs (b. 1947). Feldbergs purchased the property with privatization vouchers. His property includes a couple of 18th century manors, Firkspedvāle and Briņķpedvāle, and a lovely landscape of meadows, streams, and wooded areas.

Sculptures and installations are dispersed throughout the property. Over the years Feldbergs' persistence, energy, and ability to make friends world-wide has turned Pedvāle into one of Latvia's and the Baltics' most attractive tourist destinations. My brother, Krišjānis, and I took a long and relaxing walk around the grounds, enjoying the afternoon's warm, slanting sunlight. It was divine. At the end of our walk we sat down outside to savor some Latvian beer and snacks and enjoyed the sunset. We were able to get a room for the night at the manor.

Brother and sister in the fatherland in the summer of 1998 at Pedvāle. Photo: Krišjānis Vots.

We bid farewell to Pedvāle and meandered southward. I wanted to show my brother Buses *pilskalns* ("castle hill"), which I had stumbled upon during a previous trip. There are about 500 castle hills throughout Latvia. These fortified hills in the central part of a *novads* (region) served military, administrative, economic, and cultural functions in ancient times, before Latvia's territory was conquered by the Germans. Thousands of castle hills are scattered throughout the Baltics. Some are well preserved, such as Kernave in Lithuania. Others remain unmarked or concealed in remote areas, covered with trees and bushes. Alfrēds Stinkulis explored many of Latvia's castle hills in the 1970s and 1980s, documenting them for the sake of posterity, when Latvia's independence from the Soviet Union seemed improbable. Some castle hills were being unintentionally harmed by local people who were ignorant about their origin, purpose, and historical significance. Like Stinkulis, I was attracted to our "distant mirror." **

The Vikings once referred to the Baltic Sea's eastern lands as *Garderike* or "the land of castle hills." Castle hills include hills on which our ancestors built their wooden castles, and on which stone and mortar fortresses were built by the Germans in the Middle Ages. Castle hills have spawned many legends about mysterious entrances and passageways that have drawn people and animals in; some have returned; others have not. **

The lovely Imula winds past the Buse castle hill. Although small, it is a swift stream said to be full of fish like chub, perch, pike, and roach. As Krišjānis scrambled up and down the sides of the hill, Arvils and I sat down at the top to look out over the glorious valley flooded with sunshine and at the shimmering Imula. What was it that moved me so? Was there some otherworldly presence there that touched me? Latvians once believed in the spirit world, *veļu valstība*. Many still do. I do. A gentle breeze rocked the branches of the trees above our heads, which folded over us like the arches of a church.

Buse (also known as Matkule) was one of ancient Vanema's political and economic centers. Vanema was part of Kursa, an area spanning much of modern day Kurzeme, Latvia's westernmost region. Buse was settled by humans more than 3,000 years ago, as well as between the 10th and 14th centuries. Ernests Brastiņs (1892–1942) laid the groundwork for the exploration and documentation of Latvia's approximately 500 castle hills. He was also the founder of Latvia's religious revivalist movement *dievturība*, which sought to reconnect Latvians with their pre-Christian beliefs and traditions. The Soviets arrested Brastiņš on July 6, 1940 and deported him; he was shot on January 28, 1942. **

Vanema, Megave, Duvzare, Piemare, Bandava, Ventava: all around us stretched the lands of ancient Kursa. Primeval forests teeming with wolves, bears, aurochs, wisents, and other wild animals had once covered Latvia. I wondered what the people who had congregated at Buse looked and sounded like. Their genes lived on in modern day Latvians. Their castle hills are a mysterious legacy of Latvia's ancient past.

My brother and I: that summer we were just two Latvian American kids looking out over our fatherland and reconnecting... Sitting on top of the hill, I felt the roundness of the earth, and that life moved in a circle. More than a half-century ago our grandparents and parents had fled westward through Kurzeme to escape Soviet terror. Before us lay the magical land of our Opaps' unfettered imagination. I recalled his riveting, hair-raising tales about the vast, shadowy forests of ancient Latvia, the wild and mythical beasts, *sumpurņi* ("dog muzzles") and *vilkači* ("were-wolves"), and the horrible "floating hand"... It was so many years ago, or was it just yesterday, that we sat at our grandfather's feet in faraway New Jersey, feeling ourselves being transported to our fatherland's magical landscape. Buse, Matkule, Kursa, Kurzeme, Vidzeme, Zemgale, Latgale... For 17 years I had lived my life on a castle hill called Latvia. But now I was peering down into a mysterious, dark entrance that beckoned. I would fall into it, lose my way, and stumble through a long and dark passage that lead me back to the land of the American Indians. As I am nearing the end of my story, I long to find the passageway back to the castle hill. Latvia is just as much a fairy tale as it is real.

Left: Kurbads and the *sumpurnis* ("dog muzzle") from Rihards Zariņš's (1869–1939) print series "Ko Latvijas meži šalc" ("What Latvia's Forests are Whispering," 1908–1911.)

I left Latvia in March of 1999. Arvils died of cancer in New York City two years after our travels in our fatherland. I am grateful that I had the opportunity to show my brother Latvia, a gift and a revelation.

Chapter sources

(1)   "Jaunmoku pils." < http://www.jaunmokupils.lv/lv/par_jaunmoku_pili/>
(2)   Ozols, Otto. "Latvietis, kuram čigāni pieminekli veltījuši." TVNET. July 4, 2012; June 6, 2013. <http://www.tvnet.lv/zinas/viedokli/427870-latvietis_kuram_cigani_pieminekli_veltijusi>
*   Sources about Pedvāle: www.Talsitourism.lv; www.Pedvāle.lv; www.Pilis.lv
**   Sources about castle hills: Buses / www.visitKandava.lv
        Wikipedia / Pilskalns: <http://lv.wikipedia.org/wiki/Pilskalns>

Soviet Aggression Against The BALTIC STATES

Penned by my paternal grandfather Senator Augusts Rumpēters and published by the World Federation of Free Latvians in 1974, this tractate "analyzes how the Soviet Union, by breaking existing international treaties and by the use of force, committed its aggression against the Baltic States." (Latvians.com)

"Rita Laima has written a unique memoir that explores the experiences of the Latvian exile community during the Soviet era and the situation of Latvians in their Soviet-occupied homeland in the 1980s, as well as during the first decade of independence beginning in 1991. The author's strengths are her frankness and ability to draw conclusions. Laima describes how the post-World War II Latvian refugee's mentality developed outside of Latvia, and how a young woman with the Free World's mindset dealt with Soviet socialism and post-communist reality in Latvia. The author's escapades are supplemented with historical background notes, which enable the reader to grasp the context of events of her time in Latvia (1982–1999). Laima had the courage and strength to confront her own inherited notions of the fatherland with Latvia's real situation in the 1980s and 1990s. This memoir is not a nostalgic longing for the past but rather a truthful and sometimes harsh story about life in all its complexity and rich nuances, gleaned from the author's personal experience."

Mārtiņš Mintaurs, PhD, Assistant Professor at the Department of History and Philosophy, University of Latvia, Rīga

"Rita Laima has authored an eloquent and frequently riveting account of an extraordinary personal experience. Having made the choice to enter the prison-like society of Soviet Latvia as a young woman born and raised in the United States, she tries to comprehend, decades later, what attracted and fascinated her by the land of her parents and ancestors. What makes Laima's project especially valuable and enlightening is the skill with which she reintegrates the minutiae of daily life in Soviet Latvia within the broader context of the nation's history. By contrasting her observations and experiences in Soviet Latvia with what she knows and what she has grown to value in a free and democratic society, Laima brings to light the mindless, absurd, and dehumanizing colonizing process enveloping a once-independent nation and its people. Laima's artistic eye and sensitivity bring out the beauty of nature as well as that of musical, architectural, and other cultural achievements that both illustrate Latvia's rich and colorful past and its people's continuing creative potential. The tribute the author pays to all those who dedicated their efforts and lives to achieve independence can serve as an inspiration not only to those engaged in similar struggles around the globe but also to those who take it for granted."

Karlis Racevskis, Emeritus Professor of French, The Ohio State University

ibidem-Verlag / *ibidem* Press
Melchiorstr. 15
70439 Stuttgart
Germany

ibidem@ibidem.eu
www.ibidem-verlag.com
www.ibidem.eu